METHODS & STRATEGIES FOR
Teaching Students with High Incidence Disabilities 2ᴇ

A CASE-BASED APPROACH

Joseph R. Boyle
Temple University

David Scanlon
Boston College

CENGAGE

Australia • Brazil • Canada • Mexico • Singapore • United Kingdom • United States

CENGAGE

Methods and Strategies for Teaching Students with High Incidence Disabilities: A Case-Based Approach, **2nd Edition**
Joseph R. Boyle and David Scanlon

Product Director: Marta Lee-Perriard

Product Manager: Steven Scoble

Content Developer: Drew Kennerley

Marketing Manager: Andy Miller

Digital Content Specialist: Justin Hein

Digital Production Project Manager/Media Producer: Jackie Hermesmeyer

Customer Account Manager: Doug Bertke

Photo Researcher: Lumina Datamatics Ltd.

Text Researcher: Lumina Datamatics Ltd.

Production Management and Composition: MPS Limited

Art Director: Helen Bruno

Text Designer: Diane Beasley

Cover Designer: Helen Bruno

Cover Image: © 2015 Creativity Explored Licensing, LLC

For product information and technology assistance, contact us at
**Cengage Customer & Sales Support, 1-800-354-9706
or support.cengage.com.**

For permission to use material from this text or product, submit all requests online at **www.cengage.com/permissions.**

Library of Congress Control Number: 2017951370

Student Edition:
ISBN: 978-1-337-56614-8

Loose-leaf Edition:
ISBN: 978-1-337-56615-5

Cengage
200 Pier 4 Boulevard
Boston, MA 02210
USA

Cengage is a leading provider of customized learning solutions with employees residing in nearly 40 different countries and sales in more than 125 countries around the world. Find your local representative at: **www.cengage.com.**

To learn more about Cengage platforms and services, register or access your online learning solution, or purchase materials for your course, visit **www.cengage.com.**

Printed in the United States of America
Print Number: 10   Print Year: 2021

To Carole, Joshua, and Ashley—with love.
J. R. B.

To Candace Bos—friend and teacher.
D. J. S.

Brief Contents

Contents

Chapter 6   Early Reading: Strategies and Techniques   189

About the Authors

Joseph R. Boyle is a former special education teacher. In his special education classroom and other settings, he taught students with HI. His students included students with learning disabilities, mild to moderate intellectual disabilities, traumatic brain injury, attention deficit/hyperactivity disorder, autism, and Asperger's syndrome. As a special education teacher, he has collaborated and co-taught with general education teachers and other school professionals. He received his PhD in special education from the University of Kansas. Through his research, he has developed a number of classroom interventions for students with HI in the areas of reading, writing, and note-taking.

Joseph R. Boyle is currently an associate professor of special education at Temple University, Philadelphia, PA. He has taught or currently teaches courses for university students in undergraduate to doctoral programs. The courses he has taught include methods and materials for special education, collaboration and consultation, introduction to special education and special education law, assessment in special education, special education behavior management, language disabilities, critical issues in special education, and technology in special education classrooms. He has also taught several courses online and in other web-based formats. His current research interests include examining the effectiveness of teaching techniques among students with HI, particularly in the areas of reading, writing, and note-taking. He has co-authored three special education casebooks and numerous journal articles. He is currently co-editor of the *Journal of Special Education Technology*.

David Scanlon is a former high school and community college special education teacher. In his high school resource room, he taught students with a variety of disabilities; some were "mainstreamed" and others took most or all of their academic courses with him. In the community college, he taught basic literacy courses and assisted with advising students with disabilities. He received his PhD in special education and rehabilitation from the University of Arizona. Following his graduation, he worked as an assistant research scientist at the University of Kansas Center for Research on Learning (CRL). There, he and his colleagues developed strategic interventions appropriate to the inclusive content-area classroom context. While at the CRL, David served as director of intervention research for the National Adult Literacy and Learning Disabilities Center. The Center was funded to identify best curricular practices in adult basic education.

David Scanlon is currently an associate professor of special education in the Lynch School of Education at Boston College. He teaches courses ranging from the undergraduate to doctoral level. Among the courses he teaches are an introductory special education class, special education methods for general education teachers, methods for special education teachers of students with HI, and an advanced class on scientific and social theories on the nature of learning disabilities and special education practice. He continues to research effective interventions for children and adolescents with HI disabilities, including focuses on content-area literacy, self-advocacy, and transition. He also studies IEP dispute resolution. David Scanlon has co-authored several learning strategies, in addition to curricular materials and nearly 50 research publications and book chapters. He is the past chairperson of the Special Education Research Special Interest Group of the American Educational Research Association, past chairperson of the Research Committee of the Council for Learning Disabilities, former associate editor of the *Journal of Teacher Education*, former editor of the *Learning Disability Quarterly*, and is currently editor of the *International Journal for Research in Learning Disabilities*. He is a Fellow of the Autism Consortium as well as the International Academy for Research in Learning Disabilities.

About the Cover Artist: Anne Conway

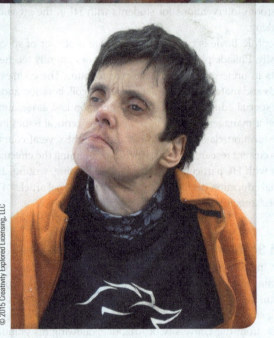

Anne Connolly was born in 1951. She worked as an artist at Creativity Explored from 1987 until 2015.

Connolly is a painter and print-maker who typically creates energetic abstractions using bright complementary colors. Her distinctive style features bold, forceful brushstrokes with overlapping layers of paint. The interactions between these layers produce interesting results: when opaque, one layer obscures the one underneath. When Connolly dilutes the paint, the layers combine, producing new colors at their intersection. These dynamic compositions give Connolly's work great depth.

About Creativity Explored

Creativity Explored is a San Francisco-based nonprofit visual arts organization that gives artists with developmental disabilities the means to create and share their work with the community, celebrating the power of art to change lives.

We are committed to supporting people with developmental disabilities in their quest to become working artists, and to promoting their work as an emerging and increasingly important contribution to the contemporary art world.

creativityexplored.org

Preface

Welcome to the second edition of our textbook, *Methods and Strategies for Teaching Students with High Incidence Disabilities*. We have combined our experiences as educators and researchers with our knowledge of evidence-based instructional practices to write this book and are excited to share this new edition with you.

Why We Wrote This Book

Our own experiences as former teachers—and now as teacher educators and researchers—have helped us shape the content, features, and pedagogy found in this book. Having taught graduate and undergraduate education students for more than two decades, we found many special education methods textbooks lacking. Some offered too few practical instructional methods, or represented dogmatically narrow approaches to teaching and learning. Most were a compendium of methods and techniques, often to the detriment of student learning. Our students often complained to us that their textbook had too many techniques that were presented in a superficial manner and that lacked sufficient depth for use in the classroom. We observed that students knew the features of the techniques, but didn't quite understand how to use them with their students. We also found texts that promoted instructional practices that lack supporting research.

We therefore developed this textbook with student learning at the forefront. We wanted to develop a text that would reflect first-rate pedagogy. The practices described in this book are supported by educational research involving pupils with HI and their teachers. We also wanted students to be able to apply their knowledge soon after learning it. As a result, *we designed this textbook around a common core of knowledge that we believe all special education teachers should know, and then designed activities and cases to support learning it.*

Who Should Use This Book?

This textbook was designed for students preparing to be either special education or general education teachers. It describes the current inclusive context of K-12 schooling. It also presents teaching practices appropriate to both roles. It addresses the continuum of placements and services for students enrolled in special education. Readers of this textbook will learn best and evidence-based instructional practices and how to participate in all aspects of the special education process (for example, RTI, multidisciplinary teams, IEPs, collaborating with families, co-teaching, providing accommodations, and progress monitoring) for students with HI.

The introductory chapters provide a link between traditional methods courses and other "introductory" special education courses. Instead of simply providing a redundant introductory text, we present an overview of the HI disabilities, with discussions of the special education process and various educators' roles, and theories of learning that influence instruction applicable across the different HIs, all from an applied perspective. Hence, this book is appropriate for methods courses that build from a general/special education foundation, those that serve as students' only exposure to practices appropriate for their students with HI, and inclusion courses that provide strategies and techniques that can be used in inclusive settings.

How This Textbook Is Different From Others

As we explain here in greater detail, our textbook is unique and innovative for the following key reasons:

1. Throughout the entire text, we link current educational research to practice.

At the heart of the book is our philosophy of *linking research to practice* so that teachers use effective strategies and techniques to constantly improve the learning (and lives) of students with disabilities. This text reflects the most current scholarship about teaching students with HI but in a way that is accessible to preservice students and novice readers. The featured practices, and details on how to teach with them, reflect both standards expected for all learners and research-based effective practice.

2. This special education textbook interweaves compelling case studies and research-based special education teaching strategies and techniques.

We integrated cases into the text to connect theory and knowledge with practice. In each chapter, two cases are presented so that students can apply their knowledge of strategies and techniques. The cases reflect realistic special and general education scenarios, lending insight into the experiences and perspectives of students, educators, and families. References to the cases illustrate key concepts and practices throughout each chapter; however, the discussion is broader so that instructors are not bound to teach the cases.

3. Instead of including every technique under the sun, each chapter focuses on several key, empirically validated teaching practices.

This text takes a focused and integrated approach to teaching methods. Each chapter presents a limited number of teaching techniques, but with sufficient detail so that students can thoroughly learn them. As we explain each technique, we discuss typical challenges for students with HI.

4. Equal attention is paid to each of the HI areas.

In every chapter, the unique learning needs of students with different HI areas are described. Effective practices and the research that supports their use with students with varying disabilities are also referenced.

5. Equal attention is paid to elementary and secondary education.

In every chapter, the learning characteristics and needs of students with HI from kindergarten to secondary school are described. Effective practices based on developmental needs and schooling level considerations are fully explained.

6. The relationship of student and family diversity to effective teaching and learning is presented.

Instead of addressing diversity in feature boxes or as a separate chapter, examples in each chapter directly show how to consider types of diversity such as sex, race, ethnicity, English language learner status, economic class, family status, and sexual orientation, in addition to disability. Empirically supported evidence of how diversity impacts schooling and learning is presented, in addition to effective inclusive practices for all.

7. As we explain in the next sections, we use reader-friendly features to alert readers to important text content and to relate content directly back to the cases.

In doing so, we try to facilitate readers' learning and understanding of the teaching strategies and techniques. The features and cases are structured to serve as examples that you can also use in your class teaching; however, they are not relied upon so heavily that you cannot make connections to your own perspectives or experiences.

Student Learning Features

Every chapter of this text offers the following features that were designed to enhance student learning. Each of these features represents effective pedagogic practices. They are designed to make this textbook not only informative, but a teaching and learning tool for your students.

Learning Objectives: To orient students to the information they are about to read, each chapter begins with learning objectives that represent the "big ideas" students should think about as they read.

Case Studies with Accompanying Case Questions, and a "Think Back to the Case" Feature: Each chapter contains two engaging case studies about real education issues for students to "solve." Each case study ends with questions about what teachers should do based on the case scenario. Those questions guide students to reflect on critical components of the cases as they read the chapter. As information appropriate to answer a case question is presented, a "Think Back" box summarizing an answer to that question follows.

Methods and Strategies Spotlight Boxes: In each of these special boxes, a specific practice is highlighted and discussed in depth.

Tips for Generalization Boxes: Because teachers need to learn how to generalize procedures they learn, we highlight examples of generalization practices. Readers can consult these boxes to learn ways that popular and validated practices can be properly generalized to meet the needs of individual students or unique setting demands.

Application Activities: To help students extend their learning of what they read, each chapter ends with three to five Application Activities. Each of these activities encourages students to apply and think about the practices they have learned. The activities are designed so that students may engage in them even if they are not in a student teaching situation when they read this book.

Coverage of the CEC Initial Preparation Standards 2015: The Council for Exceptional Children 2015 Standards for entry-level educators are listed inside the front cover of the text. In each chapter, explicit reference is made to the CEC. The purposes of the standards, how to use the standards, and ways to meet the standards are addressed throughout the entire book.

Text Organization and Coverage

Chapter Walk-Through

Chapter 1 begins with a discussion of the characteristics of students with HI, major legislation that affects today's schools and families, and current practices in the field (for example, responsiveness to intervention). Instead of being simply redundant with what many students may learn in an introduction to special education class, this chapter focuses on implications for practice. In **Chapter 2**, we describe how to plan, teach, and monitor instruction in the inclusive classroom and other special education settings. The importance of collaboration, including co-teaching, is highlighted. We take readers from the pre-referral process, through individualized education program plan (IEP) development, lesson planning, and best and evidence-based practices in special education, and end with a discussion of ways to monitor the progress of students with disabilities, all focused on the roles and activities of effective general *and* special educators. **Chapter 3** explains how to collaborate with families, including how to plan for a positive transition to life beyond high school. The IDEA expectations for collaborating with families and practical methods for collaboration are explained. The benefits of collaboration for students, families, and educators are also described. How to use those valuable collaboration skills in providing effective transition programming is highlighted. The expectation to plan and provide transition services is explained as it relates to the special educator's role. Options for transition destinations are described, along with helpful information on how to select options for individual students in collaboration with the student and her or his family. Effective transition planning and programming practices are also explained with examples. **Chapter 4** discusses current learning theories in special education and techniques or methods that are derived from those theories to aid student learning. **Chapter 5** addresses strategies and techniques for improving oral language.

Next, we move on to the reading chapters. **Chapter 6** describes early reading skills such as phonological awareness and word-attack skills. **Chapter 7** covers fluency and comprehension skills and strategies. **Chapter 8** describes how to teach written language skills and strategies to students with HI.

Chapter 9 discusses how to teach math concepts and skills to students with HI, and how to implement strategies to help students overcome difficulties with problem solving. Skills from basic to advanced mathematics are included. **Chapter 10** explains ways to facilitate learning in the content areas, including content enhancement routines and techniques for helping students understand textbook information. **Chapter 11** describes how to teach students with HI much-needed organizational skills, note-taking and study skills, as well as test-taking strategies. **Chapter 12** describes how assistive technology can be used in today's classroom to bypass skill deficits or improve student learning in basic skill areas such as reading and written language. We also discuss how teachers can enhance their own teaching through technology, including using technology to manage their time by using electronic gradebooks and electronic IEPs.

Supplements for Students and Instructors

A variety of exciting supplemental materials are also available to accompany the text.

MindTap: Empower Your Students

MindTap is a platform that propels students from memorization to mastery. It gives you complete control of your course, so you can provide engaging content, challenge every learner, and build student confidence. Customize interactive syllabi to emphasize priority topics, then add your own material or notes to the eBook as desired. This outcomes-driven application gives you the tools needed to empower students and boost both understanding and performance.

Access Everything You Need in One Place

Cut down on prep with the preloaded and organized MindTap course materials. Teach more efficiently with interactive multimedia, assignments, quizzes, and more. Give your students the power to read, listen, and study on their phones, so they can learn on their terms.

Empower Students to Reach their Potential

Twelve distinct metrics give you actionable insights into student engagement. Identify topics troubling your entire class and instantly communicate with those struggling. Students can track their scores to stay motivated toward their goals. Together, you can be unstoppable.

Control Your Course—and Your Content

Get the flexibility to reorder textbook chapters, add your own notes, and embed a variety of content including Open Educational Resources (OER). Personalize course content to your students' needs. They can even read your notes, add their own, and highlight key text to aid their learning.

Get a Dedicated Team, Whenever You Need Them

MindTap isn't just a tool, it's backed by a personalized team eager to support you. We can help set up your course and tailor it to your specific objectives, so you'll be ready to make an impact from day one. Know we'll be standing by to help you and your students until the final day of the term.

Instructor's Manual

Instructors will appreciate succinct chapter summaries, outlines, learning objectives, reflection questions, and additional suggestions for activities provided in the Instructor's Manual.

Test Bank

The Test Bank contains multiple choice, fill-in-the-blank, and essay questions, as well as readily referenced teaching tips for each chapter.

PowerLecture

This one-stop digital library and presentation tool includes preassembled Microsoft® PowerPoint® lecture slides by the authors.

Acknowledgments

We are grateful to the many reviewers whose thoughtful feedback helped make this the best textbook possible. The following experienced general and special education teacher-educators suggested content and features that they know from experience are essential to our students' learning: Roger Bass, Carthage College; Robin D. Brewer, University of North Colorado; Steve Chamberlain, University of Texas at Brownsville; Carrie E. Chapman, Indiana University; Hollie C. Cost, University of Montevallo; Carol B. Donnelly, Worcester State College; Elaine Fine, Montclair State University; Joseph B. Fisher, Grand Valley State University; Gerlinde G. Beckers, Louisiana State

University; Kimberly Grantham Griffith, Lamar University; Mary Beth Hendricks, Columbus State University; Celia E. Johnson, Bradley University; Ui-jung Kim, California State University, Los Angeles; Stephanie Kurtts, University of North Carolina at Greensboro; Loralee A. LaPointe, University of South Dakota; Robin H. Lock, Texas Tech University; Marc A. Markell, St. Cloud State University; Sharon A. Maroney, Western Illinois University; Maurice Dean Miller, Indiana State University; Yvonne Ridings Moore, Union College; Gerry Nierengarten, University of Minnesota, Duluth; Michie L. Odle, State University of New York, Cortland; Marion Panyan, Drake University; Mary B. Perdue, Oakland City University; Kathleen Puckett, Arizona State University; Barbara Ray, University of Tennessee at Chattanooga; Tess Reid, California State University, Northridge; Colleen Klein Reutebuch, Texas Tech University; Joan P. Sebastian, National University; Martha Staton, University of Delaware; Roberta Strosnider, Towson University; Lisa P. Turner, Clarion University.

We are especially grateful to Dr. Joseph B. Fisher of Grand Valley State University, our expert reviewer, who provided detailed feedback on nearly every chapter of this text. We are thankful for his contributions to the ancillary support materials that accompany this text as well. We also appreciate all of the editorial and production staff at Cengage, particularly Drew Kennerley.

Finally, we wish to express our appreciation to our families, friends, and colleagues for being patient with us as we worked on this textbook, and for providing us with support and encouragement throughout the many phases of this project.

1 Providing Special Education to Students with High Incidence Disabilities

Learning Objectives

After reading this chapter, you will understand:

1-1 What the high incidence (HI) disabilities are, and how they affect a student's academic and social skills

1-2 The principles of instructional practices that have evidence as benefitting students with HI

1-3 Where students with HI receive their education and the types of services that may be provided

1-4 The major implications of federal laws concerning how we serve students with disabilities, and the major approaches to services endorsed by those laws

CEC **Initial Preparation Standard 1: Learner Development and Individual Learning Differences**

1-1 Beginning special education professionals understand how language, culture, and family background influence the learning of individuals with exceptionalities.

1-2 Beginning special education professionals use understanding of development and individual differences to respond to the needs of individuals with exceptionalities.

CEC **Initial Preparation Standard 5: Instructional Planning and Strategies**

5-1 Beginning special education professionals consider individual abilities, interests, learning environments, and cultural and linguistic factors in the selection, development, and adaptation of learning experiences for individuals with exceptionalities.

5-5 Beginning special education professionals develop and implement a variety of education and transition plans for individuals with exceptionalities across a wide range of settings and different learning experiences in collaboration with individuals, families, and teams.

What makes special education "SPECIAL"?

This question has been asked time and again in the field of special education (for example, Bateman 2011; Dunn 1968; Will 1986). As the federal special education law states, **special education** is an educational program that is designed to meet an individual student's unique needs (Individuals with Disabilities Education Act [IDEA] 2004). **Individualizing** based on both what a student needs to learn and how that student learns best is in essence what makes it "special" (Kavale and Forness 1999). Special education instruction is typically provided in an explicit way and at an intensive pace and is more structured than general education instruction (Kauffman and Hallahan 2005). Although several other factors might contribute to the uniqueness of special education (for example, low teacher–pupil ratios, provision of therapies and services related to education, and the involvement of parents), the instruction qualified educators provide is essentially what makes it unique. That is, *you* will be the defining factor that makes a student's education "special."

To teach students with disabilities, it is important first to understand the different types of disabilities and the characteristics of each type.

1-1   Practical Descriptions of the High Incidence Disabilities

Throughout this book, we will refer to students with high incidence disabilities (hereafter HI). You may recognize this term or you might know it as mild or mild/moderate disabilities. Terminology evolves as our understanding of the thing it labels evolves. Hence, for a long time "mild/moderate" has been the accepted term, representing how much these disabilities impact a person in comparison to the severe disabilities (such as deafblindness), which are known as the "low incidence" disabilities. However, terms like "mild" can carry the connotation that these disabilities impact a person in only minimal ways; that can sometimes be true but most certainly is not universally true. "High incidence" instead simply signals that these are the disabilities that occur most often, or at a high incidence rate. The acronym **HI** refers to students who have learning disabilities, speech or language impairment,[1] attention-deficit/hyperactivity disorder, autism at the "requiring support" level, mild levels of intellectual disability, and emotional or behavioral disorders. There are 13 categories of disability served by the IDEA (Table 1.1). (States sometimes use different labels for individual disabilities, but they all correspond to the IDEA's 13 categories.) The HI disability categories account for more than half of all students served in special education under the IDEA. We present them in order of prevalence, starting with the highest percentage of students in special education.

Specific Learning Disability

Specific learning disability (LD) is the most commonly identified disability among school-age students in special education (U.S. Department of Education 2016).

---

[1] We will not directly address SLI in this text, as students with SLI are served primarily by trained speech and language pathologists.

TABLE 1.1 Disability Categories Currently Served Under the IDEA

Autism spectrum disorder
Deaf-blind
Developmental Delay
Emotional disturbance
Hearing impairment
Intellectual disability
Multiple disabilities
Orthopedic impairment
Other health impairment (includes ADHD)
Specific learning disability
Speech or language impairment
Traumatic Brain Injury
Visual Impairment

CASE 1.1   Three Elementary School Students: Maria, Sy, and Burt

Case Introduction

In this case, you will meet Emily Holcomb and three of her students with HI. Emily is a special educator who works with the students both in their inclusive classroom and in her learning center classroom. As you read the case, you will notice that each student has some difficulties in class, but so do some of their classmates. Teachers face the challenge of knowing when a learning difference is a disability and what to do when they suspect that it is. As you read the case, ask yourself what special education services the students need.

At the end of the case, you will find case questions. These questions are meant to serve as points for reflection. Of course, if you can answer them immediately, you should do so, but you may want to wait to answer them until you have read that portion of the chapter that pertains to the particular case question. Throughout the rest of the chapter, you will see the same questions. As you see them, try to answer them based upon that portion of the chapter that you just read.

Emily is a special education teacher at Gamon Elementary. She started out as a general education classroom teacher but quickly discovered her passion was for working more individually with students. She particularly likes the challenge of working with students who struggle, figuring out how to guide them in building their skills. Three of Emily's students are Maria, Sy, and Burt. She works with all of them in the classroom where she co-teaches with José Luis Ramirez. She also works with Maria in her learning center classroom.

Maria appears to be extremely shy. She seldom asks for help, volunteers to answer a question, or participates in even fun activities. Maria also tends to sit still and observe her classmates when she is supposed to be partnering with them. Sometimes she works alone, seemingly unaware she is supposed to be participating with others. She has one "friend," whom Emily has noticed usually bosses Maria around. Maria typically withdraws from other students and remains silent if they try to be social with her. In second grade, Maria had been identified as having an emotional disturbance, specifically that she was experiencing depression. Emily believed that shyness and demure behavior were common for Mexican-American girls who live in the community, so she was surprised by the diagnosis. Also, she had trouble believing that someone so young could experience depression. Maria consistently earns low grades, averaging Cs and Ds. She is particularly behind in reading, and Emily fears the gap between her reading skills and what is expected of her is growing faster than Maria is developing her skills. Emily works with Maria in the learning center twice a week to focus on any content from José Luis's class that she needs to review.

Saed, who goes by Sy, is a quiet student, but not shy like Maria. Sy's family moved to this country last year. He had learned some English when they lived in Palestine, but his mother and father tend to speak Arabic at home. Emily gets to work with Sy when she co-teaches in José Luis's classroom. Sy is not a special education student but the teachers at Gamon suspect he may have a disability. Understanding that

continued

language differences hold him back, Emily has been comfortable with the amount of work and socializing that Sy does. At the same time, she notices that he seems to have difficulty developing sight-word vocabularies (words in print that he recognizes instantly) and recognizing sounds made by letters and letter blends. Feeling that they are not meeting his needs, Emily and José Luis sought the help of a team of colleagues comprising Sy's former-grade teacher, a teacher of English as a second language (ESL) whom Sy sees three times a week, and another special educator. Together, they have tried different instructional activities and kept records of how the activities benefited Sy. Based on that team's referral, Sy was recently evaluated for a learning disability, but the testing was inconclusive because he is still considered to be an English language learner. The team agreed that Emily should continue to work with Sy and keep data on his progress when she is in José Luis's classroom. Sy seems to lack some general knowledge expected of fifth graders, but the teachers attribute that to differences in schooling between his former home and the local community.

Burt is what Emily's principal referred to as "all boy." It seems like he always finds excuses to move around the classroom; if something interests him more than what José Luis wants him to attend to—for example, the magnifying glasses on the bookshelf or manipulatives for math time—he can't resist going after them anyway. The principal made her observation about Burt in late October when José Luis commented that Burt was a very nice boy but too disruptive and distracted compared to the other children in the room. José Luis and Emily have kept careful observations of what he does and the results of different efforts they (most Emily) made to help him control his behavior. They also kept the principal informed and spoke to Burt's parents, whom they found are at their wit's end with his behavior at home as well. In early spring, Burt was identified as having ADHD. Emily suggested an aide be assigned to help manage Burt in the classroom and that he spend 30 minutes each day in the learning center going over content from class that he missed. The rest of the team disagreed with her. They said he didn't need special education and they ultimately decided that he would receive a 504 plan and José Luis and Emily would work with him in the classroom on self-regulation strategies.

CASE QUESTIONS

1. In what ways could Sy's primary language impact the process of determining whether he has a learning disability?
2. In what ways could Maria's ethnic culture impact the process of determining whether she has an emotional disturbance?
3. What are common characteristics associated with these student's specific disabilities?

While most people refer to it simply as "learning disability" or "learning disabilities," "specific" in the official name signals that it impacts individuals in specific academic skill areas. The definition cites a significant limitation in using language to acquire, think with, and/or express information in one or more of the following areas: listening, speaking, reading, writing, spelling, or mathematical calculations (Federal Register 2006).

Just as no two students learn alike, we have increasingly come to understand that no one cognitive disorder constitutes an LD; rather, LD is a "heterogeneous group of disorders" that all include difficulties in using language to acquire information, think with it, and/or express it (National Joint Committee on Learning Disabilities [NJCLD] 2016). That explains why one student with LD may have difficulty with beginning reading skills (for example, recognizing letters or letter blends), whereas another may have trouble with higher-level reading skills (such as discerning main ideas or inferring meaning), and still another might have difficulties in writing, mathematics, or organization, but not in reading. The commonality that unites all students with LD is that they process information differently than others and frequently experience low academic achievement because of it. Put simply, an LD is an unexplained difficulty with learning among students with average or above-average intelligence (Fuchs et al. 2003; Stanovich 2005).

What LD "Looks Like" and How It Is Experienced. Students with LD have significant difficulty processing information. This processing difficulty is often evidenced in poor performance in academic skill areas such as reading, written language, and math. Because LD can vary in its "severity," some will work in very disciplined ways in the area(s) impacted and achieve at levels commensurate with their peers. More commonly, however, students with LD will struggle and achieve at a below-average level in the area(s) impacted. Some students with LD have low self-esteem and low motivation for academics, if not more broadly (Louick 2017). Dropping out of school is also more common for students with LD than it is for the general school population, particularly for those who become frustrated with school (Scanlon and Mellard 2002).

Cognitive Processing Difficulties. Students with LD have been characterized as "inactive" and inefficient learners (Torgesen 1982). This is because they tend not to think proactively about a task (for example, reading a difficult word, solving an algebraic equation, planning to complete a project on schedule). Instead, if not told what to do, they may skip parts of the process, produce low-quality work, or simply give up on the task. For this reason, giving directions explicitly and periodically prompting appropriate performance are often needed.

The language-processing challenges at the core of LD include using language to store and recall information in memory. Weak working memory in particular is a common characteristic of students with LD, although it may be specific to just those academic skill areas impacted by the LD (Brandenburg et al. 2015; Swanson 2003). For students who are English language learners the challenge may be compounded by difficulty accessing working memory that is not dependent on proficiency in a language (Swanson Saez, Gerber, and Leafstedt 2004). These facts mean that students with LD need heavy prompting or additional practice to learn facts or skills they would otherwise not fully learn. As Jerman, Reynolds, and Swanson (2012) found, improvements in working memory skills are not likely to spontaneously lead to improvements in academic skills incumbent on working memory.

Students with LD also tend to have slower processing skills (the using language part of the definition), which means they can and do acquire, think with, and express information, but only if given ample time and support to do so. Thus, this characteristic also calls for explicit teaching of information and both allowing students additional time for processing (with scaffolding) and frequent and intensive instruction and/or practice to facilitate memory storage.

As a consequence of their slower learning rates and difficulties with comprehension and recall, students with LD tend to have a limited number of approaches for addressing a learning task, such as making sense of an unknown word when reading (Hallahan et al. 2005; Harris, Reid, and Graham 2004; Meese 2001). They can be characterized as *nonstrategic* (Harris et al. 2004). A strategic approach to performing a task would involve recognizing the task demands (for example, reading an unfamiliar word), identifying options for how to approach the task (using context clues or decoding), selecting an appropriate option, and following that plan for completing the task. While following the plan, strategic students monitor whether they have followed the steps of the plan and evaluate whether or not the plan is working. When necessary, the students "troubleshoot" strategy performance (for example, Pressley 2002; White and Frederiksen 2005). Being able to coordinate all of the thinking involved in being strategic is described by some as **executive functioning** (Meltzer et al. 2001).

Many students with LD also have difficulties with cognitive organization (Mastropieri and Scruggs 2007), which is related to strategic planning. This means that they are not aware of relationships among facts or concepts and they do not discern between salient and noncritical information. Recognizing relationships, which includes inferring them, is essential to storing information in memory and to comprehending concepts (Searlman and Herrmann 1994).

Academic Skills Difficulties. By definition, students identified as having LD have difficulties in one or more academic achievement areas (c.f. Scanlon 2013). You are likely to first observe evidence of problems in cognitive processes among students with LD as difficulties in listening, speaking, reading, writing (including spelling), calculating, or math problem solving.

As estimated 80 percent of students with LD have their primary difficulty in reading (Mercer and Pullen 2005). Reading comprises a complex array of skills (see Chapters 6 and 7) that relate to one another, ranging from recognizing letters, in sounds and print, to interpreting and generalizing the meaning of complex texts. Decoding words is a basic skill of reading. Many students who have difficulty with reading find it difficult to master the foundational skills involved in decoding—namely, phonological awareness, or the understanding that words are made up of sounds, and phonemic awareness, which is the recognition of the individually meaningful units of sound in syllables and words (Reutzel and Cooter 2004). Readers who have difficulty with decoding will further have problems with reading text fluently. Fluency, in turn, is a critical reading skill for comprehending (Good, Simmons, and Kame'enui 2001). Yet, some readers will be challenged in comprehension instead because of the inferential skills involved (again, LD is a heterogeneous group of disorders).

Written language and oral language skills rely on some of the same cognitive processes involved in reading. Some students with LD may have difficulties with spelling, word choice, and organization of information when expressing themselves. For these reasons, help with planning organized writing products or oral communications is helpful (De La Paz and Graham 2002). Students with LD are also likely to be poor spellers, at least until they have developed strong decoding skills, as the foundational skills of decoding are essential to being able to spell (Berninger 2003). Handwriting can also be challenging for students with LD. This may be due to poor fine motor control, but also to memory for forming letters. Extensive practice is necessary to improve handwriting (Berninger 2003). Sometimes educators encourage the use of a word processer as an alternative to handwriting, but this could put the student at a disadvantage in a world where handwriting is still a practical skill.

For some with LD the challenges are in mathematical conceptualizations and reasoning, and/or challenges in performing math calculations, which may be due in part to memory difficulties (Tolar, Fuchs, Fletcher, Fuchs, and Hamlett 2016). Similar to reading and writing, math difficulties most commonly involve basic skills but can extend to complex higher-level skills. Number sense, or an understanding of quantity and how numbers relate to one another, is foundational to mathematical thinking and operations (Compton, Fuchs, Fuchs, Lambert, and Hamlett 2012). For some students, memory weaknesses result in difficulty recalling arithmetic facts and operations. Others with LD will be challenged to comprehend mathematical processes (Compton et al. 2012; Tolar et al. 2016).

Social Skills Difficulties. There are differences of opinion about whether or not students with LD experience any more social challenges than their peers who do not have disabilities. However, it is reasonable to assume that the cognitive processing challenges they experience can occur in social situations (NJCLD 2016). Some students with LD report having few friends (Elksnin and Elksnin 2001), and observational evidence has indicated that their classmates sometimes avoid partnering with them, at least for academic tasks (Donahue, Pearl, and Bryan 1980; also see Toste, Bloom, and Heath 2014 regarding teachers' perceptions of their academic relationships with students with HI in their classrooms). Some students with LD may not be actively processing while in social situations, or processing quickly enough to keep up, and may not know how to conduct themselves in certain contexts (for example, cooperative groups, whole class participation, recess, the cafeteria, or the locker room) (Hutchinson, Freeman, and Berg 2004). Still, some students with LD are well liked, in both social and academic settings. This is because of the limited ways their LD affects them, because of their own self-regulation skills, or because they use more positive social skills (Raskind et al. 1999). Sy is an example of a student who seems to be coping well in all regards but reading.

Methods and Strategies Spotlight

Gifted and LD

Learning disabilities are often thought of in terms of deficits, or the things students cannot do well. Consequently, we can form negative views of students' potential. So much of the focus of special education for LD is on remediating what students have difficulty doing that we tend to forget LD is not an *inability*. We can even find ourselves forgetting that an LD impacts only certain areas of a student's cognition and achievement. A particular subgroup of students with LD should remind us just how heterogeneous learning disabilities are: students who have an LD but are also gifted. Such students are sometimes referred to as **twice exceptional** (Reis, Baum, and Burke 2014).

Students who are twice exceptional have the following three characteristics:

- They fit the diagnostic criteria for an LD.
- They show evidence of a cognitive processing deficit.
- They have an outstanding talent or ability (Mills and Brody 1999), such as music, writing, or mathematics.

Twice-exceptional learners have been estimated to represent between 2 and 5 percent of all school students (National Education Association, 2006). We often have difficulty recognizing the dual exceptionalities of these learners. Sometimes their cognitive and academic difficulties "compete" with their cognitive strengths and they cannot demonstrate what they are capable of. For example, a student with significant reading difficulties will have difficulty in a math class that relies heavily on reading and writing skills. In other cases, we observe the low achievement that results from their LD and fail to notice their exceptional abilities that are a sign of giftedness (Mills and Brody 1999; see also Ferri, Gregg, and Heggoy 1997).

It is relatively uncommon for schools to recognize both conditions in a student (Gardynik and McDonald 2005). This may be because school personnel do not accept that students with LD can also excel intellectually (Gardynik and McDonald 2005). Such thinking represents a fundamental misconception about LD.

Once educators get past their shortsightedness about whether LD and giftedness can coexist, they should find providing appropriate interventions easy. Many of the same intervention approaches appropriate to serving those with LD are appropriate for gifted students. Effective approaches include the following:

- Matching instructional level and pace to the individual student's interests and learning needs
- Varying instructional levels for subject or topic areas across the curriculum (for example, the student participates in an English language arts curriculum below the level of classmates and in a mathematics curriculum above that of classmates)
- Using technology to help students progress at a personally appropriate pace (see Lovett and Lewandowski 2006 for source citations and further details)

When twice-exceptional students receive services appropriate to both their giftedness and their LD, they tend to be more motivated, to have high self-esteem, and to improve academic performance (see Gardynik and McDonald 2005).

THINK BACK TO THE CASE with the three students: Maria, Sy, and Burt . . .

In what ways could Sy's primary language impact the process of determining whether he has a learning disability?

Sy demonstrated slow development of a variety of normally expected reading skills. Sy's cultural adjustments and limited English instruction could certainly have been factors in his slow reading development. Focusing solely on those factors, however, could obscure attention to any cognitive difficulties he may be having. He seems also to have memory difficulties with language tasks. That could be a sign of an LD. Language differences can confound accurate assessment of students' language and cognitive abilities (Haager 2007), which likely explains why no clear decision was reached from Sy's evaluation.

Attention-Deficit/Hyperactivity Disorder

Like LD, attention-deficit/hyperactivity disorder (ADHD) is a cognitive disorder intrinsic to the individual. It includes difficulty regulating one's own behavior, in such ways as giving or sustaining attention, and/or controlling movements, which appears as inattention, impulsivity, or hyperactivity. Individuals with ADHD vary in terms of how they are affected.

There are four subtypes of ADHD, three of them well established: (a) predominately inattentive, (b) predominately hyperactive-impulsive, and (c) combined inattentive and hyperactive-impulsive. Note the use of the word "predominately": this is to acknowledge that persons who have either of those subtypes demonstrate some behaviors of the other subtype, but not enough (six or more for children and adolescents, five or more for adults) to satisfy the criteria for "combined." Since 2013 a new subtype has been recognized: ADHD-inattentive (restrictive), which means an individual demonstrates inattention but has had fewer than two examples of hyperactivity within the past six months (American Psychiatric Association [APA] 2013). According to the most commonly accepted definition, ADHD in all of its subtypes (a) critically impacts functioning, (b) occurs in two or more settings for a period of six months or longer, and (c) has its onset before the age of 12 (APA 2013).

A common misconception is that students with ADHD cannot receive services under the IDEA. The IDEA states that students with ADHD are entitled to services under the "other health impairment" (OHI) disability category (see Sec. 300.8 (c)(9)(i), 46757). The definition for this category includes the criterion "chronic or acute" problems with functioning. Historically, that standard has caused confusion as to when students with ADHD satisfy the eligibility criteria, because judging the level of inattention or hyperactivity-impulsivity as chronic or acute is subjective (see the "Differing Perspectives on Disability" box); in fact, all students engage some of these behaviors some of the time (Hallahan et al. 2005). In response to the misconception, the U.S. Department of Education clarified that students with ADHD can be eligible for IDEA services for the condition "ADD/ADHD," when categorized within OHI or when coexisting with another eligible disability (Davila, Williams, and MacDonald 1991; Wodrich 2000). Both LD and emotional/behavioral disorders are sometimes comorbid with ADHD. Because students with ADHD are counted under different disability labels, just what percentage of the population is served can only be estimated. An estimated 3 to 7 percent of the school-age population may have ADHD (Barkley 2006). (According to parent reports of diagnosis, 11 percent of children between the ages of four and 17 had ever received a diagnosis of ADHD in 2011 [Visser et al. 2014].) Yet the National Institute of Mental Health (2006) reports that perhaps less than half of children and adolescents with ADHD meet the criteria for the IDEA. Many students with ADHD receive services under another law, Section 504 of the Rehabilitation Act (1973), because it relies on a more general definition of "disability" than the IDEA does, interfering with a major life function.

Differing Perspectives on Disability

When nationwide special education was passed into law in 1975, Congress noted that approximately six million American schoolchildren were denied an appropriate education because they had a disability. That was considered discriminatory treatment, and special education was the response. Today there are many different perspectives on disability and special education, particularly when it comes to the HI disabilities.

Each of the HI disabilities is identified in a subjective process; that is, the opinions of parents, educators, and other professionals play significant roles instead of relying on presumed scientifically objective measures (for instance, analyzing brain scans). Some criticize that subjectivity and note its relationship to the over-representation of students of color, low-income students, and English learners among other "minoritized" groups (for example, Costa-Guerra and Costa-Guerra 2016; Harry and Klingner 2006). There are also suggestions that the overall special education process is unfair to those same groups (Ford 2012; Kalyanpur, Harry, and Skrtic 2000; Skiba et al. 2008). However, there is some question of whether the disproportionate representation is instead a reflection of systemic racism and classism that extends far beyond schooling (for example, Morgan, Farkas, Hillemeier, and Maczuga 2016) and whether there might actually be under-representation (Morgan et al. 2005). Other scholars have questioned whether the subjective identification processes arbitrarily distinguish who is and is not entitled to individualized support (Siegel 2012; Stanovich 2005). An underlying question in this debate is whether disabilities and special education are either a negative or a privilege, neither of which was Congress' stated intention in passing the IDEA into law.

The prefix "dis" is considered by some to represent lowered expectations and a "blaming" of the student for her or his academic or social difficulties. The difficulties may be real, having been induced by the process of labeling the student, they would argue, or may be a false perception by those doing the labeling (Gallagher 2010). Christensen (1999), for example, points to terminology such as "special educator," "learning center," and "remediation" as evidence of a "medical model" orientation that presumes the student is "sick" and needs to be treated (Poplin 1988). The remedial education practices and curricular and physical segregation historically favored in special education are criticized as preventing students from advancing in meaningful and engaging learning (Poplin 1988). Some critics suggest that special education exists to excuse schools for failing to serve some of the population; that is, by labeling the student as "special ed" the school can be exonerated for her or his underachievement on the grounds that the student has a disability and more cannot be expected (Skrtic 2005). In response, some encourage a reframing of special education, signaled by positively worded terms such as "learning differences," "exceptional education," and "disABILITY," although even these are open to criticism for not fully renouncing the "evils" of special education as well as for using euphemisms that deny special education is different and is what some students with disabilities need (Kauffman 2002).

continued

There is also another perspective. Counter-critics argue that the intention of hold-ing the same high expectations for all learners and claims that special education is the cause of students' challenges instead of a best response to them negate the reality that some students really do have disabilities that impede their learning (for example, Kauffman 2002; Kavale and Forness 2000). It may be that critics of special educa-tion have discomfort acknowledging that some students have cognitive impairments (rarely, if ever, inabilities), whereas there is no contesting the legitimacy and impact of sensory, physical, and health impairments, for example. Hehir (2007) warns well-intentioned critics of disability and special education not to go so far that they en-gage in "ableism," which is denying human differences and pretending that everyone is equally capable if only they would be set free of the supports and services provided based on a disability. That may be the opposite of the original intention for special education and may not actually empower students identified as having disabilities. Persons with autism and their advocates make reference to "neurodiversity" to remind "neurotypicals" (those without any cognitive disability) that the spectrum of cognitive profiles extends across all humans and that they too are different and not necessarily superior or "normal" (Fenton and Krahn 2007).

What ADHD "Looks Like" and How It Is Experienced. Being easily distracted, day-dreaming during class, feeling the urge to fidget or get up and walk around, and doing so without even realizing the urge are some examples of behaviors that reflect ADHD. While the same behaviors can also be observed in "typically developing" students, in the case of ADHD the behaviors interfere with performance and the individual has difficulty regulating them. As children and adolescents grow older their ADHD profile can change. For example, by later adolescence some with ADHD-combined become less hyperactive and become identified as having ADHD-predominately inattentive (Ramsay 2010; Weyandt 2009). Table 1.2 gives examples of common behaviors of stu-dents with ADHD at different age levels. Also, while males are far more likely to be identified as having ADHD, it is a myth that ADHD is "less severe" in females (Elkins, Malone, Keyes, Iacono, and McGue 2011; Mahone and Wadka 2008).

TABLE 1.2 Sample Characteristics of Students with ADHD at Different Age Levels

Preschool		
Accidents due to acting independently Noncompliance	Resists routines Aggressive in play	Excessive talking Easily upset
Elementary/Middle School		
Fidgeting Out of seat	Interrupting Inconsistent productivity	Dependent on adults Poor social skills
Middle/Senior High		
Restless Substance use	Low self-concept Procrastination	Impulsive Difficulty following directions

Reprinted with data from M. Fowler, *C.H.A.D.D. Manual.* (Fairfax, VA: CASET Association, 1992), and S. E. Shaywitz and B. A. Shaywitz, "Attention Deficit Disorder: Current Perspectives," in *Learning Disabilities,* ed. J. F. Kavanagh and T. J. Truss (Parkton, MD: York, 1988, 369–523).

For some with the hyperactive-impulsive or combined subtype, their hyperactivity is unmistakable. They cannot seem to sit still—or to sit at all in some cases. They are restless, shift in their seats, get up a lot, and are impulsively quick to act in settings as varied as the playing field and the chemistry lab. For others, hyperactivity is more subtle, or at least not always that pronounced; these students are likely to fidget a lot. Either way, these students benefit from frequent breaks during which they are allowed to move and exert themselves (Hoza et al. 2004; also see Mulrine, Prater, and Jenkins 2008).

The distractibility and inattentiveness associated with the ADHD-inattentive sub-type can be more difficult to notice than hyperactivity. Distracted and inattentive students chronically attend to what others are doing, routinely get off task by focusing on something else, or instantaneously stop paying attention, even in the middle of one-on-one conversations, but in ways that may not be readily noticeable to others. They are the students who have difficulty focusing their attention in the first place, seem never to get started with a task, or do not pay attention to details. Research from the 1990s found that those with inattention tend to achieve at lower levels than those with impulsivity (for instance, Fergusson, Horwood, and Lynskey 1993), which may be because they were not noticed and redirected. Also, females with the inattentive subtype have been found to achieve at the lowest levels (Elkins et al. 2011). For both hyperactivity-impulsivity and inattention, redirecting students to task and providing summaries of what they may have "missed" in such simple ways as repeating information, writing it down, or conducting quick reviews for the benefit of all in the class can be helpful.

Cognitive Processing Difficulties. The unique cognitive processes of students with ADHD have been characterized as problems with *inhibition* (Barkley 2000). Typical, nondisabled students do not act on their impulses; rather, they control them—their self-regulation prevents them from acting on their thoughts. The uninhibited (or *impulsive*) cognitive processing characteristic of those with ADHD is believed to be a form of limited executive function (Gualtieri and Johnson 2006). Different from the limited executive function in those with LD, those with ADHD may have the appropriate cognitive behaviors within their repertoire, but they merely are not selected.

Barkley (2000) has suggested that people with ADHD are uninhibited specifically in the areas of *time awareness* and *time management*. He suggests that they do not consider the relation of time to themselves; instead, they act spontaneously rather than delaying or regulating their actions. Moreover, they do not organize tasks based upon priority and do not take into account the proportion of time or effort necessary to complete a task efficiently. In addition, individuals with ADHD may have difficulties with working memory (Barkley 2000). They may not retain and attend to information in working memory, or they fail to attend to salient information, which results in poor comprehension. Students with ADHD can be taught to self-regulate (Reid and Johnson 2011), which involves learning to monitor their ADHD behaviors and finding ways to manage them, such as squeezing a fidget object while paying attention to class.

Academic Skill Difficulties. The cognitive processing profiles of students with ADHD serve as an explanation for their ADHD behaviors; the learning difficulties associated with ADHD are, in effect, secondary consequences. It is the consequence of being distracted or inattentive that results in students missing important information or producing poor-quality work (LeFever et al. 2002; Salend and Rohena 2003). For example, students with ADHD tend to produce poorer-quality written products because they do not sufficiently plan and self-regulate across the three stages of writing: planning, composing, and revising (Casas, Ferrer and Fortea 2013). Academically, students with ADHD do not achieve at commensurate levels with their peers (Frazier, Youngstrom, Glutting, and Watkins 2007; Stubbe 2000) because they do not fully learn information. They often rush through assignments and do not check their work. When confronted with the consequences of being off-task or doing low-quality work, these students will often respond in a panic mode, attempting to redo and catch up on their work, resulting again in a low quality or quantity of work (see Sibley, Altszuler, Morrow, and Merrill 2014).

As the students age there is a compounding effect: they get farther behind because of what they have missed in the lower grades (Massetti et al. 2008). Overall, those with inattention get fewer interventions in the classroom than those with hyperactivity-impulsivity, perhaps because they are more easily overlooked. It may be for this same reason that females with the inattentive subtype have some of the lowest academic (for instance, grade point average) and cognitive (IQ) levels of those with ADHD, and also uniquely low academic motivation (Elkins et al. 2011). Effective intervention responses address both regulating behavior patterns and remediating academic content and skills.

Social Skills Difficulties. Socially, the status of students with ADHD depends on how the condition manifests itself. The students' distractibility behaviors may be barely noticed by their peers, or at least not be of concern to them. However, females with the inattentive subtype experience less social acceptance than males or students with any of the other subtypes; they also experience loneliness and bullying at higher rates (Elkins et al. 2011). This suggests that inattention, for females and males, is noticed at least indirectly. Students with hyperactive-impulsive behavior are more likely to be noticed. They might garner a reputation for being the class clown if their off-task and out-of-seat behaviors constantly cause them to be viewed as "goofy," or they might get a reputation as class rebel if they come across to their peers as defying the teacher's attempts to have them participate in activities. Peers are more likely to resent students with ADHD if the students' behaviors bring negative consequences to the peers (Mikami, Jack, and Lerner 2009; Olmeda, Thomas, and Davis 2003); in the case of hyperactivity-impulsivity, other students in the class may be distracted from their own work, penalized due to the student not fulfilling expected contributions to a group task, or offended or even harmed by the student's actions. Just as with academic skills, students with ADHD can learn to self-regulate their behaviors in social contexts (DuPaul, Arbolino, and Booster 2009) and also benefit from structured social situations that are responsive to their behaviors (Pfiffner, Barkley, and DuPaul 2006).

ADHD and Medication. An estimated 6.1 percent of children aged four to 17 with ADHD took medication for it in 2011 (Visser, Blumberg, Danielson, Bitsko, and Kogan 2013). These medications may be in the form of a stimulant, a nonstimulant, or in some cases an antidepressant. Students must take them at properly prescribed intervals. This may mean that a school nurse has to be available to supervise drug taking during school, and at home parents must follow the schedule. Some students use weekends and summer as "medication vacations," not taking their medications because of side effects. In a review of research on "adverse events" Cortese et al. (2013) found research does support that ADHD medications can cause appetite suppression, height and weight growth suppression (which attenuates over time for those taking the medications for multiple years), and slight increases in blood pressure and heart rate. The evidence is unclear but medication usage may be associated with difficulty falling asleep or insomnia as well. Their review found no conclusive support for an association between medication usage and tics, seizures, suicidality, or psychotic symptoms.

Prescription medications for ADHD typically have their desired effect, which is to reduce inattention (note this is not literally the same thing as increasing attention) or hyperactivity (Spencer, Biederman, and Wilens 2010). The medications suppress but may not completely remove the ADHD "behaviors," and they will not result in improved academic or social engagement or achievement unless the student is also taught positive skills. Hence, with the exception of students with the most "severe" cases of ADHD who need the medications to regulate themselves, others should use the medications to reduce the behaviors to manageable levels while they learn skills of self-regulation (Fabiano et al. 2007). Otherwise, medication only helps to reduce the impact of the student's ADHD on others without building any strengths in the student.

Autism

An autism spectrum disorder (ASD) is a "persistent impairment in reciprocal social communication and social interaction, and restricted, repetitive patterns of behavior, interests or activities" (APA 2013). As the term "spectrum" connotes, persons with autism exhibit a range of functioning levels across these areas. Some are virtually nonverbal, may rock or flap their hands excessively, and may not perform the most basic of daily functions independently. Also, some with autism have below-average IQ. However, as it is a spectrum, others appear and function so much like typically developing individuals that their autism may not be immediately noticeable.

After being identified as having autism, the person is next classified based on her or his severity level, which represents how much support she or he will need to function independently. These severity levels are requiring support, requiring substantial support, or requiring very substantial support (APA 2013; see Aljunied and Frederickson 2011). Those with autism at the "requiring support" level may be considered as having an HI disability (note that this is our suggestion, as there is no hard-and-fast rule as to how to distinguish the levels of autism as high versus low incidence).

There is also a relatively new autism designation, social (pragmatic) communication disorder (SCD) (APA 2013). It applies to those who have difficulties with social language and communication skills but none of the other features of autism (or only rarely).

Some students on the autism spectrum might be known by a different label. The classification system for ASD was updated in 2013. Anyone who had an ASD diagnosis prior to the switch is allowed to keep using the original label at her or his (or the parents') discretion. Previously, the spectrum included (in order, from the least "severe") Asperger syndrome, autism, pervasive developmental delay not otherwise specified (PDD-NOS), Rett syndrome, and disintegrative disorder. (Some chose to recognize high-functioning autism after Asperger; however, that was never an official label and some research indicates it is indistinguishable from Asperger [Prior 2003]). Those who would have been labeled as having Asperger syndrome under the old system now are most often considered to have autism requiring support (Foley-Nicpon, Fosenburg, Wurster, and Assouline 2017; also see Kulage, Smaldone, and Cohn 2013). Some may be recognized as having SCD; however, as SCD is a newer conception and the assessment tools most commonly used to identify ASD may not be sensitive to it (Foley-Nicpon, Fosenburg, Wurster, and Assouline 2017), this designation may not be widely used.

What Autism Requiring Support "Looks Like" and How It Is Experienced. Students with autism requiring support do not exactly match many of the stereotypes of autism. They often have strong vocabularies and tend to be verbose. In fact, they may talk at length, usually about topics that interest them. Also, repetitive gestures such as hand flapping are usually minimal, if they occur at all. Students with autism requiring support are likely to thrive on sameness and routines; in fact, they can become very disoriented and upset when routines as simple as the order of events for beginning class are altered. Some also have special interest areas. They may come close to obsessing on these topics (such as trains or how a lightbulb works), they spend significant amounts of time studying them, and they steer the conversation to them whenever they can.

Those with autism requiring support have difficulty interpreting idioms, sarcasm, and implied information. They can be very literal; Shore (2003), an adult with Asperger, describes how for years he could not understand how his friend could "feel like a pizza." They also tend to be very logical or rule-bound without considering sentiment, emotions, or exceptions to rules. For this reason, they may take perspectives and express themselves in ways perceived as rude or uncaring. This can lead to their being socially isolated. As you will read later, many are lonely.

Finally, very few persons with autism at any support level have exceptional talents, such as the ability to memorize everything they hear, to play a musical instrument flawlessly the first time they try, or hyperlexia (the ability to read words without formal reading instruction).

Academic Skill Difficulties. Even though students with autism requiring support typically have strong vocabulary and grammar skills, they have several problems with language. For example, they tend to read dysfluently and to have difficulties with reading comprehension, particularly when critical thinking and verbal reasoning are involved (Huemer and Mann 2010; Schaefer Whitby and Mancil 2009; Smith Myles et al. 2002). They also tend to have challenges with writing, particularly organizing information and taking into consideration what their audience needs to be told. They may not vary their sentence structure and vocabulary, and they commonly have graphomotor difficulties, likely due to poor coordination of their motor skills (Schaefer Whitby and Mancil 2009). In mathematics, skill difficulties are typically seen in problem solving; basic mathematics comprehension is a comparative strength, yet arithmetic skills and the abstract and logical thinking needed for problem solving tend to be poor (Schaefer Whitby and Mancil 2009). In all of these academic skill areas—speaking, reading, writing, mathematics—students with autism requiring support benefit from procedural facilitators and graphic organizers that help them to structure and vary their communications. They also can learn "rules" for skills for positive social interactions (Koegel 2007).

As this information indicates, students with autism requiring support tend to achieve at below-average levels. This contrasts with the erroneous stereotype that they are "little geniuses."

Cognitive Processing Difficulties. Those with autism requiring support tend to be "concrete" thinkers who are challenged to think abstractly. In addition, they have slow processing speeds (Holdnack et al. 2011), which means they will need guiding prompts and longer amounts of time than their peers to respond to questions and directions. Also, they are more likely to engage in a task when it interests them or when they understand its relevance (for example, "We have to write observation notes so that later we can consult a record of what we have observed over time").

Some research indicates that persons with Asperger[2] have weak working memory skills (Holdnack, Goldstein, and Drozdick 2011). However, their memory challenges are greatly reduced when they are cued to think about the source of the memory (Bowler, Gardiner, and Berthollier 2004) (for example, instead of asking, "What causes acid rain?" ask, "What mixes with water and oxygen in the upper atmosphere to cause acid rain?"). This may indicate that challenges with abstract and inferential thinking are at the root of their memory difficulties (Bowler et al. 2004).

---

[2] You will find several references to Asperger syndrome in this chapter because the cited resources report on persons who were identified with that label.

Students with all ASDs find it challenging to think about themselves; this interferes with tasks such as describing themselves or explaining what they are like. This is due to weak autobiographical memory (Tanweer, Rathbone, and Souchay 2010). Consequently, they find it easier to describe their traits than their identities, which is a more abstract concept.

Perhaps the most obvious indicator of autism requiring support and SCD is social communication and interaction impairments. There are at least three related reasons for this. First, these students find it difficult to read facial expressions, including eye gaze (in part because they typically avoid eye contact), gestures and body postures, and voice gestures (tone and inflection). Second, they are considered to have weak *theory-of-mind* skills (Aljunied and Frederickson 2011; Flood, Hare, and Wallis 2011; c.f. Froese, Stanghellini, and Bertelli 2013), which means they find it difficult to consider another person's perspective. For this reason they may not gauge someone else's interest in their special interest area nor consider what information a communication partner needs, or they may be so blunt that they are considered rude and insulting. Third, some theorize that they also have weak *central coherence*, which means they have the various cognitive skills to perform academic and social tasks proficiently but lack the executive function to coordinate and regulate those multiple skills (Le Sourn-Bissaoui, Caillies, Gierski, and Motte 2011). Teaching these specific cognitive skills can be effective but, they are unlikely to change the profile of the student with autism requiring support or SCD. Historically, those with ASD at all levels have been taught in very behavioral ways, especially using approaches based in *applied behavior analysis* (ABA). However, the result for those with autism requiring support has most often been limited to their learning some skills in isolation (Ryan, Hughes, Katsiyannis, McDaniel, and Sprinkle 2011).

Social Skills Difficulties. As you are now aware, social skills are a significant area of difficulty for those with autism requiring support. They tend to speak in monotones and to be repetitive, and they may fail to observe conventions such as taking turns (Shriberg et al. 2001). Their considerable challenges with making eye contact and understanding pragmatics can be further challenges when participating in social interactions. For these reasons they are sometimes more comfortable interacting with adults than with same-age peers. They also do better with someone who has shared interests.

It is important to know that at all age levels persons with autism requiring support desire socialization (Causton-Theoharis, Ashby, and Cosier 2009). While their cognitive and social skills deficits make it appear as though they are unwilling to put effort into appropriate interactions, that is not the case; rather, they have weak social perception skills (Holdnack et al. 2011) and find it challenging to interact. Further, they often feel social anxiety (Kuusikko et al. 2008). Effective interventions may teach them critical skills (for example, Koegel and Koegle 2006). Limited research evidence also supports analyzing common social scenarios and appropriate interactions, such as social stories (Ryan et al. 2011; Sansosti and Powell-Smith 2006; also see Hanley-Hochdorfer, Bray, Kehle, and Elinoff 2010) and self-modeling (Bernad-Ripoll 2007). Importantly, however, it may not be possible or ethical to "change" people with ASD. Instead, they might be taught how to think positively about themselves and to target personally feasible social goals and interactions (Bottema-Beutel, Mullins, Harvey, Gustafson, and Carter 2016).

Mild Intellectual Disability

Those not familiar with the subtypes of intellectual disability (ID) might be surprised that it can be included as an HI disability. The subtypes constitute a range of intellectual disability, divided into four levels of functioning (mild: IQ 50–55 to approximately 70; moderate: IQ 35–40 to 50–55; severe: IQ 20–25 to 35–40; and profound: IQ below

20–25). The DSM-5 (APA 2013) states that the distinctions among the four levels relate to IQ and adaptive functioning; however, in practice, the labels are typically assigned based on IQ alone. (See APA 2013 for an alternative labeling system based on levels of support needed, similar to autism, that has not been adopted in special education in the United States.) Mild intellectual disability is the highest-functioning level; it is the only one of the four considered "mild" or an HI.

A person with mild ID has overall cognitive functioning that is impaired to a degree that significantly limits age-appropriate functioning (note that "significantly" differs from "severely"). Cognitive functioning encompasses abilities such as memory, reasoning, comprehension, and abstract thinking; age-appropriate functioning refers to the range of skills involved in tasks of daily living, including participating in school.

People with ID have limitations in multiple areas of cognitive functioning. Unlike those with LD (who need support in using their cognitive skills efficiently) or those with ADHD (who are impulsively distracted from employing appropriate skills), those with mild ID are thought to have limited aptitude in terms of cognitive skills. Especially in the mild subtype of ID, the notion of limited capacity does not mean an absolute limit to what an individual is capable of learning, however. Those with ID at all levels are always capable of learning new things, but they typically learn slowly and in very concrete ways, needing constant review and support to apply their knowledge (Miller, Hall, and Heward 1995).

The label *mild* is the hardest part of mild ID to define. Those with mild ID typically function well in the general education environment and can be semi-independent in daily living. Conversely, those with profound ID perform cognitively at very low levels, including in their ability to learn, and hence need almost constant support. The difficulty in defining "mild" is in operationally defining it.

What Mild ID "Looks Like" and How It Is Experienced. Because mild ID is a cognitive disorder, physical indicators or characteristics may not always accompany it (for example, those with Down syndrome often exhibit physical characteristics such as an almond shape to the eyes, shorter limbs and digits, and protruding tongue). Indeed, students with mild ID can have such proficient social skills and independent living skills that one may not realize that they have ID.

Academically, beginning in elementary school, students with mild ID will likely be behind others in the class by roughly two or more years in skill levels such as reading or math. However, even though ID is a pervasive cognitive disorder, they will have comparative strengths and weaknesses just like any other learner and may function on grade level in some areas. In addition to academic skills, students with mild ID may also be delayed in social, emotional, and independent functioning skills. The reason for the delays is that students with mild ID learn new skills and concepts at a much slower rate than their classmates do, both academic and social skills, particularly as the complexity of the skills or concepts increases. Thus, the older the students, the further behind they will be. Students with mild ID also tend to forget skills and concepts that are not routinely reinforced by drill and practice.

Cognitive Processing Difficulties. Students with mild ID have difficulties gaining and sustaining attention, but in a different manner than the attention difficulties of students with ADHD. Because students with mild ID do not discern where to focus their attention, they may observe a procedure (for example, for an arithmetic calculation) but not identify the critical actions of each step or the order in which to perform the steps. As part of the difficulty with regulating their attention, they may shift their attention to extraneous information either because they found it interesting or could not distinguish it as unimportant information. It appears that students with mild ID do not have the executive function to remain focused on critical content.

Students with mild ID also have difficulties with the three stages of memory: short term, working, and long term. Short-term memory is particularly difficult for them (Schuchardt, Geghart, and Maehler 2010; Van der Molen, Van Luit, Van der Molen, and Maurits 2010). As a consequence of not attending to details and recognizing relationships that help give new information significance, they tend not to grasp information well. Although students with mild ID are prone to forgetting information stored in long-term memory, especially when it is not regularly rehearsed, their long-term memory capacity tends not to be as limited as their short-term capacity (Bray, Fletcher, and Turner 1997).

Academic Skills Difficulties. Due to their lack of attention to salient details and their poor comprehension, those with mild ID typically require more exposure to content and more practice opportunities to comprehend and recall information accurately (Miller, Hall, and Heward 1995). Actual processing time can be slower as well. Thus, they will require a longer time to think about an appropriate response or to recall a needed skill, as well as guidance with the processes of thinking through and completing a task in many cases.

Typically, students with mild ID need to learn new tasks in concrete ways. Tasks that require abstract reasoning, drawing complex relationships, or constructing inferences can be challenging for them. Thus, they learn "lower-level" skills more efficiently. In reading, they will be more successful with skills of word calling and reading "comfort-level" passages that do not include complex concepts than with more abstract skills such as passage comprehension beyond the recall level. In math, they will perform simple operations with greater success than problem-solving activities.

Generalization (also referred to as transfer) is also a challenge for those with mild ID. This means the ability to apply knowledge or skills to tasks similar to or different from those with which the skill was learned. Whereas other learners may learn a skill and after some practice then readily apply it (for example, generalizing arithmetic facts to word problems), students with mild ID may need to learn the skill in context so that little transfer of learning is involved (for example, after learning addition, having to learn how to use it in solving word problems).

Social Skills Difficulties. As we noted, along with cognitive and academic skills difficulties, students with mild ID can experience social skills difficulties. Some children and adolescents with mild ID report dissatisfaction with the quality of friendships they have, and adults similarly perceive them as having fewer and poorer friendships (Hughes et al. 1999; Siperstein, Leffert, and Wenz-Gross 1997). In other words, their friendships tend to lack intimate sharing and spontaneous interactions (Siperstein, Leffert, and Wenz-Gross 1997). Additionally, young adults with mild ID more commonly report negative and even aggressive encounters with persons outside of their peer group and strangers (Larkin, MacMahon, and Pert 2012). Some of their social challenges are due to how they are perceived and valued by others, but their social difficulties are also due in part to their concrete ways of thinking, which extend to their limited capacity to take into account the interests of others and to express themselves fully. Also, those with mild ID do not always present themselves in socially appealing ways—for example, coming across as stubborn or aggressive when they are frustrated with a task or social option (Cook and Semmell 1999). In addition, as they progress into the adolescent years, the social gap widens and their friendships tend to decline (Hughes et al. 1999).

Unfortunately, some peers may not wish to associate with students with mild ID for fear it will cause them to be socially ostracized. In other cases, students without disabilities will befriend those with mild ID, not so much out of personal bonding but because they wish to do a good deed. Although true friendships can flower from such arrangements (for example, the Best Buddies program [www.bestbuddies.org]), it can be the basis for an unequal relationship where the "friend" with mild ID is treated differently than a nondisabled friend. In the case of academics, classmates may not welcome working on group projects with classmates with mild ID for fear they will prevent the group from earning a good grade. Although they may have fewer friends and more strained friendships than others, those with mild ID also do have genuine friendships with peers who care about them just as they would any other friend (Siperstein, Glick, and Parker 2009). Also, despite potential obstacles to including students with mild ID in general education classrooms, their presence has increased over the years and has resulted in positive academic and social outcomes for all students (U.S. Department of Education 2015; Williamson et al. 2006).

Emotional/Behavioral Disorders

Emotional and behavioral disorders (EBD) can be thought of as distinct from one another. One concerns emotions in the forms of feelings, moods, and mental states such as hallucinating, whereas the other relates to actions a person makes. In a practical sense, however, both aspects are often present in a person with EBD. Those with EBD may have emotional disorders that manifest as challenging behaviors, for example. Therefore, an appropriate response would address the emotional needs as well as the behavioral needs.

There has been considerable professional disagreement as to the nature of this disorder. The disagreements are highlighted by the differences of opinion about what to call it. The IDEA names this disability "emotional disturbance." Although the term *disturbance* has also been criticized as pejorative and unlike the labels used for any other disability category (Kauffman and Landrum 2009b) it has not been changed in the IDEA. Also, many professionals argue that the term "behavioral" needs to be included in the label to ensure that students with primarily behavioral challenges are included in research on this disability and in receiving the rights and services associated with it. Observing that the disability may have something to do with a predominately emotional disorder, a predominately behavioral disorder, or a combined condition, the Council for Children with Behavior Disorders—a division of the special education professional organization the Council for Exceptional Children (CEC)—instead refers to the condition as *emotional/behavioral disorders*. The slash signals that the disorder is rarely only emotional or behavioral. The acronym EBD is fairly commonly used among school-based professionals.

Despite the controversy about which specific label to use, most professionals broadly recognize that students with EBD have similar characteristics. They have chronic difficulties in one or more areas involving socialization with others, unusual behaviors or emotions under normal circumstances, a general mood of unhappiness or depression, and physical or emotional reactions such as fearful responses to school or personal problems. These chronic problems adversely affect the student's educational performance and social interactions as well as put them at risk for harm, and are often not easily treated.

What EBD "Looks Like" and How It Is Experienced. Some of the indicators of EBD are far more obvious than others. The distinction, however, is not based on emotional versus behavioral type. The different types of EBD are traditionally separated into those that are primarily **externalized** (overt outward performances) or **internalized** (withdrawing and acting toward the self, including by self-neglect) (Lambros et al. 1998). Table 1.3 lists common externalized and internalized behaviors.

TABLE 1.3 Common Externalized and Internalized Behaviors of Students with EBD

Externalized Behaviors	Internalized Behaviors
Violent outbursts	Isolated play
Angry reactions	Frequent claims of being ill
Emotional mood swings	Depression
Physical or aggressive actions	Cutting or mutilation of self
Tantrums	Extreme shyness
Destructiveness	Disregard by peers
Disrespect and noncompliance	Anorexia
Sexual promiscuity	Panic attacks

Students with EBD display signs of emotional difficulties that are sometimes easily overlooked. Students with eating disorders, depression, or anxiety and those who are delusional may be skilled at hiding it from others. However, upon careful observation or by communicating with the student, you might discover that the student is not eating properly (eating disorders such as bulimia nervosa), is obsessively counting steps (obsessive–compulsive disorder), or is harboring harmful thoughts (such as suicidal ideation, a form of psychotic disorder).

As you might suspect, behavioral manifestations of EBD tend to be more readily observable. They might be in the form of major mood swings (bipolar or manic-depressive disorder, which is both emotional and behavioral), acts of aggression (bullying, rage, or explosive temper), or inappropriate expressions of sexuality.

Cognitive Processing Difficulties. Students with EBD have cognitive processing difficulties that interfere with their academic functioning. They may become so depressed, obsessed about their own body image, or filled with deep rage that they cannot focus on academic tasks. Although some students with EBD miss a large amount of school (Bauer and Shea 1999; Hodge, Riccomini, Buford, and Herbst 2006), many miss out on schooling because they do not fully attend cognitively due to their emotional or behavioral problems. Many of these students develop gaps in skills, such as performing well in reading but not math, or knowing well some content studied in history but having no understanding of other content. Students with EBD do not have limited ability to perform the cognitive skills needed for learning; rather, they have difficulty *regulating* their cognitive skill performance. They have difficulty attending, perceiving information correctly, and making logical deductions and decisions. As a result, they often score below average on tests of intelligence and achievement (Coleman and Webber 2002; Kauffman and Landrum 2009). Kauffman and Landrum (2009) report that students with EBD tend to have IQs in the low-average range, although as a "population" they have IQs ranging from very low to very high.

Academic Skills Difficulties. One indicator of an EBD is poor academic performance due to gaps in knowledge and skills (Gresham, Lane, et al. 1999). Regardless of whether they exhibit internalizing or externalizing behaviors, students with EBD miss out on instruction and skills practice because of their condition. Some with EBD are removed from the classroom because they are disruptive to other students, for their own personal safety or the safety of others, or because they need privacy to deal with their emotions or need to receive additional support or related services. Of all the students with HI, those with EBD are the most likely to be removed from the general education classroom or building because of their disability (U.S. Department of Education 2016).

However, some of the specific disabilities that fall within the EBD category include limited comprehension or memory skills. Effective instructional responses include reviewing missed information and skills practice. Some students with EBD learn better when instruction is explicit, as it might be for those with LD or ADHD for example. However, it is particularly important that instructional approaches are comprehensive for these students. In other words, they must address both the academics and emotional and behavioral characteristics, which includes controlling problematic thoughts and behaviors (Kaufman and Landrum 2009; Lane and Menzies 2010). Effective academic, cognitive, and behavioral interventions include consistent practice of skills (Walker and Sprague 2007).

Social Skills Difficulties. Students with EBD tend to be unpopular (Kauffman 1997; Panacek and Dunlap 2003) among peers regardless of whether they have internalizing or externalizing behaviors. On the one hand, those with primarily internalized behaviors might more accurately be described as *unnoticed*. For example, it may take a long time before others notice that a student with an eating disorder has a problem. Students who are depressed can be thought of as only shy, unless their shyness turns into chronic and acute withdrawal from others. Withdrawn behavior can easily be overlooked in the busy milieu of a school. On the other hand, because of the mood swings and atypical behaviors of some students with EBD, classmates may find them "odd" and not wish to interact with them; unfortunately, teachers may also avoid interacting with them (Feldman et al. 1983). Just as with academic skills, students with EBD learn effective socialization when they receive consistent instruction and practice in skills as part of a comprehensive approach that addresses their emotional and/or behavioral needs as well (for example, positive behavior supports interventions, cognitive-behavioral therapy).

THINK BACK TO THE CASE   with the three students: Maria, Sy, and Burt . . .

In what ways could Maria's ethnic culture impact the process of determining whether she has an emotional disturbance?

Cultural behaviors that differ from the school's majority population, as well as assumptions about cultures, can confuse evaluations. Just as Emily presumed there was a cultural (and possibly gender) basis for Maria's different behaviors, another educator could assume a student demonstrates inappropriate behaviors by failing to take cultural norms into consideration. Evaluators should use a variety of measures before making assumptions about disabilities, and actively take cultural (and linguistic) differences into consideration. If they lack cultural knowledge themselves, they can consult colleagues and the student's family for insights; this is something the school administration should be prepared to help them with as well. In Maria's case it would help if Emily and her colleagues knew that Latina and Native American students are sometimes reticent to assert themselves in school, even in such expected ways as answering questions, demonstrating their knowledge, or asking for help (Sparks 2000). However, they should be careful not to presume that cultural trait necessarily applies to Maria; instead, they should look for evidence that supports or refutes it. Webb-Johnson (2002) observed that culturally typical expressive behaviors of African-American students with EBD are often discouraged. As a consequence, the students either acted out more than they would in a culturally responsive environment or focused more on behavioral compliance than on academic engagement.

Students with EBD are often considered to be among the most challenging students to teach. Like all students with disabilities, they do challenge teachers who fear academic diversity and consider it beyond their capability or job description. However, when teachers collaborate with other educators, service providers, and parents and use the student's individualized education program (IEP) to guide them (see the next section of this chapter), they can be successful in including students with EBD in the general education classroom, as appropriate, and, in the process, help those students manage their disability.

Positive Behavior Supports

Many teachers have found themselves in the situation of having a student challenge their authority. The situation can quickly become a power struggle between the teacher and student, and regardless of who "wins" that one struggle, a negative relationship develops and both "sides" may be determined to fight harder to win the next time. This kind of relationship is common for students with HI who pose attentional or behavioral challenges in schools. Even in those situations where there is more tolerance for the student's behavior, it is unproductive for these routines to simply continue occurring (tolerance is not a special education goal). Of course, attention and behavioral challenges that some students with HI present in an inclusion classroom interfere with their own and classmates' learning and with the teacher's ability to teach (Lane, Menzies, Bruhn, and Crnobori 2010).

The U.S. Department of Education Office of Special Education and Rehabilitation Services encourages the use of positive behavior supports in special education and inclusion (Hehir 2009). *Positive behavior support* (PBS) (also sometimes referred to as positive behavior intervention and supports [PBIS]) is an approach to both prevent and replace undesired behaviors (Dunlap, Kincaid, Horner, Knoster, and Bradshaw 2014; Sugai and Horner 2002). Instead of reacting to students' problematic behaviors, PBS is used to instruct students in positive behaviors and encourage their use (Menzies and Lane 2011). It is proactive and preventive. Students are rewarded for what they do right instead of punished for what they do wrong.

Using PBS, educators observe for trends in a student's persistent undesirable behavior. They make note of the antecedent, or the event that triggers the behavior (for example, a student creates disruptions in the classroom when individual seatwork lasts more than 20 minutes). Then they develop a plan to either remove the antecedent (shorten the amount of time for individual seatwork assignments) or teach the student an alternative behavior that competes with the undesired behavior (taking a break after every 15 minutes of continuous work). The process can be managed fully by the educators but can be more effective when it involves the student in learning to self-regulate her or his own behaviors (as in our example) (Menzies and Lane 2011).

Conducting PBS properly involves conducting a *functional behavioral assessment* (identifying the behavior's antecedents as well as more desirable or competing behaviors) and then using that information to develop a *behavior intervention plan*. The IDEA requires that such a plan be developed and acted upon whenever (1) a student in special education has disability-related behaviors that impede her or his learning or put others at risk, (2) the student is suspended for a total of more than 10 days, or (3) another serious disciplinary action is taken, particularly if it includes a change in placement.

In this era of accountability in schools (for example, high-stakes assessments and the "challenging" curriculum standards for all learners associated with ESSA), schools

continued

are less tolerant of students who do not conform to traditional expectations. Certainly students who present attentional or behavioral challenges to school routines fall into that category. However, it is also true that students who do not reflect a school community's majority culture may be regarded critically. As Menzies and Lane (2011) explain, "teachers may view students as noncompliant or less socially competent when they interact in ways that reflect the student's home culture, but are not congruent with the school culture" (p. 181). Banks and Obiakor (2015) propose that educators adopt a culturally responsive PBS approach.

PBS can also be enacted schoolwide, with all teachers consistently applying the same practices across the school day (Lane, Kalberg, and Menzies 2009).

1-2   Meeting the Learning Needs of Students with HI

When someone asks what we do for a living and we say we are special education teachers, we commonly hear, "You must have a lot of patience." That is very telling of what people think about students with disabilities and what it takes to teach them. There might be some truth to it, but it misses by a mile what special education teaching is all about. Special educators do have some methods of teaching that are different from what general educators typically use, but for the most part we teach the same content and skills that general educators do. This is especially true in the case of students with HI, who are almost always included in general education for some or all of the school day.

Earlier in the chapter we explained each of the HI disabilities as a difference in how students process information during the stages of acquiring, constructing, and expressing knowledge, as well as differences in behaviors that impact learning. Special educators employ principles of effective practice that are based upon the processing and behavioral strengths and needs of students with HI. What is also different about special education students is that, more so than their general education peers, they exhibit gaps in skills and are less likely to benefit from the traditional teaching methods used in general education classrooms. Students with HI tend to have a limited range of learning strengths and, therefore, need to be instructed in specific ways if they are going to benefit fully from a lesson.

Researchers have identified the following practices as effective for students with HI, and their general education peers can also benefit from these practices. Therefore, both special *and* general educators can use these practices in pull-out or inclusive settings.

THINK BACK TO THE CASE   with the three students: Maria, Sy, and Burt . . .

Given the learning challenges that Maria, Sy, and Burt present, are there generally effective teaching practices Emily should use with them?

Yes. We have translated facts about the ways students with HI learn best into important **principles of effective instruction**. Even though the three students each have a different disability (a *potential* disability in Sy's case) and different learning challenges, these practices can be appropriate for each of them.

Clear and Explicit Instruction

To provide clear and explicit instruction, the teacher must be unambiguous and leave no doubt as to what he or she is communicating to students (Good and Brophy 2003). Some students with HI have poor attention and are easily distracted. They may not pick up on essential details during instruction. Even more commonly, students with HI have difficulties with short-term memory and recognizing how information is organized. They are typically not efficient at making inferences and drawing relationships between and among knowledge and skills. Students with such difficulties may become confused if content and skills are presented in a disorganized fashion or if the cues to the organization are not clear. Those students benefit from instruction that is *clear* and *explicit*.

Students in general education classrooms are expected to make assumptions about what they hear or read, to make connections to prior knowledge as well as across the new knowledge they are acquiring/constructing, and to think about the demands of the task. Students with HI perform those cognitive skills poorly in terms of both quality and consistency. Consequently, they need to be taught how to perform them and need frequent cues to help them remember to use those newly learned skills and strategies.

To be clear and explicit, first think carefully about whether your explanations or directions name a topic. For example, you could say, "You are to *write an essay* that *tells me . . .* " or "When your numerator—*remember, that's the number on the top, the one you are dividing into*—is bigger than your denominator. . . ." Also consider whether you are stating the major concepts or discussion points overtly and clearly: "Remember, an essay is at least five paragraphs and it contains . . ." or "When people started to work in factories during the Industrial Revolution they had to leave some old work skills behind. Where did they work before factories, and what kind of skills did they have that wouldn't be needed in a factory?" Get into the habit of asking yourself, "Do they know what I mean?" It can be helpful to ask students to repeat directions back to be sure they fully understand them or to restate concepts "in their own words" to check for clarity.

Frequent and Intensive Instruction

Information that is heard only once is not likely to be transferred to long-term memory. Because of memory difficulties and the complexities of building comprehension, students with HI are particularly prone to gaps in comprehending information and forgetting important facts when there are delays between exposures to content or skills (Mastropieri and Scruggs 2007). Exposure, whether to content or skills, needs to occur multiple times, and those multiple exposures should occur in close proximity to one another (Gleason, Carnine, and Vala 1991). *Frequent* instruction involves providing multiple opportunities to practice new content or skills, and those multiple opportunities should be close together in time. It could mean working on the same information for three successive class sessions instead of once per week, for example. *Intensive* instruction means that students are exposed to the concept or skill a number of times within a single lesson, including practice sessions. If instruction is intensive, within each of the frequent lessons the students will have multiple practice opportunities. Although drill and practice has benefits (Gleason, Carnine, and Vala 1991), lessons do not need to be overly repetitive. Any concept or skill can be incorporated into further iterations of the topic, and practice activities can be varied (for example, Bulgren et al. 2000).

Effective learning involves contemplating knowledge and applying it. When teachers show students a new skill, the logical next step is to have them practice it.

One purpose of multiple practices with informative feedback is so students can eliminate mistakes, develop proficiency, and encode the information to long-term memory. To have students develop fluency of skills, some special education techniques call for fast-paced, intensive practice (for example, Direct Instruction [Carnine, Silbert, and Kame'enui 1997] and the Strategy Intervention Model [Ellis et al. 1991]). Although the need for speedy practice can be debated, the benefit of providing students with HI with intensive lessons is well established. The more frequency and intensity, the more likely new lessons can build on previous lessons instead of repeating them.

Modeling and Examples

To **model** is to demonstrate a skill or task. To provide an example is to show or explain what something is like. Students with HI particularly benefit from modeling and examples because they remove one potential source of confusion about what is being learned. With a mental image in mind, the students have a better chance of replicating the skill or comprehending a concept (Uberti, Scruggs, and Mastropieri 2003). Without a mental model or concrete representation, students would have to guess at what the expectations were and would have nothing against which to judge the quality of the product (or process) they produced. For students who have difficulty monitoring their own cognitive processes, using a model as a reference can be a tremendous help.

Teaching with think-alouds is another example of effective teaching. Think-alouds are important particularly for modeling of cognitive processes, such as a cognitive strategy (Fisher and Frey 2015). In think-aloud modeling, teachers not only overtly show expected behaviors (for example, the steps of a mathematical calculation or for writing a complete paragraph), but they also demonstrate for students what they are thinking while performing the behaviors. This helps students to "see and hear" the cognitive thought processes involved in completing the task. Students with HI typically have inefficient cognitive processes, so modeling more appropriate thought processes is essential for them to learn the skill or task. A teacher modeling how to write a good paragraph might demonstrate clearing the desk and holding the paper and pen at the proper angles while saying, "Now that I have my writing space clear and paper and pen in front of me and ready, I need to plan. So first I will think of the main idea of my paragraph. Let's see, I know that I am supposed to write about the life of factory workers in England during the Industrial Revolution. That's a big topic, so I need to make a specific point about it. One thing that I think is interesting is . . ." Think-aloud modeling includes labeling the parts of the process as well. In this example, the teacher cued students to first prepare their materials and writing environment, next to plan, then to execute the plan, and so on.

Practice/Application Opportunities

Along with the principle of *frequent and intensive instruction*, providing practice through application activities is another essential component for student learning. Offering multiple exposures is not enough; students need multiple chances to practice and/or apply what they have learned. This may be the point at which learning truly occurs, because it is through their use of knowledge or a skill that students come to "own" it. Students with HI may not fully appreciate a concept that they merely read about but never discussed, and they may not understand directions or a skill that they only heard about or observed. However, through practice, they come to understand and assimilate the knowledge into long-term memory.

It is almost intuitive that students will need to practice new skills; the same is true for applying concepts they learn. Application can be a low-level cognitive process such as actively thinking about something, or it can be higher-level manipulation of information that students need to comprehend, store, and later recall. However, inclusive classroom teachers report moving on when approximately half of the class seems to grasp a concept or skill (Scanlon et al. 2006), but that leaves the other half not having fully learned.

Informative Feedback

At the very least, feedback by itself tells students whether they got something right or wrong. Even more effective is feedback that is *informative*. **Informative feedback** tells students what was right or wrong about their performance of a task, or it tells them why something did or did not work and what they should change to correct their actions. You might say to a student, "The reason you got that right was because . . ." or "What you want to do differently on your next attempt is . . ." These types of informative feedback statements provide students with clear, actionable feedback on their performance.

Because students with HI tend to be inefficient at monitoring, modifying, and abandoning inappropriate approaches to completing a task (for example, Harris, Reid, and Graham 2004), informative feedback can be valuable at helping them to correct their actions.

If you cannot provide students with informative feedback due to time constraints or other limits on their instruction, at least provide them with **consequated feedback** (that is, telling them the consequences of their performance—right or wrong, or a total score). In doing so, students can at least judge whether they are getting the content correct or not. However, whenever possible, use informative feedback with students so that they can better understand how well they are doing and take corrective actions to improve future performance.

Instruction Within the Student's Range

Effective instruction is instruction that is given on a student's cognitive and instructional level. As students with HI get older, a gap can develop between what is expected of them and what they know/can do well (Baker, Gersten, and Scanlon 2002; Bulgren and Scanlon 1997/1998). As this gap continues to grow, students with disabilities may become frustrated because the skills that they are currently learning, based upon their *grade level*, may not be the same as their *knowledge level*. In those cases, they may need first to learn prior knowledge and prerequisite skills.

Because students with HI are typically less proficient in abstract reasoning and understanding relationships among new and known information, they are less likely to benefit from instruction that is beyond their current knowledge of the topic. Instead, by working within their instructional level—what they are able to learn with supports—they can gradually increase the sophistication of their knowledge or skill. The cognitive psychologist Lev Vygotsky (1978) referred to this as the "zone of proximal development." Vygotsky suggested that students can gradually raise the "ceiling" of their capabilities, developing the potential to learn successively new and more complex information, when teachers provide appropriate supports or scaffolding.

The challenge for teachers is to try to gauge the zone for a particular student. Teachers often rely on grade-level calibrated standards and curricula to guide them;

however, this can be a challenge when teaching students with HI who differ in cognitive processing, knowledge, and skill gaps. It can be particularly valuable for teachers of students with disabilities to conduct a pretest to determine their baseline (that is, starting level) knowledge or skills. The process can be as simple as making informal observations with careful reflection, but better yet, supported by student work samples. In some cases, students could give a demonstration or explanation or complete practice exercises or a test—be it a quick probe or a comprehensive standardized measure. Information from students' IEPs should also be helpful to identify starting points for teaching them.

Structured Instruction

Often, students are not sure why they are learning certain information or skills, other than because the teacher said so. It would be far more instructive if students knew what they were learning and how it related to things that they previously learned or to events in their life (Lenz, Marrs, et al. 2005).

Because of inefficient or distracted learning traits, students with HI often have difficulty seeing the "big picture" of a lesson or reading. For them, it can seem like a collection of random facts and concepts. It can help for teachers to present an overview of what students will learn prior to teaching. Virtually any theory of learning explains how information is understood, remembered, and recalled for usage by forming associations to other information in long-term memory (for example, schema theory, information processing theories, social constructivism; Schunk 2004; Snowman and Biehler 2006). When teachers make the organization of content overt, all learners, especially those with HI, understand its relationship to prior knowledge and better understand how it links to new knowledge.

To reveal the structure of instruction, teachers can do things as simple as orienting students to what they will be learning and why (for example, Lenz, Marrs, et al. 2005). Basically, this can occur by sharing the day's agenda with students. Too often, teachers treat their lesson plans as secrets. A much better practice would be to discuss what they will learn and how it relates to previous lessons. To further improve instruction, teachers could also discuss why the day's content matters, including how it relates to previously learned information. Also, when students know what is expected of them, both in terms of actions and products, the outcomes of a lesson are more likely to be achieved.

Supporting Technologies

Students with HI can benefit from the use of **instructional technologies**. These technologies can help to make the content visible, including abstract aspects such as relationships among key concepts, through the use of maps and organizers (Bulgren and Scanlon 1997/1998; Englert et al. 2007) or through the use of grids to help them understand the concept of place value, for example.

The term *technology* here means the wide range of materials that support instruction (Edyburn 2010; Swanson and Hoskyn 1998), not just things that require a power source to operate. From this perspective, lists or figures on the chalkboard constitute technology, as do graphic devices (see Baker, Gersten, and Scanlon 2002) or laptop computers loaded with specialized hardware for reading text to students. (See more about technology in Chapter 12.)

The CEC standards for effective special educators (2015; also see the inside cover of this text) identify additional important practices for teaching students with special needs.

CASE 1.2 The Role of the Special Educator

Case Introduction

In Case 1.1, you read about three students with disabilities and their general education teacher. Now you will read about where they receive additional instruction. As you read the case, think about when Maria is and is not receiving special education. If students with disabilities are enrolled in an inclusion classroom, how can they still receive their individually appropriate special education? What is the rationale for Maria receiving reading instruction in the classroom but other services in the learning center?

Emily and José Luis had been assigned to co-teach because there were five students in special education enrolled in his inclusion class. Maria was one of the few who also spent time with Emily outside of the general education classroom. There was another student with a disability who, like Burt, was not in special education but did receive related services through Section 504 in the classroom. Emily knew her main responsibility in the class was the students in special education, but she and José Luis had agreed that they would both do their best to work with all learners in the room.

Their classroom was an RTI class. Emily was part of a group of teachers at Gamon Elementary who planned to conduct screenings of all students for reading, math, and writing three times a year, early in the fall, in the middle of the school year, and early in the spring (this made more sense than late in the spring, as that time of year would not leave much time to work with students). Even though Maria was already enrolled in special education at the beginning of the year, she was included in the screening because the educators wanted up-to-date data on how she was performing on reading tasks.

Based on the screening results, Maria and Sy were found to need Tier 1 intervention, along with a few other students. Emily and the team of teachers selected a reading intervention that had research evidence indicating its match to the Tier 1 students' needs. During English/language arts time Emily worked with those students at a table in the reading area in the back of the classroom while José Luis worked with the other students in the class. This arrangement made the most sense because Emily had trained in the reading approach and José Luis was only minimally familiar with it. Under this arrangement Emily was able to work with the few struggling readers intensively. (While Tier 1 would be successful for Maria, Sy would eventually be graduated to Tier 2, when he would receive additional reading instruction time with Emily and just two other students.) Emily sometimes addressed reading with Maria again during their time together in the learning center, but for the most part they worked on other academic skills there.

At other times in the classroom Emily was teaching both Maria and Burt to be more aware of the ways they disengaged from learning during class; she planned that once they became strong at this skill she would teach them to self-regulate those behaviors. Emily and Maria also worked on this in the learning center. (Maria also had regularly scheduled time with a mental health counselor, and Emily and the counselor periodically informed each other on their progress.)

CASE QUESTIONS

1. *Why do some students receive special education services in the general education classroom whereas others go to a separate setting for their individualized instruction?*
2. *If students have special learning needs, why are there three different options for how schools can respond to those needs (special education, Section 504, RTI)? Are the same services provided across the different options?*

1-3 Where Special Education Is Provided

In the early days of special education, students with HI were often segregated from their peers, both physically and in terms of the curriculum used to teach them. Much has changed since then, and now you are more likely to find students with disabilities in general education with their special education supports being provided to them in the classroom, such as the classroom in Case 1.2, where Emily and José Luis co-teach. Some of those students are "pulled out" from time to time to receive more intensive interventions. Interestingly, in the case of some of the HI disabilities, students spend more time in pull-out settings in secondary school than they do in elementary (U.S. Department of Education 2016). This is likely due to their needing more individualized instruction than the content-area general education classroom can provide.

The General Education Classroom

According to the U.S. Department of Education (2016), nearly half of all students in special education aged six to 21 receive at least 80 percent of their education in a general education classroom; this is a particularly common special education placement for students with HI. Among only students with HI, those with EBD are the least likely to be included (statistics for those with mild ID and ADHD are not readily disaggregated from the broader disability categories in which they are counted). For the most part, students with HI receive their instruction from the general education teacher, although others (for example, special education teachers, behavior specialists, paraprofessionals) may also be involved. As such, students with HI typically participate in the general education curriculum. (See Chapter 2 for a discussion of instructional accommodations for the general education classroom.)

Aides and paraprofessionals are often assigned to provide academic assistance in the classroom. If a student needs more intensive or unique instruction, a special educator might accompany the student to the class and provide the instruction there. The special educator might also provide instruction to others in the class at the same time.

There is no official definition and there are no criteria for what constitutes an inclusive classroom. In fact, while inclusion is common for most students in special education with HI, the IDEA (2004) prefers inclusion but does not require it ("removal . . . from the regular education environment occurs only when . . . education in regular classes with the use of supplementary aids and services cannot be achieved satisfactorily"). Individual states or districts, however, may have "inclusion policies," meaning that, with rare exceptions, students must be placed in general education classrooms and that appropriate supports for their success there should be identified and provided (Kauffman, Bantz, and McCullough 2002). Depending on the students' academic

---

THINK BACK TO THE CASE   about Emily and the Role of the Special Educator . . .

Why do some students receive special education services in the general education classroom whereas others go to a separate setting for their individualized instruction?

Students enrolled in special education who participate in the general education classroom and curriculum still have an individually designed education program that indicates what types of special instruction they need to benefit from their education. Depending on how much the IEP differs from the general education curriculum and classroom routine, the general educator might be responsible for delivering the special education components of the program, or a special educator or other specialist would be. Whenever possible, that individually appropriate education is delivered in the general education classroom. "Possible" means that it can be delivered effectively so that the student benefits from it and it is reasonable to do it that way (for example, it does not detract from the education other students receive). In the case, Maria worked on reading at a separate table in the classroom along with Sy and a few other students, even though she was the only one enrolled in special education. She had additional times in the learning center with Emily and with a counselor. This allowed her even more individualized instruction.

needs, they may be placed in inclusive classrooms for all subject areas or for only those in which they can participate with minimal support. In some cases, **inclusion schools** offer classes with a reduced number of students. If the school is truly "inclusive" and does not just offer a seat in the classroom, then the classroom teacher directly interacts with students with disabilities.

Special educators sometimes consult with general education teachers and observe in their classrooms but do not directly teach the special education students present. That is yet another way that special education can be provided in the general education classroom.

The Learning Center and Resource Room

Some students go to another setting to receive some or all of their special education. The special education classroom has no universal name. In some schools it is called the special education room, but it is most typically called the learning center or resource room. The distinction between the latter two, if any, depends on the school. Some schools distinguish between a room where students only sporadically visit for support (the learning center) and where students attend on a routine schedule (the resource room). As a general rule, the more differentiated the curriculum or instructional practice, the more likely it will be taught in a resource room.

Sometimes students in special education need to receive their education outside of the general education environment. This may be because they are working on a curriculum that is substantially different from the general education curriculum, they cannot work with peers in their general education class or even grade level, they may need to work with peers who have similar learning needs, they require one-on-one instruction, or they may simply like more privacy as they receive their specialized instruction. For example, students who are significantly behind their peers in reading may be more comfortable practicing their skills outside of the view of others.

More Restrictive Settings

Some students receive their education in "substantially separate" placements, which are often in a separate building. Typically, these students have more severe disabilities. As we noted, of students with HI, only those with EBD are highly likely (in percentages) to be placed in programs more restrictive than the general education classroom (U.S. Department of Education 2016). This usually occurs in the case of students who are prone to highly disruptive and injurious behaviors (to themselves or others) and those whose internalizing behaviors pose a significant threat to themselves, such as self-mutilation or suicidal tendencies. As distracting as a student such as Burt in Cases 1.1 and 1.2 can be, she or he is not likely to be placed outside of the general education environment. Some experts in the field of special education see this as a disparity based on the fact that those with EBD make others more uncomfortable than do those with ADHD, despite the fact that both are disruptive to the classroom (see Hallahan et al. 2005).

Even though many teachers have reported apprehension about inclusion, they have been found to be supportive of the practice (Hernandez, Hueck, and Charley 2016; Monson, Ewing, and Kwoka 2014; Vaughn et al. 1999). Indeed, research findings show that inclusive approaches can be effective (Rea, McLaughlin, and Walther-Thomas 2002).

about Emily and the Role of the Special Educator...

When students have special learning needs, why are there three different options for how schools can respond to those needs (special education, Section 504, RTI)? Are the same services provided across the different options?

It can be confusing as to why there are so many options for students with disabilities. To understand, first remember that sometimes students have a disability but don't require any special services to benefit from their education. Those students would not be in special education, nor would they receive Section 504 services. However, when a student does need an individually appropriate curriculum or approach to instruction because of a disability, then she or he should receive special education as described in an IEP. Based on the individual's needs, that special education might be only slightly different from the regular general education curriculum and methods of instruction, or there may be significant differences. Related services through Section 504 are provided if a student with a disability does not need special education but does need related services to access her or his (general) education. Of course, some students may need both special education and related services (to access their general or special education), and they would be enrolled in both special education and Section 504.

Maria had a special education goal to improve her self-regulation of participation in class, and Emily's services to Maria included instruction on that. Burt was receiving the very same instruction, at the same time as Maria (however, Maria received additional instruction on the skill in the learning center), but in his case it was as a related service. The difference is that Maria's IEP team determined this was a goal she needed to meet (an IEP goal), and she needed a different level of instruction to learn the skill. Burt didn't need special education to learn the skill; he merely needed to be taught how to do it and then be monitored and prompted to use it. So what's different? Burt didn't have an outcome goal because his teachers didn't think it would be challenging for him to learn the skill and he didn't need specialized instruction. Emily simply found it efficient to teach him the same way she was teaching Maria.

RTI may *look* like special education, but it is not. Also, RTI is not a related service, because it is instruction and not a service that enables access to instruction. RTI only requires that a student be found to perform (achieve) below an expected level. Therefore, students who show signs of beginning to struggle on an RTI screening measure immediately receive early intervening to address the "problem." It can lead to special education if students progress to the highest tier of RTI and still do not make satisfactory learning progress. Thus, any student can receive services through RTI. It is designed to speed services to students who are beginning to struggle and to prevent unnecessary referrals to special education. Students already in special education for the skill area in question (for example, reading) would be included in RTI procedures only if they were in an inclusive classroom and the educators found it helpful to get an updated screening or the IEP team agreed the instruction provided through RTI would be the most appropriate way to address their special education goal, as was the case for Maria.

1-4 Three Major Laws Pertaining to Special Education

Three major federal laws call for disability-related education services in schools. They make distinct contributions to how we provide special education. In addition, each state has its own laws governing special education practices, and the federal Americans with Disabilities Act requires schools to protect the civil rights of students with disabilities.

The three major laws that we will discuss are the IDEA, Section 504, and the Every Student Succeeds Act (ESSA).

Individuals with Disabilities Education Act (2004)

The **Individuals with Disabilities Education Act** (most recently updated in 2004 as the Individuals with Disabilities Education Improvement Act) is the primary law pertaining to special education. It is the law that dictates in the greatest detail what special education services should include. Through its regulations, this education act prescribes how special education will be provided. The IDEA complements the comprehensive ESSA (see later in this section) by requiring that all students in special education have access to the general curriculum and that they be included in accountability measures.

The Six Major Provisions of the IDEA in Practice. The expansive IDEA has maintained six major provisions since its inception in 1975, as Public Law 94-142, The Education for All Handicapped Children Act. Some of the major provisions of the IDEA deal more with protections for families and schools and less with specifically what goes on during daily instruction. Still, they are all vital to ensuring that students with disabilities are properly served and their rights to an appropriate education are protected. The following are the six provisions:

1. The **zero reject** provision makes clear that no student with a disability who needs special education may be denied a free and appropriate public education.
2. The **due process** provision provides parents with rights and recourse when decisions are being made about their child's education. School systems are required to have procedures in place that make due process available.
3. The **parent and student participation** provision ensures that parents and students are informed and invited to participate in the special education planning, implementation, and evaluation process. In fact, special education services cannot begin until parents have signed an IEP affirming their consent for the special services. There is also an expectation that students will participate on their IEP team whenever appropriate.
4. **Nondiscriminatory identification and evaluation** is a provision based on a long history of discriminatory practices in referring students to be assessed for disabilities and special education eligibility. Cases involving nonnative English speakers (for example, *Diana v. California State Board of Education,* 1970) and students of color (*Larry P. v. Riles,* 1972) who were wrongly identified as having disabilities demonstrate that both the process for identification and the actual evaluations may be biased. The nondiscrimination provision is not limited to initial identification, however: the IDEA requires regular evaluation of progress, as well as triennial assessments of the status of disabling conditions. Nondiscriminatory practices in those activities are provided for as well. Despite this provision, questions continue as to whether members of traditionally underserved groups are still overrepresented in special education (Costa-Guerra and Costa-Guerra 2016; Harry and Klingner 2006).
5. **Free and appropriate public education** means that students with a qualifying disability and who need special education are eligible for an education at public cost as long as they are enrolled in public education. Moreover, their special education must be "appropriate," which means the educational program must be designed so that the student receives meaningful benefit from it.
6. Finally, the place where special education is provided must be the **least restrictive environment** (LRE), which means the physical location closest to the classroom

the student would be in if she or he had no disability and no special education. The intent is to minimize the segregation of students with disabilities (see Lipsky 2005). The IDEA 2004 regulations emphasize that every effort should be made to have the general education environment be the LRE, but the regulations still do not *define* LRE as the general education classroom.

Section 504 of the Rehabilitation Act of 1973

When revised in 1973, the Rehabilitation Act included **Section 504**, which pertains to those with disabilities enrolled in programs that are federally provided or benefit from federal funding. Over years of reauthorization, Congress and the courts have affirmed that it pertains to students with disabilities enrolled in school, regardless of whether they have been found eligible under the IDEA.

The primary contribution of Section 504 is its provision requiring *related services*, which provide access to education for students with disabilities. Related services are not education services themselves; rather, providing them allows the student to access (hence, "related") her or his education. For instance, if an old school building has entrances only at the tops of stairs, it would be difficult for a student who uses a wheelchair to enter the building. What should the school do? Section 504 tells schools that they should find a reasonable way to ensure that student is able to participate in her or his education—that is, provide access to education.

Every Student Succeeds Act

The **Every Student Succeeds Act** (**ESSA**) was passed into law in 2015 to replace the No Child Left Behind Act (2001). It is designed to encourage state departments of education to promote and support "continuous improvements" in public education. That includes providing equitable opportunities and learning outcomes for students with disabilities (Council of Chief State School Officers, 2017). The ESSA is not a special education law but is intended to be coordinated with the IDEA. Thus, special educators need to keep it in mind when planning and providing special education for students with HI.

The ESSA affirms the IDEA expectation that individual education programs should be aligned with the same achievement outcomes expected for the general education program. That means that special education goals should be the same when appropriate and otherwise should prepare the student to progress toward achieving those same goals. It also affirms that students in special education should be prepared for postsecondary education and/or the world of work upon completion of secondary school. The ESSA also requires that all students' academic achievement be assessed annually, and it states the grade levels for assessing in reading/language arts, mathematics, and science. Students in special education must also be assessed. Results for students with disabilities must be disaggregated so that the effectiveness of special education on achievement outcomes can be monitored. For this reason, it is important that special education teams remember to consider the general education curriculum when planning a student's IEP (see Chapter 2 for more on this).

The ESSA includes several other requirements that pertain to special education and students with disabilities. Two in particular are that universal design for learning (UDL) principles must be used "to the extent practicable" in assessments, and that accommodations are provided both in instruction and during those assessments. Both UDL and accommodations are explained in this textbook.

Finally, you may be surprised that we do not name the Americans with Disabilities Act (ADA) (1990; 2008) as one of the major laws pertaining to special education.

The ADA is a civil rights law that prohibits discrimination against persons with disabilities. It applies to schools and students. Prohibiting discrimination is very important; in fact, the IDEA was created in response to a history of schools discriminating against students with disabilities (Weintraub 2005). However, both the IDEA and Section 504 state what services, and to some degree outcomes, should be provided based on disability-related needs. For that reason, they are far more significant on a day-to-day basis when we are concerned about an individually appropriate education. That said, the ADA is always available to students and parents if they believe disability-based discrimination is happening.

The IEP: The Blueprint for individualized Education

Students receive special education when they are identified as having a disability and are found not to be benefiting from "regular" education (the IDEA uses the term *regular* to describe the general education curriculum and school environment). When a student is enrolled in special education, an IEP must be designed. Through the IEP, parents and the school describe and agree to how the student's education will differ from the general education the school offers.

A team develops the IEP. The IDEA mandates who must participate on the team: (1) a special educator, (2) at least one of the student's general educators from a class where the disability poses an impact (thus, at the secondary level, not every teacher the student has throughout the day has to participate), (3) a school administrator, (4) a parent or legal guardian, (5) the student (when appropriate), (6) someone qualified to interpret assessment results if any will be considered, and (7) other service providers as appropriate (for example, related service providers or classroom aides). With their diversity of expertise and perspectives, the team has the task of identifying what needs to be different in the student's education and working out a program of services that will be provided.

A paper or digital plan must be written to keep a record of what the team decides. That document is the IEP. The IEP can be thought of as a "blueprint for special education" because it must clearly state what the special education will be.

The IEP should be written plainly enough so that parents who are not professional educators can understand it. A great variety of information must be recorded on the form. The IEP must state which disability the student has and the ways in which the disability interferes with the student benefiting from the general education (for example, "Due to Maria's clinical depression, she often misses important information in class, and she is not developing appropriate skills for socializing with peers"). That information would logically lead into what special instruction and services are planned for the student. Thus, it must also state what special education instructional goals will be accomplished in the ensuing year, and where and by whom services will be provided.

To ensure that the IEP becomes a plan that is followed, the team must recommend the nature of special instruction to be offered. It also names where the LRE is for each of the specified activities and what type of professional will provide the services (for example, special education teacher, general educator, reading specialist).

Responsiveness to Intervention

As the term **responsiveness to intervention** (RTI) indicates, how a student *responds* to instructional interventions (for example, does or does not make intended learning progress) serves as the basis for determining the student's instructional programming. It is intended as an early intervening approach—that is, to provide supports as soon as a possible learning challenge is detected, before it evolves into a more serious problem.

To detect needs as soon as possible, RTI begins with **universal screening**: all students in a class or grade level are screened. The screening tool is a quick but valid and reliable measure of skills of concern, such as grade-level-appropriate reading, mathematics, behavior, and writing.

All students who do not meet expected standards on the screening are placed in the first of three tiers of instructional intervention. Each tier represents a level of intensive intervention using interventions with a scientific evidence base as effective for similar students (for instance, by gender, age, English language proficiency). Beginning with **Tier 1**, the intervention is given time to be effective and the student's progress is monitored. For students who respond as desired, instruction continues until that performance is stable and then they are exited from RTI. Any student who does not respond satisfactorily after a reasonable amount of time or number of opportunities is placed in **Tier 2** of intervention, which involves more individualized instruction (typically in a small group), using a different evidence-based practice better matched to the student's needs. **Progress monitoring** continues and the student is either exited from RTI upon making expected gains or is moved into **Tier 3**. The third tier is even more individualized and intensive; in some schools it requires enrollment in special education, and in other schools special education follows if Tier 3 intervention is not successful. (In some RTI models students who perform particularly poorly on a screening may be placed immediately into a Tier 2 or 3 intervention; Fuchs, Fuchs, and Compton 2012). There is no one model of RTI, but the three-tier version is most common (Mellard, McKnight, and Jordan 2010).

Note that RTI is not special education, although it may lead to special education enrollment. Since 2004 the IDEA has allowed states to use an RTI process in place of the traditional aptitude–achievement discrepancy approach to identifying LD (see Berkeley, Bender, Peaster, and Saunders 2009). When it is used for LD identification it contrasts with the traditional IDEA eligibility process. Critics of the discrepancy formula and conventional IDEA referral process argue that it does not reliably distinguish learners with a true LD from other low achievers, that it is not useful for determining who needs specialized services (Stanovich 2005), that it delays providing needed services (for this reason the referral process has been nicknamed the "wait to fail" approach) (Vaughn and Fuchs 2003), and that it may be biased against traditionally underserved populations (Harry and Klingner 2006).

Universal Design for Learning

The U.S. Department of Education Office of Special Education and Rehabilitation Services encourages the use of universal design in special education and inclusion (Hehir 2009). Universal Design for Learning (UDL) promises equal access to education by all students, regardless of disability. To achieve this, lesson goals, materials used, methods of instruction, and methods of assessment need to be accessible to all learners. For example:

1. Lesson goal: A lesson goal that includes students reading for information would be altered so that it addresses acquiring the information but without presuming reading is required (this means the lesson goal is not to develop their reading skills but to learn the content of the reading).
2. Materials used: Digital readers of texts could be available, or there could be versions written for different reading levels (see Benton and Johnson 2014).
3. Methods of instruction: Students could use a reading strategy to guide the reading process (see Chapter 7) or read with a partner. The teacher could deliver the content in some format other than print text.

4. Methods of assessment: The assessment of learning should not be incumbent upon the student reading if reading is not essential to learning the content or demonstrating what is learned (assessment).

To ensure UDL is incorporated across all components of a lesson, you should plan for multiple means of representation (for instance, alternatives to printed grade-level text), student engagement (listen, strategic reading, interview an expert), and student expression (present a project, explain orally instead of in writing, teach others). By planning for multiple means, you can be confident you will provide options that are appropriate for the range of learners you are teaching. Ideally, the students will be involved in choosing from among the options. This may be both motivating and helpful to students learning to be thoughtful about their own learning.

UDL is often associated with technology and the electronic devices that are revolutionizing access. For example, a smart phone can magnify text or read it using apps that translate, look up unfamiliar words, read it aloud, or take an image that can be marked up. As valuable as such "hi-tech" methods are, "low-tech" devices (such as a ruler to slide down the page to help with visual tracking or graphic organizers to map content) and "no-tech" aids (partner reading, a teacher checking on a student) are important to practicing UDL too. The goal is to ensure that all students have meaningful access to all aspects of a lesson, from its planning and goals to the assessment of learning outcomes. UDL is not technology, but rather an approach to providing learning opportunities (Edyburn 2010). When UDL is incorporated into a lesson, the barriers presented based on a disability are removed and there is equal access to learning.

CHAPTER SUMMARY

Students with HI are a diverse group. Although certain characteristics are common among all of those with the same disability label, each individual is unique in terms of how the disability impacts her or him, as well as in what is needed for academic success. The five HIs are ADHD, autism at the "requiring support" level, EBD, mild ID, and specific learning disability (plus speech or language impairment, which we do not address).

Children and adolescents with HI are as capable of benefiting from education as any other student. However, cognitive processing difficulties distinguish them from general education students. Their academic and social development is often at a slower pace than their peers, and achievement is often documented to be lower as well. Effective instructional practices for students with HI are based upon their specific cognitive strengths and needs. Principles of effective practice include, in addition to holding them to high standards and expectations, evidence-based practices that directly respond to their unique cognitive processing and behavioral traits. Such practices include using clear and explicit instruction, providing models and examples,

and scaffolding practices that are within the student's range of abilities.

Children and adolescents with disabilities are entitled to an appropriate free, public education just like any other student. Two of the three major laws concerning the rights of students with disabilities, the IDEA and Section 504, most directly inform special education and related service practices in schools. In accordance with those laws, students who have HI typically participate in the general education curriculum and school environment. That requires that the educators involved have clearly defined roles and that they support one another in those roles. The IEP is used to devise an individually appropriate education program and to inform all parties involved of what is expected educationally for the student with the disability. In addition, students may receive related services, which provide them access to their education services, through Section 504. Schools are increasingly using RTI models as well. RTI is not special education but rather an approach to detecting possible learning needs early and intervening immediately.

KEY TERMS

Consequated Feedback, 25

Due Process, 31

Effective Instruction, 25

Every Student Succeeds Act, 32

Executive Functioning, 5

Externalized, 18

Free and Appropriate Public
   Education, 31

Generalization, 17

HI, 2

Inclusion School, 29

Individualizing, 2

Individuals with Disabilities
   Education Act, 31

Informative Feedback, 25

Instructional Technologies, 26

Internalized, 18

Least Restrictive Environment, 31

Model, 24

Nondiscriminatory Identification
   and Evaluation, 31

Parent and Student Participation, 31

Principles of Effective Instruction, 22

Progress Monitoring, 34

Responsiveness to Intervention, 33

Section 504, 32

Special Education, 2

Tier 1, 34

Tier 2, 34

Tier 3, 34

Twice Exceptional, 7

Universal Screening, 34

Zero Reject, 31

APPLICATION ACTIVITIES

The following activities were designed to help you apply knowledge that was presented in this chapter. Using information from the chapter, complete the following activities.

1. Review the first case, with Maria, Sy, and Burt. For each of the three students, brainstorm how the IDEA provisions for *nondiscriminatory identification and evaluation*, *free and appropriate public education*, and services in the *least restrictive environment* could be fulfilled in Emily and José Luis's classroom.

2. Among students with HI, those with EBD are the most likely to be removed from the general education classroom. For each internalized and externalized behavior associated with EBD listed in Table 1.3, recommend a related service that might enable a student exhibiting the behavior to stay in the regular classroom (recall that related services are different from individually designed special education interventions).

3. Develop a lesson plan for a single student or a whole class. Identify in the plan how you will incorporate each of the principles of effective practice.

4. Read Deshler et al. (2001). Thinking of a special education student you have worked with, list special education and related services you believe the student should receive and then identify which level of service from Deshler et al. is best suited to providing those services.

2 | Effective Instructional Practices in Inclusive and Co-Taught Classrooms: Planning, Teaching, and Monitoring Instruction

Learning Objectives

After reading this chapter, you will understand:

2-1   The stages of the special education process for planning and providing an individually appropriate special education

2-2   How special education plans and services can be coordinated with general education, and why they should

2-3   The skills involved in effectively collaborating and co-teaching with colleagues

2-4   What constitute "Best" and "Evidence-Based" practices and why they are so important for special education

2-5   How students can collaborate with their peers in the classroom for meaningful learning

CEC **Initial Preparation Standard 1: Learner Development and Individual Learning Differences**

1-2   Beginning special education professionals use understanding of development and individual differences to respond to the needs of individuals with exceptionalities.

CEC Initial Preparation Standard 3: Curricular Content Knowledge

3-3   Beginning special education professionals modify general and specialized curricula to make them accessible to individuals with exceptionalities.

CEC Initial Preparation Standard 4: Assessment

4-3   Beginning special education professionals, in collaboration with colleagues and families, use multiple types of assessment information in making decisions about individuals with exceptionalities.

CEC Initial Preparation Standard 5: Instructional Planning and Strategies

5-1   Beginning special education professionals consider individual abilities, interests, learning environments, and cultural and linguistic factors in the selection, development, and adaptation of learning experiences for individuals with exceptionalities.

5-5   Beginning special education professionals develop and implement a variety of education and transition plans for individuals with exceptionalities across a wide range of settings and different learning experiences in collaboration with individuals, families, and teams.

CEC Initial Preparation Standard 7: Collaboration

7-1   Beginning special education professionals use the theory and elements of effective collaboration.

7-3   Beginning special education professionals use collaboration to promote the well-being of individuals with exceptionalities across a wide range of settings and collaborators.

Did you ever wish people would leave you alone so you could work on something your own way?

We all feel that way sometimes. As a special educator you will more often be glad to have others who work with you. There is a lot to special education. It can begin with determining whether a student has a disability and needs special education. When the answer is yes, an individually appropriate special education must be planned. Then it must be delivered. Today, students with HI spend much of the school day participating in the general education classroom and curriculum. Thank goodness we special educators can collaborate with a range of colleagues to plan special education and provide it to our students with HI.

2-1   How and Why to "Plan, Teach, and Monitor" for Students with HI

Effective teachers think carefully about what they are going to teach, which involves considering the learning needs of their students and how best to teach the content. Effective teachers also collaborate with their colleagues, especially when their students are struggling. The Council for Exceptional Children (CEC) provides standards for educators working with students with special needs. These standards emphasize skills of planning and collaboration (CEC 2015; also see the inside cover of this textbook).

Collaborating When Students Struggle

Gail in Case 2.1 did the right thing by noticing that Erin was having trouble academically and socially. She was also right to be concerned and consider it her job to address Erin's challenges. A number of factors could have influenced her opinion that Erin

| CASE 2.1 | Figuring Out What the Problem Is |

Case Introduction

As you read the following case about Gail, you may recognize yourself, even if you have not taught in a school yet. The more experienced teachers seem to have insights about a student's presumed disability, even though that student, Erin, doesn't seem to have been formally identified as having a disability. Gail can't quite decide if the teachers are showing the wisdom of experience or are being presumptuous. When Erin joins Gail's class Gail finds herself thinking like the veteran teachers. She decides to seek help from colleagues to see if they can't together figure out what the "problem" is with Erin.

At the end of the case, you will find case questions. These questions are meant to serve as points for reflection. Of course, if you can answer them immediately, you should do so, but you may want to wait to answer them until you have read the portion of the chapter that pertains to the particular case question. Throughout the rest of the chapter, you will see the same questions. As you see them, try to answer them based upon the portion of the chapter that you just read.

All of last year Gail heard teachers and staff talk about Erin. "Sometimes there's just no getting through to her," one teacher would say. Fairly regularly there would be discussion of some unusual thing Erin had done. "She's one of your 'spectrum kids,' isn't she?" the school secretary would routinely ask of Mo Jenkins, the special education inclusion facilitator. Gail never liked the derogatory connotation of the secretary's question, nor that some teachers responded with a knowing laugh. Mo always replied with a polite deflection, such as, "There's more to autism than that." Gail almost never saw Erin last year but she paid attention to the conversations because she knew Erin would be entering her grade and might end up in her class. She was right.

This year, Gail is in her second year of teaching and Erin is one of her students. Gail's curiosity about Erin and her concern that Erin was being unfairly judged by the other teachers were on her mind from the start of the year. Gail quickly noticed that Erin had quirky habits, such as sometimes smiling wryly while ignoring classmates or Gail talking to her when she was engaged in a task, or never directly touching food, instead using a plastic baggie like a glove. Academically, Erin had an excellent memory and was one of the top performers in math. Indeed, she learned new math skills so quickly that Gail sometimes thought she must already know how to do them. However, reading was more challenging for Erin. When she read aloud, Erin's typically loud voice grew soft; she read unevenly, typically going a little too slow with little inflection, but often stopping to slowly decode a word she miscued and then always going back and rereading the entire sentence. She miscued a lot more often than she caught, however, and made word substitutions without realizing. Erin's reading difficulties were causing her

to misunderstand a lot of the material Gail assigned for reading. Once Erin had misinformation in her head it was nearly impossible for Gail to get her to correct it. Erin's writing was far less sophisticated in vocabulary and complexity of expression than was her spoken language. As a consequence, Gail wasn't always sure if a weak written answer reflected poor knowledge or just weak communication skills.

After teaching Erin for several weeks with mixed success, and having spoken to one of Erin's former teachers for advice a few times, Gail decided to ask Mo for help. Gail trusted Mo and felt comfortable asking her for help, although she did hope that Mo wouldn't mention it to anyone in the administration or to some of the more senior teachers. Also, Gail now also wondered whether Erin might have some level of autism. Mo said that she did know of Erin but actually didn't know much about her. She suggested that the first thing she and Gail should do is have lunch alone in Gail's classroom and discuss what help she needed.

Gail explained Erin's academic strengths and weaknesses, noting how exceptional Erin is in math compared to other students and then commenting on how her reading and writing were "nowhere near what she does in math." She infused the conversation with a number of comments about Erin's quirky behaviors, and concern that Erin was becoming socially ostracized.

It was obvious that Mo knew a lot about teaching reading. She suggested a few things that Gail might try as well as a few things to watch for. Gail was encouraged that these might help Erin. Mo also suggested that Gail keep careful records of Erin's work habits and performance over the next two weeks to try to establish a "data-based record" of how Erin was doing academically. She said that if it looked like the concerns Gail had were happening at problematic rates it would be a good idea to assemble a team to look into what was going on with Erin and to offer some advice.

Gail felt a little insulted that Mo asked her to keep data on problems she had already identified, but she liked and trusted Mo and knew that she had to do *something*, so she was willing to give that a try. She really didn't like the idea of asking a team for help. She was afraid that it would convey the message that she was not a good teacher. She also wondered why Mo didn't just provide help herself; after all, it was her job to work with students like Erin.

CASE QUESTIONS

1. *In addition to the possibility of a disability, what else could explain the academic and social challenges Gail thought she saw?*

2. *Is it reasonable to suspect that Erin might have a disability? If yes, how should the team screen for that?*

might have autism and need special education. There was a time in special education when students like Erin were hastily evaluated for a disability and enrolled in special education, before other explanations for what was observed were considered (disability evaluations are not infallible; it is possible that the subjective diagnoses used for the HI disabilities could lead to false identification) or the need for special education was established. Over successive reauthorizations of the IDEA, the special education process has been modified in response to these possible problem areas. The procedural safeguards now in the special education process overwhelmingly call for different educators and parents to work together in the best interests of the student.

There are now four stages to the traditional special education process in schools. It begins when an educator, parent, or student detects that a student may be having challenges in learning or appropriate behavior, and it concludes with creation of the individualized education program (IEP) plan for students who become enrolled in special education.

Pre-referral: The First Stage. Before a student can be enrolled in special education and receive an individually appropriate education, that student must be identified as (1) having a disability covered by the IDEA and (2) needing special education. As a preliminary step to determining whether a student such as Erin satisfies those two generic special education eligibility criteria, a pre-referral process must be completed. Pre-referral is a helpful process for determining how to provide a student with appropriate academic or behavioral supports while the student is still in the general education classroom.

In a **pre-referral** process, both theories as to why the student is having difficulties and possible instructional remedies are explored. However, the very first step is to verify that the student is, in fact, having a learning problem. A busy teacher in a fast-paced classroom can easily form a judgment based on insufficient data. The teacher might theorize the student is having difficulty based on just one or two of the student's responses that stood out over several days. The teacher could also sense work avoidance, which might not have anything to do with how challenging the work is; on more careful observation it could turn out to be the student prioritizing socializing, not actually avoiding work. In Gail's case, she compared Erin's work in math to that of other students and recognized Erin as excelling. She then compared Erin's reading abilities to her math performance but not to other students or grade-level expectations. She did notice specific problems with Erin's reading, but it was not clear how serious the problems were or if there was a quick way to resolve those skill challenges. Thus, when a teacher "suspects" that a student is having difficulty, it is important to begin by keeping observation notes or work samples, providing the student a few additional chances to perform, and looking for alternative explanations. That data will help everyone to make an informed decision.

When a learning problem is detected, the next step is to attempt instructional remedies instead of immediately looking for a possible disability (Burns 2006; Marston et al. 2003). So although Gail was right that Erin's academic and social behaviors could be symptomatic of some disability, it makes more sense first to learn more about the behaviors and determine if they are readily resolved before testing her for a disability. (Also, it is premature to assume they would know for what disability to assess her.) Observing a student's learning patterns, asking the student about the challenge, reteaching, teaching in a different way, and responding to a student's affective needs are all pre-referral activities focused on instructional remedies. A student may have difficulty learning certain content for various reasons (for example, low interest, inadequate prior knowledge, ineffective teaching for that individual, absences, or social and other personal stresses). If the source of the problem is that the student is not motivated to learn the content or that the teacher has not been effective in teaching that student, then activities should be designed to correct the learning problem. By exploring why the student is having difficulty and altering instruction, the "problem" might be addressed and an unnecessary evaluation for special education may be avoided.

In the case of Erin, in addition to Mo's advice to keep data on Erin's actual performance, Gail might also have investigated whether Erin had mastered certain pre-skills or knowledge in reading and writing; if she found that not to be the case, she could reteach in those areas or reconsider what she was teaching Erin. Gail could also have Erin use think-alouds or interviews to complete assignments. A nearly endless variety of pre-referral activities may be tried. They should be simple attempts to see if the problem truly exists and whether it can be alleviated; they are not major instructional interventions such as teaching a student a detailed learning strategy.

Observing the student's learning patterns and trying to teach in different ways are just good teaching behaviors that teachers should routinely use. However, when a student does not seem to be benefiting from instruction that is generally effective for others, teachers must seek to understand why the student is not learning and explore the use of differentiated methods to teach that student. If you find that some of your students are not learning as expected, you should immediately question whether you could be teaching differently to better meet their needs.

THINK BACK TO THE CASE of Gail and Erin . . .

In addition to the possibility of a disability, what else could explain the academic and social challenges Gail thought she saw?

First, it is possible that there is not really a "problem" at all. Erin may have some preferred ways of behaving that are just different from what Gail is used to or that she commonly sees in the other children. Erin might like to focus intently on her work and just not have a more socially acceptable way of communicating that to others. She may not be aware that it is received as odd or rude. Also, she might be highly conscious of dirt and germs; many people are. These are all behaviors that she might have learned at home, where they are considered the norm.

Also, Gail and her colleagues should consider whether Erin's reading and writing performances are truly at low enough levels to cause concern. Is she reading and writing at levels close to what is expected for her grade? Are there consistent patterns that describe any difficulties? Perhaps she just needs a bit more or varied instruction to build her skills to expected levels.

Finally, just because Erin exhibits some behaviors that may resemble autism at the requiring support level, Gail's suspicion that that is the explanation for the problems she thinks she sees may have been influenced by rumors floating around the school, not objective observations.

Your colleagues can be great resources for helping you think about ways to vary your teaching. If the problem is not quickly and easily resolved, you should follow your school's procedures for formally initiating the pre-referral process, which typically involves a team of educators who will work with you to resolve the student's problems.

The team of educators that becomes involved upon formally initiating a pre-referral process is typically known as the **Student Support Team** (other common names include Child Study Team, Pre-referral Intervention Team, Early Intervention Team, and Teacher Assistance Team) (Fig. 2.1). Members of the Student Support Team can

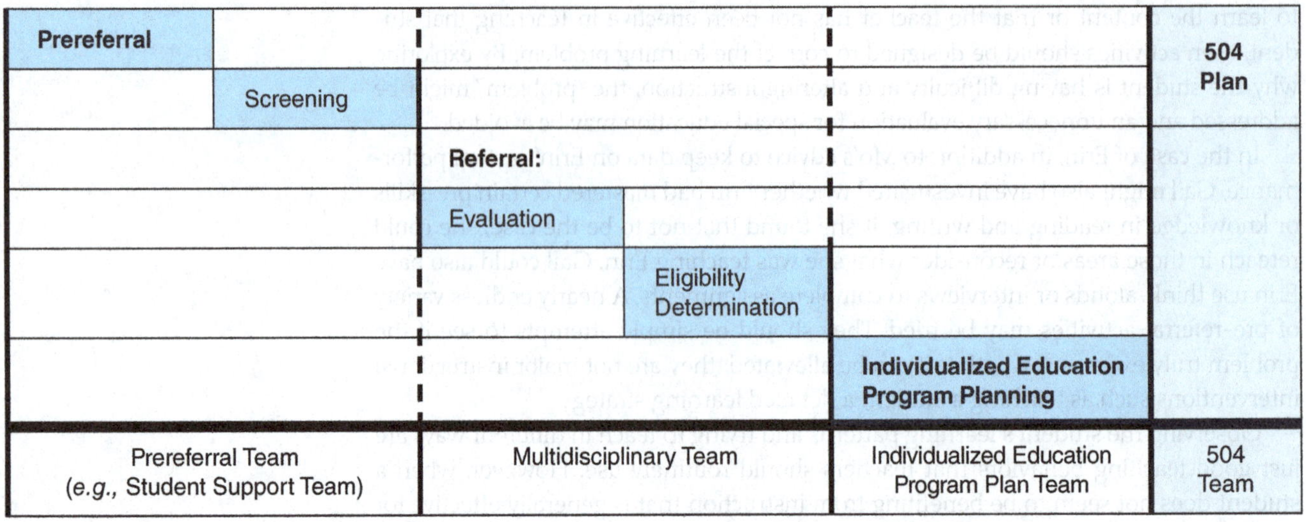

Prereferral				504 Plan
	Screening			
		Referral:		
		Evaluation		
			Eligibility Determination	
				Individualized Education Program Planning
Prereferral Team (*e.g.*, Student Support Team)		Multidisciplinary Team		Individualized Education Program Plan Team	504 Team

Note: Prereferral, Multidisciplinary, and IEP Teams are mandated by the IDEA. 504 teams are mandated by Section 504.

▲ **FIGURE 2.1**
Stages of the Special Education Process and Mandated Teams

include the classroom teacher experiencing the difficulty, a special educator, a teacher coach, behavior specialists, administrators, and others who have relevant expertise. The team should inform the parents that they are working on behalf of their child and consult the parents for their perspective on the source of the student's learning or behavioral difficulty. The parents might have ideas on how to respond to the problem as well. Throughout this process, the team documents the learning problem and offers suggestions to the classroom teacher. In individual cases, two general educators consult, a special educator may observe and offer tips, another teacher may come in to model different teaching practices, or a counselor might talk with the student.

The nice thing about student support teams is that colleagues come together to aid one another; it is not a committee judging your competence as an individual teacher, it is colleagues joining together to solve a problem. With that attitude, Gail could look forward to receiving input from her colleagues with varied experience and expertise. Indeed, the team is most successful when the participants perceive one another as collaborators instead of as administrative or authoritative experts judging each other (Rafoth and Foriska 2006).

Historically, large numbers of students have been incorrectly identified as having disabilities and subsequently placed into special education when in fact general education could have been more appropriate for them. Likewise, some students who would have qualified as having disabilities were denied special education because they were not accurately identified (Harry and Klingner 2006; Stanovich 2005). Research has shown that students of color, those from lower socioeconomic backgrounds, and English language learners have been particularly vulnerable to misidentification (Figueroa 2005; Haager 2007; Harry and Klingner 2006; Morgan et al. 2015). This misidentification is likely due to educators not understanding the student's language and culture, rather than to teacher bias. Teachers who engage in pre-referral activities are less likely to refer students for special education based on sociocultural factors; they instead are more likely to refer a student based upon learning problems (Drame 2002).

You will recall from Chapter 1 that both the Every Student Succeeds Act (ESSA) (2015) and IDEA (2004) call for teachers to use **evidence-based intervention practices**. Beginning in the pre-referral process, data should be collected documenting that evidence-based intervention practices were used and what their effects were

(IDEA 2004). This data collection is to ensure that teachers have tried research-proven teaching practices and that the learning problem persists despite teachers' best efforts. Should the teacher and team decide to proceed toward assessing whether a disability is present and whether special education is warranted, the effects of using evidence-based practices will need to be documented prior to the actual referral for special education evaluation. See the Tips for Generalization box on guidelines for identifying evidence-based practices.

You read about RTI in Chapter 1. It is a process that parallels the pre-referral stage and could lead to disability identification and special education enrollment as well. The RTI approach also calls for using evidence-based practices in each tier of intervention. For some students RTI is used as an alternative to special education for delivering differentiated interventions. Review Chapter 1 for a detailed description of that process and its implications.

TIPS FOR GENERALIZATION

How to Identify "Evidence-Based" Practices for Special Education

The ESSA (2015) defines "evidence-based" intervention practices as having "rigorous and relevant evidence" supporting their effectiveness (U.S. DOE 2016). (The ESSA's predecessor, the No Child Left Behind Act [2001], introduced the concept to education as "scientifically based practices.") Identifying evidence-based practices can be time-consuming, and it is not quite as simple as looking for practices that come with a claim of having been researched. There are standards for what constitutes "evidence-based" (Cook and Cook 2013). First, be aware that the majority of teaching practices that are promoted, both commercially and passed down by tradition, are not adequately tested through research to determine their effectiveness (Carnine 2000; Odom et al. 2005). In fact, in one study, special educators were found to more often use practices with evidence that they are not effective (Burns and Ysseldyke 2009)! To help determine which practices satisfy the standards of "evidence-based," the ESSA and IDEA clarify that research studies published in peer-reviewed publications (typically, professional journals) or otherwise reviewed by a panel of independent experts are reliable sources. The two laws specify that, ultimately, the published research should include *rigorous experimental research procedures,* including "well-conducted randomized control trials and regression continuity studies, and secondarily quasi-experimental studies of especially strong design" (Institute of Education Sciences 2006). What this means is that the "gold standard" is experimental research and that next best is quasi-experimental research, and in either case it must be well conducted. For various reasons, it can be difficult to conduct experimental or quasi-experimental research

with student populations that meets high standards. Hence, it is necessary to review the research, and not just a synopsis of the results, to get a sense of whether its reported findings are relevant to your needs; see Cook and Cook (2017) for a primer on how to read these types of research.

What to Look For

There is no simple checklist to follow when determining whether an intervention is sufficiently researched. Claims by researchers and evidence of their methodological rigor must be evaluated. However, Gersten et al. (2005) and Horner et al. (2005) have identified standards for experimental and quasi-experimental research studies in special education. Published research can be compared to these standards to judge how trustworthy its results might be. The following resources will also be helpful in learning about standards that satisfy the expectation for "evidence-based research":

Two Special Issues of Exceptional Children

In *Exceptional Children,* volume 71, issue no. 2 (2005), five articles explain what constitutes appropriate evidence of sound research practices for documenting effective special education interventions. It includes the articles by Gersten et al. and Horner et al. presenting standards for judging certain types of research. Also see *Exceptional Children,* volume 75, issue no. 3 (2009) for five studies that apply various evidence standards to special education research.

What Works Clearinghouse

The U.S. Department of Education, Institute of Education Sciences, maintains a website (http://ies.ed.gov/ncee/wwc)

continued

TIPS FOR GENERALIZATION (*Continued*)

that includes detailed guidelines that Clearinghouse evaluators use to determine if research evidence supports specific practices. A section of the website provides reports on their evaluations of specific interventions. Unfortunately, the WWC has been slow to identify practices that have been researched with students with disabilities. It is becoming a more useful resource concerning students with some of the HI disabilities, however.

Scientific Research in Education

This 2002 report by the National Research Council, edited by Shavelson and Towne and published by the National Academy Press, criticizes "evidence-based" standards as inappropriately narrow for education research and includes suggestions for additional appropriate research practices. Also see Gallagher (2004) for a critical commentary on evidence-based practices specifically in special education.

Among the challenges to finding evidence-based practices is finding research that is relevant to your intended purposes. For example, if you want research on female adolescents with autism requiring support who are also English learners, you will have difficulty finding research that speaks directly to your population (see Cook and Cook 2015). Further, we must remember that just as it can be difficult to track down highly relevant evidence and interpret its fit for your needs, it is difficult to follow evidence-based practices exactly as they are prescribed, and to know what variations will not violate its potential effectiveness (Fixsen, Blase, Horner, and Sugai 2009). Thus, as important as it is to find evidence-based practices, it is also important to practice them with fidelity. Throughout this book we describe evidence-based instructional practices that you should expect to find in quality research.

Screening: The Second Stage. During the pre-referral process, the Student Support Team may begin to suspect that the student's learning problem is due to a disability. Before rushing to assess the student for a disability in that case, the team first assesses the *probability* of the student having a disability, through the screening process. This process can also be useful for narrowing down the list of possible disabilities to consider. Even though you or other members of the team may suspect a disability even before beginning pre-referral interventions, proceeding to the screening stage should be a data-driven process. Team members should still consult one another and employ evidence-based practices with data collection to monitor whether or not the practices are effective. Anecdotal and research-based data (for example, Harry and Klingner 2006; MacMillan and Siperstein 2001) indicate that the student is more likely to be inappropriately referred and identified when educators prematurely presume the student has a disability.

In the **screening** process, indicators of a disability are looked for using the combination of informal and formal measures. For example, if a teacher suspects an attention problem, the teacher might try observation checklists, conversations with the student about attention habits, and moving the student's seat to prevent distractions. Teachers who suspect difficulty with mathematical reasoning might review the student's work samples and ask the student to model a few mathematical procedures, in addition to having the student complete a published math skills test that is normed for the student's grade level, to see if direct evidence of a reasoning problem is present. However, formalized assessments (for example, achievement tests, psychological evaluations) are not used at this stage. Screening is assessing for the probability of a student having a certain disability(s), but it is not actually evaluating for the presence of that condition. Because screening is more a continuation of the pre-referral process, the teacher should also attend to other factors such as deficits in prior knowledge that are easily corrected through instruction.

THINK BACK TO THE CASE of Gail and Erin . . .

Is it reasonable to suspect that Erin might have a disability? If yes, how should the team screen for that?

Erin does display some of the hallmark characteristics of autism. She appears to have set routines that she does not like to alter. She may have trouble reading social cues from others or at least does not practice expected social norms. She lacks affect in her tone, at least while reading. Despite stereotypes about persons with autism being savants, many persons with autism do not have strong memories. Screening should investigate all of the possibilities, not just the one that is someone's first best guess. After Gail collects observational data it may turn out that she is a busy teacher and was not fully accurate in noting how Erin was doing. As previously noted, there are many possible explanations for Erin's behaviors that are not disability based. Finally, if Erin does have a disability it might be ADHD or an LD; either one could coexist with autism, or it could be one of those and no autism at all.

Referral: The Third Stage. If attempted instructional remedies during pre-referral are insufficient and the screening evidence indicates that a disability is a reasonable possibility, then a **referral** for evaluation for (1) a disability covered by the IDEA and (2) a need for special education due to that disability is warranted. Rinaldi and Samson (2008) note that educators sometimes delay referring students who are English learners, believing they need more time to develop English language proficiency. Rinaldi and Samson note that although language development is an important factor in learning, delaying referral for those who likely do have a disability will only make the eventual task of remediation more difficult; they advocate following an RTI model (review Chapter 1) to speed needed interventions to the English learner.

The referral is made to a **Multidisciplinary Team** (sometimes known as a Collaborative Problem-Solving Team), which is composed of a variety of professionals from the school district who have professional strengths to contribute based on the student in question (IDEA 2004). (In some school districts the Multidisciplinary Team is the team that begins the special education process at the pre-referral stage. This can be appropriate because the membership of the team can match what is required for both tasks.) The team members must employ a variety of approaches to assessment, in part to ensure that the IDEA provision for nondiscriminatory identification and evaluation is not violated. The team will also review the information collected from various sources during the pre-referral and screening processes. The impact of cultural and language bias is reduced when multiple data sources are used (de Valenzuela and Baca 2004).

Once parents have been notified of the pre-referral "findings" and have provided their written consent, the **evaluation** for a possible disability may begin. The outcome of the evaluation process is a declaration as to whether the student has a disability, and if yes, what disability.

If a disability is found, a team continues the process to determine whether the student with a disability is eligible for special education. The eligibility criteria include that the student has a disability covered by the IDEA and that the student needs special education (sometimes phrased as "would benefit from" special education). Members of this team must include the student's parents and special educators (IDEA 2004). If the outcome of this **eligibility determination** process is that the student should be enrolled in special education, the team must plan an individualized education program.

The IEP: The Fourth Stage. To help ensure that you and your colleagues provide eligible students with disabilities with an individually appropriate education, the IDEA requires that a written plan for that "special" education be developed. The resulting document is the IEP. Recall from Chapter 1 that although many presume the "P" stands for "plan," it actually stands for "program." The distinction signals that the team does not just create a plan but sets in place a comprehensive program to meet the student's need. (From birth until age three, an eligible child is covered by an Individualized Family Service Plan [IFSP] that also provides services to family members necessary to support the child's development.) The purpose of the IEP is to explain a student's unique learning needs, relevant history of learning, individualized instructional goals, procedures that help that student attain those goals, and the settings where the student will participate in various services, among other things. The IEP should address the student's individual needs and participation in the general education curriculum, extracurricular activities, and nonacademic activities (IDEA 2004).

The IDEA regulations (2004) specify the minimum required content of an IEP. See Box 2.1 for a list of IDEA-required content for all IEP forms. Those most explicitly related to educational planning may be organized into four major categories: *the*

BOX 2.1

Contents of Written IEPs as Specified By IDEA 2004 Regulations*

1. Statement of child's** present levels of academic achievement and functional performance, including how disability affects involvement and progress in regular education curriculum
2. Measurable annual goals, including academic and functional goals that enable the child to be involved and make progress in regular education curriculum or meet other educational needs
3. Description of how progress toward meeting annual goals will be measured, and when periodic reports of progress will be made
4. Statement of special education and related services and supplementary aids and services; and statement of program modifications or supports to school staff to enable the child to:
   i. Advance toward annual goals
   ii. Be involved in and make progress in the regular education curriculum, and to participate in extracurricular and nonacademic activities
   iii. Be educated and participate with other children with and without disabilities
5. Explanation of extent to which child will not participate with other children while engaged in services stated in (4)
6. Statement of individual accommodations needed to participate in state and district-wide assessments of academic achievement or functional performance, and statement of why a child cannot participate in the regular assessment and attesting that the selected alternate assessment is appropriate for the child
7a. A projected date for the beginning of services and modifications, as well as the frequency, location, and duration of them
7b. Appropriate transition goals and needed services, beginning no later than with the IEP in effect at age 16
7c. Statement informing stakeholders one year in advance of rights transferring to the child upon reaching the age of legal majority

*Paraphrased from IDEA (2004) regulations, §300.320.
**The term *child* is used in the law.

present level of academic achievement and functional performance (PLAAFP), instructional goals, specially designed instruction, and the *service delivery plan.*

PLAAFP

The IEP must include a statement of the student's **present level of academic achievement and functional performance (PLAAFP)**. In the PLAAFP section, the teacher provides information describing how the student's disability relates to participation and learning progress in the general education curriculum. The content must pertain specifically to achievement in major academic skill areas such as reading, writing, and mathematics (to be consistent with ESSA expectations for achievement to be used as an index of student learning) (Gibb and Dyches 2016); however, the student's functional skills need to be considered as well. Examples of functional performance include socialization, self-care, employment skills, and ability to use public transportation.

The necessary information concerning academic achievement and functional performance includes statements of the student's current level of ability. These statements should be summarized from formal and informal assessments of the student. Observations from teachers, related service providers, parents, and the student may be incorporated. Note that this means information gathered in the pre-referral stage or through RTI will be useful as well. Both the student's current levels (typically meaning "strengths") and needs in the area(s) of concern should be documented. A useful PLAAFP statement includes specific information that can be informative for planning instruction to meet the student's needs (for example, "decodes at 3.1 grade level, on the GORT-4 scored below average for silent reading fluency and silent reading comprehends passages at 2.4 grade level" as opposed to "reads at a 2nd to 3rd grade level").

Instructional Goals

The heart of the IEP is the statement of **annual goals.** The annual goals respond to the information in the PLAAFP and are the basis for determining what accommodations and specially designed instruction will benefit the student. Simply said, the annual goals are outcome statements that name what the student will accomplish in one year. For each academic, extracurricular, or nonacademic area impacted by the student's disability (as stated in the PLAAFP), the IEP should contain at least one goal stating what the team expects the student to be able to learn in one calendar year. When written appropriately, the goal will state an observable outcome. If the goals are written with overly general wording, there is no guarantee that the teacher and everyone else who works with the student will have the same outcome in mind. Instead, a goal statement should name precisely what will be observed if the goal is accomplished.

Consider the two examples of good goal statements from Box 2.2: although there will always be room for some questioning of what a goal statement intends, all stakeholders know fairly specifically what outcomes are expected for Rena and Jae-Su. In the case of Jae-Su's goal statement, there is room to question how much the quality of her composition matters and what "*conform to* English Language Arts standards #3, 7, and 8" means, but there is enough specificity that all stakeholders can share understanding of the goal.

Historically, **short-term objective** statements have had to accompany annual goal statements; however, since 2004 IDEA only requires objectives, or benchmarks, for students who participate in alternative assessments that correspond to alternative

BOX 2.2

Examples of Good and Poor IEP Goal Statements

GOOD GOAL STATEMENTS

"Rena will recognize 50 words on sight from the second-grade level of the Dolch word list."

"Jae-Su will compose five-paragraph essays on class topics; essays will conform to English Language Arts standards #3, 7, and 8."

POOR GOAL STATEMENTS

"Stuart will improve his social skills."
[What does "improve" mean? Which social skills or how many? In what context?]

"Anwar will use grade-level math strategies."
[Which strategies? For what math skills?]

"Felicia will pay attention for five minutes without getting distracted or fidgeting."
[Pay attention to what? In what setting?]

achievement standards. When used, short-term objectives should be accomplished in the process of attaining an annual goal. In some cases, students would master the objectives sequentially, in the order they are listed under the goal statement. A traditionally worded objective statement includes an observable behavior, the condition under which the behavior will be performed, and the standard by which performance will be judged (most commonly a proficiency level). IDEA has also allowed using **benchmark** statements in place of short-term objectives. Recognizing that many goals are not accomplished by lockstep attainment of discrete skills (sequential objectives) and that progress can be assessed without discrete measurements, benchmarks instead represent markers of improvement toward goal attainment (Box 2.3). We strongly recommend that you always write objectives or benchmarks (whichever is appropriate) to accompany a goal, and that the goal also be written in the three-part format. This ensures the greatest clarity for all who must read and use the IEP.

Specially Designed Instruction

The **specially designed instruction** portion of the IEP includes descriptions of any modified skills or content instruction that the IEP team determines the student must receive to attain the IEP goals and succeed in whichever curriculums the student participates. The modifications might be to the content learned, how instruction is delivered, and/or performance criteria. *Modified* means that it is significantly different from what is provided in general education. An example of specially designed content would be a student working on decoding and reading fluency while the rest of the class works on reading for comprehension, or a student might learn about safely navigating her or his neighborhood while others study global cartography. The method of delivery of instruction can be modified to ensure the student learns in a way the PLAAFP revealed is effective for that student—for example, a multisensory approach to reading instruction. Finally, performance criteria can be altered to be more appropriate to the individual; maybe the expected percentage correct would be changed or the student could demonstrate knowledge orally instead of in writing.

It should be obvious that general education teachers responsible for teaching the student should be aware of the specially designed instruction modifications specified

---

BOX 2.3

Examples of Short-Term Objective and Benchmark Statements

GOAL

"Rena will recognize 50 words from the second-grade level of the Dolch word list, on sight in grade-level reading passages."

Objective #1: Given a list of 10 randomly selected words from the Dolch first-grade-level list, Rena will correctly read 8 of the words aloud.

Objective #2: Given a list of 10 randomly selected words from the Dolch second-grade-level list, Rena will correctly read 8 of the words aloud.

Objective #3: Given a grade 2-level controlled reading passage, Rena will read aloud sections including at least 8 Dolch second-grade-list words, without error.

GOAL

"Jae-Su will compose five-paragraph essays on class topics; essays will conform to English Language Arts standards #3, 7, and 8."

Objective #1: Jae-Su will prepare a TREE outline for essay planning that conforms to an essay topic assigned for a social studies topic.

Objective #2: Jae-Su will compose paragraph-length "essays" that conform to a TREE outline she develops.

Objective #3: Jae-Su will compose five-paragraph essays that conform to a TREE outline she develops, for a topic assigned in any of her content classes.

How Jae-Su's objectives may be rewritten as benchmark statement:

Benchmark #1: Jae-Su will compose paragraph-length essays that conform to a TREE outline she develops.

Objective #2: Jae-Su will compose three-paragraph length essays that conform to TREE outlines she develops.

Objective #3: Jae-Su will compose five-paragraph essays that conform to TREE outlines she develops, for topics assigned in any of her content classes.

---

in the IEP. Of course, they should have been involved in planning them as part of the IEP team planning process.

Even when a student will receive instruction that is planned as part of the general education curriculum anyway, it should be specified in the specially designed instruction section. That way, if the classroom teacher decides to alter the curriculum, the special education student will still be entitled to receive the needed instruction. The information in the specially designed instruction section sometimes pertains to individual goals (for example, the orthographic approach to writing would be used during instruction on the skills of writing, but maybe not during a social studies class) and other times to all instruction for the student (for example, provide feedback and praise).

Another facet of specially designed instruction is **related services**, which include transportation and developmental, corrective, or other support services that a student needs to receive and benefit from an education. The term "related" is used to signal that these services provide students with access to their education, but they are not educational interventions themselves. Examples of related services include physical or occupational therapy, secure storage and adult supervision for students taking prescription medications during the school day, psychological services such as counseling, and transportation to and from school. The only related services that may be provided under the IDEA are those that are needed for students to benefit from special education. In accordance with Section 504, however, related services must be provided to support general or special education.

The specially designed instruction section of the IEP is also the place to identify **instructional accommodations** students should receive. An accommodation is a minor change in how teachers present information to the student or in how the student learns or performs. The change does not alter overall learning expectations. Note that an accommodation is a lesser change than is a modification. To accommodate a student with attention-deficit/hyperactivity disorder (ADHD), for example, the teacher might give that student preferential seating away from distractions or the teacher might give the student a fidget object to squeeze to alleviate a desire to fidget. Other accommodations relate more directly to the teaching-learning process; the teacher might give the student print copies of directions that everyone else only receives orally, or for the sake of that one student the teacher might write the instructions on the board and everyone could benefit from the student's accommodation, or the teacher may give the student extra time on exams to compensate for distractibility. Note that, in all of these examples, the student still learns, or is tested on, the same content or skills as nondisabled peers. (For much more on accommodations, see Chapter 10.)

Service Delivery

Once the goals and specially designed instruction are stated, the IEP must include a **service plan.** This section of the IEP identifies the following:

- The types of professional(s) (for example, special educator, general educator, therapist) who will provide specific services (for example, classroom instruction, one-on-one tutoring, counseling)
- Where those services will be provided (the least restrictive environment [LRE])
- The duration of the services (for example, number of minutes per day, how frequently per week, for what portion of the calendar year)
- How each goal is addressed by one or more of the specified services

The service plan section also includes an area to specify **testing accommodations** that the student will receive during standardized and high-stakes testing, as well as during classroom testing. Just like instructional accommodations, testing accommodations are minor changes in how the student is tested or in how the student performs the test; testing accommodations do not alter the overall testing expectations. Among common testing accommodations for students with HI are extra time, a scribe, taking the exam in a study carrel or private setting, being able to use a calculator, and being allowed to write directly on the exam, even if others have to write answers on a separate answer sheet.

To be effective, the testing accommodations listed in the IEP should be consistent with the instructional accommodations the student receives (Burns 2006). The accommodations will be of limited usefulness on tests unless the student uses the accommodations daily. It makes little sense to teach a student to do a task one way (for example, completing math problems using a calculator) and then assess the student's abilities in other ways (for example, using scratch paper only).

Completing this section of the IEP is very important. In the case of some standardized and high-stakes tests, accommodations that are not certified as necessary on an official document such as an IEP may be denied to students. Some standardized exams (for example, SAT, GED, and states' high stakes achievement exams) have approved lists of acceptable accommodations. IEP teams should consider those lists for students who will eventually take those exams.

The 504 Plan

A different plan is developed for students with disabilities when they do not need special education services under IDEA but still require related services to access their education due to their disability. However, a student may have both plans if considered necessary, for example when a student needs a related service not directly related to her or his special education, or if a student is going to exit special education but will still need related services. A plan specifying needed accommodations and related services, commonly known as a **504 Plan,** is developed instead, in accordance with provisions of Section 504 of the Rehabilitation Act (1973). It is not special education; instead it provides for services related to whatever education the student with a disability receives, be it special or general education. Remember, it provides access to that education. Like an IEP, a 504 Plan needs to include sufficient information for educators to understand why specified services are needed, what those services should be, and how they should be provided (for example, who is responsible and in what settings).

To qualify for 504 services, a student must meet one of three conditions: the student has a physical or mental impairment that substantially limits a major life activity, the student formerly had such a disability but is still impacted, or the student is regarded (treated) as having a disability by others. Many students with ADHD in particular qualify for 504 services but do not meet IDEA eligibility criteria (Barkley 2000).

Section 504 does not specify what content should be included in a 504 Plan (nor, technically, that a plan be written). However, a useful 504 Plan specifies what related service(s) a student should receive, who will provide it, and how its impact will be monitored (see Burns 2006; Smith 2001). See Figure 2.2 for an example of a 504 Plan.

The Team Develops the IEP

As you can tell, every stage of the special education process, from pre-referral through planning and providing an individually appropriate special education, requires collaboration among special educators, general educators and other service providers, administrators, and parents and the students themselves. The team that comes together to compose the IEP represents the various stakeholders who play a role in the student's education. The following people are named by IDEA 2004 as members of the team:

Parent(s)
Student, whenever appropriate[1]
Special education teacher
General education teacher(s) of subjects impacted by the disability
Representative of local education agency, who is:

- Qualified to supervise provision of services
- Knowledgeable about general education curriculum
- Knowledgeable about resource availability

Professional to interpret instructional implications of evaluation results[2]
Transition agency representative[2]
Others deemed appropriate by the parent or education agency and consistent with IDEA and state and local requirements[2]

---

[1]*Must participate at least within one year of achieving legal age of majority, or if transition planning is to be discussed.*
[2]*As needed.*

▼ **FIGURE 2.2**
Sample 504 Plan

Name: _____ Albert C. _____   School/Class: _____ Fifth _____

Teacher: _____ Penny Margolis _____   Date of Plan: _____ 10–29 _____

General Strengths:

Albert performs math skills on grade level and is doing well during Math. His problem-solving skills (mathematical and otherwise) are also strong. He has excellent penmanship. Socially, he is appropriate with his peers and has made friends since moving into the district.

General Weaknesses:

Albert reads below grade level, showing difficulties with decoding as well as with comprehension. He makes frequent spelling errors in essay papers and assignments. A significant difficulty for Albert is comprehending and following directions.

Accommodation 1

Provide explicit directions for all assignments and back them up with written step-by-step directions.

Class:

All

Person Responsible for Implementing Accommodation:

Classroom teacher and any aides

Accommodation 2

Review instructions with Albert by having him paraphrase or explain them.

Class:

All

Person Responsible for Implementing Accommodation:

Classroom teacher or aide

Accommodation 3

When reading is not an instructional goal, provide easy-to-read version of materials or either read aloud or allow group reading.

Class:

All

Person Responsible for Implementing Accommodation:

Classroom teacher or aide

Individuals Participating in Development of Plan:

Penny Margolis–classroom teacher
Martha Bender–special educator

Source: Format for blank form reprinted with permission from T. E. C. Smith. Section 504, the ADA, and public schools (*Remedial and Special Education* 22(6)(2001):335–343).

Parents and students can feel like outsiders at a team meeting (see Summers et al. 2005). When teachers use professional jargon that is unfamiliar to parents or assumed to be common knowledge, it is easy for parents to feel devalued and unable to contribute (see Box 2.4 for one way schools are addressing this). Educators have an obligation to make parents feel that their input is valued, because families have valuable insights and goals for their child that can easily be overlooked in the process (Gonzalez et al. 2001;

BOX 2.4

Special Education Service Coordinators and Team Leaders

The IDEA requires that each child enrolled in early childhood special education (that is, between birth and age 3 and covered by Part C of the law) be assigned a service coordinator or case manager. There is not a similar requirement for students age 3 through 21. However, many K–12 schools do assign special education case managers. This professional's responsibilities include ensuring that all services identified in the IEP are provided in a coordinated fashion. The case manager also is responsible for communications between the school and parents and seeing that IEP proceedings are conducted in compliance with regulations. The case manager is sometimes also the individual student's special education teacher.

Similar to a case manager, many schools now have a team leader, sometimes known as the inclusion facilitator. This professional has a large caseload of special education students whom she or he oversees. This professional may or may not be the student's special education teacher. Note that Section 504 regulations specify that schools must have a 504 Service Coordinator, but that person is responsible for making sure the school is in compliance with 504 regulations and does not have direct responsibilities for individual students or their parents.

Moll et al. 1992). In the case of parents for whom English is not a comfortable language, the IDEA requires that a translator be present at the meeting and that all relevant documents be shared in translated forms, including the IEP document that the team develops.

In the same ways that parents may feel like outsiders to the IEP process, students who are present in IEP meetings tend to remain silent, with their input rarely solicited (Arndt, Konrad, and Test 2006). With preparation to participate, however, they too can make valuable contributions regarding their educational experiences and goals (Test et al. 2005). Students who participate in their own IEP meetings in meaningful ways tend to be more motivated to succeed in the education they and their teammates plan (Arndt et al. 2006). (See Chapter 3 for more on student participation on IEP and individualized transition plan [ITP] teams.)

2-2   Relating Education Plans to General Education

The IDEA requires that all students in special education participate "in the regular classroom, to the maximum extent possible, in order to . . . meet developmental goals and, to the maximum extent possible, the challenging expectations that have been established for all children" (IDEA 2004, §1400(c)(5)). When such participation is not appropriate, the goals specified for these students should focus on meeting the curriculum standards of their nondisabled peers (Allbritten, Mainzer, and Ziegler 2004).

The charge from the IDEA is clear: teams should plan an individually appropriate education that maximizes a student's participation in general education (Turnbull, Huerta, and Stowe 2006). All general education curricula have **curriculum standards.** The standards identify the learning experiences or outcomes expected of all learners who participate in that curriculum (Popham 2006). Curriculum standards shape the mandated general education curriculum at the state and local levels. In accordance with ESSA requirements, all students' performances on state-adopted "challenging" standards in English/language arts, mathematics, and science (depending on grade level) must be directly assessed, which is typically accomplished through exams. In many states, those exams are "high stakes," meaning that performance on them is tied to whether students are promoted to the next grade or graduate. Many states' standards are readily available via their Department of Education websites. For most curriculum areas, states adapt standards proposed by professional organizations in the various curriculum areas (for example, National Council of Teachers of Mathematics, National Geographic Society, Center for Civic Education, the Consortium of National Arts Education Associations). The standards reflect the opinions of experts and other stakeholders regarding what skills and knowledge students should possess. Some standards identify exact and observable skills or knowledge (for example, "As a result of activities in grades K–4, all students should develop understanding of . . . life cycles of organisms" [*National Science Education Standards*, National Research Council, 1996]), whereas others identify more global expectations (for example, "Students read a wide range of . . . texts to build an understanding of texts, of themselves, and of the cultures of the United States and the world" [*Standards for the English Language Arts*, National Council of Teachers of English and the International Reading Association, 1996]).

Standards and Students in Special Education

There are no separate curriculum standards for special education. Students with HI who perform certain academic skills significantly below grade level are expected to keep up with the general education content to the greatest extent possible while they work on those academic skills. Whenever possible, they should learn grade-level appropriate skills, even though other more basic skills proficiencies still need to be developed. Thus, if asked to read a play by Shakespeare, a student who reads well below the comfortable reading level required might be accommodated in reading the play (for example, receiving assistance with comprehension, using an alternative version of the text) while also receiving supplemental instruction in more basic reading skills. It can be challenging to teach both grade-level and more foundational skills to a student who struggles, but that is the expectation of the special education law.

Although students with HI typically benefit from the same high learning standards as other students, they do sometimes need to be taught differently or are expected to perform in ways that differ from what the standards expect. In such cases, the specially designed instruction section of the IEP is where the different content, methods of instruction, or performance criteria are recorded.

The Need for Collaboration and Co-Teaching

Clearly, special educators need to collaborate with parents, administrators, specialists (such as a speech pathologist, reading specialist, or physical therapist), and, of course, other teachers to plan special education. It should now be clear as well that they need to collaborate in providing that special education. The most common collaboration is a special education teacher pairing with a general education teacher, as Karen and Tom did in Case 2.2. These teachers commonly collaborate in inclusive general education classes to teach both students with and without disabilities.

Collaboration in its true sense means two teachers working together to plan and teach students with and without disabilities in an inclusion or collaborative setting. Friend and Cook (2000) view collaboration as "a style for direct interaction between at least two coequal parties voluntarily engaged in shared decision making as they work toward a common goal." It is referred to as a *style* because individuals can collaborate to varying degrees. For example, some teachers may choose to be more accommodating to their partner, whereas others may be more direct when

CASE 2.2   When Two Teachers Intersect to Co-Teach

Case Introduction

Now that you have worked through the first case in this chapter, you should feel comfortable addressing issues in a second case. You are going to read about how a special educator and her inclusive classroom co-teacher collaborated. They planned together and co-taught in the ways they agreed to in the classroom. However, both would prefer something about how the other one interacts to be a little bit different. Watch for ways they might improve on their already positive collaborative relationship.

"Mr. Lennon, we think the correct answer is 'isosceles triangle'," Karen De Grazia called out from where she was standing beside Sharon and Benny's desks.

"Oh, they got it!" Mr. Lennon announced to the room. "But you have to tell us why."

"What did we say, Benny?" Karen asked. When he hesitated, she prompted "about the two sides."

"That it has two equal sides," Benny replied to Mr. Lennon.

"Correct again!" Mr. Lennon congratulated. "Let's see who gets the next one."

Sharon and Benny felt pretty good about getting the correct answer. So did Karen.

Karen is Benny's special education case manager. She leads his IEP team, is the person in the school who is responsible for ensuring that his various special education services remain coordinated, facilitates communication between the school and Benny's parents, and teaches Benny. She is also his math co-teacher. The IEP team suggested she co-teach in Benny's geometry class, and it worked out as she also has two other students with IEPs in that class. Sharon is not a special education student.

Karen felt good about Benny and Sharon getting the right answer with her help because, as she confessed to Tom Lennon when he told her they would be doing a unit on shapes and angles, she recognized the various terms but it had been so long that she really didn't remember the rules for distinguishing one shape from another. Mr. Lennon assured her that "it's not that hard to get" and he would help her if she ever got stuck.

As they planned, Mr. Lennon was the lead teacher up at the front of the room where sample problems were displayed on the screen. Karen circulated throughout the room, checking progress over students' shoulders, paying particular attention to Benny and her other special education students. She was often able to help students because she paid careful attention to Mr. Lennon's demonstrations and explanations to the class. When she wasn't quite sure of her own knowledge she would signal Tom to come over if he was circulating around too, or if he was up-front she would call out, "Mr. Lennon, we have a question." While she really wasn't sure of the correct information, it appeared to the students that she was just being a helpful teacher to the whole class. This was because sometimes during Mr. Lennon's demonstrations at the board she would interrupt him and say things like, "Mr. Lennon, can you give us one more example of that," or "Mr. Lennon, is that true because ...?" Occasionally, Tom would say something like "OK, this is for Ms. De Grazia and everyone else who wasn't paying attention the first time," but most students took this as a way of keeping the mood light. Most students in the class appreciated Karen being their "voice," as she often asked about or confirmed the same things they were wondering about.

These roles were something else Karen and Tom had planned. He came to appreciate just how much clearer his teaching had become since Karen joined him in the classroom. In fact, in previous school years Karen's students had done very poorly because Tom had difficulty keeping an eye on them when he was the only teacher in the room, and he really wasn't sure how to differentiate his instruction for them. Not only that, but when those students sought help in the learning center Karen often didn't know what they were working on or how they should write their geometry proofs.

Tom felt appreciative of Karen being there to help in his classroom, in part because he felt that the special education students were not supported well enough when they had to get help in their learning center instead of his classroom. To his mind, it wasn't that he needed to do more for those students, because he was already an effective teacher, but he was glad to see them being better served. Karen wished he saw her more as an equal, but she never voiced this to him because she was embarrassed by her limited mathematics skills.

CASE QUESTIONS

1. *Karen and Tom did not have a "perfect" collaborative relationship yet it worked well. What were the strengths that helped their relationship work?*

2. *How effectively do Karen and Tom communicate with each other?*

3. *How would you describe Karen and Tom's approach to co-teaching?*

---

interacting with others. Moreover, collaboration is a shared process whereby both educators are viewed as co-equals valued for their expertise, and both support the learning of all students in the class. Successful collaboration results when the two teachers value each other and communicate effectively with one another to meet their students' needs.

For some teachers, collaboration means having minimal interactions with students in a co-taught class. For others, collaboration means becoming fully involved while teaching content in academic classes. Either way, collaboration requires teachers to work together and to share. Friend and Cook (2000) point out the following six defining characteristics of effective collaboration:

- Collaboration is voluntary.
- Collaboration requires parity among participants.
- Collaboration is based upon mutual goals.
- Collaboration depends on shared responsibility for participation and decision making.
- Individuals who collaborate share their resources.
- Individuals who collaborate share accountability.

Collaboration Is Voluntary. Collaboration works best when two teachers volunteer to collaborate. Like many initiatives imposed upon teachers, mandating that teachers collaborate rarely works. Typically, teachers who have worked together in some capacity in the past are more amenable to collaborating than teachers who have never worked together. In most cases, teachers form a natural pairing and both look forward to working together. Teachers who have already developed a bond and established communication and collaborative working skills often make an ideal pair to begin collaboration (Gately and Gately 2001).

Collaboration Requires Parity Among Participants. Simply put, parity involves viewing your colleagues as equals. Recall that Karen and Tom worked well together, but there was some tension in how he thought of her and in how they both valued the other's role. Parity is likely to develop when both teachers have respect for one another's skills as teachers. According to Friend and Cook (2000), if one teacher views the other as lacking in expertise, parity is unlikely to develop. Respect is a key component to keeping the relationship working and viable over the years.

Collaboration Is Based Upon Mutual Goals. Collaboration works best when two teachers have the same shared goals. For collaborative pairs, this means having open discussions about goals and expectations for their impending work together. When using mutually agreed-upon goals, two teachers can work together to accomplish them. Although the pair may not agree with all of the goals, Friend and Cook (2000) point out they need only to agree upon one goal to make the collaborative relationship work.

Collaboration Depends on Shared Responsibility for Participation and Decision Making. Shared participation and decision making are key components of effective collaboration. We often hear from co-teachers that their participation is limited and that they are omitted from the decision-making process. When teachers have not been trained to collaborate or when one of the teachers makes all of the decisions, the other teacher may harbor resentment or may refuse to fully accept ownership of all of the students in the class. Those teachers may still be grateful to be collaborating but simply wish for a greater role in the collaborative partnership. For some teachers, this does not necessarily mean an equal division of labor between the pair (Friend and Cook 2000). For instance, some teachers may be happy serving in a support role for the pair. One teacher may lead class in the front of the room while the other teacher records notes on the board, asks questions, and monitors students' note-taking.

Individuals Who Collaborate Share Accountability for Outcomes. As previously mentioned, not only do co-teachers share participation, but they also share accountability for outcomes. Working as a pair or group, the members work toward a common goal and share the responsibility for reaching that goal. It is a group effort to assist the students, and all members of the group work toward that end.

Individuals Who Collaborate Share Resources. Teaching resources fall into three general categories: teaching materials, classroom space, and knowledge or skills. Teaching materials include all of those materials used in the classroom, from books and worksheets to quizzes and tests to computers and electronics. Classroom space is another shared resource. We have known collaborative teachers who push a cart from classroom to classroom because they do not have a classroom or any place to store their teaching materials. These "nomadic" teachers work with different teachers and move to each new classroom ready to co-teach the next group of students. Teachers with fixed classrooms should share space so that these co-teachers can store their materials and have a place to call home.

Teachers also share knowledge and skills for teaching students with disabilities. In collaborative contexts, teachers will share what they learned from books, classes, or professional development activities with others. These skills and techniques are viewed as public property, void of any one person's ownership, and are meant to be shared and used by all.

Throughout this chapter, we use *collaborative teaching* and *co-teaching* as synonymous terms. This is because co-teaching is the commonly used term in education but we are encouraging you to always think about it at the level of collaborative partnership.

Co-teaching has a number of advantages for students, including lower student/teacher ratio, immediate available support, exposure to varied teaching styles, and access to help for *all* students. Likewise, co-teaching has numerous advantages for teachers, including shared skills and materials, exposure to varied teaching models, increased knowledge about teaching, mutual support for one another, and greater job satisfaction (Bradley and Switlick 1997; Scruggs, Mastropieri, and McDuffie 2007), just to name a few.

THINK BACK TO THE CASE of Karen and Tom . . .

Karen and Tom did not have a "perfect" collaborative relationship yet it worked well. What were the strengths that helped their relationship work?

The two did not satisfy all of Friend and Cook's (2002) characteristics of effective collaboration, but they did approximate several of them. They had some degree of parity. Each respected the other to do a job she or he couldn't. They each focused on their co-teacher's strengths and were not concerned about their co-teacher duplicating their own strengths. They also shared goals for their teaching and their students.

Additionally, they had shared responsibility for participation and decision making, even though it may not have looked like it. Each agreed to the roles they played in the classroom and in planning. Tom brought one expertise and Karen another. Thanks to their planning, they also shared in making decisions about how they would teach, including being responsive to each other in the moment, such as when Karen would prompt Tom to give the students another example. You should be able to find additional ways the characteristics of effective collaboration are met.

Lesson Planning

The first step of effective teaching is planning an effective lesson, and when teachers co-teach, co-planning is absolutely necessary. There is no one best approach to planning, just as there is no one best format for lesson plans. Planning a lesson helps to ensure that a teacher(s) has carefully thought through the following:

- What the student(s) should learn
- Why the student(s) should learn it
- What the student(s) should know or be able to do as prior knowledge
- What the student(s) will need to be able to do in the lesson to have success
- Ways the lesson may need to be modified
- Each teacher's roles and responsibilities (when co-teaching)
- How the teacher(s) will know if students have success
- How the classroom will be configured

A good plan will also guide teachers in evaluating how effectively they taught and how efficiently the students learned. Having a good plan is essential to having a good lesson.

Components of a Lesson Plan. Traditional components of a lesson plan include objectives, materials, procedures, and assessments (Albert and Ammer 2004).

Searcy and Maroney (1996) break it out further: they have identified 14 components of lesson plans that professional literature recommends teachers use. Those marked with an asterisk in Table 2.1 are the components that special educators most strongly recommended beginning special education teachers include in their lesson plans. (See Callahan, Clark, and Kellough [1998] for other recommended lesson plan components.) Ultimately, what makes a lesson plan useful is that it contains all of the information a teacher needs to get through a lesson.

The Challenge of Planning. Making time to plan is one challenge to planning. Fighting the inclination to "plan in your head" is another. Even though experienced teachers recommend that beginning teachers develop lesson plans, most novices do not; indeed, most experienced teachers report that they do not either (Arends 1998; Searcy and Maroney 1996). The greater the number of students for whom they are responsible, the more likely they are to write plans, however.

Co-Planning Skills

If you are going to co-teach you have to co-plan; in fact, co-teaching without co-planning is almost certainly going to go poorly. A well-planned lesson may not always guarantee a well-taught lesson, but it certainly increases the chances that

TABLE 2.1 14 Lesson Plan Components Recommended for Teacher Planning

Student objectives*	Materials required*	Time required
Prerequisite skills	Seating arrangement	Anticipatory set
Instructional steps*	Checks for understanding*	Guided practice*
Independent practice*	Summary/closing	Evaluation of student outcomes*
Follow-up activity*	Self-evaluation of lesson presentation	

*Components beginning special educators most need to include in their lesson plans. Reported by Searcy and Maroney (1996) as recommended by greater than 55 percent of survey respondents.

the lesson will go well. Conversely, having no plan is an invitation for disaster. Therefore, it is important to have a plan that is developed by all who will teach the lesson and that has been well thought out ahead of time. During co-planning, establish a routine and, initially, use a written guide to structure co-planning time (Table 2.2). The written guide should cover the previous lesson, break down the

TABLE 2.2 Co-Planning Guide and Lesson Plan

Evaluation of Previous Lesson

Which portion of the lesson went well?

Which portion of the lesson went poorly?

Which content should be reviewed or retaught?

Which activity could be used to review content that is being retaught?

Are there parts of co-teaching that could be improved (that is, introduction, preview, transitions, review, preparation/distribution of materials, monitoring of students, feedback to students, and so on)?

Lesson Considerations

What cognitive supports could be used in the lesson to ensure that all students learn the content?

What accommodations do students with disabilities need?

What effective teaching methods or supports are used in the lesson to enhance learning?

What classroom management components are needed for the lesson?

New Lesson Format:

Advance Organizer or Review of Previous Content or Skills

What will you say/do? Who does this? How long?

Partner-teacher does what?

Introduction to New Content or Skills

What? Who? How long?

Partner-teacher does what?

Guided Practice of Content or Skills Through Activities

Activity 1

What? Who? How long?

Partner-teacher does what?

Activity 2

What? Who? How long?

Partner-teacher does what?

Activity 3

What? Who? How long?

Partner-teacher does what?

Assessment of Learning

What? Who? How long?

Partner-teacher does what?

Summary or Review

What? Who? How long?

Partner-teacher does what?

Filler, Enrichment, or Follow-Up Activity

What? Who? How long?

Partner-teacher does what?

new lesson into sections that can be discussed, and include an area for assigning who will be responsible for carrying out each portion of the lesson. Each portion should be assigned based upon each teacher's skills or expertise as well as students' needs. It is important that both teachers are clear about their roles and responsibilities during teaching.

In middle or high school math classes, the special education teacher might be responsible for the warmup portion of the class. In the warmup, the teacher reviews problems that were previously taught and ensures that students understand previous material before moving on to new material. The general education teacher might then take over for teaching new content while the special education teacher walks around and monitors students, checking for correctness of work and understanding of new information. As we noted, each of these areas should be worked out ahead of time and assigned to the teacher responsible for that portion.

Establishing a routine ahead of time prevents teachers from having downtime during their co-planning periods. Routines are especially important for novice teachers or new co-teachers. Routines ensure that all people know what they are responsible for during planning and what materials are needed. For example, an effective co-planning routine might involve meeting in the same room every time to plan out the next day's lesson, having all of the necessary materials that will be used during planning (for example, the textbook, the teacher's guide, paper, pencils, ancillary materials related to the lesson, the teacher's gradebook, students' work, master copies of handouts), having the school secretary hold all calls during your meeting time, having a method for recording the lesson plan (for example, one person is a scribe to record notes and you switch the next time you meet), following a set procedure (see Table 2.2), and ending within a reasonable amount of time. Again, the purpose of a routine is to minimize downtime and make the meeting flow smoothly. Planning time is such an important part of co-teaching for teams that protecting it is often a *number one* concern (Dieker 2001).

The actual co-planning guide and lesson plan can serve as a record of agreed-upon components and roles. The first portion of it serves to review the previous lesson. If planning takes place in the afternoon, an evaluation of the lesson that was taught that day would be recorded in this portion. The purpose of this section is to learn from what did and did not work and then make the appropriate changes. Be sure that you base your decisions on data from the previous lesson. If students did not adequately learn a new concept or skill, to what extent did they not learn it? Is it based upon test or quiz results, or is it based upon oral questions? Similarly, if students mastered content or skills, how do you know they reached mastery? Did all or just barely a majority of students reach mastery? High-achieving students can frequently master content and skills despite the teacher's lack of skills at teaching it. Many of these students are self-motivated learners capable of learning on their own. Because you are teaching a diverse group of learners, consider whether other students (for example, average, low-achieving, and students with disabilities) also reached mastery of specific skills or content (see the HALO procedure in Chapter 10). For some students, reviewing or even re-teaching of content or skills may be needed for them to progress on to the next skill level.

The lesson considerations portion serves to remind teachers about cognitive supports (for example, guided notes, cognitive maps and organizers, outlines, mnemonics, study guides) that could be used to help students record better notes and remember the content of lectures. This section also prompts teachers to identify and include effective teaching methods (for example, differentiated instruction, direct instruction, discovery learning, mnemonics techniques, pause procedure) or supports that they could use to deliver content to students. The accommodations question serves to remind teachers to consider appropriate accommodations for students with disabilities.

The classroom management component serves to remind teachers that different management components might be needed when using different co-teaching models. For example, if using station teaching, teachers might provide additional reinforcers (such as stickers, tokens, points) for students who are quiet, transition quietly, cooperate while working in groups, and follow directions.

The last portion of the co-planning guide and lesson plan, new lesson format, is the actual lesson plan. This portion could be modified depending upon the lesson, but be sure to use the following components: advance organizer, introduction, guided practice activities, assessment of learning (for example, independent practice), and summary of lesson.

Making Use of Lesson Plans. Students will benefit from teachers who share lesson plans with them in the form of advance organizers (Ellis and Lenz 1990; Lenz, Alley, and Schumaker 1987). In the 1960s, Ausubel (1963; Ausubel, Novak, and Hanesian 1968) suggested that advance organizers help orient learners to the topic and task expectations in ways that boost participation and learning outcomes; more recent research has corroborated that idea (Bulgren and Lenz 1996; see also Swanson and Hoskyn 2001).

In Figure 2.3, a teacher completes a lesson organizer for a lesson on women in U.S. history. The teacher begins by orienting students to the lesson. First, she explains the lesson topic (similarities and differences between Harriet Tubman and Sojourner Truth) and how it relates to the larger unit (famous women in American history). Now the students have a sense of what the lesson has to do with anything else they are studying.

The web is the central feature of the lesson organizer. It identifies key concepts and vocabulary that will be addressed in the lesson, as well as how they all fit together based on the lesson topic. The teacher should walk the students through reading the web, and all portions of the organizer, by narrating the information represented. To keep the students actively involved, the narration should become an interactive dialogue in which the students share their prior knowledge about the lesson topic and web content. They can also generate questions they want to answer during the lesson, or they can predict answers to questions the teacher poses. In this way, they participate in developing the plan for what they will study. The lesson organizer serves to inform students as to what will be learned, activate their prior knowledge, preview vocabulary and concepts, indicate relationships among vocabulary and concepts, and motivate students to think about the content.

The organizer sections titled "Challenge Question" and "What questions should I ask myself?" are places to indicate the "big ideas" of the lesson. The questions cue students to the types of information and relationships among concepts they will be studying. They are also cued to which information is particularly important to attend. The questions are designed to prompt thinking. Thus, a good question on a lesson organizer does not ask a student merely to recall a fact, but rather to synthesize or otherwise act on content from the lesson (Lenz et al. 2005). The questions can be referred to periodically throughout the lesson.

Although the lesson organizer is useful to help launch a lesson by orienting students to the topic, it can also be a useful organizational tool throughout the lesson. The "tasks to accomplish" section can include a record of when assignments are due

▶ **FIGURE 2.3**

Shared Planning Lesson Organizer: Women in History

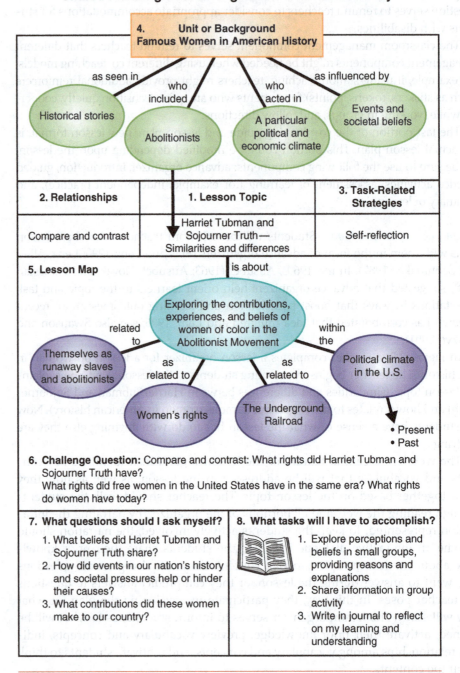

Reprinted with permission from L. R. Albert and J. J. Ammer."Lesson Planning and Delivery."
In *Teaching Content to All*, eds. B. K. Lenz, D. D. Deshler, and B. R. Kissam. (Boston, MA: Allyn
& Bacon, 2004, 205).

or when certain activities will take place. In the Figure 2.3 lesson organizer, students
can see that they will have a small group activity and a journal writing assignment
for which they are responsible. To help them remain organized, students should have
copies of the lesson organizer that they can keep in their notebooks and refer to as
needed. Co-teachers using the Lesson Organizer Routine have to use effective collaboration skills to be effective. The same is true for any other form of teaching they
went to the trouble of co-planning.

2-3 Skills Needed for Effective Collaboration and Co-Teaching

For teachers to collaborate effectively, they must possess or acquire skills that allow them to communicate clearly to their partners and that enable them to provide support to one another throughout their working relationship. Some individuals already possess these skills and are effective communicators in their own right. Others lack the appropriate communication and support skills and may benefit from professional development activities to enhance their skills. Four key skills are important for effective collaboration: (1) communication skills, (2) support skills, (3) problem-solving skills, and (4) co-planning skills.

Communication Skills

Teachers need effective communication skills to be productive and to develop healthy working relationships with colleagues. Those communication skills involve understanding both verbal and nonverbal communication, as well as effective listening. According to Friend and Cook (2000), effective communication involves active listening as well as interpersonal communication skills or verbal communication skills.

THINK BACK TO THE CASE of Karen and Tom . . .

How effectively do Karen and Tom communicate with each other?

In the classroom Karen and Tom have established a very effective communication routine. Each knows what their agreed-upon role is, and their communication patterns usually respect that. They agreed that they should not draw attention to Karen's limitations in geometry. However, Tom occasionally mocks her, but in ways that appear to the students like the two are just having fun together. In contrast, she speaks in the voice of a student when she wants him to review something for the class. In planning sessions they could discuss how this communication style feels to each of them and talk about any changes they might desire. They could also talk more about how Karen could be prepared for each lesson. Also, they should discuss more fully what role Tom can play in meeting the special education needs of Benny and the other students. They can use effective communication skills to ensure those conversations are productive.

Active Listening Skills. Active listening means that the person listening is engaged in the conversation and trying to understand what is being said. Effective listeners typically use nonverbal cues, body movements, vocal cues, posture, and verbal cues to communicate with and understand the person who is speaking. Active listeners lean forward slightly toward the speaker, maintain eye contact with the speaker, and use verbal and nonverbal cues to communicate their attention and involvement in the conversation. All of these actions are necessary to be a good listener.

Nonverbal Listening Cues. Miller (2005) reports that 93 percent of communication comes through facial expressions and vocal intonations. For collaborators, this means that paying attention to nonverbal cues is essential for understanding the message. Nonverbal cues can express feelings that are too upsetting to state and are usually a more accurate indication of the true intent of the message (Miller 2005). Nonverbal cues include body language, vocal cues, and encouragers.

Body Language. Body language includes body posture, gestures, and facial expressions that serve as cues to inform us about underlying messages that accompany verbal messages. We often use body language to add meaning to our spoken messages. The gestures and facial expressions show the speaker that the listener is attending to the conversation and doing his or her best to understand what is being said. Although body language by itself has no exact meaning, it can confirm or reject the spoken words when paired with vocal language. Hence, when communicating, teachers should be cognizant of students' body posture, gestures, and facial expressions to fully understand messages and detect any mixed signals by following up with questions or summarizing information to confirm the accuracy of the message.

Vocal Listening Cues. Vocal cues are another important component of active listening. Vocal cues help the listener detect the emotion behind the spoken message. Vocal cues are provided in the pitch, tone, and volume of the spoken word. People tend to speak in a louder tone when upset; when excited, people tend to speak in a higher pitch and louder tone; when depressed, people tend to speak in a lower and quieter tone. All of these cues can help us understand the message and help others understand our message to them. Another type of cue, called encouragers, can be nonverbal (such as nodding or smiling) or verbal ("OK," "Yeah," "Go on," or "Right").

Verbal Communication Skills. When listening to others speak or when communicating with others, it is important to be accurate in your understanding of their message; likewise, it is important for you to try to send an accurate message. When listening to someone describing a problem, you have to be in tune with the feelings and message to ensure that you understand the problem from the speaker's perspective. Remember that you are both working toward a solution from a "shared" perspective. For example, if your co-teacher asks you to take the lead in developing a behavior intervention plan for a student with disruptive behaviors but you never discuss which behaviors are of concern or the desired goal, there will be confusion that causes each of you to question the other's competence for dealing with the problem. For two people to understand the solution from a shared perspective, both must do their best to make sure the message is clear and explicit and, when necessary, use questions to clarify any discrepancies. Likewise, when co-teachers make a statement about teaching, both should use questions and summary statements to ensure that each has the same or a similar perspective about the problem.

Support Skills

Along with verbal communication and active listening skills, support skills also play an important role in collaboration. Support skills are verbal and nonverbal forms of communication to show your partner that you understand the problem and any feelings associated with the problem. Support skills are important because, along with effective listening and verbal communication skills, they aid in the development of bonds between teachers. These support skills are often the "glue" that holds the co-teaching team together. Support skills include the feedback that you provide to others.

Friend and Cook (2000) have suggested that feedback should be descriptive, specific, and concise. Moreover, it should be directed toward changeable behavior, and you should always check for agreement and understanding. Descriptive feedback refers to providing feedback in an objective, nonjudgmental form. In doing so, the observer should describe a specific event in descriptive terms and in a concise way. Rather than chat on and on about an event, describe it, check to make sure the individual understood your statements, and then move on to another area or discuss some possible solutions to the problem. When discussing solutions to problems, they should be feasible and based upon behavior that the individual can change. These guidelines allow statements to become more "objective"—that is more about the action and less about the person.

Types of Feedback Statements. There are three main types of feedback statements: positive feedback, constructive feedback, and supportive feedback. *Positive feedback* statements are those in which a teacher describes affirmative actions that the person has completed. Any meetings that involve providing feedback to teachers should always incorporate positive and constructive statements. These positive statements should address actions that can be shaped over time into more appropriate target behaviors. For example, "I noticed that you were assisting Natalie with her worksheet this afternoon. You did a wonderful job giving her explicit feedback on her answers." Again, the statement is descriptive and reflects observable behavior while providing positive reinforcement for the actions.

Constructive feedback includes statements that provide the individual with suggestions for changing actions or behavior. Constructive feedback, like the other types of feedback, should be objective and descriptive. It should describe observed events or actions and should provide recommendations for modifying those actions. According to experts, "feedback that is immediate, specific, positive, and constructive holds the most promise for bringing about change in teacher behavior" (Scheeler, Ruhl, and McAfee 2004).

Supportive feedback is the third type of feedback that you could provide to colleagues. Supportive feedback lets the individual know that you relate to the feelings or emotions that the person feels about an incident. These statements also let the individual know how much you appreciate her or his support. Statements of support might include, "I agree with your idea and will help to implement it" or "I think you handled that situation well."

Of course, the most effective feedback is feedback that has been solicited. Individuals who ask for assistance or advice are more likely to take your advice.

Problem-Solving Skills

Problem-solving skills are another important component of effective collaboration. Problem-solving skills can be used to help solve students' behavioral and academic challenges or they can be used to address issues with instruction or classroom routines. When problem solving, consider not only what the student can do differently but also what the teacher(s) can do differently to help remediate the problem.

Co-Teaching Models

The main models of co-teaching that we will discuss in detail are station teaching, interactive teaching, alternative teaching, and parallel teaching (Cook and Friend 2000; Friend and Bursuck 2006; Walther-Thomas et al. 2000). Each model can be used with different content (see Figure 2.4). Depending upon the purpose of a lesson, one model might work better than others. For example, parallel teaching might be used when teachers want to review content before a test. On the other hand, alternative teaching might be used if a portion of the class has missed content and the purpose is to catch those students up with the rest of the class.

Station Teaching. Using station teaching, depending upon the size of the class, teachers set up three to five stations around the room and students move in groups from one station to another after a designated period of time (10 to 15 minutes). As you

▶ **FIGURE 2.4**
Co-Teaching Models

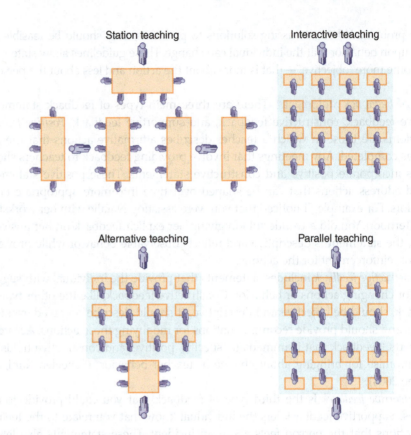

could guess, station teaching requires quite a bit of preparation on the part of the teachers. Prior to the lesson, teachers have to prepare each station with the appropriate materials and make sure that the directions are clear. If directions are not clear or if expectations for student behavior are not explicit, students may become sidetracked trying to figure out what to do or may end up using materials in an inappropriate manner. In station teaching, teachers also have to monitor the noise level and behaviors in the room.

When used in collaborative classrooms, each teacher will work at a station where teaching or direct supervision is required; at the remaining stations, students are expected to work independently. For example, if students were studying the parts of a plant, you could set up five stations: (1) a short video that shows how plants grow from a seed into a mature plant; (2) a puzzle or activity that students have to complete to demonstrate the life cycle of a plant over the four seasons; (3) a virtual reality game in which students add the proper amounts of sunlight, water, and fertilizer to make the plant grow; (4) one teacher would explain and discuss the process of photosynthesis; and (5) the other teacher would teach students about components of a plant cell (for example, cell wall, nucleus, vacuoles, and chloroplasts).

Interactive Teaching. With interactive teaching, one teacher assumes the lead, teaching in front of the class while the other teacher supports by monitoring student learning. After a short period of time, the teachers switch roles. In effective co-taught classes, teachers work efficiently so that it becomes a symbiotic relationship. Each teacher has multiple opportunities to serve in both the teaching and supportive modes. In the support role, teachers are engaged in the lesson and ask questions or rephrase when they see students having difficulty understanding a concept. The support teachers also supervise practice and monitor behaviors.

For example, while one teacher is discussing how light refracts through a convex lens, the other teacher is monitoring students' notes and checking for understanding.

Occasionally, when the support teachers see a student having difficulty, they would stop and ask questions to the lead teacher such as, "Did you say the light refracts as it passes through the lens? You also mentioned that *refracts* means to bend; is that correct?" The support teacher uses questions in this fashion rather than drawing attention to a student who is having difficulty understanding the concept. Shortly after convex and concave lenses are explained, the support teacher becomes the lead teacher and walks the class through a lab in which students project images into different types of lenses to see the effects of each. The same teacher then continues to explain how light changes when it comes from air and enters water. This teacher explains how light refracts in water at a different angle than when it is in the air. The support teacher now monitors students' notes to ensure their accuracy.

Although interactive teaching can be an enjoyable way to teach, both teachers have to know the content well and have to plan ahead of time to ensure smooth transitions between their teaching. They should be careful not to get stuck performing the same limited tasks because they might be viewed as less than equals in students' eyes. For example, if one teacher is the one who handles disruptive behavior, students may be more likely to behave inappropriately on a day when that teacher is absent. If one teacher is the one who teaches the content, then students are more likely to turn to that one for their questions. Both teachers should share the different roles, both roles that are burdensome and rewarding.

Alternative Teaching. Alternative teaching involves forming a small group of students and then teaching them in one section of the room, usually a corner or table in the back of the class. While one teacher works with the small group, the other teacher instructs the rest of the class. The purpose of the grouping is for re-teaching concepts, providing enrichment activities, helping students who were absent to catch up, or addressing special problems that students may be having (for example, students who are talkative or disruptive, who need prerequisite content, or who need extra assistance taking notes). Using this model, teachers will alternate roles on a regular basis so that they do not become cast as the person who always works with small groups (one implication being that the particular teacher cannot handle large groups or only works with a certain type of student).

Likewise, the group should be heterogeneous and should not include the same students every time, lest the small group take on the appearance of students who have behavior and academic problems. All students should be given opportunities to participate in both large and small groups. For example, if a student with a mild disability is having difficulty understanding the concept of a recessive gene, that student might be paired up with a high achiever who understands the concept well, and then both could be given practice activities in a small group. In this way, both the teacher and high achiever could explain the concept to help the student with mild disabilities understand it. The purpose of the alternative teaching configuration is still met; because the students with the highest needs have been distributed between the two teachers they will be able to receive the levels of attention they need.

Parallel Teaching. Parallel teaching involves dividing the class in half and having each instructor teach students the same content. Each group of students is heterogeneous (that is, consisting of high, average, and low achievers). This configuration provides a good format for students who are reluctant to respond in larger groups or for those times when teachers want more interaction with students. As such, it would be an appropriate format to use when teaching difficult concepts, when students need a lot of practice with skills, or when teachers want to make sure that all students have mastered a set of content or skills. Parallel teaching requires careful planning so that both teachers cover the same content, and both teachers must maintain an adequate pace to ensure that all of the designated content is covered by the end of class. Of course, having two instructors teaching in the same classroom may be more distracting and may create more noise. Some teachers may need some time to acclimate to this format, particularly teachers who are unsure of their teaching and classroom management skills.

Other Approaches to Co-Teaching Models

The previous four models of co-teaching represent the primary different configurations possible for co-teaching. Many other variations can be used with one or more of the four models. These approaches include speak and chart, speak and comment, one teach and one observe, and one teach and one assist. As you read about these four approaches, you will note many similarities and slight differences among them.

Using **speak and chart** (Garmston 1997), the lead teacher presents content and the support teacher (that is, the scribe) records notes on the board or digital projection. As the information is recorded or projected on the board or screen, students record it in their own notes. Using this approach, the support teacher remains silent and simply records notes.

A second approach is called **speak and comment**. Garmston (1997) reports that speak and comment requires the lead teacher to direct the discussion and make decisions about when to end the discussion and when to move on to new content. The support teacher adds comments, gives examples, or elicits a question about the topic for the class. The purpose of the support teacher's comments and questions is to keep the conversation lively and engaged. When using either of these methods, co-teachers should feel free to monitor and intervene in discussions and should develop signals for switching from lead to support teacher. Some of these signals may include verbal intonation, purposeful pauses, physical proximity, or eye contact.

A third approach, **one teach and one observe**, is used when one teacher instructs and the other teacher observes to see how students respond to instruction, students' behavior during instruction or intervention, or how well the teacher interacts with students (for example, does the teacher ask questions to all the students or just a select few? Does the teacher use sufficient wait-time after asking questions?) (Friend and Bursuck 2006). Through these systematic observations, teachers can accurately improve their own teaching behavior or carefully monitor changes in student behavior.

A fourth approach is **one teach and one assist**. Using this approach, one teacher instructs students and leads students through the lesson while the other teacher assists students who have questions or need additional assistance. Typically, the lead teacher is teaching content while the other teacher circulates around the room making sure that students are recording notes, are on task and paying attention, and are exhibiting appropriate classroom behaviors.

As can be the case for other approaches, this last approach can be problematic when the general education teacher is doing the actual "teaching" and the special education teacher ends up assisting the teacher or is delegated to nonteaching tasks (for example, grading papers, monitoring student behavior, or preparing materials for the lesson). A big complaint voiced by special education teachers in ineffective co-taught classes is that they are often "stuck" doing similar nonteaching tasks and often feel like a teaching assistant as a result. Of course, with better communication between teachers and the willingness of both teachers to share the teaching role, they can usually resolve many of these problems.

THINK BACK TO THE CASE of Karen and Tom . . .

How would you describe Karen and Tom's approach to co-teaching?

Their co-teaching reflects more than one co-teaching approach. One of the approaches resembled is interactive teaching; however, Karen and Tom do not switch lead roles. They also reflect speak and comment sometimes. Using a hybrid of approaches is common for co-teachers, just as most teachers use a variety of instructional approaches. They adjust their co-teaching approach to match their plan for the lesson and the instructional decision making they necessarily make in the middle of a lesson. Of course, it is important for them to communicate about their experiences with the different approaches so that they can continue to interact effectively.

Research Evidence: Collaboration and Co-Teaching

Numerous studies and reviews (for example, Dieker and Murawski 2003; Weiss 2004; Weiss and Brigham 2000) indicate that co-teaching has positive effects on student achievement and social skills. For example, Rea, McLaughlin, and Walther-Thomas (2002) compared outcomes for students with LD in co-taught inclusive classes versus pull-out programs and found that students with LD in inclusive classes (a) achieved higher course grades (in language arts, sciences, mathematics, and social studies), (b) achieved higher scores on the language and mathematics subtests of the Iowa Test of Basic Skills, (c) had comparable scores on state proficiency tests, (d) had comparable low rates of in-school and out-of-school suspensions, and (e) attended more days of school than students with LD in pull-out programs.

More recently, in perhaps the most comprehensive analysis of co-teaching research, Scruggs, Mastropieri, and McDuffie (2007) found several similar overall benefits of co-teaching. Their meta-synthesis found that co-teaching benefited teachers (both general education and special education), students with disabilities, and students without disabilities. Highlights of their findings include the following:

- General education teachers reported that co-teaching with special education teachers led to their own improved professional development.
- Both general education and special education teachers believed that co-teaching led to reciprocal learning experiences in which co-teachers learned and benefited from one another.
- Many teachers reported increased cooperative skills among students without disabilities in co-taught classes, along with increased social benefits for all students.
- Students with disabilities benefited from additional attention given to them in co-taught classes in terms of academic and social skills.

These benefits did not come about without much hard work, effective co-teaching skills, and administrative support. Scruggs, Mastropieri, and McDuffie (2007) found that co-teaching worked best among compatible teachers who volunteered to work together and were given adequate planning time, administrative support, and proper training. Put simply, when teachers are provided with the skills to collaborate and co-teach and the administrative support, not only do teachers benefit, but more importantly, their students benefit.

Using Best and Evidence-Based Practices in Special Education Teaching. All teachers, co-teachers and solo teachers alike, are expected to use the most effective practices they can. The best way to predict the effectiveness of a practice is to look for information that indicates it is a "best" or "evidence-based" practice. Both special education and RTI call for the use of "best" and "evidence-based" practices. As the term suggests, *best practices* are those instructional techniques that are considered most often to be effective for students with HI. *Evidence-based* means that there is rigorous research evidence to support using a practice. Whenever there is a choice, teachers should use evidence-based practices, as there is strong research to support the likelihood of them being successful. Educational researchers design experiments to "test" instructional practices and publish their findings; in the second half of this section, you will read how to judge the findings of such research. (Most standards recommended by professional organizations are for practices supported by research.)

Standards for Special Educators

Just as there are curriculum standards for what students should learn in school, there are standards for what teachers should know and be able to do. Standards exist for educators by school level for the lower grades; for example, the CEC's Division for Early Childhood published *Recommended Practices* for preschool through age five (2014), and the Association for Childhood Education International produced *Elementary Education Program Standards* for the elementary years (ACEI 2007). Standards also exist by subject areas for teachers at all levels. Examinations are commonly used to determine whether teachers meet the expected standards in a given state.

The CEC Standards. The CEC (2015) has identified standards of practice for special educators (the publication is commonly known as "The Red Book"). Various stakeholders in special education collaborated to identify topic areas for special educator standards as well as the standards within each of those areas. They have developed standards for entry-level special education teachers, including by certain disability categories (and gifted and talented), for special educators preparing for advanced roles such as diagnostician and administrator, and for special education paraprofessionals. (In addition, they have identified a "code of ethics and standards for professional practice for special education.")

The "preparation standards" pertains to virtually all beginning special education teachers of students with HI. This is because inclusion is so common for students with HI at all schooling levels. There are seven of these standards (see the inside cover of this book). Within each standard, there are specific competencies known as "key elements" of the standard. CEC has also published "knowledge and skill specialty sets," which are essentially standards for specific disabilities and specific special educator roles (for instance, early childhood special education).

In one survey study (Zionts, Shellady, and Zionts 2006), special educators reported that they appreciate the importance of the CEC standards but find them difficult to implement. Crutchfield (2003) identified a four-step process to use the standards to monitor and improve one's practice that may be helpful:

1. Identify the appropriate set of CEC standards (for example, for entry-level educators).
2. Rate your mastery level for each standard (using Crutchfield's self-evaluation forms).
3. Note which standard areas are your strongest and weakest.
4. Choose a domain(s) to work on and plan your professional development course of action.

2-4 Best and Evidence-Based Instructional Approaches in Special Education

Although the CEC standards represent overall knowledge and skills a special educator should possess, they are not all that a special educator needs to know to be an effective teacher. Effective special educators need to know which specific instructional practices are most beneficial for their students, as well as how to use them. As discussed in Chapter 1, most students with HI learn the same content and skills as other students. Particular instructional practices, validated by careful research on their effectiveness, are commonly used with special education students, regardless of the content or skills they are learning, however. Many of those practices are effective for all learners, but they are considered by some to be essential for students in special education (Harris and Graham 1996; Kauffman 2002; compare to Heshusius 1991).

Research Evidence: Best and Evidence-Based Practices in Special Education

Several researchers have conducted rigorous experimental or quasi-experimental design studies to identify which instructional practices have been the most effective for those with HI (for example, Swanson and Hoskyn 1998; Vaughn, Gersten, and Chard 2000; Vellutino et al. 2000). Perhaps the most comprehensive of all of these has been work conducted by H. Lee Swanson and his colleagues in the 1990s (see, for example, Swanson and Hoskyn 1998; Swanson, Hoskyn, and Lee 1999). Swanson first identified published research studies from a 30-year period that (1) satisfied rigorous criteria for identifying who the participants were (for example, documentation that they satisfied the definitional criteria for a specific learning disability and for special education enrollment), (2) studied one or more interventions, and (3) fully reported the analyzed data. The researchers then applied meta-analytic statistical procedures to identify trends across study findings (Swanson and Hoskyn 1998). They identified the following nine instructional components that the body of published research can support as effective for students with HI:

- Sequencing
- Segmentation of information
- Augmentation of teacher instruction (for instance, homework)
- Drill, repetition, practice
- Technology
- Directed questioning/responding
- Controlling task difficulty
- Small interactive groups
- Strategy cuing

In a further analysis of effectiveness for adolescents (defined as between 11 and 19 years of age), two components were found to have the most impact: advance organizers and explicit instruction (Swanson and Hoskyn 2001). Two instructional approaches that incorporate high percentages of these components, Direct Instruction and learning strategy instruction, are commonly used in special education teaching.

Direct Instruction/Explicit Instruction. Direct Instruction (commonly known as DI) is a published series of curricula (for example, Carnine, Silbert, Kame'enui, and Tarver 2009; Stein, Kinder, Silbert, Carnine, and Rolf 2018). Traditional components of DI include carefully sequenced learning goals and lesson content, teacher-cued student participation, scripted lessons, and rapid-paced student responding. Some educators consider DI to be too limiting on teachers as instructional decision makers and to promote isolated skill performances that are of limited utility for application in practice (Heshusius 1991; Poplin and Rogers 2005). For these reasons some teachers embrace some of the principles of DI but not the carefully constructed DI curricula. The critical principles of DI include the following:

- Sequenced skill objectives
- Sequenced lesson activities
- Review of pre-skills/prior knowledge
- Re-teaching
- Intensive practice
- Frequent practice
- Errorless learning
- Corrective feedback

Instructional approaches that borrow from DI principles are sometimes known as *direct instruction* (spelled with a lowercase "d" and "i") but more commonly as *directive instruction* or *explicit instruction*. Many of the principles of DI are incorporated, but some common practices are relaxed or omitted (for example, scripted lessons and unison student responding when the teacher cues). Swanson and colleagues' meta-analysis findings included that DI/explicit approaches are among the most effective for students with HI learning both academic and behavioral skills. They also found cognitive strategy instruction, or learning strategies, to be effective. "A combined direct instruction and strategy instruction model is an effective procedure for remediating learning disabilities relative to other models" (Swanson and Hoskyn 1998, p. 303) (note that they use the term *direct instruction* to mean the same thing as "DI/explicit instruction," and not exclusively the published curriculum series). You will read about instructional practices that incorporate DI/explicit instruction principles throughout this book.

Learning Strategies Instruction. In learning strategies instruction, students are taught integrated skills that address all aspects of performing a meaningful task. The focus in learning strategies instruction is on performance of the overall task instead of on individual component skills—which is what tends to be emphasized in DI/explicit instruction. For example, in the paraphrasing strategy (Schumaker, Denton, and Deshler 1984)—a classic reading comprehension strategy—students learn to identify reading tasks that call for the strategy (for example, comprehend a multi-paragraph reading and recall its key content), analyze the reading paragraph by paragraph for main ideas and important details to recall, and then paraphrase that information as a check of their comprehension (also see Ellis 1996). The strategy includes cognitive cues that remind students of what to do and why (Ellis et al. 1991).

By being taught learning strategies, students not only learn specific skills of a task (for example, reflecting at the paragraph level and identifying a main idea in the Paraphrasing Strategy), but also learn how those skills fit together into a comprehensive process. Thus, instead of building up incremental skills of the reading process to the point where fluid reading with comprehension is eventually realized, students learn the overall process.

Relationship Between DI/Explicit Instruction and Learning Strategy Instruction. Swanson and Hoskyn (1998) reported that learning strategies instruction alone was more effective than DI/explicit instruction alone, although both were rated as "highly effective." The two are not diametrically opposed approaches to teaching. Many of the principles of DI/explicit instruction are incorporated into research-validated strategy instruction models (for example, Ellis, Deshler, Lenz, Schumaker, and Clark 1991; Harris and Graham 1996). Likewise, updates to the DI curricula include application of skills to meaningful tasks even when more incremental skills of the overall process have yet to be mastered (for example, Carnine et al. 2009). In fact, Swanson and colleagues' meta-analysis indicates that the combination of DI/explicit instruction and learning strategies instruction is more powerful than either approach alone (Swanson and Hoskyn 2001).

Progress Monitoring. Teachers can enhance their use of DI/explicit instruction, learning strategies instruction, or almost any approach to teaching, by incorporating

Methods and Strategies Spotlight

C-BM for Monitoring Student Performance

Another popular instructional approach in special education for students with HI is **Curriculum-Based Measurement** (C-BM). C-BM is virtually synonymous with progress monitoring. It has its origins in Curriculum-Based Assessment (Deno 1992, 2003a, 2003b), which is an approach to assessment that relies on evaluations of student performance using content from the student's curriculum instead of, for example, standardized achievement tests. In C-BM, teachers routinely sample student performance at the end of every few lessons to inform ongoing lesson planning. A particular benefit of C-BM is that it helps teachers to chart a student's progress on long-term learning goals, not just day-to-day short-term objectives (Stecker 2006).

In the graphs in Figure 2.5, the teacher, Rosa, has drawn **goal lines** at 100 words read per minute and 80 words read correctly per minute, indicating the levels of correct performance she is working to help Paula achieve. By plotting Paula's performance data from every third lesson, Rosa can see that Paula is making good progress toward the reading rate goal (observe her accelerating **trend line**). However, the acceleration rate for word reading accuracy is too slow, as evidenced by the slope of that trend line. Rosa expected Paula's accuracy to lag behind her rate but not to remain so poor. Rosa compared Paula's rates and slopes of progress by drawing **aimlines** on the graphs. The aimlines are straight lines that begins where Paula's first performance is plotted and extend to the points in time on the goal lines above the lesson by which Rosa expects Paula to accomplish the goals. Once drawn, the data points should fall very close to the aimline, to indicate that Paula's progress is occurring as planned. By continuing to use Paula's graphs, Rosa and Paula will be able to monitor what types of learning progress ensues when Rosa modifies her instructional practices concerning reading accuracy.

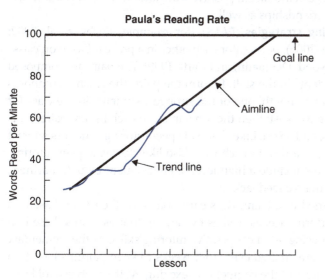
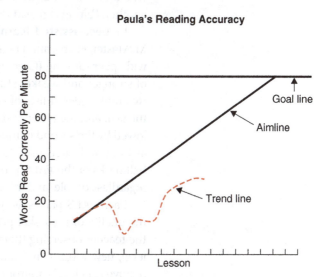

▲ **FIGURE 2.5**
Paula's Daily Reading Rate and Accuracy

progress monitoring. They will also be in compliance with legal expectations for effective practice. The ESSA requires that states document their schools' progress toward achievement standards the state sets. The premise of this requirement is that all students, including those with disabilities, can achieve the standards if progress is monitored and effective instructional decisions are driven by that data. The IDEA also requires that student progress be monitored, specifically, for individual students in a way that reflects progress toward their IEP goals. Progress monitoring can be effective in improving both teaching practices and student learning (Safer and Fleischman 2005). If data show progress to be minimal, or too slow, then changes to improve performance should be made; otherwise, the data can confirm that teachers should stick with the practice they are using.

2-5   Peer Tutoring and Cooperative Learning

Just as education colleagues collaborate to meet the special education needs of their students, so can special education students collaborate with their peers in the inclusion classroom. Two particularly effective approaches are peer tutoring and cooperative learning, but just like teacher collaboration they must be done right to be effective.

If you have ever worked with a partner or in a group where someone did all of the work and somebody else got the credit, you know that there is more to getting students to cooperate than just telling them to work together. In peer tutoring and cooperative learning, students take active roles in the learning process by helping each other to learn. The two approaches are sometimes criticized; some charge that the approaches hold back more knowledgeable peers and deprive students of the teacher's expertise. However, when conducted properly, neither is the case. We reference both of these approaches throughout this book.

Peer Tutoring

Peer tutoring is an effective way for students to practice using new skills and content. Among the benefits of peer tutoring is enhanced social standing for students with disabilities (Fuchs, Fuchs, Mathes, and Martinez 2002). By being paired, students with and without disabilities can interact in positive ways and come to appreciate one another. Pairing can lead to friendships as well.

In **peer-assisted learning strategies (PALS)** (for example, Fuchs et al. 2002; McMaster, Fuchs, and Fuchs 2006), peers tutor each other in a process based on classwide peer tutoring (Greenwood, Delquadri, and Carta 1999). The pairs are composed of stronger and weaker students in the skill. To form the pairs, the teacher composes two rank-ordered lists of equal length, one of the strongest students in the class for the skill and the other of the weakest; then the top names on each list are paired, followed by the second names, and so on. Like classwide peer tutoring, students interact as tutor and tutee, each taking a turn in each role. Also like classwide peer tutoring, hallmarks of the PALS process include a high level of engagement by both partners, regardless of role, and informative feedback.

Each PALS pair is assigned to a team. Pairs earn points for their team based on the quality of their skill performance, as well as by earning "bonus points" based on the teacher observing them using good cooperative tutoring skills. At the elementary level, new PALS pair teams are created every four weeks to keep pairings based on relative skill levels appropriate and the competition exciting. At the high school level, pairs are reformed daily, in response to both absentee rates and interests in working with a variety of peers (McMaster, Fuchs, and Fuchs 2006).

Research has demonstrated that PALS benefits both students with HI and their peers in inclusive classroom settings (Fuchs et al. 1997). Positive effects have been found for social skills as well (Fuchs et al. 2002). Those findings are reported for both elementary- and secondary-level students (see McMaster et al. [2006] for a summary). Interestingly, research into why some students do not benefit from PALS as much as their peers has indicated that limited pre-skills are likely contributing factors, but alterations to address their specific needs have only produced mixed effects (Al Otaiba and Fuchs 2002; McMaster et al. 2005). (You can read more about the PALS strategy used with reading in Chapter 7 and with math in Chapter 9.)

Cooperative Learning

The two factors that distinguish cooperative learning from peer tutoring are (a) more students are involved and (b) the task is typically a joint effort to solve a challenge or to produce a product. The benefits of cooperative learning are much the same as they are for peer tutoring, however. When cooperative learning works correctly, students with and without disabilities benefit by being actively involved in the learning process, social relationships are enhanced, and all participants learn academic content from the experience (Jones and Sterling 2011; Slavin 1991; also see Tatayama-Sniezek 1990).

However, cooperative learning does not always work (Jenkins, Antil, Wayne, and Vadasy 2003). Some students get excluded, others do a disproportionate share of the work, not everyone involved learns the same things, and social relationships are damaged. In fact, some group activities do not even qualify as "cooperative learning." It is merely "group work" if certain essential factors are not present, factors that render the process cooperative. Robert Slavin analyzed published research on cooperative learning to identify the essential factors for effective cooperative learning. The following are Slavin's (1991) **five essential factors for cooperative learning** that must be incorporated into the group process for it to be cooperative:

- Common goal—valued by both the group and individual members
- Group interdependence
- A structured schedule of instruction
- Individual accountability
- Group rewards based on individual members' achievement

According to Slavin's review, the combination of all factors is necessary for effective cooperative learning. Thus, cooperative learning activities need to be structured in such a way that all members of the group are invested in the process and that all members are accountable for their own performance as well as that of all group mates so that certain specified learning activities occur. Students with HI benefit from structured approaches to collaboration; they help the students know what to do and what is expected of them.

To demonstrate the necessity of these five factors, Slavin modified a popular approach to cooperative learning that did not satisfy all five and, hence, according to his research review, was not a consistently effective approach to cooperative learning. That original approach was Jigsaw (Aronson et al. 1978); Slavin named his revised version that incorporated the five elements Jigsaw II (Slavin 1991). In Jigsaw II, the teacher divides the topic by the number of teams that can be formed in the class. Each "home team" has the same number of members as the topic has been divided into. In the first step, all members of the home team go to a different table to become experts on their part of the topic. At each topic table is one member from each home team. For the sake of the home team, each representative at a topic table must work hard to learn the information and bring it back to the home team. While working with members of other home teams at the topic table, the student should use effective cooperative skills to be sure to benefit as much as possible from studying the topic (sabotaging other home teams' representatives will not work because the topic table members must cooperate to learn their information). When students return to their home teams, they each have to teach their teammates about the content they studied. To end the activity, each member of the home team takes a quiz on all content studied at each of the topic tables. The score for the quiz is a team score, compiled from the individual group members' performances. In this way, each home team member has an obligation to help all teammates fully learn the content that each has brought back to the team.

Based on disability-related student variations, cooperative learning or peer tutoring will not go well if students are not prepared to work well together (McMaster and Fuchs 2002). Without having a clear procedure in which each participant can feel successful and be successful in the eyes of peers, animosity may develop, the essential activities of effective cooperative learning will not occur, and poor learning will result (Gillies and Ashman 2000). As per Slavin's (1991) research documents, students must be accountable for their cooperative roles in addition to the learning outcomes. When that happens, students with HI, and their classmates, can be successful.

CHAPTER SUMMARY

Planning to provide an appropriate education to students with disabilities begins by determining their educational needs. Rushing to identify disabilities and to place students in special education has proven unnecessary and may have contributed to overidentification of some student populations and overlooking others who should have been identified and appropriately served (Harry and Klingner 2006). The pre-referral process required by the IDEA helps to ensure that teachers have collegial support to investigate the nature of a student's learning difficulties and to identify workable responses.

In the case of students for whom special education is deemed to be the right option, teachers continue to collaborate by participating in a team process to develop an IEP. The IEP document that the team generates serves as a blueprint for all educators and service providers who will work to provide the student an appropriate education. The IEP should guide the teacher's instructional planning process. Teachers still need to develop lesson plans for students receiving special education regardless of where those students receive their education (the LRE) and how many students or professionals are involved in the lesson. Lesson plans help teachers to fully prepare and can guide their process during the lesson.

When teachers collaborate in teaching, they may merely consult with one another, as can be the case when students receive some of their education in the general education classroom environment and other parts in a more restrictive setting. There are a variety of configurations for how teachers can co-teach.

Effective collaborative teaching, or co-teaching, does not happen overnight. As with any change in teaching, it takes time to develop a collaborative partnership with others. As those partnerships develop, attitudes begin to change among teachers as they co-plan and co-teach lessons. They begin to develop better communication and support skills and become more adept at problem solving and co-planning, the four key components of effective collaboration and co-teaching. As teachers become more proficient at co-planning and teaching, they begin to work not as two teachers, but as one team.

Research evidence (for example, Swanson and Hoskyn 1998, 2001) supports the notion that some instructional practices are more effective than others for students with HI. Typically, those practices include orienting students to lesson goals and tasks, providing clear and explicit instruction, keeping students actively engaged in the learning process, supporting practice, and providing informative feedback. Such practices should guide teachers' work with students who have HI. Fortunately, these practices can be applied in any setting or curriculum where a student with special needs may be placed. By committing to informed planning and following plans, all educators who serve students with HI can participate in providing them with an appropriate education.

Finally, students can collaborate with their inclusion classroom peers. Student collaborations are most effective when they include structured activities and the students are suitably matched. Peer tutoring and cooperative learning are particularly beneficial approaches to student collaboration.

KEY TERMS

504 Plan, 51
Aimline, 73
Annual Goals, 47
Benchmark, 48
Collaboration, 54
Co-Teaching, 54
Curriculum-Based Measurement
    (C-BM), 73
Curriculum Standards, 53
Eligibility Determination, 45
Evaluation, 45

Evidence-Based Intervention
    Practices, 42
Five Essential Factors for Cooperative
    Learning, 75
Goal Line, 73
Instructional Accommodations, 50
Multidisciplinary Team, 45
Peer-Assisted Learning Strategies
    (PALS), 74
Pre-referral, 40

Present Level of Academic Achievement
    and Functional Performance
    (PLAAFP), 47
Referral, 45
Related Services, 49
Screening, 44
Service Plan, 50
Short-Term Objective, 47
Specially Designed Instruction, 48
Student Support Team, 41
Testing Accommodations, 50
Trend Line, 73

APPLICATION ACTIVITIES

Using information from the chapter, complete the following activities that were designed to help you apply knowledge that was presented in this chapter.

1. Gather three different blank IEP forms (for example, from local school districts or from the education websites of various state departments of education). Using a completed IEP (for good examples, see Gibbs and Dyches [2016]), transfer the content onto each of the three forms. Note differences in criteria for recording the same information, what information is not required across all forms, and any features or content unique to one or two that you consider to be appropriate for all IEP forms.

2. As a student preparing to become a special educator, you should not expect to be a proficient special educator yet. Using Crutchfield's (2003) evaluation guides, self-identify the CEC standards on which you are close to competence and those you most need to work toward.

3. Work with another student and develop a co-taught lesson. List what each person will be doing during the lesson.

4. Using the four models of co-teaching—station teaching, interactive teaching, alternative teaching, and parallel teaching—design a lesson for each. Note the different responsibilities for individual teachers depending on which model is being used.

5. Review the procedures for Jigsaw II (p. 69). Identify how each of the five essential factors for effective cooperative learning (Slavin 1991) is accounted for in the process.

American Images Inc/Digital Vision/Getty Images

3

Working with Families and Transition

Learning Objectives

After reading this chapter, you will understand:

3-1 Why parent–school partnerships matter

3-2 Effective qualities of school–parent partnerships

3-3 IDEA expectations for involving families

3-4 What rights, responsibilities, and roles are available to parents throughout the stages of the special education process

3-5 Why there should be a transition initiative for students in special education, and how it relates to the "outcomes" of special education

3-6 The demands various post-school settings put on students with HI, and how those demands should be taken into account when planning for successful transitions

3-7 Why transition is supposed to be a "results-oriented" process and the types of planning that lead to positive transition "results"

3-8 What the appropriate process for transition planning is, and what role students should play in preparing for their own transitions

CEC Initial Preparation Standard 1: Learner Development and Individual Learning Differences

1-1 Beginning special education professionals understand how language, culture, and background influence the learning of individuals with exceptionalities.

CEC Initial Preparation Standard 4: Assessments

4-3 Beginning special education professionals, in collaboration with colleagues and families, use multiple types of assessment information in making decisions about individuals with exceptionalities.

4-4 Beginning special education professionals engage individuals with exceptionalities to work toward quality learning and performance and provide feedback to guide them.

CEC Initial Preparation Standard 5: Instructional Planning and Strategies

5-1 Beginning special education professionals consider individual abilities, interests, learning environments, and cultural and linguistic factors in the selection, development, and adaptation of learning experiences for individuals with exceptionalities.

5-5 Beginning special education professionals develop and implement a variety of education and transition plans for individuals with exceptionalities across a wide range of settings and different learning experiences in collaboration with individuals, families, and teams.

Do you think there is more to special education than helping students achieve academically?

Yes, there is. Special education certainly is about ensuring that students with disabilities achieve academically, but it is also about their success in functional behaviors that impact their daily functioning and participation in society. The individually "appropriate" education that special education offers is intended to provide students the supports that will result in their becoming school leavers who live as independently as possible, participate in education and employment as adults, and lead healthy and satisfying lives that include participating in their communities. Special education is about much more than only helping students to pass their classes. Parents are vital partners in planning and delivering a special education student's individually appropriate education; this is true for academics, functional behaviors, and transitioning to life beyond the schooling years. The ultimate outcome schools and parents should work together toward is the good life that special education students will lead as young adults. Students with HI have particular needs for strong family–school collaborations and for preparing for transitions to life beyond their school years.

3-1 Forming Collaborative School–Family Partnerships

Although family involvement in education is important for all students, it is particularly important for students in special education. In recognition of the important roles families play in education for students with disabilities, the Individuals with Disabilities Education Act (IDEA) requires that parents[1] have the opportunity to participate fully in all phases of the special education process. In the case of early childhood special education, the entire family may be involved in receiving and providing special education services that benefit the child.[2] Parent involvement requires much more

---

[1] The IDEA and this book use the term *parent* to mean whomever is a primary caregiver to a child or adolescent. One, two, or more people may fit the label *parent*. In the same regard, families may not be limited to blood relatives or those who live in the same household.

[2] When referring to students of any age, the IDEA makes reference to *child*. To avoid confusion between referencing laws and regulations and recommended practices, we also use the term *child* in the section on working with families. Unless otherwise stated, the term is intended to include adolescents as well.

than inviting parents to individualized education program (IEP) meetings and having an open-door policy. True parent involvement requires forming a partnership between school and parents (Winter 2007).

Conformance with the IDEA requirements for parental involvement is the minimum expectation for partnering with parents. Although the law serves to protect educators from having to respond to unrealistic expectations or meet needs that fall outside of the responsibility of schools, truly partnering with parents means engaging in a positive and reciprocal relationship. The trust and respect that Rhonda and Mrs. Waters in Case 3.1 have for each other is an example of such a relationship. They communicated well, they respected and trusted each other, and each listened to the other's contributions and gave useful input—all of which were to Charlie's benefit.

CASE 3.1　Charlie's Individualized Education

Case Introduction

As you read the following case, ask yourself what evidence indicates whether Charlie's parent, Mrs. Waters, and the special educator, Rhonda, have a good relationship. Think about how you could replicate the factors that contribute positively to their relationship. Also consider how their relationship impacts Charlie's education.

At the end of the case, you will find case questions. These questions are meant to serve as points for reflection. Of course, if you can answer them immediately, you should do so, but you may want to wait to answer them until you have read the portion of the chapter that pertains to a particular case question. Throughout the rest of the chapter, you will see the same questions. When you come to them again, try to answer them based upon that portion of the chapter that you just read.

When Mrs. Waters received an invitation to her son Charlie's IEP annual review meeting, she called Rhonda, Charlie's special education teacher. Mrs. Waters and Rhonda had a good relationship. She told Rhonda that she was generally pleased with how Charlie's homework was going. She and Charlie's father had both been monitoring the quality of Charlie's work, and signing off that he had shown it to them seems to be working well. At last year's IEP meeting Mrs. Waters and Rhonda agreed that Charlie's homework habits were very poor and that his schoolwork was suffering because of it. At that meeting, Charlie insisted that he didn't ever have much homework and that he rarely failed to work on assignments he really did have. Following Rhonda's suggestion at that meeting to institute an assignment notebook and calendar, Charlie's teachers and parents now know to expect him to present his notebook to them daily for signatures. Shortly after they began using the assignment notebook, Charlie revealed to his mother that he was often overwhelmed by his homework.

Rhonda had met with the Waterses and shared some procedures with them for helping Charlie through his homework. The Waterses found her tips helpful, because Charlie's

difficulties with following their directions had been frustrating them.

On the phone, Mrs. Waters said that she thought Charlie's writing assignments expected too much of him. She was worried that he was working on too many different skills at once. Rhonda assured Mrs. Waters that they would be able to discuss this at the IEP meeting.

On the day of the meeting, Mrs. Waters arrived a little bit late, due to unexpected traffic. Mr. Waters did not attend; in fact, he had never attended any of Charlie's special education meetings. Rhonda and the director of special education were still in the director's office, meeting about another matter, so Mrs. Waters had to wait several minutes for them.

Once the meeting began, Charlie introduced everyone and, with some prompting from Rhonda, summarized his progress for the year and stated his goals for the upcoming year. Everyone agreed that the homework monitoring system had been going well; Mrs. Waters and Rhonda both praised Charlie for the effort he was putting into monitoring his assignment completion. Even though Charlie argued that he no longer needed the monitoring system, the team agreed to continue its use.

When the subject of writing assignments came up, Mrs. Waters expressed her concern that Charlie was having difficulty doing all that was expected of him. Melinda Orafaci, the English language arts teacher, explained that she wanted her students to appreciate the complexity of composition, so although the students worked on specific skills in class, she wanted them to practice integrating all skills when they did their twice-weekly homework writing assignments. Mrs. Waters also expressed that she thought the expectation for a full-page composition each time was too much for Charlie. Melinda responded that students in Charlie's grade should be able to write "at least" that much. Rhonda broke into the conversation and suggested that she would meet with Melinda to review the writing curriculum expectations and together they could come up with guidelines for how the Waterses could support Charlie's writing at home. She then initiated a discussion about appropriate accommodations for Charlie.

continued

All agreed that, if needed, after two months of monitoring Charlie's comfort level and the quality of his writing, Melinda would meet with them again to consider alternatives to the standard assignment. They all agreed to this proposal, as well as to writing messages to one another about Charlie's progress in his assignment notebook.

Rhonda took over a week longer than she promised to write up the IEP following the meeting. Once Mrs. Waters received it in the mail, she was happy to sign and return it.

CASE QUESTIONS

1. What are the indicators that the Waterses have taken a positive view of Charlie's academic potential?
2. Did Rhonda's interactions with Mrs. Waters reflect professional standards for how special educators should interact with parents?

Although partnerships between schools and parents often go well, at other times, the parties cannot seem to come to agreement or do not communicate at all. The "systems" of schooling and special education can sometimes seem daunting to parents, primarily because of the imbalance of power between families and schools, especially for families that are not from the majority culture (Kalyanpur, Harry, and Skrtic 2000).

How Family and Disability Impact Each Other

Expectant parents typically do not anticipate having a child with a disability. Although standard medical procedures can detect many forms of intellectual disability in utero, they cannot reliably detect it in all cases, and none of the other HIs is detectable even through infancy (advances in early detection of autism have yet to lead to reliable identifiers in children this young, and it is not clear whether promising experimental practices

BOX 3.1

The Concept of Family

Remember that families come in many different forms. Today's average American household is dramatically different from what it was 100 years ago (Hodgkinson 2002); however, the concept of an extended family having responsibility for children is still accurate. Families are not as likely to be the "nuclear family" of the 1950s, which was typified by a married mother and father and 2.5 children per household. Today, approximately 50 percent of children in America live with a single parent for at least part of their childhood (Hodgkinson 2002). The numbers of children being raised by unmarried parents, single fathers, same-sex parents, and grandparents have increased significantly (Pew Research Center 2015). The percentage of children raised by single mothers is declining. Just as was the case 100 years ago, extended family members such as grandparents, aunts and uncles, and older siblings may all have central roles in childrearing, or they may be the primary caregivers in place of parents. Adoption agencies that arrange placements for children and adolescents with disabilities are more likely to place them with gay and lesbian single adults and couples (Brodzinsky, Patterson, and Vaziri 2002). Some children and adolescents legally are not in the care of any family member at all; they are instead wards of the state, and a foster family or a caseworker has legal responsibility for interacting with the school and making legal decisions on their behalf; these include immigrant children who have entered the country without a parent or adult family member.

would capture autism at the "requiring support" level). Thus, news of a child having a disability most often comes as either a surprise or a dawning realization. How parents and other family members react to the news of a disability varies (see Box 3.1). Some consider the diagnosis "tragic," regardless of whether the disability is mild or severe; others welcome it as an explanation for phenomena they have been observing (for example, hyperactivity, persistent learning difficulties, restrictive and repetitive behaviors, obsessive phobias); and some acknowledge its significance while accepting it as simply another life condition (Ho and Keiley 2003; Roberts, Stough, and Parrish 2002).

How a mild disability manifests itself strongly relates to family members' reactions (Poehlmann et al. 2005). Children with hyperactivity or inattentiveness can aggravate others in the household because they often seem unfocused, forcing others to complete tasks for them. Communicating with a family member with attention-deficit/hyperactivity disorder (ADHD) can also be cumbersome if the individual frequently strays off topic. Likewise, a child with an emotional or behavioral disability (EBD) can cause a great deal of concern for family members, but may also be exasperating either because of withdrawal or acting-out behaviors. Lardieri, Blacher, and Swanson (2000) found that the academic and communication problems of children with learning disabilities (LD) did not pose a significant problem to either sibling or parent relationships. They did find, however, that when those with LD also had behavioral problems, siblings reported being less comfortable interacting with them and less accepting of them, and parents reported higher levels of frustration.

Just as the occurrence of a disability in a family can be a source of stress for the family, it can also be an occasion for family readjustment. Families that include a member with a disability have been found to:

- Adjust emotionally,
- Adjust to the reactions of peers,
- Access community resources,
- Adjust emotionally in relation to the nature of the disability,
- Adjust family and caregiver roles, in accordance with the child's skill development,
- Realize the need for continuous family involvement and care,
- Respond to the financial ramifications of the disability on the family,
- Plan for transitions, including future vocational preparation, and
- Arrange for socialization beyond the family unit (as summarized by Lustig 2002).

These family readjustments can be either positive or negative.

THINK BACK TO THE CASE   **about Mrs. Waters . . .**

1. *What are the indicators that the Waterses have taken a positive view of Charlie's academic potential?*

The fact that the Waterses actively participate in Charlie's special education is a strong indicator that they believe in his potential to learn (however, even though some families are not active participants in their child's education, they may still be interested). Mrs. Waters has goals for Charlie. Even when she was concerned that the writing assignments were too complex for him, she did not suggest that too much was expected of him, only that it was too much all at once. She believed that Charlie could learn the expected skills. If the Waterses had held any pessimistic views of Charlie because of his disability, they have clearly reframed them into more optimistic views of his potential with their support.

Research Evidence

Positive Family Relationships. Parents and other family members can benefit from adopting positive perspectives about disability in their families. Many do once they get over any initial negative reaction (Muscott 2002; Poehlmann et al. 2005). Muscott (2002) explains that some families have to progress through stages of **coping** similar to those Kübler-Ross (1969) proposed for how people grieve a death.

Parents who advocate on behalf of their child with a disability develop both a sense of purpose and a realization that they can participate with schools and other service agencies in responding to their child's needs; through such activities, parents come to develop a positive sense of their role as caregiver (originally cited in Lustig 2002). According to Scorgie and Sobsey's (2000) findings from interviews and surveys with parents of children with disabilities, most became more confident, assertive, and compassionate; developed stronger relationships with others (including marital bonds and friendships) and empathy in those relationships; and experienced positive adjustments in personal and social perspectives (for example, acceptance of others). Of course, those parents likely also experienced stresses not common to parents of children without disabilities. Parents of children with disabilities uniquely worry about finding services for their child, providing care for their child, and determining how their child's needs will be met in the future (Lustig 2002).

Effective Responses.   How resilient family members are when a family member has a disability relates to how well they cope and solve problems (Lustig 2002). According to Lustig (2002), **problem solving** is "the family's ability to define . . . stressors in terms of manageable components, identify alternative courses of action, and begin to take steps to resolve the component problems and, ultimately, the problem." Consider the family members who become frustrated with the child with ADHD-inattentive who never seems to participate in games or chores without getting distracted. Awareness that the disability is the cause of the child's behaviors will likely not prevent the family members from becoming frustrated, although that information may be useful for tolerating the behavior. However, the family members who have problem-solving skills might realize that the length of time waiting to take a turn in a game or the time needed to complete a chore is long enough that the inattentive child can become distracted. They can examine distracters that may "tempt" the child's inattention. In the case of the game, for example, the child might easily become distracted because of long wait times between turns, enticing game pieces, a nearby electronic device, or other fun objects in the area that divert attention from the game. With this realization, family members can learn to help the child select strategic seating to avoid focusing on the distracters, have some neutral object such as a squish ball to manipulate, or select games that do not require long intervals between taking turns.

In addition to developing routines that take into account the child's disability, the family can also collaborate with the child and the school to develop preferred behaviors for the child. In the case of children with ADHD-inattentive, interventions might include teaching them to self-monitor and self-regulate their attention to task by learning to set performance goals, monitor their productivity or attention to task, and self-administer breaks at appropriate times. The family members can also learn to monitor and regulate their reactions to the child's inattentive behaviors. They might, for example, discuss their emotional reactions to the behaviors, and set personal goals for how they respond to the behaviors. The child with HI will be more successful in using such routines if they are the same at school as at home.

Methods and Strategies Spotlight

Effective Methods for Communicating with Parents

Parent–teacher conferences are just one way that parents and teachers stay connected. Materials can be viewed together, and there are benefits to face-to-face interactions, such as reading one another's expressions and receiving someone's full attention. Although these face-to-face meetings can be beneficial, they can also be inefficient. Scheduling often presents one of the biggest challenges for teachers. These meetings usually have designated end-times, which may preclude having the fuller conversation that everyone would have liked. Also, distractions are bound to occur during the session.

Parents may be willing to converse by telephone or even voicemail messages (Bauer and Shea 2003), in which case prearranged times for conversations should be established. These options allow for more flexibility in scheduling meetings. Bauer and Shea also suggest that the educator ask the parents if they are willing to communicate via email. All parties should remember that email is not a secure medium, however. School districts may also prohibit certain identifying information from being communicated over such a public channel. Also, check with the school's policy on retaining copies of email communications.

3-2 Families' Relationships with School

Positive home–school partnerships are characterized by "reciprocity, trust, and respect" (Beveridge 2004). Creating welcoming environments or just putting educators and parents in contact with one another is not enough (Salas et al. 2005). Parent participation has a positive impact on student achievement, in both special and general education (Salas et al. 2005). In addition, parent involvement has been reported to:

- Increase parents' understanding of school,
- Increase parents' understanding of their involvement in their child's education,
- Promote confidence in parents,
- Increase parental involvement,
- Engender more positive feelings in parents about their own parenting role,
- Increase parents' willingness to participate in school activities, and
- Increase parents' interactions with teachers and administrators. (Salas et al. 2005)

"Low-income parents are often perceived by educators as resistant to school efforts to involve them, as poor participators in school events, and as not as committed to their children's school achievement and success as middle-class parents" (Lott 2003). Other common perceptions of low-income parents include that they are "apathetic and disinterested in their children's education, do not encourage school achievement, and are not competent to help with homework" (Lott 2003). In truth, low-income parents are interested in their children's achievement and wish for involvement in their schools just as much as parents from other income groups. Further, they typically cite school achievement as the basis for their children's success in life (Lott 2001).

Despite the desire for involvement by low-income parents, their relationships with schools are often fractured. Calls for parental involvement in schools often appear to be targeted toward middle-class families (Lott 2003). Lott (2003) proposes the following five "prescriptions for change" in how schools relate to low-income families:

- Replace stereotypes with attention to strengths.
- Help parents reduce obstacles to school involvement.

- Expand the role of parents in schools.
- Increase informal communication.
- Help administrators in providing leadership. (Lott 2003)

There are specific mindsets and practices schools and educators can follow to fulfill the prescriptions. Salas et al. (2005) identified six areas of "best practices" for schools to follow to foster better home–school partnerships with Mexican American families. They apply to families of other ethnicities and cultures as well:

- Do not assume or make stereotypes about the family's linguistic abilities, acculturation, socioeconomic status, education, experiences, and the like.
- Develop credibility and trustworthiness.
- Understand the literacy proficiency of families, both for English language and special education jargon (see also Smith 2001).
- Determine parents' language of comfort for communications and use it.
- Consider the family's acculturation and how that may account for their goals and interaction styles.
- Do not assume that parents know what educators expect of them or that they are comfortable partnering with the school.

Salas et al. (2005) note that developing such bonds of trustworthiness and credibility takes time.

Parents who feel welcomed by schools say that they were invited to be involved, were treated with respect (including communicating in a comfortable language), and had their opinions valued (summarized from original sources cited in Lott 2003).

BOX 3.2

Parent Checklist for Home–School Communications

It's important to establish and maintain strong home–school communications to get the best help for your child. Use this checklist as a guide to get you started.

- Keep communications open with your child's teacher, and listen carefully if he or she describes problems with aspects of your child's learning. If you think the problems are serious enough to require special attention, ask the teacher if alternative instructional approaches might help address the problem and ask if any have been tried.
- Keep track of the instructional practices used to help address your child's problems and record how well they assisted your child's learning.
- Ask about the availability of research findings that show the effectiveness of the instructional practices or behavioral programs being used.
- Discuss whether there are cultural factors that might make a difference. If so, explain your child's background so the teacher and other educators can understand your child's behavior and actions. The information provided by parents and family members can be crucial to understanding a child's learning difficulties.
- Try to understand the way your child learns and be able to communicate what you think will help the teacher better understand your child's specific learning style. Observe and provide all the information you can to help the educators develop a better understanding of it.
- Find out if supplementary educational services such as tutoring are available at your child's school and investigate the programs to see if any would benefit your child.

Source: Reprinted with permission from C. Cortiella, IDEA Parent Guide: A Comprehensive Guide to Your Rights and Responsibilities Under the Individuals with Disabilities Education Act (IDEA 2004). New York: National Center for Learning Disabilities, 2006.

Smith (2001) warns that education jargon can discourage parents from meaningful participation in the special education planning process. He notes that parents may be confused by everyday terminology for special educators, such as *ITP*, *accommodations*, and *inclusive classroom.* Statistical information from standardized testing and assumed common knowledge, such as what *percentile* means, might also be confusing.

To help confront the many barriers to productive relationships between parents and schools, the IDEA (2004) requires that a designated **service coordinator** be provided to families of all students in special education. That individual is responsible for facilitating communication between the family and the multidisciplinary team and for informing families about service agencies in their state that may provide services to them and their child (NJCLD 2007).

Cortiella (2006) has provided a useful checklist for parents to facilitate effective home–school communications (Box 3.2). Schools could share the checklists with parents as one way of indicating they are open to parent involvement. Educators should be aware of the types of information parents may wish for and reasons for parents to communicate with them. With that knowledge, they can help the parents keep track of needed information and be prepared to respond to parents in ways consistent with the parents' purpose for communicating.

TIPS FOR GENERALIZATION

Collaborating with Culturally and Linguistically Diverse Parents

Many parents are not actively involved in their child's education due to language and cultural barriers. To build positive relationships with parents from culturally diverse backgrounds, educators must both prevent and remove barriers to parent participation and respond to the parents' needs for support (Matuszny, Banda, and Coleman 2007).

Matuszny et al. (2007) propose that teachers develop a "progressive plan" to establish and maintain such a relationship. That plan is enacted over the cycle of the school year. In *Phase 1: Initiation*, the educators and parents should meet each other in a social context. Matuszny et al. suggest that the meeting be relaxed and festive, with the goal to create a personal relationship, not to "get down to business." They suggest that the event include food and music, but remind planners to be considerate of cultural and religious orthodoxies when planning. Ideally, Phase 1 will occur before the school year begins.

Following establishment of initial acquaintanceships at the start of the school year, the focus in *Phase 2: Building the Foundation* is on building trust between the family and educators. Useful activities include providing and sharing information, giving parents choices, and inviting parental input to the decision-making process (Matuszny et al. 2007). Families should visit their child's classroom to observe how it is organized and run. The educators and parents should also discuss how to communicate with each other and what arrangements will be convenient when meetings are required. Importantly, activities for building the foundation should focus on learning from the parents about how the classroom culture does or does not coincide with their culture (for example, as Matuszny et al. point out, some religions do not include celebrating birthdays or particular holidays).

In *Phase 3: Maintenance and Support*, the relationship that has been established is both maintained and nourished. This phase requires that the educators continue to respect the culturally based traditions and preferences of the parents as they interact. Part of doing so is to maintain "informational equity," which means that educators share information (such as new and relevant test data or evolved insights about the child's learning) as soon as they have it.

Although the progressive plan never ends but rather continues year after year, the final phase, *Phase 4: Wrap-Up and Reflection*, involves the teacher and parents jointly reflecting on their relationship and considering what worked well and what needs to be changed. With all of the focus on the student, it is easy to neglect the quality of the relationship between the mutually concerned adults. Even parents who will not be affiliated with the same teacher the following year will benefit from the wrap-up assessment, as it will yield useful information for them to carry to the next educator with whom they should collaborate.

3-3 IDEA Expectations for Involving Families in Special Education

Students benefit from collaborative partnerships between their parents and school. "Parent involvement in children's education has been correlated with higher academic achievement, improved school attendance, increased cooperative behavior, and lower dropout rates" (Bryan and Burstein 2004). Prior to passage of the special education law, there were no nationwide provisions for inviting parents to provide valuable information about their child's performance at home. In some cases, parents were not consulted before drastic measures such as medication, sterilization, or institutionalization were taken (D'Antonio 2004). More commonly, their children were tracked into a lower-expectations curriculum in a segregated setting with no input from the parents as to its appropriateness.

In response to this history of parent exclusion, when Congress was preparing the bill that became the Education for All Handicapped Children Act (and after many reauthorizations is now referred to as the IDEA), parent advocacy groups were invited to participate in establishing its parameters. Consequently, the IDEA has been characterized as promoting "family-centered care, whereby families are fully involved in assessment and intervention decisions for their children" (NJCLD 2007).

Although all six of the major provisions of the IDEA (review Chapter 1) relate to families, two particularly emphasize the role of the family in special education: *due process* and *parent and student participation*.

The **due process provision** is a safeguard of parents' (and schools') rights (Bauer and Shea 2003). The legal term "due process" means a process for protecting rights that is not arbitrary and is consistent with the law, and a set of formal proceedings that adheres to legal rules and principles. In great detail, the IDEA regulations specify the due process rights for all parties in all stages of the special education process.

Parents must be informed of their due process rights by the school district. As the wording **parent and student participation** indicates, this IDEA provision specifies that parents must be invited to participate in every stage of special education. Therefore, beginning with the question of whether the child has a disability and may need special education, the parents must give consent for special education procedures and must be invited to join in the process. The IDEA regulations for parent and student participation are just as extensive and involved as those for due process. Parents' rights, such as to be included on the IEP team and consent for special education actions, are spelled out in the regulations.

The IDEA protects the rights of families by setting expectations for informed consent before a child is assessed for eligibility for special education. The same protection is available in deciding if a child will be evaluated for the presence of a disability, if a child will be enrolled in special education, or if major changes are to be made to the student's special education (for example, annual IEP review, change of placement). **Informed consent** requirements in the IDEA are intended "to ensure that the parent:

- Has been fully informed of all information related to the proposed activity (in his [sic] native language, or other mode of communication),
- Understands and agrees in writing to carrying out the activity for which his consent is sought,
- Understands that giving consent is voluntary and may be revoked at any time, and
- Understands that revoking consent will not apply to an activity that has already occurred." (Cortiella 2006)

3-4 Opportunities for Parent Involvement in the Special Education Process

Family-centered approaches to education and social services are commonly advocated (Hoffman et al. 2006). As we have noted, parents should be involved at every stage of the special education process. They are valuable information resources, and they have the capacity to make important education decisions (for example, Dewey, Crawford, and Kaplan 2003).

The Special Education Process

Table 3.1 presents the major stages of the special education process and identifies ways in which parents can be involved at each stage. Both legally required participation and pedagogically and socially appropriate practices are listed. (Table 3.2 later in this chapter represents parallel information for responsiveness to intervention [RTI] models—review Chapter 1.) However, even before pre-referral, the first stage of the special education process *in* schools, there are ways that special education programs are responsible for serving children and collaborating with their families.

The very first opportunity for some parents to become involved in special education is through the **child find** activities of a state or local school district. In accordance with the child find requirements of the IDEA, state-level education agencies have an obligation to "identify, locate, and evaluate" (NJCLD 2007) children who may eventually require special education or related services. Many states, in turn, require local education agencies (for example, school districts) to participate. The intent of the child find mandate is to ensure that interventions are provided to a child as soon as possible. Although the benefits of early intervention can only be estimated, they include minimizing the negative impact of a disability on a child and the family (Heward 2006). Children with emotional disorders may receive instruction in coping strategies, and their parents can be informed of pharmaceutical options in the early childhood years, for example. Those with mild intellectual disability may begin to receive intensive instruction in literacy and functional skills so that they may have initial successes in both of those areas. In the case of children under the age of three, services may also be extended to family members, when they will benefit the child with a disability. Without child find, parents may not realize that their child has a disability or that special education supports are available before the child enters school; thus, some children may not realize the benefits of early intervention.

As we noted previously, with the exception of some instances of intellectual disability and EBD, the mild disabilities cannot be detected prenatally or in infancy. However, because some disabilities co-occur with others, the risk for specific HIs can be noted for some children and early detection can occur (see Roberts, Stough, and Parrish 2002). The child find requirements include a responsibility on the school agency's part to partner with pediatricians, daycare and preschool providers, and social service agencies to be on the lookout for children at risk for disabilities or with probable special education needs. This responsibility includes informing the service providers with guidelines on what may indicate a disability.

Early Childhood Special Education

Special education services can begin as early as birth. From birth until age three special education is provided through Part C of the IDEA, and is known as **early intervention**. (Beginning at age three traditional special education is provided, through Part B of

TABLE 3.1 Parent Information and Participation in the Traditional Special Education Model

Early Intervening*	Parent consultation Participation at home Progress reports
Child Find	Information and resources about disabilities Information and resources about special education
Pre-referral	Parent consultation Progress reports
Referral	Written notification Procedural Safeguards document
Screening	Written notification Parent consultation Written parent consent
Evaluation	Written notification Procedural Safeguards document Parent consultation Written parent consent Data and information shared is comprehensible to parents Information and resources about disabilities Information and resources about special education
Determination Meeting	Written notification Procedural Safeguards document Advance invitation to schedule the meeting Advance invitation to identify need for language interpreter or accommodations Data and information shared is comprehensible to parents Parent collaboration
IFSP/IEP/ITP Development	Written notification Procedural Safeguards document Advance invitation to schedule the meeting Advance invitation to identify need for language interpreter or accommodations Data and information shared is comprehensible to parents Parent consent Parent collaboration
Exploration of Alternatives to Special Education (for students found ineligible for special education)	
Intervention and Progress Monitoring	Participation at home Homework monitoring or assistance
Annual Review/Triennial Reevaluation	Procedural Safeguards document
ITP/SOP Development	Procedural Safeguards document

*Although not a special education service, up to 15 percent of special education funds may be used to support early intervening. The intention of early intervening is to support struggling students in general education environments, with particular emphasis on grades K-3 (IDEA 2004).

the IDEA.) IDEA (2004) includes the mandate that services for children from birth to age three are provided in a "natural environment" whenever possible. Home and childcare settings are typically thought to be natural environments, particularly for children with mild disabilities (remember, HIs are not commonly identified in this age group). The purpose of this mandate is consistent with the overall purpose of early childhood education, which is to ensure that young children receive the best educational foundation they can early on, to minimize the negative effects of disabilities and delayed education.

Early childhood special education needs to take a comprehensive approach, because the impact of most disabilities across childhood and adolescence can only be estimated. Evaluations should be conducted to determine areas that require targeted intense instruction in an overall comprehensive curriculum. A comprehensive evaluation of a young child's status and needs related to education involves an integrated assessment of functioning in:

- Cognition, including perceptual organization, memory, concept formation, attention, and problem solving;
- Communication, including speech/language form, content, and use for receptive and expressive purposes;
- Emergent literacy, including phonological and print awareness, and numeracy, including number recognition and number concepts;
- Motor functions, including gross, fine, and oral motor abilities;
- Sensory functions, including auditory, haptic, kinesthetic, and visual systems; and
- Social-emotional adjustment, including behavior, temperament, affect, self-regulation, play, and social interaction. (NJCLD 2007)

Young children have limited attention and sitting tolerance, so it is impractical to think of administering the types of testing batteries that may be used in elementary or secondary education. Furthermore, a more accurate assessment of young children's knowledge and skills will come from observing them in their normal routines. Systematic observations conducted in the early childhood years may include both formal (for example, standardized protocols) and informal procedures. Multiple observations should be made, using multiple procedures and instruments, and in multiple contexts. In fact, the accuracy of observations improves when multiple observers are involved. Children should be observed in their natural environments; this suggests that home and daycare and similar settings should all be included. Accordingly, parents and other caregivers with whom children normally interact should be involved in collecting the data. With knowledge of the young child's needs within the functioning areas identified by the NJCLD, educators, caregivers, and parents can partner to address the child's most crucial needs.

Parents collaborating with educators or caregivers can use early childhood special educators' knowledge of effective curricular practices to determine jointly how to develop the child's skills within natural contexts. This process will involve parents' direct participation in planning, intervening, and monitoring progress. For example, the National Early Literacy Panel (2008) has identified the following areas as indicators of appropriate literacy development for young children:

Oral language	*Phonological sensitivity*	*Concepts about print*
Alphabetic knowledge	*Invented spelling*	*Rapid naming*
Write own name		

Children can develop skills in those literacy areas by engaging in conversation and games with parents and caregivers who know how to model, prompt, and correct a child's performance. The parents also need to understand the literacy goals for their children, so that they can gauge what skills are a priority, how long skill development may take, and when it will be time to introduce new skills of concern to them, for example.

The IDEA includes requirements for assessment of family outcomes for early intervention special education programs. Areas of appropriate outcomes from effective early intervention include families' (a) understanding of their child's strength and needs, (b) awareness of their rights, (c) ability to advocate for themselves and their child, (d) participation in their child's education, (e) receiving of needed support, and (f) ability to access community services beyond (but including) public special education (Bailey et al. 2006).

Early Intervening. Early intervening should not be confused with "early intervention." (Caution: Many educators and parents do not observe the technical distinction between these two terms. The conceptual difference, and its implication for services, is important, however.) As you just read, the latter refers to services provided to infants, toddlers, and young children. The IDEA specifies that early intervention cover children from birth to age three; some states extend early intervention services until kindergarten (remember that children are eligible for traditional special education when they turn three). *Early intervention* is intended to help children get off to the best start possible in life. Specifically, early intervention services are intended to minimize the impact of a disability. IDEA stipulates that early intervention services should address five forms of development: physical, cognitive, communication, social or emotional, and adaptive. Head Start is an example of an early intervention program. When early intervention is provided as a special education service, the child must be enrolled in special education.

The concept of *early intervening* is quite similar, so it is easy to confuse the two terms, especially when early intervening is applied to preschoolers. **Early intervening** means to provide intervention as soon as a possible need is detected. Instead of waiting to collect extensive documentation of a learning difficulty or for an evaluation to document that a disability exists, educators intervene immediately upon detecting a possible need. Technically, early intervening is not a special education service—in fact, it may be thought of as a step to prevent the need for special education (for example, Fuchs et al. 2003). The most common example of early intervening is RTI, which may lead to special education but is not itself special education (review Chapter 1 and see ahead). You could also think of the pre-referral stage of the traditional special education process as early intervening, as part of the intention of pre-referral activities is to determine if there is a simple way to resolve a child's learning challenge.

Parents can play a vital role in early intervening. They can help to provide services at home, or at least support those that educators use. Parents often will need to be trained in the procedures they are asked to follow at home (Kutash et al. 2002; Zhang and Bennett 2003). In fact, an important aspect of early intervening, or any stage of education involving parent participation, is preparing parents and supporting them in their roles. In the spirit of collaboration, parents should be asked to identify the level and types of involvement to which they may be able to commit (Bauer and Shea 2003). Periodically, an educator should review the parents' activities to make sure they continue to be consistent with what had been planned.

So that parents can fully contribute to the collaborative effort on behalf of their child, they should receive progress reports throughout the early intervening process. The educator and parents can set the schedule for the reports as well as discuss an appropriate format. The reports might be in the form of casual conversations when the parents come to pick up the child, they may be scheduled phone conversations or one-on-one meetings, or they may be written notes or summaries of curriculum-based measurement (C-BM) data collected across sessions. In addition to providing parents with data they need to participate in the early intervening collaboration, progress reports are a useful tool to demonstrate to parents that the school cares about their interests in their child. Remember, among the reasons that parents report low levels of involvement in their child's education is that they did not believe school staff valued their input or even believed that the parents were concerned about their child's education (Salas et al. 2005).

Now that we have considered how parents and schools may collaborate in early childhood and activities that may lead to special education, we focus on the stages of the formal special education process and how they provide opportunities for collaboration in the best interest of the child.

Pre-referral. When a parent, teacher, or student perceives a difficulty with academics or functional performance, pre-referral is an appropriate response. Recall from Chapter 2 that the **pre-referral** process includes trying to resolve the difficulty by collecting information about the student's difficulties and modifying instruction based on that data to see if the"problem"can be resolved. By engaging in pre-referral activities, you may realize that you simply need to modify instructional practices somewhat or revisit concepts and skills assumed to be prior knowledge.

The IDEA does not require that parents be notified when educators engage in pre-referral strategies and conferences. Still, informing the parents may be appropriate. Should the pre-referral indicate that a referral is warranted, parents would be surprised to learn that educators had a concern and they were not informed. This could result in the start of a poor relationship between parties. Further, the information gathered during the pre-referral process may be useful in the referral stage; however, if the parents did not participate in contributing, selecting, or reviewing the data it will be less comprehensive for making plans.

Just as parents should be informed of pre-referral strategies and consulted about their child, they should also be informed and consulted about the progress of pre-referral activities. Collecting parents' valuable insights should not end when interventions begin (in this case, pre-referral strategies). Parents can report on how pre-referral activities are impacting a student at home. Of course, parents may also have suggestions on alterations to attempt based on the progress being made in the pre-referral stage.

When parents are informed about pre-referral activities, they can also be consulted as information resources. Family background and child history information can be very valuable to understanding the profile of an infant, child, or adolescent. Parents will be able to report on events that happen outside of school. They may have insights on their child's social status, or they may see evidence of cognitive processing and literacy skills not commonly exhibited in school settings. The family may be experiencing economic hard times, the parents may be going through a divorce, or the child may only begin homework late at night, due to the family's routine. All such factors could cause a professional to suspect a disability when in fact the student does not have one. Conversely, professionals may not believe they are seeing indicators of a disability if they are not familiar with factors outside of schooling.

Referral. For the same reasons parental consultation is a good idea in pre-referral, parent consultation is also beneficial during the referral stage. At the **referral** stage, someone—an educator or a parent, typically—makes an official declaration that a disability is suspected or known to exist and that the option of special education should be investigated. Parental input can be useful for narrowing down the probable type of disability.

In addition to being a good idea, parental notification is a requirement of the IDEA at this stage. Educators must provide written notice to the parents that they have made a referral for an evaluation. No action may be taken toward disability evaluation or consideration of special education enrollment until the parent has provided written consent. This requirement is in keeping with the due process and parent and student participation provisions of the IDEA.

Screening. "The [disability] identification process includes (1) screening, (2) examination for the presence of risk indicators and protective factors, (3) systematic observations, and, if indicated, (4) a comprehensive evaluation" (NJCLD 2007).

A **screening** in special education is an informal assessment of the child's *potential* for having a disability (Pierangelo and Giuliani 2009). In addition to indicating whether a more formal investigation of the presence of a disability may be warranted, the information screening yields can inform instruction.

Screening should include looking for both risk indicators and protective factors (NJCLD 2007). **Risk indicators** are situations such as low Apgar[3] scores, living in poverty, and failure to meet or delay in meeting developmental milestones. The child find requirements require screening children for possible disabilities or at-risk status when necessary. **Protective factors** are those that may help prevent the onset of a disability or buffer its impact; examples include quality healthcare, language-rich home environments, and related services. The information on risk indicators and protective factors will be useful to the educators and parents as they consider whether there is reasonable concern about the presence of a disability. Parents are primary sources of information about risk indicators and protective factors. They should provide information related to the prenatal development of the child and perinatal events relevant to disability status (for example, premature birth, anoxia). School districts may have forms listing questions about the birth experience, home environment, and developmental milestones. Also, meeting with parents to interview them can provide valuable information (Bauer and Shea 2003). A meeting can also begin a positive relationship between the two parties.

Evaluation. When a screening indicates the probability of a disability, a more formal evaluation for the presence and nature of the disability is usually warranted. Once again, the parents can be helpful collaborators in selecting evaluation tools, scheduling evaluations at optimal times, providing data, and interpreting the significance of what is found. To protect parents, the due process and parent and student participation provisions of the IDEA provide explicit guidelines on how they must be involved and informed throughout the evaluation process.

Parents can provide information on the child's English language ability and likely sitting tolerance for certain tests; they can even advise as to whether the test administrator should be male or female. Informed parents might have opinions about the evaluation instruments used; it is best to discuss those opinions before getting to the stage of trying to interpret the evaluation data. The same types of background information on birthing events, early milestones, and the home environment that may have been provided at an earlier stage can be essential information in evaluating for

---

[3] The Apgar test is given to newborns immediately after their birth to assess their physical health and whether immediate medical intervention is needed. It is named for anesthesiologist Virginia Apgar, who developed it in 1952, but the name also stands for activity and muscle tone, pulse, grimace response, appearance, and respiration.

the presence of a disability, as can prior evaluations and diagnoses. Dewey, Crawford, and Kaplan (2003) found that when parents contributed observational data, the accuracy of psychometric testing-centered evaluation for ADHD in children was improved. They noted that the parents assessed for different aspects of child functioning than the tests could be used to measure.

Once evaluation data has been collected, it must be analyzed consistent with the operational criteria for specific disabilities referenced in the IDEA. The student will be eligible for special education services only if the criteria for one of the 13 disability categories served by the IDEA are met, regardless of the child's educational needs (see Stanovich 2005) (Section 504 services may be an option for students with disabilities who are not found eligible for special education). Although parents should supply data and participate in reviewing it, they may not understand the operational criteria or agree with what a narrow reading of the evaluation data indicates. Parents should be informed about the specific disability in question and related conditions (for example, the distinctions between LD and intellectual disability are minor in cases of students who are close to cutoff levels).

Eligibility Determination. At the **eligibility determination meeting**, the parents are joined by professionals knowledgeable about the child's possible special education needs. The educators typically include a school administrator, a school psychologist (or other individual qualified to interpret evaluation results), special educators, and general educators. Thus, the participants in an eligibility determination meeting are typically the same as those who may participate in IEP meetings. Other individuals may also attend at the invitation of the parents or school district if they have knowledge or expertise regarding the child. A translator is provided if needed. The purpose of the meeting is to determine if the child (a) is eligible for special education and (b) needs or would benefit from special education. If all agree the child is eligible, they may then begin to plan for that special education (that is, begin to plan the IEP, assuming the required members of an IEP team are present). The IEP meeting does not have to be rushed into, however. The IDEA (2004) requires that, once eligibility is determined, the school district must provide written notification of that and an IEP meeting must be scheduled so that an IEP can be developed within 30 days.

When There Are Disagreements. Disagreements are almost inevitable in a group planning process, especially one as complex and emotional as planning a student's special education. Smith (2001) suggests that the "best, fastest, and least costly" resolution of a conflict is via informal problem solving. An impartial third party can sometimes bring disagreeing parties back to the process (Scanlon, Saenz, and Kelly 2017). However, the IDEA calls for a more formal dispute resolution process when needed (Fig. 3.1). **Due process hearings** follow when less formal mediation procedures are unsuccessful. The IDEA regulations provide very specific guidelines for due process hearings (see Cortiella [2006] for a useful summary of the process, including major activities and obligations at each stage). Although parents and schools never lose their legal rights, the IDEA now requires that parties engage in a **resolution session** after

Less formal ⬅————————————————————➡ **More formal**
Mediation > Due process complaint > Resolution session > Due process hearing > Civil suit

◀ **FIGURE 3.1**

Stages of Due Process

Source: Reprinted with permission from C. Cortiella. IDEA Parent Guide: A Comprehensive Guide to Your Rights and Responsibilities Under the Individuals with Disabilities Education Act (IDEA 2004). New York: National Center for Learning Disabilities, 2006.

a **due process complaint** has been filed by either party, but before proceeding to a due process hearing. The decisions arrived at through the resolution session may be legally binding.

Development of an IEP/Individual Family Service Plan. Parent consent to enrolling a child in special education is a required first step in developing an IEP or individual family service plan (IFSP). However, educators should not think of obtaining parental consent as a mere formality.

In inviting parents to the determination meeting, school staff should extend the same courtesies and legally required rights that they have in other interactions with the family. Thus, educators should provide written prior notice; inquire as to whether a language translator or accommodations will be needed; and inform the parents of the purpose of the meeting, its time and location, their rights (the Procedural Safeguards document), who will be in attendance, and their right to include others who are knowledgeable about the child's educational needs (for example, a special education advocate). As Smith (2001) notes, the communication to the parents must be in a language and format they can comprehend. When parents participate in identifying goals for their child, the chances that they will be able to support those goals at home increases (Smith 2001).

Once the IEP team has identified educational goals (and objectives) and corresponding instructional plans, they next need to discuss where services will be provided and by whom—the placement decision. School staffs may think of placement for services in terms of efficiency for scheduling and professional expertise. Parents are likely to be more concerned with their child's safety, social status, transportation, and implications for future placements, in addition to being concerned with educational processes and outcomes (Smith 2001). Note that although it may seem efficient to first think of where a child in special education will be placed, that discussion of the least restrictive environment should not take place until the special education itself is first decided on because the team cannot know the least restrictive environment for a service before it has identified what that service is.

Intervention. Many parents are interested in supporting their child's education. They want a say in whether their children are enrolled in special services and updates on how well their children are progressing, as well as to more literally participate in educating their children.

Parents should be told about the education services their child will receive. In special education, that communication is partially accomplished through the requirements for parent participation in IEP development and for their written consent to enact the IEP. Parents should also be informed as to how well their children are performing in their education. Special education personnel respond to this need by providing required progress reports and an annual IEP review, but much more can be done to enhance parents' participation.

Supporting Interventions at Home. Ample research evidence supports that students benefit from multiple practice opportunities to learn new skills or information (Kame'enui et al. 2002; Swanson and Deshler 2003). Ideally, the practice will be distributed over time and integrated with related skills or content (Kame'enui et al. 2002). Working on academic content at home can be a useful way for students to get the additional practice they need. Parents can monitor their child's practice. They can quiz children, ask children to model and practice think-aloud skills, and participate with the child to work on assigned tasks.

Methods and Strategies Spotlight

Interviewing Parents about their Participation in their Child's Education

The word *interview* connotes one person answering questions that another person reads off a clipboard, but the interview with parents should be far more conversational. As Salas et al. (2005) note, the teacher should give information during the "interview conversation" too, and should welcome the parents to ask questions and raise other topics.

Bauer and Shea (2003) advise that an interview with a parent can function much like an "intake interview," where educators seek necessary information about students. They note that the initial interview can include the following:

- Establish a positive working relationship between teacher and family members;
- Review and discuss the child's program;
- Review and discuss related services and accommodations;
- Review and discuss the role of parents;
- Introduce the parents to engagement in their child's education. (Bauer and Shea 2003, p. 71)

If parents are uncomfortable participating in interviews, the teacher can ask if they would be willing to complete interest forms on which they indicate their interest and comfort level discussing a variety of topics, such as their feelings about their child and the disability, how children develop and learn, and areas in which help is desired.

Progress Monitoring. Although the IDEA requirements for progress reports call for periodically informing parents of their child's progress toward achieving goals, progress monitoring presumes an ongoing process of collecting and analyzing data to indicate how well a student is progressing in all lessons. Progress monitoring is not necessarily distinct from intervention. The data collected for progress monitoring comes from interventions and should be used to inform intervention practices.

Perhaps the best established example of progress monitoring in special education practice is C-BM (Deno 1985, 2003a, 2003b). Using C-BM procedures, samples of the student's progress in a lesson or unit are collected at regular intervals. When a child is working on literacy, numeracy, or dressing skills, for example, the educators can assess and record how well, how consistently, or how quickly he or she performs targeted skills. For academic interventions, quick one-minute "probes" of skill performance are typically administered every third lesson or weekly (review Chapter 2). The data collected is plotted on a graph so that the teacher, parents, and student can all monitor progress.

Parents can participate in administering C-BM probes and charting their child's performance. When they do so, a chart of home performance can supplement a chart of in-school performance.

Of course, sharing C-BM data with parents is a useful way to communicate with them about their child's progress. Specific data points and trends can be discussed, which should help both parties feel certain they are talking about the same phenomena. It also enhances the probability that both parties will interpret the data in the same way. In addition, when parents have access to C-BM data, they are better informed about skills and content to practice with their child beyond the homework assignments the student receives.

Progress Reports to Parents

To be involved in a child's special education, parents must be informed as to how their child is progressing. In recognition of this need, the IDEA requires that parents be informed of their child's progress on IEP goals and objectives/benchmarks at least as often as parents in general education receive a progress report. Therefore, as often as report cards and/or progress reports are sent home, so too must parents receive reports related to how well their child is progressing on IEP goals and supporting activities. Sending a report card is not enough. Although grades over the school year should be indicative of overall progress and parents of children in special education should still receive report cards, report cards are not likely to directly reflect progress toward an IEP or transition goal (see ahead in this chapter for more about transition planning).

The progress report needs to address academic achievement as well as functional performance. Recall that the IDEA and the Every Student Succeeds Act (ESSA) both focus on achievement as an outcome of special and general education. The portion of the progress report addressing academics should base progress on academic goals within a profile of academic achievement. For example, a report may indicate how well a child is progressing in specific goals for composition, accompanying objectives if the team has elected to write them, and how well the child is achieving in the language arts curriculum. For example:

> *Despite difficulties with generating main ideas and topic sentences, which reflects a continuing problem with organizing his thoughts, Charlie has mastered brainstorming content before he begins writing and predetermining the order in which to express that content. Quality of written expression accounts for one-fourth of his quarter grade in language arts; he is averaging C⁻ work in written expression this quarter. Combined with his performance in other aspects of language arts, his quarter grade is C⁺, an improvement over the previous quarter.*

Reports of progress toward goals should be based on multiple objective measures (IDEA 2004), not just teacher observations or test results. The reports should also be in conformance with any format and content expectations agreed upon in the IEP document.

Annual Review and Triennial Reevaluation. As discussed in Chapter 1, in addition to the annual review of the IEP, a triennial review must be conducted to update the IEP team on the child's current disability condition and how it impacts his or his academic learning and functional performance. In advance of the meeting, parents should be consulted regarding the agenda and the major topics for discussion (Cortiella 2006). They should be advised to identify their level of satisfaction with the child's education to date and their goals for the coming year. Having this type of information can facilitate devoting more of the meeting time to planning. Parents should also be clearly informed that they will be able to state their information within the meeting and that no decisions will be made in advance of the session. According to the IDEA, parents additionally need to be informed as to who will be present at the review meeting, by both name and position. The parents are welcome to bring along professionals knowledgeable about their child's education needs (for example, a special education advocate). Remember, the balance of power in the special education process can seem to pit the school against the parents (Kalyanpur, Harry, and Skrtic 2000; Salas et al. 2005); thus, parents might bring an advocate or support person with them so that they feel comfortable collaborating.

RTI. For students who participate in an RTI approach (review Chapter 1), the parents must be furnished with a **written intervention plan** (Table 3.2). The purposes for

TABLE 3.2 Parent Information and Participation in the RTI Model*

Universal Screening	
Tier 1: Class-wide or School-wide Intervention	Written intervention plan Parent consultation Progress reports
Tier 2:	
Tier 3:	
Evaluation**	Written notification Procedural Safeguards document Parent consultation Written parent consent Data and information shared is comprehensible to parents Information and resources about disabilities Information and resources about special education
Determination Meeting	Written notification Procedural Safeguards document Advance invitation to schedule the meeting Advance invitation to identify the need for language interpreter or accommodations Data and information shared is comprehensible to parents Parent collaboration
IEP/ITP Development	Written notification Procedural Safeguards document Advance invitation to schedule the meeting Advance invitation to identify the need for language interpreter or accommodations Data and information shared is comprehensible to parents Parent consent Parent collaboration

*RTI model based on NJCLD (2007).

**Parents may request a formal disability evaluation for special education determination at any time in the RTI process.

providing an intervention plan parallel the purposes of various communications to parents in the pre-referral, referral, and IEP planning stages of the traditional special education process. That is, it is designed to inform the parents of what is being done with their child and why, as well as to provide advance notice of how the parents will be informed throughout the RTI process. Contents of a written intervention plan should include the following:

"A description of the specific intervention;

The length of time (such as number of weeks) that will be allowed for the intervention to have a positive effect;

The number of minutes per day the intervention will be implemented (such as 30 to 45 minutes);

The persons responsible for providing the intervention;

The location where the intervention will be provided;

The factors for judging whether the student is experiencing success;

A description of the progress monitoring strategy or approach, such as C-BM, that
will be used;
A progress-monitoring schedule." (Cortiella 2006)

Although RTI models do not typically require providing progress-monitoring
reports to parents when their children enter into Tier 2 or 3 interventions, common
sense dictates that parents would value being informed and that they may have useful
input. Furthermore, knowing that interventions at a particular tier have not been successful may be important to parents, because they have the right to refer their child for
traditional evaluation of a possible disability at any time.

Parents also need to be informed of their right to request a formal evaluation for
the presence of a disability at any stage of the RTI process. The Procedural Safeguard
document should make this option clear to the parents, including informing them on
the implications of both RTI and full evaluation. Parents may be confused as to whether
participation in RTI is the same as enrollment in special education. It is not, except in
the case of versions where one of the tiers constitutes special education enrollment
(typically Tier 3, or following the child's failure to respond to effective interventions in
Tier 3, although special education enrollment is not an automatic outcome). Although
the IDEA does allow states to incorporate RTI data into the formal evaluation process,
designation of a disability and enrollment in special education still require parental
consent and participation. Remember that RTI as a route to identification is only available for those with possible LD, not the other HIs.

Standards for Working with Families

Now that you have read about the many ways schools and parents should collaborate and why they are so important, reflect on how you, the educator, can be a good
collaborator.

Competent educators are sensitive to the needs of their students and their students' families, including having an appreciation for diverse cultures (Sileo and Prater
1998). Competent educators possess knowledge, skills, and attitudes that facilitate
their interactions; they also acknowledge the contributions that families make to their
own understanding of the child and the school environment (Sileo and Prater 1998).

All educators need to be aware of factors that can inhibit effective interactions with
families. Typical barriers to parents' participation in their children's schooling include
being uncomfortable with the school's conceptualization of parent involvement; limited English proficiency; few experiences with accessing resources to inform their
decision making on their child's behalf; and prior negative experiences with schools
based on ethnic, racial, and cultural backgrounds (Hughes, Schumm, and Vaughn
1999; Salas et al. 2005; Sileo and Prater 1998). In contrast, professionals who are competent in interacting with parents are aware of their own experiences, values, and
attitudes toward diverse groups; aware of the varied cultural, linguistic, and familial
backgrounds of their students' families; and culturally responsive in both communications with families and their pedagogical practices (Sileo and Prater 1998).

There are particular needs for, and challenges to, collaborating with families from
different cultures from one's own or the school's majority culture. However, the above
points are equally relevant for effectively collaborating with families that "look" very
similar to your own.

The Council for Exceptional Children (CEC) (2015) standards for special education
teachers do not include a separate set of standards for working with parents and families; rather, they integrate them among the standards areas (see the inside cover of this
book). Many of the standards relate to working with families; several explicitly name

the expectations for special education teachers to do so. Other standards concerning language and cultural differences, education planning, and collaboration relate to educator–family relationships as well.

THINK BACK TO THE CASE about Mrs. Waters . . .

2. *Did Rhonda's interactions with Mrs. Waters reflect professional standards for how special educators should interact with parents?*

Case 3.1 does not speak to all of the CEC standards related to working with parents, but it does give several indications of how well Rhonda performed these aspects of her role. Over time, Rhonda learned about the Waterses' home environment. She found out about Charlie's study habits at home and she learned about how the Waterses were willing and able to support Charlie's education at home. She did not just provide the Waterses with periodic progress reports and otherwise ignore them; rather, she invited Mrs. Waters to contribute ideas about Charlie's education. She listened to Mrs. Waters's concerns and suggestions and worked to incorporate them into her practice. Thus, we do have some indicators that Rhonda exhibited expected skills for collaborating with parents.

However, Mrs. Waters was kept waiting several minutes when she arrived at the school for the IEP meeting, and this was after she was delayed in arriving. The fact that neither Rhonda nor the special education administrator greeted her reflects poorly on them. This behavior can send the message that they are more important than the parent is or that they are in control of the process. Rhonda was also over a week late in sending the final version of the IEP to Mrs. Waters. Although we can all understand getting behind on paperwork, the Waterses could have interpreted that tardiness as Rhonda's not being as invested in their son's education as she indicates she is in their presence.

3-5 Transition

Among the reasons parents are involved in special education planning and service delivery is that disabilities do not go away when the school day is over. Of course, disabilities also do not go away just because a student[4] graduates or leaves school in some other way. School–parent collaborations include working together to plan for the student's transition to life beyond school. And that partnership must include the student, as it is his or her future that is being planned. Students with disabilities are among those who are uniquely vulnerable to difficulties in life upon leaving school (Osgood et al. 2005).

Since the 1990 reauthorization of the IDEA, **transition** has been defined as being about preparation for leaving school. However, the importance of transition was stated prior to that version of the law. It was first identified in the 1983 Education of the Handicapped Amendments (Public Law 98-199), which addressed the need for coordinated education, training, and related services to prepare students for post-school experiences, with employment as the ultimate goal.

---

[4] At this point in the chapter we revert to using the term "student." While the IDEA uses "child," here it is more appropriate to use "student" as the transition period is mostly about preparing adolescents for moving beyond secondary school. However, transition planning and services can be appropriate for young children as well, as you will read in Box 3.4—for example, to ensure a successful transition from an early intervention program to kindergarten.

The 1990 reauthorization was the first version of the IDEA to require that transition planning and services be provided, when needed; it included the requirement that transition goals and objectives be written. **Transition planning** is the process of identifying and addressing the needs of a student in special education associated with successfully moving to post-school experiences. Unlike the 1983 Amendments, the goal of transition has been broadened to consider school outcomes in addition to work.

Trends in Post-School Outcomes

Students with HI are a diverse group. Many of them are academically and socially successful in school and generally have positive lives. Likewise, as a benefit of special education, the majority go on to lead fulfilling adult lives, which may include employment, further education, and successful transitioning through the stages of adult living (see, for example, *Federal Outlook for Exceptional Children* [CEC 2007]; Hamill 2003). However, the statistics indicate that individuals with disabilities are more likely to have a diminished quality of life upon leaving school compared to their nondisabled peers (Morningstar, Trainor, and Murray 2015; Newman et al. 2009; Wagner et al. 2006; see also Jenkins et al. 2006; Rusch and Loomis 2005). They can have diminished experiences and achievements in the areas of education, employment, and daily living.

Education. Students with HI are more likely than their general education peers to leave school without graduating. This likelihood includes dropping out (Edgar 2005; Scanlon and Mellard 2002), "aging out," and abruptly leaving by expulsion or entering a correctional system (Baltodano, Harris, and Rutherford 2005; Cavendish 2014; Horowitz, Rawe, and Whittaker 2017; Quinn et al. 2005). Students of color or from low-income families and communities are also more likely to leave school before completion (see Murray and Naranjo 2008); as those students are disproportionately represented among students with HI, they are effectively at "twice the risk" of unsatisfactory outcomes (Osgood et al. 2005). Even those with HI who do complete school by traditional standards are more likely to complete lower-track curricular options or meet minimal standards for passing (Rojewski and Gregg 2017; Skinner and Lindstrom 2003), which leaves fewer post-school options available to them.

Once out of school, students with HI are also less likely than their peers to participate in the range of postsecondary education options, which include adult basic education, correctional education, vocational training, community college, and baccalaureate and graduate programs (Madaus, Banerjee, Merchant, and Keenan 2017; Murray et al. 2000; Stodden and Dowrick 2000).

When students with disabilities do enter postsecondary education, they are more likely to leave the program without completing it, whether it is an adult basic education or college program (Madaus et al. 2017; Milsom and Hartley 2005). In fact, within 10 years after graduating from high school, the majority of nondisabled adults will have graduated from either a community or four-year college, while the majority of those with LD will not have (Mellard and Lancaster 2003; also see DaDeppo 2009 and Horowitz et al. 2017), and those with EBD and mild intellectual disability are even less likely to have attended and graduated from postsecondary education (McEwan and Downie 2013). Among the two biggest hurdles that postsecondary students with HI experience are not being prepared for the academic demands of their new setting (Lowery-Corkran 2006) and not being equipped to deal with the demands of daily living (for example, lacking transportation, family and social relationships, organization) (Troiano 2003; see also Mull, Sitlington, and Alper 2001).

Employment. The employment trend upon leaving high school for young adults with HI has steadily improved; however, those with HI continue to be unemployed and underemployed after leaving high school (Newman, Wagner, Cameto, Knokey, and Shaver 2010). Do not be fooled by the fact that young adults with HI have been found to earn more than their peers without disabilities in the initial years after leaving secondary school: the probable explanation is that fewer students with HI enter college, instead entering the workforce. Beginning the fifth year after leaving high school, those without disabilities begin to earn more, and the gap between the two populations only widens after that (Wagner et al. 2005; see Madaus 2006). Adults with disabilities who complete postsecondary education typically earn more than adults with disabilities who do not (Dickinson and Verbeek 2002; Madaus 2006).

Daily Living. Reports on daily living for young adults and adults with HI indicate that they experience limited independence and social satisfaction (Barkley et al. 2006; Coutinho, Oswald, and Best 2006). As young adults, those with HI more commonly remain single and live with their parents (Newman et al. 2009). They also have been reported to have fewer friends or close relationships (Elksnin and Elksnin 2001; Margalit and Al-Yagon 2002; Newman et al. 2009; Stacy 2001). Sometimes, they lack the social competence to use social skills effectively in varied contexts (Gresham, Sugai, and Horner 2001); they may have difficulty interacting appropriately with peers versus adults or in academic or work situations where tasks must be completed efficiently. As Hill and Coufal (2005) report, communication disorders are often associated with general social difficulties, particularly when they are linked with EBD. Psychosocial factors appear to influence adolescents with LD or ADHD to participate in risk-taking behaviors such as delinquency, sexual activity, and gambling (McNamara, Vervaeke, and Willoughby 2008).

However, not all students with HI have social skills difficulties. In fact, they may have social challenges at a rate similar to their same-aged peers without disabilities; it is simply that traits associated with their disability may relate to their challenges (see: Smith and Wallace 2011; Weiner 2004). Some students with HI have particularly positive social status and satisfaction in online environments (e.g., Bargh and McKenna 2004; Eden and Heiman 2011; Raskind, Margalit, and Higgins 2006). Also, despite these overall trends in daily living, Morningstar et al. (2015) found a generally positive sense of well-being among youth with ADHD, EBD, and LD.

Expanding the Transition Focus Beyond Employment

The original intention of transition planning and services was to prepare students with disabilities to enter the world of work (see Will 1984, 1986). Critics of that emphasis argued that work alone was too narrow a goal (see especially Halpern 1985). They suggested that other aspects of adulthood and well-being also needed to be addressed to achieve successful post-school outcomes (Halpern et al. 1995). **Wellbeing** refers to physical and mental health, including one's personal satisfaction with life (see, for instance, Biggs and Carter 2016; also see Annie E. Casey Foundation [2014] for comparisons of children's well-being across the United States). Halpern (1985, 1993) suggested that, in addition to employment, those leaving school need to be secure in three domains—*physical and material well-being, performance of adult roles,* and *personal fulfillment*—for a satisfactory **quality of life** (Box 3.3).

BOX 3.3

Halpern's Quality of Life Domains

PHYSICAL AND MATERIAL WELL-BEING

Physical and mental health
Food, clothing, and lodging
Financial security
Safety from harm

PERFORMANCE OF ADULT ROLES

Mobility and community access
Vocation, career, employment
Leisure and recreation
Personal relationships and social networks
Educational attainment
Spiritual fulfillment
Citizenship (for example, voting)
Social responsibility (for example, doesn't break laws)

PERSONAL FULFILLMENT

Happiness
Satisfaction
Sense of general well-being

Source: Reprinted from A. Halpern, "Quality of Life as a Conceptual Framework for Evaluating Transition Outcomes (Exceptional Children 59 (1993):486–98).

CASE 3.2 — The Challenge of Planning for the Most Appropriate Options

Case Introduction

As you read the following case, ask yourself what options are appropriate for Adam at the end of ninth grade; also consider what his needs are likely to be if he stays in school through 12th grade, and what supports he might need after that.

At the end of the case, you will find case questions. These questions are meant to serve as points for reflection. Of course, if you can answer them immediately, you should do so, but you may want to wait to answer them until you have read the portion of the chapter that pertains to a particular case question. Throughout the rest of the chapter, you will see the same questions. When you come to them again, try to answer them based upon that portion of the chapter that you just read.

Adam's ninth-grade year at Monroe High School was quickly coming to an end. Mary Alice had been looking forward to his IEP meeting. As the high school director of special education services, she had participated in his eighth-grade IEP meeting

when he was preparing to come up from the Sumner Middle School. This year, she had a high level of direct involvement with Adam and his family, due to several incidents of inappropriate behaviors by Adam. Adam was one of Mary Alice's favorite students, and she often thought that students like him made her enjoy special education work so much.

Adam came to Monroe High School with a thick special education file. The year he entered elementary school, he was permanently placed to live with his aunt's family, after suffering an early childhood of neglect and sexual abuse. Mary Alice could never get a clear answer from Adam's aunt or caseworker as to where Adam's mother is or how involved she is in his life. All she knows about the father is that "he is no longer on the scene," but that he attempted to contact Adam once or twice but never followed through. She knows that Adam's life with his aunt is not ideal; his aunt had taken him in out of a sense of obligation. She sometimes commented in front of him that she is glad to model the importance of family for him even though he poses a burden on her

continued

family. Adam had told Mary Alice that his aunt routinely favored his two younger cousins, whom she referred to as her "real children."

Because of his diagnosed EBD, Adam has been receiving counseling services. He also has yearly IEP goals related to social skills and academics. He has two friends with whom he spends time, but they often argue, and Mary Alice doubts they would be friends if each had someone else with whom to spend time. Adam generally gets along well with other students while sitting next to them in class; however, most students seem to avoid interacting with him. Mary Alice presumes this is due to his sullen and sometimes aggressive behavior. It is commonly rumored in the school that Adam has attempted suicide at least once.

Adam's last IEP meeting was a challenge, with much of the time spent discussing his behaviors and recent incidents that occurred in middle school and at home; almost no time was spent discussing his academic needs that result from his comorbid EBD and LD or how to help him successfully move to the high school.

Mary Alice looked forward to this meeting because in scheduling it everyone talked about the importance of developing "really clear" IEPs for Adam's final years of schooling. Mary Alice even sent all parties an advance agenda: 15 minutes to discuss academic goals, 15 minutes to discuss behavior and counseling goals, 15 minutes to discuss other family goals or concerns, and 15 minutes to identify transition plans. She thought that this order of topics would ensure that all important topics would be discussed before the session could be derailed by focusing on some recent incident.

Despite her planning, Mary Alice wasn't prepared when, at the start of the meeting, the school counselor stated that he was afraid Adam was feeling "lost" at the large high school and that he would be better off attending a smaller vocational program. He suggested that the smaller vocational school would be more conducive to Adam making progress on his social skills. Adam's aunt immediately endorsed the transfer as a good idea. Despite Mary Alice's best attempts to discuss Adam's academic and behavior goals before contemplating a change in placement, the conversation never recovered. The rest of the meeting was spent discussing what Adam could do by attending the vocational school. Adam wasn't present at the meeting, but his aunt was sure that he would like the switch.

Mary Alice felt as if she had lost a fight. Everyone else in the room was satisfied with virtually repeating academic goals from this year's IEP; instead of developing a transition plan, they agreed that Adam simply needed to transfer to the vocational program, and that they would have a better idea of transition needs based on how the year went.

CASE QUESTIONS

1. When in the course of Adam's schooling should discussion of his transition needs have begun?
2. What evidence may indicate that a student, such as Adam, needs a transition plan?
3. What post-school options should a transition plan address?

The discussion of Adam's transition needs in case C.2 did not go well, nor did his IEP meeting in general (review Chapter 1). Transition planning is done within the IEP planning process and should progress from a discussion of interests, strengths, and needs to identifying goals and steps to meet those goals. Even if moving to the vocational school was the right decision for Adam, the IEP/transition meeting did not go well. Participants focused too much on reacting to Adam's behaviors. By beginning with a focus on why the high school may not be appropriate for him, the team negated careful discussion of what transition goals should be addressed and how best to address them. Without that information, it is hard to know if Adam would be better off in a vocational curriculum. Do the vocational options available at the school even interest Adam? Also, Adam has important academic learning needs and social-emotional needs. Only "reacting" to him instead of planning for his future in those realms will not lead to successful adulthood. Note too that the focus was only on his short-term transition. The discussion also should have addressed post–high school options for Adam, how those options should be explored, and what experiences he should begin to have to be ready for leaving school.

THINK BACK TO THE CASE   about Adam . . .

1. *When in the course of Adam's schooling should discussion of his transition needs have begun?*

When Adam was still in eighth grade, there was reason to be concerned about his transition to high school. The IEP team should have developed transition goals and a plan for him while he was still in eighth grade. The IDEA 2004 regulations call for teams to develop transition plans as soon as they anticipate the student will have a transition need. Therefore, had the team members anticipated a need for transition support even earlier than eighth grade, they should have begun preparing for the transition then.

If Adam is likely to need counseling or personal living supports after high school, the team should begin planning for that. Likewise, it is time to plan for Adam's post-high school goals for employment or education. If the team members anticipate that he will have difficulty finding success in those new settings, they should begin planning for his transition. These are decisions Adam and his IEP team members should make. Without a doubt, the team members should have been more thoughtful in discussing Adam's transition to the vocational school, beginning with identifying his interests, strengths, and needs.

Current IDEA Requirements for Transition Planning and Services

The IDEA requires that an **individualized transition plan (ITP)** (note that here the "P" stands for "plan," unlike in "IEP") be developed by members of the IEP team and other appropriate parties, who make up the transition planning team. Their task is to set transition goals and plan the services that will support a student in meeting those annual goals, just as is done for the academic and functional behavior goals on an IEP.

THINK BACK TO THE CASE   about Adam . . .

2. *What evidence may indicate that a student, such as Adam, needs a transition plan?*

In reviewing evidence that a student will need any type of transition planning, educators should take into account whether the student has the functional skills for academic tasks and other demands associated with the quality-of-life domains. Likewise, the team members should consider whether the student has realistic goals or any goals at all. As need be, transition planning can focus on helping the student to determine personal goals. When the team members consider what is required to succeed at a particular goal, they can next consider whether the student will need support to be prepared to succeed.

Relying on population statistics about students with HI is a dangerous way to make plans about transition. Although it is useful to know that students with EBD, like Adam, are among the most likely to drop out of school (Cobb et al. 2006) and have difficulty holding jobs (Wagner and Cameto 2004), educators must first look for evidence that the student is at risk for such experiences before presuming that transition efforts should focus on preventing certain scenarios.

According to the IDEA regulations, **transition services** "means a coordinated set of activities"(§300.43(a), 46762) to improve both the academic and functional achievement of a student, with the intent of facilitating transition to post-school activities. Those post-school activities include the following:

- Postsecondary education,
- Vocational education,
- Integrated employment (including supported employment),
- Continuing and adult education,
- Adult services,
- Independent living, or
- Community participation. (§300.43(a)(1), 46762)

Therefore, transition planning and services must address postsecondary training and/or education, employment, and independent living or community participation.

Note that the IDEA regulations plainly state that transition services need to address a student's academic and functional *achievement*. That phrasing not only supports the ESSA (and the No Child Left Behind Act before that) and IDEA emphases on achievement as school outcomes, but also indicates that transition services are not merely about identifying the student's next "placement" upon leaving school. Transition is also about preparing for the student to succeed in that placement (see Box 3.4 for transition intentions and policies for early childhood education).

The IDEA (2004) identifies transition as part of a "results-oriented process" (§300.43(a) (1), 46762). If a high school graduate gets a job, for example, but soon finds that he or she lacks critical entry-level skills or the ability to self-advocate as an adult with a disability, that placement may soon be a failure. It is too late for the former student to return to the school for further assistance, because transition services end when the student leaves special education (for example, by graduating or completing school, dropping out, or no longer being identified as needing/benefiting from special education). Effective transition planning, however, involves anticipating the demands that different settings and contexts will place upon transitioning students, and preparing them to meet those demands.

BOX 3.4

Transition in Early Childhood Special Education

IDEA Part C is the portion of the special education law concerning early childhood special education, covering ages birth up until the child's third birthday. That section of the law requires that necessary transition planning be done for children aging out of early childhood services. Thus, at least 90 days before an infant or toddler who is "potentially eligible" for preschool special education services turns three, the agency serving the infant/toddler must notify the state and local education agencies (for example, the respective departments of education) that the child may be eligible for services. The intention is that the child can seamlessly make the transition from early childhood services through an IFSP to preschool special education services via an IEP, if appropriate. (Some states have "opt-out policies" that allow parents the right to block the agency from notifying the state and local agencies. This is another example of how schools and parents partner in special education planning and services, similar to the parents' right to refuse to enroll their child in special education.)

Part C regulations require that a "transition conference" be held for potentially eligible infants/toddlers. Required participants include a representative of the agency

continued

currently providing early childhood services, a parent, and a representative of the local education agency that may receive the child. (In the case of a child who is not potentially eligible, participants must be the currently providing agency, the parent, and providers of other appropriate services.) At the transition conference the parties must review program options for the child through the end of the school year when he or she turns three. A transition plan must be written, just as it must for students in special education with an IEP (Part B of the IDEA). That transition plan must specify what transition services will be provided, and because the infant/toddler is still in early childhood special education, the parent and other family members may be eligible to participate in the transition services as well.

IDEA Part B requires that IEPs for children age three and older preparing to enter K–12 must address school readiness, pre-literacy, language, and numeracy skills. Therefore, it is likely that the early childhood ITP will make reference to these skills.

3-6 Addressing the Demands of Various Transition Settings

Upon leaving secondary education, students with disabilities may not realize that, unlike in primary and secondary education, they must be "otherwise qualified" to gain access to most post-school placements (see Americans with Disabilities Act of 1990; Section 504 of the Rehabilitation Act of 1973 [both of these laws have since been amended]). This is quite different from K–12 education, where the emphasis is on determining how to make the education accessible to the student. As we will explain further in this chapter, students must learn to self-advocate for their rights. Whether they are exiting special education but remaining in K–12 education or preparing for their life after high school, students may also need transition support specific to their destination.

Exiting Special Education

Some students exit special education while still enrolled in school because they no longer require special education services to benefit from their education. They may receive related services in accordance with Section 504, if needed. In deciding whether to discontinue special education, the IEP team should not only consider whether the student still needs supports to make academic and functional performance achievements but must also address whether a student may, nonetheless, have disability-related needs for a supported transition to beyond high school (see Mull and Sitlington 2003). Keeping a student enrolled in special education with an education plan solely to address transition goals is appropriate. When students leave the familiar environment of secondary school, they may immediately be confronted by situations they are not ready to navigate, due to their disability. For example, a former student with an emotional disorder may not be able to adjust to the changes in daily routine, or someone with ADHD may not have learned self-regulation strategies that are feasible on the job. Such students could have benefited from transition services to prepare them for post-school circumstances.

Dropping Out, Removal, and Expulsion

Some students leave school without having completed their education. Prematurely leaving school, via dropping out, temporary removal, or expulsion, is almost always detrimental and is also more common for students with disabilities (Scanlon and Mellard 2002; Smith, Manuel, and Stokes 2012). It can result in a number of problems.

Dropping Out. A number of intractable factors such as race/ethnicity, sex, and socio-economic class increase a student's risk for dropping out (Horn, Peter, and Rooney 2002; Murray and Naranjo 2008). Having a disability is also an intractable risk factor for dropping out of school. Other factors, such as school attachment, academic success, and positive attitudes toward school, are also related to dropping out, but each of these can be adjusted (Dunn, Chambers, and Rabren 2004; Eisenman 2007; Scanlon and Mellard 2002). Four adjustable factors long known to contribute to dropout prevention are (a) academic success, (b) students' belief that adults in the school care about them, (c) support for immediate and pressing personal concerns, and (d) an appreciation of the relation between schooling and personal goals (McPartland 1994). The most effective interventions will address the constellation of factors that may contribute to dropping out, and not just one or two in isolation (see Eisenman 2007). Thus, IEP teams concerned that a student is at risk for dropping out should plan to address these four areas to prevent the student from actually dropping out. For example, Cameron and Bartel (2009) found that 35 percent of students with LD who dropped out were failing and believed they would only get further and further behind. They not only needed support to begin to have more academic success, but they needed to feel cared about, that they belonged in the school community, and that school was relevant to their interests and goals. The other 65% of dropouts needed those things too.

Temporary Removal. Some students may be removed from schooling, either voluntarily or involuntarily, for reasons such as substance abuse, mental or physical health interventions, or pregnancy. Students may also be temporarily suspended from school for disciplinary reasons. Unless the cause for removal is related to a disability, such as a student with HI who placed others at risk due to an impulsive decision, students are not protected by the IDEA from being removed from school. IDEA regulations stipulate that special education students involuntarily removed from school must continue to receive special education services; however, the students may be removed to an alternative setting to receive those services.

The length of time a student is removed can vary. Even when it is short term, removal represents a transition. Whenever possible, IEP and transition teams should anticipate such transitions as plausible events (for example, teams can often be aware of whether a student with EBD is at risk for needing full-time placement out of school) and plan to help the student avoid getting to the point of removal (for example, by teaching self-regulation skills) and to help with successful transitions when necessary. The team (including the student) should know what circumstances could cause the removal and what the alternate placement will be like. They should be prepared to plan for how education and transition curricula and services will follow the student. Of course, the team also needs to evaluate whether and how transition plans and services will need to be altered for a student returning to school from an alternative setting.

Expulsion. Although students typically cannot be expelled if the cause is based in their disability, in some cases the school can successfully argue that the disability was not substantively related to whatever caused the expulsion. Once expelled, students must continue to receive their special education (IDEA 2004). However, it is likely they will receive those services in an alternative setting. Just as in instances of temporary removal, the IEP/ITP team should work to prevent the expulsion by teaching the student positive skills and help the student prepare for life following expulsion. The student may not be able to access in-school services once the expulsion is finalized. At-risk students should understand their rights, responsibilities, and options for entering another school system. They should also have an idea of alternative options to pursue once out of the school system (for example, employment, GED preparation) and procedures to activate them.

The World of Work

Transition planning should include consideration of work goals, even for students who plan on postsecondary education, military enlistment, or some other option prior to entering the world of full-time work. Part of the challenge of identifying work goals and setting transition plans for students is that they have so many options for employment. Many adolescents are not prepared to identify their career preferences.

Lindstrom and Benz (2002) identified three phases of career development based on studies of young women with LD: *unsettled, exploratory,* and *settled.* Adolescents are often limited in their knowledge of career options; being asked what career they would like to prepare for can result in no reply or a forced choice that is based on limited information, at best. Those adolescents would be beginning in Lindstrom and Benz's *unsettled* phase. To help adolescents identify promising work directions, consider their interests, capabilities (including potential to develop capabilities via training or education), and potential for opportunities (for example, ways they can pay for postsecondary tuition). The many students who do not yet know what they would like to do can still specify information related to what they would enjoy, would be good at, and realistically could accomplish in work. From there, work options can be *explored.* Based on the results of exploration, students can enter into the *settled* phase by becoming stable in a work routine and finding work fitting within a positive quality of life. However, entering the settled phase does not ensure the worker will *stay* settled.

Disabilities in the Workplace. Identifying potential work directions is merely the first step in preparing for transition into the world of work. In addition to possessing job-seeking skills such as searching for and applying for work, and the necessary skills for holding a job (for example, personal conduct, technical skills), persons with disabilities must also employ appropriate skills related to managing potential disability influences. Most adults do not disclose their HI at the initial job interview, fearing it would harm their prospect of being hired (Gerber et al. 2004). Most do not request accommodations in the job interview process either, even when those accommodations may be needed as part of the interview (Gerber et al. 2004). Gerber et al. (2004) offered the example of a job applicant who claimed he did not need accommodations during the job interview "because I could bring [the paperwork] home, and my mom will help me" (p. 287). Once on the job, most adults with disabilities do not request accommodations either. This is often due to fear of embarrassment or retribution, including being fired (Gerber et al. 2004). Thus, transition planning for many students needs to include preparing them to know their disability rights and how to self-advocate.

The Military

The decision to join the military involves weighing a variety of factors, which may pose a challenge for those with HI. Because of the commitment involved, it is particularly important to help adolescents make informed choices. A common misperception among teens is that they can easily resign if they regret enlisting (see Ayers 2006). Undocumented immigrants should be informed that they are not eligible for military service, even though males are required to register with selective services, and that the accelerated pathways to citizenship that are available via enlistment are not open to them (National Immigration Law Center 2004).

To be considered eligible for military service, Department of Defense (DoD) standards must be met for "age, citizenship, education, aptitude, physical fitness, dependency status, [and] moral character" (DoD Instruction 1304.26, March 23, 2015). Interested students should know that rights and protections under Section 504 of the Rehabilitation Act are not available to military personnel, beginning with entrance requirements (although they are available to civilian employees).

Postsecondary Education Options

Even though most high school students with HI have traditionally been directed toward vocational education more often than four-year colleges (Janiga and Costenbader 2002), and HI disability labels have the effect of disproportionately reducing opportunities based on race, class, and sex (Reid and Knight 2006), students with HI are participating in postsecondary education in increasingly higher percentages (Madaus et al. 2017). Indeed, the percentage of young adults with mild ID enrolled in community college is increasing (Hart et al. 2004). Often these students are "dual enrolled" in secondary and postsecondary education, which means they take some life-skills instruction in the postsecondary setting before completing high school (Hart et al. 2004). Part of the reason for the increase in enrollment is the success of transition planning (Skinner and Lindstrom 2003). The varied postsecondary education options place different demands on students, beginning with admission and extending through accessing services, to the academic and social expectations of the student.

Adult Basic Education. Estimates of the percentage of participants in adult basic education who have disabilities have ranged from 50 to 80 percent (Taymans 2012). Adult basic education tends to be more learner-centered and individually paced than K–12 education (Beder and Medina 2001). Thus, in adult basic education placements, enrollees with disabilities (some adult education agencies avoid the label *student* because older adult participants may take exception to it) can expect to spend a significant portion of their time working alone and progressing at their own pace (Mellard et al. 2005; Smith and Hofer 2003).

The curricular focus in adult basic education programs is almost exclusively on basic skills like reading, writing, and mathematics (Mellard et al. 2005). Adults enrolled in these programs should, therefore, be prepared to work intently on some of the same skills by which they were challenged in their K–12 education (Zoino-Jeannetti 2006). Some programs also offer services in job preparation and academic skills preparation for transitioning into community college.

Participation in adult education can require particular fortitude. Transition preparation for entrance into these programs should also help students to clarify their goals and their understanding of what adult basic education will require, so that they will be better prepared to participate and continue if they feel overwhelmed by the demands.

Two- and Four-Year Colleges. Students with a variety of "learning, cognitive and intellectual disabilities" are increasingly participating in postsecondary education, including college (DaDeppo 2009; Hart et al. 2004; Hurst and Hudson 2009; see also Harbour 2004). In 2011–12, 11 percent of college undergraduates had a disability (US Department of Education, National Center for Education Statistics, 2016).

As we noted, college programs are sometimes linked to high schools, so students may enroll in postsecondary education while still enrolled in (and served and protected by) special education (Hart et al. 2004). When deemed appropriate by an IEP/ITP team, the young adult between the ages of 18 and 21 may receive transition supports in the postsecondary setting while still technically enrolled in secondary education. Enabling students to participate in college settings as part of transition services greatly expands their prospects for successful transition in all of the quality-of-life areas (Hart et al. 2004).

Young adults who enter two-year and four-year college settings will find the demands on them as students quite different from most high school experiences. College students are expected to assume responsibility for keeping up with academic expectations, such as budgeting their time, taking notes, and seeking accommodation resources (Lowery-Corkran 2006). To be successful, college students with LD must be motivated, academically prepared for college, and able to act as self-advocates (Madaus et al. 2017); the same can be assumed for successful students with other HIs. ITP teams need to be sure that students planning to go to college or another postsecondary education option are motivated and prepared for the learning routines expected in college.

Skinner and Lindstrom (2003) identified the following as influential to college success for students with HI:

Knowledge of the nature of their disability,
Awareness of degree of impairment,
Knowledge of compensatory strategies,
Ability to proactively manage a disability (for example, self-advocate),
Available emotional and academic support,
Motivation, and
Willingness to persevere when conditions are adverse.

Disability services coordinators at 74 postsecondary institutions reported in a survey that they were least satisfied with how prepared students with LD were to engage in self-advocacy (Janiga and Costenbader 2002). Madaus et al. (2006) reported that many special education students who transition to postsecondary institutions do not even know their disability label.

Despite the increasing participation of students with HI in postsecondary education, transition preparation for postsecondary options remains limited. Cummings, Maddux, and Casey (2000) reported six problems that persist in transition planning: (1) inadequate transition planning, (2) inconsistencies between secondary and postsecondary curriculum requirements, (3) failure to coordinate activities between schools and postsecondary institutions or community agencies, (4) inadequate transition services, (5) beginning transition planning too late, and (6) transition initiatives that do not begin early in the K–12 years. All these years later, their findings seem equally relevant. In a published research study, Hitchings, Retish, and Horvath (2005) noted that only four of more than 100 IEPs they reviewed included transition planning for postsecondary education. They also reported that almost half of the 10th graders with IEPs who expressed interest in postsecondary education did not express the same desire three years later. Transition planning should serve to support students in maintaining their education goals. In a study of urban students of color with LD, Kenny et al. (2007) found that most students did not adjust their transition aspirations across four years of high school even when critical milestones had not been passed. Cobb and Alwell (2009) found that most students with HI did not participate in any transition planning while in high school.

The following important strategies can help prepare high school students to have successful transitions to college:

- Teach students about their disability and personally effective compensatory strategies and accommodations.
- Teach students to self-advocate.
- Teach students about legal rights and responsibilities, including those that pertain in secondary as well as postsecondary education.

- Help students select postsecondary schools wisely.
- Work with students and parents to develop a timeline for preparation for college.
- Encourage students to self-identify and seek appropriate assistance during their freshman year.
- Teach students how to organize for learning and living.
- Facilitate a support network—family, social, professionals, and educators.
- Assist students in obtaining a comprehensive psychoeducational evaluation in high school.
- Encourage participation in postsecondary preparation programs. (Skinner and Lindstrom 2003)

Documentation Needs. Students with HI should have up-to-date psychoeducational evaluations so that planning for transition needs is accurate. IEP/ITP teams may need to be reminded of this, as they are not required to complete a three-year reevaluation for those graduating with a regular diploma or aging out of special education services. Further, the teams should realize that secondary school evaluations are sometimes limited to documenting academic weaknesses and not cognitive processing needs (for example, memory or auditory recall) (Madaus and Shaw 2006). Postsecondary institutions may not accept outdated information, and information focused on documenting weaknesses will not adequately inform institutions about appropriate accommodations—which is the primary service they would offer, in accordance with the Americans with Disabilities Act and Section 504.

The IDEA (2004) requires that the IEP/ITP team provide a **summary of performance (SOP)** statement for students who do not receive a reevaluation prior to exiting secondary education. The SOP document must include a summary of the student's academic achievement and functional performance, as well as state recommendations on how to support the student in meeting his or her postsecondary goals. The National Transition Assessment Summit (NTAS)—a coalition of professional organizations concerned with effective transition practices—notes that the document should include sufficient documentation to establish a student's eligibility for accommodations in postsecondary settings, as well as useful information for appropriately determining accommodations in those settings. The NTAS further notes that the SOP is most useful when linked to the IEP/ITP process and when the student actively participates in its development. Kochar-Bryant and Izzo (2006) have proposed a template for an SOP form, and Madaus et al. (2006) have recommended the nature of content to include on that template (Box 3.5). For additional suggestions on developing useful SOPs, see Association on Higher Education and Disability (AHEAD) (2008).

In light of the experiences of students with HI in postsecondary education, Mull, Sitlington, and Alper (2001) recommend that while still in high school, students determine which accommodations they will likely need in their postsecondary setting and how to arrange for them. In addition, their teachers need to provide them with practice and experiences in the demands of postsecondary education. Students may also need to become familiar with assistive technologies prior to entering postsecondary settings. The following is a list of resources that students with HI may need in college settings:

- Preferential registration,
- Counseling,
- Accommodations,
- Assistive technology,
- Notification of rights and responsibilities,
- Skills for daily living (including social skills, personal safety) and academics, and
- Organizational skills.

BOX 3.5

Recommended Content for a Summary of Performance (SOP) Report: For Students with HI

PART 1: DEMOGRAPHIC INFORMATION

To establish the student's history as a person with a disability and eligibility for services:

State the student's primary disability.

State the date of initial diagnosis.

List formal and informal assessment methods conducted with the student.

Include all that clearly contribute to identifying the student's disability and functional strengths and needs.

Attach only the most recent formal and informal assessment reports.

PART 2: STUDENT'S POSTSECONDARY GOALS

Restate the student's postsecondary transition goals from the IEP form.

PART 3: SUMMARY OF PERFORMANCE

The Summary of Performance section is divided into three sections; Present Level of Performance and EAMAT information should be provided in each of the three sections.

TIPS ON THE TYPES OF INFORMATION TO INCLUDE:

Present Level of Performance

- *Do not just list scores or reference an "attached report."*
- *Be sure content corresponds to student's postsecondary transition goals (Part 2).*
- *Include strategies and skills the student knows and uses.*
- *List gaps between student's knowledge/skills near secondary school exiting and targeted postsecondary path.*

Essential Accommodations/Modifications and Assistive Technology (EAMAT)

- *List accommodations and modifications currently used by the student in secondary school.*
- *Accommodations recommended on an IEP but not actually used may not need to be included.*
- *State the rationale for why particular accommodations are needed, particularly for standardized testing.*

ACADEMIC CONTENT AREAS

(Reading, mathematics, written language, and learning skills)
Provide specific and objective information.
Provide information based on formal and informal measurement sources.
Use multiple sources of assessment data to fully represent the student.
Provide indicators of the student's strengths and needs.
Use age-level appropriate data.
List recommendations based on what student currently needs/will need in future (consult transition goal).
Provide essential supports for student to access information or help, and share information.
Provide information separately for each academic content area.

continued

> ## COGNITIVE AREAS
> ## (GENERAL ABILITY AND PROBLEM SOLVING, ATTENTION AND EXECUTIVE FUNCTION, AND COMMUNICATION)
>
> *Do not include information for cognitive areas that are not areas of need.*
> *It is imperative to provide a range of information instead of a single score.*
> *State sources of information, include a cautionary statement for subject information.*
>
> ## FUNCTIONAL AREAS
> ## (SOCIAL SKILLS AND BEHAVIOR, INDEPENDENT LIVING, ENVIRONMENTAL ACCESS/MOBILITY, SELF-DETERMINATION AND SELF-ADVOCACY, AND CAREER/VOCATIONAL/ TRANSITION)
>
> *State information based on current functional skills and the context of intended transitions.*
> *Provide data collected near the end of the student's high school experience.*
> *Include both adaptive and problematic behaviors.*
> *You may include anecdotal information.*
> *Provide a summary of student's interests regarding career/vocation/transition.*
> *Include results of functional or career/vocational assessments.*
> *Provide key content of an individualized behavior intervention plan.*
> *Provide results of assistive technology needs and usage assessments.*
>
> Note: Content in italics is adapted from Madaus et al. (2006). Nonitalicized content represents section headers of an SOP form proposed by Kochar-Bryant and Izzo (2006).

Independent Living and Community Participation

Many adolescents have unrealistic expectations for independent living. They may not grasp the costs associated with daily living, how long the money in their pocket will last, or how high a debt they accrue using payment apps. They are also unlikely to be realistic about the responsibilities and expectations that come with living autonomously. Adolescents with HI have been found less successful than their peers in the areas of maintaining a home (for example, managing bills, preparing meals, cleaning, and maintenance), community involvement (socializing, participating in recreational activities, not getting in trouble with the law), and personal and social relationships (having friends, not feeling lonely or awkward) (Scanlon, Patton, and Raskind 2017).

Halpern's quality-of-life model can be useful for thinking about preparing for the many dimensions of independent living. Physical and material well-being, performance of adult roles, and personal fulfillment are all essential to independence. The IDEA expectations for education and transition plans to address functional performance concern independent living needs. Thus, special education and transition curricula should include such skills as counting money and making change, personal healthcare and hygiene, and transportation skills such as navigating public transportation (for example, reading schedules, dealing with missed connections) or driving a car.

Independent living does not necessarily mean that young adults with disabilities will live self-sufficiently outside of their parents' homes; indeed, that standard for independence has been characterized as a white European American value (for example, Tang 1995) and as inconsistent with the economic realities of lower- and middle-class America in the 21st century (for example, see Sarkisian, Gerena, and Gerstel 2007). In some cultures, communal living—remaining in the family home until marriage or caring for elders—is valued over living on one's own. In such instances, independent living refers to having personal responsibilities and contributing to the household.

3. What post-school options should a transition plan address?

A transition plan should be comprehensive, but it does not have to target activities for every aspect of a student's life. The needs identified and the goals and plans to address those needs should focus on the quality-of-life domains that the team anticipates will be problematic for the student. As with academic and functional performance IEP goals, ITP goals should focus on priorities. Accordingly, an ITP may address goals and plans related to further education, employment, self-care, and independent living, as appropriate.

3-7 Transition Planning

According to the IDEA (2004), transition planning should begin no later than the IEP year in which the student turns 16. Ideally, transition planning will begin as early as the elementary school years, when students begin to become aware of options for adulthood and pathways for accomplishing them (Blalock et al. 2003; see also Madaus and Shaw 2006). The planning should be done in a collaborative process with the student (IDEA 2004), taking into account the student's interests and preferences. The IDEA further states that in order to facilitate positive outcomes, transition goals should be based on the student's "strengths."

Because many secondary school students will reach legal adulthood (the "age of majority") while still in school or soon after, the IDEA requires they be notified one year before attaining that age of the rights that will transfer over to them as adults (these include the right to sign or reject the IEP and ITP). Despite the logic of planning for transition and including the student in that process, few parents, or students, actively participate in transition planning (NLTS2 2004).

The IEP team is responsible for anticipating if a student will have transition needs, as well as for developing and implementing the transition plan. Just as an IEP document is developed in a team process, so too is an ITP. In fact, the ITP is required to be a part of the IEP, so that the programming and planning for the two can be coordinated. Also, as is the case with an IEP, progress toward stated transition goals must be monitored, and the plan must be updated at least annually.

The Transition Planning Team

The members of the IEP team (special educator, general educator[s], administrator, parent, student, appropriate others [review Chapter 1]) are also members of the ITP team, because transition planning is done in concert with planning and providing a special education. The IDEA stipulates that the ITP team should invite the participation of representatives of other service agencies when they are relevant to the student's transition needs (for example, counselors, related service providers, representatives of agencies to which the student will transition, such as an employer, a job coach, a residential specialist, a postsecondary institution's accommodations manager).

The CEC has identified a number of knowledge and skill standards for special education transition specialists. Many school districts employ **transition specialists**, who are responsible for coordinating transition efforts and would serve as members of the ITP team. As with other special educator standards identified by the CEC (see inside cover of this textbook), transition specialists are expected to have specific knowledge and skills in all seven standards areas (see CEC 2015, or visit www.cec.sped.org for lists of the standards and corresponding knowledge and skills).

The ITP

The transition plan is typically developed as part of the IEP meeting. Although technically those individuals who serve on the IEP/ITP teams solely for transition purposes are not needed for IEP development, their input into the IEP is appropriate to ensure coordination and integration of the two initiatives. For example, when IEP team members are considering which high school English courses are most appropriate for a student with low literacy skills, they may need the input of a college representative to tell them which courses would be more appropriate if the student will be seeking college admission.

The IEP and ITP documents should be one and the same. Indeed, because transition goals and activities should be enacted in concert with the student's academic education, it makes sense to plan, document, and act on both types of information in a unified process, if for no other reason than so the goals and activities for education and transition will not contradict one another. Proper ITPs include statements of need, profiles of a student's relevant strengths and weaknesses, annual goals, and service delivery plans for addressing those goals—all categories of information that can also be found on an IEP.

3-8 Transition Practices

Mellard and Lancaster (2003) summarized the research on transition and identified the following as best practices in transition preparation:

- Individualized transition planning and plans,
- Parents' involvement in transition planning,
- Interagency collaboration,
- Social skills training,
- Vocational training, and
- Paid work experience during school.

Before students become engaged in activities such as vocational training, work experiences, or selecting electives intended to facilitate a transition, the goals for such activities should be clearly articulated. Remember, those goals should emanate from the student's strengths and interests, and the student should be involved in planning them.

Identifying Transition Goals and Plans

The process for identifying a student's transition goals and plans is essentially no different than that for identifying academic and functional performance goals and plans for an IEP. With the student's and family's interests in mind, as well as the student's strengths and needs, the team collaborates to identify annual goals that are obtainable. Of course, those annual goals must contribute toward realizing an ultimate transition goal. Thus, the team members should not limit themselves simply to planning for where a student will transition to next. They should also consider why the student will go there (for example, does a student entering the military plan to become a career soldier or move on to something else after one term of enlistment? Would Adam be better off in a technical college or entering the world of work?). Transition goal planning should take into account the students' goals and needs in relation to each of the quality-of-life domains.

Self-Determination

Self-determination is the process of taking the lead of one's own life by setting personal goals and making decisions about one's own quality of life. It involves one's ability to set goals, make choices, and self-assess, as well as to act on those abilities by problem solving and self-advocating (Eisenman 2007; Trainor 2005). Certainly others may give input into that process, but self-determined individuals have primary control (Mithaug, Mithaug, Agran, Martin, and Wehmeyer 2003). Self-determined individuals know, for example, what living arrangement they want, what type of occupation and lifestyle they desire, and what pathways are involved in getting there (for example, Kenny et al. 2007). Having positive self-determination skills is essential to setting realistic goals and succeeding (Eisenman 2007).

In light of the importance of self-determination, promoting it has become an important special education practice, endorsed as an integral part of transition preparation (for example, Carter et al. 2006; Skinner and Lindstrom 2003; Trainor 2005; Wehmeyer 2007), and it has been required since the 1999 IDEA regulations.

At any life stage, knowing what you want to accomplish in each of the quality-of-life domains and having the disposition needed to be successful can be a challenge. This assessment poses a particular challenge to the many high school students who do not know what career they want to embark upon to start their adult lives. Even when they do know, or think they do, they still need to understand their own strengths and needs in relation to attaining that goal, in addition to having realistic self-dispositions for success.

The many young adults with HI who have diminished qualities of life upon exiting high school (Scanlon et al. 2017) would likely benefit from improved skills of self-determination. For example, often students with HI who drop out understand the negative consequences associated with dropping out but do so anyway (Kortering, Braziel, and Tompkins 2002). They would benefit from self-determination interventions that instill in them the foresight and wherewithal to commit to remaining in school, which might include choosing electives to investigate potential interests or to pursue a vocational school option, for example. "Teaching self-determination skills can be an effective prevention activity aimed at reducing students' involvement in risky behaviors and tipping the scales toward their persistence in school" (Eisenman 2007).

Factors that improve the effectiveness of self-determination programs for students with HI include (1) using curricula for teaching self-determination, (2) teaching and coaching students to participate in their education planning (for example, the IEP/ITP process), and (3) student practice in choice and decision making outside of instructional contexts (Karvonen et al. 2004).

Various validated curricula, such as the *Self-Determined Learning Model of Instruction* (Wehmeyer et al. 2000), *Take Action* (Martin, Marshall, Maxon, and Jerman 1999), and the *Steps to Self-Determination Curriculum, Second Edition* (Hoffman and Field 2005) stress stages of planning and action that begin with a student's self-assessment of interests and abilities in order to set proximal and distal goals, followed by action steps to progress toward goal accomplishment, including assessment, reflection, and adjustments to both the goals and plans to accomplish them. Thus, they commonly include three components: setting goals, setting and acting on plans, and modifying goals and plans.

Wehmeyer (2007) has identified the following 10 guidelines for promoting students' self-determination skills, which are consistent with the three components:

- Model problem solving for your students.
- Tell students you believe they are capable of making things happen in their lives.
- Emphasize students' strengths and uniqueness.

- Create a learning community that promotes risk taking.
- Promote choice making.
- Empower students to make decisions and set goals.
- Teach self-determination skills.
- Encourage self-directed learning.
- Involve peers without disabilities to provide social and academic support.
- Use technology to support self-direction.

These guidelines identify steps that special and general educators can take to promote self-determination within the general education classroom and curriculum. As Wehmeyer notes, self-determination skills can be taught in isolation, yet students' ability to apply them should be enhanced by experiencing them within the curriculum.

Most states' curriculum standards include problem-solving skills (Wehmeyer 2007). In addition, content-area teachers have identified problem solving as an essential skill for comprehending content and for participating in classroom learning routines (Bulgren et al. 2006). Still, many students are not taught procedures to follow for effective problem solving. Generic steps of problem solving include "(1) identifying and defining the problem, (2) listing possible solutions, (3) identifying the impact of each solution, (4) making a judgment about a preferred solution, and (5) evaluating the efficacy of the judgment" (Wehmeyer 2007). Skills such as problem solving are learned in part by the steps of the process being explicitly taught, and in part by teacher and peer modeling, but they are also learned through application (review Chapter 2 for more on these instructional techniques). Classroom learning communities are one effective venue for promoting problem-solving skills. When a classroom or a cooperative group becomes a learning community, students work together in a respectful way, guiding and relying on one another. In a learning community, students are able to take risks, explore decision options, apply their strengths, and receive support and encouragement from others. Self-determined learners are, by definition, learners who are responsible for planning, executing, and evaluating their own decisions, but that does not mean they need to perform those skills in isolation.

Effective promotion of self-determination includes adults (for example, teachers and parents) ceding control and responsibility to students for goal setting and success (Skinner and Lindstrom 2003). Adults need to guide students in possessing and using the skills necessary for success, as well as in recognizing their own proactive abilities. In addition to gaining a stronger sense of self, students who develop self-determination skills will actually commit positive actions such as self-advocacy, which will have a direct, positive impact on their transition success.

The **self-determined learning model of instruction** (SDLMI) (Wehmeyer et al. 2000) is a curriculum used to teach students with HI to effect positive "self-determined" outcomes, in part by setting and meeting goals to change inopportune experiences. The model was designed in recognition that students may be able to set goals and work toward them but that environmental factors (for example, others' attitudes, policies, limited opportunities) may prevent their full attainment of desired outcomes (see Kenny et al. 2007; Wehmeyer et al. 2000).

The SDLMI curriculum involves a three-phase problem-solving sequence. At each phase, students are guided in identifying and solving problems. In the first phase, the students determine what their goal is (Box 3.6). This leads to the second phase, developing a plan to accomplish the goal. Based on the plan developed, which includes recognizing potential barriers and planning to act on the plan, the students take stock of what they learned in attempting to accomplish the goal and make appropriate adjustments to the plan; all of this occurs in phase three. Thus, students must set goals, set

BOX 3.6

The Three-Phase Problem-Solving Sequence of the SDLMI Curriculum

INSTRUCTIONAL PHASE I FOR SELF-DETERMINED LEARNING MODEL INSTRUCTION

Set a Goal
Problem for Student to Solve: What Is My Goal?

Student Question 1: What do I want to learn?

Teacher Objectives

- Enable students to identify specific strengths and instructional needs.
- Enable students to communicate preferences, interests, beliefs, and values.
- Teach students to prioritize needs.

Student Question 2: What do I know about it now?

Teacher Objectives

- Enable students to identify their current status in relation to the instructional need.
- Assist students to gather information about opportunities and barriers in their environments.

Student Question 3: What must change for me to learn what I don't know?

Teacher Objectives

- Enable students to decide if action will be focused toward capacity building, modifying the environment, or both.
- Support students to choose a need to address from prioritized list.

Student Question 4: What can I do to make this happen?

Teacher Objectives

- Teach students to state a goal and identify criteria for achieving goal.

Note: Educational supports include (a) student self-assessment of interests, abilities, and instructional needs; (b) awareness training; (c) choice-making instruction; (d) problem-solving instruction; (e) decision-making instruction; and (f) goal-setting instruction.

INSTRUCTIONAL PHASE 2 FOR SELF-DETERMINED LEARNING MODEL OF INSTRUCTION

Take Action
Problem for Student to Solve: What Is My Plan?

Student Question 5: What can I do to learn what I don't know?

Teacher Objectives

- Enable student to self-evaluate current status and self-identified goal status.

Student Question 6: What could keep me from taking action?

Teacher Objectives

- Enable student to determine plan of action to bridge gap between self-evaluated current status and self-identified goal status.

Student Question 7: What can I do to remove these barriers?

Teacher Objectives

- Collaborate with students to identify most appropriate instructional strategies.
- Teach student needed student-directed learning strategies.
- Support student to implement student-directed learning strategies.
- Provide mutually agreed upon teacher-directed instruction.

continued

Student Question 8: When will I take action?

Teacher Objectives

- Enable student to determine schedule for action plan.
- Enable student to implement action plan.
- Enable student to self-monitor progress.

Note: Educational supports include (a) self-scheduling; (b) self-instruction; (c) antecedent cue regulation; (d) choice-making instruction; (e) goal-attainment strategies; (f) problem-solving instruction; (g) decision-making instruction; (h) self-advocacy instruction; (i) assertiveness training; (j) communication skills training; and (k) self-monitoring.

INSTRUCTIONAL PHASE 3 FOR SELF-DETERMINED LEARNING MODEL OF INSTRUCTION

Adjust Goal or Plan
Problem for Student to Solve: What Have I Learned?

Student Question 9: What actions have I taken?

Teacher Objectives

- Enable student to self-evaluate progress toward goal achievement.

Student Question 10: What barriers have been removed?

Teacher Objectives

- Collaborate with student to compare progress with desired outcomes.

Student Question 11: What has changed about what I don't know?

Teacher Objectives

- Support student to reevaluate goal if progress is insufficient.
- Assist student to decide if goal remains the same or changes.
- Collaborate with student to identify if action plan is adequate or inadequate given revised or retained goal.
- Assist student to change action plan if necessary.

Student Question 12: Do I know what I want to know?

Teacher Objectives

- Enable students to decide if progress is adequate, inadequate, or if goal has been achieved.

Note: Educational supports include (a) self-evaluation strategies; (b) choice-making instruction; (c) problem-solving instruction; (d) decision-making instruction; (e) goal-setting instruction; (f) self-reinforcement strategies; (g) self-monitoring strategies; and (h) self-recording strategies.

and follow plans related to those goals, and adjust actions based on evaluation of progress within each of the three phases of the curriculum.

In each phase there are questions the students answer to guide the process. Although these questions are written in the first person, the teacher guides the students through the process (e.g., "Ask yourself . . ."). The teacher introduces the students to each of the questions and may paraphrase them in some instances. The teacher objectives (see Box 3.6) guide the teacher in helping the students to understand and respond to each of the student questions. Across all phases, the teacher guides the students, gradually ceding control of the process to the students (that is, scaffolding) (Wehmeyer 2000).

Self-Advocacy

Self-advocacy builds from self-determination. Students use **self-advocacy** to express and work toward their own goals. In doing so they are negotiating for their own interests, needs, and rights (Milsom and Hartley 2005; Skinner and Lindstrom 2003). Self-advocacy activities may be as simple as selecting classes, arranging one's own accommodations, or naming a career path.

It takes a lot to be self-determined and then to self-advocate for oneself. Students who are able to self-advocate have self-awareness, self-acceptance, awareness of their rights and resources, assertiveness, and problem-solving skills (Eisenman 2007). They "become self-advocates when they (a) demonstrate an understanding of their disability; (b) are aware of their legal rights; and (c) can competently and tactfully communicate their rights and needs to those in positions of authority" (Skinner 1998, as cited in Skinner and Lindstrom 2003).

Furthermore, they must be aware of effective accommodations and strategies (Skinner and Lindstrom 2003; see also Milsom and Hartley 2005). And, to be effective self-advocates, they must know how to actually secure the services to which they are entitled (Milsom and Hartley 2005). Like any other skill, students with HI must be taught why and how to self-advocate. Unfortunately, many postsecondary students with HI are not aware of their own disabilities and needs (Madaus and Shaw 2006). Also, persons with LD have been found reluctant to self-disclose their learning disability status and needs in the workplace for multiple reasons, but principally due to a lack of knowledge about their own disabilities (Price, Gerber, and Shessel 2002). The self-esteem and social skill difficulties can also challenge persons with disabilities attempting to self-advocate (Skinner and Lindstrom 2003).

Because employment is a central aspect of adult living, many transition and self-determination curricula address it. However, career development curricula are often developed based on the aspirations of middle-class European Americans (for example, independent living, career-oriented) (Rojewski 2002). For that reason, career guidance often prioritizes career advancement over family and community, and focuses narrowly on attaining a high income. Guidance that reifies middle-class values may clash with the quality-of-life aspirations of students from cultures other than middle-class European American. Effective transition and self-determination/self-advocacy curricula must be responsive to cultural differences. African American and Hispanic American male students, for example, are more likely to solve problems and discuss imminent academic concerns (for example, attendance) when talking about transition at home (Trainor 2005). Therefore, effective planning for traditional African American and Latino students in particular should directly involve the family and build from the skills the students would actually use.

Schreiner (2007) suggests that self-advocacy goals be written into IEP/ITPs; she recommends, for example, that the annual goals include that "the student will describe the nature of his/her special education program services . . . the student will access appropriate helpers and resources to address challenges presented by the disability" (pp. 302–303). Writing self-advocacy goals into the IEP/ITP is a way to ensure that they are addressed, she suggests.

Van Reusen et al. (2007) have validated a strategy for students to identify their own goals and advocate for them. This Self-Advocacy Strategy can be used to guide participation in IEP/ITP planning as well as in transition settings such as the workplace, living environment, or postsecondary institutions. The mnemonic I PLAN (Van Reusen et al. 2007) reminds students of the steps of the process:

Inventory strengths, weaknesses, goals, and learning choices.
Provide your inventory information.
Listen and respond.
Ask questions.
Name your goals.

The *inventory* step takes place prior to an IEP/ITP meeting or other situation that calls for students to self-advocate. In that step, the students identify their goals, needs, and desires that are appropriate to communicate in the upcoming meeting. For the sake of an IEP/ITP meeting, the areas addressed should span the three quality-of-life domains (Halpern 1993). In a meeting related to securing college or workplace accommodations, students should be prepared to focus on just the priority goals and needs for success in those contexts. To inventory goals, needs, and desires, students should consider their (a) strengths, (b) areas to improve or learn, and (c) goals, options, and preferences for (d) learning and (e) accommodations.

Once students have created an inventory, the content needs to be communicated effectively. Following the I PLAN steps, students share their goals (the *provide* step), and so on, with others. Van Reusen et al. note that each step of the I PLAN strategy calls for specific skills that must be learned and practiced with an educator familiar with both the I PLAN strategy and the planning/transition situation in which the student will make use of the strategy. Students who learn and use the self-advocacy strategy participate more in their IEP/ITP meetings, have more to contribute, and report more satisfaction with the education and transition plans that result.

Methods and Strategies Spotlight

Using Ear Buds to Guide Students' Self-Advocacy in the Transition Planning Process

Preparing students to participate in transition planning meetings is essential but still does not guarantee they will participate successfully when the time comes. Discussing the meeting in advance and preparing for specific scenarios are helpful preparation activities that are commonly used (for example, Test and Neale 2004; Van Reusen et al. 2002). Goodman and Duffy (2007) have studied an effective approach to coaching a student *during* the transition meeting.

Using bug-in-ear (BIE) technology (Goodman and Duffy 2007), a student can receive telecommunicated prompts from a coach observing the actual transition meeting. The student wears an earbud and the coach speaks into a transmitter. Because the student is using a personal listening device and the coach communicates via microphone (possibly a cellphone) outside of the meeting group, their interactions are not observed by other members of the team. The coach's role is to prompt the student, not to provide the student with specific content. Thus, if a student has difficulty naming goals, the coach might offer the prompt, "read the rest of your goals" or "tell them about the job exploration you want to do this summer."

Using BIE technology does not replace preparation activities. Students should still identify their strengths, needs, and goals in advance of the meeting, as well as discuss the format of the meeting and even rehearse (Test and Neale 2004; Van Reusen et al. 2002). Advance preparation reduces student anxiety during the meeting. When that preparation includes practice using BIE procedures, student anxiety during the actual meeting is further reduced, as the student feels supported and knows how to make use of the coach's prompts during the meeting (Goodman and Duffy 2007).

CHAPTER SUMMARY

Collaboration between parents and schools is required to meet the needs of students with HI in schools and to prepare for positive transitions. When they work together, special educators and families can provide a student with HI with an appropriate education. The IDEA provides for the involvement of parents in their child's special education. Families can provide valuable information to educators about their child's development and learning experiences at home. Families can also partner with educators to help students extend learning to home, including supporting them in succeeding at homework.

True family involvement is a complex process. Ideally, schools and parents will enter into a collaborative partnership where they truly value one another's skill and expertise. By partnering at every stage of the special education process, students are more likely to receive a successful education that is relevant to their life in school and beyond.

Transition initiatives were developed in response to the limited successes that students with disabilities have had beyond their school years. Although, overall, the quality of school outcomes has improved for students with HI since the beginning of the transition initiative in the mid-1980s, the results for many are unsatisfactory. In education and employment sectors, those with HI are underrepresented and less accomplished when they do participate. In their personal lives as young adults and adults, many report limited independence and personal satisfaction.

Transition planning and services need to address areas such as health, having and meeting personal goals, and being satisfied with one's own circumstances, or the overall quality of one's life. The concept of transition now considers both the paths to successful employment and other dimensions of living. Consistent with this expanded view, transition teams must be aware of the contexts into which a student might transition. That awareness includes anticipating the knowledge and skills the student will need to select that destination and to thrive in that context. One of the most challenging transition preparation activities is identifying appropriate goals with students.

Setting goals and plans for transition, as well as acting on those plans, requires collaboration among the student, the school, and parents. IEP teams are responsible for determining if students will need help with transitions. Beginning with an awareness of the demands of various post-school options and of the students' interests, the IEP/ITP team needs to work with the student to plan experiences that will result in the student making a successful transition. The entire process should be "results-oriented" (IDEA 2004).

Transition success is not limited to a student simply making it into whatever institution or circumstances come next; rather, it includes the student thriving there. Students are enabled when they have the self-determination skills to think carefully about their own interests and the self-advocacy skills necessary to ensure their disability-related needs will be met.

KEY TERMS

Child Find, 89

Coping, 84

Due Process Complaint, 96

Due Process Hearings, 95

Due Process Provision, 88

Early Intervening, 92

Early Intervention, 89

Eligibility Determination Meeting, 95

Individualized Transition Plan (ITP), 106

Informed Consent, 88

Parent and Student Participation, 88

Pre-referral, 93

Problem Solving, 84

Protective Factors, 94

Quality of Life, 103

Referral, 93

Resolution Session, 95

Risk Indicators, 94

Screening, 94

Service Coordinator, 87

Self-Advocacy, 122

Self-Determined Learning Model of Instruction, 119

Self-Determination, 118

Summary of Performance (SOP), 113

Transition, 101

Transition Planning, 102

Transition Specialists, 116

Well-Being, 103

Written Intervention Plan, 98

APPLICATION ACTIVITIES

Using information from the chapter, complete the following activities that were designed to help you apply knowledge that was presented in this chapter.

1. Select an instructional activity that you know well (or one of the many presented in this text). Develop a "lesson plan" for teaching the procedures to a parent so that she or he may support the student in using it at home (for instance, for homework).

2. Review the CEC standards (see the inside cover of this text) and identify those that relate to parent and family partnerships. For each standard you locate, list at least one skill from this chapter that you are sure you can do to meet that standard.

3. Role-play an IEP meeting with your classmates (or attend an actual meeting if that is possible) and observe how, even in the simulation, the parent(s) and educators interact. Pay particular attention to the power dynamics (see, for example, Kalyanpur, Harry, and Skrtic 2000) and consider ways that parents may have felt valued or intimidated in the process.

4. Locate an IEP form. Determine where on the IEP form to record the content called for in transition planning. (Hint: Think about the information for Adam or a case student from another chapter in this textbook, or think about yourself preparing to exit from high school.) Based on this activity, think critically about whether transition planning can be satisfactorily addressed based on the IEP planning process.

5. Meet with a special education student preparing to transition either to a different educational setting or out of school. Talk with that student about his or her concerns and goals.

6. Think about a transition you will be making in the next one to three years. Follow each of the steps of the SDLMI question asking/answering process to plan your transition goals and activities (remember that the latter steps are done after you have taken some action, so you will not be able to do this activity all at once). If your transition activities include advocating for your needs or rights, follow the I PLAN steps.

Racorn/Shutterstock.com

4 Learning Theories: Understanding What Works

Learning Objectives

After reading this chapter, you will understand:

4-1 Why theories are used in education

4-2 Different theories that are used in education

4-3 Theories that can help teachers understand how students learn and the practical aspects of theories that teachers can use in their classes

CEC **Initial Preparation Standard 1: Learner Development and Individual Learning Differences**

1-0 Beginning special education professionals understand how exceptionalities may interact with development and learning and use this knowledge to provide meaningful and challenging learning experiences for individuals with exceptionalities.

Why do educational theories matter—especially in an era when achievement outcomes seem to be what is most important about education?

The No Child Left Behind (NCLB) Act and the Individuals with Disabilities Education Act (IDEA) both stress the importance of students *achieving* high standards. How students are taught influences how they learn and how well they achieve, and theory guides how you teach. Some educators disdain their theory courses as the least valuable part of their teacher preparation program, and do not consider theory as relevant to their day-to-day practices. Education theories, however, explain why certain effective teaching practices work as they do. Education theories also represent our best explanations as to how students learn. Whether we are conscious of them or not, our theories guide how we teach. Whenever you read about a strategy or technique in this book that you like, your theories of teaching and learning are informing your opinion. Theories also drive the work of researchers and policymakers and, in turn, the techniques that are used in classrooms.

4-1　Why Learn About Theories?

As the very first CEC (Council for Exceptional Children) standard for entry-level special education teachers states, effective educators of students with HI need to know "models, theories, and philosophies that form the basis for special education practice" (forthcoming). Because theories serve to inform teachers and guide their teaching, effective educators need to be familiar with major theories and how they influence their practices.

What Is a Theory?

A **theory** is a framework that is used to describe an event or set of events; it makes generalizations about observations and consists of an interrelated, coherent set of ideas and models. Nicolaus Copernicus developed a theory that the sun is the center of our universe, Sigmund Freud asserted theories of conscious and unconscious minds, and a number of cognitive psychologists and educators have evolved theories about how people learn. A theory is testable. If one aspect of the theory, a *hypothesis*, is confirmed through research or testing, the theory is strengthened. If a hypothesis is rejected, the theory is weakened and may need revising. Hypotheses are tested and confirmed through research. Continual hypothesis generation and testing helps theorists to revise, modify, or eventually reject a theory.

In his book *A Brief History of Time* (1988), Stephen Hawking wrote that "a theory is a good theory if it satisfies two requirements: It must accurately describe a large class of observations on the basis of a model that contains only a few arbitrary elements, and it must make definite predictions about the results of future observations." He went on to state that "any physical theory is always provisional, in the sense that it is only a hypothesis; you can never prove it. No matter how many times the results of experiments agree with some theory, you can never be sure that the next time the result will not contradict the theory. On the other hand, you can disprove a theory by finding even a single repeatable observation that disagrees with the predictions of the theory" (p. 43). Sound and solid one day, a new theory can rock our world; it can literally change the way that we see things. In the history of educational theory, some theories have forever impacted educational practice, whereas others have influenced us for a short period of time and then were quickly discarded.

What makes for a "useful" theory? A useful theory should summarize or explain observable events, generate hypotheses that can be empirically verified, and create new research (Hergenhahn and Olson 2001). A good theory should help teachers explain how learning occurs and, when used with students, should result in improved learning or teaching (see Case 4.1).

CASE 4.1   The Heart of the Highway

Case Introduction

In this case, you will read about a health sciences teacher, Ned Massori, who used theory to help shape his teaching. He thinks about the learning objectives for his lesson; in that way, he arrives at effective teaching practices to use. As you read the case, you will see how he uses both direct teaching and an analogy to help students learn new content.

At the end of the case, you will find case questions. These questions are meant to serve as points for reflection. Of course, if you can answer them immediately, you should do so, but you may want to wait to answer them until you have read that portion of the chapter that pertains to the particular case question. Throughout the rest of the chapter, you will see the same questions. As you see them, try to answer them based upon the portion of the chapter that you just read.

Ned Massori taught a unit on the functions of the human heart last year, and was very disappointed with the outcome. Last year, his students first drilled on the key vocabulary associated with the heart (for example, *ventricle, artery, muscle*), and students had to write definitions for the terms. Following that drill, he used an oversized plastic heart model to point out the various parts of the heart on which students had been drilled. While the students watched his demonstration, they labeled parts of the heart on a diagram he had passed out. Finally, they viewed a short movie that showed both how cartoon and real hearts operate. The video narrator repeated many of the things Ned had said while he taught students with the plastic heart model.

As he reflected on last year's lesson, Ned recalled that a few students couldn't memorize the key terms and their definitions. A few more knew most of the terms but had mixed up which definitions belonged with which terms. He was most vexed that although the majority of the class correctly learned the heart vocabulary, they had little understanding of what it all meant. Test questions that required students to explain how the heart works or to problem-solve common heart ailments proved to be too challenging for most.

Ned realized that his teaching activities did not match the types of comprehension outcomes he had planned for the unit. He also realized that although he did want his students to memorize key concepts—on the assumption that

memorization is necessary for fully thinking about them—he also wanted them to be able to think *with* those concepts.

After careful reflection on what happened during last year's lesson, as well as on what he wanted students to know, he was ready to begin anew. This time he did not start with drill and practice of key vocabulary; instead, he wanted his students to learn about them in context right from the start. He thought that the terms would be better recalled if students could relate them to the functioning of the heart.

So Ned Massori began this class with, "Today we are going to discuss the human heart, so I thought I would bring along my map of the Beltway around Washington, DC, to help me explain it."

As students at Kennedy High School, in a Virginia town not far outside the Beltway, Ned's students were all too familiar with the highways around Washington, DC. As he drew the Beltway, Ned highlighted the main roads around the DC area. It looked like this:

He began asking the students to think of the cars as red blood cells traveling on the highway, or major arteries. He told them, "I-95 South represents the inferior vena cava. I-270 represents the superior vena cava. Route 97 represents the aorta. Routes 295 and 267 are pulmonary arteries, and Routes 50 and 66 are the pulmonary veins." As he went on, the students filled in the same handout he had used last year.

continued

"What happens when we have plaque buildup in an artery?" he asked them. Yosef raised his hand and said, "There is a blockage."

"Yes, you're correct," replied Mr. Massori, "just like a blockage that is caused by a car accident."

Mr. Massori then explained that an ambulance comes to help when there is an accident, just as humans have white blood cells to help. He made several other analogies between parts of the heart and the highway system. As the class filled out the diagram, he questioned students around the room, checking for accuracy of the diagram and asking about analogous parts.

Following this lesson, he asked students to work on memorizing the concepts by writing definitions in their own words. Ned theorized that they needed to memorize the concepts to master them and that they should do better than last year's students because they learned how the heart relates to a highway system and how the different components of the heart function.

CASE QUESTIONS

1. In his revised lesson, Ned Massori still wanted his students to memorize key concepts about the heart. How could this help them to "think *with*" the concepts?

2. Why would an analogy serve as an effective method for teaching students the names of the heart's parts and their functions?

3. If Ned had instead given his students a list of key concepts and definitions, and then asked them to apply them to a drawing of the DC Beltway without explaining the analogy for them, could the students have figured out the analogy?

Knowledge about how to teach comes from multiple sources. These sources can be personal experiences, advice or testimonials from others, or knowledge from learning theories or research. These sources of *teaching knowledge* are often deeply ingrained in our "belief system." These beliefs support our acceptance of a technique or theory and explain a teacher's continued use of a technique. Likewise, to encourage teachers to use a new technique, personnel preparation trainers must demonstrate to teachers that the new technique is worth replacing their current method. How well the new method matches teachers' personally held theories of teaching and learning influences whether they will adopt the practice (Gersten, Chard, and Baker 2000; Scanlon et al. 2005). Of course, teachers can decide to use new techniques for any number of reasons, but perhaps the best reason is that the new techniques have been shown through research or learning theory to be more effective than prior methods.

Origins of Our Own Teaching Knowledge

One of those sources of how to teach probably comes from how we were taught as children and from our own personal experiences (Good and Brophy 1994). In their first teaching situations, novice teachers often rely on their own knowledge and experiences of how they were taught, though these memories may be distant. For many, this is a reflexive response and does not reflect the best methods for teaching students or managing their behavior.

A second source of teaching knowledge is advice or testimonials from others. Novice educators are recipients of many bits of wisdom passed down from veteran teachers. The teachers' lounge serves as the perfect environment for stories and lessons learned from others. Some of this knowledge may be effective, but new teachers should be wary of any suggested teaching method unless it is backed up by research, rather than just hearsay. Although experienced teachers do have practical wisdom, many practices employed in classrooms have little research backing (ibid.). Similarly, testimonials from producers of educational materials should be viewed with caution. Some of these new techniques or materials may be accompanied by testimonials from other teachers or administrators who used them and vouch for their effectiveness. You should remember that manufacturers of educational materials are in the business of sales and, although a new technique may follow common logic, it may not be effective unless it is accompanied by research.

Learning theories or research are the third source of teaching knowledge. This is the best source when looking for effective teaching techniques. Research-based techniques typically have been well scrutinized and have gone through extensive reviews by professionals in the field (see, for example, the What Work's Clearinghouse; http://ies.ed.gov/ncee/wwc). Typically, such teaching methods have research studies to back up their use, and the procedures for using them are explicitly described so that teachers can use them correctly in the classroom. Moreover, teaching techniques drawn from sound theories provide a basis for developing a wide variety of other new techniques. In addition, teachers who use techniques that are drawn from theory and research can understand how they work, and these methods can represent the best hope of remediating skills or behaviors in their students.

4-2 Theories of Learning Influential to Special Education Practices

The number of teaching theories that have been generated may never be calculated with any accuracy. Some theories are better known than others, some have been quickly rejected following hypothesis testing, while still others are slight variations of earlier theories. In this section, we describe several theories and models of learning. Over the years, some of these theories have been more useful than others; at any one time, however, each theory was used to explain how individuals learn and grow. Furthermore, each of these theories has been particularly influential to twentieth- and twenty-first-century special education practices in North America. Although some theories have been discredited or are no longer widely used, other new theories have spun off from the original. Read each carefully and try to understand how each explains the process of learning.

Although the theories featured here are only a small sample of the many theories that have influenced special education, they represent three major domains of education theories: behavioral, cognitive, and constructivist. Historically, each of the three domains influenced an era of educational practice, in the order we name them; each, undoubtedly, influenced the theories that followed.

Behavioral Theory

A very influential theory that has guided much of education practice in the past 50 years is **behavioral theory**. Behavioral theory looks at the effects of different external stimuli to help us understand why we behave the way we do. Its application to teaching is often referred to informally as *behaviorism*. There are multiple facets to behavioral theory, some focusing on reinforcing behaviors, others on extinguishing behaviors. The various facets may be employed in teaching individually or in combinations.

From a behaviorist viewpoint, all behavior is learned and has been learned through the use of reinforcement, punishment, or extinction. Singing, talking, walking, and determining one's political perspectives are all learned behaviors developed to produce positive effects in our environments. Toddlers who take a few steps find walking fun and expedient; they also receive praise for it, so the behavior is reinforced and continues. Based on experiences people have had, they form political views that earn them labels such as "liberal" or "conservative," and that process explains why they support certain candidates. Educators can capitalize on the effects of reinforcers, punishers, and extinction to shape students' learning and behaviors.

Behavior modification is a technique based on the work of renowned psychologist B. F. Skinner. Using behavior modification, teachers extinguish an undesirable behavior and replace it with a desirable behavior. Based upon Skinner's principle of **operant conditioning**, any response that is followed by a reinforcing stimulus tends to be repeated, and any response that is followed by punishment or by being ignored tends not to be repeated (Hergenhahn and Olsen 2001). In other words, individuals learn a behavior to *operate* in their environments (make a certain response to their environment) to acquire or avoid a consequence—hence the term *operant*. Skinner believed that to understand behavior, we should look only at overt responses to find out why the behavior is occurring, has decreased, or has stopped. It is not that Skinner did not believe in cognition and thinking as mediating factors to explain why people behave as they do, but he believed that the best way to understand behavior was to examine it in terms of overt responses and consequences (Hohn 1994). The following explanations of components of operant conditioning include examples of behavioral principles in action.

Reinforcement. According to Skinner, a consequence is a reinforcer when it serves to increase the probability that the response will recur. A **reinforcer** is anything that increases the rate with which an operant response occurs. Praising a student for good work (for example, solving a math problem, conjugating a verb, behaving appropriately) is very likely to be reinforcing to the student; in turn, the student will repeat the behavior to receive more praise. However, what is reinforcing to one person may not be reinforcing to another person. Also, what was reinforcing at one point in time in a person's life may not be reinforcing at another time. It is important to remember that a reinforcer works only when it increases the probability that the response will recur. One other important fact about reinforcement is that if you want the response to occur again, you must provide the reinforcer only when the response occurs—this is known as **contingent reinforcement**.

Reinforcers can be either negative or positive. A **positive reinforcer** increases behavior when presented immediately following the response. A **negative reinforcer** increases behavior when removed. Therefore, a negative reinforcer is not punishment; it is instead removal of something (relief) that the student does not appreciate (for example, erasing the student's name from a list of students at risk for being kept after school, or decreasing the number of homework problems for students who achieve a high percentage of correct performances during in-class practice).

THINK BACK TO THE CASE   **about Ned's lesson about the heart . . .**

In his revised lesson, Ned Massori still wanted his students to memorize key concepts about the heart. How could this help them to "think __with__" the concepts?

We most often think about behaviorism as applied to "behaviors" such as sitting appropriately in class and speaking politely, but the same principles apply to learning content. From a behavioral theorist's perspective, students need to be reinforced for thinking about concepts, including their definitions, accurately. They can also be reinforced for applying them, or thinking *with* them.

Types of Reinforcers. A **primary reinforcer** is something that is needed for survival, like food, water, or sex, and increases a response rate (Skinner theorized that breathing, seeking food and drink, and sex drive are the only innate human behaviors). Primary reinforcers work because they are not taught or learned: everyone needs them for survival. When a neutral stimulus is paired with a primary reinforcer, the neutral stimulus begins to take on the reinforcing value of the primary reinforcer. The neutral stimulus (now reinforcing) is known as a **secondary reinforcer** or **conditioned reinforcer**. Points or tokens that can be traded for a primary reinforcer are secondary reinforcers. Praise and attention can also serve as secondary reinforcers when paired with a primary reinforcer. When a secondary reinforcer has been paired with more than one primary reinforcer, it becomes a **generalized reinforcer**. Money is the best example of a generalized reinforcer because it can be used for many different types of primary reinforcers. Even when the primary reinforcer is gone, generalized reinforcers usually remain strong reinforcers. For example, students may respond to money even though they cannot use it. Students may respond well to praise even though the primary reinforcement is no longer present. Teachers can use a variety of secondary reinforcers or make new ones such as praise, pats on the back, or smiles, if paired with primary or even generalized reinforcers such as money.

Punishment. Whereas reinforcement increases behavior, punishment decreases the probability that a behavior (response) will occur temporarily. According to Hohn (1994), punishment can occur in one of two ways: it can present an aversive reinforcer (for example, spanking, yelling, incarceration) or remove a positive reinforcer (for example, removing tokens, points, or recess time). In order to be considered punishment, punishment has to *decrease* the student's behavior when applied. If the punishment is applied (for example, a spanking) and the child continues the inappropriate or dangerous behavior, either the punishment is not punishment (that is, it is a neutral stimulus) or another reinforcer may be present that is maintaining or increasing the behavior. An example would be if a parent were to slap his child on the back after the child burped, yet other people in the room laughed at the child. If the child continues "burping" behavior, it could be that the behavior is actually being reinforced (that is, laughing), rather than decreased (that is, slapping). Remember that unlike punishment, negative reinforcement *increases* the response, whereas punishment *decreases* the response. Another distinction is that with negative reinforcement the teacher removes the stimulus (for example, nagging) once the behavior increases. Punishment occurs when the teacher applies an aversive stimulus to decrease behavior. Keep in mind that punishment reduces the behavior only temporarily. Even Skinner claimed that punishment suppresses the response only while it is being applied, and that it is likely to reappear after withdrawing the punishment (Hergenhahn and Olson 2001).

Punishment may also have deleterious side effects:

1. Punishment may lead to avoidance behaviors. Students who are constantly punished for inappropriate behavior may avoid coming to class or may try to escape from the situation or setting when it comes time to receive the punishment.
2. Punishment may lead to retaliation or negative feelings toward the punisher. Teachers who give punishment may be the target of retaliation or, at the very least, may be viewed negatively by students. Students who are punished by being given extra English assignments may then develop negative feelings toward English.
3. Punishment teaches a student *what not to do* rather than teaching what to do. In some cases, students may become confused and frustrated because they do not know what to do to receive positive reinforcement or feedback.

4. Punishment may generate negative emotions. Emotionally, students may develop feelings of fear, sadness, or depression, or may learn that inflicting pain on others is acceptable (ibid.).
5. Punishment may not generalize across settings. Although punishment may work for a teacher during math, it may not work during other subjects or in other settings.

Again, just think of punishment as suppressing the behavior. Under what conditions should punishment be used? Probably never. Punishment is really not a viable solution to addressing inappropriate student behavior. In certain situations, you may feel a need to punish a student because alternative behaviors for reinforcement are not apparent, the student has clearly broken a policy, or you are afraid of the precedent that may be established by not publicly punishing the student. Punishment is potentially legitimate in such circumstances, but the effects will be short term at best. The better solution is to arrange the situation so that you are able to reinforce the student for behaving appropriately in ways that prevent the student's inclination to act inappropriately. Some students seek punishment because punishment is better than receiving no attention at all.

In the following sections, we discuss the use of differential reinforcement of incompatible (DRI) behavior or differential reinforcement of alternative (DRA) behavior as useful alternatives to punishment.

Time-Out. Time-out is another procedure that attempts to decrease the probability or the occurrence of a behavior (response) temporarily. **Time-outs** are the withholding of reinforcement for all behaviors. Typically, they are used with younger students. In some cases, the child may be moved to a quiet area of the classroom; in other cases, the child may be removed from the classroom. When using time-outs, teachers should avoid nagging or scolding children, speaking to them in an angry voice, or looking at them while in time-out.

Just as there are problems associated with punishment, there are also problems with time-outs:

1. Removal from the classroom may constitute a change in placement for the child and may require administrative approval. In some cases, if time-outs are overused, they become seclusion. Teachers should always check with their supervisors before using time-outs.
2. If the classroom is not a positive reinforcing environment, removing the child may serve no purpose. Hence, the teacher can expect the inappropriate response to continue in the time-out setting. Also, the child has no incentive to come back to a classroom that is not a positive reinforcing environment. Teachers have to be certain that leaving the classroom is not a reinforcing experience in itself. If a child is placed in the principal's office and the principal or other office staff inadvertently provide reinforcement while the child is in the office, the child may want to leave the classroom on a more frequent basis to go to the office. The same might be true of using the hallway as a time-out setting.
3. Similar to punishment, time-outs may only teach the child *what not to do* rather than what to do.

Extinction. **Extinction** means to eliminate a behavior by withholding reinforcement. Whereas time-outs involve removing the student from a reinforcing environment, extinction involves withholding reinforcement for an inappropriate response. With extinction, it helps to identify the reinforcement that is associated with the student's response. For example, when students call out answers to questions rather than raising their hands, the teacher probably inadvertently reinforced calling out the answer by giving attention to those students (or even using positive reinforcement in the form of responding to their answers). In this case, to use extinction, teachers must make it clear that they will not accept any answers that are called out; instead, they will only accept answers from students who raise their hand.

Alternatives to Punishment and Time-Out. **Differential reinforcement of incompatible (DRI)** behavior and **differential reinforcement of alternative (DRA)** behavior serve as good alternatives to punishment. With these techniques, teachers reinforce appropriate behaviors. With DRI, the teacher identifies the inappropriate behavior and an incompatible or mutually exclusive behavior as a replacement behavior. For example, if the inappropriate behavior is getting out of the seat, an incompatible target behavior would be sitting in the seat. Similarly, DRA looks for alternative behaviors—these are *not* mutually exclusive, and it might be possible for both incompatible and target behaviors to occur at the same time, like raising a hand and calling out an answer. However, teachers should identify target behaviors that are unlikely to occur simultaneously, such as teasing and complimenting. All students have appropriate behaviors in their repertoire—it is simply a matter of finding them and reinforcing them. Again, be sure that you have reinforcers at your disposal that are reinforcing for the student. Just because you view an item or event as reinforcing does not necessarily mean that your student will find it reinforcing.

DRI or DRA involves the following steps:

1. Identify the inappropriate behavior and then identify an incompatible (target) behavior (for DRI) or an alternative (target) behavior (for DRA) with which to replace it. In other words, an incompatible behavior is one that cannot occur simultaneously with the inappropriate behavior or a mutually exclusive behavior.
2. Try to use a target behavior that students already have in their repertoire.
3. If possible, choose a behavior that can be maintained by environmental reinforcers (for example, smiles or conversations).
4. As soon as you observe the target behavior, reinforce it. Use extinction with the inappropriate behavior.

Methods and Strategies Spotlight

Targeting Behaviors for Change

Not all rule-breaking behaviors that students exhibit need to be changed. For example, wearing a hat, tapping a pencil or pen on the desk, chewing gum or eating candy, expressing anger, fidgeting in the seat, or speaking without permission are some behaviors that may violate school rules; however, not *all* teachers would agree that they need to be obeyed. In the case of students such as those with EBD, teachers may view getting through the school day as enough of a challenge that they will relax certain rules.

So just how do you know if a behavior needs to be targeted for change? Kaplan (1995) devised a set of guidelines to help teachers determine if a questionable behavior needs to be changed.

Classroom Rules. Teachers love rules—some teachers more than others, particularly those who either have too many rules for students to follow or have rules that shouldn't be rules at all.

Are students allowed to chew gum? Are students allowed to swear in the classroom? (If so, which words constitute a "swear" word?) Are students allowed to disagree with a teacher? These are just some of the rules that might be called into question. In other words, choose your rules carefully, and be prepared to defend them.

Control Issues. Some teachers enjoy total control in their classroom. We have been in classes in which students were not permitted to talk or even whisper to other students. For some teachers, controlling the behavior of others can be an obsession. Many of these teachers use too many rules (both written and unwritten) to control the behavior of others. Although control is an important aspect of classroom management, overly controlled classrooms can be stressful learning environments for both the students and the teacher. When you develop a rule, consider whether it benefits the students.

The So-What Test. Kaplan defines the "so-what" test as a measure to determine whether a student's inappropriate behavior interferes with his or her physical, emotional, social, or academic well-being. If it does interfere, it might be a behavior to target for change. When applied to each individual, a behavior may be acceptable for one student but unacceptable for another student. For example, if a student taps a pencil on her desk so loudly that it disrupts other students, the other students may get angry and pick on her. This behavior might be appropriate for changing. Conversely, if a student has a nervous habit of tapping his pencil on his desk, others are not bothered by it, and the student is academically performing well in the class, then it is probably not a behavior that needs to be targeted for change.

Sociocultural Considerations. For all students, it is important to consider the individual's culture when deciding whether to change behavior. Some behaviors may be bound by the student's particular culture. For example, in certain Asian cultures, when a youth has used inappropriate behavior and is being reprimanded, it is customary for him or her to turn away from the person doing the reprimanding because he or she feels ashamed. Therefore, it may not be appropriate to have the child look at you (that is, maintain eye contact) while being reprimanded for an inappropriate behavior. Time is a concept that differs from culture to culture for students. Certain children may have difficulty coming to class at a specific time each day, and it may take a while for them to adjust to the new culture's sense of timeliness. Reprimanding is not an appropriate response in such a case.

Cognitive Behavior Modification

Cognitive psychologists and education theorists valued many of the principles of behaviorism offered by Skinner and others but rejected the notion that we should restrict ourselves to addressing observable behaviors. They believed that we are capable of theorizing cognitive activities, and that understanding how the mind works is essential to addressing fully the thinking and learning process. They proposed and tested a second behavioral theory, cognitive behavior modification.

Cognitive behavior modification (CBM) refers to using cognitive skills to help control one's behavior. Cognitive behavior modification grew from the belief that people do in fact use cognitive skills and that psychologists and others can modify or change behavior by having individuals think about their behavior. CBM represents a merging of the cognitive field with the behavior field. CBM incorporates self-talk or self-monitoring for students to monitor their own behavior. The two main types of CBM are self-instructions and self-monitoring.

Donald Meichenbaum (1977) developed one of the earliest studies that used self-instruction training to teach coping strategies to children with attention-deficit/hyperactivity disorder. Self-instruction includes several steps for students to verbalize statements of self-coping, self-evaluation, and self-reinforcement. These steps are meant to help students think through and solve problems. Meichenbaum taught children with hyperactivity the following skills:

1. Define the problem ("What is it that I have to do?").
2. Focus attention and response guidance ("Carefully . . . draw a line").
3. Use self-reinforcement ("Good, I'm doing fine").
4. Use self-evaluative and coping skills ("That's OK. Even if I make a mistake, I can keep going").

After students were trained in these skills, they used them with various fine motor and problem-solving tasks. Meichenbaum (1977) reported that this training was successful at helping children with hyperactivity and children with impulsivity to improve their performance on complex and time-consuming cognitive tasks.

This early research has helped establish countless studies involving the use self-instruction and is still used today for students with HI (Ennis and Jolivette 2014; Smith, Ayers, Alexander, Ledford, and Shepley 2016)

Teachers should use the five-step sequence for training students to use self-instructions (Rivera-Flores 2015). The crucial first step (now called think-alouds) is frequently used in strategy programs and helps students in understanding the teacher's internal thoughts while they are performing the task. The following are the five steps of the Meichenbaum and Goodman model:

1. Cognitive Modeling—An adult model performs a task while thinking aloud.
2. Overt External Guidance—The student performs the same task while the model verbalizes the steps and provides guidance.
3. Overt Self-Guidance—The student performs the task while saying the steps aloud.
4. Faded Overt Self-Guidance—The student whispers the steps while completing the task.
5. Covert Self-Guidance—The student performs the task while silently reviewing the steps.

Another CBM technique is called *self-monitoring*. When teaching students to use self-monitoring, there is initially a cuing system (for example, a bell or tone) that prompts the students to stop what they are doing to record self-behavior on a self-monitoring card (Fig. 4.1) (Boyle and Hughes 1994). The tone or bell sounds at random intervals from 15 seconds to 120 seconds. Once students hear the tone, they stop the task and ask, "Am I working?" (or "Am I on task?"). If on task, students place a mark under the "Yes" and keep working. If the answer is "No," students record a mark under "No" and tell themselves, "I need to get back to work." This self-monitoring training program was used with elementary students with intellectual disabilities. Figure 4.2 presents a self-monitoring card used with older students. Using this card, students record a + or 0 when the tone sounds. Figure 4.2 also includes a "cheat sheet" to remind students of examples of on-task and off-task behavior.

Cognitive Theories

Building on the sentiments of CBM theorists, other psychologists further rejected behavioral theories that refused to consider cognitive processes. Cognitive theorists believe that we can understand cognitive processes and

▼ **FIGURE 4.1**
Self-Monitoring Card

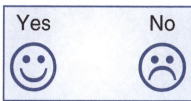

▶ **FIGURE 4.2**

Self-Monitoring Cheat
Sheet and Cue Card

Source: J. Kaplan, *Beyond Behavior Modification: A Cognitive-Behavioral Approach to Behavior Management in the School* (Austin, TX: PRO-ED, 1995).

even theorize thinking operations based on careful examinations of how people go about completing various cognitive tasks. We present five influential cognitive theories: working memory, schema theory, metacognitive theory, social learning theory, and perceptual theory.

Perhaps the most influential model to describe how learning occurs and the cognitive processes associated with it is that of the Baddeley and Hitch **working memory** (WM) model (Baddeley 2006). This model (Fig. 4.3) has been effective at describing the components of WM, along with its interacting subsystems, and its role in a wide range of cognitive activities, including how learning occurs in the

▶ **FIGURE 4.3**

Baddeley and Hitch's
multicomponent model of
working memory

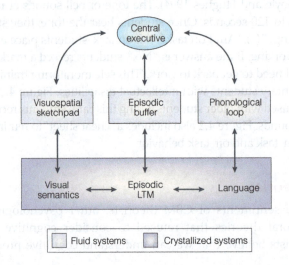

classroom (Gathercole 2008). WM is the part of the brain where information is held to be worked upon, organized, and shaped before it is stored in long-term memory (LTM) (Johnstone 1984).

During learning, the various components of this model work in an orchestrated manner and sequence. Perhaps the most important element of WM is the central executive. The executive is responsible for a wide variety of tasks that include regulating information in WM, retrieving strategies and other forms of information from LTM, directing attention for both encoding and retrieval of information in LTM, and task shifting (Gathercole, Alloway, Willis, and Adams 2006). Sometimes the executive is referred to as a "homunculus—a little person who runs things and whose activity could be used to explain all the issues that lay beyond the limits of the two systems" (Baddeley 2006, p. 16).

One of the most important roles of the executive involves controlling and directing attention. The central executive is assisted by two systems. The first system is the *phonological loop*, which is capable of holding and rehearsing verbal and speech-based information in temporary storage. Information fed through the loop allows the individual to temporary store this information indefinitely or use the information (Baddeley 2006). The other system, the *visuospatial sketchpad*, performs a similar holding and rehearsal function for visual information. In this system, any visual or spatial information is processed and encoded for storage. Visuospatial tasks typically include learning visual images and spatial information and include learning tasks such as reading maps, recognizing letters, numbers, and words by their shape, learning the shapes of objects (such as a circle, square, or triangle), learning colors, and remembering the location of objects (for instance, squares on a checkerboard or tic-tac-toe board) (Dehn 2008). Whenever the phonological loop (or visuospatial sketchpad) is used in concert with the central executive, only a limited amount of information can be processed before information is lost.

Finally, the ***episodic buffer*** is thought to combine multiple sources of information (such as the senses, short-term storage, and LTM) as episodic chunks (Baddeley, Hitch, and Allen 2009). Rather than simply passing information on to the activated LTM, the buffer is thought to play a more active role in constructing and binding information together into organized chunks that can be stored more efficiently (Baddeley 2000). In the buffer, long-term representations (that is, schemes or scripts) are manipulated and reconstructed. The episodic buffer allows for direct encoding of information to LTM, as well as searches in LTM and retrieval of specific information (Dehn 2008).

Working Memory Problems and Students with HI

A number of researchers have proposed that students with learning disabilities, as well as other HI disabilities, have problems associated with various aspects of WM (Daneman 2001; Gathercole, Alloway, Willis, and Adams 2006; Gathercole, Durling, Evans, Jeffcock, and Stone 2007; Geary, Hoard, Byrd-Craven, and DeSoto 2004; Siegel and Ryan 1989; Swanson and Beebe-Frankenberger 2004; Swanson and Saez 2003).

Swanson and Saez (2003) point out several reasons why it is important for researchers to focus on WM research as it relates to interventions for students with LD. For students with HI, these include the following:

1. WM problems interfere in learning and, ultimately, students' achievement.
2. Several studies have shown that students with HI do not appear to use up or exhaust their WM abilities, thereby presenting researchers with the challenge of identifying strategies or techniques that would help students make better use of their WM.

3. WM research represents the field's attempt to apply cognitive research to help students solve real-life learning problems in all aspects of learning, not just cognitive tasks in clinical settings.
4. Several cognitive intervention programs rely heavily on principles derived from memory research (Swanson, Cooney, and O'Shaughnessy 1998).

WM problems of students with HI have been examined extensively in both math and reading.

In the area of reading, several recent studies have shown that differences between less skilled readers and skilled readers on measures of cognitive function are related to WM limitations (De Jong 1998; Passolunghi and Siegel 2001; Swanson 2003). For example, deficits in WM have been linked to deficits in word recognition (Siegel and Ryan 1989) and reading comprehension (Swanson 1999) in students with reading disabilities (Siegel and Ryan 1989; Swanson 1999). Other studies have suggested that limitations of WM in students with LD are attributed mostly to an isolated storage system (that is, verbal short-term memory) that holds and maintains phonological codes (Shankweiler and Crain 1986; Siegel 1994; Stanovich and Siegel 1994) and is responsible for phonological (verbal) memory (Gathercole, Tiffany, Briscoe, and Thorn 2005). Moreover, other studies (Bull, Johnston, and Roy 1999; De Jong 1998; Passolunghi and Siegel 2001; Swanson 1993) have suggested that difficulties in executive processing are the cause of poor WM performance in students with reading disabilities and that verbal WM (that is, includes controlled attention), rather than short-term memory (in the phonological loop), was related to growth in reading comprehension and reading fluency (Swanson and Jerman 2007).

In mathematics, the role of WM performance has been also studied, and WM has been found to play a pivotal role in calculation and solving arithmetic word problems (Bull and Sherif 2001; Geary, Hamson, and Hoard 2000; Passolunghi and Cornoldi 2000; Passolunghi and Pazzaglia 2004). In addition, WM has been identified as a main cause of deficits in students with mathematical disabilities (Geary 1993; Passolunghi, Cornoldi, and DeLiberto 1999; Passolunghi and Siegel 2001; Siegel and Ryan 1989; Swanson 1993). Perhaps the most consistent finding in the literature is that students with LD in mathematics have difficulty retrieving basic arithmetic facts from LTM (Garnett and Fleischner 1983; Geary 1990, 1993; Jordan and Montani 1997; Ostad 1997, 2000) and that this problem is often associated with the central executive.

In terms of performing tasks that placed a heavy load on WM, Gathercole, Durling, Evans, Jeffcock, and Stone (2007) asked students with HI (that is, students with poor WM) to perform memory tasks that required them to both process and store information: one task involved detecting and recalling rhyming words in spoken poems, and the other involved listening to a sentence and counting the number of words. Their results indicate that the children with low WM had problems that were associated with the central executive. The tasks used in their study relied upon students using both the phonological loop and the central executive (whose main function is to allocate and direct attention during processing of information). According to these researchers, students' errors represented deficits that were indicative of failures of both WM and sustained focused attention.

In another explanation of learning problems relating to WM, Gathercole and colleagues (Gathercole 2004; Gathercole, Alloway, Willis, and Adams 2006) suggest that learning difficulties among students with HI result because information in WM tends to "bottleneck" during learning tasks (Gathercole 2004). As a result, these students process or store information more slowly, and new information is often lost while they are processing incoming information, particularly when working on complex learning tasks that require heavy memory loads (Gathercole, Lamont, and Alloway 2006). This leads to frequent task failures, which represent missed opportunities to learn, resulting in a snowball effect when learning subsequent skills. This viewpoint is also supported by Swanson, Zheng, and Jerman (2009), who speculate that children with HI perform well in some academic domains or on specific cognitive tasks because those domains or tasks do not place heavy demands on WM operations, or that these students compensate for WM demands by using domain-specific knowledge (prior knowledge), or that these students compensate through the use of classroom (teacher) supports. Likewise, researchers have found that while students rely heavily on WM during the initial stages of skill acquisition (Ackerman and Cianciolo 2000), it is less important once skills are committed to LTM and automatic retrieval is occurring (Geary, Hoard, Byrd-Craven, and DeSoto 2004).

Memory Span. Memory span refers to the capacity of either the phonological loop or visuospatial sketchpad to hold information. It is believed that unless information is acted upon (that is, rehearsed or linked to prior knowledge), it will be lost within a couple of seconds lost. When rehearsed, the information can remain in the loop indefinitely, depending upon the rate of decay or rehearsal rate (Dehn 2008). Because of the limited span, there are techniques that teachers can use to assist students with rehearsal or linking new information to previous knowledge.

Psychologists believe that phonological memory span can hold seven plus or minus two bits of information. This came to be known as Miller's magic number, after the famous psychologist who performed his experiments in the 1950s and 1960s and found that individuals can remember between five and nine bits (or items) of information (Miller 1956). Despite this magic number, psychologists today believe that the capacity may be closer to five plus or minus two bits of information when trying to remember information. Bear in mind that this depends upon the familiarity of the information and whether we are able to manipulate or rehearse the information to keep it in WM or encode it to LTM. For example, if we were given a list of 12 items, we might be able to categorize or group them so that we could remember the information longer and remember all 12 items (that is, associate them via a story or a rhyming method such as peg word) (Krinsky and Krinsky 1996; Scruggs, Mastropieri, and Levin 1986), or by chunking them, such as when we remember the phone extension "1-1-8-0" as "11-80."

What exactly is a *bit* of information? A bit can be thought of as a small amount of information. In some cases, one bit equals one number, such as those found in telephone numbers. In other cases, a bit can be a word, phrase, or small chunk of information. As you could guess, the larger the bits the fewer of them that can be held in phonological memory. Because of its limited capacity, new information may often bump out information already in this store, or it may simply drop out as time progresses. For students with disabilities, short-term memory is even more limited than seven plus or minus two bits of information. The belief is that students with certain types of disabilities (for example, intellectual disabilities or LD) have poor or limited short-term memory. For these students, therefore, we need to break information down into smaller chunks and practice rehearsal strategies to transfer or encode this information into LTM.

Rehearsal. Rehearsal serves two purposes: for short-term use and for longer use so that we transfer the information over to LTM. In the first case, we can use **maintenance rehearsal** to keep information in memory for a short period of time—such as repeating a telephone number until we can dial it. In the latter case, we typically use **elaborative rehearsal** to encode the information into LTM. Elaborative rehearsal works by elaborating on information from LTM to associate it with new information. To do this, we must bring information from LTM into WM and then connect the two together by adding (or elaborating on) bits of new information with the previously learned concept. When teaching older students, connecting new with prior knowledge may not be a problem because older students have lots of experiences and knowledge already in LTM. However, younger children may not have much prior knowledge about the new concept you are about to teach; therefore, you need to find ways to tap into the limited knowledge they do have about the concept you are teaching.

Chunking is another strategy that we use to remember information. Like rehearsal, we can use chunking to keep information in short-term memory longer, or we can use it to transfer information into LTM. With chunking, we look for common associations between and among the items being learned so that we can clump similar items into groups or chunks. The organized information is now easier to remember, in part because of the similarities in each group and in part because each item in the group serves to cue us to remember other items in a group. Teachers can help students clump information together to remember it by organizing it ahead of time and then showing students the relationships among the items in each group. We often cluster information without realizing we have done so. For example, if we go shopping without our grocery list, we may have trouble remembering the items. One technique to recall the items is to compartmentalize the store into sections such as meats, produce, bakery, and dairy products. We then use these areas to remember items from our grocery list—such as milk and eggs in dairy, oranges and pears in produce, hamburger and lunch meats in meats, and bread and donuts in bakery.

Long-Term Memory. Once information is encoded to LTM, it is stored there forever. Psychologists believe that it never fades or is lost except for injuries, such as stroke, traumatic brain injury, or other brain traumas. Anecdotal evidence from a neurologist named Wilder Penfield (1969) suggests that this is, in fact, true. Penfield was a neurosurgeon who performed thousands of procedures on patients. During his operations, he would use an electronic probe to stimulate different parts of his patients' brains. Having done this, his patients reported back that they recalled long-forgotten memories that they believed had been lost. The same is true for us. Often when given the proper recall cue such as an odor, sound, or picture, we remember a flood of memories from long ago. For some people, walking into a school for the first time since they graduated and smelling that distinct "school smell" brings back memories, both pleasant and unpleasant. These memories have not been lost but were simply stored away in LTM.

The levels-of-processing theory has provided some research to attest to the fact that we actually "know" more than we can easily recall. According to this theory (Craig and Lockhart 1972), information can be processed at varying levels of depth. Information that is remembered for its meaning is stored deeper than information that is stored based upon visual (seeing it) or acoustic (hearing it) cues. Thus, the deeper the level of processing, the more the person would remember the information. This means that if you want to ensure deep processing of information in students, you need to make it meaningful to them. Rather than just explain and tell them about a concept, the levels-of-processing theory tells us to have students elaborate on the concept and relate it to what they already know about the concept and to organize new information with prior knowledge from LTM.

Long-Term Memory Units. According to cognitive psychologists, knowledge is stored and arranged in units (Anderson 1990). These units can be defined as declarative knowledge, procedural knowledge, or conditional knowledge. **Declarative knowledge** is knowledge about facts and things—the knowledge of *what*. When we learn that Christopher Columbus sailed to the New World in 1492, we are creating declarative knowledge. **Procedural knowledge** is knowledge about steps or procedures—the *how* of knowledge (for example, how to throw a football and the steps involved in long division). **Conditional knowledge** is knowledge about *when* to use certain bits of declarative knowledge with procedural knowledge. Some theorists believe that learning strategies are part of conditional knowledge (Mayer 1987); others consider them part of procedural knowledge (Gaskins 2005). It is quite possible that the strategies are initially learned as procedural knowledge, and as students become more proficient at using them with different types of content and material over time, the strategies become conditional knowledge.

Schema Theory. Cognitive psychologists also theorize that information in LTM is arranged into knowledge structures. Each knowledge structure is called a **schema** and contains information about a particular concept. Schema theorists believe that we possess schemata (the plural of schema), and that these schemata consist of both declarative knowledge and procedural knowledge (Gagne 1985). For example, if you discussed golf with another person, you might be discussing popular PGA players and the rules of golf (declarative knowledge), as well as how to swing a driver versus how to swing a wedge (procedural knowledge). According to schema theory, when students have a well-defined schema about a concept they are learning, they can easily access the schema, elaborate on it, and become more knowledgeable about the concept. On the other hand, when they have a poorly developed schema, learning becomes slow and tedious as they try to grasp the concept.

Regardless of which theory you espouse, it is important to remember to tap into prior knowledge before teaching new knowledge. Remember, learning involves making connections between what is known and what is being learned.

THINK BACK TO THE CASE **about Ned's lessons about the heart...**

Why would an analogy serve as an effective method for teaching students the names of the heart's parts and their functions?

Both information processing theories and schema theory suggest that students learn concepts by forming relationships among them. Ned Massori's analogy to the DC Beltway should therefore help his students to relate the functions of the heart to something already familiar to them. Likewise, they will be able to relate the parts and various functions of the heart to one another because they all relate to each other to tell the story of the Beltway/heart functioning.

Executive Function. Knowing when to use a strategy or procedure based upon the type of task requires knowledge beyond the memory stores presented in our model. Using planning and goal-setting skills, being flexible when solving problems, directing attention to the appropriate parts of the task, and using self-regulatory behaviors to control emotions and impulses during tasks all require control from a larger, overarching system (Meltzer and Krishnan 2007). In the information processing system, this overarching, supervisory mechanism is typically referred to as **executive function**. There has been a lack of clarity between the use of the terms *executive function* and *metacognition* (Meltzer and Krishnan 2007). For some, they mean the same thing (Snowman and Biehler 2006). Keep in mind that, to date, there is still no clear distinction made in the professional literature between the two concepts (Meltzer and Krishnan 2007). For the sake of clarity in this textbook, we will use the term *executive function* as a broad umbrella term that describes how to control many different cognitive processes and encompasses metacognition, self-regulation (for example, planning and self-monitoring), attention, and regulation of our memory systems. Although executive functioning involves metacognition, it also refers to attention and self-regulation of learning in general. When applied to students, executive function refers to selecting appropriate goals, beginning work, organizing information, prioritizing tasks, memorizing information for later use, shifting strategies dependent upon the tasks and situation, and self-monitoring and checking (Meltzer and Krishnan 2007). Conversely, we will use the term **metacognition** to mean knowledge of tasks and strategies, and the flexible use of a strategy. We will intentionally limit this term as it applies to tasks, strategies, and strategy use.

Another way to think of executive function is as a mechanism that "orchestrates cognition" in the brain. The main purpose of the executive function is to direct the traffic of managing multiple tasks, particularly when WM becomes taxed from trying to complete too many tasks at once or from trying to complete complex, difficult tasks. Executive function is responsible for allocating and directing attention to tasks when too many demands are made on memory and processing. Think of executive function as the dispatcher in a taxicab company. The cabs are analogous to strategies, and the dispatcher decides when and where to send them as the calls (that is, learning demands) come in. The dispatcher must match up the best strategy with the demands of the task. For instance, if the task is to remember someone's telephone number long enough to dial it, the dispatcher might send a rote memory strategy, whereby the individual simply verbally repeats the number several times until it is dialed. If, on the other hand, the learning task is to remember all five Great Lakes, then the dispatcher might send a first-letter mnemonic strategy, whereby the individual remembers the names using the acronym HOMES (Huron, Ontario, Michigan, Erie, and Superior). The dispatcher must pay attention to feedback and self-monitor the strategies that are used to determine if the best, most efficient strategy has been dispatched and if the strategy led to successful task completion.

Metacognitive Theory and Strategy Use. Flavell (1976) claimed that metacognition involves how to use a strategy, where to employ a strategy and support its use, and when to employ a strategy based upon the task or situation. A **strategy** is a set procedure or series of steps for successfully completing a task. Ellis et al. (1991) define it as "an individual's approach to a task." More than likely, these strategies are stored in LTM as procedural knowledge or conditional knowledge (Ellis et al. 1991; Mann and Sabatino 1985). As procedural knowledge, the strategy allows the student to work through a series of steps and substeps on the task. As conditional knowledge, the student is able to modify and adapt the strategy for different learning situations.

Students with HI have several problems associated with executive functioning in general, and more specifically with metacognition and strategy use. These students often lack effective strategies, or, in some cases, they know about effective strategies but fail to use them for the task at hand (Mann and Sabatino 1985). Indeed, students with HI have problems in strategy selection and use (Butler 1998). In terms of metacognitive skills, these students do not know when and where to use certain strategies. It is not that they lack metacognitive skills, but they simply use less sophisticated ones (Wong 1996). For example, a student might be aware that she needs to study for an upcoming test on Friday; however, the night before the test, she decides simply to read over her notes (a common study strategy used by students with HI). Although this strategy has worked well in the past on quizzes, there is too much content to remember for this particular study strategy to be effective on the upcoming test. In this case, the student has failed to recognize that the task demands have changed and to adjust accordingly (that is, to use a more effective strategy). Some students with HI may have problems selecting appropriate strategies to match task demands or have problems actually implementing the strategies that they set out to use (Butler 1998). At other times, they do not monitor task performance and fail to make adjustments in strategy use based upon feedback and performance (Wong 1991, 1996). Some of these problems are the result of weak or inadequate metacognitive skills, but others are due to poor attention and self-regulation of cognitive skills (Meltzer and Krishnan 2007).

Social Learning Theory. A third theory builds on ideas present in both behavioral theory and information processing theory. This model, developed by Albert Bandura (1977), is called **social learning theory**. According to this theory, learning occurs as the result of an interaction of three factors: physical characteristics of the person (P), environmental contingencies (E), and the person's behaviors (B) (Fig. 4.4). From this perspective, students learn new behaviors by observing others and then responding to those observations. Much of Bandura's early work, referred to as **observational learning**, examined how young children would change their behavior after observing a model who was either reinforced or punished for the behavior. Bandura believes that, through observations, students see and learn the consequences of the behavior of others and then decide whether to use this information to change their own behavior when they are placed in similar situations.

The following is an example of how social learning theory works, based on how a person's expectation might affect how he would respond in a given situation. George, a poor math student (P), is working on a math worksheet (E) with a good student, Sandra. George's expectation (P) might be that he will not do well, so he gives up easily when he comes to difficult problems (B). Sandra, however, intervenes and shows him a strategy for solving the problems (E). As a result, George can solve the difficult problems (B) and feels better about his math skills (P).

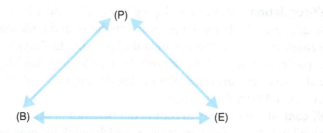

(P) Person The physical characteristics (for example, race, gender) of the person include expectations, beliefs, knowledge, and values. The physical characteristics also include metacognition or the ability to plan and monitor learning.
(E) Environmental contingencies Environment refers to the student's social and physical environment. This component includes interactions with and influences of others, as well as the nature of the task.
(B) Person's behavior The person's behavior refers to how the person responds to and modifies behavior in light of what is learned. This component not only includes current behaviors, but the ability to regulate behavior based upon self-observations and self-evaluation.

According to Bandura, the following components are essential to observational learning:

1. **Attention** is needed to observe a model and determine which actions and responses are important to remember. It helps to break down complex tasks into subtasks so that attention can be focused on the salient parts of each subtask.

2. **Retention** is crucial for remembering information from observations. Bandura claims that we store observational information in two forms: verbal descriptions or images. Physical activities, such as how to roll a bowling ball or form letters when writing, are probably stored as images. On the other hand, how to balance a checkbook might be stored as verbal descriptions, as this procedure is usually a series of steps. Despite the distinction between the two types, representations of observed events more than likely contain both verbal descriptions and images.

3. **Production** refers to the translation of stored images and verbal descriptions into actions. In some cases, we may rehearse in our mind before we actually perform the actions. During production, we frequently compare our actions with a model and then use self-observation and self-correction to modify our actions or behaviors. If a student is demonstrating a new behavior or skill, it is important to have a teacher observe and give immediate feedback to the student. During later stages, students use self-observations and self-correction to further correct their actions.

4. **Motivation** occurs through reinforcement in observational learning. Bandura believes that reinforcement serves to motivate people in three ways: (1) people see the model reinforced for his or her actions and they like it; (2) people believe that, if they act like the model who was reinforced, they too will be reinforced; and (3) people perform the actions and enjoy (that is, internal reinforcement) performing the actions. The belief is that these three ways serve to motivate students to perform the same or similar actions.

The "Self" Components.   As you can see, the "self" components are important in Bandura's view of social learning theory. Self-regulation, self-control, self-reflection, and self-efficacy all serve to help us better understand and use new skills, actions, and behaviors.

Self-regulation involves developing personal standards to evaluate our performance, deciding whether we met those standards, and deciding whether we should be rewarded for meeting those standards. For example, Tom just learned how to play golf, in particular how to drive the ball. He has decided that his goal is drive the ball 300 yards. After one successful night at the driving range, 15 of the 30 golf balls that he drove went 300 yards or longer.

Self-control is our ability to control our behavior or actions, even when others are not around to judge us (with rewards or punishment). In some cases, we delay gratification for our actions until we can earn a larger reward. For example, after earning an "A" on a quiz, Nerbay decides to continue studying hard for the next few nights until he takes the test. After he takes the test and finds that he has earned an "A," he decides to take a couple of nights off from studying and watches TV.

Self-reflection is an important skill to possess because it encourages us to reflect and judge past actions. In doing so, we are able to adjust our actions to improve our behavior or performance. In some cases, our self-reflection and judgments help us improve our actions, but we might also use moral standards to judge our actions or behaviors. In some cases, our self-morality keeps our behavior and actions in check, particularly when dealing with other people. For example, Marcy has just yelled at her class for being too loud. Upon reflection, Marcy realizes that she was upset about a fight she had this morning with her boyfriend and that according to her moral code, she was wrong to take out her frustrations on her students.

Self-efficacy is a person's beliefs about what he or she is capable of doing. How successful the people perceive themselves to be at a particular task often determines whether they will persevere through tough times or give up on the task. Comparing our performance to that of others and failing or succeeding at a task often determines our *level* of self-efficacy (for example, I'm good at golf) but not necessarily the *accuracy* of our self-efficacy (for example, I actually shoot 120 per game). In other words, one's perceived self-efficacy may or may not match real self-efficacy (Hergenhahn and Olson 2001). Accordingly, people who have low perceived self-efficacy but are actually doing well may become overwhelmed and give up on difficult tasks. On the other hand, people with highly perceived self-efficacy may get in over their heads on tasks because, in fact, they are not good at the task.

Constructivist Theory

Each of the previously mentioned behavioral and cognitive theories has been influential in the fields of special and regular education, and they continue to be prominent, particularly in special education research and practice. Perhaps indicative of the differences between special education and regular education (see Poplin and Rogers 2005), one theory has been considerably more influential in regular education research practice than in special education. The current preeminent theory of learning in regular education is **constructivism** (sometimes more formally known as social constructivism) (see Moll 2004). Constructivists focus less on the behavioral and cognitive aspects of learning and instead address the social nature of learning and comprehending, including the importance of meaningfulness for learning.

The Russian psychologist Lev Vygotsky first proposed the principles of constructivist theory. According to Vygotsky (1978), learning is a social process in which learners interact with others in their environment to learn concepts and skills and gradually internalize them. Constructivist theory also has its origins in the work of Jean Piaget, with contributions from other education theorists (Poplin 1988). Constructivists believe that students learn through a process of *actively constructing knowledge*. Whereas constructivist principles have been commonplace in regular education classrooms for the past couple of decades, it has only been within the past decade that special education has begun to apply these principles to develop teaching techniques for students with disabilities (Poplin and Rogers 2005).

This construction process involves making connections between new information and prior knowledge (Good and Brophy 1994). More specifically, the construction of new knowledge comes about through the processes of transformation and self-regulation (Poplin 1988). **Transformation of knowledge** occurs when students learn new knowledge (or new experiences), and their prior knowledge is then transformed into new knowledge. This construction of new knowledge occurs not simply by adding new information, but by assimilating the new knowledge and, in doing so, changing the way the student understands the concept. For example, early on, a child learns the concept of a cow as a large creature with horns. Living next to a dairy farm, the child sees many different types of cows. Then one day while on a walk in the woods with his father, a boy sees a deer foraging on small bushes and immediately calls the deer a "cow." The father corrects him, telling him that a deer is skinnier and has antlers, not

> **BOX 4.1**
>
> ### Constructivist Principles
>
> 1 All students are active learners. Always search for constructing knowledge.
> 2 The best predictor of what is learned is based on what students already know.
> 3 Form follows function in learning.
> 4 Learning occurs best when it goes from whole to part to whole.
> 5 Errors are essential to learning.
> 6 The end goal is construction of knowledge, not transmission of it.
>
> *Source:* Adapted from M. Poplin (1988). Holistic/Constructivists Principles of Teaching/Learning Process: Implications for the Field of Learning Disabilities (*Journal of Learning Disabilities* 7(21): 401–16).

horns. According to constructivist theory, the child must now reconstruct his knowledge about cows as he learns more about deer. This new experience with a deer transforms his knowledge about cows. However, if the concept of a deer is too much for the child to accept, the child may reject the notion of deer and continue to call deerlike animals cows. In this case, the child self-regulates what he learns and refuses to learn.

Box 4.1 illustrates six principles of constructivist theory (Poplin 1988). The following paragraphs elaborate upon the six constructivist principles.

In the first principle, according to constructivists, students are always active learners, always searching to learn new information, as long as it is of interest to them. Constructivists believe that students are always trying to make sense of the world around them. In doing so, students first judge whether the topic/concept is of interest or value to them. If it is something worthwhile to learn, they will then construct knowledge of this topic.

In the second principle, the best predictor of what people will learn is often what they already know. As self-regulated learners, students will search out to learn more about those topics that interest them and about which they have prior knowledge. If students have no prior knowledge about a topic, learning about the topic will be very difficult unless it is linked to some related prior knowledge.

The third principle states that form follows function in learning. This tenet refers to the fact that students will learn some new skill or topic in their own manner because they are more concerned with the function of the skill or content than the exact form; that will come later. For example, when students learn to write, they often follow natural developmental or emergent stages (Lipson and Wixson 1997); however, they will scribble on paper and, when asked what they are writing, they will read back to you a logical-sounding message, despite the fact that what was written is illegible (or nonsense). Over time, students begin to use letters that are parts of the word, and, still later, the correct letters (in the correct order) to form actual words that make up a "real" message. Only over time and with much practice will students master the correct form (that is, writing legible letters/words) of the message (function).

Under the fourth principle, learning occurs best from whole to part to whole. Some constructivists claim that, when teachers reduce a task to its individual components, the task itself loses its meaning; it simply becomes a collection of parts or steps. Moreover, teachers should try to help students understand the meaning or purpose of concepts or skills first so that when broken down, the students can scaffold the parts to something that is meaningful. Constructivists claim, and rightly so in many cases, that teachers are often so busy teaching the specifics of learning tasks that they forget to explain to students why they are learning the task in the first place (Poplin 1988).

TABLE 4.1 Transmission of Information Versus Social Construction of Knowledge

Transmission View	Social Construction View
Knowledge as fixed body of information transmitted from teacher or text to students.	Knowledge as developing interpretations co-constructed through discussion.
Texts, teacher as authoritative sources of expert knowledge to which students defer.	Authority for constructed knowledge resides in the arguments and evidence cited in its support by students as well as by texts or teacher; everyone has expertise to contribute.
Teacher is responsible for managing students' learning by providing information and leading students through activities and assignments.	Teacher and students share responsibility for initiating and guiding learning efforts.
Teacher explains, checks for understanding, and judges correctness of students' responses.	Teacher acts as discussion leader who poses questions, seeks clarifications, promotes dialogue, helps group recognize areas of consensus and of continuing disagreement.
Students memorize or replicate what has been explained or modeled.	Students strive to make sense of new input by relating it to their prior knowledge and by collaborating in dialogue with others to co-construct shared understandings.
Discourse emphasizes drill and recitation in response to convergent questions; focus is on eliciting correct answers.	Discourse emphasizes reflective discussion of networks of connected knowledge: questions are more divergent but designed to develop understanding of the powerful ideas that anchor these networks; focus is on eliciting students' thinking.
Activities emphasize replication of models or applications that require following step-by-step algorithms.	Activities emphasize applications to authentic issues and problems that require higher-order thinking.
Students work mostly alone, practicing what has been transmitted to them in order to prepare themselves to compete for rewards by reproducing it on demand.	Students collaborate by acting as a learning community that constructs shared understandings through sustained dialogue.

Source: Reprinted with permission from T. Good and J. Brophy, *Looking in Classrooms* (New York: Harper Collins College Publishers, 1994).

The fifth principle states that learning errors are important. Rather than penalize students when they make errors, constructivists claim that we should help students understand their errors so that they can correct them and, in the process, learn.

In the sixth principle of constructivist theory, teachers are no longer the ones who *transmit* facts or other bits of unrelated knowledge to students; instead, teachers help students construct knowledge—knowledge that is *meaningful* to each student (Table 4.1). Because students personalize and make the information meaningful as they learn, they will remember it longer and recall it when needed. In this type of learning, teachers move away from having students remember facts and other unrelated bits of knowledge and instead focus on reflective discussions and the implication of content or skills learned (Good and Brophy 1994).

THINK BACK TO THE CASE   about Ned's lessons about the heart . . .

If Ned had instead given his students a list of key concepts and definitions, and then asked them to apply them to a drawing of the DC Beltway without explaining the analogy for them, could the students have figured out the analogy?

From a constructivist perspective, the students could have used their expert knowledge about the DC Beltway to construct an understanding of the functions of the heart, about which they are currently novices. Ideally, they would problem-solve the analogy in a social context. For example, they could work in small groups, or Ned could be an expert who gives them hints and answers questions they ask. Through dialogue, students would model their ideas for each other and refine the analogy they construct by talking it through. Seeking how to solve an authentic problem, such as Beltway congestion or heart disease, might help the students.

4-3   Using Theories in Teaching

Now that we have discussed several theories of learning, we will discuss their applications to learning. Think back to each theory as you read about the applications, and try to understand how the application was derived from that theory.

Applications of Behavioral Theory

Applications of behavioral theories rely upon stimulating the learning processes that behaviorists believe underlie cognition. We provide examples of some the most commonly utilized practices in special education (see Swanson and Hoskyn 2001, for example): reinforcement, task analysis, and group contingencies.

CASE 4.2   Math Problem Problems

Case Introduction

Now that you have worked through the first case in this chapter, you should feel comfortable addressing issues in a second case. In this case about math teacher Vernon Jackson and his student, Linda, see if you can find evidence of how the various education theories described in the first half of this chapter are enacted in an everyday teaching scenario. Ask yourself what the implications are of Vernon's and Linda's thoughts and actions for the type of learning that results for Linda.

Vernon Jackson told students to read the first problem on the worksheet as he handed it out. He then told them, "I will tell you how to do the first problem, and you will do the rest." In front of him, Linda looked over the 10 problems on the worksheet and let out a depressed sigh.

"Not again," she said to herself. "I hate doing these problems."

When Mr. Jackson reached the last row, he continued, "OK. Read the first problem while I tell you how it's done." Writing it on the board, he was cognizant of his students' general dislike of word problems and listened for disparaging remarks about the assignment. Linda didn't attend to the directions and instead began to write a note to her friend Cory Franks.

Mr. Jackson then described how to complete the problem: "For this problem, you will need to use only the important information and disregard the rest of the information." As Linda glanced at the first problem, which was about camping, she remarked to herself, "Great, I don't even like camping."

"Linda," Mr. Jackson asked, "How many campers like hotdogs?"

Linda, surprised that he called on her, responded with a blank look on her face.

"OK," Mr. Jackson continued, "look at the problem and tell me how many campers are eating hotdogs out of 20 campers?"

Linda responded, "12?"

continued

"Good," Mr. Jackson remarked, while leaning against his desk. "If each student eats three hotdogs, how many hotdogs are needed?"

Linda looked around and saw that students were busy writing down what Mr. Jackson had said. Because she missed what was said, she scribbled out her own computation. "Uh . . . 27?" Linda responded.

"No, Linda," Mr. Jackson replied. "Blaine, how many hotdogs are needed?" Blaine correctly responds "36," and Mr. Jackson smiles and tells him he is correct.

"Finally, if hotdogs are 30 cents apiece, how much money is needed to purchase hotdogs for the campers?" Mr. Jackson asks the class.

In a chorus of voices, they respond, "$10.80."

"Now, you do the rest," he instructs his class, despite the fact that many students have already begun working on the second word problem. It's not surprising that many of the students are working independently because they have been reviewing word problems for the past two weeks.

Mr. Jackson then lets the students work on the remainder of the problems while he sits at his desk and looks for worksheets for the next portion of his lesson. Mr. Jackson likes to tell students how to complete problems. He feels that students understand his directions because he is a verbal person who believes that all students need to become auditory learners if they hope to progress into the higher grades.

To Linda, a student with a learning disability, completing math word problems is just about the worst thing. In addition to her reading problems, she does poorly in math, often failing to pick up concepts that other students easily understand. Over time, despite having different math teachers, Linda has grown to dislike math and often avoids anything relating to it. For example, when Mr. Jackson informs students that they can complete one extra worksheet per week for bonus points, Linda flatly refuses in spite of her borderline grade of a "D."

CASE QUESTIONS

1. From behavioral theory, what could you do to help Linda improve her math skills?
2. What components of social learning theory could you use to teach this math lesson?
3. What could you do to help Linda with her self-efficacy for solving word problems?

Reinforcement. Reinforcement serves as a strong tool for teachers to use in the classroom. You can use various forms of environmental reinforcers such as smiles, verbal comments, winks, or pats on the back to initiate or maintain appropriate behaviors in students. In many cases, your attention serves as a form of reinforcement for students. However, be cautious because there may be times when your attention inadvertently serves to reinforce a student's inappropriate behavior. Pointing out misbehaviors in some students can serve to reinforce a particular behavior and maintain it or even increase its frequency. When introducing new behaviors to a student's repertoire, reinforce those new behaviors immediately and frequently. Once the behaviors are established, you can use reinforcers less frequently, as well as use less intense reinforcers (that is, move from primary to secondary reinforcers). Whenever you use primary reinforcers, always pair them with a secondary reinforcer, such as praise or attention, so that you can begin using more natural reinforcers that are commonly found in the student's environment.

Steps for improving behavior involve the following:

1. Choose an inappropriate (that is, undesirable) behavior that needs to be changed.
2. Decide which new or alternate behavior you want to see increase in frequency and replace the inappropriate behavior.
3. Decide how to measure the new target behavior, and begin gathering data to determine its current level.
4. Decide when and how you will begin reinforcing the target behavior, and determine which reinforcers you will use.
5. Gather data to ensure that the target behavior is increasing. Once you see increases and know that the behavior has been established, decide how you want to change, if any, the reinforcement or the frequency of reinforcement.

6. Once the behavior has been established over a long period of time, decide how you want to fade out external reinforcers or move to a self-monitoring system.

Task Analysis. Using a **task analysis** to examine complex behavior changes or complex tasks often helps students. A task analysis involves breaking down a large task into smaller subtasks or steps. Once tasks are broken down, students are taught to perform these smaller steps before being asked to complete the larger overall task. Typically, students must master each step before being taught the next step. For example, washing your hands involves several smaller steps: turn the water on; wet your hands; put soap on your hands; lather the soap in your hands; rinse off the soap; turn off the water; dry your hands. In this example, each step would be taught individually or in conjunction with other steps. Some children can learn multiple steps, whereas other children need to be taught each individual step.

Group Contingencies. A group contingency is a system in which the receipt of reinforcement for the entire group depends upon the behavior of its group members. A group contingency is a behavior management technique that is used to control the behavior of large groups of students. For example, the "marbles in a jar" technique has been used to help control group behaviors. Using this technique, the teacher has two jars, one full of marbles and one empty. The first jar should contain a sufficient number of marbles so that you can give periodic reinforcement over a few days. Periodically, you will reinforce positive classroom behaviors by moving a marble from one jar to the other. In some cases, you will explain why you are moving marbles from one jar to the other; at other times, no explanation is given. Initially, explain to students which positive classroom behaviors are being reinforced (for example, quiet behavior, on-task behavior, using cooperative skills with one another). Although this group reinforcement technique might be a consistent technique, you should supplement this form of management with other types of reinforcement, such as verbal praise or smiles for appropriate classroom behaviors.

THINK BACK TO THE CASE   **about Linda's math skills...**

From behavioral theory, what could you do to help Linda improve her math skills?

From a behavioral perspective, Mr. Jackson could break down the skill of solving word problems into steps and then list these steps so that Linda could refer to them while working on word problems. He could also use positive reinforcement to shape Linda's behavior until she begins to use the problem-solving steps correctly.

Applications of Cognitive Theories

As we have discussed previously, cognitive theories attempt to explain how students think and learn. As you read each section on the application of cognitive theories, think about how each could improve the thinking and learning skills of students with HI. We begin with *cognitive* aspects of learning and end with more *social* aspects of learning.

Application of the Information Processing Model in Teaching. Several applications have derived from the information processing model. While reading this section, think about how each application might assist your students in storing new knowledge in

LTM—the ultimate goal of learning. Of course, this involves pulling down knowledge from LTM into WM so that new knowledge can be encoded and then stored in LTM.

Attention

Attention is a process used to decide what is critical to remember and process and then send this information on to the next memory store. Prior to any lesson, direct students' attention to the task at hand (for example, see the "lesson grabber" activities described in Chapter 10). If giving oral directions, first have students stop what they are doing and look at you as you describe the directions. Using selective attention, students pay attention to you and your words as you describe each step.

 Gaining their attention is one aspect of attention; the other aspect is *sustaining* their attention over a period of time. Sustained attention is a difficult process for some students with disabilities. Teachers can improve students' sustained attention by using activities such as "20 Questions" or "I Spy." For students with attention problems, it is important to reduce distractions (for example, excessive noise or visual clutter), break large tasks into manageable parts, present multistep directions one step at a time, emphasize key parts to a task or key information in a learning unit, and reinforce students when they focus and sustain attention to task.

Chunking

Chunking involves combining similar or like items together for the purpose of learning or remembering them. Chunking is a particularly helpful strategy with unorganized information or lists of items. Students can learn to organize lesson content into a web or other graphic that depicts how discrete concepts are related and then use the category label to recall them, for example. Of course, prior to presenting it to students, teachers can organize information into helpful chunks of knowledge based upon a category. These useful chunks of related knowledge will help students remember the information better, particularly if the chunks are distinct categories. For example, you can chunk types of triangles into equilateral, isosceles, and scalene, and you can chunk types of polygons into rectangle, quadrilateral, parallelogram, and rhombus.

Meaningfulness

Meaningful learning occurs when students link new knowledge with prior knowledge (that is, from LTM). They are not just chunking the information but are forging schematic relationships. With the technique KWL (know, want, learn), students determine what they already know about the topic prior to learning and then linking it up with new information as they learn. Figure 4.5 is an example of a KWL Plus chart. This chart includes the letter "S," which represents *things you STILL want to know about.* Other ways of connecting new with prior knowledge involve using an advance organizer. An advance organizer is given at the beginning of a lesson and involves tapping into prior knowledge in the form of a review of content already learned, a discussion of information about a known topic, or a review of recently learned information. For example, prior to learning about double-digit addition with carrying over, students might review math problems that do not involve carrying over. Once they practice a few of these, students then learn the new concept of carrying over.

Analogies

Analogies represent another method of tapping into LTM to bring the prior information into working memory so that new knowledge can be encoded to it. For example, biology students often use the analogy of the cell function with that of a

K	W	L	S
In this column, list things you already **know** about estuaries.	In this column, list things you **want** to know about estuaries.	In this column, list things you **learned** about estuaries.	In this column, list things you **still** want to know about estuaries.
• _____ _____ _____	• _____ _____ _____	• _____ _____ _____	• _____ _____ _____
• _____ _____ _____	• _____ _____ _____	• _____ _____ _____	• _____ _____ _____
• _____ _____ _____	• _____ _____ _____	• _____ _____ _____	• _____ _____ _____

▲ **FIGURE 4.5**
KWL Plus Chart on Estuaries

factory (Table 4.2). Of course, students have to be familiar with the first part of the analogy or they will be learning two new concepts.

Strategies

Strategies are a set of procedures or steps that are used to complete a task. With any given task, some strategies may be more successful than others. We often use strategies without even consciously thinking about them. However, for many students, particularly those with disabilities, strategies must be directly taught. The most effective strategies are those that are tied to a specific task (for example, reading comprehension, solving math story problems, or studying lists of items) and/or content area. The strategies that need to be taught to students are those that are more than mere rote rehearsal strategies.

Effective strategies are tied to a specific learning task and are taught along with metacognitive skills (that is, knowing when and where to use the strategy). Rather than use rote rehearsal to remember vocabulary words and their definitions, students could use specific study strategies, such as the IT FITS strategy (King-Sears, Mercer, and Sindelar 1992; Box 4.2) or the LINCS strategy (Ellis 1992; Box 4.3), for example. A number of other strategies are described throughout this book.

TABLE 4.2 Analogy Between Cell Functions and a Factory

Plant Cell	Factory	Function
Cell wall	Border fence	Protection
Nucleus	Copy room	Makes DNA copies
Endoplasmic reticulum	Conveyor belt	Transports materials
Ribosomes	Assembly line	Assembles proteins
Mitochondrion	Power station	Makes energy
Chloroplast	Solar panels	Gathers energy
Vacuole	Waste pond	Stores wastes

TIPS FOR GENERALIZATION

Metacognition and Strategy Flexibility

Any strategy training should include metacognitive components. In particular, Wong (1996) pointed out that training should promote self-awareness and self-regulation. That means teachers should nurture their students' self-awareness by making them aware of the task demands and how the strategy will help them address these demands for success. Self-awareness of task demands means that students know why they are completing the task (that is, the purpose of the task) and are also aware of the steps needed to achieve the goal. Self-regulation, on the other hand, refers to self-monitoring of accurate strategy use and self-checking of work for accuracy. Other researchers go beyond these definitions and suggest that metacognitive skills should include *flexibility* of strategy

use for new situations and *internalization* of the strategy steps so that students can put into their own words why the strategy is effective for them.

In terms of training for *generalization* of a strategy, teachers should train students to use the strategy with new, similar tasks (for example, use the reading strategy with a newspaper article and with a textbook, rather than just with short passages) and should teach students to internalize the strategy by helping them understand why the strategy works for them. Through internalizing (Wong uses the term "mediating student mindfulness"), students can understand which aspects of the strategy lead to their success. By practicing the strategy with novel materials, students learn how to use it in a flexible manner.

BOX 4.2

IT FITS Strategy for Remembering Vocabulary

I Identify the term.
T Tell the definition of the term.
F Find a keyword.
I Imagine the definition doing something.
T Think about the definition doing something with the keyword.
S Study what you imagined until you know the definition.

BOX 4.3

LINCS Strategy for Remembering Vocabulary

L List the parts.
I Imagine a picture.
N Note a reminding word.
C Construct a LINCing story.
S Self-test.

Application of Social Learning Theory. Whereas information processing models address the mechanisms of cognitive processing, social learning theory is applied by focusing on both social interactions and the cognitive processing that students engage to navigate and learn from those social interactions. Social learning theory relies on modeling and various opportunities to learn in cooperation with others.

Models

As you read about social learning theory, you probably saw that the use of models is an important component in changing behavior. The use of peer models is particularly helpful for students when they are learning new tasks or need feedback about incorrectly performed tasks. Models serve to show students how to perform a task and provide a concrete and realistic example of performance. Whenever possible, teachers should try to model a behavior for students rather than just describe it. Although descriptions are important prior to modeling, modeling provides students with an explicit example of the behavior or performance. Once teachers model a behavior, it is important for students to practice that new behavior while receiving feedback. Using guided practice, students can practice modeling the behavior for each other while the teacher circulates around room providing feedback on their performance.

Cooperative Learning and Peer Tutoring

Cooperative learning and peer tutoring are often associated with one another. Although both involve students working together to learn, there are typically differences between the two sets of approaches. Cooperative learning involves students working to complete a task in groups, in which they can be dependent on one another in several possible ways. In peer tutoring, two students take turns performing the roles of tutor and tutee.

Cooperative learning consists of organizing students into heterogeneous groups of four or five students. Within each group, students are responsible for achieving both an individual and a group goal (Putnam 1993; Slavin 1990). Individual efforts within a cooperative learning group help contribute to the group goal. By contributing positively to a group goal, individuals develop self-efficacy. Moreover, as others in the group are rewarded for their actions, students may become confident that they too are capable of successfully completing the task. Teachers can also provide encouragement and feedback to students as they work in groups. Teacher feedback serves as another source that will enable students to develop accurate self-efficacy skills about the task they are working on.

Classwide peer tutoring (CWPT) is a popular peer tutoring method to help students learn from one another. In peer tutoring, students directly assist or teach other students skills or knowledge. The act of teaching others often builds self-confidence in students, because they must know the material well enough to teach it. In doing so, students remember the content in meaningful ways that help them retain and recall the information in long-term memory. To get the most out of the tutoring experience, teachers should take care to match up tutors with tutees. Good models have appropriate coping skills to deal with the demands of the task. Those skills, such as verbalizations (for example, "I need to calm down to complete this task" or "I need to go slower over the tough parts"), serve to improve the self-efficacy skills of those being tutored. Even though adults can model the correct completion of tasks for students, students may wonder whether they are capable of performing like an adult to complete the task. Instead, peer models can provide a more realistic example of how to complete a task for the student being tutored (Hohn 1994).

THINK BACK TO THE CASE   about Linda's math skills...

What components of social learning theory could you use to teach this math lesson?

From a social learning perspective, Mr. Jackson could pair Linda up with a model who could show her how to solve word problems. He could then reinforce the students who correctly model the problem-solving steps. Another option would be to place Linda within a cooperative learning group where other students would work together to help her solve word problems.

What could you do to help Linda with her self-efficacy for solving word problems?

Linda needs to develop higher levels of self-efficacy for solving word problems and better self-regulation skills. Mr. Jackson can help with these "self" skills by making sure that she completes problems successfully. He can model for her by thinking aloud while he solves problems. He could use positive self-talk and self-reinforcing statements to help her with self-regulation skills.

Application of Constructivist Theories

As we noted, students participating in general education classrooms are likely to encounter constructivist-based teaching and learning, and certainly it can be found in popular special education practices today as well (for example, Mariage 2001; Montague 2003). Constructivist lessons very often involve a social component such as dialogues with a teacher or a peer, teaming, or group work. Because the process of constructing knowledge relies on active cognitive engagement, constructivist lessons tend to be focused on meaningful or authentic tasks, such as solving a problem of interest to students (for example, using mathematics to determine a plan for equitable distribution of relief resources following a natural disaster as opposed to "mindlessly" solving practice problems).

In a social, or dialogic, process, the student receives information and tries to construct meaning about the new information, which can include trying to use it (for example, you might ask questions or try to explain new information to someone who is helping you learn about it). Through an exchange in which the learner is actually problem-solving how to comprehend new concepts, understanding is constructed. The student less familiar with the information is termed a **novice**. The more knowledgeable partner(s) is the **expert**. Vygotsky (1978) referred to the range between a student's present problem-solving developmental capability and what the student is capable of when guided by an expert as the **zone of proximal development (ZPD)**. Through social interactions with experts, the novice gradually becomes an expert on a particular concept. This theory of how people learn is often thought of as distinct from behavioral practices that emphasize drill and practice to mastery (for example, Direct Instruction), although the two can work together (Harris and Graham 1996; Poplin and Rogers 2005).

Social interaction during constructivist lessons is only a vehicle for the process of knowledge construction within a student's ZPD. Through such social activities as peer editing and presenting one's writing from the "author's chair" (Englert and Mariage 1991), students interact with experts to think actively about content. Sharing ideas and attempting to comprehend others' perspectives cause students to grow in their understanding.

To be effective experiences, constructivist lessons cannot simply be open-ended opportunities for teams of students to explore whatever interests them. Without direction, students may not think about the critical aspects of a concept or may simply elect to not investigate things that are not of interest to them. Without guidance, students may even come to firmly "learn" misinformation (Mayer 2004). Scaffolded instruction is an effective approach to supporting students' learning as they gradually assume "ownership" of ideas (Hogan and Pressley 1997). By **scaffolding**, teachers support students by directing their learning. Teachers might provide the students with specific questions to answer, outline the process the students are to follow for their own knowledge construction, or model procedures when scaffolding (Baker, Gersten, and Scanlon 2002; Reiser 2004).

When constructivist lessons include scaffolded support, they can be effective for learners with HI, who have been found to benefit most from explicit instructional practices (review Chapters 1 and 2). Typically, students with HI benefit from explicit instruction to help them firmly master foundational concepts and skills (Gersten 1991; Swanson and Hoskyn 2001). Others have noted that a balance of constructivist and more explicit instruction is more likely to benefit those with HI (for example, Harris and Graham 1996; Poplin and Rogers 2005).

CHAPTER SUMMARY

We hope that you now have a new appreciation for learning theory and can approach learning tasks from different perspectives after reading this chapter. Because a sound theory is a framework used to describe events, it can be used to describe how students with HI learn and why they exhibit certain behaviors—both appropriate and inappropriate. Theories serve to help you become a better teacher. We have described different theories and provided applications of each to help you understand how they are used in teaching.

In the field of special education today, behavioral (including cognitive behavior modification) and cognitive (including the use of strategies and metacognition) theories represent the predominant theories, and constructivist theories are becoming increasingly influential. Special education teachers and their colleagues use applications of these three theories daily. If you visit any classroom that includes students with HI, you will see popular techniques derived from these theories, such as learning strategies, mnemonic instruction, self-monitoring, self-instructions, peer tutoring, and cooperative learning. The rest of this book will discuss different teaching techniques and strategies that have been derived from the theories and that are research-based techniques. We hope that this book will not be the first or last time that you read about these theories, because many of them are much too complicated to be presented in a few short pages; instead, we hope that you will read other sources for expanded views on the different theories.

KEY TERMS

Attention, 146
Behavior Modification, 132
Behavioral Theory, 131
Chunking, 142
Classwide Peer Tutoring (CWPT), 156
Cognitive Behavior Modification (CBM), 136
Conditional Knowledge, 143
Conditioned Reinforcer, 133
Constructivism, 147
Contingent Reinforcement, 132
Cooperative Learning, 156
Declarative Knowledge, 142
Differential Reinforcement of Alternative
    (DRA), 135
Differential Reinforcement of
    Incompatible (DRI), 135
Elaborative Rehearsal, 141

Executive Function, 143
Expert, 157
Extinction, 134
Generalized Reinforcer, 133
Maintenance Rehearsal, 141
Metacognition, 144
Motivation, 146
Negative Reinforcer, 132
Novice, 157
Observational Learning, 145
Operant Conditioning, 132
Positive Reinforcer, 132
Primary Reinforcer, 133
Procedural Knowledge, 143
Production, 146
Reinforcer, 132
Retention, 146

Scaffolding, 157
Schema, 143
Secondary Reinforcer, 133
Self-Control, 146
Self-Efficacy, 147
Self-Reflection, 146
Self-Regulation, 146
Social Learning Theory, 145
Strategy, 144
Task Analysis, 152
Theory, 128
Time-Outs, 134
Transformation of Knowledge, 147
Working Memory, 138
Zone of Proximal Development (ZPD), 157

APPLICATION ACTIVITIES

Using information from the chapter, complete the following activities that were designed to help you apply the knowledge that was presented in this chapter.

1. You have a student who constantly curses in your classroom. Because this is a behavior that you have targeted for change, describe what you could do to change this behavior. Describe the new behavior, how you will reinforce it, what you would do if cursing continues, and how you will monitor the student's performance. Review your answers and identify which theory(s) they most reflect.

2. Using the information processing model, describe one concept and how you could teach it using an analogy. Describe what information would tap into prior knowledge and how you would link new knowledge about the concept with prior knowledge.

3. Think of a concept or skill that you will teach when you become a teacher (or if you cannot think of one, use the concepts: theory and hypothesis). Identify how you could teach the same thing from each of the three domains of behavioral, cognitive, and constructivist theories.

5 Oral Language: Strategies and Techniques

Learning Objectives

After reading this chapter, you will understand:

5-1 Components that make up oral language

5-2 How models are useful in describing how language develops in children

5-3 Common problems students with HI encounter with oral language

5-4 How language normally develops in children and common language difficulties among students with HI

5-5 Strategies and techniques that are effective for improving language skills of students with HI

CEC Initial Preparation Standard 5: Instructional Planning and Strategies

5-2 Beginning special education professionals use technologies to support instructional assessment, planning, and delivery for individuals with exceptionalities.

5-4 Beginning special education professionals use strategies to enhance language development and communication skills of individuals with exceptionalities.

5-6 Beginning special education professionals teach to mastery and promote generalization of learning.

5-7 Beginning special education professionals teach cross-disciplinary knowledge and skills such as critical thinking and problem solving to individuals with exceptionalities.

Do you think language problems are common among students with disabilities?
If you answered *yes*, you are correct. Among students with disabilities, 96 percent had one or more types of a communication deficit; of those students, 90 percent had a language impairment, and 23 percent exhibited articulation disorders (Gibbs and Cooper 1989; Wagner and Blackorby 2002). The American Speech-Language-Hearing Association (ASHA) 2006 Schools Survey confirms these numbers by reporting that approximately 70 percent of speech language pathologists (SLPs) regularly serve students with HI (for example, learning disabilities and mental retardation) in public schools. In addition, in a 2008 ASHA survey, SLPs identified 45 percent of their caseload as having moderate communication impairments, 21 percent severe/profound impairments, and 29 percent mild impairments.

In this chapter, you will learn how to teach oral language skills to students with HI. We will present information about components of language, models of language development, and milestones for normal language development. In addition, we will discuss the language problems of students with HI and techniques, skills, and activities for improving the oral language of students.

CASE 5.1	Short Supply of Words

Case Introduction

In this case, you will read about a student who has language difficulties. As you read the case, you will see how his problems affect his communication with others and his academic skills. Think about how you could help him if you were his teacher.

At the end of the case, you will find case questions. These questions are meant to serve as points for reflection. Of course, if you can answer them immediately, you should do so, but you may want to wait to answer them until you have read that portion of the chapter that pertains to the particular case question. Throughout the rest of the chapter, you will see the same questions. As you see them again, try to answer them based upon the portion of the chapter that you just read.

Sammie Mattati grew up in the suburbs of Philadelphia, Pennsylvania. His parents, Kakie and Sabot Mattati, work in center-city Philly as successful lawyers at a large law firm. When Sammie was born, his parents didn't really notice that anything was different about him at first. Often too busy to spend much time with him during the day, they relied upon their nanny, Sophie, for reports of Sammie's progress. Even Sophie didn't notice problems as she cared for him. In all, his first two years of life were rather uneventful. During the latter part of Sammie's second year, however, Sophie and his parents began to notice that while other children Sammie's age were speaking, he remained void of words and instead communicated using gestures and sounds. Despite the delay, Kakie and Sabot didn't worry because Sabot himself did not speak until he was almost three years old. Even when Sammie began to use words, he still relied heavily on gestures to help him communicate. When he turned four, his parents noticed that his speech was still behind that of his playmates and decided it was time to seek help.

Working with their local school district, the Markel School District, Sammie's parents scheduled him for a speech and language evaluation. It was determined that Sammie was delayed in the areas of language and sound production. Within a few weeks, Sammie was receiving speech services from the SLP at his local preschool. These services continued when he entered kindergarten and are continuing even today, now that Sammie is in fifth grade. In addition to receiving special education services for speech and language, he also qualified under the category of specific learning disabilities in third grade because of reading problems. To receive assistance in reading, Sammie leaves his fifth-grade class and walks to the special education resource room twice a week.

Sammie's language problems continue, particularly in the area of word recall. On one recent day, Mrs. Laptia, his special education teacher, asked him to identify some common objects found around the room. Sammie had particular difficulty with certain objects, such as the wall clock. When his teacher asked him to name the object, he first had to describe its shape, size, and characteristics before finally calling it by its name: a clock. He has similar problems recalling specific vocabulary words and uses this technique whenever he cannot immediately think of the name. Often, he has similar problems in his written assignments. In addition, class discussions are particularly difficult for Sammie because he has trouble keeping track of who is talking and has difficulty contributing to the discussion. In reading, he also has some difficulty recognizing new vocabulary words, particularly those that have multiple syllables. When he comes to a word that he can't pronounce, he will either skip it or replace it with a similar-sounding word.

During his language services, his SLP works with him in the speech clinic. In the room, they review worksheets to

continued

improve his vocabulary, particularly for vocabulary words in upcoming chapters or stories, and work on his reading aloud. She also works with Sammie on writing stories from memory and using synonyms when he can't come up with the correct word. His classroom teachers also help by using word walls and allowing Sammie to use technology to aid his writing. Although these techniques help Sammie, he still has problems writing stories or with on-the-spot responses.

CASE QUESTIONS

1. What area of remediation would you target for Sammie?
2. In addition to oral language, what other skills would you, as the teacher, address?
3. Name and describe two types of oral language activities or techniques that you could use to remediate Sammie's language problems.

As you can see from Case 5.1, Sammie's language problems interfere not only in how he communicates, but in other academic areas as well. Oral language serves as the primary means of communication in most classrooms, particularly elementary ones, yet it is rarely part of the formal curriculum. Typically, teachers only address oral language skills when students have speech and language difficulties. At other times, teachers simply refer the child to an SLP for services. In this chapter, you will learn about oral language and methods that you can use to improve the oral language skills of students with HI, like Sammie.

5-1 The Importance of Oral Language

Oral language skills are important for several reasons. Oral language skills allow students to communicate effectively. Oral language skills are used on a daily basis in the classroom and are essential skills as they are the primary means by which teachers and students communicate for learning. Language skills are also useful as students answer teachers' questions about information that is learned, participate in classroom discussions, initiate and maintain conversations with peers and adults, and express ideas and feelings about various topics. Language skills have been linked to academic development, particularly in the areas of reading and written language (Catts and Kamhi 2005). Among bilingual students, oral language skills play a critical role in reading (Miller et al. 2006). Language difficulties can be discouraging for a student like Sammie, because the difficulties affect both him and those with whom he is trying to communicate. For students like Sammie, communicating with others can be a frustrating experience.

Oral language is not addressed directly in the classroom, despite its importance, for varying reasons, some of which include the following:

- Some believe that most children develop language skills naturally and do not require remediation.
- It may be difficult to determine language proficiency in children who are shy or withdrawn.
- Oral language skills may be difficult for teachers to break into subskills that can be taught effectively.
- Most schools emphasize academic skills and may not consider oral language as part of the academic curriculum.
- Most educators believe that children will simply outgrow language difficulties. (Polloway and Smith 2000)

Although emphasizing academic skills over oral language skills may be valid for prioritizing content taught in classrooms, oral language skills remain the primary means of communication in elementary classrooms. Whether teachers are giving verbal directions for completing worksheets or students are listening to a lecture on science, oral language skills form the basis of classroom communication. Because of the importance of these skills for school and beyond, language skills should be incorporated into the curriculum, especially for students with HI.

Oral Language and Its Components

Language is defined as "a socially shared code, or conventional system, that represents ideas through the use of arbitrary symbols and rules that govern combinations of these symbols" (Bernstein and Tiegerman-Farber 1997, p. 6). Not only are most people familiar with the written symbol *B* in the English language by its name *bee*, but most are also familiar with the letter–sound association of it: *ba*. The letter name and letter sound both represent a "shared code" that two people need to understand for effective communication. The same is true of spoken words and sounds (that is, phonemes) that we use.

Furthermore, to communicate, there must be a **sender** of a message, a **receiver** of the message, a **shared code** of understanding of the message, and a shared **intent** of the message (Kuder 2013), as illustrated in Figure 5.1. Typically, when two people are having a conversation, a sender and receiver are trying to convey a message. For these two to understand the message, both need to understand the shared code (that is, both speak English), and both should understand the subtle nuances of the message or intent of the message. For example, if you were speaking to a child as she pulled out a bag of cookies and began eating them, you might say, "Mmm . . . those cookies look good." If the child responded, "Yes, they are good," then there would be a misunderstanding as to the intent of your message. In this case, your intent was that you wanted to eat one of the cookies. Lastly, speech, although not necessary, is useful for communication to occur. Speech is "the neuromuscular act of producing sounds that are used in language" (Kuder 2013, p. 8).

Categories of Language

Language is typically broken down into two categories: expressive or receptive. **Expressive language** refers to spoken words that are produced from speech. **Receptive language** refers to an understanding or comprehension of spoken words. Children can have problems in either expressive or receptive language, or both. Expressive language problems can occur in a person's ability to pronounce phonemes, words, or sentences, or to express thoughts or feelings. One of the most common expressive language problems is with articulation. For people with articulation disorders, speech can be difficult to produce.

Students with receptive language difficulties typically have problems with tasks that involve the understanding of sounds, words, or sentences. For example, children

▶ **FIGURE 5.1**

Parts of Communication

Sender   Message   Receiver

may exhibit problems with (1) discriminating between similar phonemes (for example, *mat* and *nat*), (2) determining the correct ending of spoken words (for example, is it correct to say, "we goed to the store"?), (3) determining the correct sentence structure (for example, which would be better to say, "hitting Sue" or "Bill hit Sue"?), (4) knowing the correct meaning of spoken words (for example, "He was a precocious boy. What does precocious mean?"), or (5) understanding the rules of a conversation (for example, if you are having a conversation with another person and he begins to check his watch and speak less often, what might he want to do? Bring the conversation to a close?).

Components of Oral Language

In addition to classifying language problems as receptive and expressive, oral language is also divided into five components: phonology, morphology, syntax, semantics, and pragmatics. The five components of oral language are illustrated in Table 5.1.

Phonology refers to the system that defines each sound and the rules for how the sounds can be combined together. A **phoneme** "is the smallest linguistic unit of sound that can signal a difference in meaning" (Kuder 2013, p. 15). To determine if a sound is a different phoneme, simply change the phoneme in a word. If the sound creates a new word that you recognize, then the sound is a different phoneme from the original.

Morphology refers to how words are constructed from morphemes. A **morpheme** is "the smallest linguistic unit that has meaning" (ibid.). In other words, a morpheme is the smallest part of a word that has meaning and cannot be broken down further because it would lose its meaning. For example, *boy*, *run*, and *bat* are morphemes because each has meaning by itself. This type of morpheme is commonly referred to as a **free morpheme** because it can stand alone and has meaning. Another type of morpheme is called a **bound morpheme** (for example, *-ly*, *pre-*, and *-ed*). A bound morpheme only has meaning when connected to a free morpheme or another bound morpheme that is connected to a free morpheme. Prefixes (for example, *re-*), suffixes (*-tion*), past tenses (*-ed*), present tenses (*-ing*), possessives (*-'s*), and plurals (*-s* or *-es*) all represent examples of bound morphemes.

Syntax is the system of rules that help us determine the correct structure of words and phrases to form sentences. Syntax also guides how to transform sentences into new similar sentences or completely different sentences. For example, a child could say, "Billy and Natasha were playing with the toy," or "The toy was played with by Billy and Natasha." Both sentences have similar meaning, yet the sentence structure has changed slightly. If the child said, "Billy hit Natasha with the toy," then the sentence

TABLE 5.1 The Five Components of Language

Component	Expressive Example	Receptive Example
Phonology	Showing a child a picture of a rabbit, the child says the word (*rabbit*, not *wabbit*).	You ask the child to tell you if the words *bat* and *back* are the same or different.
Morphology	*I am kicking the ball. Yesterday, I ___ the ball.*	*Look, there is a wolf. Now look, there are two wolfes.* Is that correct?
Syntax	Use the words *tall*, *is*, *Matt*, *boy*, and *a*. Make a sentence using these words.	Does this sentence make sense? *The jumped in and boy swam.*
Semantics	*Which word means to jump very high?* (leap)	Show me what you would do if I asked you to *scrawl* something on a piece of paper.
Pragmatics	*I once saw a snake and it scared me. Have you ever seen something scary?*	*Can you circle the cat in the picture and draw a line under the dog?*

structure changed, as well as its meaning. As children grow older, they use syntactic rules to form new, complex sentences. Children begin to use interrogation and negation to form sentences to ask questions and state sentences in the negative.

Semantics refers to the meaning of language and is usually measured by looking at a student's use of vocabulary. Semantics also involves the set of rules that determine whether certain words can go with other words and still make sense. For example, because most teachers are adults, the *three-year-old teacher* would not make sense. Nor do the words *north cars rain and walk,* when arranged in this order. Although the words may be structurally correct (that is, noun plus verb), they simply do not make sense the way they are stated. Moreover, the *context* in which words are used helps us to understand the meaning of the sentence. Take the sentence *Roger was flying today.* Depending upon the context in which it is used (or what has already been said about it), it could mean that Roger flew on a plane, Roger ran really fast, or Roger was driving very fast. The meaning of the sentence depends upon whether we were talking about his flight, talking about seeing Roger at a track meet, or talking about seeing Roger at a car race.

The last element of language is pragmatics. **Pragmatics** refers to language use in social contexts "to express one's intentions" (Gleeson 2009, p. 22); it "includes . . . the rules that govern the use of language for social interaction" (Kuder 2013, p. 23). Pragmatics refers to the use of language during conversations, during narratives or stories, or in everyday situations to understand and make requests for our wants and needs. Pragmatics involves knowing the rules and skills for using language in social situations. Knowing when to take turns in a conversation, how to initiate and end a conversation, and when to ask questions for clarification are all important aspects of pragmatics. Moreover, because students use pragmatic skills in a wide variety of social situations, they will need to draw on their knowledge of language conventions (for example, sentence structure and grammar) as they adjust their speech to respond to the needs of specific audiences, purposes, and situations (IRA/NCTE 1996). (See the National Council of Teachers of English [NCTE] website at www.ncte.org for more on teaching standards relating to speech and writing.)

Implications for Diverse Students

Within the English language are dialectic traditions that vary by culture. African-American children who speak African-American English at home, for example, at school are confronted by expectations that they will comprehend and use different rules for the five components of language (Washington 2001). They may use nonstandard rules for syntax that hinder their communication skills in school. Further, African-American children from low-income households have learned different language traditions than those expected in traditional classroom learning—for instance, they may not be familiar with responding to "wh" questions (who, what, when, where, and why) (Washington 2001). As Washington suggested, students who are not familiar with the dominant language or dialect must be supported when using language for learning. Teachers should consider all five language components when examining the oral language skills of children, particularly students who have language difficulties due to disabilities, English language learner (ELL) status, and/or cultural variations.

5-2   Different Models of Language Development

The following four different models describe how language develops in children: behavioral, psycholinguistic, semantic-cognitive, and pragmatic. Although no one model seems to account for all language development, each model makes a contribution to our understanding of language development. A shortcoming in one particular model can often be explained by another model.

Behavioral Model

According to the behavioral approach, language is learned (Skinner 1957) like other skills and behaviors. That is, learning occurs through modeling, imitation, reinforcement, punishment, or extinction. As children learn sounds and words, reinforcers in the environment help to shape those sounds into words; when reinforcement is applied for an approximation or the correct pronunciation of words, those words are repeated. Slowly, children begin to acquire more phonemes and use them as they pronounce words. According to this theory, children's use of verbal language is reinforced, usually by natural reinforcers such as smiles, pats on the back, or other environmental or natural stimuli. Hence, as language skills are reinforced, they are used more frequently. Accordingly, teachers and parents can provide positive reinforcement to a young child if they are interested in increasing the child's use of language. For example, some parents do not give their child food or drink (reinforcer) until they use words like *juice* or *drink* (behavior).

Psycholinguistic Model

According to this model, all children are born with a universal learning mechanism called a **language acquisition device** (LAD). Analogous to RAM memory that is built into a computer, the LAD is "built in" and allows children to learn language easily. The LAD consists of the rules or general set of principles for sentence structure and a mechanism for discovering how this set of sentence structure rules applies to a child's particular language. According to this theory, the LAD explains why children are capable of learning language so quickly and why children can learn such large amounts of language within a short period of time.

Semantic-Cognitive Model

According to the semantic-cognitive model that came from the work of Jean Piaget and Lois Bloom, the language development of young children is very much dependent on their cognitive development. Similarly, as children acquire more experiences about a particular topic, their language about that topic becomes more complex and sophisticated. Therefore, when building vocabulary, teachers should focus on providing rich experiences from which children can draw meaning. In the same manner, concepts should be learned through rich experiences. In some cases, teachers may look for "learning moments" to stop the class and teach a particular concept. For example, if children find a caterpillar during recess, the teacher might encourage them to bring it back to the classroom and then teach children about the stages of metamorphosis as it applies to the life cycle of a butterfly.

Pragmatic Model

According to this model, children develop language through the need to communicate and interact with others. Children also learn that communication can direct the behavior of others in their environment to have their own needs met (Bruner 1983). Under this model, language develops through the more functional aspects of language such as making and understanding requests. Early on, as parents attempt to meet the needs of their children through communication, children begin to use language to have their needs met. Social interaction, particularly through language, is self-rewarding. With young children, parents very often adjust their language by using "motherese." Parents using "motherese" often speak to children slowly, in short, concrete sentences. In this way, parents adjust their language so that children can understand the intent of their communication.

5-3 Typical Language Development

In most children, language follows a natural course of development. Generally, we say that children have typical language development if they are following a developmental path defined by a set of language milestones aligned in a hierarchal order based upon age. However, milestones simply provide a range of skills and are more or less a general approximation of where a child's language should be by a certain age. The Learning Disabilities Association of America (1999) has defined milestones using the chart provided in Table 5.2. However, the authors of the chart also caution that children do not typically master all of the items in each box until reaching the upper age in the range.

How Do I Know When a Child Has a Language Problem?

Although milestones may provide an approximation of a child's language development, teachers should consider other factors to determine if language difficulties are problematic enough to warrant a referral for a speech and language evaluation (Kuder 2013). The first factor relates to academic difficulties that the child might be having. Is the child's oral language problem interfering with any other academic skills such as reading and writing? If so, the child's language problem may be contributing to these difficulties. The second factor concerns how the child's language problems affect his or her relationships and interactions with peers and others. Because language problems may interfere in the child's ability to communicate clearly, they could affect the child's ability to make friends and socialize. The third factor is the child's ability in the classroom to interact with the teacher or other professionals who work with the child. For example, if the child does not follow verbal directions or participate in discussions, this may hinder his academic performance. The fourth factor is a lack of progress in language and one of the previously mentioned areas. ELL students can present some of the same difficulties due to language differences (Swanson et al. 2004); thus, educators should use multiple and dynamic approaches to assess whether they are observing English language learning difficulties and/or more generalized language difficulties (Laing and Kamhi 2003). As a rule, if the child's language problem is getting progressively worse and the child has a problem in one or more of the three areas previously mentioned, then the child should be referred for a speech and language evaluation. ASHA provides useful resources on its website (www.asha.org), such as "Your Child's Communication Development: Kindergarten Through Fifth Grade," which details the speaking, listening, reading, and writing skills that students should have at each grade level.

Language Difficulties and Implications in the Classroom

Language disorders are especially prevalent among students with HI. Despite documented evidence of language problems, only 6 percent of these students receive services by an SLP (Gibbs and Cooper 1989). Whether in comprehension or production, language problems can prevent students from being successful in the classroom and may interfere with academic skills (Seidenberg 1997). In the classroom, these students may not feel comfortable in social situations and may not want to participate in groups. At other times, they may be reluctant to speak or may speak in a quiet voice when interacting with peers. ELL students and others for whom English is not

TABLE 5.2 Hearing and Talking Milestones

Hearing and Understanding	Speaking
Birth to 3 Months	**Birth to 3 Months**
Startles to loud sounds Quiets or smiles when spoken to Recognizes parent voice and quiets if crying Increases or decreases sucking behavior in response to sound	Makes pleasurable sounds (cooing and gooing) Cries differently for different needs Smiles at familiar faces
4 to 6 Months	**4 to 6 Months**
Moves eyes in direction of sounds Responds to changes in tone of voice Notices toys that make sounds Pays attention to music	Makes babbling sounds more speech-like (includes *p*, *b*, and *m*) Vocalizes excitement and displeasure Makes gurgling sounds when left alone and when playing with you
7 Months to 1 Year	**7 Months to 1 Year**
Enjoys games like peekaboo and patty-cake Looks in direction of sounds Listens when spoken to Recognizes words for common items like "cup," "shoe," "juice" Begins to respond to requests ("Come here," "Want more?")	Makes babbling sounds with both long and short groups of (consonant-vowel) sounds, such as "tata upup bibibibi" Uses speech or non-crying sounds to get and keep attention Imitates different speech sounds Has one or two words (*bye-bye, dada, mama*), although they may not be clear
1 to 2 Years	**1 to 2 Years**
Points to a few body parts when asked Follows simple commands and understands simple questions ("Roll the ball," "Kiss the baby," "Where's your shoe?") Listens to simple stories, songs, and rhymes Points to pictures in a book when named	Says more words every month Uses some one- or two-word questions ("Where kitty?" "Go bye-bye?" "What's that?") Puts two words together ("more cookie," "no juice," "mommy book") Uses many different consonant sounds of the beginning of words
2 to 3 Years	**2 to 3 Years**
Understands differences in meaning ("go/stop," "in/on," "big/little," "up/down") Follows two requests ("Get the book and put it on the table")	Has a word for almost everything Uses two- or three-word "sentences" to talk about and ask for things Speech is understood by familiar listeners most of the time Often asks for or directs attention to objects by naming them
3 to 4 Years	**3 to 4 Years**
Hears you when called from another room Hears television or radio at the same loudness level as other family members Understands simple "who, what, where, and why" questions	Hears you when called from another room People outside family usually understand child's speech Uses a lot of sentences that have four or more words Usually talks easily without repeating syllables or words
4 to 5 Years	**4 to 5 Years**
Pays attention to a short story and answers simple questions about it Hears and understands most of what is said at home and in school	Voice sounds clear like other children's Hears and understands most of what is said at home and in school (e.g., "I like to read my books") Communicates easily with other children and adults Says most sounds correctly except a few like *l, s, r, v, z, ch, sh, th* Uses the same grammar as the rest of the family

Source: Adapted from Learning Disabilities Association of America, "Speech and Language Milestone Chart" (http://www.ldonline.org/article/6313, 1999).

their primary language face similar learning challenges and consequences, regardless of whether they have a specific language impairment. Approximately 69 percent of ELL students at the middle and secondary levels are second- or third-generation immigrants who have been enrolled in American schools since at least kindergarten (Calderon 2007). Like students with HI who have language difficulties, ELL students need intensive support, as well as recognition of their language learning needs across several school years. Of course, some students are both HI and ELL students (Baca and Cervantes 2003). Just as annual individualized education program (IEP) goals should address language development for students with HI, the No Child Left Behind Act (2001) requires that schools make progress in developing the English language proficiency of all students.

For students with disabilities, language or communication may prove to be a difficult or frustrating task. Among students with mental retardation, language problems are considered one of the most detrimental aspects of adaptive behavior (Owens 1997). These students exhibit both quantitative and qualitative differences in their language that affect their communication and interactions with others. According to Bernstein and Tiegerman-Farber (1997), the language development of students with mental retardation before the mental age of 10 is similar to the development of nondisabled students; it differs only in **mean length of utterance** (for example, quantity of language). After the mental age of 10, the language of students with mental retardation differs qualitatively; their sentences are shorter, more concrete, and may be difficult to understand. According to Owens (1997) and Kuder (2013), some of the general difficulties that students with mental retardation exhibit include the following:

1. Problems understanding phonological rules
2. Delayed acquisition of morphological rules
3. Poor vocabulary
4. Lack of understanding of pragmatic rules

Problems in Phonology, Morphology, and Syntax

As noted, many students with HI have difficulties with phonological awareness, particularly in processing language sounds. Research has also shown that students who have difficulty with phonological awareness also have problems with reading. Students with HI have problems with morphological knowledge, particularly word parts. In addition, these morphological problems often occur with more complex or higher-level morphological components such as irregular word endings, noun derivatives, and understanding of prefixes (Wiig and Semel 1984). In regard to syntax, students with HI often use shorter, less complex sentences with fewer elaborations. In fact, their syntactic development may plateau at a certain age and may limit their use of sentence structure and sentence length (Kuder 2013).

Problems in Semantics and Pragmatics

As you could guess, students with HI also typically have problems in semantics, particularly in the area of expressive and receptive vocabulary. Often they use limited vocabulary, use more concrete vocabulary in conversations, and have difficulty understanding abstract or figurative language (Owens 1997). In the area of pragmatics, students with HI have delayed understanding of requests and commands, take a less active role in conversations, and show poor understanding of conversational rules (for example, taking turns, making significant contributions to a conversation, and using conversational repair strategies).

THINK BACK TO THE CASE

THINK BACK TO THE CASE **with Sammie...**

1.   What area of remediation would you target for Sammie?

As you have read, oral language encompasses five main areas: phonology, morphology, syntax, semantics, and pragmatics. From the case, you can see that Sammie has problems in word recall that could be considered an aspect of semantics. He also has trouble with tracking speakers during class discussions, which could be considered an aspect of pragmatics. These two areas would be appropriate for remediation.

5-4   Oral Language and Reading and Writing

The association between language problems of students with HI and reading and writing problems is complex; however, a link does exists between language disabilities and reading or written language disabilities (Friel-Patti 1999). Deficits in oral language could result in problems in reading and written language (Sturm and Clendon 2004), as illustrated by Table 5.3. Longitudinal studies have found that children who develop language impairments at an early age often have continued problems during adolescence in oral language, literacy, and academic achievement (Aram and Hall 1989). In particular, children who lack phonological awareness appear to have problems in early reading (Adams 1990). In addition to this link, researchers have found other skills, both oral language and print skills, that correlate with later reading skills. For example, the language skills of expressive vocabulary, oral language proficiency, and recall of sentences or stories are three skills that have been shown to predict reading achievement. All of this information points to the role that oral language skills, including phonological awareness, play in reading development, as well as other literacy aspects such as awareness of print (for example, concepts of print and letter identification) (Scarborough 2005).

As children get older, other skills beyond phonological skills contribute to decoding and comprehension. For example, students who have difficulty with semantic skills also have problems with vocabulary words and reading comprehension (Nation 2005). Other language skills such as listening comprehension are also related to reading skills. Students with poor listening comprehension also performed poorly on measures of reading comprehension (Nation and Snowling 1997). Moreover, weaknesses in certain aspects of oral language may lead to or be causally linked to problems in reading and written language (Nation 2005); students with language disabilities or spoken language delays often perform poorly in other areas, such as spelling and vocabulary (Snowling 2005).

THINK BACK TO THE CASE **with Sammie...**

2.   In addition to oral language, what other skills would you, as the teacher, address?

Because word recall could create problems for Sammie during written language, it might be a good area to address. In terms of written language, Sammie's word recall problems might create frustrating situations for him when he is asked to write responses to short-answer or essay questions on worksheets or tests, or to compose written essays or compositions. Keep these problems in mind as you read about oral language skills and techniques.

TABLE 5.3 Oral Language and Reading and Written Language

Language Domains	Implications for Reading	Implications for Writing
Phonology		
• Demonstrated delays in phonology (e.g., Berninger and Gans 1986; Vandervelden and Siegel 1999)	• Phonological skills are related to the development of phonemic awareness and decoding.	• Phonological skills are related to spelling development.
Morphology		
• Difficulties with production of morphemes (e.g., Binger and Light 2002; Kelford Smith, Thurston, Light, Parnes, and O'Keefe 1989; Sutton and Gallagher 1993)	• Knowledge of morphology is needed to comprehend sophisticated meaning changes in text.	• Morphology is critical to conventional writers who communicate subtle word meanings through text.
Semantics		
• Restricted experiences and background knowledge (e.g., Carlson 1981; Light 1997) • Vocabulary delays (e.g., Berninger and Gans 1986; Udwin and Yule 1990)	• Background knowledge and vocabulary are needed to effectively comprehend text. • Vocabulary is needed to communicate during a range of reading lessons.	• Background knowledge and vocabulary are central to content generation. • Categories of knowledge support retrieval of content. • Vocabulary is needed to communicate during a range of writing lessons.
Syntax		
• One- or two-word utterances predominate (e.g., Harris 1982; Udwin and Yule, 1990) • Prevalence of simple clause types, word order deviations, and word omissions (e.g., van Balkom and Welle Donker-Gimbrere 1996)	• Knowledge of sentence structure and sentence connections is needed to process the range of sentences encountered in text.	• Knowledge of sentence structure is needed to compose simple, compound, and complex sentences and to support cohesion between sentences.
Pragmatics		
• Impaired pragmatic skills (e.g., Light, Collier, and Parnes 1985a; O'Keefe and Dattilo 1992; von Tetzchner and Martinsen 1996) • Typically respondents (e.g., Basil 1992; Harris 1982; Light et al. 1985a; O'Keefe and Dattilo 1992; von Tetzchner and Martinsen 1996) • Restricted range of speech acts (e.g., Light, Collier, and Parnes 1985b; Udwin and Yule 1991)	• Pragmatic skills are related to understanding the author's intention. • Pragmatic skills are needed to understand classroom participation structures of reading activities.	• Pragmatic skills are related to understanding the audience. • Writing requires children to generate text independently, often with an absent audience. • Pragmatic skills are needed to understand classroom participation structures of writing activities. • Children ask questions and comment on peers' compositions.
Discourse		
• Greater number of communication experiences with conversational discourse (e.g., Nelson 1992) • Restricted experiences with classroom discourse (for example, narrative discourse or expository discourse) (e.g., Nelson 1992; Sturm et al. 2003a)	• Knowledge of the discourse structures of text is needed to support text comprehension. • Knowledge of the discourse structures of reading lessons (e.g., small group reading, large group discussion) is needed to participate effectively in the classroom.	• Knowledge of the discourse structures of text is needed to organize a coherent composition. • Knowledge of the discourse structures of writing lessons (e.g., peer and teacher conferences, large group lessons, sharing) is needed to participate effectively in the classroom.

Source: Adapted from J. Strum and S. Clendon, "Augmentative and Alternative Communication, Language, and Literacy: Fostering the Relationship," *Topics in Language Disorders* 24(1):77, 2004.

5-5 Strategies and Techniques for Teaching Oral Language Skills

Using the four previously discussed models, the following are some basic principles for teaching oral language. These practices can and should be used both when directly teaching language skills and when teaching for content learning, as oral language skill is essential for learning and using content knowledge (Moje et al. 2004).

1. From the behavioral perspective, use imitation and modeling for the proper use of language. Provide a sentence or word, and ask the child to say it. Provide positive reinforcement in the form of a smile or praise if the student says the word or sentence correctly. If a student is using incorrect syntax in class, the teacher should simply rephrase aloud what the student was trying to say. For example, the response to a student who says, "We goes to the car now?" should be "Yes, we are going to the car now."

2. From a semantic-cognitive approach, teach language skills in context whenever possible. If you are discussing concepts or vocabulary, teach them in context. For example, if teaching students about different animals, teach them by visiting the zoo.

3. From the psycholinguistic perspective, teach rules for using language. If teaching sentence structure, teach students first to differentiate between complete and incomplete forms of sentences (for example, *She in the yard played* versus *she played in the yard*), then to finish partially completed sentences (for example, *The dog ate the ___*), and, finally, to produce their own complete sentences.

4. From the pragmatic approach, teach language within a group dynamic. Use other children as models for the correct use of language and to encourage the target child to participate with others during small-group discussions. When using groups, be careful that you promote tolerance for language differences among others in the group. In fact, exposure to language differences makes others more tolerant and open (Wilby 2004).

5. Use games or other activities to teach target skills. Students enjoy learning and are more engaged when they are taught using games or other motivating language activities.

6. Focus on expressive and receptive language skills. Language involves more than just speaking words and sentences. Receptive skills are often overlooked and include following oral directions, listening for new vocabulary words, reading a story and having the students predict the ending, playing listening games (for example, Simon Says), or playing a song and having the children listen for verses to sing aloud.

7. When teaching younger children, gain their attention before beginning an activity, and use tactile and fun materials to maintain their attention throughout the activity.

8. Use sufficient wait-time when you ask questions and after a student responds to your question (Rowe 1986). Allow at least three seconds of wait-time after asking a question and before prompting a student for more information (Rowe 1986), particularly for young children (Medcalf-Davenport 2003). Wait-time allows children time to consider the question, search their long-term memory for information, and formulate an appropriate response. When teachers wait three seconds or more after asking a question, the amount and quality of discussion increases

(Roberts and Zody 1989). Similarly, when teachers wait three seconds or more after the student has responded to the question, there are also improvements in the student's use of language and logic (Rowe 1986).

9. Use structured lesson plans that include aspects of Direct Instruction. If teaching a new skill, model the proper response, use guided practice so students can perform the skill while you provide feedback, and then assess by having the child demonstrate the skill independently.

10. Teach for generalization. If children are taught a language skill in school, have them practice the skill for homework and report back when and where they used the skill.

Improving Language Skills in the Classroom

To improve oral language skills, children must be given opportunities to practice and use the skills that they have been taught. Often, classrooms are tightly controlled environments in which students are expected to work quietly with very little interaction with other students. However, scheduled breaks during the day (for example, lunch or recess) could serve as opportunities for students to practice and use language skills. Throughout the day, teachers could use routines as opportunities for students to practice communication skills (Creaghead 1992). Many of these routines are typically accompanied with scripts that students use to communicate. Routines include the following:

1. Beginning the day
2. Transition between subjects
3. Lunch
4. Recess
5. Free choice time
6. Ending the day
7. Classroom lessons
8. Reading groups
9. Tests
10. Getting, doing, and returning homework
11. Working independently
12. Studying from workbooks

During these times, students could be taught the scripts (that is, a set of typical communication skills) that could be used on a daily basis. For example, as students enter the classroom at the beginning of the day, they should say, "hello," and use other appropriate greetings for the teacher such as, "It looks like a cold/hot day today, Mrs. King." These routines provide cues for students to use communication skills. Of course, teachers may have to use more explicit prompts to get students to use communication skills (Creaghead 1992). Over time, many of these prompts could be phased out.

Students from underrepresented communities in the school and school district, including those with limited English proficiency, can benefit from the literacy instructional activities previously described, merged with critical literacy practices. For example, they can be asked to use language to describe experiences unique to their identity group (Herrero 2006). Examples include discussing family activities, community traditions, or ways in which American society reacts to their group(s) (Harry, Klingner, and Hart 2005).

Methods and Strategies Spotlight

Supporting Speech and Language in the Classroom

If possible, classroom-based language interventions should be a collaborative effort between the SLP and the classroom teacher. A collaborative effort provides advantages for everyone involved in the class. SLPs often can advise teachers on what materials and methods to use to help students develop language skills. Classroom teachers can provide an ideal teaching environment for the SLP because of the ample supply of models (that is, students who can correctly use language skills) and because the classroom can provide plenty of interaction among students. In other words, the classroom is a natural environment for language development to occur.

The following template is useful for teaching communication lessons in the classroom (Dodge 2004):

Target skill: Identify a specific target skill. Use a previous assessment to help identify a specific language skill or language-related social skill the student needs to develop.

Opening question: Use an opening or intriguing question to gain students' attention. This question should be tied into the content or activities of the lesson. For example, "You are busy working on a science worksheet and you want to know what the term *igneous* means. What could you do to find the information?"

Model: The teacher should model the appropriate script (that is, the language and actions). Show students a few different examples of correct and appropriate responses to this situation (for example, how to ask the teacher a question).

Role-play: As with learning any new skill, students should practice. One of the best ways to simulate reality is to practice the skill through a role-play scenario. Pair up students and allow them to practice role-playing the example.

Carry over: Plan with students how they could be reminded to use their script. In some cases, the teacher could cue the student to use the script. In the same case, the teacher could use a nonverbal cue, such as a raised finger, or a verbal cue such as "wait and think" to remind students to use the appropriate script before responding.

Wrap-up: During wrap-up, ask students to think about one time during the day that they will be able to use their new communication skills. Ask them to remember the situation and script to be used during that time, and state that you will check with them tomorrow to see how well they used their new communication skills.

Challenge and follow-up: Challenge your students to use the new skills in the agreed-upon situation and in other situations. Follow up by checking to see if students actually used the targeted communication skills and if they need to make modifications in the script that they used.

Creating Opportunities for Students to Use Communication Skills

Teachers should try to *create* opportunities for student interaction by forming cooperative learning groups during class. As discussed in Chapter 2, cooperative learning involves having students work in small groups of three to five students. Each student works toward a common goal, and each student is individually accountable as well. During cooperative learning, students are interdependent (Johnson, Johnson, and Holubec 1990; Putnam 1993) upon one another to complete the task and achieve the goal.

The following is an example of a cooperative learning lesson that encourages language-based interactions. The teacher has assigned students to write a report about a dinosaur and then present it to the class (**goal interdependence**). They need to present where the dinosaur lived, its diet, and its characteristics, an illustration, along with other facts. One group chose Tyrannosaurus. Each student is assigned a role (**role interdependence**). Nathan was designated the illustrator; Jacob, the researcher; Sammie, the writer; and Kaytlyn, the presenter. All students need to complete their parts with the help of others. Jacob needs to research (**task interdependence**) the dinosaur with the help of others. Jacob might begin looking on the Internet for information and then ask the others in the group to go to the library to find information. Before Sammie can write the report, he needs the research from his classmates. Jacob needs to use the computer for research (**resource interdependence**), but must share it with Nathan to find pictures to illustrate and with Sammie to write the report. Each student receives a grade for individual contribution, and the group will also receive a group grade for the report and presentation (**reward interdependence**).

Listening Skills

Language, like other academic areas, should be taught to students with HI. Some students may require intense instruction, whereas other students may simply need direct instruction in language skills only when they encounter problems. When teachers consider language skill instruction, they should think broadly to include language skills such as listening skills as well as more traditional language skills such as words and word endings.

Because most of the information given in classrooms, particularly elementary, is in verbal form, listening skills are important for students to learn. Listening requires focusing attention on the speaker, selecting the important parts of the message, and remembering those parts. Listening is more than just hearing; it involves processing and understanding the message. Because these skills are so important, they should be taught directly, particularly to young children.

When providing directions to a child, Wiig and Semel (1984) suggest strategies such as asking the child to *repeat the steps overtly* and *rehearse* the directions by repeating them silently, *printing* critical words from the directions on cards that the child can use while carrying out the task, or having the child *write* them down as the directions are given aloud.

To aid students with HI in remembering components of effective listening skills, use the acronym in Box 5.1.

A teacher can also facilitate the effectiveness of giving directions to a student by (1) gaining the child's *full attention* prior to giving any directions, (2) maintaining *eye contact* while giving directions, (3) keeping directions *short* and straightforward, (4) using *vocabulary* that is commensurate with the child's cognitive level, (5) *pointing* to objects

---

BOX 5.1

PLAN to Listen

P **P**ay close attention to what is being said.

L **L**isten to the message and remember the steps or parts.

A **A**sk questions if you don't understand.

N **N**ame the steps or parts of the message.

Say them again to yourself or write them down.

Whole Class Directions

Use the following suggestions when providing directions to the entire class:

- Begin by gaining everyone's attention. Prompt students to stop working and watch you. Use verbal prompts such as, "Eyes on me" or "Watch and listen."
- Do not give directions until you have everyone's attention, even if that means standing quietly in front of the class until everyone is watching you.
- Provide verbal reinforcement for students who are paying attention (for example, "Good, Lashonda is watching me and paying attention").
- Write the directions on the board prior to giving them verbally and then point or refer back to the directions as you give them.
- Be very explicit and provide examples to illustrate each point in your directions.
- Before students begin the task, ask them if they have any questions.
- After students begin the task, monitor to make sure they are following your directions correctly. If they are not following the steps, stop everyone and review or model the directions again.

or pictures to help the student understand parts of the directions, when appropriate, (6) *modeling* what the child should do, (7) asking the child to *show* you what to do, (8) *asking* the child if he or she understands the directions or has any questions, and (9) using *cues* to prompt the child to the most important parts of the directions (for example, "The most important part to remember is . . ." or "The three things you need to remember are . . ."). When providing directions to the *entire class*, the suggestions in Box 5.2 might be useful.

Listening Activities

The following listening games and activities could be used to strengthen students' listening skills:

- **Teacher Says** This game is similar to Simon Says. The teacher asks students to complete different motor skills, such as jumping up, walking around the room, or jumping up and down. Students have to listen closely and should perform only those skills that are preceded by the words *Teacher says* (for example, "Teacher says, touch your toes"). The purpose of this game is to train the students to listen to and follow your directions.
- **Same or Different** Students listen to the teacher read a pair of words to determine whether they are the same or different. Begin with words that are discernibly different when spoken (for example, rock and ball); gradually use word pairs that are similar (for example, ran and rat).
- **Last Is First** The teacher says a word aloud and the child says a new word that begins with the last letter (for example, *bag, girl, lost, top, pan, now*).
- **Scrambled Story** The teacher reads the scrambled-up parts of a story and asks students to put the parts in the correct order.
- **Story Chain** Elementary students love this activity. Start by giving students a story starter such as, "One day I was flying my rocket home and . . ." Next, ask a child to add a part to the story. Once the first child adds a part, another child does so, and so on, until everyone has participated in the story.
- **Word of the Day** Teachers choose a "word of the day" for students, particularly students in secondary classes. Students then try to use the word correctly in as

many different sentences as possible. Students who can correctly use the word in the most sentences and can use the word in the best sentence (that is, provide the best example for use of the word) are awarded prizes.

- **Oral Reports** Older students can present information to other students in small groups or in class. These reports can be tied into content-area subjects, such as science, history, or literature. Working in small groups, each student is responsible for completing a portion of a report and then presents that portion verbally to others in the group or to the entire class.
- **TV Newscasts** Older students listen to an evening newscast. The students write down three to five unknown words from the newscast, bring them to school, and find out the meaning of the words from either a dictionary, a student workgroup, or the teacher. The student then has to use the term correctly in a sentence.

Directed Listening-Thinking Activity

To improve listening comprehension, teachers should use a directed listening-thinking activity (DLTA) (Cramer 2004). This activity can be used whenever the teacher reads or explains content to students. Using a DLTA, teachers tap into students' prior knowledge about the topic to make predictions, check for comprehension while reading or explaining, and discuss or elaborate on the topic after teaching.

The DLTA has the following three main components:

1. **Before listening**, teachers establish a purpose for listening. Teachers ask questions about the topic and elicit predictions based upon student input.
2. **During listening**, teachers periodically stop the activity (such as lecturing or reading) to ask students questions about what they are being told. These questions involve checking the accuracy of predictions and then modifying the predictions or confirming the accuracy of these predictions based upon supporting evidence.
3. **After listening**, follow-up activities are used to review vocabulary, check comprehension, or check the accuracy of predictions.

Phonemic Skills

Phonemic awareness is the understanding that spoken words are made up of phonemes. Although phonemic awareness deals solely with sounds or phonemes, it is not the same skill as phonics (Rasinski and Padak 2004). **Phonics** refers to letter and sound correspondence. Phonics links the written symbol with phonemes. Phonemic awareness is the precursor to phonics and has been identified as an important pre-reading skill. Before children can understand sounds with their corresponding written symbols (phonics), they must first learn to recognize, remember, segment, and blend phonemes. (Chapter 5 also presents phonemic awareness activities for students.) Following are several phonemic awareness skills that Yopp and Yopp (2000) have identified for students to master:

- **Sound Matching** In sound matching games, students determine if two words that are spoken begin (or end) with same sound. Do *pass* and *pot* begin with same sound? Do *sat* and *tap* have the same middle sound? Do *fat* and *cot* have the same end sound?
- **Sound Isolation** In sound isolation activities, children identify the sound that a word or words begin with. What sound do you hear at the beginning of the word *mat*? At the end of the word *man*? In the middle of the word *fast*?

- **Sound Substitution** In sound substitution activities, children substitute a sound within a word. What word would you have if you changed the *pa* in *past* to *ma*? If you changed the *nd* in *hand* to *rp*?
- **Sound Blending** In sound blending activities, children pair parts of words to make new words. What word would you have if you put these sounds together: *par- ty*? *man – a – ger*? *f – a – st*?
- **Sound Segmentation** In sound segmenting activities, children segment letters or word parts into sounds. Which parts do you hear in the word *cost*? What sounds make up the word *cat*? How many different sounds do you hear in *sat*?
- **Sound Deletion** In sound deletion activities, children tell the teacher parts of words. Say the word *baseball* without the *base*. Say the word *power* without the *er*. What sound do you hear in *will* that is missing in *ill*? What would be left if the *r* sound were missing in *track*?

Teachers should make these skills into games and activities that students can enjoy (Yopp and Yopp 2000). See which students can get the most correct, or pair students up and see which pair can get the most correct. Some tasks are easier than others, so begin with easier tasks and move on to more difficult ones. For example, sound matching using the initial phoneme is easier than blending phonemes to produce words. If students are having problems, say the words more slowly and exaggerate the target sound that you want students to practice (for example, LLLLLLLittle). In some cases, students can tap out or clap the number of sounds in words to help them discriminate.

Understanding Word Parts

When teaching word parts or morphemes, remember that there are two types of morphemes: bound and free. These are often taught to students as part of spelling or language arts, and both free and bound morphemes can be taught to students with disabilities. Recall that a free morpheme can stand on its own as a word (boy, bat, can), and a bound morpheme only has meaning when attached to a free morpheme (-ly, -s, -ed, -est, anti-). Bound morphemes can change the meaning of words when added to them. Wiig and Semel (1984) have categorized bound morphemes into three groups: prefixes, suffixes, and infixes:

1. *Prefixes* include *sub-* and *trans-*. In American English, the most common prefixes are *un-, in-, dis-,* and *non-*.
2. *Suffixes* include *-er, -ly, -ed, -ness, -ing, -ate,* and *-tion*.
3. *Infixes* are words that have been changed by inserting or adding a morphological element, such as an affix. An *inflectional affix* adds a particular grammatical function to a word without changing the category of that word, but results in a variant of the word. Examples of inflectional affixes include noun plurals (*-s* or *-es*), possessives (*'s*), present progressive (*-ing*), and past tense (*-ed*).

Teaching children with disabilities about free morphemes is important because understanding word parts can help them break down spoken and written words to pronounce them or understand their meaning. Infixes with inflectional endings (for example, *-es, -ing, -ed*) should be taught first because they tend to be the easiest to learn. Next, teach the affixes through activities where children learn the affix, the meaning, and how to use them with real words. If possible, tie these activities in with reading or writing affixes in context.

Different sources will list common prefixes and suffixes; however, lists both overlap and differ. In Tables 5.4 and 5.5, we have combined different lists to provide a list of prefixes and suffixes to teach students with HI.

TABLE 5.4 List of Recommended Prefixes

Prefix	Meaning	Examples
ab-	from; away	absolve; abnormal
de-	opposite; remove	deflate; demote
dis-	opposite; not	disgrace; disagree
en-, em-	cause to; into	emboss; enclosure
in-	in; not	install; indirect
mis-	bad; wrong	mistake, misplace
non-	not	nonresident; nonprofit
pre-	earlier than; before	prepare; preamble
re-	again; backward	recount; rewind
sub-	under; lesser	subject, submit
super-	above; greater	supersonic; supervisor
trans-	across; to change	transatlantic; transplant
un-	not	unskilled; uncover

TABLE 5.5 List of Recommended Suffixes

Suffix	Meaning	Examples
-able, -ble	having much skill at; capable	acceptable; credible
-al	relating to; action	personal; rehearsal
-er	one that performs; comparative	reporter; hotter
-ful	full of	peaceful
-ic	relating to	idiotic
-ion, -tion	act; process; condition	demolition; perfection
-ious, -ous	full of; having	cautious; poisonous
-ize	cause to be	visualize; specialize
-less	lacking	careless; joyless; homeless
-ly	like; similar	lovely; motherly
-ment	state of; process	amazement; involvement
-ty, -ity	condition of; degree	safety; rarity
-y	made of; state of	muddy; truly

Teaching Syntax and Morphology

Along with morphological skills, syntax is another area of oral language that may be a concern for students with disabilities (Polloway and Smith 2000). The following suggested guides for teaching morphological and syntactic aspects of oral language might be useful to cover (Wiig and Semel 1984):

1. Regular noun plurals
2. Noun–verb agreement of singular and plural regular nouns and verbs in present tense
3. Regular noun possessives in the singular and plural forms (for example, *cat, cats*)
4. Irregular noun plurals (*leaf, leaves*)
5. Irregular noun possessives (*geese's food*)
6. Regular past tense of verbs (*walked*)
7. Irregular past tense of verbs (*fall, fell, fallen; eat, ate, eaten*)
8. Adjectival inflections for comparative and superlative forms (*big, bigger, biggest; good, better, best*)

9. Noun and adverb derivation (*sing* to *singer*; *slow* to *slowly*)
10. Prefixing (*write, rewrite*)

When teaching syntax or sentence structure, begin with short, simple, direct sentences before moving on to more complex ones. Use concrete objects or pictures to illustrate sentences that students are having difficulty understanding. Provide plenty of examples for students to understand the new sentence structure. Wiig and Semel (1984) suggest that teachers use at least ten examples when teaching sentence formation. For example, because children with disabilities have difficulty understanding passive language (for example, "The ball was thrown by Judy"), you may need to present many examples that include illustrations or stick figures drawn on the board to help students understand passive sentences. Once students learn a new sentence structure, use drill and practice (with feedback) to ensure that they master it. After students understand your examples of the new sentence structure, you can ask them to choose (discriminate) between two or three sentences to choose the new form. Once they can do this, you can ask students to give you examples of new sentences that they created. Often, oral language activities can be paired with written exercises.

Building Vocabulary and Improving Word Find

Because students with HI learn vocabulary at a slower rate than nondisabled students (Baker, Simmons, and Kame'enui 1998), teachers need to use a variety of techniques and activities to remediate deficits in this area. When teaching vocabulary, here is the suggested order of activities:

1. Introduce vocabulary words in context (for example, "*Erosion* is wearing down the granite on the statue").
2. Provide students with definitions that use examples in context. For example, you might use *erosion* in the following sentence: "The rain caused erosion that took the dirt down the hill and left a bare, muddy bank."
3. Use pictures or real-life examples to illustrate the vocabulary word.
4. Whenever possible, present multiple examples so that students master the word before introducing non-examples. For example, present examples of erosion (such as pictures of the Grand Canyon, mudslides, and smooth granite surfaces like the Washington Monument) before presenting non-examples (such as the sun fading the color on a piece of paper or cloth).
5. Relate vocabulary words to students' prior knowledge to make deep connections during learning.

Other teaching techniques include using semantic maps, mnemonic strategies, or visual imagery, and teaching children to categorize items.

Semantic Classification and Categorization

To improve storage of information, students can cluster information in semantically related categories (Wiig and Semel 1984)—in other words, they can list similar words under one category. Students can be given review activities in which they have to categorize information such as parts of a cell, different types of biomes, or different types of cells. While lecturing, the teacher can present information that has been organized in different categories for students to record in their notes. Teachers should explain why items in a category are related and how, discussing the similarities and differences. In early grades, teachers could ask students to categorize pictures and, in later years, words.

▼ **FIGURE 5.2**

Word Map for Chlorophyll

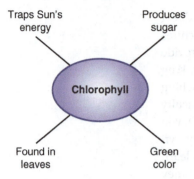

▼ **FIGURE 5.3**

Mnemonic Method for the
Vocabulary Word *Chlorophyll*

Phyllis Green making sugar
cookies.

▼ **FIGURE 5.4**

Visual Imagery for *Decibel*

Jenny Solomon/Shutterstock Images

Semantic Maps. A *semantic map* (Bos and Anders 1990) or *word map* (Schwartz and Raphael 1985) is a type of map that helps students to understand a vocabulary word and its characteristics. The visual display shows how words are related. To create a map, students use a vocabulary word and related words. A vocabulary word is placed in the center circle and then the students use words to describe the concept by drawing lines to it (see Scanlon, Duran, Reyes, and Gallego 1992). When students first create word maps, it is best to keep them simple (Fig. 5.2).

Mnemonic Strategies. Keyword and mnemonic methods are used to help students remember new information such as vocabulary because they link new words or concepts to familiar words and images (Mastropieri, Scruggs, and Fulk 1990; Scruggs and Mastropieri 1990; Uberti, Scruggs, and Mastropieri 2003). By linking unfamiliar vocabulary with familiar information, the vocabulary words become more meaningful and concrete and thus can be more easily remembered. For example, to remember the word and function of chlorophyll (a green pigment that makes sugars) students might pair up a picture of Phyllis Green making sugar cookies (Fig. 5.3).

Visual Imagery. Visual imagery is another effective technique to increase recall of vocabulary, particularly if paired with keywords or mnemonic techniques. Using this technique, teachers provide students with a vocabulary word, a definition, and a keyword. Using imagery, students form an image in their minds of the keyword interacting with the definition. For example, if students are trying to study what the term *decibel* (a unit for intensity of sound) means and are given the keyword *bell,* they might imagine a large bell ringing so intensely that their eardrums are about to burst (Fig. 5.4).

Word Find Activities

Children with HI often have word retrieval problems. These problems can plague students well into adulthood. How information is stored in long-term memory often determines how well it can be retrieved. Remembering information from memory depends upon three things: acquisition, retention, and retrieval (Norman 1982). Acquisition refers to how you acquire or learn information. If you never really hear important information, then you have not really acquired it. The second component, retention, relates to how well you studied or learned the important information. Once you learned the information, did you rehearse or practice it? If so, you are more likely to recall it. Another way to retain information, and probably the best way, is to relate or link new information with information that is already stored in your long-term memory. Linking new information this way will provide more cues for you to recall it later. The last component, retrieval, refers to cues that are present when you need to recall information. If the cues, keywords, are present at the time of recall, then you are more likely to be able to retrieve information. Using these three components will not only help you recall more information, but will help your students as well.

Teachers can use the following techniques to help students with disabilities retrieve information more quickly and more successfully (Wiig and Semel 1984):

1. Help a student retrieve a word (for example, *armadillo*) by providing *word cues* that belong to the same semantic class (type of animal with a hard covering).

2. Use phonemic cues to assist students. The teacher can say or "mouth" the first phoneme or syllable of the word.

3. Use associative cues (for example, *army*) or synonyms to help the student retrieve the target word (*military*).

4. Provide multiple cues to help the student retrieve the target word. For example, if the child were trying to retrieve the word *tanker*, the teacher could say, "Is it a ship, barge, or boat?"

5. Provide cues that are used to study the word to help with retrieval of a target word. For instance, if the child learned that a *pathogen* is an *agent* that causes a communicable *disease*, the teacher can cue the student by asking, "What is an *agent* of *disease*?" or state, "It has to do with a communicable *disease*."

THINK BACK TO THE CASE with Sammie ...

3. *Name and describe two types of oral language activities or techniques that you could use to remediate Sammie's language problems.*

As you have just read, teachers can provide students with word cues to assist them in word recall problems. As was discussed in this case, the teacher can use a word bank to help a student like Sammie. Teachers can also use semantic or mnemonic strategies that are discussed later in the chapter.

Improving Pragmatic Skills

As stated previously, students must be given opportunities to practice oral language skills in the classroom. Teachers can create opportunities by changing the response format of assignments (for example, from written to oral presentation) or by creating activities that encourage students to use oral language skills with others. For example, after reading a passage, teachers can ask students to tell orally what they read instead of having them write a summary. Or they have students do oral reports or presentations to demonstrate their knowledge of content.

Another activity that allows students to practice oral language skills with other students is *role-playing*. There are two types of role-playing exercises: individual and interactive. During **individual role-playing**, students must take a side or play a role. In some cases, students can practice new language skills (that is, scripts) that they have recently learned. Typically, one student practices the skills with another student. For example, two children could role-play using persuasion to voice their feelings about something that they feel strongly about—say, water conservation, recycling, or attending a rally. The target child could be on one side, and the other child could play the role of someone with an opposing view. The second role-play type is **interactive role-playing**. In this type of role-playing, a few students assume a role and act out or improvise it. If the subject is a social skill, students could play roles in which the target student responds using the newly learned social skill. For example, a child could practice giving instructions to a group of students about how to play a new game, or an older student could explain to others how to complete an assignment.

Conversation Skills. As children grow older, they learn the art of "holding a conversation." Conversation, like other aspects of language, has rules that most children learn incidentally. The rules for having a successful conversation include taking turns when speaking, choosing an agreed-upon topic, contributing bits of information about the topic, listening to the other person's contributions to the topic, and using appropriate nonverbal cues. Nonverbal cues that are used in conversations provide feedback to the speaker and listener about how the conversation is progressing and whether to end the conversation. These cues include facial expressions, eye contact, and distance between the speaker and listener. If one person becomes distracted or does not understand what the other person is saying, either one can use **conversational repair strategies** to get the conversation back on topic or to change topics. Conversational repair strategies include asking for clarification, asking the other person to repeat something, or asking for more information (Konefal and Folks 1984). When the conversation is not progressing or is coming to a close, either party can provide verbal and nonverbal cues to end the conversation, such as looking at a watch, yawning, or ending eye contact, or one party may simply say, "I have to get going."

If children with disabilities are experiencing problems with conversations, teachers may have to teach rules explicitly and then practice those rules through role-playing.

Discussion Skills. Very often, teachers hold class discussions hoping to provide an engaging format in which students will make educated contributions and learn from the knowledge that is shared. However, for a lot of teachers, class discussions often do not succeed because students fail to listen or make meaningful contributions, or they are distracted by irrelevant activities occurring in the class. Likely, two key factors to the success or demise of a class discussion are the topic of discussion and how well students prepare (including having knowledge about the topic). Choosing familiar and interesting topics can increase the chances that the discussion will be successful. During discussions, students must use active listening to focus on the topic and follow who is speaking. Active listening involves leaning slightly forward toward the speaker, maintaining eye contact, and providing nonverbal feedback to the speaker, such as nodding one's head to agree and providing verbal feedback like, "Yes, I agree" or "I see how you could feel that way."

One technique that has been shown to be effective at increasing student participation is the SLANT strategy (Box 5.3) (Ellis 1989; also see Paxton-Burrsma and Walker 2008 for more information). Students first *sit up* in an upright but relaxed position. Students then *lean forward* slightly in their chairs. The next step, *activate your thinking,* reminds students to activate the discussion by asking clarifying questions such as, "What is this about?" or "What do I need to remember?" As students are completing this step, they also need to answer their question, and ask the teacher questions about what they don't understand. The *name key information* step cues students answer the teacher's questions, share their ideas or comments, and add to other students' statements. The last step, *track the talker,* cues students to keep their eyes on the teacher as he or she speaks and to look at other students as they talk.

Training for the SLANT strategy occurs through the following steps (Deshler et al. 1981; see also Lidgus and Vassos 1996):

BOX 5.3

SLANT Strategy

S **S**it up
L **L**ean forward
A **A**ctivate your thinking
N **N**ame key information
T **T**rack the talker

1. The teacher introduces the SLANT strategy and students discuss the rationale or positive outcomes of using SLANT, discuss when and where to use the strategy, and discuss what happens to students who choose to participate versus those who choose not to participate.

2. The teacher describes the five steps that make up the strategy.

3. The teacher models the strategy steps for students. During modeling, the teacher demonstrates the steps and slowly involves the students in the demonstration while providing feedback about their performance.

4. In the verbal practice step, the teacher rehearses the strategy with students and then assesses each student for mastery of the steps.

5. In the practice step, students target an academic class in which they will use the SLANT strategy, and they observe one another while providing feedback to each other.

6. Students are assessed on their knowledge of the SLANT steps. The teacher instructs students to apply the SLANT strategy to a new class and periodically checks to see how they used the strategy.

CASE 5.2   Manolo's Concussions

Introduction

...orked through the first case in this chapter, ...able addressing issues in Case 5.2. In this ...fourth-grade student who has receptive ...stly in the area of listening skills.

...orn to Julia and Mario Raba in Slidell, ...orks about 30 minutes away at a university and ...ks in town at a restaurant. His parents are from Cali, ...olumbia, and moved to Texas shortly before Manolo was born. Both still speak Spanish in the home and use broken English when they have to communicate with the school.

Manolo attends the local elementary school and is in Mrs. Katy Kanner's fourth grade. Manolo's first few years at the elementary school were a struggle for him because he had difficulty with many aspects of literacy, such as reading, spelling, and written language. His poor verbal skills hindered his academic growth during these early years and he received additional instruction in an after-school program where teachers worked on verbal and written skills with him.

His parents blame his learning problems on early brain injuries from a car accident during which Manolo suffered his first concussion and a second concussion he had when he fell of the roof of their shed (he had climbed up on the roof to retrieve his drone plane, which had gotten stuck there due to his careless maneuvering). Manolo's pediatrician also diagnosed him with attention-deficit/hyperactivity disorder (ADHD), and he currently takes medication. His parents believe that this diagnosis of ADHD is backed up by his teachers' claims that Manolo never seems to pay attention.

In third grade, Manolo was formally diagnosed with learning disabilities, mostly due to his poor language skills. His language evaluation by Ms. Pena found that he had several areas of concern relating to receptive vocabulary and language, listening comprehension, and written language deficits. In addition, Manolo was found to have difficulty following multistep verbal directions. Ms. Pena has been working with Manolo for the past year and a half, but he has made little noticeable progress.

Likewise, in Mrs. Kanner's fourth-grade class, Manolo has made slow progress. Mrs. Kanner and the special education teacher, Mr. Ryden Davis, meet frequently to discuss how to improve his literacy skills. To accommodate Manolo's difficulties paying attention, Mrs. Kanner has tried various techniques such as moving his desk closer to her and calling his parents on several occasions, but these efforts often fail. Mr. Davis pulls Manolo into his resource room to provide one-on-one tutoring to help Manolo with literacy assignments, but it is still a struggle to get him to keep up with his classes.

Mr. Davis has also found that Manolo has difficulty following verbal directions, understanding complex vocabulary, and expressing his thoughts during verbal discussions on topics from science and social studies. Mr. Davis has been working on syntax and grammar to help him write compound sentences and short essays, but Manolo continues to struggle to get his ideas down on paper and/or writes run-on sentences.

CASE QUESTIONS

1. What specific skill would you try to remediate first, and would you want to explore Manolo's use of English versus Spanish in his daily communications?

2. Name and describe two types of activities/strategies that you would use with Manolo.

Although the SLANT strategy enables students with HI to interact effectively in class discussions, it is also important to structure activities (for example, cooperative learning activities) so that students without disabilities develop positive attitudes about their peers with HI (Nowicki and Sandieson 2002). For teachers, this structuring means modeling and coaching students about how to work cooperatively with others, as well as making regular education students feel comfortable when interacting with students with disabilities. Maintaining positive attitudes may involve disclosing the nature of the disability to enhance social interactions between students with and without disabilities (Maras and Brown 2000). If regular education students view the interaction (that is, structured activity) as a threat to their social status or self-image, these students might very well reject or develop negative feelings toward students with HI (Hastings and Graham 1995).

Response Cards. Another effective procedure to increase student responding during discussions and lectures is response cards. Randolph (2007) conducted a meta-analysis and found that compared to hand raising, response cards had a significant impact on test and quiz achievement and participation. More recent studies (Clarke, Haydon, Bauer, and Epperly 2016; George 2010) that used response cards among students with HI found that they were more effective than hand raising/calling out answers on measures of test scores and on-task behavior.

TIPS FOR GENERALIZATION

Linking Oral Language Skills with Reading and Writing

When teaching oral language skills, teach these skills directly in lessons, but also integrate them into written language and reading. Because of the overlap of language skills in these areas, you can teach crossover skills in many different contexts. For example, if students have learned a new vocabulary word, you could integrate this word into a written language assignment, and they could read it in context in one of their textbooks.

Remember, there is no single method for teaching vocabulary; instead, combine methods and techniques. First, limit the number of vocabulary words to teach per class. Decide if the words are critical to learn or if students may never see the words again. Second, try to actively engage students during vocabulary instruction. Rather than just learn vocabulary through rote drill and practice, students should learn words in ways in which they can gain a deeper understanding of them. Using visual imagery, understanding word parts (for example, prefixes and suffixes), and tying the word to context are different ways of learning vocabulary that provide for a deeper understanding of words. Third, provide students with multiple exposures to the vocabulary words. Students should see the words in multiple contexts and used with a variety of activities. You may need to discuss and explain the vocabulary word in the new context because it may take on a slightly different meaning based upon its usage.

Last, do not forget about using computer software and technology to assist students in learning vocabulary. A variety of software programs can be used to increase student vocabulary knowledge. Some software programs even allow teachers to enter their own vocabulary words.

Research Evidence

Semantic Organizers and Cognitive Maps. Semantic organizers have long been shown to be effective at increasing students' vocabulary use and comprehension. In studies by Bos and others (Bos and Anders 1987, 1990; Bos et al. 1989; Scanlon et al. 1992), researchers demonstrated that students who used semantic maps outperformed students who learned vocabulary using a traditional approach (for example, a dictionary approach). These researchers also demonstrated that children who used semantic maps and organizers while reading showed increased recall of vocabulary and reading comprehension. Moreover, a recent synthesis of research on semantic organizers and cognitive maps (Kim et al. 2004) supported the use of these techniques as effective tools for increasing reading comprehension; they were particularly effective on comprehension measures among children with HI. Likewise, a meta-analysis by Dexter and Hughes (2011) found that organizers were more effective than traditional methods in terms of both comprehension and maintenance.

Keyword and Mnemonic Strategies. The keyword or mnemonic strategy has been used in numerous studies to improve vocabulary learning in students. Veit, Scruggs, and Mastropieri (1986) used the strategy to improve dinosaur vocabulary in students with learning disabilities. In this study, students trained to use the mnemonic technique outperformed all other groups on immediate recall and delayed recall tests. In another study, Mastropieri, Scruggs, and Graetz (2003) taught students with learning disabilities to remember and recall vocabulary and facts about chemistry using the mnemonic strategy; they outperformed students in the traditional learning group. In yet another study, Mastropieri, Scruggs, and Fulk (1990) taught students with learning disabilities to remember and recall abstract words using the keyword method. The keyword method resulted in the highest level of recall and comprehension of vocabulary words.

THINK BACK TO THE CASE **with Manolo...**

1. *What specific skill would you try to remediate first?*

For Manolo, it would seem appropriate to address his ability to follow directions.

2. *Name and describe two types of activities/strategies that you would use with Manolo.*

For the skill of following directions, the teacher should show Manolo how to establish and maintain eye contact when someone is speaking to him. She could also teach Manolo to repeat the directions to her verbally, step by step, before actually completing the task. She could then reinforce him for using these skills.

CHAPTER SUMMARY

Oral language often forms the basis for learning other subject areas such as reading, writing, and content areas. Oral language is important because it is the main form of communication in young children and is needed as children enter school. Early on, children learn language skills from their parents or other caregivers, but over time, teachers become the primary facilitators for teaching language skills to students. Typically, teachers instruct students in one or more of the following five oral language components: phonology, morphology, syntax, semantics, and pragmatics. Models are useful for describing how language develops in children and can serve as a basis for teachers when teaching language skills in the classroom. In children, formal language (that is, words) normally develops along a continuum that was described in Table 5.2. Students with HI often have a variety of language problems, from lack of phonology to word recall and higher-level language problems (that is, difficulty understanding abstract or figurative language). Teachers should ensure that instruction in language skills occurs daily or every other day to build a base for future learning. Teachers could use many of the language techniques that we discussed (for example, word recall techniques or the SLANT strategy) or develop their own based upon the student's individual needs. Whenever possible, language skills should be taught in context and in environments that allow students to practice these skills.

KEY TERMS

Bound Morpheme, 165

Conversational Repair Strategies, 184

Expressive Language, 164

Free Morpheme, 165

Goal Interdependence, 176

Individual Role-Playing, 183

Intent, 164

Interactive Role-Playing, 183

Language, 164

Language Acquisition Device, 167

Mean Length of Utterance, 170

Morpheme, 165

Morphology, 165

Phoneme, 165

Phonemic Awareness, 178

Phonics, 178

Phonology, 165

Pragmatics, 166

Receiver, 164

Receptive Language, 164

Resource Interdependence, 176

Reward Interdependence, 176

Role Interdependence, 176

Semantics, 166

Sender, 164

Shared Code, 164

Syntax, 165

Task Interdependence, 176

APPLICATION ACTIVITIES

Using information from the chapter, complete the following activities that were designed to help you apply the knowledge that was presented in this chapter.

1. Design a language lesson comprising different activities that will help children develop oral language skills. Be sure to include lesson objectives and one or two state standards in your lesson.

2. You are assigned a new first-grade student who has language deficits in syntax. Describe some activities that you could do in your classroom to improve her syntax.

3. Take one of the strategies/techniques that was presented in this chapter and describe how you would teach it to a child with a disability.

6 Early Reading: Strategies and Techniques

Learning Objectives

After reading this chapter, you will understand:

6-1 Different models of reading that explain how children read

6-2 Stages of reading development in children

6-3 Common problems students with HI encounter in early reading

6-4 Techniques for improving sight words, phonological awareness, word patterns, and syllabication skills for students with HI

6-5 How reading skills can be incorporated into a lesson to improve the reading skills of students with HI

CEC **Initial Preparation Standard 5: Instructional Planning and Strategies**

5-2 Beginning special education professionals use technologies to support instructional assessment, planning, and delivery for individuals with exceptionalities.

5-3 Beginning special education professionals are familiar with augmentative and alternative communication systems and a variety of assistive technologies to support the communication and learning of individuals with exceptionalities.

5-4 Beginning special education professionals use strategies to enhance language development and communication skills of individuals with exceptionalities.

5-5 Beginning special education professionals develop and implement a variety of education and transition plans for individuals with exceptionalities across a wide range of settings and different learning experiences in collaboration with individuals, families, and teams.

5-6   Beginning special education professionals teach to mastery and promote generalization of learning.

5-7   Beginning special education professionals teach cross-disciplinary knowledge and skills such as critical thinking and problem solving to individuals with exceptionalities.

What do you think is the number-one academic problem for students with HI, particularly students with LD?

If you guessed reading, you are correct. For students with LD, approximately 80 to 90 percent have problems with reading (Fletcher et al. 2007). Students with LD commonly have deficits in phonological processing skills, which are critical to acquiring beginning reading skills (Ackerman et al. 2001; Schatschneider et al. 2000).

This astonishingly high percentage of students who encounter reading problems means that teachers should have knowledge of powerful reading interventions to address students' problems on a daily basis. Furthermore, teachers should have knowledge of the responsiveness to intervention (RTI) approach to special education. We describe several interventions in this chapter; with careful monitoring, the interventions in this chapter could be used within RTI tiers, particularly Tier 2 and 3. Although we have discussed RTI in detail in Chapter 1, we would encourage special education teachers to review other resources such as the RTI Action Network (http://www.rtinetwork.org). The RTI Action Network website serves as an excellent resource for teachers looking for additional information about RTI and associated tiered interventions. Finally, a number of professional organizations (such as the Council for Exceptional Children, International Reading Association, and National Council of Teachers of English) require teacher education programs at universities to focus heavily on the "teaching of reading" as part of their program requirements for pre-service teachers. With all of the emphasis on reading, it is critical for teachers to know how to teach reading and how to implement reading interventions for students with HI.

CASE 6.1   What's Wrong with Latasha?

Case Introduction

In this case, you will read about a student who has trouble with early reading skills. The case will begin with some background information and then move on to a discussion of her specific reading problems. As you read, you will see that her teacher has tried a number of different teaching techniques and yet Latasha is still falling farther behind.

At the end of the case, you will find case questions. These questions are meant to serve as points for reflection. Of course, if you can answer them immediately, you should do so, but you may want to wait to answer them until you have read the portion of the chapter that pertains to the particular case question. Throughout the rest of the chapter, you will see the same questions. When you come to them again, try to answer them based upon the portion of the chapter that you just read.

Latasha is in first grade and has problems with reading. She also has been diagnosed with attention-deficit/hyperactivity disorder (ADHD) by her pediatrician. Her mother, Cici, feels that Latasha is doing fine in school, and really does not do much at home to assist her with reading. Cici also had problems with reading when she was a child, yet she feels that she outgrew them with age, despite still being a poor reader.

Latasha is still in the early stages of learning how to read, even though most of the children in her class have already become fluent readers. Latasha reads from a basal reader, but struggles to read even the easiest words unless she has memorized them as sight words. She has particular difficulty with novel words because of her lack of phonological awareness. She knows about 75 percent of her letter sounds and can segment simple three- or four-letter words with success, but has difficulty if asked to blend those sounds back together and pronounce the word.

continued

In terms of comprehension, Latasha has great difficulty comprehending the short sentences that she reads, unless there are pictures in the book to aid her. She often spends so much time sounding out words that she does not remember what she has just read. As a result, she is a slow, laborious reader.

Her special education teacher, Mr. Coleman, has been working on State Standard 1.6 with Latasha: "the student will apply phonetic principles to read and spell." In accordance with this standard, Latasha is to use phonetic principles to use short vowel sounds to decode and spell single-syllable words; blend beginning, middle, and ending sounds to recognize and read words; use word patterns to decode unfamiliar words; and read and spell common, high-frequency sight words.

When reading a recent story, Latasha made several errors or miscues. Prior to having the children read, Mr. Coleman reviewed the majority of the sight words that were found in the short story. Even with the review, however, Latasha still made several miscues. For example, when she came across the word *spot*, she sounded out each letter sound, but when she blended the sounds together, she said *stop*. She also pronounced *word* for *very*, *sister* for *list*, *stop* for *lot*, *and* for *have*, and *ready* for *every*.

On another day, Mr. Coleman was teaching the State Standard 1.6 skills of blending beginning, middle, and ending sounds to recognize and read words, and using word patterns to decode unfamiliar words. He decided to use a game called "Add Them or Lose Them" to cover this standard. In this game,

students substitute an initial letter sound to form a new word (given the word *rat*, change the first letter to "s" and pronounce the new word: *sat*). This activity proved especially difficult for Latasha, as she made several errors substituting *v*, *n*, and *p* to form new *at* words. In another activity, "Name That Letter," Latasha had mixed results. In this activity, when given a word (for example, *fast*), students were to name the phoneme in the beginning, middle, or end. The teacher gave the word and asked students to repeat it and then asked either beginning, middle, or end, at which time the students had to name the corresponding phoneme. Latasha was successful at naming the beginning phonemes about 90 percent of the time and the ending phonemes about 65 percent of the time, but when asked to name the middle phoneme she was correct only about 20 percent of the time.

Mr. Coleman is concerned; despite his best efforts, Latasha has fallen farther behind her classmates. Even though she is in the lowest reading group, she is still having the most difficulty.

CASE QUESTIONS

1. Latasha has difficulty with several of the most basic skills of reading. What two specific skills would you address first with Latasha?
2. Latasha needs to improve her phonological awareness. What are some activities that will help Latasha to recognize and name phonemes?

In this chapter, you will learn about early reading methods and strategies. The content of the chapter includes information about reading models, stages of reading, and reading techniques, strategies, and activities for students with HI. Although beginning reading problems are most common among preschool and elementary-age students, you will find many of the techniques in this chapter useful with older students as well.

As you may gather from Case 6.1, Latasha's problems in early reading can prove to be a challenge to even the most skilled teacher, yet research shows that teachers can use techniques, strategies, and skills to help improve Latasha's reading problems. In this chapter, you will learn about methods and techniques for remediating reading problems like Latasha's.

6-1 Models of Reading

Reading models and theories serve an important purpose in understanding the process of reading (Tracey and Morrow 2012). They seek to explain how children learn how to read. Strategies and techniques are derived from models and, in turn, these models or theories help guide teachers as to how to teach students to read. As you read about each model, think back to when you learned to read and consider the role of each model in your own reading development. Special education teachers may use one model at a particular reading stage and then eventually shift to a different model at later stages. Some teachers may rely more heavily on one model (for example, using the top-down model to help students gain meaning of what they read), yet incorporate components of another model (using work-attack skills for unknown multisyllabic words) as the situation arises. These models reflect components of information processing and cognitive processing theories (Tracey and Morrow 2012).

Bottom-Up Model

According to the **bottom-up model** of reading, young readers rely heavily on translating *print* to *letter sounds* to *meaning* as an approach to comprehending text. In other words, children must hear each letter sound (or each word) before they can gain meaning. During silent reading, readers translate words first to inner speech, before gaining meaning. This process of determining what sounds are present in a word is known as **decoding** (Box 6.1 gives a detailed listing of reading terms). In the bottom-up model, *attention* plays a major role in learning to read words. Skilled readers use

BOX 6.1

Common Reading Terms

- **Phonemes** refer to letter sounds. Each letter has one or more letter sounds.
- **Phonological awareness** refers to breaking down (segmenting) an unknown word into phonemes and then blending those sounds back together to pronounce the word.
- **Word-attack skills** refers to the ability to "attack" a word by identifying its phonemes and putting them together to form the word.
- **Segmenting** refers to breaking down a word into phonemes (for example, the word *dish* is segmented into the phonemes *d-i-sh*).
- **Blending** refers to combining phonemes to form a word (for example, the phonemes *t-a-p* combine to make the word *tap*).
- **Sight words** are sometimes referred to as high-frequency words, words that appear frequently in print and are likely to appear in published print such as basal stories.
- **Basal reading series** are a series of preplanned, sequentially organized books that contain short passages or stories. Typically, sight words are introduced a few at a time in each story, and new ones are added in each successive story, resulting in a cumulative effect as the stories become more complex.
- **Decoding skills** involve breaking down unknown words into phonemes and syllables.
- **Structural analysis** refers to breaking down unknown words into prefixes and suffixes, and then breaking them into syllables. This process is more sophisticated than decoding.
- **Digraphs** refer to two letters that represent one phoneme.
  - **Vowel digraphs** refer to two letters that represent one phoneme (for example, *ai*, *ay*, *oa*, and *ee*). These are usually one of the phonemes in the digraph (you may remember from your schooling that the first letter does the talking and the second letter does the walking).
  - **Consonant digraphs** refer to two letters that create a single phoneme or unit (for example, *ph*, *ch*, *sh*, *th*, and *wh*).
- **Diphthongs** refer to the vowel sound that cannot be represented by either sound, but forms a unique sound together, such as *au*, *aw*, *oi*, *oy*, and *ou*.
- **Consonant blends/clusters** refer to blends in which each letter can be pronounced by saying each letter sound (for example, *bl*, *str*, *cr*, *spl*).

decoding skills automatically (Samuels 1994). That way, readers shift attention from one aspect of reading to another. In some instances, readers rely heavily on decoding text to make sense of it and, at other times, automatic decoding enables students to focus on comprehension. Many believe that students must first be fluent and efficient in decoding skills to become proficient in comprehension. Moreover, these skills must become "automatic" before students can begin to focus the majority of their attention on the meaning of text.

Top-Down Model

Using the **top-down model** when teaching young students in the early stages of reading, teachers focus on a combination of decoding skills, sight words, and connected reading activities to gain meaning (such as reading sentence strips or forming sentences from known words). According to this model, students use background knowledge to generate hypotheses about what they are about to read shortly before reading or shortly after reading (Chall and Stahl 1982). This model assumes that students have prior knowledge about the topic. Moreover, research shows that prior knowledge plays a major role in comprehension (Pressley 2002). As information is processed (that is, as the student reads), the reader confirms, disconfirms, or refines earlier hypotheses or generates new ones. Many top-down theorists believe that a skilled reader goes directly from *print* to *meaning*, without transferring the information to *speech* (Chall and Stahl 1982). This model espouses that reading is very much an "active process," whereby the reader uses background knowledge, including personal experiences, to form or shape meaning while reading the text. According to this model, reading is not merely a collection of ideas that are organized into something that makes sense; rather, reading is a process in which the reader constructs meaning and creates new meanings from text. In a sense, each new idea that readers come across in print transforms their knowledge of the topic.

To use this model, teachers should focus on activating students' background knowledge prior to, during, and after reading the story. This involves using activities that tap into their knowledge of the topic before reading the story (for example, using a KWL activity; see Chapter 7), previewing the text, and then discussing the previewed material and how it pertains to students' current knowledge about the topic. The gist is that activating the students' prior knowledge will help them to connect their ideas with newly learned information as they read. Next, students read the text, confirming or disconfirming prior statements that they made during the preview process. Finally, the teacher checks to see that students have an accurate meaning of the text by asking questions and probing students on what they read. Although top-down models seem to work well for skilled readers who intuitively incorporate decoding and other rudimentary skills into their reading repertoire, for students with HI, lower-level skills must be taught first or along with higher-level, top-down processing skills.

Interactive Model

As theorists began to examine the different models, it was clear that neither the bottom-up nor the top-down model sufficiently explained the entire reading process. As a result, the interactive model (Bos and Anders 1992; Chall and Stahl 1982) was developed. According to this model, theorists believe that information is derived from both kinds of processing (top-down and bottom-up), and is combined to determine the most likely interpretation of print. In other words, an interaction of these two models results in comprehension of text. At times, readers may use top-down processing, particularly with familiar material; yet, when readers encounter difficulty, they may switch to bottom-up processing to read the information slowly and methodically.

This interactive model means that if the purpose of a reading activity is to reinforce or practice word-attack or phonological skills, then teachers should de-emphasize comprehension and emphasize phonological skills as the child reads. However, if the purpose of a reading activity is comprehension, then the teacher should focus on comprehension strategies, such as asking students to pause periodically to check if they understood what they just read, paraphrase information, or identify main ideas or details. Teachers should be cognizant of teaching skills for monitoring comprehension as children read. Many of these skills could first be taught in isolation using explicit instruction (for example, practice finding the main idea), and then these skills could be practiced within the context of reading.

6-2 Stages of Reading

As children learn to read, they go through several stages (Chall 1983). Chall refers to six stages that describe how reading progresses from what Chall terms *pseudo-reading* in early readers to its most mature form in adults. In each stage, readers focus on different aspects of reading as they interact with printed material. In other words, they attack reading differently in each stage. Although they may revert to earlier stages with different types of reading materials, they essentially progress through each successive stage as reading becomes more complex, technical, and abstract.

Stage 0: Pre-Reading (Birth to Age 6)

This stage covers the greatest period of time, from birth to first grade. In the pre-reading stage, students expand and master their use of language, particularly as it pertains to morphology (or word parts), semantics (understanding the meaning of words), and syntax (sentence structure or grammar).

As they begin to master their language, they also begin to understand various aspects of early reading. They begin to understand that words are composed of letters, and these letters represent sounds. They also begin to understand that books are made up of words and that, in part, they can use visual cues (that is, pictures) in the book to tell a story.

During this stage, children rely heavily on contextual knowledge and information that is derived from pictures in the book to learn how to read. Children often pretend to read, or use **pseudo-reading**, as they tell the story in a book aloud to others. Watch young children read and, regardless of the words, they will look at the sequence of pictures and tell the story, frequently relying on memory of the story. This stage is very much considered by some to be an emergent stage of reading, whereby children begin to recognize letter names, print some letters, and perhaps even know a few words by heart. The child's description of the actions often mimics his or her own spoken language.

During this stage, the child begins to understand the process of reading. In other words, the child begins to realize that words are made up of sounds, and that when these sounds are segmented and blended together, they form words. This phonemic phase of reading development helps the child begin to recognize segmentation, blending, and rhyme. For students to be successful at this stage of learning, they need to be provided a print-rich environment, one that allows for experimentation with language and an opportunity to make connections between language and reading (Wolf 2007).

A top-down approach to teaching reading is usually used during this stage as children begin to interact with print.

Stage 1: Initial Reading or Decoding Stage (Grades 1–2, Ages 6–7)

Students enter Stage 1 of reading when they are successful in the pre-reading stage and have progressed from pure reliance on picture cues and memory of the story line to reliance on phonological skills and recognition of sight words. In doing so, students can confidently read some words by sounding out the letters and eventually progress to the more complex decoding phase of a Stage 1 reader.

In this stage, students attempt to "crack the code." This means that students can no longer rely solely on memory or knowledge of certain words in the story; instead, they must learn phonological awareness skills and be able to apply these skills to read words. Instead of using pictures to make sense of the story, as was done in the previous stage, students must now search for words that make sense both in terms of what is occurring in the story and in terms of how well they match with the printed word.

During this stage, students rely heavily on (that is, are glued to) the printed word to pronounce words properly and focus attention on visual information. For some students, this can very much be a trial-and-error approach, relying on teacher feedback for confirmation of their phonic or sight-word skills to pronounce words. Even though students may have been able to pronounce words easily during the previous stage, they now sound out many of these words. Only through the realization that letters (both consonants and vowels) are made up of letter sounds do children fully progress through this stage. This "realization" has been described as "interiorizing of cognitive knowledge about reading" (Chall 1983). For students in this stage, using those interiorized phonological skills is essential. Difficulty specifically with phonological memory can result in problems learning vocabulary in a first and second language learner (Swanson, Howard, and Sáez 2006).

A bottom-up approach to teaching reading may be more applicable for this stage of reading development. Teachers need to teach phonological awareness and word-attack skills explicitly through modeling, providing practice with feedback, and allowing students to use the skills on their own. As students progress, their word-attack skills move from sounding out simple (monosyllabic) words to syllabication of longer words.

Stage 2: Confirmation, Fluency, and Ungluing from Print (Grades 2–3, Ages 7–8)

This stage involves the consolidation of word-attack skills learned in Stage 1 while at the same time moving away from this reliance on decoding skills. Continued teaching of decoding skills is an important activity that continues during this stage, even though students are becoming more fluent readers (Harris and Sipay 1990). Students who rely too heavily on decoding skills become "word callers," those who are still glued to text. To move successfully through this stage, students need to leave the page and reflect on whether the words that are being read make sense in the context of the storyline. Chall (1983) refers to this as being able to read "inside out" (that is, using phonological and decoding skills) while switching to an "outside in" mode of reading (that is, making sure the words make sense). For this to occur, students need to be confident in their decoding skills and must feel comfortable switching back and forth between reflecting for meaning and reflecting for proper pronunciation. To become fluent readers, students in this phase should be permitted to make mistakes, and the teacher should provide general rules for correcting such mistakes. Also, you should remember that automaticity of decoding skills is critical, because automatic decoding of words frees up working memory for comprehension.

During this stage, readers begin to develop comprehension skills and begin to become more concerned with the text "making sense," while at the same time becoming less reliant on it (unglued from it). These new phonological awareness and decoding skills enable students to become more fluent and expressive during reading. Because fluency requires practice, activities that permit practice, such as recreational reading (reading for pleasure) and repeated readings (reading the same text multiple times, to build comfort), will help students progress smoothly through this stage and on to Stage 3. Keep in mind that this stage is not necessarily for learning new information through reading, but to confirm what is known by practicing those skills that students have already acquired. Thus, stories with familiar content are typically used so that students can hone their word-attack and decoding skills while matching what they read to their knowledge of the topic. In this stage, readers must use all of their prior skills and strategies in an efficient and effective manner to gain new knowledge from what they read. Prior to getting there, however, teachers should provide students with multiple opportunities to read (that is, through structured repeated readings of stories or less structured "free" reading time), so that they can master skills while building confidence in reading at the same time. Once students can move efficiently between using context clues, sight words, word-attack skills, and making sense of the story, they are ready to move on to the next stage.

Stage 3: Reading for Learning the New—A First Step (Grades 4–8, Ages 9–13)

In earlier stages, students read to acquire rudimentary reading skills. During this stage, readers use previously learned reading skills to acquire new facts and concepts, and to gain an understanding of how things work (Harris and Sipay 1990). They develop strategies for attacking different types of text. Stage 3 is typically known as the "reading to learn" phase. At the same time, there is a shift in the purpose of reading activities. No longer is reading restricted to basal readers or storybooks, but now reading involves learning facts and concepts from textbooks and other expository text. Therefore, teachers need to provide students with new strategies for reading this type of text.

During this stage, reading skills begin to focus on finding information in the chapter or book, learning new vocabulary, and approaching reading tasks in a strategic manner. Rather than reading sight words in isolation, vocabulary and word meanings now take top priority as students use these words on tests and in their writing. To acquire new information, students must relate new knowledge with prior knowledge, understand how the two relate, and then store that new information for later recall. Teachers may need to expand pre-reading activities so that students have sufficient background knowledge to acquire successfully new information that they read. Informational materials and fictional books are also introduced during this stage, and these materials require students to apply new comprehension monitoring strategies. Reading during this stage at times follows a top-down approach, as students begin to rely more on background knowledge about the topic to connect new knowledge with prior knowledge. At other times, reading follows a bottom-up approach, as students must stop periodically to read multisyllabic words and technical information (Chall 1983). Although some students may still be using decoding skills for new words, instruction in structural analysis will become more prominent as students begin to read multisyllabic vocabulary words, particularly those longer words containing affixes. In addition, as their working memory becomes more taxed with facts and bits of knowledge, students will need to rely on more efficient comprehension strategies.

What's more, children at risk for reading difficulties have greater difficulty performing short-term memory tasks in learning a second language than do others (Swanson, Sáez, and Gerber 2004), so any strategies that allow them to search out, remember, and recall information will be useful. These strategies include various aspects of comprehension monitoring such as finding main ideas, details, and vocabulary; summarizing text; and drawing conclusions. At this stage, be aware that both native speakers and second language learners appear to exhibit the same types of reading difficulties across languages (Swanson, Sáez, and Gerber 2006). Although sophistication of vocabulary and idioms may differ, for example, core underlying reading processes like phonological processing skills are typically consistent. However, in their study of monolingual English-speaking children compared to bilingual Spanish-speaking children learning English, Swanson, Howard, and Sáez (2006) found that phonological processing problems in Spanish (but not in English) predicted limited growth in reading skills over three years; at the same time, difficulties in working memory for reading in both languages were found correlated with slow English-reading development.

Stage 4: Multiple Viewpoints—High School (Ages 14–18)

In Stage 4, students begin to read materials that are from another view or even multiple perspectives on topics and issues. This presents new challenges in reading textbooks and literature stories. Social studies, history, and even science textbooks begin to present information from multiple viewpoints. For example, students may learn about the Revolutionary War from the perspective of the merchant, the soldier, and the slave. These points of view, sometimes conflicting, present challenges for students and often go beyond factual conflicts; they may present moral and ethical issues that run counter to their own current views. They also learn more in-depth concepts and must deal with the layering of facts and concepts. Chall (1983) claims that students can acquire these more difficult concepts from multiple points of view because they previously learned "simplistic versions" of them. When students become successful with this type of critical comprehension, they have progressed from Stage 3 to Stage 4. Often, discussions and writing assignments help students sort out the details of multiple views and help them to accommodate this new knowledge more easily.

Stage 5: Construction and Reconstruction—A World View (College and Adult)

Chall (1983) claims that passage from Stage 4 to Stage 5 is perhaps the most difficult because moving forward depends upon "the reader's cognitive abilities, accumulation of knowledge, and motivation." In Stage 5, college students and other young adults rely heavily on prior knowledge and multiple comprehension strategies. Skilled readers in this stage not only have multiple strategies for reading (based upon the purpose for reading), but they have also developed the metacognitive skills necessary to determine when and where to apply each strategy. Inherent in their strategy development, these experienced students can also use strategies flexibly, depending upon the type of text and the purpose for reading or studying.

In Stage 5, students become selective in what they read and what they choose not to read. This selectivity depends upon the purpose of reading and determines the degree of detail needed while reading. Students use multiple comprehension strategies (for example, reading in depth or skimming) to construct and reconstruct knowledge about the topic of interest.

Also during Stage 5, reading becomes more critical as students use analysis, synthesis, and judgment to construct their own "truth" of the topic from multiple sources (or as Chall puts it, "from the 'truth' of others"). Students must not only feel confident about the topic, but they must feel a certain "entitlement" to use the knowledge of others to create new knowledge about the topic. Prior knowledge of a topic allows for a faster reading rate because knowledge has already been constructed about the topic, and comprehension occurs more easily from previously constructed schemata. As such, students may read at Stage 5 for selected topics (for example, those topics in which they have a special interest or specialization) because they have previously constructed a schema for the topic; yet, for other topics, students may still read in Stage 4, or even Stage 3.

6-3 Common Reading Problems Among Students with HI

When we look at how reading skills develop in students, we see that most children enter school with some pre-reading or prerequisite reading skills. Once in the school system, they often begin an intense immersion in the process of learning how to read. Teachers discuss initial letter sounds, sight words, and listening comprehension. Concurrently, students also learn other skills such as rhyming words, discriminating vowel sounds, pronouncing blends and clusters, and matching letter names with their sounds. Some students, particularly those with HI, experience difficulty in learning how to read. These problems range from beginning reading problems, such as phonological awareness, to later reading problems, such as problems with comprehension (which we will address in Chapter 7).

Basic Reading Skill Problems

Research has shown that reading is the primary academic area of difficulty for students with HI (Fletcher et al. 2007), and that an estimated 80 to 90 percent of students with LD are referred to special education because of reading problems (Kavale and Forness 2000; Welsch 2007). Mather (1992) states that students with reading problems or HI do not intuitively learn how to read and therefore may require more explicit instruction in "letter-sound relationship"; without it, they do not learn how to "crack the code" of reading. According to some, students with HI fail to crack the code of reading because they have a specific deficit in the phonological language domain (Liberman, Shankweiler, and Liberman 1989). Similarly, researchers (Rack, Snowling, and Olson 1992) have proposed that these problems represent a **phonological deficit hypothesis** and that this deficit explains why students fail to acquire reading skills during their first few years of school. However, as you read the following sections, be mindful that it is important to assess reading difficulties as distinct from more general abilities with first language and English as a second language. In some cases, deficits in short-term memory may underlie observed working memory difficulties for bilingual children learning to read in their second language, although the same short-term memory deficits are not always found for both languages (Swanson et al. 2004).

Fluency and Comprehension Problems

Although a lack of phonological or **word-attack skills** has been linked to poor reading of words, the secondary effects of these skills deficits are exhibited in a student's poor comprehension of text. Because students with HI spend much of their intellectual resources (that is, attention and working memory) trying to pronounce words, they have few resources left for constructing meaning of text (Adams 1990). Thus, although phonological awareness is important for students to read individual words successfully, other factors may contribute to successful reading fluency and comprehension, namely recognizing orthographic patterns, rapid naming, and word-reading skills (Katzir et al. 2006). For students with disabilities, these are difficult skills to acquire. Specifically, students with HI have trouble recognizing words accurately and quickly (Jenkins et al. 2003; Rack, Snowling, and Olson 1992). Reading comprehension for these students is affected by weak word-attack and fluency skills. Yet, other students may have adequate word-attack skills, but still have poor reading fluency and comprehension (Wolf and Bowers 1999), because they lack fluency with reading words in context or they lack effective comprehension strategies in some cases.

In terms of specific comprehension problems, students with HI may have difficulty with both word-level comprehension and sentence-level comprehension (Pressley 2002). Moreover, many students with disabilities have a great deal of difficulty making inferences in passages (Cain and Oakhill 1999), resulting in poor comprehension. For some students, poor working memory may interfere with their comprehension (Yuill, Oakhill, and Parkin 1989). For these students, learning novel vocabulary from context is a difficult task (Cain, Oakhill, and Lemmon 2004). For others, managing and coordinating cognitive and attentional resources becomes a problem. These problems, often referred to as metacognitive problems or executive function disorders, may prevent students from understanding ambiguous vocabulary, drawing inferences, and processing redundant information in text (Meltzer and Krishnan 2007). Moreover, when reading becomes difficult, these students are less likely to shift strategies to use different, more effective comprehension strategies (Phillips 1988; Pressley 2002). As a matter of fact, this weakness in *cognitive flexibility* is often a trait of students with learning and attentional disorders (Meltzer and Bagnato 2010).

6-4   Teaching Reading Skills to Students with HI

When teaching students early reading skills, the natural progression of skills (Fig. 6.1) would be from lower-level skills such as reading readiness activities (prereading skills), to phonological awareness, to syllabication, to word patterns and word attack, to more complex skills such as fluency, vocabulary, and reading comprehension. Despite these skills being listed as separate skills, there is overlap as they are taught (for example, when teaching children to pronounce words, we often ask them

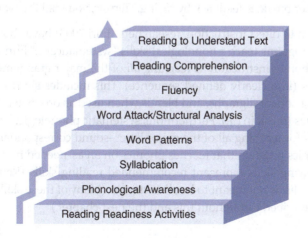

◄ **FIGURE 6.1**

Progression of Reading Skills

to comprehend short sentences that they read). In most cases, reading lessons include activities from a variety of these skill areas. In this section, we will discuss reading readiness activities, phonological awareness activities, syllabication, word patterns, and word-attack skills. Reading fluency, reading comprehension, and reading to understand text will be discussed in the next chapter.

Early reading instruction includes teaching students a number of reading skills. For example, many children with HI benefit not only from phonics skills but also from *reading readiness* skills such as listening comprehension. Likewise, research has shown that good reading programs also incorporate other important early reading skills such as phonics skills, sight-word knowledge, and spelling patterns of sight words (Ehri 2003; Share and Stanovich 1995). In addition, the National Reading Panel (2000) concluded that early reading should focus on the "big five" areas of reading: phonemic awareness, phonics, fluency, comprehension, and vocabulary.

How these skills are taught is almost as important as *what* is taught. Research has shown that early reading instruction for students with HI should consist of explicit instruction (Pressley 2002; see Chapter 2 for a more detailed discussion on this topic). For example, using an explicit instructional method such as direct instruction in reading (Carnine et al. 2006), the teacher models the skill, uses guided practice with feedback, and uses independent practice to assess the effectiveness of the skills taught during the lesson. During instruction, teachers should provide immediate and frequent feedback on errors made while reading or during training of reading skills. For instance, in this example of direct instruction, a teacher is working with a small group of students on the word *sit*:

- First, the teacher models for students. The teacher points to each letter in the word and says to students, "Sssssiiit. Sit."
- Next, the teacher uses guided practice and asks all the students to say it with her. The teacher points to each letter in the word and says, "Everyone, say it with me, ssssiiit." Students and teacher say the word together. The teacher asks, "Class, what is the word?" Students respond together "sit" as the teacher says it with them. The teacher provides feedback, "Great! Everyone read *sit* correctly."
- Finally, the teacher uses independent practice and asks one student at a time to say the word. The teacher points to the word and says, "Zane, what is the word?" Zane responds, "sit." The teacher provides feedback and says, "Zane, great job reading the word." The teacher asks another student, "Kera, what is the word?" Kera responds, "sat." The teacher provides feedback, saying, "No, Kera, the word is *sit*." The teacher points to the word and says to Kera, "Ssssssiiit. Sit." The teacher says to Kera, "This time, say it with me: 'ssssiiit, sit.'" Kera and the teacher say the word together. The teacher says to Kera, "Your turn. What is the word?" Kera says, "sit." The teacher provides feedback by saying, "Terrific, you read the word *sit* correctly."

In addition to direct instruction, researchers (Ehri 2003) have shown that successful reading programs teach phonological skills "systematically." Ehri (2003) describes systematic phonics instruction as teaching *all* of the major grapheme–phoneme correspondences (in a clearly defined sequence). This includes short and long vowels, vowel and consonant digraphs, and blends when used as onsets (such as the *c* in *cat*) or with rhymes (the *at* in *cat*). Furthermore, systematic phonological instruction incorporates plans for teaching all of the major letter–sound correspondences, rather than a casual phonics program that teaches phonics on an as-needed basis.

The following skills represent recommended reading skills (Reutzel and Cooter 2004), but this list is not meant to be all-inclusive. (Many of these skills, as well as others, will be described throughout this and the next chapter.)

- Pre-reading skills
- Comprehension
- Phonological awareness
- Phonemic awareness
- Phonics
- Vocabulary
- Fluency
- Story structure
- Text structure
- Comprehension monitoring strategies
- Finding main ideas and details
- Making inferences
- Summarizing

THINK BACK TO THE CASE with Latasha...

1. *What two specific skills would you address first with Latasha?*

You could remediate a number of different skills with Latasha, particularly in the area of phonological awareness. These skills could include recognition of short vowel sounds; blending beginning, middle, and ending sounds; using word patterns to decode unfamiliar words; and reading and spelling common, high-frequency sight words.

Teaching Reading Readiness and Sight Words to Students with HI

Reading readiness activities represent those activities that prepare students for reading. Many of these activities are also referred to as *print awareness* activities. Print awareness activities are those tasks that help students understand the

---

Methods and Strategies Spotlight

Data-Driven Teaching

Teaching should be data-driven. The effectiveness of a student's learning ability for a particular skill determines *how* you teach (what teaching method you use), as shown by the student data that you gather. Whether special education teachers teach students how to read new words or teach phonological awareness skills, they need to keep track of students' progress on a daily or every-other-day basis. Using student data should assist teachers in determining *how* to teach.

Teachers can start by choosing one skill: the number of times the child used phonological awareness to determine new words, the percentage of words pronounced correctly, or the number of words read correctly per minute in a story. Once a baseline or starting point has been established, the teacher can graph the data or use curriculum-based measurement (C-BM) to determine the goal and aimline. C-BM involves assessing one child on one skill over time. C-BM typically assesses easy-to-measure skills such as the percentage of sight words identified or words read correctly per minute, because these skills are part of the student's reading program, can be assessed as the student works on activities, and are easily measured.

▶ **FIGURE 6.2**

Monitoring Mastery of Sight
Words via Curriculum-Based
Measurement

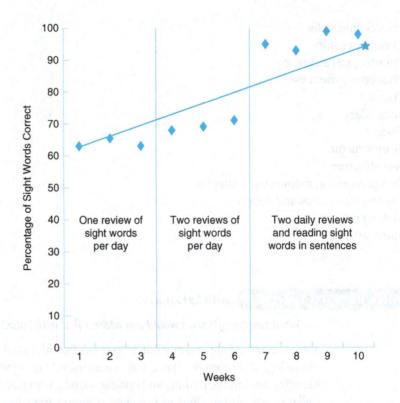

In the graph in Figure 6.2, the special education teacher is assessing the percentage of sight words pronounced correctly from flashcards once a week. First, the teacher needs to determine the student's current level (baseline point). Next, she decides upon a goal of where to expect the child to be after *x* number of weeks. This goal can be determined by assessing nondisabled peers on the same skill, using charts that have been developed by experts, or determining where she wants the child to be. In this case, the teacher has chosen 95 percent correct as the goal.

After deciding on this point, the teacher can connect the goal with the baseline point. This line is known as the *aimline*. Once the assessment data is plotted, any data points above the aimline mean that the child will eventually achieve the goal; in other words, the technique or method the teacher is using is working. If three or more data points are below the aimline, however, the technique/method is not working and needs to be changed. Notice how this teacher changed the technique until the child's data was above the aimline. The teacher should continue changing or adding techniques or interventions until the child's data is consistently above the aimline.

connection between print in written language or reading and using it as a form of communication. Many young children simply do not make the connection between the printed word and its meaning and, therefore, view reading and writing as very mysterious processes. Only over time do they begin to see the link that each letter has meaning (unique phonemes), particularly when blended together to form words. For children with disabilities, this process remains a frustrating mystery for many years until they too are able to unlock the "code of reading." Through using reading readiness activities, teachers can help students to see the link between "words" and "meaning." Many parents use reading readiness activities without ever knowing that they are building initial reading skills. For example, when a parent reads to a child and moves his finger from left to right (in the English language) while reading the words, he is in fact showing the child the directional aspect of reading.

Reading Readiness Activities

Reading readiness involves teaching students prerequisite skills for beginning reading. The following are a few skills:

- **Place names on seats, desks, or other objects.** This shows children that words are used for a specific meaningful purpose.
- **Show pictures with brief titles.** This activity represents one of the earliest reading comprehension activities, that words or phrases represent a picture.
- **Post simple reports/notices.** Again, this is an activity that links words with actions or events. Simple reports could be daily weather reports or simple notes about the day's upcoming activities, such as a schedule that is written on the board.
- **Use predictable stories.** From predictable stories, students learn that events are linked to one another and usually have a predictable outcome based upon a sequence of events. This activity serves as a precursor to reading comprehension.
- **Read decodable books.** These books use text that incorporates rhyme and frequently stories that contain words with similar spelling patterns. The sentences are usually short and contain many rhyming words, usually of the same pattern.
- **Read picture books.** These are stories without words. These books link events to an outcome, and children can look at the pictures to create their own version of the story. These books serve as precursors to listening and reading comprehension.
- **Have adults read stories to children.** When parents, teachers, or other adults read stories to young children and periodically ask questions, they are teaching children listening comprehension. This type of comprehension serves as a precursor for later reading comprehension.
- **Encourage children to label objects.** As children begin to label objects, they also begin to realize the communicative function of print.
- **Use a language-experience approach.** By writing out stories from students' experiences, teachers put their words and ideas into print. Often this experience creates memorable stories for students because they are drawn directly from their past experiences.

Sight-Word Approach

Using a sight-word or whole-word approach teaches children to learn and recognize words as a *whole*. This approach often incorporates the use of "high-frequency" word lists (Table 6.1 gives an abbreviated list). Over the years, several lists have been developed, usually consisting of words in English that children would frequently encounter in printed materials. These lists do not always match up, nor do they match up when ranking the importance of words. Some reading experts (Johns 1981) claim that 13 words (*a, and, for, he, is, in, it, of, that, the, to, was, you*) account for over 25 percent of the words that children will encounter in printed materials. Others (Fry, Fountoukidis, and Polk 1985) claim that 100 words account for over 50 percent of all words in print. (Teaching sight words will also be discussed in Chapter 7.)

TABLE 6.1 Sight Word Lists

Dolch Basic Sight Word Lists[1]			
the	at	do	big
to	him	can	went
and	with	could	are
Fry Sight Words: First Hundred Words[2]			
the	or	will	number
of	one	up	no
and	had	other	way
Functional and Survival Word List			
exit	hot	cold	open
closed	emergency	warning	caution
keep out	power	water	safety

[1]From Dolch, E. (1936). A basic sight word vocabulary. *Elementary School Journal*, 456–460. Copyright © 1936 by The University of Chicago Press. Reprinted with permission.
[2]From Fry, E. *Reading Teacher.* Copyright 1980 by International Reading Association. Reproduced with permission of International Reading Association in the format Textbook via Copyright Clearance Center.

Teaching Sight Words

Many teachers introduce these words in initial reading lessons, yet others wait until children have acquired some phonological skills before introducing children to sight words. The main purpose of teaching sight words is to have children use them as they are beginning to read actual stories. Teachers commonly choose sight words from basal readers or beginning reading books so that students can experience "reading" and not become bored with reading-related activities such as phonemic awareness or phonics activities. Teachers usually transfer sight words from lists to index cards or use flashcards. Using index cards, teachers and students can either review sight words prior to reading words in text (for example, basal reading stories) or use the words as review after certain reading activities. When teaching sight words, teachers need to ensure that students know the words "on sight" (within three seconds); therefore, students need to memorize sight words. When sight words were used with peer tutoring, the rate of sight word acquisition and fluency was shown to improve for three students with HI (Fasko and Fasko 2010). In another study, Kupzyk, Daly, and Andersen (2011) found that students read more words correctly when a strategic incremental rehearsal procedure was used that consisted of a prompt delay, corrective feedback, and error correction when teaching sight words to students.

When teaching sight words, keep in mind the following:

1. Use sight words during the initial stages of reading. Often teachers use these words to help students as they begin to read and then use them to supplement their vocabulary development as students become more advanced readers.
2. Decide which words will become sight words, and teach only a few words each week. Teachers can choose from multiple sources (for example, word lists, basal readers, or spelling words) to develop sight words for the week. When teaching sight words, students should be introduced to 10 or fewer new words per week.
3. Present sight words before or after reading. Teachers should decide when and how often they will review sight words with students. Teachers can write sight words on index cards, and then students can store their sight words in an index box. Students can also refer to these words when writing essays or compositions.

4. Sight words should be known to mastery and "on sight" (within three seconds of presentation). Students who spend more than three seconds determining the correct pronunciation of the word are probably using phonics or word-attack skills.

One of the oldest but still most frequently used word lists is the *Dolch Basic Sight Vocabulary* (see Table 6.1 for an abbreviated list). Originally developed in 1939, the Dolch Word Recognition Test (Dolch 1939) is a list of 220 words of increasing difficulty that are grouped by basal reading levels. This list has been revised over the years, but the original list still accounts for over 50 percent of words found in reading materials (Johns 1981).

Table 6.1 also includes a list of functional and survival words. For students with more moderate to severe disabilities or older students who have not mastered reading, these words may be essential words to learn for life in the community and workplace.

Teaching Phonological Awareness to Students with HI

Phonological awareness is a broad term used to describe the manipulation of language skills such as segmenting of written words, blending of letter sounds, rhyming, alliteration, and the manipulation of onsets/rhymes (Reutzel and Cooter 2004). *Phonemic awareness* is considered a subskill of phonological awareness (Reutzel and Cooter 2004). Phonemic awareness is the awareness that spoken words are made of phonemes and that these phonemes can be segmented into individual sounds. This also involves understanding that, if given a word and asked to replace the first phoneme with another phoneme, the student would form a new word ("Say the word *mop*. Now take off the *mmmm* sound and replace it with *tttt*. What would the new word be?"). **Phonics** refers to letter and sound correspondence. Phonics links the written symbol with phonemes.

Reutzel and Cooter (2004) suggest eight phonemic awareness skills that should be taught to students:

- Phoneme isolation: teaching students to identify phonemes in words. *What sound does the word* cat *begin with?*
- Phoneme identity: discriminating phonemes in words that begin with the same phoneme. *Is the beginning sound the same in the words* hot *and* help?
- Phoneme categorizing: discriminating phonemes in words that begin with a different sound. *Which word begins with a different sound:* tap, toe, *or* sit?
- Phoneme blending: blending phonemes that are presented as separate phonemes. *What word does* C-A-T *make?*
- Phoneme segmentation: segmenting a word into individual phonemes. *What sounds are in the word* sssssiiitttt?
- Phoneme deletion: removing an initial phoneme and being able to pronounce the word. *If you take away the* S *sound from* STOP, *what word is left?*
- Phoneme addition: adding a phoneme and creating a new word. *If you add an* S *sound to the beginning of* cat, *what would the new word be?*
- Phoneme substitution: changing one phoneme in a word. *If you change the* H *sound in* HAT *to an* S *sound, what would the new word be?*

When using these skills, present them in games and activities for students. Make them enjoyable and fun. Model a few examples first before asking students to try them. If students have a difficult time, exaggerate certain phonemes that you want students to focus on, as in the previous phoneme segmentation example. In some cases, teachers can use plastic letters to show students how spoken words are broken down into phonemes. Making oral language more concrete through the use of manipulatives often helps students better understand phonemic concepts.

Phonological Awareness Activities

Phonological awareness activities vary in degree of difficulty, so some children may find that some of the activities are easy whereas others are more difficult (see the following list for three activities). For example, rhymes and rhyming games may be easier for most children than a phoneme substitution activity. For first and second language learners, difficulty specifically with phonological memory can result in problems learning vocabulary (Swanson, Howard, and Sáez 2006). Chard and Dickson (1999) make some suggestions that might increase student success rates when teaching phonological awareness activities:

- Model each activity so that students can see the skill being demonstrated.
- Move from easier tasks to more complex tasks.
- Consider using manipulatives (chips or blocks) to help represent sounds in words.
- Move from larger units (words) to smaller units (phonemes).
- Start with continuous sounds (s, m, f) that can be exaggerated (sssssss) rather than stop sounds (b, p, k).

A signaling procedure (Carnine et al. 2006) can also be helpful for teaching students to focus on specific letter sounds in words. Using the signaling procedure, the teacher first points in front of the first letter of a target word (for example, *cat*). The teacher gets the student's attention with a prompt, such as "get ready." While still pointing in front of the first letter, *c*, the teacher moves a finger under the *c*, pronounces the sound, and sweeps the finger in a loop to the next letter, *a*. Once a finger is under the letter *a*, the teacher pronounces the letter sound, and sweeps to the last letter. Once under the letter *t*, the teacher pronounces the letter sound and removes the finger from the word. Once students are able to use this procedure, they can take turns pronouncing the sounds of each letter in other words.

The following are phonemic awareness activities to assist young students:

- **Rhyme Time.** The purpose of this activity is to have children identify words that rhyme with the targeted word. For example, go around the room and ask children to think of a word that rhymes with *cat*. When you have exhausted the possible rhyming words, move on to another rhyming word. Another suggestion would be to use pictures and have children produce a word that rhymes with the object in the picture. Once children can name rhyming words, move on to easy printed words. Tell the children the target word (for example, *hen*) while pointing out the rhyme part (*en*) of the word and having the children think of other words that have different onsets (*p–en* or *d–en*). Keep score of who gets the most rhyming words and award the winner a prize.
- **Clapping Words and Phonemes.** The purpose of this activity is to teach segmentation. At first, teach segmentation of words from sentences, move to segmenting syllables, and eventually move to segmenting phonemes from words. Begin by using words from familiar children's rhymes, and have them clap their hands for each word they hear. For example, "One for the mouse, one for the crow, one to rot, one to grow." After children master monosyllabic (one-syllable) words, move on to rhymes or songs with multisyllabic words and have them clap out each syllable they hear. Finally, move on to clapping out the phonemes to simple words. The purpose of this game is to eventually teach segmentation of words into phonemes.

- **Rubber Band Man Blending.** The purpose of this game is to teach children to blend phonemes to pronounce words. Using their "slow motion" voice, children begin by exaggerating words in a sentence. Then ask them to repeat the sentence at their normal speed. Once they can do this, use pictures of objects that they can exaggerate the phonemes (*ffffannnnn*) to form the word. Finally, provide them with an exaggerated word (*sssstarrrr*) and ask them to name the word.

In addition to traditional phonological awareness activities, technology is quickly becoming an alternative avenue to teach phonological awareness to children with disabilities. Chai, Ayers, and Taylor (2016) developed an iPad app for teaching phonological awareness called "Touch Sound." The intervention pairs motivating activities with reinforcement for students learning initial phonemes. Their study found that three students with disabilities who used the app improved their correct responses of target phonemes.

Phonological Awareness Strategy

The phonological awareness strategy (Boyle and Seibert 1997) is used to teach students phonological awareness skills. The purpose of this strategy is not to teach initial letter sounds (students should already know most of their letter sounds) but rather to teach the next logical step—segmenting and blending. As a prerequisite step, students are required to know at least 80 percent of the initial letter sounds (phonemes) from a list of phonemes (consonant and short vowel sounds).

The phonological awareness strategy incorporates both segmenting and blending skills through the mnemonic STOP (stare, tell, open, put; Box 6.2). These keywords are familiar and easily understood. The first step, *stare*, cues students to look at each letter of the unknown word (the first step of segmenting). In the second step, *tell*, students are asked to tell themselves each letter sound (the second step of segmenting). The third step, *open*, cues children to verbalize aloud the segmented sounds. The fourth step, *put*, cues students to blend letter sounds together to say the word.

The specific steps of the strategy were developed for the following reasons:

1. Previous studies demonstrated that segmenting and blending are two skills essential for pronouncing words (Rack, Snowling, and Olson 1992).
2. Training students in one subskill (for example, segmenting) did not result in increases in other subskills (for example, blending) (O'Conner et al. 1992).
3. Segmenting and blending must be taught together to assist students in pronouncing words (Torgesen, Morgan, and Davis 1992).
4. Phonological awareness training that explicitly linked phonological awareness skills with reading and taught specific strategies to implement those phonological awareness skills was proven to be more effective than a "skill-and-drill" approach (that is, teaching skills in isolation and out of context) (Cunningham 1980).

BOX 6.2

STOP Strategy

S Stare at the unknown word.
T Tell yourself each letter sound.
O Open your mouth and say each letter.
P Put the letters together to say the word.

Strategy instruction consists of introductory and mnemonic practice training, during which the teacher instructs students on the components of the strategy. Initially, the teacher describes and models the strategy to students, and then they begin using the mnemonic STOP while the teacher provides feedback to them. Once students are proficient at using the strategy steps, they begin using the strategy with actual words. The initial phase involves using the strategy with 10 monosyllabic words (three- or four-letter words that contain short vowel sounds) per training session. Place each monosyllabic word on an index card. Use 10 new words in each subsequent session. During each session, use two or three words that are nonsense words that students pronounce using phonetic rules. These nonsense words should be used to ensure that students are applying the strategy steps and not just remembering the words as sight words. Once students master the strategy with monosyllabic words, introduce two-syllable words. These words follow similar phonetic rules as monosyllabic words. As with the monosyllabic word phase, include two or three multisyllabic nonsense words in each session.

The PHonological And Strategy Training Program (PHAST)

The PHAST program (Lovett, Lacerenza, and Bordern 2000) was developed to help students remediate their phonological skills and combines a number of phonological skills that we have previously mentioned. The five main components of the PHAST program are as follows:

- The *sounding-out strategy* teaches children letter–sound correspondence and segmentation and blending of words (oral segmentation and blending at first, then print-based segmentation and blending of sounds). Initially, children say the segmented sounds slowly, from left to right, and then practice saying them fast.
- The *rhyming strategy* teaches children to recognize words by analogy. Children are taught the rhyming rule: words with the same spelling pattern usually rhyme. Children are then taught to recognize rhyming pairs of words and are asked to generate their own rhyming words. A keyword is introduced (for example, *and*), and then students are introduced to words that contain the spelling pattern (*hand, band, brand,* and so on). Students are next taught to use a keyword to pronounce unknown words (for example, *strand*) by recognizing the spelling pattern of the keyword (*and*) to pronounce the unknown word.
- The *peeling-off strategy* teaches students to use their knowledge of affixes to "peel off" the prefix and suffix of an unknown multisyllabic word (for example, *pre-* and *-tion* in *presumption*) to get to the root word. Once students do this, they pronounce the root word, and then blend the affixes back with the root word to pronounce the entire word. Throughout the entire PHAST program, as many as 75 affixes are taught to students at a rate of about one or two per day. Students review their list of affixes in isolation and practice recognizing them in multisyllabic words.
- In the *vowel alert strategy*, students are taught to try to pronounce the vowels in a word using different pronunciations. For example, if two vowels are present such as in *tread*, the student is taught to pronounce the word with the *ea* sound as in *eat*. If that effort does not yield the correct pronunciation, students are taught to try a second sound, such as the *ea* sound in *head*.
- Using the *"I Spy" strategy*, students are taught to look for small, familiar parts of an unknown multisyllabic word. Specifically, children are taught to look for words within words, particularly in larger words such as compound words. For example, if students come across the word *daytime*, they are taught to "I Spy" *day* and then "I Spy" *time* to pronounce correctly the entire word, *daytime*.

Initially, each strategy is taught separately. After learning each, students are taught to use all of the strategies together to read unknown words. In this phase, called the *game plan,* students are taught to use four steps: *choose, use, check,* and *score/rechoose.* When students are given a word to decode (for example, *contender*), they first choose a strategy or strategies; the student might *choose* the peeling-off strategy and the rhyming strategy to pronounce the word. In the *use* step, the student would peel off the *con-* and *-er* to get to the root word *tend*. Next the student would use the rhyming strategy to recognize the spelling pattern *end* of the keyword *bend*. Because students recognize *bend*, they pronounce *tend*. In the *check* step, students stop to think if they are using the strategy correctly and, if so, they put the parts back together to pronounce the word *contender*. Finally, during the *score/rechoose* step, if the students correctly pronounced the word, they *score* and congratulate themselves. If the strategies did not work, they go back to *choose* and begin again.

> **THINK BACK TO THE CASE**   **with Latasha . . .**
>
> 2. *What are some activities that will help Latasha to recognize and name phonemes?*
>
> A number of different phonological activities could be used with Latasha. For example, to assist her with recognizing short vowel sounds, the teacher could use "Rhyming Word Bingo." Or, to help her recognize initial letter sounds, the teacher could use "Clapping Words and Phonemes." Likewise, the teacher could use the phonological awareness strategy or PHAST to teach phonological skills such as segmenting, blending, rhyming, and other skills.

Wilson Reading System

The Wilson Reading System is a commercial reading program that is used to teach students how to decode words fluently and accurately (Wilson 1996). The program was designed for students who are reading and/or spelling below grade level, including students who have poor auditory skills and English-as-a-second-language (ELL) students. The program is based upon the principles of the Orton-Gillingham model and includes direct instruction and multisensory components (Yampolsky and Waters 2002). For a more detailed description of the Wilson Reading System, see Wilson (1996), or see Ritchey and Goeke (2006) for a more detailed description of Orton-Gillingham–based instruction.

In the Wilson Reading System, the lesson is broken down into 10 parts that can be taught all in one session or can be broken into two sessions (for example, parts one through eight in session one and parts nine and ten in session two). The 10 parts to each lesson are as follows:

1. Quick drill sound cards. The teacher shows students a sound card (that is, a letter), and the students say the letter name and corresponding sound.
2. Teach and review concepts for reading. The teacher makes words with sound cards (letters), and the student segments the words using a finger-tapping procedure and blending sounds. In more advanced lessons, syllable and suffix cards can be used.
3. Present word cards. Instead of creating words from sound cards, the teacher presents entire words on word cards, and the student reads words as fluently as possible.

4. Read word lists. The student reads words in a word list from the student reader, which contains short stories with easy-to-read words.

5. Conduct sentence reading. The student reads sentences in the student reader, silently at first and then aloud, and incorporates *scooping* of a few words at a time to improve fluency. Scooping involves breaking sentences into meaningful phrases in which students move (or scoop) their finger under a few words at a time as they read sentences (Reutzel and Cooter 2005).

6. Quick drill sounds. The teacher says a sound, and the student finds the sound card with the matching letter. This might also include having the student make letters on the table surface or in sand for tactile-kinesthetic support.

7. Review concepts for spelling. The student spells words from word cards using the finger-tapping procedure. In more advanced lessons when using multisyllabic words, the student names and spells affixes, syllables, and/or base words.

8. Complete written work. The teacher orally presents sounds (single words or sentences) that the student repeats, spells aloud, and writes in a composition book.

9. Read passages. The student silently reads a short passage, visualizes and retells the passage information, and then reads orally.

10. Check listening comprehension. The teacher reads a passage while the student visualizes the story; the teacher asks questions to aid visualization, and the student retells the story.

Teaching Word Patterns and Syllabication to Students with HI

The ability to use word or spelling patterns in words as a decoding strategy helps children to decode unknown words (Ehri et al. 2001; White 2005). This technique, sometimes referred to as *analogy-based phonics* (White 2005), teaches children to decode an unknown word (for example, *clap*) by using a known word (*nap*). When taught systematically as part of phonics instruction, children can use the technique to decode unknown words in isolation and in context, particularly when it is taught in context. In fact, research has found that reading by using analogy is easier for children with disabilities because it eliminates the need to blend segmented phonemes (Ehri and Robbins 1992; Walton, Walton, and Felton 2001).

Word Pattern Activities

Teaching students word patterns helps them break down polysyllabic words into recognizable parts. The following are two activities that help students become proficient at recognizing word parts:

- **Home Run Patterns.** The purpose of this activity is to help students recognize patterns in words. Prior to the game, the teacher cuts out a small baseball bat from brown construction paper and cuts out small (2-inch by 2-inch) blank squares on white paper. On these white squares, the teacher writes one-letter consonants. The teacher also constructs baseballs (about 5 inches in circumference) from white paper with two-letter words (for example, from word groups such as *at*, *an*, *et*, *en*, *ot*, and *on*) written on them. The game begins when the teacher places a baseball to the board and explains to students that the ball will change when they hit the ball with the bat. Prior to each hit, the teacher temporarily tapes a consonant square. As students make a hit, the teacher removes the consonant square and places it next to the ball to spell a new word (for example, using the bat with an *s* taped to it, the teacher swings and hits the *at* ball to form the word *sat*). The teacher then removes the *s* square, adds a different consonant square to the bat, and then asks a student to hit the next one. Once the child hits the ball, by adding the square to the baseball, the child says the newly formed word. A variation of this would be to add consonant blends or clusters to the consonant squares (for example, *st* added to the baseball *op* would form the new word *stop*), so that students are now pronouncing more difficult words. This game is especially popular in spring when T-ball and baseball season begins.

- **Changing Words.** The purpose of this game is to help children understand that changing one letter in a word changes the entire word and that recognizing patterns in word can help them pronounce unknown words. Begin by writing a short word on the board (for example, *pin*). Challenge the students to change the word by substituting only one letter in the word to create a new real word. For example, if we change the *i* in *pin* to an *a*, the new word becomes *pan*. If we then change the *n* in *pan* to a *t*, the new word becomes *pat*. If we change the *p* to a *c*, the new word becomes *cat*. Once students run out of variations of new words, the teacher can suggest that students change two letters in the word (for example, *cat* can change to *that*). Encourage them to use consonant blends and clusters to make the game more challenging.

Syllabication of Words

Syllabication is considered an important skill for children to learn to read large (polysyllabic) words (Shefelbine, Lipscomb, and Hern 1989). In fact, poor readers often rely too heavily on segmentation and blending skills, as opposed to using syllabification structures (Bhattacharya 2006), leading to the incorrect pronunciation of polysyllabic words. The two skills that serve as a means for determining unknown words involve using context clues and syllabication strategies. When students use context, they are instructed to skip over the unknown word and try to determine the word based upon the context of the sentence and the preceding sentence. When students use syllabication strategies, they try to break the word into recognizable "chunks" to pronounce the word. The assumption is that children have a store of words that they can use to match up with parts of the unknown word. Several studies have been conducted in which students with and without HI were taught syllabication techniques to successfully read polysyllabic words (Bhattacharya and Ehri 2004; Cunningham 1980; White 2005).

Analogy Strategy

Cunningham (1980) suggested using a compare/contrast process (or analogy strategy) to help children determine unknown polysyllabic words. This technique is based on the premise that students can determine the unknown word by using similar known words. For example, when students come across an unknown word from their reading, they should ask, "Are there parts of the word that look like words that I already know?" If so, students should apply a known part of the word to the unknown word. For example, for the word *cantankerous*, students would look for parts of similar-sounding words within the unknown word. The child might see the familiar words *cant*, *tank*, *er*, and *us*. The belief is that children already have these known words in memory and can find them using this compare/contrast process. If students do not have a store of known words, then the teacher would review or provide familiar words to help the child pronounce an unknown word.

To practice this skill, Cunningham (1980) gave students a "mystery word" that consisted of the number of letters from the word (that is, the mystery word *resolution* was given as 10 blanks), along with familiar words (*absolute*, *rebellion*, *attention*). The teacher pronounced each word, gave its definition, and used each in a sentence.

The goal of the game was for students to determine which clue word contains the beginning, middle, or end part of the mystery word. Next, students were to guess the unknown word by using the familiar words (that is, the student would ask, "Does the mystery word end like *attention*?"). If yes, the teacher would fill in the end part of the mystery word (*-tion*), and the students would continue guessing (middle like *absolute* and beginning like *rebellion*). After two weeks of training (or after solving 78 different mystery words), students were successful at increasing their decoding skills of unknown polysyllabic words.

Cunningham (1987) also suggests the following three games: Mystery Word Match (compare/contrast as previously described), Word Construction and Demolition, and Guess My Consonants. In the Word Construction and Demolition game, students begin with a root word (say, *nation*) and add affixes to build the word into a large polysyllabic word. For example, students add *-al* to create *national*, add *-ize* to create *nationalize*, add *inter-* to form *internationalize*, and finally add *-tion* to create *internationalization*. The purpose of this game is to help students understand that large polysyllabic words can be broken down (that is, by demolition) into smaller known words.

In another game, students can be given a sentence that contains a mystery word with blank spaces (one space for each missing consonant) but with the vowels written in the correct location among the blanks. Next, students read the sentence and guess letters (one at a time) to determine the word.

Graphosyllabic Procedure

Bhattacharya and Ehri (2004) taught students a graphosyllabic procedure for determining unknown words. The following rules were used:

1. Every syllable has a vowel in it, and there is only one vowel sound per syllable.
2. Each letter can go with only one syllable. (In other words, you cannot use the same letter in two different syllables.)
3. The vowel sounds of the syllable should be as close as possible to the whole word (for example, *mustard* should be pronounced like *must-ard* or *mus-tard*, not like *muse-tard*).

The training consists of the teacher explaining and modeling the correct way to segment a word into syllables. In doing so, the teacher presents students with a model word (say, *finish*) on an index card, reads the whole word aloud, says the word in syllables (*fin-ish*), and raises one finger for each syllable. Next, the teacher tells students that the word has two syllables; she tells students to use their fingers to spell the letters for each syllable, and finally, blend the syllables together to say the whole word. Students then practice breaking down words into syllables while the teacher provides feedback. Several different ways of dividing words are considered acceptable (*finish* could be pronounced *fin-ish* or *fi-nish*). Many of the syllabication rules can be learned using the mnemonic CLOVER (Learning Disabilities Association of Minnesota 2004).

First, students should check the unknown word for prefixes and suffixes and remove any prefixes or suffixes that are present; in some cases, students should be formally taught affixes and their meanings. Then students should use the CLOVER method to break the remaining word into syllables. CLOVER is an acronym for the six major syllable types found in the English language:

1. **C: Closed syllable.** A closed syllable has a short vowel sound and is followed by a single or double consonant (for example, *at, ex, un, ment, ness, black*). Keep double consonants together with the vowel and divide them off as a unit (*ex/pect, dis/tress*).

2. **L: -*le* syllable.** An *le* syllable represents a consonant before *le* (for example, *ble*, *tle*, *dle*, *zle*). Divide off at the beginning consonant along with the *le* syllable (*bot/tle*, *puz/zle*, *bat/tle*).

3. **O: Open syllable.** If an open syllable has a long vowel sound and ends in a vowel (for example, *o, a, be, re, tri*), divide off after the vowel sound (*mo/ment, ti/ger*).

4. **V: Vowel pair or double vowel.** For syllables with a vowel combination that makes a long vowel sound (*ai, ay, aw, oa, oo, oi, ou, ow, ee, ea, ie, ei, ue*), keep vowel pairs together, keep consonants before or after it, and divide off after the ending consonant (*train/er, con/geal, bea/gle*).

5. **E: Vowel and consonant with silent *e*.** This syllable has a long vowel sound and the *e* at the end is silent. Divide off as one unit (*re/mote, com/pete, des/pite, re/late*).

6. **R: R-controlled.** This is a syllable containing an *r*-controlled vowel (for example, *ar, or, er, ir, ur, ear, our*). Keep vowel(s) and *r* together and divide off (*chapt/er*).

Word Identification Strategy

The word identification strategy was developed by Lenz et al. (1984) and is meant to assist students in identifying unknown words. The keywords are action words that prompt students to perform a specific step. An important part of the strategy training involves teaching students an extensive lists of affixes (prefixes and suffixes) and the meaning of each. Like other strategies from the University of Kansas Center for Research on Learning, this specific methodology for teaching strategies involves an eight-step process:

1. Pretest and make commitment
2. Describe the strategy
3. Model the strategy
4. Verbal practice of strategy steps
5. Controlled practice
6. Advanced practice
7. Posttest and make commitment
8. Generalization, with substeps of orientation, activation, adaptation, and maintenance (Ellis, Deshler, Lenz, Schumaker, and Clark 1991; Schumaker and Deshler 2006)

The mnemonic DISSECT (Box 6.3) should prompt students to dissect or cut words apart to read them:

1. *Discover*: Skip the unknown word, read the rest of the sentence, and then use the information to guess the unknown word. If you still have difficulty, proceed to the next step.

2. *Isolate*: Look at the first few letters; can you identify a prefix? If so, draw a box around the prefix. If not, and you still can't identify the word, go to the next step.

3. *Separate*: Box off the suffix, if any.

4. *Say*: Try to say the stem. Then say all three parts (prefix, stem, and suffix), if recognized, together. If you cannot pronounce the stem, move to the next step.

5. *Examine*: Examine the stem using the "rules of twos and threes" (see Box 6.3). If you can now read the stem using these rules, combine the prefix, stem, and suffix together to pronounce the word. If you can't, go to the next step.

6. *Check* with either the teacher or, if appropriate, another student. If no one is available, go to the final step.

7. *Try* a dictionary: Look up the word and use the pronunciation guide to say the stem.

> ### BOX 6.3
>
> ## Word Identification Strategy—DISSECT
>
> **D** <u>D</u>iscover the context.
>
> **I** <u>I</u>solate the prefix.
>
> **S** <u>S</u>eparate the suffix.
>
> **S** <u>S</u>ay the stem.
>
> **E** <u>E</u>xamine the stem using the "Rules of Twos and Threes":
>
> > Rule 1: If a stem begins with (a) a vowel, divide off the first two letters; or (b) a consonant, divide off the first three letters.
> >
> > Rule 2: If you can't make sense of the stem after using Rule 1, take off the first letter of the stem and then use Rule 1 again.
> >
> > Rule 3: When two different vowels are together, try making both of the vowel sounds (*diet*). If this does not work, try pronouncing them together using only one of the vowel sounds (*believe*).
>
> **C** <u>C</u>heck with someone.
>
> **T** <u>T</u>ry a dictionary.

CASE 6.2   Trouble with Casey

Case Introduction

Now that you have worked through the first case in this chapter, you should feel comfortable addressing issues in a second case. In this case, two teachers work together in an inclusion classroom to meet the needs of all the students, but, in particular, the learning needs of young Casey.

Karen Watson currently works as a first-grade teacher at Rosewood Elementary School in North Carolina. Karen has been working with Lucy Taylor, the special education inclusion teacher, in her classroom for only a month. Still fairly new to each other, they are both working out the "kinks" in the classroom. The inclusion classroom is a mix of general education first-grade students and six special education students.

After undergoing some educational testing last month, Casey Percy was identified as having ADHD under the "other health impairment" (OHI) category. Casey's main academic difficulties continue to occur in reading, but her inattention and hyperactivity also affect other academic areas. In reading, she has specific problems with phonological awareness. For example, Casey knows her initial letter sounds but often forgets how to blend sounds together or confuses words with similar spellings (for example, *can* for *cat*). After her parents complained this year that she could not "sit still" and was "always bugging neighborhood children," along with teacher concerns, the school decided to move forward in testing Casey to see if she were eligible for special education services. Now Casey can receive special education services in the inclusion classroom, eligible under OHI.

Because Casey is in the lowest reading group, she has peers who have similar problems. This group typically works on early reading skills as they begin to learn to read. During a recent reading class, Casey seemed to be having an especially difficult time during the "Cap Game." In this game, students were working with "word groups." The word group that particular day was *at*. Students were given a cap (each contained a new consonant sound: *c, h, r, m,* and so on) and were to place it on the head to form a new word. Casey could pronounce the first combination (*cat*) but had a difficult time pronouncing new combinations. Although she knew each initial letter sound, she had difficulty blending them to pronounce the new words.

At the end of the day, Karen and Lucy met to recap the day and plan for the next day. Karen brought up Casey's difficulties and said, "Casey really had a rough time during reading. Do you think she'll ever catch on?" "Let's hope," said Lucy. The two teachers began brainstorming ideas to help Casey improve her phonological awareness skills. As the two began to co-plan lessons for the next day, they talked about how they could better integrate some of their ideas to help with Casey's reading problems.

CASE QUESTIONS

1. What early reading area would you target for remediation with Casey?
2. Name and describe two types of phonological awareness activities that you would use with Casey.

6-5 Putting It All Together: Incorporating Reading Skills into Lessons

As we have mentioned before, teaching students with HI to read involves teaching them multiple skills over time. For example, teaching sight words should be part of a larger reading lesson that might involve phonological awareness activities, reading in context activities, and listening comprehension activities. Torgesen et al. (2001) developed an instructional reading program in which students with LD, ages eight to 19, were introduced to a variety of reading activities, all within two 50-minute lessons (Box 6.4). Within one year following the training, 40 percent of them no longer needed special education services.

Basal Reading Series

Special education teachers regularly use basal readers or a **basal reading series** to teach children to read. Basal readers are books that contain short passages or stories that progressively become more difficult from the first few stories in each book to those at the end. The books are highly organized and typically arranged on levels that correspond with grade levels. Similar to basal readers, leveled books are written to follow a specific "leveling criteria" (for example, based upon the number of words, sentence length, complexity, predictability, and so on), which results in a graduated level of increasingly more difficult stories from one level to the next.

BOX 6.4

Sample Reading Lessons

LESSON ONE
- Sight words practice (10 minutes): Students practice new sight words.
- Spelling sight words (5 minutes): Using the same sight words, students practice spelling them while the teacher points out common patterns in them.
- Sight word games (10 minutes): The teacher uses the sight words in a game format. For example, the teacher uses pairs of matching sight words in a memory game such as Concentration.
- Phonics activity (10 minutes): The teacher teaches students common consonant and vowel combination in words by decoding and spelling the words.
- Oral reading (15 minutes): Students spend about 15 minutes reading either a graded series trade book or basal reader. This activity is based upon the student's current sight word knowledge and phonological awareness level.

LESSON TWO
- Sight words practice (10 minutes): Students practice recently introduced sight words or review previously taught sight words.
- Spelling practice (5 minutes): Students practice spelling sight words or other words that could be spelled phonetically.
- Silent and oral reading (20 minutes): Students practice reading a passage silently and then read the same passage orally to improve their fluency and accuracy.
- Writing activity (15 minutes): Students write sentences using sight words from current and previous practice sessions. The teacher monitors students for proper meaning of sentences, correct grammar, and correct spelling of words.

TIPS FOR GENERALIZATION

Connecting Skills Together

Reading involves more than just a collection of phonics-based activities; it is a combination of skills that are built slowly over time. A combination of phonological awareness activities (learning the code), sight words, and connected reading activities (that is, using words in context) will enable children to practice reading. Along with listening comprehension activities, such as teaching students to answer questions about a story that the teacher reads to them, students will slowly learn to read simple stories.

Early on in reading development, sight words are introduced and are often memorized, particularly during the first few lessons. Because sight words (sometimes referred to as "high-frequency" words) are seen in text repeatedly, students need exposure to them on a frequent basis. Essentially, basal readers are designed so that sight words are present in each story. Words from the first story repeat themselves in the next story (with a few more added), and words in successive stories are a reiteration of earlier learned words.

Although the use of sight words is useful in learning how to read, students cannot learn by sight all of the words needed to be a successful reader. Therefore, we teach phono-logical awareness skills so that students can segment (sound out) new words and blend those sounds together to pronounce the word. Segmenting skills also play a useful role in helping children determine vowel sounds for unfamiliar words. Rhyming also plays a supporting role as children sound out "vowel-sounding words" (rhyming words) and try to pick a match from long-term memory. Furthermore, using word patterns, children can match known words from prior knowledge with either matching words or word parts to decode unknown words.

The key to reading seems to be frequent exposure to reading skills, particularly those skills that can cross over or generalize from one activity to another. For example, if working on the phoneme *p* during a phonological awareness activity, teachers can use it in context in words as children learn sight words and as they read *p* words in a basal story. The more generalizing that can occur in class, the easier it will be for the child to use skills in a new context. Of course, using drill-and-practice activities with immediate feedback will ensure that children master skills, and constant feedback will prevent students from practicing errors or learning miscues.

Beginning teachers usually prefer basal readers because the teacher guides come with preplanned activities that correspond with each story and include pre-reading and post-reading activities. An advantage of using a basal reader is that new sight words (or vocabulary) are introduced in small increments in each story and, typically, the stories build on sight words learned in previous stories. Basal readers have been used in the United States since the 1860s, beginning with the McGuffey Readers. Over the years, others have included the once-popular Dick and Jane series. Despite the popularity of basal readers, some have criticized them as being too structured, focusing too much on teaching students isolated skills rather than encouraging children to read for the simple joy and love of reading (Shannon 1993).

THINK BACK TO THE CASE   with Casey . . .

1. *What early reading area would you target for remediation with Casey?*

Like Latasha in the first case, you could target a number of phonological skills for remediation with Casey, such as segmenting letter sounds, rhyming words, or blending letter sounds.

2. *Name and describe two types of phonological awareness activities that you would use with Casey.*

As mentioned earlier in the chapter, any number of phonological awareness activities, such as segmenting, blending, or rhyming activities, could benefit Casey, as well as any of the phonological awareness strategies.

Research Evidence

Phonological Awareness Strategy. This strategy was used with second-and third-grade students with HI (Boyle and Seibert 1997). The results indicated that from pretest to posttest, these children increased the number of monosyllabic and multisyllabic words that they were able to pronounce, and increased the correct pronunciation of words used during generalization, nonsense words, and unknown words.

Word Identification Strategy. This strategy was used with seventh-, eighth-, and ninth-grade students with LD (Lenz and Hughes 1990). The results indicated that trained students were able to reduce the number of errors from baseline (range was 6.3 to 20.5 errors) to post-training (range was 0 to 6.4 errors). The average baseline score for the group's reading ability level materials was 39 percent; it increased to 88 percent after training. The baseline average score for students on grade-level materials was 39 percent; it increased to 58 percent after training.

In a research brief, Bremer, Clapper, and Deshler (2002) reported the results of two studies. In the first study, ninth-grade students who were identified as struggling secondary readers were taught to use the word identification strategy. The results demonstrated that students with LD made large gains in word recognition, as did African American males and Hispanic males when compared to a comparison group of students. In the second study, sixth-grade struggling readers made impressive gains in both decoding and reading comprehension.

Finally, video lessons were used to teach the word identification strategy to students with HI, and the results showed that these video lessons were effective at increasing students' oral reading rates (Fitzgerald, Miller, Higgins, Pierce, and Tandy 2012).

Syllabication Techniques. According to Cunningham (1980), students who used the compare/contrast method improved their ability to pronounce words in isolation and in context more than those in a control group. They were also able to read polysyllabic words one week after testing. In the study by Bhattacharya and Ehri (2004), third-grade students with reading problems who were trained to use the graphosyllabic procedure outperformed students who were taught to read polysyllabic words as whole words. They also outperformed a control group of students on measures of segmenting words into syllables by counting and segmenting words by circling syllables.

CHAPTER SUMMARY

How students read can be explained by one of three models: top-down, bottom-up, or interactive. As students learn to read, they often use one or more of these models. Depending upon the difficulty of the text and the student's background knowledge of the topic, students may use different models at different times. As they learn to read, they progress through several stages, from initially understanding that spoken words are related to text, to learning *how* to read words, to later stages where they read to understand different viewpoints and read for the enjoyment of learning. Although most students transition smoothly through these stages, students with

HI often encounter problems as they learn to read. Some students lack phonological awareness, while others lack reading fluency and/or comprehension strategies.

Throughout this text, we have described not only reading skills that should be taught to students, but also strategies and techniques that teachers can use to help students remediate skill deficits in reading. We have emphasized that teaching reading should be more than just teaching disparate skills. Instead, reading skills should be combined into literacy lessons that teach students components of several related skills, such as sight words, phonics, fluency, and comprehension. An initial early reading lesson might involve teaching sight words for five minutes, having students practice in a "connected reading" activity for 10 minutes, listening to a story read by the teacher and answering questions for 10 minutes, and reading a worksheet on one initial letter sound for 10 minutes. Only through a variety of skills and applications of skill combinations do students with HI learn how to read.

KEY TERMS

Basal Reading Series, 215

Blending, 192

Bottom-Up Model, 192

Consonant Blends/Clusters, 192

Consonant Digraphs, 192

Decoding, 192

Decoding Skills, 192

Digraphs, 192

Diphthongs, 192

Phonemes, 192

Phonics, 205

Phonological Awareness, 205

Phonological Deficit Hypothesis, 198

Pseudo-reading, 194

Segmenting, 192

Sight Words, 192

Structural Analysis, 192

Top-Down Model, 193

Vowel Digraphs, 192

Word-Attack Skills, 198

APPLICATION ACTIVITIES

Using information from the chapter, complete the following activities that were designed to help you apply the knowledge that was presented in this chapter.

1. Visit a reading website such as www.readwritethink.org (or other reading website), and review an *early reading lesson plan*. Identify the early reading skills being taught. List two other activities from this book that could be used to teach one of the skills described in the lesson.

2. Design a literacy lesson composed of different reading activities that will help children develop reading skills. Be sure to include lesson objectives and one or two state standards in your lesson.

3. You are assigned a new first-grade student who has reading deficits in word attack. Describe some activities that you could use in your classroom to improve his word-attack skills.

Steve Smith/Photodisc/Getty Images

7 Later Reading: Strategies and Techniques

Learning Objectives

After reading this chapter, you will understand:

7-1 Components that make up fluency

7-2 Reading comprehension and the different types of comprehension questions

7-3 Common problems students with HI encounter in reading

7-4 How to monitor reading and comprehension

7-5 Strategies and techniques to improve the vocabulary skills of students with HI

7-6 Strategies and techniques to improve the fluency skills of students with HI

7-7 Strategies and techniques to improve the reading comprehension skills of students with HI

CEC **Initial Preparation Standard 5: Instructional Planning and Strategies**

5-2 Beginning special education professionals use technologies to support instructional assessment, planning, and delivery for individuals with exceptionalities.

5-4 Beginning special education professionals use strategies to enhance language development and communication skills of individuals with exceptionalities.

5-6 Beginning special education professionals teach to mastery and promote generalization of learning.

5-7 Beginning special education professionals teach cross-disciplinary knowledge and skills such as critical thinking and problem solving to individuals with exceptionalities.

How proficient are secondary-level students with HI in the area of reading?

On average, students with HI can read only at the fourth-grade level when entering high school (Deshler and Schumaker 2006). Others have found that, compared to students' actual grade level, secondary students with disabilities are on average 3.6 years behind their grade level in reading, with 26 percent of those being 5 or more grade levels behind, and another 41 percent who are 3 to 4.9 grade levels behind in reading (Wagner et al. 2003). Moreover, the 2015 National Assessment of Educational Progress (NAEP 2017) in reading indicated that among 12th-grade students with disabilities, 63 percent scored below the *basic level**, compared to only 19 percent of nondisabled students. Similar distributions were found for eighth-grade students who took the 2015 NAEP, with 63 percent of the students with disabilities scoring below the *basic-level* reading (NAEP 2017). Thus, students with disabilities who have reading problems will more than likely have difficulty gaining information from textbooks and other school resources. At the secondary level, achievement of three to five years behind in reading is likely to hinder students' ability to access the general education curriculum and to tackle the increasingly complex academic content called for by most state standards tests (Wagner et al. 2003).

In Chapter 6, you learned about reading models, stages of reading, and reading techniques, strategies, and activities for addressing the early reading problems of students with HI. In this chapter, you will learn about later reading methods and strategies. This chapter is mainly about reading fluency and comprehension; yet, we will weave into this content information about various reading models to help you better understand how students learn to read. We will also discuss skills and strategies for addressing students with reading fluency and comprehension problems. Finally, we describe numerous reading interventions (for example, class-wide peer tutoring); however, if searching for additional reading interventions, including commercial reading programs (for example, Reading Recovery), please access the What Works Clearinghouse website (http://ies.ed.gov/ncee/wwc).

Just as with Habib in Case 7.1, reading can be an exasperating experience for students with disabilities. Despite having general proficiency in the basic skills of reading, many students find reading a laborious process, and fluency and comprehension remain challenges for them. Because students with HI have processing and memory problems that interfere with learning, acquiring reading skills can often become a discouraging and frustrating experience. Further, even when English is not an elementary student's primary language, reading instruction in school typically begins with English phonics instruction (Reese et al. 2000; Swanson, Sáez, and Gerber 2006). Such children develop conversational proficiency in one language but begin to develop reading proficiency in another. Although they may appear proficient at the basic skills of reading, fluent reading and comprehension can be more challenging. It is up to you, as their special education teacher, to help students develop effective reading skills so that reading can become an enjoyable activity.

7-1   The Role of Fluency in Becoming a Skilled Reader

As illustrated in the case about Habib, fluency and comprehension go hand in hand in terms of reading difficulties. They are probably the most common reading problems for older students with disabilities. These two components are inextricably tied

---

*Of the three categories (basic, proficient, advanced), basic represented the lowest category of performance. Under the basic category, students should be able to identify and relate aspects of the text to overall meaning, make simple inferences, recognize interpretations, relate text ideas to their own personal experiences, and draw conclusions.

CASE 7.1   I Give Up!

Case Introduction

In this case, you will read about Habib, a student who has trouble with later reading skills. As you read the case, you will see that his teacher has tried a number of different teaching techniques, and yet Habib is still having problems.

At the end of the case, you will find case questions. These questions are meant to serve as points for reflection. Of course, if you can answer them immediately, you should do so, but you may want to wait to answer them until you have read the portion of the chapter that pertains to the particular case question. Throughout the rest of the chapter, you will see the same questions. As you see them, try to answer them based upon the portion of the chapter that you just read.

Habib is a third-grade student who was recently classified as having high incidence mental retardation. He was classified due to his low cognitive and achievement scores. The reading specialist and a member of his eligibility committee, Niki Gersten, has been working at his school, Poole Elementary, for several years. During her recent assessment, she found that Habib mainly had problems with fluency and comprehension. His fluency problems stem from the fact that Habib stumbles over many of the second- and third-grade-level words found in his literature reading series. He also has problems recalling facts and details from stories and cannot stay on task for long periods of time.

Two weeks after his eligibility determination, Niki began working with him. Niki has tried a number of different activities, including reviewing sight words prior to reading the story, having Habib spell his sight words, alternating between reading aloud to him and having him read aloud to her, and having Habib take the story home to read to his parents. Despite her best teaching efforts, Habib's current average reading rate is 57 correct words per minute (cwpm). This is well below the recommended reading rate of 79 cwpm for a third-grade student.

During a recent reading session, Niki had Habib read the story "Best Wishes, Ed," by James Stevenson (2003). The story is about a wayward penguin that floats off on an iceberg that has split in two as he sleeps. As Habib read the passage, he made numerous errors. The passage went as follows:

One night when Ed was asleep, he heard a loud noise, like ice cracking. Ed thought it was a dream. When he woke up, he saw that the island of ice was cracking in two. He was all alone on an island of his own. Ed's friends looked very little as his island floated away. Ed watched until he couldn't see them anymore.

As Habib was reading the passage, he made several miscues, including mistaking *nose* for *noise*, *creek* for *cracking*, *isand* for *island*, and *wake* for *watched*. He also skipped the word *until*, and did not seem to notice or self-correct. Niki recorded his miscues and, when he finished this passage, asked Habib two questions. The first was, "When Ed heard the ice cracking, what did he think was happening?" Habib answered that Ed seemed to be having a bad dream. Next, Niki asked, "When Ed's ice split, who else was with Ed as he drifted off?" Habib answered that his brother was with him when he floated off. Immediately, Niki told Habib that his answer was wrong and that Ed was alone when he floated away.

He then read the next passage:

Then he walked all over the island. There was nobody on it at all. At last, he came to his own footprints again. Some birds flew over. Ed waved, but they did not wave back. "I think I will be here the rest of my life," Ed said. When the day was over, Ed wrote the words "I GIVE UP" in the snow. Then he went to sleep.

During his reading, Niki again recorded errors. This time, Habib made fewer miscues. His miscues on this reading included mistaking *none* for *nobody*, *against* for *again*, and *wave* for *waved*. During this brief intermission, Niki again asked two questions. "Was there anyone else on the island?" Habib answered. "No." When Niki probed further as to how he knew that nobody else was on the island, Habib responded, "It said there was nobody on it." The next question Niki asked was, "Why did Ed write the words, 'I GIVE UP' in the snow?" Habib answered, "Ed was sleepy." Niki quickly restated her question: "Why did Ed give up?" Habib answered, "Because he was sleepy and wanted to go to sleep." (The answer Niki was looking for was that no one else was on the island, and Ed was tired of looking.) "Not really," said Niki, "Ed was tired of looking for everyone else and finally gave up."

As Habib read the rest of the story, he made several more miscues and responded incorrectly to several of Niki's comprehension questions. With only two pages to go, Habib was at the end of his rope and was too exasperated to read anymore. Finally, he said to Niki, "I give up!" He soon followed with the statement, "Now I know how Ed the penguin felt." Niki realized that, despite her best prodding and rewarding, she may have pushed Habib too far, and she felt badly. She gave him a sticker (of a penguin), told him he did a great job, and walked him back to his class.

CASE QUESTIONS

1. What skill area would you target to remediate for Habib in reading?
2. What other skills would you, as the teacher, address?
3. Name and describe one type of fluency activity that you would use with Habib.

together when students read. Although it may be possible for a student to read fluently and lack comprehension, it is nearly impossible for a child who has fluency problems to have successful comprehension.

Fluency is not necessarily a skill that first comes to mind when teachers think about teaching reading skills. In fact, some have called fluency the "neglected goal" of reading programs (Heitin 2015). Fluency began to gain national attention from the National Reading Panel's (2000) findings that identified fluency as one of the five essential areas in teaching children to read (the five areas being phonemic awareness, phonics, fluency, comprehension, and vocabulary). Prior to this report, other researchers have known the importance of fluency in helping children to become proficient readers, yet little was done to include it in the daily staple of activities found in reading programs. For example, LaBerge and Samuels' (1974) seminal research discussed the role of automaticity in reading and posited that fluent readers are those children who have mastered decoding subskills at an automatic level. Because of their mastery of decoding skills, their attention during reading is free to focus on meaning and comprehension. Because of their mastery of word recognition, fluent readers can chunk information into larger units that aid them in comprehension. Still, more recent studies have begun to parse fluency into its basic components and have reported an additive effect of having students use prosody during reading for improved comprehension (Veenendaal, Groen, and Verhoeven 2015).

Components of Reading Fluency

Being a fluent reader is more than just being able to read fast. In fact, when someone reads fluently, he or she does not necessarily speak quickly, but the words sound natural and language-like (Stahl 2006). With this in mind, consider the three components of **reading fluency**: accuracy, rate, and prosody (Hudson, Lane, and Pullen 2005):

- **Accuracy** As students read, they need to read accurately (or read the words correctly) and in a smooth motion to understand the text. For readers to read words accurately, they must have the prerequisite skills of phonological awareness, word knowledge, and word-attack skills.
- **Rate** When we think of reading fluency, *rate* is perhaps the most common term associated with it. Rate typically refers to automaticity when reading words, such as reading sight words (in isolation or in connected readings), and is often associated with the "speed" at which students can read these words. Reading at an appropriate rate also involves reading quickly and effortlessly (Rasinski 2003). Usually teachers measure rate based upon the number of correct words read per minute or the amount of time it takes to complete a story.
- **Prosody** This term refers to reading "with expression." The belief is that students who can read with expression understand the author's message and tone (Prescott-Griffin and Witherell 2004). When reading with prosody or expression, students break sentences into *phrases* and correctly use stress, intonation, and duration as they read each phrase (Schreiber 1991). Readers who break sentences down into phrases are able to gain a deeper understanding of the text, rather than just reading individual words in the text. These students can use larger phrases and are then able to focus their attention on the meaning of the text. Good readers use both textual cues, such as punctuation, as well as other cues, such as knowledge of phonological and morphological rules. These rules enable students to place the proper stress while reading multisyllabic words, proper intonation (that is, high or low pitch) when pronouncing words, and proper duration (that is, saying a word quickly or elongating its pronunciation) when speaking these words.

Fluency Development and Its Role in Chall's Early Stages

As you recall from the previous chapter, Chall (1983) refers to one of the first stages of reading as **Stage 1: Initial reading or decoding stage**. During this stage, students focus on breaking the code of reading through the acquisition of phonological skills and knowledge of sight words. At this stage, students are immersed in texts that have stories that use *narrative text*. Stories with narrative text are rich in dialogue and imagery. Next, children move through **Stage 2: Confirmation, fluency, and ungluing from print stage**. During this stage, children master their decoding skills and automaticity with text. As they learn to read words with automaticity, they also learn how to read using text features, such as punctuation and chunking of words into phrases (Kuhn and Stahl 2000). Using these prosodic features, children now move one step closer toward understanding the author's message and intent. Fluency now becomes the main focus of reading with children so that they can practice their word attack and gain meaning from the text. Somewhere in Stage 2 or Stage 3, children are introduced to *expository text*. In the next stage, **Stage 3: Reading for learning the new**, children become fully immersed in expository text. In reading expository stories, children now face a new challenge, as the structure of the text changes from narratives that dealt with plot, characters, and sequences of events to passages that deal with main ideas and details (Kuhn and Stahl 2000). Prior comprehension skills and newly developed ones become even more critical in this stage, as text becomes more difficult to understand and children are introduced to increasingly more difficult vocabulary from content-area textbooks.

Ehri's Phases of Development in Sight-Word Learning

Although Chall's stages describe reading in broad terms, Ehri's phases describe the skill of reading *sight words*. As students move from Stage 1 through Stage 2 of Chall's model, they go through a series of phases to learn words by sight (Ehri 1995, 1998; Pikulski and Chard 2005). According to Ehri (1995), students learn all words—irregularly spelled as well as easily decodable words—through a process of reading that occurs throughout phases of development. As children progress through these phases, they begin to learn words by making multiple connections based upon a word's spelling, pronunciation, and meaning. Eventually, the most skilled readers learn words by breaking them down into chunks of letters. Ehri believes that grapho-phoneme knowledge is essential in learning how to read and that, along with early phonological and word-attack skills, learning to spell words is also critical because the two are intertwined as children learn to read words quickly and accurately. Ehri's four phases are *pre-alphabetic, partial alphabetic, full alphabetic*, and *consolidated alphabetic*, and are illustrated in Figure 7.1.

The first phase that children go through is the **pre-alphabetic phase**. In this phase, beginners connect visual attributes of the word and its letters to pronunciations and the meaning of the word. Children may learn *pasta* because the *S* in the middle looks like a pasta noodle. These visual cues are learned early for children and, although helpful in this phase, become unreliable as children become exposed to other similarly spelled words. For most students, this first phase occurs through paired associates learning. As such, the cue is paired with the pronounced word and stored in long-term memory, rather than learning letters with their associated letter sounds.

In the next phase, the **partial alphabetic phase**, children begin to learn that certain letters are associated with letter sounds. In this phase, children begin to use phonological awareness skills to associate certain letters in the word to pronounce the word. When children first learn to read words, they often rely on the first and last letters of a word to pronounce it (Bowman and Treiman 2002). For example, as former teachers,

▶ **FIGURE 7.1**

Ehri's Phases of Sight-Word
Learning

Pre-alphabetic Phase

bed

Child learns bed *because he thinks
it looks like an actual bed.*

Full Alphabetic Phase

stop

"s" "t" "o" "p"

*Child segments each sound and
blends back together.*

Partial Alphabetic Phase

boot

b - - t

Child learns boot *by pronouncing "b" and "t"
and remembers this word because it begins
with a "b" sound and ends in a "t" sound.*

Consolidated Alphabetic Phase

stop

"st" "op"

Child uses knowledge of word parts.

Adapted from Ehri, L. 1998. Grapheme-phoneme knowledge is essential for learning to read words in English. In *Word Recognition in Beginning Literacy*, ed. J. Metsala and L. Ehri, Mahwah, NJ: Lawrence Erlbaum.

we can remember children in this stage trying to pronounce the word *out*. They would open their mouths for the *o* sound and the *t* sound and then say the word *out*. They would use partial cues because they had not yet mastered all of the phonemes with graphemes. Although these students were well on their way toward developing phonological awareness, they often had difficulty with similarly spelled words.

Next, as children become more proficient with letters in words and their associated phonemes, they move into the **full alphabetic phase**. As children encounter familiar and new words, they are able to apply their phonological awareness skills to segment the word into letter sounds and blend these sounds back together to pronounce the word. In addition, children in this phase can now correctly discern between similarly spelled words. As children are able to read words as sight words, they can now alternate their attention between reading words on the page and constructing meaning from those words.

Finally, in the last phase, the **consolidated alphabetic phase**, children are able to pronounce words by recalling word parts or letter patterns. Typically, children learn word parts such as *ing, ion, est, ent,* or *able*. Children then use their knowledge of word parts when they encounter multisyllabic words in their reading. According to Ehri (1998), these letter patterns become part of the student's knowledge about reading and spelling. As such, spelling becomes part of the reading process. Accordingly, if children can spell words that they read, then it would make sense that these words would be stored rather strongly in memory and should improve their reading. As it turns out, research has confirmed that spelling instruction improves students' abilities in phonological awareness and reading (Graham and Santangelo 2014).

Why Is Reading Fluency Important?

Fluency is important in learning to read for two main reasons. First, fluency is deeply intertwined with reading comprehension. For children to have the mental resources to comprehend the meaning of the text, they must be fluent readers. Fluent readers are able to switch their attention instantaneously back and forth from word recognition (or decoding) to understanding the meaning of the text being read. They not only have a store of sight words and efficient decoding skills, but they use comprehension monitoring strategies that help them to detect when the text does not make sense. Moreover, from a large-scale data analysis completed by NAEP for reading, Pinnell et al. (1995) found a positive correlation between reading fluency and comprehension. Their work demonstrated that those students who rated higher on a fluency scale performed better on the NAEP reading assessment. Likewise, other researchers have found that fluency is highly correlated with reading comprehension (Deno 1985; Jenkins, Fuchs, et al. 2003a, 2003b), and that interventions that increased fluency also increased reading comprehension (Kuhn and Stahl 2000).

Second, fluency helps readers understand the subtle or hidden meanings associated with an author's intent. Prosody enables readers to understand if the author is using irony or has stated things incorrectly in the text. A combination of background knowledge and prosody also probably helps students to fully understand an author's intent. Lack of fluency leaves little room for comprehension. In turn, this "inadequate capacity for comprehension robs reading of its inherent enjoyment because few resources are left for processing meaning, reflecting, becoming absorbed in a narrative, understanding humor, and using one's imagination" (Nathan and Stanovich 1991).

7-2 Understanding Reading Comprehension

Reading comprehension is the ability to understand what is read. Although other skills such as phonological awareness, phonics, fluency, and vocabulary are important skills to teach children, teachers should remember that the end goal of teaching children to read is comprehension. For readers, understanding text is a constructive process whereby readers use the text, prior knowledge of the topic, and comprehension skills and strategies to decode the text into meaningful units of connected knowledge. The keys to reading involve not only being able to say the word and know its meaning, but also connecting it to prior knowledge throughout the process.

In reading, some view each unit of organized knowledge as a schema (plural is schemata) for a particular concept (Gunning 2000; Reutzel and Cooter 2005). A schema is defined as an "organized knowledge structure" (Gagne 1985; Liu, 2015), and can be thought of as a three-dimensional spider web. The topic is in the center of the web and is linked to features that characterize it. Schema theory attempts to explain how information is stored in long-term memory for different topics or concepts. For example, a simplified schema of the concept "fish" might look like the example in Figure 7.2. Each schema is linked to other schemata to form a complex of networks within one's long-term memory. When students read information, they use prior knowledge of the topic to construct meaning. As the students read, they retrieve information from long-term memory into working memory. They then read and parse or chunk information that is read. This new information is then added to the retrieved schema to form a newly reconstructed or elaborated schema that can be stored in long-term memory. This process occurs repeatedly until the students have completed the story (Gagne 1985). In doing so, students fill in new information from reading with existing information in the schema.

Types of Reading Comprehension Questions

In the last chapter, we discussed the different kinds of comprehension questions found in basal readers and textbooks. Authors use three main types of questions to check a student's comprehension of text (Applegate, Quinn, and Applegate 2002). The first type is **textually explicit** or **literal comprehension** questions. A factual recall question

► **FIGURE 7.2**

Schema of a Fish

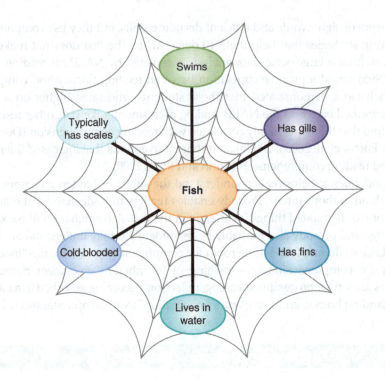

is a type of textually explicit question. These types of questions are typically derived directly from the printed text on the page. For example, read the following sentences about a fictitious alien species:

Breggs raffled on the carbet squod.
Breggs raffled loudly and quirked precociously.

Now, answer the following questions:

1. Who raffled?
2. Where did Breggs raffle?
3. What did Breggs do?

Even though you knew nothing about this alien species, you were able to answer the questions by directly reading the text. These are known as textually explicit (or literal) questions. The answers can be found directly from the text or passage.

The next type of comprehension question is **textually implicit** or **inferential**. With this type of question, your students are required to think and make conclusions about information that might not be readily evident from reading the passage or text. In other words, the students read "between the lines" to answer the questions. As you could guess, these questions are more difficult. Students find information to answer textually implicit questions by reading different parts of the story (textually derived) and then piecing together those parts to answer the question.

Read the following excerpt:

> *Mr. Johnson opened his umbrella and decided to head home. The weather outside was beginning to turn ugly. His slow stroll turned into a run as the dark clouds opened up to dump their wet contents. The heavy wind banking off the tall buildings made the weather even worse. Even the sidewalks themselves took on a cascading effect. Finally, Mr. Johnson could barely see a few feet in front of him and had no choice but to hail a taxi.*

Now, answer the following textually implicit questions:

1. What was the weather doing?
2. How was Mr. Johnson traveling before he caught a taxi?

Finally, the last type of question is **scriptally implicit**. This type of question requires students to use their script (or schema) of the topic to answer the question (Liu 2015; Pearson and Johnson 1978). Using background and long-term memory of the topic, students must use this information to answer the question (Lipson and Wixson 1997; Pearson and Johnson 1978). In some cases, students may have to defend their responses by explaining how they derived their answers. Read the excerpt again and answer the following scriptally implicit questions:

1. What locality (for example, farm, home, city) was Mr. Johnson coming from?
2. Do you think Mr. Johnson got wet? Why or why not?
3. When Mr. Johnson began to run, what would other people on the same street be doing?

Other Elements of Reading Fluency and Comprehension

Not to be overlooked, other factors play a role in acquiring fluency and comprehension skills. These include prior knowledge of the topic, knowledge of text elements and text structure, language skills, "practice" with easy reading materials, and vocabulary development (Perfetti 1985).

As described by schema theory, prior background knowledge does make a difference in how students comprehend information. Students with prior background about a topic seem to attack the reading task differently and comprehend better than students who lack prior knowledge (McNamara and Kintsch 1996). The more background knowledge a student has about a topic, the more the student can connect with the ideas being read in the text. When key words or concepts are encountered, students are able to access this information from long-term memory and make connections to create "meaning" in working memory (Pardo 2004). Moreover, active processing during reading (via drawing on knowledge stored in long-term memory) seems to be critical in achieving high levels of comprehension (Gilabert, Martinez, and Vidal-Abarca 2005). This means that teachers should activate prior knowledge before reading, so that this knowledge is available for students to use for making connections with ideas from their reading.

If students do not have adequate prior knowledge about a topic, it might be useful for teachers to build knowledge about an upcoming topic well beforehand; doing so immediately prior to reading may not help students to make "meaningful" connections (Gilabert, Martinez, and Vidal-Abarca 2005; McNamara and Kintsch 1996), because their new background knowledge will not have been adequately assimilated into long-term memory. Therefore, teachers should prepare days or weeks ahead of time by using informational books and having discussions on various topics (concepts). These planned-out *knowledge-building sessions* will better prepare students to use new information and build a storehouse of knowledge about the concept.

Knowledge of text structures and elements of text is also useful for students to increase reading comprehension. With narrative text, knowledge of common **text elements** such as setting, characters, problem, solution, and outcome have been found to be useful to aid reading comprehension (Hall, Sabey, and McClellan 2005). In expository books, authors organize information using typical structural patterns called **text structure**. The following common text structures can be found in most expository text: description (or enumerative), problem/solution, comparison/contrast, cause/effect, and sequence (Hall, Sabey, and McClellan 2005; Pardo 2004). Pointing out these text structures before children read will enable them to organize the information during reading and, if accompanied by a visual organizer or framework, will enable students to understand the content of the passage better. The following are the common types of text structure:

- **Description** This type of text provides specific details about a topic, person, event, or idea.
- **Problem/solution** This type of text presents a problem, perhaps explains why it is a problem, and then offers possible solutions, usually settling on one solution as most appropriate.
- **Comparison/contrast** This type of text points out differences and similarities between two or more topics, including ideas, people, locations, or events. This text structure can be signaled by key words and phrases such as *like, as, still, although, yet, but, however,* and *on the other hand.*
- **Cause/effect** This type of text links events (effects) with their causes. Such text usually includes key words and phrases, called causal indicators to signal a cause-and-effect relationship structure. Some common causal indicators are *because, for, since, therefore, so, consequently, due to,* and *as a result.*
- **Sequencing** This type of text presents information in terms of a time or order sequence, such as the actions that led to an important historical event or the steps in a scientific process. This kind of structure most often includes signal words such as *first, second, last, earlier, later, now, then, next, after, during,* and *finally.*

Some experts (Perfetti and Marron 1995; Stahl 2006) also claim that language skills play a major role in the comprehension of text. Reading comprehension appears to be one subcomponent of language skills. In turn, language skills help students understand what they read. These language skills and experiences help frame our knowledge of a topic and help guide us as we read. Weaver (2002) suggests that, when we read, we use language skills and experiences, along with the syntactic and semantic cues in text, to help make sense of the text and to monitor comprehension. In fact, learning to read and write is highly correlated with oral language in English-speaking, as well as English-language-learning (ELL) students (Miller, Heilmann, Nockerts, Iglesias, Fabiano, and Francis 2006).

Vocabulary represents another important area that relates to fluency and comprehension skills. Unfortunately, students with HI are at a real disadvantage when learning new vocabulary because they often lack strategies for learning words "in context," often do not engage in much independent reading (that is, where they would encounter new vocabulary words and be able to use them in new contexts) (Jitendra et al. 2004), and often lack background knowledge about the new vocabulary words. Therefore, before reading, teachers should consider spending time discussing and teaching vocabulary words, including finding what students already know about the vocabulary word or related words. In addition, having students learn vocabulary from text glossaries may not necessarily enable students to make meaningful connections that can be stored in long-term memory (Blachowicz and Fisher 2000). As such, teachers should use a variety of techniques to engage students when learning new vocabulary words.

Finally, practice makes perfect, or at least enables students with HI to become better readers. Reading a lot *does* matter (Adams 1990). Children need to read to practice the reading skills that they have learned. This may mean restricting students to certain books based upon individual reading levels, and showing children how to choose books based upon readability and text features. These steps will help students to have success and avoid frustration during reading. Highly effective teachers also find ways to maximize the amount of time their students have for easy reading by providing regular "blocks" of time when students can engage in independent silent reading or partner reading (Allington 2002). DEAR or "drop everything and read" time is one way to accomplish this in the school day.

7-3 Reading Fluency and Comprehension Difficulties of Students with HI

Research has shown that students with HI have numerous problems related to reading fluency and comprehension: they often (1) have slower reading rates—up to three times as slow when compared to their nondisabled peers (Jenkins et al. 2003a); (2) make more miscues (Jenkins et al. 2003a); (3) read in a slow, halting manner that impedes reading accuracy (Katzir et al. 2006); and (4) have a difficult time recognizing many words and acquiring word-reading proficiency (Idol 1988; Jenkins et al. 2003a), making inferences in text (Cain and Oakhill 1999), and with general reading comprehension when compared to peers (Jenkins et al. 2003a).

Other research shows that these students perform poorly (when compared to peers) in reading rate and accuracy of words from a list and in context (Jenkins et al. 2003a). Many students with HI perform 1.5 to 2 grade levels or more below average on reading measures when compared to peers (Jenkins et al. 2003a), and, as time progresses, frequently fall farther behind as they struggle to keep up with their peers and as they encounter fewer grade-level words (Al Otaiba and Rivera 2006).

As mentioned earlier, these inefficient word-recognition skills tax attentional resources and consume memory resources that are much needed for comprehension (Jenkins et al. 2003b). As a result, many students with HI have reading comprehension problems due to poor fluency, as well as due to other reading difficulties such as poor reading-comprehension strategies. In one particular study, reading words in context (versus reading words in isolation) was the best predictor of comprehension (Jenkins et al. 2003b). It is surmised that when students read words in context, they are able to chunk words into meaningful phrases and are also able to use other cues from the context that assist them at reading (Jenkins et al. 2003a).

In addition to fluency problems, students with disabilities may also have problems with weak vocabularies, grammatical awareness, and background knowledge; may have poor retrieval strategies; and may lack knowledge of text structure, all of which lead or contribute to poor comprehension (Gersten et al. 2001; Venable 2003). Other researchers claim that these students exhibit executive processing deficits and strategy deficits (Pressley 1991; Swanson 1999; Wong 1991) that contribute to or cause reading comprehension problems.

Finally, in terms of strategy knowledge, experts sum it up nicely when they point out that students with HI either do not have an appropriate reading strategy for a particular situation, may not know when to use the strategy (that is, lack metacognition of strategy use), or may not be willing to use a particular reading strategy even if they are taught it (Gersten et al. 2001). Moreover, from an Executive Function perspective, students with HI have difficulty using strategies flexibly and shifting between strategies as the nature of the text changes (Meltzer 2010). All three of these issues present challenges to teachers. However, teachers can take steps to ensure that students learn a strategy or technique, implement it with appropriate reading materials, generalize it to new settings and materials, and use it on a regular basis.

THINK BACK TO THE FIRST CASE with Habib . . .

1. What skill area would you target to remediate for Habib in reading?

Fluency would be one skill that you could target with Habib. More specifically, you could target fluency of words in context. You might also want to assess Habib's knowledge of words presented in a list. It would also be useful to assess his word-attack skills to determine whether he is using them appropriately.

2. What other skills would you, as the teacher, address?

Reading comprehension is another area that you could address. His fluency problems might be related to his comprehension problems. If so, you might want to target both fluency and reading comprehension.

7-4   Monitoring Reading Fluency and Comprehension

To know what kind of help your students need with fluency and comprehension, you need accurate information about their performance, not just your general impressions. Assessing fluency can be accomplished in any number of ways. Perhaps the most common is to select a starting point in a passage where you want your student to begin reading aloud and then time the student for one to three minutes. Count the number of words read correctly and divide by the total number of minutes read. This gives you the student's contextual reading rate in correct words per minute (cwpm). Complete this procedure a few times and average the cwpm rate. Of course, you should also note the reading level of the passage selected. (For an example, see the graph in the Methods and Strategies Spotlight.)

Methods and Strategies Spotlight

Using Curriculum-Based Measurement for Monitoring Reading Fluency

As we stress throughout this book, good teaching is data-driven. This means that you will determine how you teach (what teaching method you use) by the method's effectiveness for the target student, as shown by the student performance data that you gather. Recall that C-BM involves assessing one child on one skill over time. In the following case, this teacher chose to target correct words per minute (cwpm) because reading rate is highly correlated with reading comprehension. He set a goal cwpm based on the student's baseline performance and the expected rate for typical readers the student's age.

First, the teacher determined the student's current reading rate, which serves as the starting point or baseline (48 cwpm). Next, he determined a goal from the chart of oral fluency rates (see Table 7.1) and from averaging reading rates from nondisabled peers (for example, 90 cwpm).

Once the teacher decided upon 90 cwpm as the goal, he then connected the baseline point to the goal and drew in the aimline. Using different reading instructional methods, he determined that the student was not making adequate progress, so changes were needed in instruction. The rule of thumb is that a change in teaching methods or techniques should occur if data from three consecutive days fall below the aimline (Salvia and Hughes 1990), and should continue until the child's data is above the aimline.

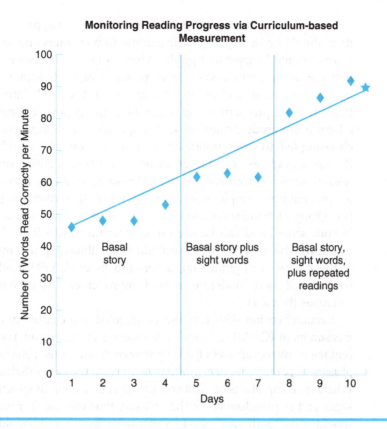

Monitoring Reading Progress via Curriculum-based Measurement

Because oral reading rates vary among sources, we developed a table (Table 7.1) that was derived from multiple sources (adapted from Hasbrouck and Tindal 1992; Hudson, Lane, and Pullen 2005; and Rasinski and Padak 2004). This table should serve as a guide to help teachers determine appropriate levels of fluency. Students who fall below the lower of the two numbers in a given range are probably experiencing problems with fluency and should receive assistance in improving their fluency. The middle or upper portions of each range (per grade level) can be used as goals for students to achieve (for example, 70 to 90 cwpm for a second grader).

TABLE 7.1 Oral Fluency Rates of Words Read in Context

Grade	Correct Words Per Minute
1	25–50
2	50–90
3	70–110
4	95–125
5	110–140
6	125–150
7	130–160
8	135–170

Please keep in mind that this table represents an approximation of where children should be in terms of their reading fluency rates and, as with other fluency charts, should be used as a guide. When using any fluency chart that illustrates a national norm group, always develop and incorporate local norms. In most cases, because your goal will be to integrate a child with HI into the general education's reading program, using students in the general education class as part of a local norm group makes sense. For special education teachers, this could mean choosing five to seven nondisabled students from general education (who are in the same grade as your target student) and then eliciting one- to three-minute reading samples from each of them. These general education students should be a representative sample of students from the class. Averaging the cwpm rates for this group of nondisabled students may give you a better feel for reading rates in your school and can be used in combination with Table 7.1 to determine the extent to which a child with disabilities has fluency problems. Although the use of these tables can guide you, others (Fuchs et al. 1993; Fuchs and Fuchs 2004) recommend more moderate rates of improvement, based upon words-per-week increases (Box 7.1).

Comprehension skills can also be targeted and charted using curriculum-based measurement (C-BM) techniques. To assess comprehension, you could monitor percentage of correct answers to comprehension questions, percentage of correct paraphrases of paragraphs, or performance on cloze measures (Salvia and Hughes 1990). Whatever comprehension skill you monitor, be careful in selecting the reading passages and standardization of the measure that you use. For example, your student should consistently read passages of similar length and should slowly move up to higher readability level passages in an incremental fashion (for example, from third-grade readability level passages to fourth-grade readability level passages to fifth-grade readability, and so on). On each level, students should not advance to the next level until they have met a criterion for mastery (for example, 80 percent comprehension). Moreover, comprehension questions should remain constant in terms of the number and the type of questions (for example, textually explicit, textually implicit, and scriptally implicit).

Finally, an alternative way to assess reading fluency and other early reading skills is called Dynamics Indicators of Basic Early Literacy Skills (DIBELS). DIBELS are short (one-minute), standardized measures used to assess early reading skills (that is, initial sound fluency, letter naming fluency, phoneme segmentation fluency, nonsense word fluency, oral reading fluency, and retell fluency) for students in kindergarten through sixth grade. These measures are meant to be used frequently to monitor the early reading performance of students throughout the school year. When students' scores are compared to benchmark goals, teachers can quickly determine if the student has a deficit or is at risk, or whether the skill

---

BOX 7.1

Average Cwpm Increases Per Week

First Grade: 2–3 words per week increase
Second Grade: 2.5–3.5 words per week increase
Third Grade: 1–3 words per week increase
Fourth Grade: .85–1.5 words per week increase

is well established in the student's repertoire of early reading skills. (For more information about DIBELS, visit the University of Oregon's website at http://dibels .uoregon.edu/index.php.)

Deciding upon Appropriate Reading Materials and Textbooks

When teachers choose texts for students with HI to read, care has to be taken not to exacerbate their fluency and comprehension problems. In many cases, students have had embarrassing moments when reading aloud from books that were beyond their current readability level. Such experiences reinforce the idea that the student is a poor reader, and recurring failure further solidifies negative feelings toward reading. These experiences decrease the willingness to read and deflate motivation for future reading. Therefore, special education teachers should consider those texts that are interesting and well within the student's readability level, using readability formulas as a guide. For those texts that are especially challenging for students (for example, higher-grade-level textbooks), teachers should provide students with plenty of supports such as teacher assistance during reading, cognitive or semantic organizers, digitized text, or recorded readings.

Other factors to consider in text selection include the *type* and *frequency* of words contained in them. To build fluency skills, students must have repeated exposure to reading the same or similar words. Less fluent readers spend most of their attentional resources on decoding or word attack, to the determent of comprehension. Thus, teachers should select texts at the students' current reading level and texts with features that promote fluency. Hiebert and Fisher (2005) identified key features in texts that promote fluency. These include a small number of rare words, a high percentage of the most frequently used words, and frequently repeated critical words (that is, those words that influence the meaning the most). These features are often cited as the critical factors in the success of repeated readings (Faulkner and Levy 1994). If a text has many different unique or rare words, students end up stopping to focus attention on each one; these present challenges because every rare word within a text, particularly those that show up only once, can require attention that may divert resources for comprehension. Conversely, books with high-frequency words—either sight words or words with phonetically similar patterns (for example, *cat, at, mat, rat*)—are easier for students to read and thus increase fluency. Finally, critical words are important vocabulary words that carry a great deal of meaning throughout sentences and paragraphs.

Determining Readability of Textbooks and Materials

When choosing materials for reading instruction or choosing textbooks for students to learn from, teachers should consider the interest of the passage, as well as the **readability level** of the passages. Determine readability levels of passages beforehand to ensure that the reading material does not frustrate students. Most formulas determine readability based upon a combination of frequency of multisyllabic words and sentence length. Usually, the result of using a readability formula is a quantifiable readability score based upon specific grade levels or ages. For example, the Fry Readability Graph (Fig. 7.3) determines readability based upon the number of multisyllabic words (syllables per 100-word sample) and number of sentences per 100-word sample.

▶ **FIGURE 7.3**

Fry Readability Graph

A. Select samples of 100 words. Choose the beginning, middle, and end of the passage, chapter, or book for your three 100-word samples.

B. Find the average number of sentences per 100-word passage (calculating to the nearest tenth).

C. Find the average number of syllables per 100-word sample.

D. Use the Fry Graph to determine the reading age, in years.

The curve represents normal texts for students. Points below the curve represent longer-than-average sentence lengths. Points above the curve represent text with a more difficult vocabulary (content-area textbooks).

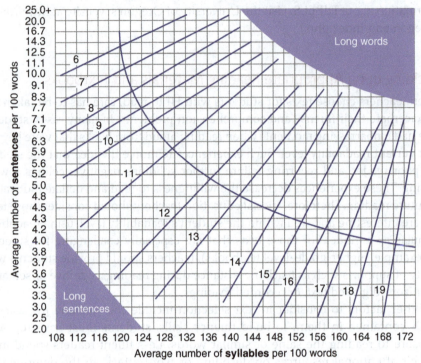

Reprinted with permission from Edward Fry, "A readability formula that saves time" (*Journal of Reading* 11:513–7. International Reading Association, 1968).

7-5 | Strategies and Techniques for Improving Vocabulary

As we discussed previously, teaching vocabulary as pre- and post-reading activities is useful because students with disabilities have a difficult time understanding vocabulary they read in text, and this vocabulary aids fluency and comprehension. Prior to vocabulary instruction, teachers should consider the purpose of students' learning the vocabulary. If the purpose is to teach a new vocabulary word and its definition, then a direct instructional approach might work best. If the student already knows a definition for a vocabulary word and the purpose is now to teach multiple meanings, then a semantic approach, such as mapping, might be a better approach (Jitendra et al. 2004).

Whatever the purpose, teachers should try to tap into prior knowledge to help students make meaningful connections between new knowledge (vocabulary) and prior knowledge. Teachers should also keep in mind that children have different levels of "processing information," particularly for vocabulary. Stahl (1986) defines three levels of processing. The first level is *associative*. On this level of processing, students simply make an association between a word and another word. This is a rather weak level of processing; if students do not use the vocabulary frequently, they will soon forget the word. The second level is *comprehension*. During this level, children have a better understanding than on the first level, but still cannot generalize the word to new sentences. During this level, children understand the meaning and can use the word for activities such as fill in the blanks or categorizing. The final level is the deepest level of processing and is referred to as *generational*. During this level, children have mastery or ownership of the word and its meaning, and can now define the word in their own words. They can also use the word easily during writing activities and discussions. To attain this level, students must move from rote recall of the term to using it in thinking and discourse. Through facilitating discussions, providing engaging vocabulary activities, and using multiple presentations of vocabulary words, teachers can bring their students to this deepest level of understanding. Other principles of vocabulary instruction include:

- Teaching a small number of vocabulary words at a time;
- Using distributed practice to learn words;
- Presenting new vocabulary in context, typically in simple sentences; and
- Matching the vocabulary taught with word meanings that are used in a story or textbook.

For more information about research-based techniques used to teach vocabulary to students with disabilities, see Bryant et al. (2003) or Jitendra et al. (2004).

Word Maps

A **word map** (Schwartz and Raphael 1985), similar to a semantic map (see Chapter 6), helps students to understand the meaning of vocabulary words. A word map provides students with a target vocabulary word and synonyms of it in the form of a visual display. Given a vocabulary word and using this map (Fig. 7.4), students ask three questions about the word: What is it? What is it like? What are some examples? Students answer these questions on the map and, if they cannot answer a question, they search for the remaining information from supporting materials (Schwartz and Raphael 1985).

Teachers can create partial maps that students can work on prior to reading and then complete after reading. We feel that students should be allowed to fill in part or all of a map during the activity because this allows them to become actively engaged in the task. Furthermore, research supports this notion that students have better comprehension when they create their own maps, as opposed to when the teacher gives them a completed map (Boyle and Weishaar 1997). Not only are students actively engaged in the task, but they also physically link ideas together (main ideas with details) as they create a semantic map.

Keyword and Mnemonic Strategies

Keyword and mnemonic methods are effective techniques to help students learn abstract vocabulary words (Mastropieri, Scruggs, and Fulk 1990; Scruggs and Mastropieri 1990; Uberti, Scruggs, and Mastropieri 2003). Through making connections

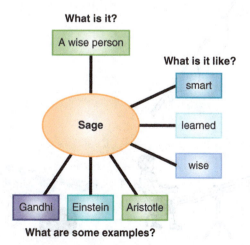

◀ **FIGURE 7.4**
Word Map for Vocabulary

▼ **FIGURE 7.5**

Symbolic Reconstruction
insular = narrow-minded

between new vocabulary and prior knowledge, students are better able to recall the vocabulary word, and the unfamiliar word becomes more meaningful and concrete.

To aid memory, the **keyword technique** links up a target vocabulary word with a similar-sounding keyword. Many keyword techniques also use visual images to help students make more concrete connections between the vocabulary word and its definition. Researchers claim that, based upon reconstructive elaboration theory, the keyword method elaborates and reconstructs a vocabulary word, thereby making it more meaningful and concrete (Mastropieri, Scruggs, and Fulk 1990; Scruggs and Mastropieri 1990; Terrill, Scruggs, and Mastropieri 2004). The reconstructions described by Scruggs and Mastropieri (1990) are based on the principle that the more familiar, concrete, and well elaborated the information, the better it will be learned and remembered. This model employs three types of reconstructions that teachers can use separately or in combination:

1. **Acoustic reconstruction** links a vocabulary word with a similar-sounding keyword (for example, *denominator–demons*).
2. **Symbolic reconstruction** links an abstract vocabulary word with a picture to make the information more memorable (for example, *insular* means *narrow-minded*; Fig. 7.5).
3. **Mimetic reconstruction** uses literal pictures for familiar, concrete information. For example, if students were studying simple machines in science and had to remember an example of the three classes of levers, a mimetic reconstruction of the levers might be illustrated as in Figure 7.6. To enhance memory, you could tell the children to visualize the fishing rod (class 2 lever) physically hooking the boy, picking him up from the seesaw (class 1 lever), and dropping him in the wheelbarrow (class 3 lever).

The following are three steps (Terrill, Scruggs, and Mastropieri 2004) for developing good keyword links for vocabulary words:

1. Develop a similar-sounding word from the vocabulary word. For example, if we want to develop a good way to remember the word *dinoflagellate*, which means a type of plankton that propels through water in a whirling motion, a good keyword for *dinoflagellate* might be *dinosaur* (because it sounds like the vocabulary word).

▶ **FIGURE 7.6**

Mimetic Reconstruction:
Three Classes of Levers

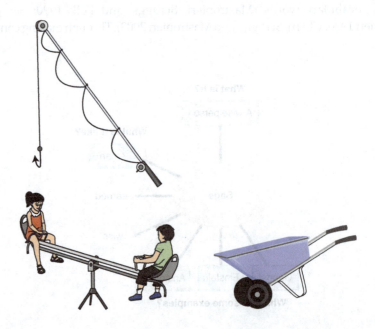

2. Create a picture in which the keyword and the definition of the keyword are combined. The picture should be interactive, linking the keyword with the definition. For example, the picture could be a *dinosaur whirling through the waves*.
3. Students are then asked the meaning of dinoflagellate and are prompted to think of the keyword, what is happening in the picture, and the definition (Fig. 7.7).

Content Acquisition Podcasts (CAPs) integrate multimedia technology with effective principles of vocabulary instruction (for example, keyword, morphemic analysis) to create short movie clips of content-area vocabulary (Kennedy, Deshler, and Lloyd 2013). These CAPs have proven to be an effective technique for helping students with and without disabilities learn important vocabulary.

7-6 Strategies and Techniques for Improving Fluency

Although teaching vocabulary has been shown to promote reading comprehension in students with learning disabilities (Bryant et al. 2003), building fluency is an even more influential skill that should be a consistent part of any reading program to improve comprehension, particularly for students with HI. Because of the link between fluency and comprehension, it is critical to teach students how to read fluently and then have them practice fluency skills using the following interventions.

Experts recommend that teachers should include the following in fluency programs: model good fluent reading, encourage fluency through phrasing, provide plenty of practice, and provide oral support for readers (Rasinski 2003):

- Modeling fluency is important because teachers can show students how to derive meaning from the text by matching the author's words with proper fluency. By reading aloud, teachers can model the detriments of reading too slow and too fast, and then demonstrate the benefits of reading at an appropriate pace.
- Meaning is often determined through phrases, not individual words. Phrasing involves chunking text into syntactic units while reading. Attending to punctuation is a useful guide to proper phrasing. Through repeated reading of a passage, students can begin to chunk text into appropriate phrases. Taking turns reading the same text also helps students to understand and use the phrasing of the text.
- Practice allows students to master those skills that they have already acquired. Opportunities to practice can occur through partner reading, repeated readings, or other activities.

- Finally, students with fluency problems need plenty of support during oral reading. This support can come in the form of a paired reading partner or through the use of recorded texts. Simultaneously hearing the text read while actually reading has increased both fluency and comprehension in students with disabilities.

Repeated Readings

Using **repeated readings** is a simple technique whereby teachers have students read one passage several times or until they reach a predetermined level of fluency. O'Shea, Sindelar, and O'Shea (1985) report that four readings appear to be the optimal amount because, by the fourth reading, children have reached maximum gains in reading speed, error reduction, and expression. Repeated readings have been used since the late 1970s (Samuels 1979), and have been proven effective for increasing fluency on passages that students read more than once and on new passages as well. Repeated readings have been shown to be successful when a teacher or another higher-level peer monitors a child's oral reading. In a review of repeated reading research, Therrien (2004) found that repeated readings were effective for increasing both fluency and comprehension. Moreover, repeated readings have transfer effects to new readings. In other words, increases in fluency and comprehension were found not only for the current passages that students were repeating, but for new passages as well. The effects were more pronounced for those new passages that contained common words from the previous passage. Like any skill, it appears that practice makes perfect (or at least improves reading skills).

Repeated reading works best when the text is matched with the child's reading level. Some suggest that students practice repeated reading with easier texts that are below their readability level, and others suggest that repeated readings be used with more instructional-level texts that are on the student's current reading level (85 to 90 percent word-recognition accuracy). You can determine which approach is most appropriate for individual students by monitoring their progress across repeated reading sessions. Remember the C-BM rule of thumb: if you see no progress toward the goal after three lessons, it is time for a change in the intervention.

Teachers using repeated readings should prepare by allotting 15 to 30 minutes each day for them, using the same passage three or four times, and choosing short passages with reading levels that have been predetermined using a readability formula (Therrien 2004). If the passages are too difficult, students will struggle to read them and read too slowly. If passages are too easy, students may not be practicing newly learned sight words or vocabulary words.

Once students are ready to read, Rasinski (2003) recommends the following guidelines: use 50- to 500-word passages and have students orally read the passage until they reach a predetermined reading rate. The passages can come from a variety of sources, including basal stories, newspapers, or textbooks. As discussed earlier, predetermined rates can be ascertained by using available reading rate charts, as well as past performance on C-BMs. Once students achieve the criteria, move on to a new passage that is as difficult as or slightly more difficult than the last. Finally, be sure to track reading rates (as well as prosody) while the child is reading.

Paired Reading or Peer Tutoring

Paired Reading. Paired reading is another technique for improving fluency. Paired reading can be used with any two people, as long as one is a more proficient reader than the other. It can occur with a parent and child, teacher and child, or student and student. When using paired reading, the pairs find a comfortable area in the class, sit side by side, and begin reading aloud together. Each paired reading session can last from 10 to 20 minutes and should take place daily or every other day. As with repeated reading, the materials that are used should be on the student's instructional reading level (85 to 90 percent word-recognition accuracy).

Paired reading also benefits proficient readers because it allows them to practice good reading skills too. As the pair begins to read together, they should match each other's reading rate, slowing for difficult parts and moving quickly through easy sections. During this activity, both students should read naturally, look at their own text while using a finger to follow along in the reading. Because the purpose of the activity is to increase fluency and comprehension, a "word supply" method should be used when a student makes an error, whereby the more proficient reader supplies the correctly pronounced word for the other student's miscue. If a student becomes "stuck," the helping student should allow the other student two to three seconds to see if he or she can correctly pronounce the word or self-correct any miscues. Then, the helping student should supply the missing word or correct pronunciation. Using a "word supply" method, rather than phonetically sounding out the word, minimizes any interruptions in the student's comprehension.

As the student begins to feel more comfortable reading aloud, have the more proficient student eventually phase out supports by reading in a softer voice, eventually whispering, and then allowing the other reader to read independently. At the end of each session, provide oral or written comprehension questions for students to answer. Finally, if possible, try to keep track of miscues and reading rates by recording or charting the cwpm rate. Students can learn to perform the data collection by marking miscues in a print copy of the text while their partners read aloud.

Peer Tutoring. Peer tutoring is a technique that pairs students together for the purpose of tutoring each other as they read. In peer tutoring, students are matched up based upon reading ability, with a higher-performing student matched with a lower-performing student. Pairs then take turns reading orally to each other for about 5 to 15 minutes each (total reading time for the group is 10 to 30 minutes).

Fuchs and Fuchs (2005) developed three reading activities that occur during the peer-tutoring program called PALS (peer-assisted learning strategies). The three activities that are integrated into the 35-minute program are *partner reading, paragraph shrinking,* and *prediction relay.*

Every session begins with five minutes of *partner reading.* During this activity, the higher-performing student reads first using a connected text. Once done, the other student rereads the same material. Each student then retells the events that occurred in the story for two minutes each.

Next, students read one paragraph at a time and then name the main idea in each paragraph. Once students decide the "who" and "what" of the paragraph, they report the main idea in statement of 10 words or fewer. This activity is referred to as *paragraph shrinking* and lasts for five minutes, after which partners switch roles for an additional five minutes.

Finally, with the *prediction relay,* partners make predictions about what they will learn on the next half-page. The lower-performing reader reads the passage first to confirm or disconfirm his or her predictions and states the main idea. After completing this activity for five minutes, the partners switch roles.

PALS has been documented as effective for Hispanic bilingual students, because the program incorporates culturally responsive practices such as peer tutoring that resemble culturally traditional familial and social learning contexts (Calhoon et al. 2006; Saenz, Fuchs, and Fuchs 2005).

THINK BACK TO THE FIRST CASE with Habib...

3. Name and describe one type of fluency activity that you would use with Habib.

You could use any or all of the previously mentioned fluency techniques: repeated readings, paired reading, or peer tutoring. Each accomplishes the goals of practice with modeling and feedback, using suitable-level reading materials. Habib's teachers can observe to determine which he is more comfortable using, and they have flexibility in how to address his reading fluency as they teach in an inclusive classroom.

7-7   Strategies and Techniques for Improving Comprehension

Reading comprehension represents another area of difficulty for students with HI. A number of factors contribute to difficulties in overall reading comprehension, such as lack of prior knowledge of the topic, difficulty making inferences, poor comprehension monitoring, and poor understanding of text structure (Cain and Oakhill 1999; Gersten et al. 2001; Pressley 1991; Wong 1991). A number of effective reading techniques and strategies have been identified as useful at improving reading comprehension for students with HI, particularly for students in secondary classes (Mastropieri and Scruggs 1997; Pressley 2002). More importantly, experts advocate that teachers should use explicit instruction to teach students comprehension strategies, and not just assume that students are already using comprehension-monitoring techniques when they read (Pressley 2002). The reading strategies and techniques presented in this book should be taught to students using explicit instruction.

Collaborative Strategic Reading

Collaborative strategic reading (Boardman, Vaughn, Buckley, Reutebuch, Roberts, and Klingner, 2016; Klingner, Vaughn, and Schumm 1998) is a multiple-component reading procedure that incorporates cooperative learning groups through scaffolding and peer-mediated learning. Its main components are preview, click and clunk, get the gist, and wrap up. During "preview," students read the title, headings, and keywords, and make predictions about what the expository passage is about and tie their ideas to prior knowledge of the topic. Next, working in small cooperative groups, students are given roles (for instance, leader, cluck expert, gist expert, question expert) and are asked to use these roles as they read the passage. During reading, students use both "click and clunk" and "get the gist" to monitor comprehension and find the main ideas of the passages. Using "click and clunk," students identify difficult words and concepts and use fix-up (e.g., context clues and morphemic analysis strategies) for information that doesn't make sense. Students also use "get the gist" to identify the main idea in each paragraph and then share it with the group. Finally, when they have finished reading the passage, students use a two-step process to "wrap up" and summarize the passage. First, students generate question about important ideas in the text, write down important ideas from the text, and share them with the group. Second, the question expert guides the group through answering and discussing the questions. (See Klingner, Vaughn, Boardman, and Swanson 2012 for more details about how to teach collaborative strategic reading.)

Paraphrasing Strategy

The paraphrasing strategy (Schumaker, Denton, and Deshler 1984) is a reading comprehension strategy that asks students to find main ideas and details from each paragraph that is read and then to paraphrase orally that information. The purpose of the strategy is to help students become actively engaged in reading through searching for main ideas and details in paragraphs and then transforming that information through paraphrasing to make it personally meaningful. The three steps of the paraphrasing strategy are represented by the acronym RAP (Box 7.2); students can remember that they need to "rap" or talk to themselves as they read for recall and comprehension.

Students use the strategy with short passages that are at least five paragraphs in length. For example, published reading materials such as *Timed Readings* are frequently used with this strategy. Similar to other strategies from the University of Kansas Center for Research on Learning, this follows the eight-stage *Strategy Intervention Model* (SIM; Deshler et al. 1981). SIM is a model that promotes effective teaching and learning of critical content in schools through the use of strategies and other techniques.

The eight-stage SIM begins with the teacher pretesting the students to see if they qualify for the strategy. The results of the pretest are reviewed with the students to encourage them to make a commitment to learn the RAP strategy. If students need the paraphrasing strategy, the teachers describe the strategy for them. Following the description of how and why the strategy works, teachers model using the strategy for the students. In this stage, teachers "think aloud" how they perform the strategy (for example, "Let's see, to find the main idea I know that I should look at what the first sentence is about").

Next, students move on to verbal practice of the strategy steps. This practice involves naming the RAP mnemonic and stating what each letter stands for at an automatic level. Upon mastery of the steps of the strategy, students advance to controlled practice. In controlled practice, students begin reading passages that are on their current *reading ability level* and, upon reaching mastery (80 percent paraphrasing and 70 percent comprehension scores), progress on to *grade-level* passages in the advanced practice phase. They begin with controlled-level passages so that they may initially concentrate on the RAP procedures; once comfortable with them, they move on to applying them with more challenging content.

Once students reach mastery in the grade-level phase, they take a posttest. Ideally, the posttest will be on the same passage they read at pretest to demonstrate their need to learn the strategy. The marked improvement in performance should be motivating to students.

In the final stage of the SIM model, students proceed to the generalization phase. In this phase, students are instructed on how to use the strategy with other materials and settings.

Throughout the strategy training, teachers keep a record of students' paraphrasing and comprehension scores as they silently read passages but paraphrase each

---

BOX 7.2

Paraphrasing Strategy

R *Read* a paragraph.

A *Ask* yourself, "What were the main idea and details in this paragraph?"
   Finding the main idea:
   1. Look in the first sentence of the paragraph.
   2. Look for repetitions of the same word or words in the whole paragraph.

P *Put* the main ideas and details in your own words.

paragraph aloud. This explicit comprehension strategy, once mastered, enables students with weak comprehension skills to read below-grade-level and grade-level materials.

Story Map

A story map presents a basic framework for understanding important elements found in narrative stories. For students, general knowledge of these story elements such as setting, problem, goal, attempts, internal response, and resolution results in improved recall and comprehension (Gordon and Braun 1983). Because some students need a more concrete model of these story elements, researchers (Idol 1987; Idol and Croll 1987) developed a story map that contained these components (Fig. 7.8).

▶ **FIGURE 7.8**
Story Map Example

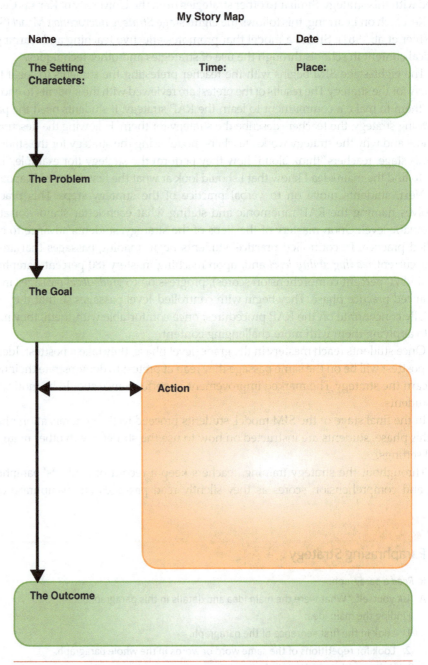

Adapted from L. Idol, "Group story mapping: A comprehension strategy for both skilled and unskilled readers" (*Journal of Learning Disabilities* 20(1987):199).

Using direct instruction procedures, students are taught to use story maps as they read narrative stories. Students should be matched to appropriate reading levels based upon their reading rates. Story maps are used with short reading passages (100-plus words). First, teachers model how to use the story map. During modeling, the teacher should familiarize students with the different components found in the story map. Next, the teacher should have the students read the passage and periodically stop at points where information needed to fill in the map is provided. At this point, students should write information directly onto the story map. Throughout this early training, the teacher should provide immediate feedback for errors. Upon reading each story, students should also answer comprehension questions of varying levels (textually implicit, textually explicit, and scriptally implicit). Throughout the training, students should be taught to rely less on the teacher and should eventually be able to complete the map independently. As students reach a set level of mastery in comprehension, teachers should gradually phase out the use of the map while continuing to check comprehension.

Another version of a story map, developed by Boulineau et al. (2004), contains seven main areas for recording a narrative's story: setting/time, characters, problem, solution, outcome, reaction, and theme. These researchers used basal stories with the map and had students read portions of the story orally until they read the entire story. Prior to reading, students were taught each story element individually. Once they read the entire story, each student completed a story map. Once students were able to complete maps with 90 percent accuracy, they were no longer instructed on story elements prior to reading. Instead, students read each passage and completed a story map independently.

POSSE Strategy

The POSSE strategy (Englert and Mariage 1990, 1991) was developed to enhance the reading comprehension skills of students with disabilities through reciprocal teaching and construction of maps. The strategy itself incorporates a variety of strategies that include predicting, organizing, searching, summarizing, and evaluating expository reading passages. The strategy can be used before, during, and after reading. Using POSSE, students predict ideas based upon background knowledge, organize predicted textual ideas and background knowledge based upon text structure, search/summarize by searching the text structure in the expository passage, summarize the main ideas, and evaluate their comprehension. As the students complete the steps, the teacher simultaneously constructs a cognitive map to display visually the text structure and organization of ideas. The POSSE training consists of two pre-reading strategies (predict and organize) and three strategies to use during reading (search, summarize, and evaluate).

The POSSE steps include the following:

Predict what ideas are in the story.
Organize your thoughts.
Search for structure.
Summarize the main idea in your own words.
Evaluate: compare, clarify, and predict.

In the *predict* step, students use cues from the book such as the title, headings, pictures, and the initial paragraph to predict what the story will be about. This brainstorming activity allows students to tap into their prior knowledge. During this step, the teacher guides students to relevant responses and records responses on the strategy sheet. Englert and Mariage (1990, 1991) recommend that teachers make a transparency and record responses on it.

▶ **FIGURE 7.9**
POSSE Strategy Sheet

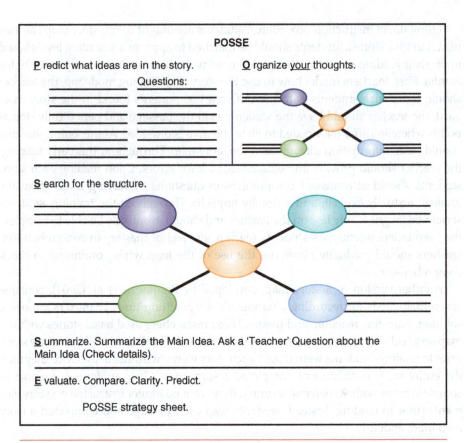

POSSE

<u>P</u> redict what ideas are in the story.   <u>O</u> rganize <u>your</u> thoughts.

Questions:

<u>S</u> earch for the structure.

<u>S</u> ummarize. Summarize the Main Idea. Ask a 'Teacher' Question about the Main Idea (Check details).

<u>E</u> valuate. Compare. Clarity. Predict.

POSSE strategy sheet.

Reprinted with permission from C. Englert and T. Mariage, "Making students partners in the comprehension process: Organizing the reading 'POSSE'" (*Learning Disability Quarterly* 14(1991): 123–138).

During the *organize* step, the teacher directs students to choose ideas that are similar, so that they can be organized (Fig. 7.9). Once the ideas are arranged, the teacher then organizes them into a cognitive map with the students.

Next, in the *search* step, students begin reading the passage as they search for the ideas to map out in the next step.

In the *summarize* step, students identify the main idea for a portion of the passage (such as a paragraph). This is done through group discussion and consensus. The teacher then records the agreed-upon main idea and places it in the circle of the cognitive map. The group leader—the teacher or student who has been assigned to lead the group—then takes the main idea and converts it into a question. As students answer this question, their responses become the details that the teacher records on the map. At the end of the passage, the students have now created a second cognitive map.

In the *evaluation* step, the students compare the two maps, clarify by asking questions about unknown vocabulary or unclear information, and predict what would be in the next section of the text. This starts the process all over again for the next chapter or passage.

Cognitive Mapping Strategy

The cognitive mapping strategy was developed to enable students with disabilities to independently map out information that they read from expository passages (Boyle 1996; Boyle and Weishaar 1997). Each passage used was approximately 400 words long and contained about five or six paragraphs.

TIPS FOR GENERALIZATION

Effective Strategy Components

Training students to use a strategy, technique, or intervention requires explicit instruction. This means that teachers should set a clear goal when teaching the strategy and that students should master the strategy steps before actually using the strategy with materials. Adapting the eight-step instructional sequence described by Deshler et al. (1981), and using effective intervention components from Mastropieri, Scruggs, and Graetz (2003), we will describe the general steps for training students to use most techniques and strategies.

When teaching a strategy, teachers should use the steps of direct instruction (model, guided practice with immediate feedback, and independent practice) to show students exactly how to perform each step of the strategy. While performing these steps, teachers should use think-aloud techniques whereby they verbalize what is occurring in each step. When teachers verbalize their thoughts and actions, students can clearly see what is occurring during instruction. As students begin to understand the strategy steps being demonstrated, the teacher can slowly integrate them into the demonstration. As students become more involved in the strategy demonstration, they can begin to use the components with actual materials. As students use the strategy and materials, the teacher should be cognizant to give students immediate and corrective feedback to ensure that they are performing the strategy steps properly. If students are using a cognitive strategy, they should next practice the strategy steps until they can recite strategy steps to mastery.

Once students reach mastery on the strategy steps, they can begin using the strategy or technique with "easy" materials. The purpose of this portion of the training is to ensure that they can use the strategy steps properly, not necessarily reach mastery with content materials. Again, teachers should provide immediate and corrective feedback so that students can master the use of strategy steps with easy materials. Monitoring performance ensures that students successfully use the strategy or technique.

Next, students can begin using the strategy or technique with grade-level materials. Again, the teacher needs to monitor performance and provide feedback. Once students have mastered this step, they are ready for the last and perhaps most important step: generalization. Whenever teachers instruct students in a strategy or technique, one of the most important components of training is training for generalization. Although it is important for students to learn a strategy and demonstrate its effectiveness with the teacher, it is crucial that they can then use the strategy with new people and in new settings. In this last step, students think about how the strategy or technique can be applied to new settings or materials. This step may require students to modify the strategy or technique. In some cases, the teacher can begin to fade out materials (for example, teacher cues) so that students no longer rely on these supports. Once students can use the strategy or technique with new materials, they should be monitored periodically to ensure that they have properly integrated the strategy into their daily routine.

These steps ensure that, from start to finish, students will be able to use successfully the strategy and techniques that you teach them.

To teach the strategy, a teacher needs to model it for students while thinking aloud in each step. Next, the teacher should encourage students to use the strategy steps with the passage to create the map (that is, use guided practice). Finally, after providing students with feedback while they are reading the passage and creating a map, the teacher should check for accuracy of the content in the map. If students reach mastery of the content in the map and can use the strategy steps independently, they can now begin to use cognitive mapping independently (that is, independent practice). Initially, students read passages that are matched to their readability level. They then map out each readability-level passage. Once they complete these passages with mastery, they are given grade-level passages to map out.

The purpose of each step in the cognitive mapping strategy is to have students become actively engaged in reading by searching for pertinent information and creating a map of the information (Box 7.3).

In the first step, *topic*, students are instructed to search for the topic, state where and how they find it, write it down, and circle it. Next, during the *read* step, students

BOX 7.3

Cognitive Mapping Strategy

T   Write down the <u>t</u>opic.
R   <u>R</u>ead a paragraph.
A   <u>A</u>sk for the main idea and three details, and write them down.
V   <u>V</u>erify the main idea by circling it and linking its details.
E   <u>E</u>valuate the next paragraph, and <u>a</u>sk and <u>v</u>erify again.
L   When finished, <u>l</u>ink all circles.

are instructed to read a paragraph. During this step, students read one paragraph silently. At the end of the paragraph, they move on to the *ask* step. During the *ask* step, students go back to the paragraph to find the main idea and three details, and write them down. Students then *verify* the main idea by circling it and linking its details to the main idea. In the next step, students are to *examine* the next paragraph, read it, and then *ask* and *verify* the main idea and details. The *read, ask,* and *verify* steps are repeated for each successive paragraph until the student comes to the end of the passage. Finally, after mapping out the last paragraph, students review the map, search for similar main ideas (in circles), and link up these main ideas. Figure 7.10 shows a map created by a student who used the TRAVEL strategy while reading a passage about the Statue of Liberty.

KWL

The KWL strategy (Carr and Ogle 1987; Ogle 1986) consists of three components or steps to help students tap into prior knowledge, set a purpose for reading, and summarize what was read. The **K** step is what we **<u>know</u>**, the **W** step is what we **<u>want</u>** to know, and the **L** step is what we **<u>learned</u>**. Students list this information in chart form (Box 7.4) and complete it before reading, during reading, and after reading.

▶ **FIGURE 7.10**

Student Map Using the Cognitive Mapping Strategy

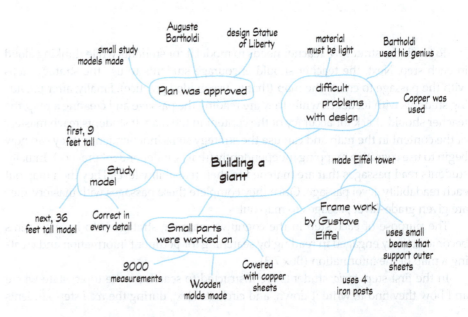

KWL Chart About Hurricane Katrina

K: What we know	W: What we want to find out	L: What we learned and still need to learn
Fierce winds	What made the wind so powerful?	Strong winds near the eye Category 3 hurricane at landfall Winds were 125 mph
Heavy rain	Where did all the rain come from?	Warm water from the Gulf fueled it to a Category 5
Flooding	Why did it kill so many people?	Storm surge was 28 feet New Orleans is like a bowl
Loss of electricity and drinkable water	How did it form?	Circulating mass of air over Gulf's 80°F water
Destruction of buildings	Could we have stopped it?	No, too powerful
Left people stranded	How did they survive?	Rough time at first and then eventual evacuation

During the pre-reading stage, children describe what they know about the topic. This stage involves a brainstorming session about ideas that they already know about the topic. The teacher should be very specific about the topic to be read (for example, information about monarch butterflies, not butterflies and moths) to delve into the specific schemata of students (Ogle 1986). As the students respond, the teacher records responses on the board or overhead. After students have finished responding with what they know about the topic (monarch butterflies), the teacher then leads them into categorizing the topics that are listed. Finally, the teacher records information in the "What We Know" column of the chart, and students do the same on their own charts.

Next, students develop questions about "What We Want to Know." The teacher and students discuss these questions and then all students record what they personally want to know from the passage on their charts. The purpose of having students write their own questions is so that all students can personally focus on their own goals for reading. After students finish reading the passage, they are told to write down what they learned from the reading in the "What We Learned" column, as well as what they still need to learn. If the passage did not answer their questions, the teacher can provide new passages that students can read to find information that will answer their questions.

Research Evidence

Semantic Organizers, Cognitive Maps, and KWL. Semantic organizers have long been shown to be effective at increasing vocabulary and comprehension of students who use them. In studies by Bos et al. (Bos and Anders 1987, 1990; Bos et al. 1989), students who used semantic maps outperformed students who learned vocabulary using a traditional approach (for example, dictionary approach). These researchers also demonstrated that, when students used semantic maps and organizers while they read, they increased recall of vocabulary and reading comprehension (Scanlon et al. 1992). Moreover, a recent synthesis of research on semantic organizers and cognitive maps (Kim et al. 2004) supported the use of these techniques as effective tools for increasing reading comprehension, pointing out the particularly large effect size (a statistical measure of effectiveness) of them on comprehension measures among students with HI. Similar positive results were found when students used the cognitive mapping strategy TRAVEL. Students who used this strategy to create their own maps while reading expository text outperformed control-group students on both literal and inferential comprehension (Boyle 1996;

CASE 7.2   Helping Lancer to Comprehend Better

Case Introduction

Now that you have worked through the first case in this chapter, you should feel comfortable addressing issues in a second case. In this case, two teachers work together in an inclusion classroom to meet the needs of all the students, but in particular the learning needs of Lancer.

Lancer, a student in Jen Timson's 10th-grade class, was recently diagnosed with learning disabilities (LD). Jen and Karen Hopkins work side by side most of the morning in English class. Karen is the special education teacher who co-teaches in History class. Jen and Karen have been collaborating for about two years. On two days during the week, they have an opportunity to sit down for about 20 minutes to co-plan during their free period.

Lancer has been experiencing a number of reading problems over the past two years but, with help from his teachers, he has been able to avoid a full referral for special education services. However, this year, his lack of substantial progress and a request from his parents led to full referral and diagnosis of LD.

During a recent literature lesson, students were reading the story *The Adventures of Huckleberry Finn*. Unfortunately Lancer struggled to read the chapter as Jen was working with him one on one, quietly reading along with him when it was his turn to read in class. She noticed that he struggled over some words, like formal names (for example, *Navarre*) and some vocabulary words (such as *infernal, rapscallions, victual, delirium*) and had particular problems with comprehension questions dealing with inferences or providing details.

When Lancer read, Karen and Jen began to hear some of the students giggling, but quickly warned those few students that their behavior would not be tolerated. Upon finishing his paragraph, Lancer gave out an audible "whew." For Lancer, reading is a daily struggle and often an embarrassing one. Even when he reads silently, Karen and Jen can tell that it is a similar struggle. During silent reading, Lancer often has his hand raised, asking about the parts of the story that he does not understand.

Naturally, his problems pronouncing some words hinder his comprehension, but Karen feels that he also lacks solid reading comprehension strategies. But even when his teachers use word supply as he reads, Lancer still has trouble with inferential and critical comprehension questions. Karen has kept a close eye on Lancer and frequently notices that he appears "lost in space" as other students read or when his teacher reads part of a story aloud to the class. Lancer's distractions seem to get worse as the day progresses. Jen has often complained that she has to "walk him through" his biology class (which takes place after lunch).

To counter his difficulty with vocabulary, Karen recently began reviewing vocabulary words with him prior to class. Lancer hates these preview lessons because he hates reading. Initial results have been mixed. On some days, Lancer makes fewer miscues, yet on other days he still makes many miscues. Despite the number of miscues, whether few or many, comprehension still poses a problem for Lancer.

History also presents challenges for Lancer and his teachers. Lancer has difficulty reading the textbook chapters and answering questions. During independent seatwork, such as worksheets, Lancer also has problems remaining on task and completing his work correctly. At home, his parents have also noticed problems. Lancer has problems reading his textbooks and answering questions. His parents really struggle to keep him working and on task. For example, as soon as he gets home, he begins working on his homework. This works out fine when he doesn't have much homework but, on a typical day, it takes him three hours to complete his homework because it is so difficult for him.

CASE QUESTIONS

1. What specific skill would you try to remediate with Lancer?
2. What other skill would you, as the teacher, address?
3. Name and describe one fluency technique and one comprehension technique or strategy that you would use with Lancer.

Boyle and Weishaar 1997). Furthermore, Boyle and Weishaar (1997) found that students who created their own cognitive maps while reading performed better on inferential comprehension than students who were supplied with completed maps (expert-generated maps).

Finally, the KWL technique is based upon the schema model of reading, whereby students need to activate background knowledge to make new connections to information that they are learning and to fill in those slots in schemata as they read (Gammill 2006). Research findings (Cantrell, Fusaro, and Dougherty 2000) support that students who were trained using KWL outperformed students who wrote summaries on a measure of reading comprehension.

Keyword and Mnemonic Strategies. The keyword or mnemonic strategy has been used in numerous studies to improve the vocabulary learning of students. Veit, Scruggs, and Mastropieri (1986) used it to improve the learning of dinosaur vocabulary for students with learning disabilities. In another study, Mastropieri, Scruggs, and Graetz (2003) found that students with learning disabilities who were taught to remember and recall vocabulary and facts about chemistry using the mnemonic strategy outperformed students in the traditional learning group.

Repeated Readings. Over 100 studies have been conducted on repeated readings since Samuels introduced the strategy in 1979. The findings from studies have consistently shown that repeated readings lead to improvements in reading speed, word recognition, and comprehension (Samuels 2002). In addition, Dowhower (1989) summarized the findings from several studies and reported that, among students with reading problems, repeated readings resulted in decreased reading miscues, improved processing of text and retention of factual information, improved fluency, enhanced deeper questioning and insights, and improved recall of pertinent content from passages, such as main ideas and vocabulary.

Paired Reading, Peer Tutoring, and Collaborative Reading. Paired reading is another technique that has shown to be very effective at increasing fluency in students. Studies that examined paired reading and peer tutoring have shown benefits for both high-level students (tutors) and their tutees, particularly when students are carefully matched and progress is continuously monitored (Topping 2005). Mastropieri, Scruggs, and Graetz (2003) reported from their review of peer-tutoring research on reading that when compared to conventional teaching methods, peer-tutoring methods increased reading comprehension among students with disabilities. Several studies have been conducted on the effectiveness of collaborative strategic reading in inclusive classrooms and have shown it to be particularly effective for improved reading comprehension among students with HI (Boardman, Vaughn, Buckley, Reutebuch, Roberts, and Klingner, 2016).

Paraphrasing Strategy. The paraphrasing strategy has been shown to be effective at increasing reading comprehension among students with disabilities. Ellis and Graves (1990) reported that teaching the paraphrasing strategy was effective at increasing reading comprehension among 68 fifth- through seventh-grade students with disabilities. Similarly, Katims and Harris (1997) reported that the paraphrasing strategy was effective at increasing the reading comprehension for middle-school students with and without disabilities.

THINK BACK TO THE SECOND CASE with Lancer . . .

1. *What specific skill would you try to remediate with Lancer?*

A number of systematic approaches to teaching reading fluency would benefit Lancer. Karen and Jen should review his specific reading strengths and weaknesses and then select from among possible reading strategies to find approaches that are successful for Lancer. Because of his embarrassment, they should select activities he can do away from his peers, or when matched with peers with whom he is comfortable.

2. *What other skill would you, as the teacher, address?*

Lancer's other reading problem is with comprehension of the story.

3. *Name and describe one fluency technique and one comprehension technique or strategy that you would use with Lancer.*

For fluency, teachers could use repeated readings or paired reading. For comprehension, teachers could use a number of different strategies or techniques, such as RAP, POSSE, TRAVEL, collaborative strategic reading, or story maps.

CHAPTER SUMMARY

As we have shown, fluency is a critical skill for students with HI to learn if they are ever to become skilled readers. Fluent readers not only read words accurately and with sufficient speed to gain meaning, but they are able to use prosody to chunk information into larger units that aid them in comprehension. When reading fluently (that is, with expression), students break sentences into phrases and correctly use stress, intonation, and duration as they read each phrase (Schreiber 1991). In doing so, they break down sentences into phrases that allow them to gain a deeper understanding of the text than when just reading individual words in the text. This deeper understanding aids students in answering not only lower-level comprehension questions (such as textually explicit or literal questions) but, perhaps more importantly, higher-level questions (textually implicit and scriptally implicit questions).

Unfortunately, because students with HI have problems with fluency and comprehension, they constantly struggle to understand what they read. The good news, however, is that these students can improve their fluency and comprehension by learning instructional techniques and strategies. Like nondisabled students, students with disabilities can improve their reading skills and use them more effectively and efficiently through practice. Teachers can assist students in learning reading skills by giving them immediate feedback while they learn the skill and monitor their progress on a frequent basis via curricu-

lum-based measures. Teachers should also be certain that reading materials are matched to the students' reading levels by using readability measures. If the materials are too difficult for a particular student's reading level, then teachers should either teach students strategies and techniques that could help compensate for the difference or modify the material so that the students can comprehend what they are reading. Some of these techniques or strategies, such as word maps and mnemonic techniques, can help students better understand vocabulary, and others, such as repeated readings or peer tutoring, can help improve students' fluency.

Finally, because students with disabilities do not effectively monitor their comprehension when they read, teachers should instruct students in how to use comprehension strategies.

As with Habib in the first case and Lancer in the second case, reading can be a painful and traumatic experience for your students. It is up to you to help your students. Think back to the last time you read a good book. Do you remember how it felt to get through some of the more exciting chapters or how it felt to read a book that was so good that you just couldn't put it down? Do you remember how good it felt to finish it? Maybe you felt a sense of accomplishment?

Every time you work on reading skills with students with disabilities, don't just think about helping the child to complete the task; instead, think that one day these students could feel the same sense of accomplishment upon reading an article or book, if you are willing to assist them through the reading process. The reading skills that you teach today may become their life skills of tomorrow. Students with disabilities need to learn how to read as part of the schooling process, but reading is much more than that.

KEY TERMS

Acoustic Reconstruction, 236
Consolidated Alphabetic Phase, 224
Full Alphabetic Phase, 224
Inferential Question, 226
Keyword Technique, 236
Literal Comprehension Questions, 225
Mimetic Reconstruction, 236

Partial Alphabetic Phase, 223
Pre-Alphabetic Phase, 223
Readability Level, 233
Reading Fluency, 222
Repeated Readings, 238
Scriptally Implicit, 227
Symbolic Reconstruction, 236

Text Elements, 227
Text Structure, 227
Textually Explicit Question, 225
Textually Implicit Question, 226
Word Map, 235

APPLICATION ACTIVITIES

Using information from the chapter, complete the following activities that were designed to help you apply knowledge that was presented in this chapter:

1. Design a reading lesson composed of different activities that will help readers to develop fluency and comprehension skills. Be sure to include lesson objectives and one or two state standards in your lesson.
2. Use a textbook from a middle- or high-school classroom. Review the questions at the end of the chapter and determine what type they are (that is, textually explicit, textually implicit, or scriptally implicit).
3. Use the TRAVEL strategy to summarize any one major section of this chapter (for example, Strategies and Techniques for Improving Vocabulary). Next, create a story map for the case about Habib. List similarities and differences in the content of these expository and narrative comprehension summaries.

8

Written Language: Strategies and Techniques

Learning Objectives

After reading this chapter, you will understand:

8-1 The process approach to writing

8-2 Common problems that students with HI encounter in written language

8-3 Teaching handwriting skills to students with HI

8-4 The strategies to teach spelling skills to students with HI

8-5 Teaching writing techniques and strategies to students with HI

CEC Initial Preparation Standard 5: Instructional Planning and Strategies

5-2 Beginning special education professionals use technologies to support instructional assessment, planning, and delivery for individuals with exceptionalities.

5-4 Beginning special education professionals use strategies to enhance language development and communication skills of individuals with exceptionalities.

5-6 Beginning special education professionals teach to mastery and promote generalization of learning.

5-7 Beginning special education professionals teach cross-disciplinary knowledge and skills such as critical thinking and problem solving to individuals with exceptionalities.

Do you think most regular education students are good at writing essays?

If you answered *yes*, you might want to reconsider your answer. When students in grades 8 and 12 from across the nation were asked to write essays as part of the National Assessment of Educational Progress (NAEP) for writing in 2011, only 27 percent passed at or above the *proficient* level (U.S. Department of Education 2011). These students scored lower than students who participated in the 2007 version, and the scores of these students remain low in terms of the percentage passing at the proficient level (that is, the proficient level was the desired goal of those administering the test) (U.S. Department of Education 2011).

Do you think students with disabilities did much better?

As you probably guessed, students with disabilities who took the NAEP writing assessment performed worse on this measure when compared to national peers. For students with disabilities (that is, students with an individualized education program [IEP]) in grades 8 and 12, only 5 percent passed at or above the proficient level (U.S. Department of Education 2011). Even more astonishing, 60 percent of 8th-grade students with a disability scored *below* the "basic" level in writing, and 62 percent of 12th-grade students scored *below* basic. As reflected by NAEP tests, written language is an area in which all students, especially students with disabilities, need to develop better skills. The NAEP writing assessment scores were derived from students' writing of three types of essays: narrative, informative, and persuasive.

In this chapter, you will learn in detail how to teach handwriting, spelling, and composing skills to students with HI. We present information about the Hayes-Flower model, which addresses writing as a process; the stages of writing; and writing difficulties of students with HI. We begin the chapter by discussing the case of Juan's writing problems.

Have you ever had a bad writing experience? Think about writing papers for classes. Perhaps you know students who have experienced some days that were similar to Juan's. Writing can be a frustrating experience for students with disabilities. Often, they lack adequate prerequisite skills to be able to compose paragraphs and essays. Or, if they have the skills, they may lack writing strategies for planning and composing. As you read this chapter, you will learn how writing develops and how you, as a teacher, can facilitate students' writing in the classroom.

8-1   The Process of Written Language

There are three main components to written language: handwriting, spelling, and composing. **Handwriting** involves teaching children how to write manuscript and cursive letters. **Spelling** involves teaching students how to spell words from a list or spelling book. **Composing** involves teaching students how to write sentences, paragraphs, and essays. The process approach to writing addresses all three in an integrated way. After we explain the process approach, we will identify common problems with writing for students with HI.

Product Versus Process

For many years, writing was viewed simply as a product whereby writers would transcribe their thoughts onto paper to create end products such as essays or papers. Using this **product approach**, the product would be proofread, corrected, and turned in to the teacher for a grade. This product approach placed a great deal of pressure on students to produce a "perfect draft" that would allow them to meet the

CASE 8.1   Bounce Back

Case Introduction

In this case, you will read about a student named Juan who has trouble with writing. As you read the case, you will see how he actually writes an essay. Think about how you could help him if you were his teacher.

At the end of the case, you will find case questions. These questions are meant to serve as points for reflection. Of course, if you can answer them immediately, you should do so, but you may want to wait to answer them until you have read the portion of the chapter that pertains to the particular case question. Throughout the rest of the chapter, you will see the same questions. As you see them, try to answer them based upon the portion of the chapter that you just read.

Juan Luis Diaz was identified in seventh grade with learning disabilities. While he scored within the average range on IQ and cognitive measures, he scored well below average on the written language areas of spelling, logical sentences, sentence combining, and syntax. Juan has difficulty planning, translating, and writing coherent essays of various genres (e.g., descriptive, expository, persuasive). Juan is currently enrolled in a 10th-grade inclusive literature class but continues to have difficulty with his writing, as evidenced by his "D" average. His current assignment is to write a 400-word persuasive essay on whether music with curse words should be allowed at school dances.

It was now 11 p.m. and Juan was just beginning on his paper that was due at 8 a.m. in English class the next day. As Juan wrote the paper, he had his earphones in while listening to *Bounce Back* by Big Sean. As Juan listed to the lyrics, which contained curse words, he began his paper. Without any planning, he decided that he would support the viewpoint that music with curse words should be allowed at school dances. He felt that curse words in lyrics were the key to a good tune.

He wrote the following essay (with errors):

This paper is about music with course words. Music with course words make up many good songs that need to be play at school dances. Many of these songs go with pacific dance moves that are

made for the song. These moves is cool. Get the booty shaking too. So the songs for school dances need to be aloud. And then there might be other times when music with course words aren't aloud at school dances.

When Juan was finished, he thought he had written a pretty good persuasive essay. Rather than proofread or even read it, he packed it in his notebook and handed it in the next day.

Unfortunately, Juan had forgotten the key elements that make up a good persuasive essay, as well as some basic writing skills. The rubric that his teacher, Mrs. Saxon, developed assigned 4 points to each of the following components—thesis/claim, reasons, conclusion, organization, spelling/punctuation—resulting in 20 total points. When he got back his graded essay, out of a possible 20 total points, Juan ended up with only 10 points. Mrs. Saxon decided to give students a chance to improve their papers by asking them to rewrite them on their own.

That night, Juan added a few more sentences and proofread his paper but missed many of his grammatical errors, and his paper still contained incomplete sentences. The lines that he added were:

Curse words is found everywhere in our socity. Everyone curses everyday and it adds flavor to our conversions just like flavor to soup. If I don't curse everybody looks at me like I am weard or something.

Again he handed in his paper, but this time Mrs. Saxon decided to have a writing conference to help Juan improve his paper. Together they worked on not only his grammatical and mechanical errors but also his ideation.

CASE QUESTIONS

1. What aspects of Juan's approach to writing his essay may indicate that he is not likely to produce a quality essay?
2. What specific writing skill or skills of Juan's would you try to remediate first?
3. Name and describe two types of writing activities or techniques that Juan could use prior to handing in his paper to improve the quality of his writing.

length requirements of the assignment and move on to the next paper. As students worked on papers using this product approach, they often placed excessive pressure on themselves and, as a result, "blocked" when it came to putting ideas down on paper. As you can see, the product approach is often a poor way to approach writing assignments.

Employing this product approach, students would often use weak writing strategies as they wrote. According to Flower (1985), this approach commonly includes the following weak strategies: *trial-and-error, perfect draft strategy, words looking for ideas,* and *waiting for inspiration.*

Trial-and-Error Strategy. Students who write using trial and error are trying out different combinations of words and phrases with the hope that one combination will result in an acceptable form. When using trial and error, students are often so busy juggling different sentences and phrases that they lose track of previous attempts and end up writing previously rejected versions. Using this trial-and-error method, students work slowly and produce products that contain minimal ideas and content.

Perfect Draft Strategy. Using the perfect draft strategy, students write their papers from start to finish in one slow laborious process. Using this weak strategy, students strive to perfect each sentence before moving on to the next one. Usually, students use this strategy with introductory sentences or paragraphs as they try to produce the perfect beginning paragraph to a paper. As you can guess, this strategy may lead to writer's block during the beginning stages of writing and, in turn, may lead to procrastination on future writing projects.

Words Looking for Ideas Strategy. In some cases, students may use certain words that they hope will trigger ideas as they write the paper. Typically, students may rely upon transition words (for example, *first, second, third,* or *next, now, soon*) to trigger ideas about the topic. Although the use of transition words to bridge ideas is a good tool, using these words by themselves to trigger ideas is an unreliable procedure.

Waiting for Inspiration Strategy. Some students may simply wait until the "writing mood" strikes and then begin a paper or continue their work on a writing project. Although effective for some students, it may be a risky procedure to use and may cause unwarranted stress as deadlines approach. For many students, the deadline itself is the inspiration or motivation to begin the writing project; however, it may also increase stress levels and actually lead to writer's block.

More recent views of writing have led to a **process approach** to writing that ultimately results in a better product (this will be discussed later in this chapter). The Hayes-Flower model of writing (Hayes and Flower 1980) strongly influenced this shift in thinking in the academic field. When students use a process approach, the quality of their products, completed essays, or compositions is typically much improved.

Hayes-Flower Model

The original Hayes-Flower writing model is perhaps the most popular model used to describe how writing occurs within a cognitive framework (please review cognitive theories in Chapter 4). Since its inception in 1980, its designers have reworked it. The new model (Fig. 8.1) differs from their old model in several aspects; most noticeably, the new model (1) has a heavier emphasis on working memory, (2) incorporates visual-spatial and linguistic components, (3) includes motivation and affect as factors that influence writing, (4) rearranges text interpretation (formerly called revision), (5) has reflection replacing planning, and (6) subsumes translation under text production.

In the new model, the two major components are the *task environment* and the *individual.*

Task Environment. The task environment refers to outside influences on the students' writing. The social environment, one component of the task environment, refers to social aspects of writing, such as the audience and collaborators. Hayes (1996) believes that writing is purely a social activity. He views writing as a form of communication with others in our social environment. For example, when students write, they need to consider the intended receiver of their message, or the audience. Students write

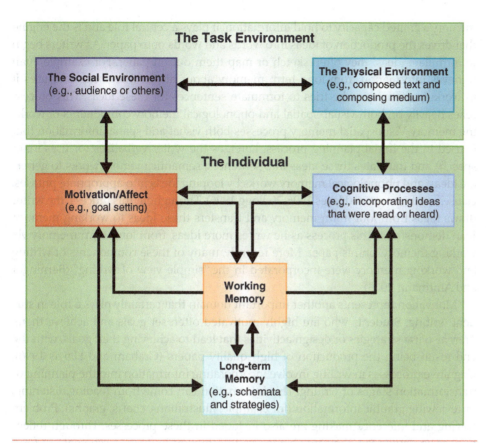

◀ FIGURE 8.1

Modified Hayes-Flower
New Writing Model

Adapted from J. Hayes, "A New Framework for Understanding Cognition and Affect in Writing" in *The Science of Writing*, ed. C. M. Levy and S. Ransdell (Mahwah, NJ: Lawrence Erlbaum, 1996, p. 4).

differently based upon whether their audience is the teacher, who will assign a grade for a formal writing assignment, or friends, who are looking for more information and are less concerned about the "formality" of the information. In addition, if a student works with another student or collaborator on a written assignment (for example, a research paper), the collaborator will influence how and what is written. Peers influence the writer and, in turn, the peers are influenced by what the writer has written.

The task environment also includes the physical environment, which refers to the text that has already been written and its effects on changing the direction of future writing. Also included under this physical environment domain are the composing medium and its influence on writing. Within the past decade, this component has taken on added importance, as much of our writing is now completed with the assistance of computers. With the help of computer software, students can write papers, compose emails, or develop other media products such as websites, text messages, and other forms of communication. According to Hayes (1996), computers have drastically changed the way that students plan and write compositions when compared to paper-and-pencil compositions. For example, word-processing programs have allowed students to revise text more easily through "cut-and-paste," spell-check, and grammar options. Computers have aided countless students with disabilities who otherwise would struggle to spell words or edit papers because of their writing disabilities.

Individual Component. The individual component looks at how different factors within the writer influence the final product. Central to the individual is working memory. Within the Hayes-Flower model, motivation, cognitive processes, and long-term memory all have two-way interactions with working memory. Despite working memory's limited capacity to hold information, it plays a central role and is the engine that drives the production of ideas into words and words onto paper. As writers begin to formulate ideas, they often sketch or map them out on paper. For example, Juan retrieves information from long-term memory about his favorite songs and uses it in working memory as he tries to formulate sentences for these ideas. This process relies heavily on both visual-spatial and phonological memory components of working memory. Visuospatial memory processes both visual and spatial information that is used in the initial planning process. Later, as the writer verbalizes (or uses inner speech) and translates these ideas into sentences, semantic memory works to generate ideas, and phonological memory works by looping ideas into appropriate phrases, clauses, and sentences (Hayes 1996; Kellogg 1996). Throughout this process, the writer draws ideas from long-term memory and transfers these ideas to working memory. Juan demonstrates this process as he writes more ideas, from long-term memory via working memory, on his paper. More recently, many of these components of writing and working memory were incorporated in the "simple view of writing" (Berninger and Amtmann 2003).

Motivation represents another important domain that certainly plays a role in student writing. Students who are highly motivated often set goals and achieve them. They also use strategies or design activities that lead to achieving their goals, with the end result being the production of high-quality papers (Graham and Harris 1996). Cognitive processes in writing involve incorporating information into the planning or transformation stages of writing. This information can come from reading, listening, or reviewing graphic information (for example, illustrations, charts, graphs). Problem solving and inference making are also included in these processes. Through reflection, as students read, they are able to use information in existing schemata to form new schemata; then, through text production, they transcribe these ideas/concepts on paper or through spoken language.

Planning, Translating, and Reviewing

According to the Hayes-Flower model, as students compose essays or papers, three main processes occur in writing: **planning**, **translating**, and **reviewing.** Writing is viewed as a recursive process whereby students write, revise, and edit at multiple stages during their writing. In the Hayes-Flower model, planning is the process that is dedicated to generating ideas, organizing ideas, and setting goals. As students begin to plan, they may map out ideas and build upon them, they set one or more goals (that is, a specific number of words or points written), and, eventually, they organize those ideas. During the next process, translating, students take ideas and translate them into sentences and paragraphs.

Berninger et al. (1995) have further defined two specific subcomponents during this translating process: text generation and transcription. In their research, they noticed that most younger students could use text generation to translate ideas into oral language, but found that only a small number were able to use transcription of these oral ideas into written text (graphic symbols). In addition, these researchers also saw that students not only organize ideas during the previous process, planning, but they often change the organization and revision of ideas as they write during the translating process. As a result, a second reorganization step may occur as students draft ideas, and a preliminary revising step may occur during the translating step.

Finally in reviewing, students evaluate and revise their writing. The purpose of the reviewing stage is to improve the quality of the text that they wrote during the translating process (Hayes and Flower 1980). During this process, students detect weaknesses in writing conventions, determine the accuracy of the written text based upon their "intent," and determine if they have met their writing goals. These actions occur through various activities such as revising the text by moving large chunks of text to appropriate sections; clarifying meaning in certain parts of text; and revising the text by looking for grammatical errors, incorrect words, and missing content. Hayes and Flower (1980) point out that any editing that occurs earlier may interfere in other processes. This is an important point to remember.

THINK BACK TO THE FIRST CASE **with Juan . . .**

1. *What aspects of Juan's approach to writing his essay may indicate that he is not likely to produce a quality essay?*

Based upon the Hayes-Flower model, Juan either omits or does not spend enough time in the planning, translating, and reviewing stages. For example, spending more time planning out his ideas would help him so that, once he is in the translating phase, he could elaborate more on his ideas that were planned out. He could also spend more time in the reviewing phase by revising and editing his paper more often.

8-2 Problems with the Writing Skills of Students with HI

As shown by Juan (from Case 8.1) and the NAEP scores reported in the chapter's opening paragraphs, learning to write is a difficult process for students with disabilities. It involves more than simply translating inner thoughts or conversations into written words. A developing writer must master lower-level spelling and grammar skills while at the same time using higher-level processing skills to plan out thoughts and ideas on paper. Unfortunately, when students with HI compose, they devote little attention to higher-order processes and often rely on weak lower-level skills to get them through the writing process.

Students with disabilities have writing problems that range from lower-order mechanical problems to higher-order strategic problems (Wong 1997). Moreover, their lower-level problems often consume cognitive resources that could be used for higher-level metacognitive skills such as the recognition of ambiguities in essays. Students with HI make both qualitative and quantitative errors in their written products; that is, their compositions are shorter than their peers', and they have more problems with coherence in paragraphs (Chalk, Hagan-Burke, and Burke 2005; Nodine, Barenbaum, and Newcomer 1985).

In terms of the different stages of writing, students with HI experience difficulty at all stages of the writing process (Lewis et al. 1998). Their problems generally include low levels of productivity; weak mechanical skills; and difficulty in planning, generating, organizing, revising, and editing (Graham et al. 1991; Lewis et al. 1998; Mayes, Calhoun, and Lane 2005).

Some students experience difficulty in the initial stages of writing, such as planning. Research shows that students with disabilities do very little advanced planning and do not use effective strategies even when prompted to during the planning stage (Ellis and Colvert 1996; MacArthur and Graham 1987). In terms of generating ideas during this stage, students with HI have difficulty writing multiple statements for a familiar topic, even though they have much more information about the topic in their memory (Englert and Raphael 1988). Also during the planning stage, students have a difficult time categorizing ideas into sets of related ideas and ordering them into a coherent overall presentation (Englert and Raphael 1988). Essays are more likely to be personal accounts by the student rather than including a developed story line or story schema (Nodine, Barenbaum, and Newcomer 1985).

During the drafting process, many students with HI use a "retrieve-and-write" approach that results in a paper that is full of personal accounts and devoid of relevant and related ideas (Troia and Graham 2002). These students also have little understanding of the structure of paragraphs (Englert et al. 1988) and use a plan-as-they-write approach in which they use preceding ideas to generate new ideas, regardless of the relevance of the new ideas (Troia and Graham 2002). This approach often results in an essay in which students ramble on and on about whatever ideas come to mind. In one study, students with learning disabilities had greater difficulty generating compositions that could be classified as stories when compared to nondisabled peers, and their stories were inordinately short and lacked coherence (Nodine, Barenbaum, and Newcomer 1985). Graham and Harris (1993) have theorized that students with HI have writing problems because they have difficulty transcribing ideas into words and limited knowledge of the writing process, and they fail to use effective writing strategies; instead they rely upon less effective strategies that hinder their progress during the writing process. Other production errors include more mechanical errors (spelling, punctuation, and capitalization errors), errors with word usage, and less legible handwriting (Graham and Weintraub 1996).

Students with disabilities have additional problems during revising and editing stages. Typically, students with HI often fail to monitor their own writing and detect errors made during or after writing (Ellis and Colvert 1996). They have a poor concept of revision, whereby they view it as correcting spelling errors, and they use limited strategies for revisions (MacArthur, Schwartz, and Graham 1991). As a result, students with HI are often more dependent on external resources, such as the teacher, to help them monitor the completeness and correctness of their writing (Englert and Raphael 1988). Even when given time to revise and edit essays, students with HI make only surface changes (for example, changes in conventions—free from mechanical errors and sentence fluency—for carefully constructed sentences) rather than deeper structural changes (changing ideas, supporting them with details, and reorganizing ideas) (Crawford, Helwig, and Tindal 2004).

Finally, students with disabilities have many problems in terms of writing different types of essays (persuasive, comparative, and so on). They have difficulty using genre-specific knowledge to frame their writing of a particular type of composition, and have a difficult time monitoring the quality of text and regulating their writing (Graham et al. 1992). It could be that students lack knowledge of text structure, which hinders their proper construction of essays and compositions (Englert and Mariage 1991). For example, in one study (Gleason 1999), students with learning disabilities had trouble with persuasive writing and instead wrote essays in a narrative style, using unsupported or nonexistent evidence; in some cases, they presented an argument that agreed with the other side.

Across the stages of the writing process, students with HI often have problems with legible handwriting and producing neat products (for example, writing on a straight line, staying within margins, cleanly erasing), which can impede effective communication to their readers and even to themselves as they try to read what they wrote.

As you can see, students with disabilities have problems that cut across many areas of writing, from problems with handwriting and spelling to problems composing and editing essays and papers. Next, we look at ways that teachers can remediate problems in these areas.

8-3 Teaching Handwriting Skills to Students with HI

Handwriting represents an important skill for students with HI because it is one means of communicating with others. Students use handwriting skills to express ideas, record important information, and share their own ideas and feelings. Students spend up to an estimated 50 percent of each day on writing tasks (for example, note taking, writing stories or summaries, answering questions) (Amundson and Weil 1996; Tseng and Cermak 1993). For many students, handwriting can be a challenge (Rosenblum, Weiss, and Parush 2004). One study found that, among children with learning disabilities, 30 to 40 percent had handwriting difficulties, and these rates are often higher for students with more severe types of HI (Cratty 1994). Interestingly, certain letters are particularly difficult for students to write. One study (Graham, Berninger, and Weintraub 1998) found that about half of the handwriting errors (that is, omissions, miscues, and illegible writing) for children in grades one through three could be accounted for by the following six letters: *q, j, z, u, n,* and *k*. It appears that these letters are either the most difficult to recall or the most difficult to produce.

The importance of how handwriting skills fit in with later composition skills cannot be overlooked. When students have to attend to lower-level writing skills as they transcribe their ideas onto paper, they are often diverting resources from high-level cognitive processing to do so. As we have discussed, these higher-level skills are essential during planning, content generation, and other aspects of the composing and writing process (Graham and Harris 1992). Mastery of handwriting skills allows students to become fluent writers who can shift their attention away from transcribing words and letters to expressing their thoughts and ideas. The reason students learn handwriting skills in the first place is to be able to convey messages to others in written form (stories, answers, ideas, feelings, and so on). However, if their messages are to be read and understood, they must be legible. Legible handwriting may not seem like an important aspect as children grow older, but these skills are used on an everyday basis. For example, studies have shown that students with disabilities often have a difficult time reading their own recorded notes from class lectures because the notes were not legible (Suritsky 1992). As you can guess, this often leads to trouble as students begin to review or study their notes from class. Moreover, students who have a difficult time with handwriting (that is, students with disabilities) often place too much emphasis on lower-level skills, and this results in shorter essays and compositions that habitually lack coherence and ideation (Isaacson 1989). Therefore, it is essential that teachers provide formal instruction in handwriting early on as part of the students' daily or every-other-day routine so that students can eventually become fluent writers.

Handwriting as Part of the Curriculum

When teaching handwriting, teachers should coach skills within a model of direct instruction. Direct instruction is particularly appropriate when teachers want students to replicate specific skills. First, teachers should model for students how to write letters and numbers. Not only should teachers show children how to produce letters on the board, an overhead, or a whiteboard—commonly referred to as **far-point copying**—but students also need an example or model on their desk that they can refer to as they write the letters—**near-point copying**. Teachers can also visit each child's desk to model how to make the letter, showing each student where to begin and the direction that lines should go to form the letter correctly. Next, as students begin practicing letters, the teacher should circulate around the room and provide guided practice with feedback to catch errors immediately, before students have a chance to practice errors. As teachers

▶ **FIGURE 8.2**

Letter Formation with Cues

will tell you, once students practice a skill incorrectly, particularly in the area of motor skills such as handwriting, correcting it later becomes extremely difficult. Moreover, students should be given specific feedback so that they know which parts of the letter were formed correctly and which parts were formed incorrectly. Once a teacher catches a student making an error, the teacher should model the skill correctly; the student should practice the corrected skill multiple times while the teacher looks on and provides feedback, and then the student should practice the skill on his or her own.

During this early stage of handwriting, teachers should use visual cues on students' papers to describe and model where to begin and which direction to go when forming the letter (Fig. 8.2). Providing visual cues, such as starting points and arrows, along with writing the letter from memory, was found to be a very effective handwriting technique among young, at-risk students (Berninger 2003). In one study, Berninger et al. (1997) taught students to examine carefully numbered arrows in a model of a letter, cover it with an index card, and then write it from memory. In terms of growth rate, students who used the visual cues plus memory technique performed better than those using other treatments (for example, motor, visual cues alone, copy). Over time, these cues should be faded as the students become more fluent at producing letters. Typically, students move from tracing over fully formed letters, to tracing over partially formed letters, to copying letters on lined paper. Ideally, good handwriting skills will be mastered at an early age, but older students with poor handwriting can correct bad handwriting habits and can also benefit from these same techniques, even though they may not be appealing to students (Graham 1999).

Some experts have used **backward chaining** with students to expedite their training of certain skills, particularly motor skills (Smith 1999) and complex community skills (McDonnell and Laughlin 1989). Backward chaining involves breaking down a skill into substeps. In the first step, the teacher completes all but the last step of the process; the student must complete only the *last* portion of the task. Next, the student completes the *last two* portions and so on until the student completes the entire portion. In Figure 8.3, the letter L is provided for the student to trace. First, the student simply traces all of it. Next, the student traces three quarters of the letter and must complete the last quarter independently. As the example illustrates, the student completes longer sections of the last portion of the letter. Unlike forward chaining, in which the student would be given the beginning or entire portion in dashes, backward chaining involves giving the student the last portion in dashes to complete with subsequent letters in which the child must complete longer and longer portions.

Finally, once students have mastered the skill, they should practice it independently for the teacher to assess. Previously learned letters should also be practiced periodically to make sure that students can recall these skills and produce them

▶ **FIGURE 8.3**

Example of Backward Chaining

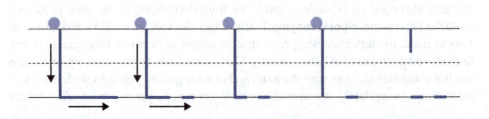

Manuscript Alphabet

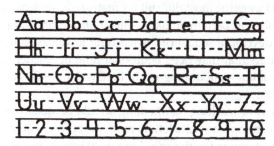

▸ **FIGURE 8.4**
Zaner-Bloser Handwriting

Cursive Alphabet

Manuscript/cursive card by the Zaner-Bloser Company (Columbus, OH).

correctly when needed. This type of maintenance is needed to ensure that students will be able to recall and reproduce all of the letters of the alphabet.

Typically during handwriting activities, teachers use commercial writing programs such as the Zaner-Bloser program (Fig. 8.4) or others. These programs provide models and samples of the correct formation of letters and numbers. Even though teachers use commercial programs, they may want to incorporate or modify some material to provide additional cues or practice for students with disabilities. As with any subject to be taught, teachers need to allocate time to teach it. This may involve listing it on the class schedule or writing it in lesson plan notebooks. When allocating time for handwriting, it is important that sessions be distributed throughout the day and week for students to practice their skills. This is known as **distributed practice** (Kame'enui et al. 2002). Rather than assign page after page of letters to practice in one large block of time, present basic skills (particularly those that require memory or drill, such as handwriting) in short (that is, 10 to 15 minutes), distributed lessons and practice throughout the day and week along with previously mastered letter skills. Also, remember that these lessons should incorporate some fun activities such as writing letters on the chalkboard in chalk or, if letters are already written in chalk, dipping a paintbrush in water and tracing over them so that no chalk lines appear when the letter is completed. Teachers could also incorporate other media and drawing instruments, such as using a paintbrush to write letters on paper; writing letters in sand, clay, or other media; or using permanent markers to trace over letters on laminated sheets (aerosol hairspray will clean the laminated sheets). Graham (1999) points out several other important aspects of handwriting, such as incorporating spelling words into handwriting, using traditional manuscript letters (that is, there is a lack of evidence that using a special style of manuscript such as D'Nealian benefits students), knowing the names of the letters in the alphabet, and paying close attention to student errors. In particular, among lowercase letters, eight letters (*q, z, g, u, n, k, j,* and *y,* in that order) were the most difficult for first-grade students to produce legibly (Graham, Weintraub, and Berninger 2001). This information is important because it can help teachers develop a sequence for teaching lowercase letters, can point out those particular letters that may need additional time or teacher attention, and can help the teacher monitor student progress in handwriting skills (Graham, Berninger, and Weintraub 1998).

Initially, the focus of teaching handwriting should be quality over quantity. Students should first learn how to write letters properly, both upper- and lowercase, and then they can work at improving the speed or rate at which they write them. In addition, some in the field of education have advocated that students should be taught letters based upon groups of associated letters. For example, they might begin practicing capital letters from the "circle" group (that is, O, C, Q, and G) and eventually move to the "line" group of letters (that is, L, I, T, F, H, E). Next, the students might move on to the group of manuscript uppercase letters that have "lines and circles" (that is, D, P, B, and R). Following this group, students might next work on the "slanted line" letters (V, X, Y, N, M, W, K, A, and Z) and then the "hook" letters (J, U, and S). Finally, students should be taught handwriting in meaningful contexts. Children (or older students correcting bad habits) should be shown that the payoff for their hard work is that good handwriting skills eventually lead to creating messages, whether they are short notes to Mom or Dad or other small meaningful phrases or sentences that convey the student's thoughts or feelings.

When providing feedback on students' handwriting, teachers should focus on the following aspects of writing letters: pencil grip, letter formation, letter size and proportion, spacing, alignment, and line quality (Hackney 1993).

- *Pencil grip.* Students should hold a pencil in their hands with a reasonable grip, not too tight that cramping occurs and not too loose that the line quality is too light. As a rule of thumb, teachers should be able to pull the pencil easily out of the students' hands while they are writing.
- *Letter formation.* Teachers should check students' letters, looking for proper formation when compared to a model letter. If a student is practicing a letter C, for example, the student should compare it to the model after writing each letter. After completing the entire page, the student should go back and circle those letters that most closely resemble the model.
- *Letter size and proportion.* Letters should remain the same proportion and not increase or decrease. For example, students practicing lowercase manuscript *e* should write between the bottom and middle line on lined handwriting paper. Letters that do not fall between these two lines are either too big or too small in proportion. Demonstrating how certain letters fall between the lines will help students understand letter size and proportion.
- *Spacing.* Letters should be spaced out properly on the student's paper, as determined by the teacher. The main concern is that the student uses a consistent amount of spacing between each letter.
- *Alignment.* Alignment refers to how letters are presented on the page in relation to the lines. For example, for properly aligned letters (manuscript uppercase letters), each should fall between the two lines, with its top touching the upper line and the bottom of the letter resting on the lower line.
- *Line quality.* Line quality refers to the thickness or thinness of the line of each letter or number. Aside from the aesthetic aspect, if a student's grip and pressure produce a thick line quality, it could cause the student's hand to cramp or quickly fatigue.

Manuscript Versus Cursive Handwriting

Manuscript handwriting is an important skill for students to learn because most children and adults use manuscript handwriting as part of their daily life, and manuscript letters form the basis of the text that we read. Traditionally, manuscript has been taught before cursive handwriting and is thought to be an easier form of handwriting for children to learn and produce. Cursive handwriting is typified by the use of letters that are connected by flowing strokes. Some experts claim that cursive handwriting is easier for children with HI because students have to see the entire word before writing it down, as opposed to manuscript, which uses a letter-by-letter approach. Yet, for some students with disabilities, cursive handwriting remains a struggle all of their lives, or at least until they are no longer required to write in cursive.

Teachers often debate whether to teach cursive handwriting, especially for students with writing or motor difficulties. When deciding whether to teach cursive handwriting to a particular student, teachers should consider the form of writing that the student's peers use, as well as the form the student's teachers use. If peers use cursive in notes or other written products, you may want to teach this form because it may serve as the primary form of communication between the student and her or his peers. Teachers who decide not to teach cursive handwriting to students should consider teaching them to read cursive handwriting, at the very least, because this may be the form that other teachers or peers use in class notes, written directions, or everyday communication. On a final note, research has shown no difference in the speed and legibility among students (in grades four through nine) who used manuscript versus cursive handwriting. Moreover, students with HI who used a combination of both manuscript and cursive often had the fastest and most legible handwriting (Graham, Berninger, and Weintraub 1998).

Transitional Handwriting

When transitioning from manuscript to cursive handwriting, Mann, Suiter, and McClung (1992) recommend using a transitional writing technique (Fig. 8.5). This technique uses students' prior knowledge about the formation of manuscript letters to assist them in the formation of cursive letters. Using this technique, students move from writing words in manuscript to writing manuscript letters in words (using connecting lines) to writing words in cursive.

Using this technique, students trace over words that are in manuscript. These words typically slant slightly to the right so that they resemble cursive letters. Next, students trace over the letters that are connected, using dots. Finally, students trace over words that are written in cursive. For more difficult letters, teachers should use more cues (for example, dots) for students to trace and follow. Initially, teachers should

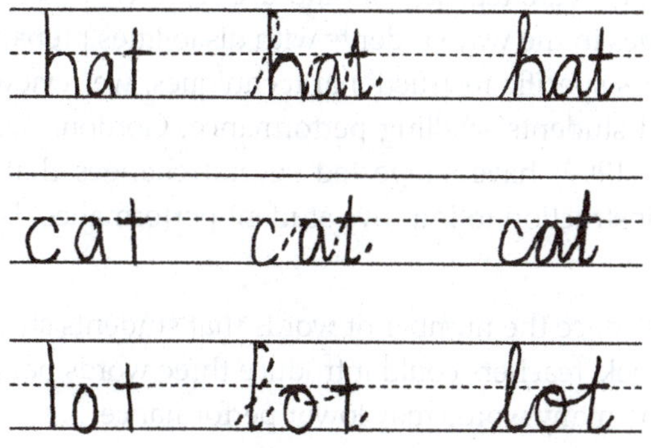

◀ FIGURE 8.5
Transitional Handwriting

use those letters that easily connect, without adding extra lines or humps, such as those shown in the example. Certain cursive letters (that is, *b*, *e*, *f*, *k*, *r*, *s*, and *z*) must be taught separately because they do not closely resemble their manuscript counterparts. Also, certain letters (for example, *m* and *n*) will require extra spacing for the added humps that are used when these letters are written in cursive (Mann, Suiter, and McClung 1992). Eventually, teachers should phase out the use of cues.

8-4   Spelling Skills and Strategies for Students with HI

Spelling can be a challenging task for even the most proficient students. We personally know professors who rely on the spell-checker that is built into their word-processing program to help them write and edit articles, books, or simple emails. Spelling involves knowledge of countless rules, word structure, and irregularly spelled words. Of course, it does not help that many letters (or graphemes) have more than one phoneme associated with them (see Chapter 5 for more details about these terms). This lack of one-to-one correspondence can create difficulties even for typically achieving students, let alone students with disabilities. Spelling is a complex memory, visual, and, sometimes, verbal process. First, students must search their memories to recall target words to be spelled. If the search is unsuccessful, students may try to segment or use phonological awareness to try to spell the word verbally. If this step proves unsuccessful or if the spelled word is still not recognized, students might consult a teacher, another student, or, usually as a last resort, the dictionary to determine the correct spelling.

Spelling problems begin in elementary school and often deteriorate as students progress to higher grades, where words become longer and more complex (Dixon 1991). Studies have found that students with disabilities typically misspelled two to four times as many words as their nondisabled peers, resulting in 10 to 20 percent misspelled words in writing (Deno, Marston, and Mirkin 1982; MacArthur and Graham 1987). Not only do these misspellings cause problems when students spell vocabulary words, but spelling difficulties slow down the writing process and interfere in the transcription and flow of putting ideas onto paper. Moreover, as we have mentioned in earlier chapters, improved spelling is often linked to improved reading (Ehri 2003).

Over the years, a number of techniques have been developed that were proven to be effective at augmenting the spelling performance of students with HI. In typical classrooms, students may be given between 15 and 20 words per week to study. In most of those classrooms, teachers use commercially prepared materials that often advocate a study-test method whereby students are given their spelling words on Monday and are tested on Friday (Brown 1990; Fulk and Stormont-Spurgin 1995). One of the problems with this approach is that students often postpone studying until the night before the test, and using this traditional approach, particularly for students with disabilities, may not be the most effective method of preparation (Murphy, Hern, and Williams 1990). Instead, teachers should use research-based spelling techniques that advocate changes in the way students with disabilities prepare for spelling tests.

Before we discuss specific instructional techniques, we review general principles that have improved students' spelling performance. Gordon, Vaughn, and Schumm (1993) and Brown (1990) have suggested several changes that could be incorporated into spelling instruction to improve student performance. They recommend the following:

- *Assess unit size.* Reduce the number of words that students study. Instead of 12 words for the week, teachers could introduce three words per day. Overloading students with too many words may lower performance.

- *Consider distributed practice.* Students should study daily or twice daily in short sessions (10 to 15 minutes per day).
- *Provide immediate feedback.* Students should be given immediate feedback for words that are misspelled.
- *Review response format.* When studying, students should write their responses on paper to simulate the format of the spelling test. If teachers use a different format, they should match their practice to the actual administration and response format used in the classroom.
- *Develop spelling lists.* Some experts (Graham 1999; Graham, Harris, and Loynachan 1994) have advocated developing spelling lists from several sources that include commonly misspelled words from students' writing assignments; vocabulary or important words from students' academic areas (for example, reading, science, social studies); words that students plan to use in compositions (or future writing assignments); and words that follow similar, but different, patterns, such as *see* and *sea*, so that students can compare patterns and learn the correct spelling of each word.
- *Teach for transfer.* Teach students to transfer words to writing and reading activities in other classes (Gettinger, Bryant, and Fayne 1982).
- *Use computer-assisted instruction (CAI).* A variety of software programs are on the market that aid students in practicing spelling and make spelling an entertaining activity.

Study Techniques for Spelling

The spelling techniques presented in this chapter incorporate a variety of methods, and students may favor them over traditional study techniques. They all incorporate a critical element in spelling study techniques: immediate feedback and correction of misspelled words. Providing students with immediate feedback of misspelled words, followed by extended practice in which students practice the correct word several times, regularly results in improved performance. All of the following techniques have been used with students with disabilities and were proven effective in research studies.

Class-wide Peer Tutoring. Class-wide peer tutoring (CWPT) is a technique that has been shown to be effective at increasing the number of correctly spelled words for students with HI (Burks 2004; Mortweet et al. 1999). During CWPT, students are assigned in pairs to be either the tutor or tutee for 10 minutes, and then they switch with one another for an additional 10 minutes (for 20 minutes total). Each pair is given a list of spelling words, paper on which to write their spelling words, and a sheet to keep track of points earned. The tutors begin by reading the spelling words, one at a time, to the tutees, who write the words. As tutees write each word, they also say the letters aloud. The tutors award the tutees two points for each correctly spelled word. If a word is misspelled, tutors tell the tutees how to spell the word correctly and the tutees practice spelling the word correctly three times while saying the letters aloud. If the tutees spell the word correctly three times, the tutors award one point. If the tutees still spell the word incorrectly, the tutors do not award any points. The tutors continue through the list of words and repeat them as necessary until the timer sounds to end the first 10-minute session. Once the timer sounds, the students switch roles so that the tutees are now the tutors and the tutors are now the tutees.

They proceed for 10 minutes, spelling words from the same list. After the second 10-minute session ends, the teacher collects materials and students report on the total number of points. The pair with the most points is rewarded with a prize or special privilege (for example, five minutes' extra free time, lining up first). Throughout the tutoring, the teacher circulates around the room and awards bonus points for students who are working correctly and cooperatively.

Analogy Technique. Using the analogy strategy in a study (Englert, Hiebert, and Stewart 1985), students were taught to spell new words using familiar spelling patterns from known words, and outperformed students in a control group who used a traditional spelling study method. Using words that rhymed and were spelled the same as the last part of the word, students were taught to use known words that rhymed with an unknown word in order to spell the unknown word. First, students were taught to spell common words (for example, *hot, bat, rake*), referred to as spelling bank words. These spelling bank words rhymed with missed words from a pretest (for example, *rot, mat, snake*). During this portion of the training, students spelled the spelling bank words aloud while looking at the written version. Next, students wrote each word from memory three times. In doing so, students had to write the word correctly twice from memory and then a third time after a one-minute delay. Once students could correctly spell these common words, they moved on to the transfer phase. In that phase, students were presented with practice transfer words. These transfer words were a set of four unknown words that rhymed with common words (for example, *cot, dot, got, not*). Once students were presented with a transfer word, they would perform the following three steps:

1. They found the printed spelling bank word that rhymed with the orally presented word.
2. They identified the portion of the word that rhymed and was spelled alike.
3. They spelled the new word using the rhyming part from the spelling bank word.

Once students could successfully practice these skills with a set of words, they moved on to the final training phase. In this phase, students read a list of words from the previous transfer phase and were asked to write/spell these words from memory. If they could not, they were to follow the three steps from the previous phase.

Spelling Package. The spelling package (Frank et al. 1987) involved a variety of practice and study skills to help students spell a set of 10 words written on numbered index cards. Five of the 10 words were words that the students could already correctly spell. Students who were trained to use this spelling package improved their spelling of unknown words. During training, students followed a five-step procedure for spelling their set of words:

Step 1. Students opened their envelopes and arranged their cards in numerical order.
Step 2. Students traced over the word on the first card with a pencil until they felt that they could spell the word. Once they stated they could spell the word, the card was removed from sight and the student wrote the word from memory.
Step 3. Students checked their spelling by comparing the spelled word with the word from the card. If correct, students drew a star or happy face next to it. If incorrect, they would draw a line through it, and erase the misspelled word. Next, the student was to copy the word from the card and write it an additional four times.
Step 4. Once students correctly spelled the word, they were tested on it by spelling the word from memory. Steps two through four were repeated until all 10 words were spelled.
Step 5. In this step, students marked on their spelling chart the correct number of words spelled (that is, self-graphing) for that particular day (during step four).

Other researchers (Murphy, Hern, and Williams 1990) have used a similar technique called a **copy, cover, and compare approach** with special education students to improve their performance on lists of 14 to 18 words. Using this approach, students would (1) check the spelling of the word by saying the word aloud while looking closely at the letters, (2) copy the word from the list, (3) cover the word with a card and write the word from memory, and (4) compare the second spelling of the word against the word list to check its accuracy.

Five-Step Word-Study Strategy. Graham and Freeman (1986) developed a kinesthetic method for students with HI to use for studying spelling words. Students who used this strategy in the study spelled more words correctly than students who used their conventional study procedure. Using the five-step strategy, students participated in a 20-minute training session during which the strategy was taught using direct instructional procedures. The five-step strategy consisted of the following:

1. Say the word.
2. Write and say the word.
3. Check the word.
4. Trace and say the word.
5. Write the word from memory and check.

Initially, the teacher modeled the strategy to students. Next, students practiced the strategy with several words while receiving assistance and feedback from the teacher. Finally, the students had to demonstrate proficiency in the strategy by using it correctly with two consecutive words before being permitted to use it in the study session.

Visual Imagery. Berninger et al. (1995) used a visual imagery (or orthographic imaging) method to help students imagine words and practice spelling them for a test. Using this procedure, students were to complete the following directions:

1. Look at the spelling word and say its name.
2. Close your eyes and imagine the word in your mind's eye.
3. Name the letters from left to right with your inside voice.
4. Open your eyes and write the word.
5. Compare your spelling to the correctly spelled word.
6. Repeat the above steps if the word is misspelled.

This method is similar to a visual imagery method that Sears and Johnson (1986) developed to improve spelling among elementary students. Using this procedure, the teacher introduced a spelling word on a transparency and then asked students to use visual imagery to remember the word. This involved (1) seeing the image in your mind, (2) imagining the word displayed on a large outdoor screen, (3) imagining each letter being pasted on the screen to spell the word, and (4) imagining nailing each letter into place with fantasy nails.

8-5 Teaching Writing Techniques and Strategies to Students with HI

In a 2003 article, Jean Schumaker and Donald Deshler asked the question, "Can students with LD become competent writers?" Given the data that we have for students with disabilities, researchers have shown that they have many obstacles to overcome to gain competence in writing. In an earlier portion of this chapter, we discussed these problems in detail. Despite these challenges, research has consistently shown that, once students are taught strategies and techniques, they can improve their writing performance, in some cases to the point where their performance is comparable to nondisabled peers (McNaughton, Hughes, and Clark 1994).

Before we discuss specific strategies for improving composing skills, we discuss some common principles for teaching writing skills. Graham and Harris (1988) have recommended several principles that should serve as a framework for writing programs for students with disabilities. These principles, many of which reflect practical ideas, will enhance any teacher's writing program and are drawn from research. First, allocate time for writing. It has been reported that students spend very little time working on composing skills in the classroom. As always in education, if you plan to teach skills, you must first allocate time to it. This means writing out schedules that block or dedicate time to composing. Composing, particularly drafting, is a skill that requires **massed practice**, large blocks of time (for example, 45 minutes or more), because it involves getting ideas down on paper and relating ideas back to the main topic or theme. Once students start writing, it is difficult to stop and then start again. Graham and Harris recommend that at least four times per week should be dedicated to writing, along with teaching writing skills.

Second, good writing programs should expose students to a broad range of meaningful writing tasks. The sources for deciding different writing tasks can be determined from end-of-the-year tests (for example, essays on different genres), state standards, content areas that classes demand (for example, report writing), goals for writing (for example, journal writing may best accomplish this goal), social/recreational purposes (for example, personal letters, letters of complaint), or functional reasons (for example, applications). Whenever possible, writing activities should serve a meaningful purpose. If students are practicing forming letters, teachers should make the activity meaningful by having students write sentences with words that have that particular letter in them.

Third, integrate writing with other academic subjects. General instruction in reading and oral language does little to improve a student's writing skills; however, specific targeted writing-related skills can influence writing skills. For example, an oral discussion about a topic prior to writing can influence the student's planning and development of the topic during writing. To influence the effects of writing in other subject areas, students must be taught task-specific skills or strategies (for example, a strategy for responding to specific types of essay questions, or a strategy for writing a research report).

Fourth, automatize lower-level skills or disregard lower skills until the latter stages of writing. Adopting this principle has several benefits. One, just as fluency is an important skill for comprehension during reading, automatizing of lower-level writing skills, such as mechanics, is an important precursor of higher-level skills during writing. For example, mastery of mechanics prevents cognitive overload during the drafting stage of writing (Graham and Harris 1988). Students should practice these lower-level skills to mastery so that putting ideas onto paper is an automatic process. Two, even if students lack some of these lower-level skills, they can still use higher-level processes by bypassing them. For example, instructing them not to pay attention to mechanics while writing will often result in higher-quality compositions. In fact, when the physical requirements of mechanics are removed (for example, by using dictation), students with HI composed better stories (MacArthur and Graham 1987).

Fifth, expose students to different genres for writing. Many students with disabilities lack knowledge of story genres for writing and often use a narrative or story genre when assignments require other types of genres (for example, persuasive or comparison/contrast) (Gleason 1999). For example, NAEP writing tests require students to produce three different types of essays: narrative, informative, and persuasive. Narrative essays should be imaginative, creative, and speculative, allowing students to express thoughts and emotions. When writing informative essays, students must analyze information and report in essay form about what they learned from it. Lastly, persuasive tasks require students to make an argument for a certain perspective or against an opposing perspective.

Sixth, help students develop goals for improving their written products. Because students with disabilities seldom use goals during the planning stage, teachers need to assist in goal planning and, eventually, teach students to plan for goals during the early stages of writing. Writing conferences or peer evaluations might help students to identify and set goals. Several studies have shown that students who set goals improve their monitoring of those goal areas and reach those goals in their writing. Such goals can include increasing the amount and type of vocabulary used, better use of transitional words in paragraphs, and a greater variety of sentence types, such as compound and complex versus simple.

The seventh and perhaps most important principle of good writing instruction involves using a **process approach** as a framework for writing (Graham et al. 2012). We discuss this framework in detail later. All of the principles previously mentioned should be integrated into any writing program for students with HI. Many of these principles are also described in the IES Practice Guide *Teaching Elementary School Students to Be Effective Writers* (Graham et al. 2012).

Methods and Strategies Spotlight

Computer-Assisted Writing

In terms of using computers in the classroom, the following statement best sums up what teachers should remember about technology and writing: "The computer is not a magical writing tool that will transform the way in which exceptional students write; neither is it a writing curriculum or an instructional method" (MacArthur 1988). MacArthur goes on to write that, despite these statements, computers are "powerful" and "flexible" tools for use in the writing process. Like other technologies and CAI, computers can assist students in learning but can never fully teach students all of the aspects of writing. When we look at the components of the process approach to writing, computers can readily assist students (1) in the planning stage through the use of brainstorming software such as Inspiration©, (2) in the drafting stage through the use of word-processing programs such as Microsoft Word©, (3) in the revising stage through the use of "cut-and-paste" functions, (4) in the editing stage through the use of spelling and grammar checking programs, and (5) in the sharing and publishing stage through word-writing programs or print publication programs such as Microsoft Publisher©.

Despite all of these wonderful options, students must still generate ideas, organize those ideas in a determined order, write the ideas down on paper (or enter them in the computer), and revise and edit those ideas so that sentences are meaningful and paragraphs/essays are coherent and meet their writing goals.

The research is mixed as to the effectiveness of word processing on the written products of students with disabilities (MacArthur 1988); however, studies do seem to indicate that the effectiveness of word-processing programs depends upon how the teacher chooses to use them during writing activities (Rubin and Bruce 1985). Computers can aid students in several areas: editing the paper, producing a polished product, providing a motivating medium, and providing access to Internet resources and other assistive software (Cramer 2004; MacArthur 1988). Obviously, the editing capability of spelling and grammar programs is appealing to students who may have problems with proofreading skills. However, spelling and grammar checkers may not detect missing words, incorrect but similarly spelled words, sentence meaning as determined by the writer, choice of punctuation, and other variables that only proofreading by humans can detect.

Computers can, however, print out a relatively smudge-free finished product, one that is ready to be displayed or published. Motivation is still another advantage; students are often very motivated to use the computer to write essays and compositions over drafting with paper and pencil. The last advantage of computers is that they allow students to access other Internet resources for research and technology for assistance in writing. Using computer technology and software, students can use speech-to-text programs to produce a written product and readers that read text aloud to assist students in proofreading.

Computers offer students an active tool for writing; however, technology can also frustrate students if they lack the skills to use the technology. Part of using technology properly involves learning how to use it and how it can (and cannot) help. For teachers, this may involve teaching students keyboarding skills and how to use software programs and peripherals (for example, printer, touchscreens, external memory drives). In addition, teachers should remember that computers can assist with teaching but are not meant to be the teacher. Teachers should integrate computers into their writing programs so that the technology becomes an integral part of writing and not the writing program itself.

An Instructional Framework for Teaching Writing Skills

Derived from the Hayes-Flower model, the following instructional framework evolved to become one of the most commonly used frameworks in today's classrooms (Bisaillon and Clerc 1999). This process approach (De la Paz and Graham 2002; Graham and Perin 2007; Graves 1983) consists of the following five stages: planning, drafting, revising, editing, and sharing/publishing. Often, teachers break these stages into distinct activities so that students essentially work on one distinct stage at a time. This is an important point because students with disabilities may become overwhelmed or confused working on more than one stage at a time.

Planning. During the planning stage, students map out ideas and organize them. This stage involves selecting topics, choosing goals for writing, identifying an audience, brainstorming ideas related to the topic, and organizing ideas into a framework for drafting (Bos 1988; Troia 2008). In some cases, the teacher helps students through these components and, in other cases, students work independently. Teachers often incorporate cognitive maps or other visual displays to help students structure and expand on ideas. Inspiration© and similar software can also be used to help students arrange ideas and expand on details of the composition. Although this stage may not seem essential to writing, some believe that storing the writing plan externally frees up cognitive resources for other higher-level processes (Torrance and Galbraith 2008). In addition, Trioa (2008) points out that students who spend time planning prior to writing produce higher-quality written products. In addition, sufficient planning time seems to help with ideation of student essays (ideation refers to how students develop and express their ideas in a clear and understandable fashion).

Drafting. This stage consists of putting previously generated ideas into written sentences. During this phase, students work to craft sentences and paragraphs by juggling various versions of them from brainstormed ideas. Just as decoding problems can interfere with reading comprehension, spelling errors and handwriting problems may interfere in the writing process (see Suritsky and Hughes 1996). Recall that working memory is limited in its capacity to hold information; therefore, if ideas are not written down quickly enough in rough draft form, they may be lost forever. Students who lack prerequisites, such as an understanding of sentence or paragraph structure, may also have difficulty during the drafting stage because they may have to recall the rules and procedures for sentence formation, using precious resources needed for ideation. For other students, using a weak strategic approach to writing may interfere in effective drafting of ideas.

Revising. Revising usually involves proofreading a writing product for meaning. While reading, students check to see whether the written draft makes sense on a micro level (sentences and paragraphs) and macro level (does the paper as a whole make sense and does it fit the intent?). From a cognitive perspective, revising involves detecting differences between what was originally written and the actual meaning (MacArthur 2007). Revising may involve moving chunks of text around to improve the transition between sentences and to develop the coherence of the paper as a whole. In other cases, revising might be as simple as filling in missing words. Finally, revising provides students with an opportunity to check if their papers meet their goals.

Editing. Editing primarily involves proofreading for grammatical and mechanical errors in the paper. Grammar refers to the system of rules by which words are arranged into meaningful units. Some rules are implicit and we may not be able to state them, but we know when they have been violated. Other rules are explicit, such as subject–verb agreement, and are taught to students as a tool to check their writing during proofreading.

In terms of mechanics, most teachers focus their attention on the basics of mechanics such as spelling, punctuation, and capitalization. Punctuation, specifically commas and periods, has been identified as the most frequent problem for elementary-school students (Porter 1974).

Sharing and Publishing. This last stage is sometimes omitted from the writing process, but we feel that it should always be part of it. We feel that if students spend the time to produce a written product, then it should be shared with others. Sharing can be as simple as posting a report (for example, a weather report) with young children, or more involved, such as having students read poems or other works aloud to the class. In some cases, the writing product can be posted on the bulletin board, read to the class, read to parents, compiled into a collection of works that is bound together, posted in the class newsletter, or posted on the class website. In some cases, teachers could model written products to show students how they wrote during the different stages of writing from drafting ideas to the final, polished product.

THINK BACK TO THE FIRST CASE with Juan...

> *2. What specific writing skill of Juan's would you try to remediate first?*
>
> Juan has quite a few problems in his writing. Perhaps the two biggest areas for improvement are writing complete sentences and proofreading. Although there are others, these two areas provide a good place to begin.

Strategies for Composing Sentences, Paragraphs, and Essays, and Monitoring Errors

Because writing is much more than just the mechanical aspects that have been addressed thus far in this chapter, we now address more complex tasks of writing as communication, composing, and error monitoring. As you will see, many of the writing strategies featured in this section incorporate one or more of the five stages of the process approach framework into their steps. As you teach writing skills to students, consider carefully how you can structure writing programs so that students participate in each stage of writing or use strategies that will cover each stage. With effective teaching, students will internalize the process approach to writing and begin to view writing as a recursive process rather than as a perfunctory task that results in a written product that meets the required assignment. Keep a variety of writing strategies in mind when you review Case 8.2 as you decide what is the best approach to helping this student improve his writing.

CASE 8.2   Crayon Colors

Case Introduction

Now that you have worked through the first case in this chapter, you should feel comfortable addressing issues in a second case, which is about the student Myles Faircloth. In this case, Mrs. Awar Hall and Mr. Henry Brown work in a collaborative classroom for science, math, and possibly language arts. Myles's eighth-grade teacher is working on Standard 8.7 that deals with writing skill. This standard states the following:

8.7 The student will write in a variety of forms, including narrative, expository, persuasive, and informational. Use prewriting strategies, organize details, use specific vocabulary and information, revise writing for word choice, sentence variety, and transitions among paragraphs, and use available technology.

Read the case and see if you can suggest skills to target for remediation and techniques or activities to help remediate the targeted writing skills.

"All right class, listen up!" Mrs. Awar Hall said to her eighth-grade students in language arts. She continued, "This is the famous 'Creative Writing Crayon Paper' that you've heard so much about. Your creative writing assignment will be to choose a color of crayon that you want to be and describe why you would be that color of crayon." The students, who had been sitting quietly in their seats until now, began cracking jokes about different colors.

"Mrs. Hall. What did the blueberry ask the sick banana?" Terry yelled out.

"I don't know," said Mrs. Hall.

"How are you peeling today?" replied Terry.

Randi next yelled out, "Did you hear about the girl who wanted to color her hair?"

Mrs. Hall couldn't resist and said, "No."

"She wanted to, but she couldn't find a blonde crayon," Randi quipped back. With that, the class began to laugh and become noisy.

Realizing that she was about to lose control, Mrs. Hall began to settle them down. "Alright, now. Settle down, settle down, settle down," she repeated to them. She handed out the assignment directions and told students that it would be due in two weeks. As she whisked by Myles Faircloth, placing an assignment sheet on his desk, she noticed that he had a very despondent look on his face.

"Myles, what's wrong?" she said to him.

"Nothing," he responded in a flat, less-than-enthusiastic voice. As she continued down the aisle handing out the assignment sheets, Mrs. Hall remembered that Myles had a difficult time with writing. Because this was his first assignment, she suspected that he might need a lot of help. Even though they were only six weeks into the new school year, Myles had already exhibited problems with spelling and writing that concerned Mrs. Hall, but she knew that Henry Brown, the special education teacher, was assisting him. Despite her concerns, she was certain he would be fine because of Mr. Brown's support.

Myles had been identified as having HI mental disabilities about two years ago when he first entered Mapleview Middle School. The committee found that Myles had problems in written language, specifically composing, spelling, and handwriting. Myles had always been a hard worker since coming to Mapleview from Parkview Catholic School. Although he had been held back a year in second grade at Parkview, Myles continued to struggle to maintain a minimal grade point average to pass from grade to grade. "Would this be the year that they moved him permanently to the self-contained special education class?" Mrs. Hall thought. It was not that she wanted him moved, but she felt that she did not have the "special skills" necessary to teach him. Mrs. Hall really liked Myles, but she had 24 other students to attend to and could not work one on one with him to complete this assignment as she had done in the past.

Later that day, Mrs. Hall caught up with Mr. Brown to alert him of the language arts writing assignment.

"I know we have collab [collaborative teaching] math and science, but you may want to try to work collab language arts into your schedule," she remarked to Mr. Brown. After giving her a blank look, he said, "OK. I'll see what I can do." Mr. Brown had his schedule set for the year; however, once again, he had to rearrange it so that he could assist his three special education students in Mrs. Hall's class. Mr. Brown knew that, if he did not fit collab language arts into his schedule, Myles and the two others would end up getting poor grades or failing the class.

continued

Myles dreaded this assignment. He hated writing, in no uncertain terms, and had already begun thinking that he was going to fail the assignment. When he brought the assignment paper home for his parents to sign, they too dreaded another writing assignment; however, they knew that, if he could begin early enough, he might have a fighting chance at passing it. Despite the best efforts of both Myles and his parents, they waited to begin working on it until the weekend before it was due. Their five-day business trip to Japan had distracted them from his school assignments. Now, with the assignment due in 24 hours, Myles sat down and began working on it.

As Myles sat down to write a rough draft, he started with, "If I were a crayon. . . ." After several minutes, he became distracted with his dog, and his mother prompted him to get back to work. In the next hour, Myles struggled to write down several sentences, most of which were poorly written and riddled with spelling errors. Myles decided that he wanted to be the color fuchsia. After a while, his mother came in the room to check on him and told him to finish up upon seeing his lack of progress. She decided to help him by giving him some sentences. "Here, write this down," she said to him. "I want to be fuchsia because it is the color of plums, my favorite food. I want to be fuchsia because my favorite shirt is that color. OK, now clean up and get ready for dinner," she continued. As Myles scribbled down those lines, he again made spelling and grammatical errors. After his mother called him again a few minutes later, he squeezed his paper into its folder, placed the folder in his backpack, and zipped it up ready for school the next day.

When Myles handed in his paper, Mrs. Hall just looked at it in amazement. He had erasure marks on it from where he had made corrections, and his paper had various folds in it after being removed from his stuffed folder in his backpack. As Mrs. Hall tried to straighten the corners, she thought that the paper would earn one of the lowest grades in the class, and now she was in a quandary. Here is what she read:

If I Were A Crayon
By: Myles Faircloth

If I were a crayn I'd be fuchsia. I would be this color cause is it my favorites. This color is a mix of pirple and blue. These colors got mix up one day and made fuschia. It can hide at nite and not seen by other color crayens. Use yellow crayen to lite my way at nite. Protect me would be color gray crayen. I want to be fuchsia because it is the color of plums, my favorite food. I want to be fuscsia because my favorite shirt is that color. Fushie it is!

"Wow," Mrs. Hall exclaimed. She thought to herself, "Should I give him time to revise it before I grade it? Or should I just grade it along with the rest of the class?"

CASE QUESTIONS

1. What are two other writing skills that you, as the teacher, would address?
2. Name and describe two types of writing activities/strategies that you would use with Myles.

Sentence Writing Strategy. The sentence writing strategy (Schumaker and Sheldon 1985; Box 8.1) was developed to assist students in writing a variety of sentence types. Ellis and Colvert (1996) provide an adaptation of this strategy, as well as additional examples of the different types of sentences that students create with the strategy. Because most students with disabilities rely on simple sentences for the majority of essays and compositions, the sentence writing strategy enables them to produce not only simple sentences, but also compound, complex, and compound-complex sentences (Deshler and Schumaker 2006). This variety is not meant to make their writing more complicated, but is meant to help them express their ideas more fully and to make the written product more readable.

BOX 8.1

Sentence Writing Strategy—PENS Strategy

P Pick a formula.
E Explore words to fit the formula.
N Note the words.
S Search and check.

> **BOX 8.2**
>
> ### Formulas and Sample Simple Sentences
>
> S = subject and V = verb
>
> S V = Tom ran home.
>
> SS V = Tom and Judy walked home together.
>
> S VV = Haja ran and kicked the ball.
>
> SS VV = Yogi and Sevin ate three pizzas and drank soda.

Using the steps of the PENS strategy, students pick a formula (Box 8.2) and explore (that is, choose) words (subjects and verbs) that fit the formula. In the next step, note, students write down the sentence from the formula that they chose. In the last step, search and check, students examine the sentence to make sure that it is a complete sentence, identify the subject(s) and verb(s), determine whether the sentence has proper capitalization and punctuation, and read it to determine whether it makes sense.

Applying the PENS strategy to actual sentences, students first learn how to use the four formulas with simple sentences, next with compound sentences, then with complex sentences, and finally, with compound-complex sentences (Ellis and Colvert 1996). Once students can successfully create the four types of simple sentences, they move on to compound sentences. As shown in Box 8.3, students create compound sentences by using a comma and a coordinating conjunction such as *and*, *so*, or *but* with two independent clauses. Variations of these sentences are created using one or two subjects and verbs from the formulas.

Once students master compound sentences using the PENS strategy, they move on to complex sentences and compound-complex sentences.

In some cases, prior to using the PENS strategy, students may need to be taught prerequisite sentence writing skills such as identification of subjects and verbs, use of proper punctuation, and rules for capitalization. Frequently, students need much practice to master these different types of sentences. Initially, they are taught first to identify a particular type of sentence before they are asked to create and write their own (Ellis and Colvert 1996).

PLEASE Paragraph-Writing Strategy. The PLEASE strategy (Welch 1992) was developed by addressing writing deficits that students with disabilities frequently made. This strategy incorporates components of the process approach into a strategy format using the mnemonic PLEASE. In other words, students learn to write all of the parts of a paragraph using the planning, composing, and revising components of the process approach. Each step is meant to elicit a specific action associated with writing. The steps are illustrated in Box 8.4.

> **BOX 8.3**
>
> ### Formulas and Sample Compound Sentences[1]
>
> S V = Tom ran home and he ate dinner.
>
> SS V = Tom and Judy walked home together, *so* they could talk to each other.
>
> S VV = Haja ran and kicked the ball, *but* it was caught by Tucker.
>
> SS VV = Yogi and Sevin ate three pizzas and drank soda; they were still hungry.
>
> [1]*And*, *so*, *or*, *for*, *nor*, *yet*, and *but* are coordinating conjunctions and are used with punctuation separating independent clauses. The sentence formulas use subject(s), verb(s), and a semicolon (with no coordinating conjunction).

BOX 8.4

PLEASE Paragraph Writing Strategy

P <u>P</u>ick a topic.
L <u>L</u>ist your ideas about the topic.
E <u>E</u>valuate your list.
A <u>A</u>ctivate the paragraph with a topic sentence.
S <u>S</u>upply supporting sentences.
E <u>E</u>nd with a concluding sentence.
AND
Evaluate your work.

In the first step, pick, students are taught to pick a topic and decide on their audience. Once students have chosen the topic, purpose, and audience, they continue in this step by choosing the proper format (for example, enumerative, compare/contrast, cause/effect) to use to write the paragraph. In the list step, they are taught techniques to generate and list ideas about the topic. Generating ideas can include asking various questions about the topic and then answering them, as well as listing or mapping out ideas (Kytle 1970). These ideas include topic ideas and related (that is, supporting) ideas. In the next step, students are taught to evaluate their list in terms of completeness, organization, and sequencing of ideas that will be used to generate supporting sentences. In the next step, students are taught to activate the paragraph with a topic sentence. During this stage, students are also taught how to write a short declarative topic sentence. In the fifth step, students are instructed on how to supply supporting sentences for their topic. During this step, students generate supporting sentences from their list of ideas. Over time, students are taught to enhance ideas by generating clarifying or expanding sentences. Finally, in the last step, students are taught to end with a concluding sentence and evaluate their work using the COPS strategy (see the Error Monitoring Strategy later in this chapter).

The training for this strategy took place over 20 weeks, with 30-minute sessions occurring three times per week. The training incorporated video presentations that consisted of seven steps: stated learning objectives, lead-in activities, focused viewing activities, segmented viewing activities, post-viewing discussion, follow-through activities, and evaluation (Welch 1992). These presentations demonstrated to students what each step entailed and how to use it.

THINK BACK TO THE FIRST CASE **with Juan...**

3. *Name and describe two types of writing activities or techniques that Juan could use prior to handing in his paper to improve the quality of his writing.*

To assist Juan in writing complete sentences that contain at least a noun and verb, his teacher could use the sentence writing strategy. Using this strategy would enable Juan to write sentences that contain both nouns and verbs. A second strategy is the TREE writing strategy (or Essay Planning Strategy). This strategy would enable Juan to use a process approach to writing that should improve his writing. This strategy also contains the COPS proofreading strategy (discussed further in this chapter) that would teach Juan to proofread his paper by looking at specific aspects (for example, capitalization, punctuation, and spelling) prior to handing it in.

Self-Instructional Strategy for Essays. Graham and Harris (1989) developed a strategy that was designed to assist students with HI with generation, framing, and planning during writing. Throughout the teaching of the strategy, teachers are cognizant of self-regulation of cognitive processes used in writing (Graham et al. 2012). Specifically, this strategy sought to improve argumentative essays. An example of an argumentative essay prompt is, "Do you think children should be allowed to have their own pets?" The general framework for the arguments consists of a premise, reasons and data to support the premise, and a conclusion. The premise represents the student's statement of belief (for example, "I think I should be allowed to own a dog"). Reasons are explanations as to why the student believes in this premise (for example, "If I owned a dog, I would take care of it every day by feeding it and walking it"). The conclusion is a closing statement that ties everything together (for example, "Because I would love and care for my dog, I think I should be allowed to own one"). In addition, elaborations are encouraged and count toward the student's final score if they are sentences that expand on the premise, reasons, or conclusion.

Prior to strategy training, students are taught about the components of a good argumentative essay through the mnemonic TREE (Box 8.5). The mnemonic and its prompts correspond to the components of a good argumentative essay.

Using this mnemonic, students have to generate ideas about the topic, support for the topic (that is, reasons), and a conclusion. As Graham and Harris (1992) explain, in the topic step, students had to think about the topic (for example, "Do you think children should give some toys to children who do not have them?") and generate a written statement that supports their belief (for example, "I believe that children should give some toys to other children"). Next, students need to generate reasons that support their premise statement. During this stage, students should try to generate at least three or four reasons to support their premise (for example, "It would be nice, it would make them happy, and we should share what we have with those who have less than we do"). Next, during the examine stage, students should examine those reasons to determine if the reader would believe them. Students should cross out those that are unbelievable and generate other more reasonable ones. Finally, during the last stage, ending, students should come up with a good ending statement (for example, "Because of the following reasons, I think kids should share their toys with others").

During the actual strategy training, students were taught the following three-step strategy for writing good essays: think, plan, and write:

1. *Think:* Who will read this? And why am I writing this?
2. *Plan:* Plan what to say using TREE (determine topic sentence, note reasons, examine reasons, and note ending).
3. *Write:* Write and say more.

The strategy steps require students to generate ideas and reasons for writing the essay, evaluate ideas based upon the potential readers of their essay, generate notes

---

BOX 8.5

TREE Mnemonic for an Argumentative Essay

T Topic: note the *topic* sentence.
R Reasons: note the *reasons*.
E Examine: *examine* your reasons (will the reader buy them?).
E Ending: note an *ending*.

about their essay during planning, and continue generating notes and ideas as they write the essay. Throughout the training, instructors model for students and use "think-aloud" techniques to facilitate strategy instruction and demonstration. Following modeling, students are required to practice the three-step strategy and mnemonic TREE until mastery. The main purpose of the strategy is for students to spend increased time on the planning stages (that is, think and plan) and draft (that is, write) sentences from their ideas only after they thoroughly develop their ideas. More recent research (Cuenca-Carlino and Mustian 2013) shows that when the mnemonic TREE was combined with POW (Pick my idea, Organize my notes, Write and say more), middle-school students with emotional and behavioral disorders improved their persuasive essays on measures of number of words, transition words, sentences, and paragraphs written, as well as essay parts and overall holistic scores.

The Essay Planning Strategy. Through a refinement of the self-instructional strategy, De La Paz (1997) developed an essay planning strategy that assisted students in examining an issue from multiple perspectives before taking a side. This essay planning strategy incorporates the two mnemonic prompts STOP and DARE (Table 8.1).

In the first session of teaching this strategy, the teacher discusses with students the purpose of the strategy and how it helps during the planning stages of writing. This discussion should include the benefits of the strategy and the goal of learning to write better essays. After obtaining a commitment to learn, the teacher describes the strategy steps and informs students that the STOP strategy is meant to have them

TABLE 8.1 The Essay Planning Strategy

Planning Strategy: STOP	Instructions for Each Planning Step:
1. <u>S</u>uspend judgment	Consider each side before taking a position. Brainstorm ideas for and against the topic. When you can't think of more ideas, see the first three cue cards: (a) Did I list ideas for each side? If not, do this now; (b) Can I think of anything else? Try to write more ideas; and (c) Another point I haven't considered yet is . . .
2. <u>T</u>ake a side	Read your ideas and decide which side you believe in, or which side can be used to make the strongest argument. Place a "+" on the side that shows your position.
3. <u>O</u>rganize ideas	Choose ideas that are strong and decide how to organize them for writing. To help you do this, see the next three cue cards: (a) Put a star next to the ideas you want to use. Choose at least (_) ideas; (b) Choose at least (_) argument(s) to refute; and (c) Number your ideas in the order you will use them.
4. <u>P</u>lan more as you write	Continue to plan as you write. Use all four essay parts (see the last cue card if you can't remember **DARE**): <u>D</u>evelop your topic sentence <u>A</u>dd supporting ideas <u>R</u>eject at least one argument for the other side <u>E</u>nd with a conclusion

Note. In the third step, "<u>O</u>rganize ideas," the number of supporting ideas and arguments should be adjusted for each writer, based on initial writing ability. Remind students that their primary goal is to be convincing, so they may include more (or even fewer) items as they write.

Source: S. De La Paz, "Strategy instruction in planning: Teaching students with learning and writing disabilities to compose persuasive and expository essays" (*Learning Disability Quarterly* 20(1997):227–248).

stop, reflect, and plan before writing. After reviewing all of the steps, the teacher models them for the students. Students will slowly become involved in this demonstration and contribute ideas and formulate sentences during the writing portion. Once this session ends, students work together to practice the steps to write essays. Finally, once students have successfully used the strategy with feedback, they begin working independently. During collaborative and independent practice, students rehearse the strategy and have to recall to mastery.

When using the essay strategy, the first step, suspend, cues students to consider each side of the argument before taking a position on the topic. The students brainstorm ideas for each side and record them on paper. During the second step, take, students evaluate the merit of both sides, choose a position for the topic, and record it on paper. The next step, organize, cues students to choose the strongest ideas from their paper and choose ideas that could be refuted. During this process, the students indicate which ideas they will use with a star, make sure that they have ideas for both sides of the argument starred, and number the ideas in the order that they will be presented. The last stage, plan, cues students to write down ideas and reminds them to make changes as needed. Also during this step, students are prompted to use the DARE strategy to develop their topic sentence, add supporting details, reject at least one argument for the other side, and end with a conclusion.

The Error Monitoring Strategy. The purpose of the error monitoring strategy is to teach students to detect and correct errors in written products (Deshler and Schumaker 2006; Schumaker, Nolan, and Deshler 1985). The strategy stresses the importance of proofreading written products before handing them in. The error monitoring strategy uses the mnemonic WRITER and incorporates the COPS acronym within the strategy (Box 8.6).

In the first step of the strategy, write, students are told that they should write on every other line of the paper when writing a rough draft of a composition or essay. Writing on every other line allows them to write corrections on the blank lines of the paper. Once the paper is written, students move on to the next step to read the paper for meaning. While reading, students should check each sentence to make sure it relates to the paragraph topic and that the wording is correct. In the third step, interrogate, students review their paper, sentence by sentence, using the following COPS questions:

- Have I capitalized the first word and proper nouns?
- Have I made any overall errors (in handwriting, margins, neatness, or spacing)?
- Have I used punctuation correctly (periods, commas, and semicolons)?
- Do the words look like they're spelled right? Can I sound them out or should I use a dictionary? (Schumaker et al. 1982).

BOX 8.6

Error Monitoring Strategy

W Write on every other line.
R Read the paper for meaning.
I   Interrogate yourself using the COPS questions.
T Take your paper to someone for help.
E Execute a final copy.
R Reread your paper.

Beginning with the first sentence, students ask all of the COPS questions and then move on to the second sentence and ask all of the COPS questions, and so on until they finish all of the sentences in the paper.

In the next step, students take their papers to someone if they have questions (or are unsure) about aspects of it or if they just want someone to double-check it. Once students are fairly certain that they have caught mistakes, they move on to the execute step. In this step, students write the final copy on a new piece of paper (or they make corrections on a computer and print out a final copy). In the final step, students reread their paper a final time before handing it in.

The following strategies are supported by research.

THINK BACK TO THE SECOND CASE with Myles...

1. What are two other writing skills that you, as the teacher, would address?

Myles has problems with planning his writing and proofreading for errors (particularly spelling). You might want to begin with planning and brainstorming for writing and discuss what to do during the prewriting stage.

2. Name and describe two types of writing activities/strategies that you would use with Myles.

Myles could benefit from using a planning strategy (perhaps the self-instructional strategy for writing by Graham and Harris [1989]). You could also try using the error monitoring strategy to help Myles improve his proofreading skills.

Sentence Writing Strategy. In one study, students who were taught the sentence writing strategy improved their performance on measures of sentence type and grammatically correct sentences. Before training, students wrote mostly incomplete sentences and simple sentences; after training, students wrote more sophisticated and complete sentences. Their sentences were more varied and included compound, complex, and compound-complex sentences (Deshler and Schumaker 2006; Ellis and Colvert 1996).

PLEASE Paragraph Writing Strategy. Students with HI were trained to use the PLEASE strategy over 20 weeks. Student essays were scored based upon each containing a topic sentence, a minimum of three supporting sentences, and a concluding sentence. In addition, the sentences had to be grammatically correct, functional, as well as related to the topic, and the concluding sentence had to be accurate. Results from the study (Welch 1992) indicated that trained students not only improved their performance from pretest to posttest, but also outperformed a comparison group.

Self-Instructional Strategy for Essays. Students with HI were trained to use the self-instructional strategy to improve their planning time and quality of essays. Results from the study (Graham and Harris 1989) showed that students who were trained increased the total number of functional elements (premise, reasons, conclusions, and elaborations) for essays (from 7 percent to 82 percent), exhibited higher coherence scores, increased prewriting time, and exhibited higher holistic scores on their essays.

TIPS FOR GENERALIZATION

Explicit Instruction

Writing strategies, like other strategies, should be taught using explicit instruction. As you read the description of several writing strategies, you probably noticed that teachers used direct instruction steps. In most of the interventions, teachers modeled the strategy while thinking aloud and, over time, involved students in the strategy training (that is, while providing feedback). As students become involved in strategy demonstrations, they can begin to use the steps to help create sentences or paragraphs. Once students are shown all of the steps, they should be permitted to use the strategy or parts of the strategy with easy material. For example, if students are using the PENS strategy, the teacher may want to first have them identify one type of sentence (for example, compound). Next, students would finish partially completed compound sentences and, eventually, students would create their own compound sentences (Ellis and Colvert 1996).

This type of instruction introduces sentence construction in incremental steps as the teacher provides feedback on student performance. In other cases, if providing think sheets or organizers, teachers might consider fading out these sheets as students reach mastery on certain aspects of writing. Furthermore, because we want students to generalize this strategy to new settings, material, and people, teachers should consider ways to fade out cues and prompts so that these techniques could be used in general education classes. As always, students' progress should be monitored to determine that they have internalized the strategy steps and are properly using the strategy in new settings. Teachers can check students' strategy use by asking them which parts of the strategy they used with a specific composition and for some evidence of its use.

Essay Planning Strategy. After training in the strategy, all students improved their essays by increasing the number of functional elements, the essay length, and the quality rating of essays. In addition, students produced essays that were highly coherent throughout the training. Equally important, students maintained these improvements after the training ended.

Error Monitoring Strategy. Students with HI who were trained to use the error monitoring strategy were able to improve their detection and correction of errors (Schumaker et al. 1982). Results from the study showed that, prior to training, no students were able to detect more than 25 percent of the errors; after training, they were able to detect more than 90 percent of the errors. In other studies (Deshler and Schumaker 2006; Shannon and Polloway 1993), students with disabilities who used the COPS acronym improved in their ability to detect errors.

CHAPTER SUMMARY

Juan (from Case 8.1) presented some challenges much like the students with HI whom we find in today's classes. Despite the many obstacles that students face, instruction in writing strategies and techniques can improve their skills and written products. The main approach that teachers can take is to help students understand that writing is a process, not a product. Using the steps of the process approach allows students to spend more time planning and organizing their writing, as well as spending time drafting, revising, and editing their work. The research has shown that students with disabilities have difficulties with writing that include low levels of productivity; weak mechanical skills; and difficulty in planning, generating, organizing, revising, and editing (Graham et al. 1991; Lewis et al. 1998). These students also have difficulty monitoring their writing (Crawford, Helwig, and Tindal 2004; Ellis and Colvert 1996; MacArthur, Schwartz, and Graham 1991). Despite these problems, the research has also shown that, once they learn specific handwriting, spelling, or composition/essay strategies, these students can improve their writing, in some cases as well as nondisabled students (McNaughton, Hughes, and Clark 1994).

Likewise, once they receive explicit instruction in handwriting, these students can improve their legibility.

As in other areas of instruction, when teaching students with HI, it is often best to model the skill, use guided practice with feedback, and finish by having students use independent practice to demonstrate that they have mastered the skill.

KEY TERMS

Backward Chaining, 262

Composing, 254

Copy, Cover, and Compare
    Approach, 269

Distributed Practice, 263

Far-Point Copying, 261

Handwriting, 254

Massed Practice, 270

Near-Point Copying, 261

Planning, 258

Process Approach, 256

Product Approach, 254

Reviewing, 258

Spelling, 254

Translating, 258

APPLICATION ACTIVITIES

Using information from the chapter, complete the following activities that are designed to help you apply the knowledge from this chapter.

1. Drawing on your knowledge of reading instructional practices (Chapters 6 and 7), identify activities that will help students develop writing skills.

2. You are assigned a new 11th-grade student who has problems with spelling. What activities or strategies could you teach her to improve her spelling skills?

3. Take one of the strategies/techniques presented in this chapter and use it to write an essay or story. Next, write a description of how you applied it and how you would use it with students with disabilities.

Hasan Shaheed/Shutterstock.com

9 Math: Strategies and Techniques

Learning Objectives

After reading this chapter, you will understand:

9-1 That basic concepts and skills are foundational to all mathematics, and how they can be taught to students with HI.

9-2 The challenges that problem solving and advanced levels of mathematics pose for students with HI, as well as effective instructional responses.

9-3 Essential features of effective mathematics curricula for students with HI.

CEC Initial Preparation Standard 3: Curricular Content Knowledge

3-1 Beginning special education professionals understand the central concepts, structures of the discipline, and tools of inquiry of the content areas they teach, and can organize this knowledge, integrate cross-disciplinary skills, and develop meaningful learning progressions for individuals with exceptionalities.

3-2 Beginning special education professionals understand and use general and specialized content knowledge for teaching across curricular content areas to individualize learning for individuals with exceptionalities.

3-3 Beginning special education professionals modify general and specialized curricula to make them accessible to individuals with exceptionalities.

CEC Initial Preparation Standard 5: Instructional Planning and Strategies

5-2 Beginning special education professionals use technologies to support instructional assessment, planning, and delivery for individuals with exceptionalities.

We often think of math as quite different from reading and writing, but can you think of some ways that they are similar?

How your students learn mathematics is similar to how they learn to read and write. It involves mastering "pre-" math concepts (for example, number sense). They have a variety of basic skills to learn, as well as many processes that range from simple to complex. Students must receive explicit instruction in—and practice with—a variety of basic concepts and operations. They also need guidance in thinking about and performing mathematical procedures. Yet, although the learning processes for mathematics, reading, and writing mirror one another, the underlying difficulties that some students have with learning mathematics are often of a different nature from those for reading and writing (Jordan, Hanich, and Kaplan 2003; Robinson, Menchetti, and Torgesen 2002).

9-1   Developing a Foundation in Mathematics

Just as humans naturally observe language and begin to develop language systems in infancy, we also observe and begin to make use of mathematics in infancy. That is, we learn the foundational concepts and skills of mathematics in much the same way we learn language for communication. Parents, toys, television, and daily experiences all help developing children to recognize mathematical concepts such as proportion, shape, time, linearity, and additive properties. For example, *take two more bites, you may pick out the next story we read,* and *oh, that's just a tiny boo-boo* all convey mathematical concepts to young children.

Once children arrive at school, effective instruction helps their mathematical literacy to grow. When students have difficulty with mathematics in school, a common cause is a weak foundation in mathematical literacy. Sometimes, however, ineffective mathematics instruction is part of the explanation for their difficulties. Math instruction is not always matched to how individual students need to learn (for example, students' prior knowledge may not be assessed and arithmetic procedures might be taught globally instead of delineating major and minor steps), and students do not always receive sufficient guided practice to master mathematics (Bottge 2001). In addition, mathematics involves complex language; a single term can represent an entire mathematical concept (for example, *solve, estimate*), which can be uniquely challenging for English language learners (ELs) with HI (Freeman and Crawford 2008; Garrison, Amaral, and Ponce 2006).

Each of the HI disabilities may be a cause of mathematics difficulties. To be "literate" in mathematics requires learning a variety of mathematical processes and how to apply them. An estimated 4.6 to 6.5 percent of school-age students actually have a "mathematics disability" (Geary 2011; additional sources cited in Seethaler and Fuchs 2006). Mathematics difficulties problematic enough to constitute "mathematics disabilities" should be evident by third grade (Fuchs et al. 2008).

Mathematics Difficulties for Students with HI

Observations of Rodney's mathematical performances in and out of school are good indications of the mathematical literacy and computation skills he has acquired. From sorting the laundry, determining the number of loads, and pouring the right amount of detergent per load, we can note that he is able to classify, recognize relative

CASE 9.1 Rodney's Mathematical Abilities

Case Introduction

In this case, you will read about a student who has trouble with math skills. As you read the case, you will see that he appears to know a variety of basic math concepts and skills; he just doesn't seem to use them consistently—inside or outside of school.

At the end of the case, you will find case questions. These questions are meant to serve as points for reflection. Of course, if you can answer them immediately, you should do so, but you may want to wait to answer them until you have read the portion of the chapter that pertains to the particular case question. Throughout the rest of the chapter, you will see the same questions repeated. As you see them, try to answer them based upon the portion of the chapter that you just read.

Rodney is a sixth grader who studies math in Ms. Abbott's resource room. This is the first year Rodney has been scheduled for the resource room since he was identified for special education in third grade. Previously, he received his special education for mathematics in the general education classroom, occasionally going to the resource room with Ms. Abbott for intensive one-on-one review. Math is the only academic area addressed on Rodney's IEP. According to his performance on the Key Math Diagnostic Arithmetic Tests-Revised/Normative Update at the end of fifth grade, he was performing at 2.7 grade level for basic concepts, 2.1 for operations, and 1.7 for applications.

In the resource room with Ms. Abbott, Rodney routinely drills the basic math facts for addition, subtraction, multiplication, and division. He and Ms. Abbott also do a variety of activities where he must show that he understands how to perform the basic operations. Every three days he attempts timed drills for one of the four types of math facts. Rodney is making steady progress in mastering performance of the facts for single-digit calculations. He has reached approximately 70 percent accuracy in timed drills, and he has steadily increased the number of problems he attempts as well. He has less than 40 percent accuracy rates for two-digit addition and subtraction, however, and has not begun to address multiple-digit multiplication and division. Rodney has persistent difficulty with explaining the basic mathematical operations, even for the single- and two-digit operations he performs well.

When he wrote, *2 + 4 = 6*, Ms. Abbott asked him to now write it the "tall" way. He wrote the following:

$$\begin{array}{r} 4 \\ +2 \\ \hline 6 \end{array}$$

After Ms. Abbott probed him with several questions, he explained that the four belongs on top because "it is bigger than the two."

In another problem, he wrote the following:

$$\begin{array}{r} 9 \\ -5 \\ \hline 3 \end{array}$$

Ms. Abbott asked him to explain what it said. He replied, "You get three."

Ms. Abbott then asked him to explain how he got the answer. Just as he had done when solving the problem, he held up nine fingers and counted down as he lowered each finger; forgetting to lower his thumb, he produced three fingers and said, "see, three."

Despite a 70 percent accuracy rate for one-digit addition, he wrote 16 when recently given the following problem:

$$\begin{array}{r} 14 \\ +22 \\ \hline \end{array}$$

When asked to explain how he got that answer, he could not.

Then when asked to try again while speaking out his process, he said, "Four plus two is six [writing 6], and two plus one is" [writing 3].

Each day when Rodney gets home, he gets his key from Mrs. Davis, who lives across the hall. Once in the apartment, Rodney finds a note with the chores that he has to complete before his mother gets home from work. On days when his chore is laundry, he first has to sort the dirty clothes by type. Then, based on how many loads he observes that he has, he needs to take the correct amount of money from the cookie jar down to the building's laundry room. There he loads the washer, fills the detergent cup to one of the lines his mother has marked for him ("small load," "big load"), and then tries to load enough coins to start the machine. He can never remember how much a load costs, and the sticker on the old machine is long gone, but remembering what combinations of coins make the right amount is even harder. Rodney's strategy is to load the washing machine cartridge with a combination of coins and push it in, trying different combinations until it doesn't pop back out. The drawback is that the coins will be accepted if he overpays, but this approach works for him. Fortunately, the dryers have a different type of cartridge, with an exact-size slot to lay the coins into for each coin that he needs. He finds that easy.

Rodney doesn't have to wait in the laundry room for the washing and drying to be finished but he typically does. Although he can tell time, he can never seem to figure out when to go back downstairs to get things out of the dryer, and his mother yells at him if she comes home and finds she has to retrieve the laundry.

continued

CASE QUESTIONS

1. What do the examples of Rodney's in-school and out-of-school mathematics performance reveal about his mathematical strengths and weaknesses?

2. What types of activities will help Rodney to think about why and how basic math operations work?

3. Will Rodney be able to learn the types of mathematics other sixth graders study if he is still working to master basic computation facts?

proportions, and, in some ways, estimate. From his schoolwork, we can see that he knows how to add and how to subtract single digits at least. Noting how he lines up addends, operation signs, and sums, we can see he has not mastered lining up numerals in an equation by place value; however, these examples do not make clear whether he appreciates the concept of place value. Likewise, he has confused rules for setting up equations (always putting the larger number on top in addition) and is at least inconsistent in following the rules for solving equations (subtracting the tens place digits in two-digit addition and failing to apply skills of estimation when reviewing his calculations). It also appears that, although Rodney is able to perform basic calculations correctly on worksheets, he may not be able to perform the same skills so well in everyday contexts. In addition, Rodney has difficulty making combinations with money, despite the fact that he recognizes different coins and bills. Also important to note is that, despite using certain amounts of money on a routine basis, he has no memory for how to "make" those amounts from the coins available to him. Although Rodney can tell time, he cannot calculate the ending of a set period of time using a clock (for example, how long the dryer cycle runs).

Rodney's performance in and out of school is representative of the mathematics difficulties that many students with HI encounter in their lives. They are literate in some concepts, but not all that we would expect. Based upon their age and grade, they can perform certain operations with moderate proficiency at least, but routinely make errors and have little understanding of what they are doing (Bryant, Bryant, and Hammill 2000). Teachers sometimes characterize these students as "careless," when, in truth, they have only partially mastered certain concepts and skills before the teacher moved on in instruction without supporting the development of those basics. Ms. Abbott is pleased that Rodney has begun to make steady progress with his skills since beginning in her resource room this year, but she knows that they must aggressively address his basic skills needs.

Foundational Concepts and Skills. Children learn concepts such as sets, one-to-one correspondence, and number names and values through instruction, games, and daily experiences. These foundational concepts are essential to comprehending the mathematical concepts and skills addressed in math instruction from elementary through high school (Bryant, Bryant et al. 2011). Because EL and underprivileged students may be less familiar with foundational concepts and skills (Andrews and Slate 2002; Garrison, Amaral, and Ponce 2006; Morgan, Farkas, Hillemeier and Maczuga 2016), they may benefit from being directly taught the new vocabulary prior to learning the mathematics concept or skill that is the focus of the day's lesson (for example, learning to say "one, two, three, four, five" before beginning instruction in counting to five) (Miller and Hudson 2006). Just as phonemic and phonological awareness are essential "pre-" skills for reading (review Chapter 5), foundational concepts of **number sense** are essential pre-skills of mathematics (Berch 2005; Gersten and Chard 1999).

Inadequate learning of number sense pre-skills is readily evident in children who have difficulty learning to count or perform simple addition (Geary 2004; Robinson, Menchetti, and Torgesen 2002). Often, children who have not mastered the pre-skills nonetheless make progress in performing basic math skills. These are students like Rodney, who cannot perform those skills consistently and who have limited knowledge of what math operations mean. However, students from underprivileged and underserved backgrounds, including poverty, are more likely to be steered into less demanding secondary school courses if they do not master basic literacy and numeracy in the early grades (Thomas-Presswood and Presswood 2008). Most minority students have consistently achieved below their peers in mathematics (Kloosterman and Lester 2004; Perie, Grigg, and Dion 2005).

The National Council of Teachers of Mathematics (NCTM 2000) has identified standards in ten areas of mathematics that have been widely adopted and should be addressed across mathematics curricula (Table 9.1); they are closely aligned with the Common Core State Standards (CCSS) for Mathematics, although the CCSS standards promote introducing some skills earlier and are more explicit about learning outcomes (Achieve 2010). Among the basic numeracy knowledge and skills identified in the ten areas are understanding and applying one-to-one correspondence, number, grade-level appropriate vocabulary, relationships, and counting. When students of any age have difficulty with these concepts and skills, they require intervention that addresses them directly. The appropriateness of interventions you use to address basic number sense will vary based on the developmental age of the students and the types of mathematical skills they have already begun to address, and their specific HI disability as well (Berch 2005).

One-to-one correspondence is one of the very first math concepts students should learn (reflected in the NCTM's Numbers and Operations Standard) because it is essential for much of mathematical understanding. It simply means recognizing that units have numerical values. In the lower grades, students can participate in activities in which they distribute objects, one per peer in a group, for example. Older students can perform sorting and matching tasks that require one-to-one correspondence, including for values greater than one. You can assign them to add five drops to each of three test tubes or identify how many problems are in each section of a workbook page. However, these occasional practice opportunities alone will not suffice for school-age students such as Rodney. They need explicit instruction and sustained intensive intervention to master this and other foundational concepts and skills. The methods described in this chapter will help you in planning and providing that instruction.

TABLE 9.1 NCTM's Ten Areas of Mathematics Standards

Content Standards	Process Standards
Numbers and operations	Problem solving
Algebra	Reasoning and proof
Geometry	Communication
Measurement	Connections
Data analysis and probability	Representations

Reprinted with permission from National Council of Teachers of Mathematics, *Principles and Standards for School Mathematics* (Reston, VA: National Council of Teachers of Mathematics, 2000).

Closely related to one-to-one correspondence is the **vocabulary for numbers.** Memorizing the names of various digits can be helpful for developing number sense but is insufficient by itself (Gersten and Chard 1999). Students should be encouraged to name *whole numbers* (numbers zero and greater that do not include a fraction [decimal]; these are also known as *integers*, which can include their opposite negative numbers; by the way, both whole numbers and integers are also *rational numbers*), both for sets of objects and for their written forms. Likewise, to master vocabulary for numbers when shown or told a number, students should be able to count it off on a number line, count out objects, or make hash marks to represent the number. Note that teaching mathematics vocabulary should always occur in relation to teaching the concept that the vocabulary represents. Therefore, vocabulary for numbers should be linked to students' understanding of the value of each digit (how much is "one," how many is "two") and the *magnitude* of numbers, for example appreciating that two is more than one and that twenty is more (greater) than ten (they will eventually learn that two and twenty are both "twice as much as" one and ten, respectively). Appreciating numbers' magnitudes is, in turn, instrumental in comprehending the *sequence* of numbers.

Vocabulary for relational concepts should also be developed. Teachers can instruct students to name and demonstrate which sets are the same and different, as well as which sets or numbers are greater than or less than others. Students just beginning to form basic number sense will need some work on each of these concepts and skills in isolation. Students who have progressed further in their mathematics learning, like Rodney, can benefit from addressing multiple numeracy skills at once. They can, for example, sort objects by type (for example, protons, electrons, and ions in science), count and record how many are in each set, and estimate or compute how many must be added to certain sets to make each equal in proportion.

> **THINK BACK TO THE CASE** about Rodney . . .
>
> *What do the examples of Rodney's in-school and out-of-school mathematics performance reveal about his mathematical strengths and weaknesses?*
>
> Rodney is likely a student who demonstrated proficiency in one-to-one correspondence and vocabulary for numbers but has only begun to develop relational concepts. His prior math instruction did not sufficiently address his understanding of the vocabulary he could apply by speaking and writing, however. This would partially explain why he is generally able to add single digits on a worksheet but cannot add coins whose values he recognizes or count forward on a clock.

To truly understand the proportional relationships among numbers, students need to understand the relative values they represent. For example, a student might readily note that both 5,876 and 5,786 are greater than 90, but not be able to identify which of the four-digit numbers is greater than the other. Don't be surprised if the student has the same difficulty with much more "manageable" numbers such as how 21 and 23 relate to 26. To determine which of the numbers is greater, students need to master foundational concepts of place value. **Place value** identifies the value of each digit in a numeral. Our number system is a decimal system, which means that each numeral is meaningful based on its relationship to ten; therefore, we use a *base 10* system. Each digit's value in a number is based on its power of 10. Until students appreciate place value, they may not recognize that the numeral 23, for example, is a combination of the digits 2 and 3, but that the 2 and 3 must be written in that order not because it represents "2 and 3"

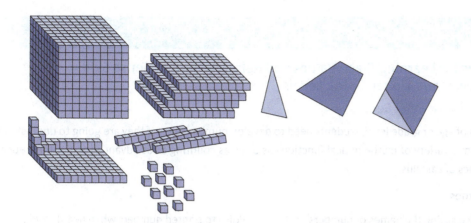

◀ **FIGURE 9.1**

Base 10 Blocks and Fraction Blocks Base 10 blocks include individual blocks, rods equivalent in length to 10 blocks, and squares equivalent to 10 rods. Fraction blocks are cutouts of fractional portions of *pattern blocks*. They may be laid atop the pattern blocks to demonstrate how much ½, ⅔, etc., of a shape is.

but as written they represent two tens and three ones. Students can practice composing numbers by the place values of their digits—for example, 253 is composed of 3 ones, 5 tens, and 2 hundreds. They can also learn to decompose numbers by their possible combinations of addends (for example, 4 = 1 + 3, 2 + 2, 3 + 1, and 4 + 0).

When students work on performing mathematical calculations, they need to understand place value so they can set up a problem correctly (note in Case 9.1 that Rodney did not make consistent use of place value columns when writing addition problems or their sums). Failure to use place value appropriately in calculations can indicate that students do not sufficiently appreciate the meaning of place values, and that they perform calculations more as rote operations than as thought out for what they represent. This is a common challenge for students with HI (Jordan, Kaplan, Ramineni, and Locuniak 2009). Using manipulatives such as base 10 blocks (Fig. 9.1) and connectable cubes (most commonly known by the brand name Unifix Cubes; you can also find websites that students can use to move digital "cubes") or place value charts can be helpful to students with HI as they transfer their knowledge across three stages of mathematical concept and skill learning, the C-S-A stages (see ahead to Basic Computation Concepts and Skills), first counting out, then drawing and eventually writing the numerals they represent.

Students can learn the meaning of place value by discussing what the digits in a numeral represent. They can be asked what the digit *2* represents when written as "2" versus when written in "20," for example. Initially, students should attend to place value for two-digit numbers. The basic concept of place value is less confusing when students focus only on ones and tens places, both because students are likely to be familiar with the amounts represented by up to two-digit numerals, and because focusing on those two establishes the value of the tens place. Understanding units of tens will in turn be useful for appreciating the hundreds, thousands, and so on place values. Note that the "teen" numbers (11, 12, 13, 14 . . .) can be particularly challenging for students with HI as they learn place values. Once the students have grasped the ones, tens, and hundreds places they can concentrate on composing the teen numbers and comparing them to one another.

Understanding **classification** will prove useful for students as they learn to comprehend the meaning of the tens place. When students classify, they group objects by like properties. Students' initial attempts at classification can consist of grouping objects by colors or shapes; then they can group sets of objects or written numbers themselves. They can progress to sorting objects into groups of tens to represent the concept of ten being the accumulation of ten ones. By seeing demonstrations, practicing with manipulatives, and writing numerals in the ones and tens places, students can come to appreciate the value of multiples of ten and its written form. (See the following Methods and Strategies Spotlight for useful activities for teaching number sense and place value at different grade levels.)

Methods and Strategies Spotlight

Activities for Learning Place Values and Related Number Sense Skills at the Lower and Upper Grade Levels

Activities for Number Sense

Regardless of age or grade level, students need to develop number sense if they are going to understand and perform a variety of mathematical functions as basic as counting or as advanced as the theoretical mathematics of calculus.

Lower Grades

Practice saying the names of numbers.

Speak the names of numbers printed in numerical form.

Count objects to 10.

Write the numbers 1 to 10 in order (in numerical form).

Organize objects by size.

Point to printed numbers when heard aloud.

Identify which of two sets of objects contains more objects.

Write numbers (in numerical form).

Match the written (spelled-out) form of numbers to their numerical forms.

Although students in upper grades who still need to develop number sense would benefit from many of the same activities used in lower grades, they are not likely to be willing to engage in such "childish" activities. They will benefit from exercises in number sense that are directly related to the more advanced types of mathematics they are exposed to in the upper grades. However, it is equally important that they get frequent and intensive practice to ensure they finally comprehend and recall skills of number sense.

Upper Grades

Count $1 bills into piles to exchange for $5 and $10 bills (or use pennies and other coins).

Follow directions that involve counting units (for example, 1 egg in recipes, add 3 drops in lab procedures, walk 10 paces and turn right in a scavenger hunt).

Number the main points represented in an outline for writing a paper.

Organize assignments from the lowest to the highest grade earned.

Compare sets for numbers of components and then overall size.

Sort piles of materials into sets of equal number.

Activities for Place Value

Lower Grades

Use graph paper to line up digits in the ones and tens places.

Sort sets of objects by whether they represent numbers filling the ones place or tens plus ones places.

Upper Grades

Rename a numeral as high as possible by successively adding one more 0 to the ones place.

Marking a decimal point, shade squares of graph paper to represent whole numbers and their decimal fractions.

Maintain a checkbook or account ledger.

Convert piles of ten objects into sets of ones; repeat with piles of 100 objects into sets of tens.

Line up numerical representations of money amounts or weights of objects (in decimal units) by decimal points.

At least three additional pre-skills are prerequisite to learning computation. Like the other pre-skills, students may ultimately master them by moving on to computation, but learning computation will be greatly eased if the student is already comfortable in these pre-skills. **Counting** is a vital skill for computation. Students should be comfortable with counting to at least 10 or 20 before they will be ready for addition. Younger students will enjoy many counting games, and older students are more interested in counting out cards, or parts or objects related to an academic activity. Once students are fluid in counting to at least 10, they should practice "counting by." **Counting by** twos, fives, and tens (for example, 10, 20, 30, 40) is particularly useful for calculation operations. Students who learn to count by twos, fives, and tens relatively easily would benefit from learning to "count by" for all of the numbers between 1 and 10, for the same reason that this will facilitate operations during calculations. Students who have difficulty mastering the "counting by" strategy can be expected also to have difficulty when they begin practicing calculating, but waiting for them to first master the "counting by" technique may delay needed practice in calculations, and beginning calculations practice can provide another avenue for practicing the "counting by" technique.

When students are comfortable with counting and counting by 2, 5, and 10, they should learn to **count backwards**. A countdown or challenge to write numbers in descending order can provide practice in this skill, which will be useful when estimation or subtraction is involved in a calculation. As with counting up, students may first master **counting down** from 10 and then might attempt it from 20 or even higher numbers. Ideally, they will master counting down from 100.

Basic Computation Concepts and Skills. **Computation** includes addition, subtraction, multiplication, and division. Initially, each of these forms of equations is taught in isolation, and typically in the sequence named, as this order is considered to be easiest to most difficult for comprehending and mastering; also, comprehension and skill in each is useful to the form that follows. Instruction for each should begin with single-digit problems. Once students have begun to master the procedure, they will be ready to progress to two-digit and other multi-digit examples (that is, progress to **algorithmic computation**), which can involve operations from the preceding calculation type for borrowing, reducing, and estimating. So, for example, students attempting $5\sqrt{15}$ can count up by fives to estimate an answer, and then use multiplication (5×3) and subtraction ($15 - 15$) to check the answer.

Effective mathematics instruction also progresses from **concrete** concepts and skills to **semi-concrete** (sometimes referred to as *representational*) and, eventually, **abstract** representations (C-S-A) (NCTM 1991; Strickland and Maccini 2013; Witzel, Riccomini, and Schneider 2008). Therefore, you should move students from using strictly manipulatives to represent a calculation, to drawing the problem or representing it with hash marks, to eventually representing the problem only by writing numerals or performing the calculation in their heads. This instructional sequence should be applied to each of the various mathematical concepts and skills students learn. Math is sometimes said to become increasingly abstract as students progress to higher grade levels; even for abstract/higher-level mathematics, the progression from concrete to abstract phases of learning should be used, especially for students with HI who are less likely to grasp concepts that are initially presented solely in abstract form (Strickland and Maccini 2013).

A first skill of learning computation is learning the vocabulary of computation, which may be taught as a pre-skill. The **vocabulary of computation** includes the terms *add*, *subtract*, *multiply*, and *divide*. It also includes terminology for the outcomes of those operations: *sum*, *difference*, *product*, and *quotient*, respectively. Furthermore, students must learn to read symbols such as +, −, ×, ÷, and =. In one study, Powell and Fuchs (2010) found students with HI were likely to mistake "=" as signaling an operation instead of representing a relationship. Students should practice associating the vocabulary for the operations and corresponding outcomes, in both oral and written forms. They can be asked to do matching exercises when the terms and symbols are randomly ordered in adjacent columns. You can also have them read aloud an equation such as 5 + 6 = __. Being comfortable with the vocabulary of computation will enable your students to concentrate on the numerical task of computation without second-guessing what the task is asking (Lee and Herner-Patnode 2007).

THINK BACK TO THE CASE   **about Rodney...**

What types of activities will help Rodney to think about why and how basic math operations work?

In the sections that follow you will read about specific instructional practices that should help Rodney to master the four types of computation. The previously named activities will help prepare Rodney for success in those upcoming lessons. He should practice the foundational concepts and skills of mathematics with a combination of games, drill and practice, and opportunities to speak and write about them. He will benefit most if he receives intensive instruction in the foundations (Fuchs et al. 2008; Maccini, Mulcahy, and Wilson 2007; also see Chapter 2).

Addition

Having developed familiarity with counting, students can learn that addition is counting by set amounts. In the concrete phase of learning, students will benefit from demonstrations and practice attempts using manipulatives. They will be able to see that four chips plus three chips, added together, equals seven chips. Students should practice narrating the process themselves, using sets of manipulatives they have counted and then counting the sum when the two are added together. Using a number line is also helpful to make the addition process apparent. Students can use their "counting up" skill to move from the first digit of the equation to the sum by counting up the equivalent of the second digit.

For initial practice, have students perform calculations that are easy for them to get correct. Although counting on fingers slows the process of adding, allow students to use their fingers or some form of manipulative during initial attempts to help make the abstract process concrete. As they begin to comprehend the addition process, continue progressing through the C-S-A stages, with the ultimate goal to count up from memory. Eventually, discourage counting up and similar practices in favor of more automatic recall of addition facts.

When students progress to solving written addition problems and writing their own, they should practice writing them both horizontally and vertically so that they appreciate how to read and perform computations in both formats. The vertical format is easier for working the problem when a student has difficulty tracking place values, and it can also be more helpful in observing whether an answer is accurate (estimating); however, students will eventually need to get used to the horizontal orientation for when they read word problems and algebraic equations.

To help students develop initial proficiency in counting, encourage them always to start from the larger of the two addends, regardless of whether it appears first or on top. As stated, multiple-digit addition should be practiced once students become comfortable with single-digit problems. Because renaming is a more complex skill, begin practice in multiple-digit addition only with addends that do not include increasing an additional place value in the sum (for example, 2 + 9 would not be appropriate).

Students benefit from learning the *commutative property* of addition. This means that numbers added in one order can be moved around and will still add up to the same sum (for example, 2 + 3 = 3 + 2). Understanding the commutative property enables students to rearrange problems from the order in which they are presented to one that is more efficient to solve and, therefore, less likely to result in error. A student presented with 2 + 8 should know that solving it as 8 + 2 when using counting up will be easier and quicker, for example. Understanding of and skill with the commutative property will also be useful in solving algebraic problems.

Subtraction

Subtraction will make more sense to a student who is already familiar with addition. The same logical practice sequences apply: solving sample problems of the concept with manipulatives, solving simple to more challenging practice problems, and solving single-digit before multiple-digit equations. To practice subtraction, begin with subtracting a smaller whole number from a larger one; encourage students to count down digit by digit from the larger number. In Case 9.1, Ms. Abbott might encourage Rodney to say "seven take away three means seven, six, five, four; seven take away three is four." Just as with addition, students can use manipulatives, fingers, or a number line during their initial attempts at subtraction. If the students learned that in addition they may elect to begin from the larger addend no matter its position in the equation (the commutative property), you will need to overtly explain to them why that same practice does not apply to subtraction.

Students should practice solving addition problems by converting them to subtraction, and vice versa for learning subtraction problems. Ms. Abbott could ask Rodney to fill in the blanks on the following exercise:

$$3 + 4 = \underline{} \quad 7 - 4 = \underline{}$$
$$7 - 3 = \underline{}$$
$$8 - 2 = \underline{} \quad 6 + 2 = \underline{}$$
$$8 - 6 = \underline{}$$

Multiplication

Although addition and subtraction may be somewhat intuitive concepts to students, multiplication is less likely to be so. To understand the purpose and function of multiplication, students need overt examples to grasp the concept behind it. Saying, "It's a faster way to do addition" is technically true, but this is not particularly useful for explaining what it means to multiply. To grasp the concept of multiplication, students can rely on their skills of counting. They can again use sets of manipulatives, this time to represent multiplying (the concrete stage of learning). A student could lay out three sets of four chips to represent 3 × 4; by adding the total number of chips, the student can see that she or he has represented three, four times, and that 3 × 4 = 12. Although any type of easy-to-sort manipulatives may be used, students might particularly benefit from practicing with base 10 blocks (see Fig. 9.1). As they graduate to multiple-digit problems, students will find the blocks' representation of place values useful.

Counting by can also benefit students in learning to multiply, just as it is useful for learning addition and subtraction. Using counting by, students can learn to count efficiently by multiplicands to solve calculations. They will learn that 3×3 is 3 . . . 6 . . . 9, for example. If students have not mastered the "counting by" technique, performing the same task will be more involved, requiring counting 1, 2, 3 . . . 4, 5, 6 . . . 7, 8, 9, while holding the highest digit from each set of three (3 and 6) in working memory and counting up by three more.

As part of learning math facts, students may find it easier to learn certain patterns. **Patterns** for multiplying by twos, fives, nines, and square numbers may be easier for students to recall than memorizing all possible multiplication facts (Chambers 1996; see also Woodward 2006). Those patterns will in turn be useful in solving multiplication problems that are close to the memorized fact.

Another useful approach to multiplication, which relies on knowing patterns, is **derived facts** (Woodward 2006). By using well-rehearsed facts, and relying on number sense skills, students can readily derive the product for a multiplication calculation. If, for example, a student is asked to solve 7×8, the student can recognize that she or he already knows that 7×7 is 49 and that by adding one more 7, the total becomes 56. The derived facts students can use depend on (a) which multiplication facts they have committed to memory, (b) recognizing that a known fact is close to the one called for, and (c) not turning the problem into a more complex algorithm (for example, $7 \times 10 = 70$, . . . -7, . . . -7), although $[7 \times 10] - [7 \times 2]$ is a simple subtraction problem for some students).

Woodward (2006) notes that many students can perform a procedure similar to derived facts. By recognizing the value of a multiplicand, a student may perform a **"split-add"** to simplify the problem. So, for example, 6×4 could be recognized to be the same as $6 \times 2 + 6 \times 2$.

The purpose of practices such as split-add and derived facts is to simplify the mental calculations involved in determining the product. Although students must grasp the concept of multiplication in order to understand the operation, and memorizing facts speeds their processing, multiplication is generally a more complex task than either addition or subtraction. Thus, students learning multiplication should benefit from learning a variety of approaches so that they may use the most expedient one for a given task, or even integrate them. For example, to solve 4×7, a student could first recognize that 4×6 is personally easier because she is more familiar with counting by with even numbers, and then separate the problem into $(2 \times 6) + (2 \times 6)$, and, finally, add 4.

Just as they learned for addition, students should learn that the commutative and associative properties apply to multiplication. Then they will come to appreciate that 3×6 and 6×3 will yield the same product. This will be useful to students who know how to multiply by threes more readily than by sixes. Likewise, learning that the numbers in a string of multiplication tasks can be regrouped (the *associative property*) can make a problem easier to solve. For example, $(3 \times 5) \times 8$ can become $3 \times (5 \times 8)$.

Division

Similar to learning multiplication, students need to learn the concept of division. That is, they need to realize that to divide is to partition a quantity into sets. They also need to consider why they would want to do that. You can ask them to think of objects or sets they might wish to break into portions and ask them to explain why (cutting a pizza is a classic example). Having established the concept of division and its utility, they should also be cognizant of how it relates to other operations they know about.

Memorizing simple division facts, including the consequences of dividing a number by zero, one, or itself, will help students to develop efficient division practices. Likewise, learning that dividing a number by two will result in a product that is one half of the dividend will be helpful to students who have a firm command of number sense and also are efficient at multiplication.

Do not neglect to use manipulatives when teaching division. Concrete representations of the operation will help students appreciate what they are actually doing. Using base 10 blocks, individual objects, or other manipulatives, students should perform the division task (for example, divide a set of 14 chips into two piles by putting equal numbers in each pile) and be able to narrate what they are doing. They should also learn to use manipulatives to represent written problems that are presented to them. With mastery of concrete representations and good number sense, they will be able to graduate to semi-concrete representations and then performing calculations written out in numerals (abstract representations).

For many students, division is complicated by the fact that problems are organized differently than are the columnar addition, subtraction, and multiplication problems they are used to. They will need to learn to read the four following problems, for example, as the same:

$$7\sqrt{14} \qquad \frac{14}{7} \qquad 14/7 \qquad 14 \div 7$$

The first of the four examples represents division problems in a format that may be most useful to students beginning to understand the concept and operations involved. They can easily see that the divisor "goes into" the dividend; the layout of the problem also facilitates writing a quotient in the correct place and aligning numbers in multistep division equations. Because some students have spatial or graphomotor difficulties aligning numbers they write, or simply do not fully grasp the importance of place value, using graph paper or drawing their own place value columns on a sheet of paper before beginning can be useful. Students can also turn lined writing paper sideways for this purpose. Then, they can readily observe the appropriate place to print each numeral in the problem as they show their work and answer.

Students who know that the **distributive property** applies to division calculations can simplify a problem such as $(6 + 12) \div 3$ into $(6 \div 3) + (12 \div 3)$. Thus, skills such as using number patterns and the "counting by" technique that students learned for other forms of calculations will help them learn division as well.

Learning that division is the inverse of multiplication may be useful for students curious to understand the operation they are performing. Learning that division and multiplication are inverse operations will also provide students with options for solving both types of equations. By applying the inverse operation, students can check their work on division problems (for example, use 7×3 to check whether the answer $14 \div 7 = 3$ is correct). It is important to remember that students who understand the inverse nature of the two operations will be more facile at using multiplication and division to check their work on the other problem type than will students who know only by rote that they can perform the inverse function as a check -they are less likely to be able to "diagnose" any errors they detect.

Methods and Strategies Spotlight

A Strategy for Systematically Teaching Math Facts
Curriculum-Based Measurement for Mathematics Learning

Curriculum-based measurement (C-BM) (Deno 2003a, 2003b) is particularly well suited to the teaching of basic facts. Using C-BM, teachers identify which specific facts (or fact skills) students are proficient at and which they need to study more. There are five basic steps to employing C-BM. Addition with renaming is used in this example, but C-BM could be used with either more basic or more advanced mathematics.

STEP 1: Prepare Materials

Identify the specific skill students are to learn (for example, addition with renaming in the tens column). Considering the sequence of prerequisite skills the students either should have mastered or have minimal proficiency in, determine if they are ready for the present lesson (following the procedures of Step 2 is one way to determine this).

Prepare a series of practice tests containing problems of equal difficulty, long enough that no student could complete all problems accurately within one minute (longer time intervals may be used).

STEP 2: Teach Lesson

Using effective mathematics teaching practices, provide students with opportunities to comprehend what is being represented by renaming, and to practice calculations requiring renaming in the tens column. Don't include problems that do not require renaming in the tens column or that extend to the hundreds column (that is, don't require adding more than 1 to 8, 2 to 7, and so on, and don't use problems that yield a three-digit sum). Once students have mastered renaming in the tens place, they may graduate to renaming that extends to the hundreds column.

STEP 3: Administer a Progress Probe

As often as every three days or once a week, have students complete one of the practice tests prepared in Step 1. Inform the students that they are being graded on the number of correctly added problems and that they should attempt to complete accurately as many as they can within one minute, but that they will lose points for all attempted problems they do not complete correctly.

STEP 4: Score and Graph Individual Test Performance

For each student, tally the number of problems attempted and the number correct. Plot the two data points on a bar or line graph that will be shared with the students (students can learn to plot the data points themselves). Over time, connect the data points for problems attempted with a dashed line, and connect the data points for problems correctly solved with a solid line.

Students and teachers can use the graph to observe learning progress. By drawing a goal line indicating the targeted level of proficiency (for example, 80 percent, 100 percent), students and teachers can observe how efficiently students are progressing toward outcome goal.

STEP 5: Use the Data to Inform Instruction

Using the plotted data points, consider whether students' levels of progress and rates of progress are satisfactory, or whether your instructional practices should be changed. As a general rule of thumb, don't make changes based on fewer than three data points (Deno 2003b).

For more on C-BM, review Chapter 2.

Memorizing Calculation Facts. Rodney's math performances in Case 9.1 indicate that he makes computation errors and is not clear on the processes of various computation operations. He could reduce his error rate and improve his comprehension of the processes if he were to memorize computation facts. It may seem counterintuitive to have students recall calculation outcomes from rote memory when we stress conceptual understanding of the operations, but dong so frees them to think in more engaged ways about problems (Gersten and Chard 1999; Woodward 2006). Fact memorization also reduces instances of random error due to calculation mistakes that even proficient calculators make from time to time (Woodward 2006). Students who know from memory that $3 + 7 = 10$ do not have to count up, count by threes and add one, or stop to consider whether 3 or 7 is the greater number. Although rate (speed) of performance is less critical than accuracy, it does matter to correct performance.

Students should not *begin* learning calculation procedures by memorizing facts. Memorization for automatic recall can result in their failing to develop conceptual understanding of mathematics problems if they are not also provided with opportunities to think about the operations they are performing (Sherin and Fuson 2005). Inattention to task and the particulars of a problem contribute to the difficulty that students with HI have in developing skills for algorithmic computation and word problem solving (Fuchs et al. 2005). Once they develop conceptual understanding of the procedures, however, fluent performance depends on facts memorization.

TIPS FOR GENERALIZATION

Calculation Facts Memorization for Students with Attention or Memory Difficulties

When memorizing a set of facts, students should drill on a number of sample facts (10 to 20 for younger students; 20 to 40 for older students; or based on an individual student's fatigue rate). The following are factors to keep in mind when using fact drills.

Fact drills should be begun once students begin to develop proficiency in performing the basic operation. If they drill on facts before they begin to understand the operation (for example, single-digit multiplication) and the fact set being drilled (for example, × 5), they will learn the facts as a rote process with limited understanding of how to apply the operations they are performing mechanically.

Students with HI effectively recall math facts when they are drilled at frequent and intensive intervals (Burns 2005). When drilling students on facts, the drills should be conducted as often as daily, or even twice a day (for instance, at the beginning and end of a lesson). Drills should include sufficient problems that students can observe and ingrain the processes. There should be enough problems presented in one sitting that students consistently perform the tasks correctly (for example, accurately multiplying by five on 80 percent of the problems, or better yet, both to 80 percent and at least five times consecutively). Whatever the correct performance rate you set (percent correct, accurate consecutive performances), students should demonstrate it on at least three consecutive timed drills before you presume the skill is "mastered." Even then, periodically revisiting the skill with another drill practice is appropriate.

Just as basic math facts and concepts do not need to be mastered in a rigid order, practice drills do not have to be achieved to mastery in a strict order either. All students, including those with HI, benefit from distributed practice (Kame'enui et al. 2002). In distributed practice, students practice subsets of like problems within the same drill. For example, they may practice two or three different "fact families" (for example, × 1, × 5, × 10) within the drill. If fact drills occur at frequent intervals, the like problems may be distributed across the drills that are close together in time.

Because many students with HI are "inactive learners" (Torgesen 1982), don't presume that mastery of fact drills alone will result in proficiency at applying those facts to other mathematics tasks. A combination of facts drill and instruction in mathematical strategies is more likely to result in the successful application of facts to more complex operations for students with HI (Woodward 2006) than is either alone. Students with HI will benefit from a balance of mathematics instruction that also addresses strategic application of those facts to simple calculations, problem solving, and more advanced mathematics.

Students with HI are particularly likely to engage in inefficient calculation practices, rather than to memorize and automatically recall math facts (Hanich et al. 2001; Koscinski and Gast 1993). Memory storage and retrieval difficulties may prevent some students with HI from developing automatic fact retrieval (Geary 2011). It can be a challenging task: there are 400 calculation facts for the numbers 1 through 10, 100 each for addition, subtraction, multiplication, and division. Through regular practice or drills, students with HI can learn to recall the facts automatically. Throughout math drills, it is important to remember that the quality of the drill matters as much as the skill being taught. See the Tips for Generalization box on teaching facts memorization to students with HI.

Using a Calculator. The working memory and short-term memory capacity of some students with HI (Gersten, Jordan and Flojo 2005; Swanson and Beebe-Frankenberger 2004; Zentall 2007), as well as the attention difficulties some experience (Fuchs et al. 2005), can make performing mathematical operations difficult. These students often face difficulties with memorizing facts and keeping track of content as they perform calculations on paper or in their heads. They may need to drill routinely on the facts to retain them in memory, whereas others will get sufficient practice by progressing to applying the facts in other forms of mathematical learning. Students for whom fact memorization is challenging will benefit from routine, lifelong math drills (as well as from mastering such skills as the "counting by" technique). However, because that is unrealistic for many students, they should be taught how to use a calculator.

Learning to perform mathematical operations on a calculator should be viewed as a compensatory skill. Using a calculator can be facilitative for students for whom memory or attention is a persistent block in practicing calculations or performing more advanced mathematics. They may always have to rely on a calculator to perform some of those operations. For others, it can be a useful learning tool, just like manipulatives or drawing.

These students must still learn number sense pre-skills to understand what buttons to push when performing the operation, to understand what they are doing via that operation, and determining its outcome. Calculator use does not reveal the concept or procedural steps, as does using manipulatives or writing out problems, so calculators are not particularly effective for introducing mathematical procedures. An exception would be if a student is being introduced to a new operation (for example, division) without first attaining proficiency in other needed forms of calculation (for example, subtraction), using a calculator to perform steps within the equation would be helpful.

Perhaps because the virtues of using calculators for basic math are often debated (Maccini and Gagnon 2006; Thurlow et al. 2005), calculators are sometimes not introduced until students exhibit persistent difficulty with operations. With the availability of low-cost calculators and ready access to them on electronic devices, most people should learn how to operate them anyway. The NCTM standards recommend incorporating calculator use in math curricula beginning at the elementary level (also see Steele 2007). In the case of students for whom using a calculator may be an appropriate accommodation during standardized testing, using the calculator to learn and practice the same types of operations that will be on the test is essential (see Thompson, Morse, Sharpe and Hall 2005).

Skills That Build Upon Numeracy and Calculation

Among the concepts and skills requiring facility at calculation are fractions and decimals, using money, and measurement, including telling time. Students use each of these skills frequently in daily living and may not recognize them as mathematics. Number sense is both needed to comprehend each and reinforced by the learning of each (Gersten and Chard 1999; Gersten et al. 2005; Seethaler and Fuchs 2006).

Fractions. Young children first become aware of the concept of fractions as they learn about proportions and parts of wholes. Parents may tell them that they must eat "three more bites" of a vegetable they dislike, which helps them recognize that the pile of vegetables on their plate is composed of parts (in essence, a set). Likewise, sharing a cookie requires dividing it. Learning that the numerical unit represented by a whole number is composed of other whole numbers (for example, 10 is a set of ten ones or two fives) enhances the concept of relations among whole numbers and their number value. Thus, activities that develop number sense (estimation, mental calculation, approximation, and generally thinking with and about numbers; Gersten and Chard 1999) and computation skills are also introductory to the concept of fractions.

Just as students learn numbers and their values, they must learn fractions and their values (for example, recognizing that when a sibling does not break a cookie exactly in half, it does not result in getting "the smaller half" but rather "less than half"). You can teach this to your students in some of the same ways that you taught whole number values. Your students may, for example, divide manipulatives into fractions such as one half and one third (they might divide a set of Popsicle sticks or use Cuisenaire rods to construct half of a base 10-block next to it). Learning the concept of fractions and how to manipulate them in mathematical problems in turn helps students to master related mathematical areas such as proportion, ratio, and probability.

Fractions can be particularly difficult for students with HI because of their abstract nature. Even for students who grasp the concept of fractions as parts of a whole (fractions are relationships to a whole amount but are not themselves amounts), being able to manipulate fractions mathematically can still be abstract. In fact, many students who are successful in mastering number sense and calculation first exhibit signs of mathematical difficulties when beginning to learn about fractions (see Hecht, Vagi, and Torgesen 2007). Following the C-S-A sequence can help. Fraction strips and fraction blocks can also be used to depict various fractions (see Fig. 9.1). Like much of mathematics learning, students should learn about fraction concepts and operations in a progression from simple to complex. That is, using simple fractions and operations should be familiar to students before they progress to mixed fractions (for example, ½ before 1½ and ¾). To fully grasp fractions, students should learn to compare them to each other and not only to rational numbers. They will have to realize that one third is more of something than is one quarter (comparing the magnitude of three to four is not helpful here; conceptually understanding division is).

Once students have a solid conceptual understanding of fractions they can proceed to learn to perform the basic operations (addition, subtraction, multiplication, division) with fractions, in order. Middle-school students with LD benefit from learning to represent and solve fraction problems using manipulatives; learning with manipulatives improves their ability to recognize and solve fraction problems embedded in word problems as well (Butler et al. 2003). See Siegler et al. (2010) for more evidence-based practices for teaching fractions across grade levels.

Decimals. Decimals may make more intuitive sense to students than do fractions. Certainly performing calculations with decimals will be more familiar to students who can comfortably perform calculations with whole numbers. Decimal place values can be taught and practiced in the same way that whole number place values are taught. The appreciation of place value is critical to comprehending decimals, however. Students should learn to pay particular attention to the alignment of decimal points when writing calculations.

Other Basic Skills for Mathematical Operations and Daily Living

The basic operations of addition, subtraction, multiplication, and division are essential forms of mathematical literacy. They are used in daily functioning and are integral to a variety of more complex mathematical operations for problem solving, algebra, geometry, calculus, and the like. However, a variety of other basic mathematical concepts and skills must be mastered for daily living and more complex mathematics as well. Measuring, telling time, and recognizing shapes are examples of these other types of mathematics. Just as is the case for computation basic operations, children should begin to learn the essential pre-skills and concepts for these other skills prior to elementary school.

Estimating. To **estimate** is to approximate an outcome to a problem. Students use estimation skills when they make an "educated guess" about an answer. However, an estimate is not an out-and-out wild guess; an estimate comes close to ("approximates") the actual outcome. Estimating speeds mathematics performance and is indispensable in checking one's own work. Estimation is commonly used in daily life to approximate distance, time, and costs. It can be used before or after performing a calculation or other operation as well.

To do estimation, students must first have fluency in numeracy and place value. The abilities to calculate and estimate rely on one another, and in students with HI, performance abilities for the two skills tend to be similar (Dowker 2003; Seethaler and Fuchs 2006). Students who have difficulty with mathematical calculations commonly have difficulty estimating, regardless of whether they have been identified as having a mathematics-related disability (Jordan and Hanich 2003; Montague and van Garderen 2003).

A simple approach to estimation is rounding. Students can **round up** or **round down** numbers to convert them to numbers that they are good at counting by. In other words, students can round (up or down) to **compatible numbers**. Compatible numbers are numbers that are easy for a given student to calculate, so they depend on which numbers she or he is good at counting by. For example, to solve 13×7, the student can use rounding down to convert the problem to 10×7 (13 can be rounded down to 10). This tells the student that (a) the correct sum is greater than 70 and (b) the problem can be solved by calculating $(10 \times 7) + (3 \times 7)$. In this example, 10 and 7 would be the compatible numbers.

Students can use a variety of approaches to estimate the answer. Faced with a multiple-digit calculation (for example, $5,363 + 4,295$), the student can estimate the answer using **front-end estimation.** To do front-end estimation, the student needs to observe the numerals on the "front" (those that are leftmost). In this example, the student observes that the 5 and the 4 must be added, and also that the digits are in the thousands place. Now the student knows that the correct sum will probably be in the nine thousands. To be more accurate, the student may wish to front-end estimate the two front digits; now the student can see that the correct answer will likely begin 9,5_ _. Note that if the problem were $5,763 + 4,895$, front-end estimating for two digits would yield a more accurate estimation of the sum.

Sequencing of Math Concepts and Skills

As suggested earlier, although there is an appropriate sequence for teaching math concepts and skills that build off one another, those concepts and skills do not need to be taught and mastered exclusively in a lockstep order. In fact, appreciation for the relevancy of certain concepts and skills can be enhanced by linking them to other mathematics concepts and skills. The same is true for students developing the ability to apply them. To begin, students should achieve a comfort level for understanding and using the numeracy pre-skills before they can be expected to have success in basic operations (Gersten and Chard 1999). In turn, those basic operations—addition, subtraction, multiplication, and division—are best *introduced* in that sequence, as (a) they each rely on pre-skills emphasized in the procedures of the preceding calculation form, and (b) the operations for each are incorporated into the successive skills (Seethaler and Fuchs 2006). Continuing practice is when it is appropriate to integrate in practice in various skills and concepts (Kame'enui et al. 2002).

THINK BACK TO THE CASE about Rodney...

Will Rodney be able to learn the types of mathematics other sixth graders study if he is still working to master basic computation facts?

The answer is *yes*. Rodney's teachers will have to follow the logical sequence for introducing and practicing concepts and skills. However, working on other math skills, such as measurement and using money, and proceeding to learn about operations with fractions and decimals can all interact to reinforce conceptual understanding and skill proficiency for the variety of basic math topics he still needs to master. Further, his teachers can be thoughtful about providing him additional practice by giving him mathematical tasks to do in the classroom (for example, dividing up materials to hand out to cooperative learning groups).

The approaches to calculation described in this chapter by no means exhaust the lists of procedures that teachers can employ to help students learn to add, subtract, multiply, or divide. Harniss et al. (2007) advocate teaching the myriad concepts and skills of numeracy and the four basic calculations by centering instruction on "big ideas."The **big ideas** of mathematics are the concepts that make major or foundational mathematical operations meaningful. Equivalence, for example, is a big idea that is essential for appreciating what many mathematical procedures indicate. Understanding the big idea of equivalence means understanding that the information on the left and right sides of the equal sign are the same (Harniss et al. 2007). Students who do not understand equivalence may fail to appreciate why $(5 + 2) - 3 = (equals)$ 4, for example. Without understanding equivalence, students will have difficulty solving the task other than on a drill sheet, will have an insufficient knowledge basis for estimating, and will not appreciate what more complex mathematical tasks such as problem solving and advanced algorithms ask of them. Harniss et al. (2007) have proposed seven big ideas related to performing basic calculations; they are listed in Table 9.2.

As Harniss et al. suggest, the variety of mathematical procedures that students learn for even a single operation will be more meaningful if they understand the big ideas behind them.

TABLE 9.2 The "Big Ideas" That Can Anchor Math Instruction

• Place value	• Expanded notation	• Commutative property
• Associative property	• Distributive property	• Equivalence
• Rate of composition or decomposition		

Source: Reprinted with permission from M. K. Harniss, D. W. Carnine, J. Silbert, and R. C. Dixon, "Effective Strategies for Teaching Mathematics." In *Effective Teaching Strategies that Accommodate Diverse Learners*, ed. M. D. Coyne, E. J. Kame'enui, and D. W. Carnine, 3rd ed. (Upper Saddle River, NJ: Pearson Prentice Hall, 2007).

9-2 Problem Solving and Advanced Mathematics

The NCTM's 2000 publication *Principles and Standards for School Mathematics* (an update of their influential 1989 *Curriculum and Evaluation Standards for School Mathematics*) calls for an increased emphasis on conceptual understanding and problem-solving skills in mathematics curricula. Referred to as *reform-based mathematics* (and sometimes standards-based), this approach to mathematics emphasizes conceptual understanding, problem solving, and mathematical thinking and expression over rote computation alone (Schoenfeld 2002). Students with HI who have difficulties learning computation or other basic skills have sometimes been denied instruction in problem solving or more advanced forms of mathematics (Schoenfeld 2002; Woodward and Montague 2002). They may have been denied participation because they had yet to master pre-skills or computation (see Wilson and Sindelar 1991), or educators may have considered higher-level mathematics to be beyond their abilities or simply unnecessary for them. Although those who continually struggle may need more work on lower-level skills, they also need instruction in higher-level mathematics. Mathematics educators and scholars refer to this as the "equity principle" (Woodward and Brown 2006).

Problem Solving

Problem solving could describe what is done in many types of mathematics. The geometer solves for angles and missing sides, and algebraic and quadratic problems are solved; likewise, those who are measuring, telling time, or comparing the properties of two entities are "solving for" the answer to their question. Typically, however, the term **problem solving** is used in mathematics to refer to tasks that have calculations imbedded in them. Problem solving is an essential life skill (Woodward et al. 2012). Students with math-related disabilities often have difficulty with problem-solving tasks (Jitendra, DiPipi, and Perron-Jones 2002). Sometimes their problems are an extension of more basic difficulties with calculation, and sometimes they are due to the particular challenges problem solving poses. Parmar, Cawley, and Frazita (1996) found that the problem-solving proficiencies of third- through eighth-graders with LD decreased as they progressed from addition, to subtraction, then multiplication. and, ultimately, division problems.

To be prepared to be successful in problem solving students must have a conceptual understanding of rational numbers and operations involving rational numbers, because they need to apply that knowledge in understanding the problem and performing the algorithm to solve it. In some cases, students with HI have difficulty "unlearning" rules that do not hold as they advance to higher-level operations—for example, when adding two negative numbers, the sum is an even smaller number (Karp, Bush, and Dougherty 2014).

Word problems (also sometimes referred to as story problems) can involve a math problem as simple as single-digit addition, yet they may strike the student with HI as far more complex. The student can be challenged by the linguistic structure of the narrative, word meaning, and extraneous information (van Garderen and Scheuermann 2014). Consider a student who is given the following problem:

$$\begin{array}{r} 4 \\ +2 \\ \hline \end{array}$$

The student may be able to solve the math problem but may not recognize the problem when asked the following question:

When Ivan returned to his video game he had already solved four of the quests on the current level. He didn't have much time to play before his mother made him quit and start his homework. But in the short time he did play he completed two more quests. Even though the game was almost "too easy" for him, Ivan felt good about the fact that the next time he played he would be starting at the next level. How many quests are there in a level?

Problem solving requires recognizing the mathematical problem and solving it, relating the outcome or solution (in this example, a sum) to the context of the problem (that is, the sum is six but the answer is "six quests"). In addition to recognizing and solving the addition problem, processing the information in the problem's story requires suspending information in working memory while reviewing the task (Swanson and Jerman 2006). For many students with HI, attending to various details and organizing the necessary information is overwhelming.

In addition to lacking prerequisite skills for computation operations, students with HI may find word problems to be uniquely difficult for at least four other reasons: motivation, mathematical and other literacy (for example, reading), confounded word problems, and complex math tasks.

The first factor is **motivation.** Instead of recognizing its relevancy to everyday life and academics, some perceive mathematics as a "school" task that they are required to suffer through to receive their diplomas. Some abstractly assume it "builds their minds" (Scanlon and Mellard 2002). Many students with HI are unmotivated to practice and learn math because of the confusion they experience during lessons and their unrewarding high failure rates (Royer and Walles 2007). Also, culturally and linguistically diverse students can be more motivated by mathematics when the tasks seem more relevant to them. A change as simple as switching the focus of a word problem from hotdogs to tacos can make the problem seem more relevant to Latino students (Cartledge, Gardner, and Ford 2009), for example, or students may be more motivated by exploring "the numeracy system from different cultural perspectives [and] games from different cultures" (Thomas-Presswood and Presswood 2008).

As noted, to address motivational learning factors, students with HI should receive explicit instruction on the purposes and utility of learning the specific mathematics practices they are studying. Although becoming prepared for math (and other) courses at higher grade levels may be motivating for some students, more practical motivations such as enhanced daily functioning should be emphasized as well. Likewise, because some math lessons can focus on micro aspects of larger operations (for example, drills on reducing fractions), using lesson advance organizers can remind the students of the relationship of any one lesson to the overall mathematics curriculum and can help them to appreciate the purpose of the individual lesson (Lenz, Marrs, Schumaker, and Deshler 2005; see Chapter 2 also).

Motivational practices such as reward systems for lesson participation and progress in skills can also be effective. (Review the previous Methods and Strategies Spotlight, and Chapter 2, for tips on using curriculum-based measurement in mathematics, which has been documented as motivating to students with HI across grade levels.) In a study comparing the impact on women's and men's spatial reasoning task performance, being told positive attributes enhanced performance for both genders (Wraga et al. 2006). In addition, students who learn to think of positive affirmations before beginning a task can improve and sustain their motivation during a lesson (Morgan and Sideridis 2006).

Word problems such as the example of Ivan's video game are sometimes daunting to students, not because of the mathematical problems they ask students to solve, but because of the **embedded literacy tasks** involved in discerning the operation(s). Students who have learned mathematics vocabulary such as "plus" and "minus" and print symbols such as "+" and "−" have not necessarily learned how to recognize when those operations are called for if none of the familiar vocabulary or symbols is used in the word problem. **Mathematical literacy** in such situations requires that addressing the word problem include the skill of inferring implied operations and answer units. This also involves the skill of recognizing a problem type when it appears in an unfamiliar format (Fuchs et al. 2004). Remember the principle of beginning skill instruction with tasks that are relatively easy when students are new to navigating word problems, and begin with ones that incorporate familiar math vocabulary. For example, consider the following:

> *Ivan already finished four video game quests; today he finished two more. Add Ivan's two new quests to the four he already finished to tell all together how many quests Ivan has now.* Total = _____ *quests*

In this example, the student's primary challenge is to discern the math question. For initial word problem practice, ask students to write only the math calculation instead of solving for the outcome.

Research Evidence

Recognizing Cue Words to Comprehend and Solve Word Problems. Research evidence indicates that when students are taught to recognize **cue words** for mathematical operations, they are better able to identify the calculation asked of them (Kercood, Zentall, Vinh, and Tom-Wrigt 2012; Verschaffel and de Corte 1997). They may engage in drills of math vocabulary or other activities that emphasize recognizing and using cue words. *Add, plus,* and *sum* are all cue words, but students should also learn the meanings of less obvious math terms such as "all told," "how many," "together," and "combined."

When students with HI learn to search for cue words, they often make calculation errors. This may be because they do not carefully focus on what the problem is asking of them (Willoughby 1990). Therefore, instruction in cue words should focus on having the students learn to recognize various mathematical words and symbols and knowing their meanings, but not as a shortcut to discerning problems. Various researchers (for example, Jitendra 2002; Miller and Mercer 1993; Montague and Bos 1986; Woodward 2006) have documented that students with HI also need strategies to help them understand the mathematical questions and operations the problem requires.

Of course, in addition to mathematical literacy, students need to have appropriate levels of **reading literacy** to comprehend word problems. As is discussed in Chapters 6 and 7, for reading comprehension students need to be able to recognize and recall most of the vocabulary they encounter in a passage, as well as have strategies for decoding and comprehending when confronted by unfamiliar vocabulary, complex sentence structures, or conceptually dense verbiage. Students who are still developing their mathematical literacy and are also confronted with taxing reading literacy demands are given a far greater learning challenge than their peers face. For example, in the word problem about Ivan's video game, a student who struggles with reading could get confused by the phrase "before his mother made him quit and start," even though that is not pertinent to the math problem. For just this reason, English language learners have demonstrated greater math proficiency when taught in their native language (Harry and Klingner 2006).

Reading word problems can, nonetheless, be looked upon as an efficient approach to providing students with practice at both mathematics and reading. In such cases, reading instruction and mathematics instruction should be coordinated so that they support one another. However, when the instructional task is to teach students how to respond to a word problem, the required reading task should be on their comfort reading level so that extraneous reading challenges do not confound learning the skill of understanding word problems.

Confounded word problems—those that include extraneous or confusing content—can compound students' mathematical and reading literacy difficulties. Some word problems can include so much narrative that the portion relating to the task is difficult to discern. Anecdotal information that makes for a more interesting story but is not relevant to the mathematical question can needlessly distract students. The word problem about Ivan could have been a distracting problem if it included information about how many times he had played to solve the first four quests, points he had deducted for errors, etc. Word problems with such excessive or diverting content should be avoided. Scaffolded practice can gradually build to working on confounding narratives. Students will need skill at solving confounded word problems when they apply their skills to math tasks in civics, history, and earth science classes, for example.

Finally, complex math tasks are part of the fourth category of factors that can make word problems uniquely difficult for students with HI. Often, solving word problems requires more than identifying and solving for a simple calculation. The same is true for other advanced levels of mathematics. Multiple calculations can be involved, and more than one approach may be possible to solve the task. **Complex math tasks** like these require students to perform multiple operations to arrive at a solution. Students are expected to read and comprehend the problem in the ways previously described while they identify the order of multiple operations and perform them, keeping track of their solution in process. A student who is adept at each of the required mathematical operations and who could readily identify any of the steps in a simple word problem faces a number of challenges to finding the solution to a complex problem.

CASE 9.2 Is Felice Benefiting from Effective Math Instruction?

Case Introduction

Now that you have worked through the first case in this chapter, you should feel comfortable addressing issues in a second case. You are going to read about the challenges Felice has in learning to apply calculations in geometry class. You will also read about the approach to teaching that Mr. Truffaut, her geometry teacher, uses for the whole class. As you read the case, ask yourself whether Felice might be inadequately prepared to learn geometry problem solving. Also ask yourself whether Mr. Truffaut's teaching sufficiently supports students' understanding and skill at geometry problem solving. These are the same questions Andrea, a special education teacher who is asked to consult, is considering.

As a special educator and member of her school's Student Study Team (SST), Andrea was asked to observe Martin Truffaut's ninth-grade geometry class. Their school has begun to experiment with the responsiveness to intervention (RTI) approach to investigating learning difficulties, specifically using the problem-solving approach. This means they work to identify the nature of an individual student's needs and select an individually matched evidence-based intervention (see Chapter 2).

Mr. Truffaut had asked for help with a girl named Felice. The first step was for the SST to help Mr. Truffaut determine the nature of any learning problem. Mr. Truffaut told Andrea and the other team members that he had observed Felice routinely make simple calculation errors and have difficulty recalling the correct order of steps for what should now be simple algorithms. He realized this as he considered why Felice was having persistent difficulty mastering new mathematical operations, which most of her classmates had mastered readily.

Using the RTI model, Andrea's first task was to observe whether Mr. Truffaut was providing effective instruction to Felice and her classmates. In a pre-observation meeting, Mr. Truffaut explained that he taught geometry skills in a three-stage process. First, on Mondays, he modeled them by narrating the steps as he performed problems projected on the whiteboard (for example, finding the circumference of a circle). In the second stage, on Tuesday, he provided scaffolded support of student practice by circulating around the classroom while students completed 10 practice problems that first day; they then completed 10 more for homework, and 20 more in class. Finally, in the third stage, on Wednesday, he had students apply their developing knowledge to solve word problems and other "real-world" math tasks of appropriate difficulty. He gave more practice examples for homework that third night.

continued

Mr. Truffaut also explained to Andrea that he was following the sequence of the ninth-grade geometry textbook. In the book, each new skill is introduced with an engaging story example, and the operation is illustrated with graphics. Next, the book walks students through the operation one step at a time, showing geometric drawings translated into numerical problems, and then numerals being reduced, renamed, and so on, step by step. Then there are several small sets of progressively more difficult problems for the students to complete. As homework to reinforce the first day of his instruction (Monday), students read the textbook introduction and do the first 10 problems from the book's practice sets.

In response to Felice's problems, Mr. Truffaut has her practice drills of the basic calculation facts for ones, fives, tens, and zeroes (for example, +1, −1, ×1, ÷1). She does this for homework every Tuesday night instead of the regular class assignment—Mr. Truffaut reasons that she "is better off" doing the drills than attempting the new operations for the week without him present to scaffold her work. She repeats the drill every Thursday night; the other students do not have math homework on Thursday nights.

As a member of the SST, Andrea observed Felice in her class. Andrea noticed how the teenagers in the room were benefiting from the instruction they were receiving. Following two weeks of occasional observations, she observed that many of them did not seem to grasp the purpose of the operations they were learning or why the steps of the operations progressed as they did. She also noted that most students steadily increased in the percentage of problems they

performed correctly across the week; in fact, by Friday, most students achieved above 75 percent accuracy on the practice activities Mr. Truffaut assigned. She also collected practice problems from Felice each Tuesday and Friday, and found that her percentage correct on each one was below 50 percent.

Based on the four times Andrea sat with Felice in class and asked Felice to explain how she was solving the problems, Andrea was able to corroborate Mr. Truffaut's observation that Felice could not reliably perform basic calculations, and that she had difficulty remembering the steps of the operations she was supposed to be learning, in addition to not understanding the purposes of the operations. All of those factors contributed to the problems Felice was having with Mr. Truffaut's instruction.

Andrea expressed to the other SST members that in addition to proposing a Tier 1 intervention for Felice, she thought there were some instructional modifications Mr. Truffaut could make for the entire class. She was uneasy about making that suggestion to her colleagues on the SST, let alone to Mr. Truffaut.

CASE QUESTIONS

1. How could Andrea help Mr. Truffaut determine whether Felice was benefiting from effective mathematics instruction?
2. Was Mr. Truffaut's approach to teaching both concepts and skills truly focused on students developing proficiency in both areas?
3. What specific instructional practices would benefit Felice and her classmates more?

Responding to the Challenges of Problem Solving and Advanced Mathematics

Consistent with NCTM's 2000 revisions to its math teaching standards, Mr. Truffaut was teaching basic skills as well as focusing on conceptual understanding and application of skills to problem solving. Andrea had noticed that many students did not have any conceptual understanding of what they were doing, however. Felice was having difficulty with all three aspects of the lesson. Unfortunately, like many secondary school math teachers, Mr. Truffaut was not using instructional practices particularly appropriate for students with HI (Maccini and Gagnon 2006). Two important practices that are commonly neglected are (1) controlling the difficulty level of tasks students attempt and (2) attending to the conceptual foundations of mathematics (Fuchs et al. 2008). The following approaches are effective for any teacher wishing to help students with problem solving and other advanced mathematics (see Foegen 2008).

Task Analysis. A starting point for effective instruction is understanding what knowledge and skills a task demands of students. Once teachers determine this, they can match that with a student's knowledge and skills. Both types of information are determined through task analysis. The Methods and Strategies Spotlight presents explanations for two main foci for task analysis: lesson expectations and student learning.

Methods and Strategies Spotlight

Task Analysis of the Learner and the Lesson

Task analysis is a useful approach to analyzing both what a lesson demands and how a student learns. It is particularly well suited to math instruction because math, from basic facts to advanced problem solving, involves hierarchies of knowledge and skills.

Using **task analysis for a lesson**, teachers identify prerequisite knowledge and skills, as well as co-requisite knowledge and skills, needed to accomplish the lesson goal (what is to be learned). They then determine the level of detail by which the topic must be broken out to address the co-requisite content (for example, teaching multistep calculations is typically broken out by each individual step of the operation). In the case study, Mr. Truffaut does not appear to have used an analysis of Felice's learning needs when he planned his whole class lesson.

To understand how students approach a learning task, **task analysis of student learning** can be performed. By means such as observations, student think-alouds, interviews, or performance probes, teachers can ascertain what a student knows and does when attempting a task. When Andrea sat with Felice, she completed task analyses of Felice's learning to understand why Felice was having difficulty with Mr. Truffaut's lessons.

Both general and special education elementary teachers are stronger at identifying errors in students' subtraction calculations, both common and unconventional errors, than they are at identifying appropriate instructional responses (Riccomini 2005). This seems to indicate that they are unsure of what processing difficulties their students have in completing an operation, as opposed to having a generalized misunderstanding of how to teach subtraction concepts and processes. In fact, only 17 percent of their instructional responses included attending to nonobservable student performances such as sustained attention to task or self-checking. Because of these teachers' incomplete task analyses, their instruction is devoted to the practice of skills that either carry little meaning to students or are not the specific skills or concepts that are difficult for the students.

When researchers used task analyses for subtraction with regrouping errors for eighth graders with LD (Woodward and Howard 1994), they discovered that most of the students had systematic error patterns. The patterns reflected misunderstandings of both mathematical concepts and basic computational procedures. With this information the teachers could reteach background knowledge and skills instead of merely increasing drills of subtraction with regrouping.

THINK BACK TO THE CASE   about Rodney...

How could Andrea help Mr. Truffaut determine whether Felice was benefiting from evidence-based mathematics instruction?

By using task analysis of student learning, Andrea and Mr. Truffaut could observe for patterns in Felice's mathematical abilities. This could involve reviewing her work samples and ideally would include having Felice narrate problem solving for them as well.

Teachers have been found to focus reteaching almost exclusively on basic facts instruction, neglecting other aspects of the process, including comprehension and the variety of approaches possible for addressing the task (see Riccomini 2005). Reteaching basics without helping students to understand their connection to the more advanced concepts and operations they are learning can result in improved rote performance of the basics but continued limited understanding of both the basics and the more advanced mathematics.

Strategies and Techniques for Improving Problem Solving

When students have difficulty with mathematics tasks, the difficulty may be in their ability to (a) analyze the task (for example, determine the question and identify the operations to perform), (b) perform the basic operations accurately (in correct sequence, without simple errors), and (c) manage the process. That is, they may lack strategic ability to perform the collective tasks involved. In one study, third graders with LD who learned word problem-solving procedures using a direct instruction strategy learned more in a nine-day period than did those who learned the same procedures but in a nonstrategic format (Wilson and Sindelar 1991).

Students can apply a simple arithmetic strategy to solve a variety of mathematics tasks, simple or complex. They can follow the mnemonic DRAW to remember the process:

Discover the sign.
Read the problem.
Answer, or draw and check.
Write the answer. (Miller and Mercer 1991a, 1991b)

This strategy is for math problems written out in numerical form. Students begin by looking at the problem and isolating the sign for the appropriate operation; students who are inattentive or who have poor memory for procedures often begin to solve a problem before checking to see what operation is called for. Then, they can read the problem, already knowing what operation is required. Performing this step requires that they are literate in the signs for arithmetic operations ($+$, $-$, $\times$, $\div$, $=$). Already having identified the operation, students can attend more fully to the number values involved when reading the problem. In the third step, they answer the question if able to do so. If they cannot, then they draw a graphic representation of the problem. If the problem is part of a word problem, students can draw the pertinent information from the problem's story. Some students with HI will draw *pictorial* images (for example, Ivan playing the video game) instead of the *schematic* pattern or relationships among the objects (a graphic showing six quests per level), however. They must practice depicting the problem, not the narrative story, before drawing will be helpful to them (Edens and Potter 2007). Alternatively, students can draw each numeral as a set of dots or tally marks, or they could use graph paper and shade in the appropriate number of squares for each number. If they cannot immediately answer the question, it is reasonable to presume that they have a higher potential to make errors. Therefore, students who draw the problem to understand and answer it should always check their work, by such procedures as estimating or redoing the entire calculation. Finally, students should be sure to write down the answer to the problem. This is a common omission for students with HI who have memory challenges.

Students who have mastered DRAW may benefit from proceeding to learn the FAST DRAW strategy (Miller 1996). Because the DRAW strategy is appropriate for problems presented in their numerical forms, many students will need a strategy to help them "translate" a word problem into its numerical representation. Students can perform the FAST steps to ascertain the numerical problem, and then follow with the DRAW steps when they need them:

Find what you're solving for.
Ask yourself, "What are the parts of the problem?"
Set up the numbers.
Tie down the sign. (Miller 1996)

When answering word problems students should remember to write down the unit as well (for example, "six quests").

Even the DRAW and FAST DRAW strategies presume students' facility with the processes of problem solving. The SOLVE strategy (Miller and Mercer 1993) gives more guidance on the overall process to follow. In this strategy students learn the following:

See the sign.
Observe and answer; continue if you cannot answer.
Look and draw.
Verify your answer.
Enter your answer. (Miller and Mercer 1993)

The "verify" step reminds students to use practices such as estimation to check the accuracy of their work; in other words, they learn that math problem solving involves more than rote performance of steps.

As already noted, some students' difficulties with solving word problems relates to their inability to comprehend the story scenario and the embedded problem. Montague and Bos (1986) offer a strategy designed to guide students who have difficulty conceptualizing the problem. The verbal problem-solving strategy guides students through verbally stating the problem and the appropriate solution process. This strategy acknowledges that, for many students with HI, poor language skills interfere with efficient cognitive processes (Montague and Bos 1990). The steps of the strategy are as follows:

Read the problem aloud.
Paraphrase the problem aloud.
Visualize the information.
State the problem aloud.
Hypothesize and think the problem through aloud.
Estimate the answer.
Calculate and label the answer.
Self-check by using self-questioning to ask if the answer makes sense. (Montague
    and Bos 1986)

You might presume that these problem-solving strategies overlap in their purpose and design, and that any one is as suitable as another. Careful review of the steps for each will reveal subtle differences in the problem-solving processes they address, however. Conducting a task analysis of an individual student's math learning strengths and needs should indicate the strategy that might be most appropriate for her or him.

Math instruction for students with math-related disabilities should include a focus on detecting errors and reteaching those skills and concepts (Riccomini 2005). However, that instruction alone will not necessarily produce students who are strategic in their ability to apply the skills they have mastered (for example, Calhoon and Fuchs 2003). Problem solving relies upon cognitive and metacognitive strategies

(Impecoven-Lind and Foegen 2010; Montague, Enders, and Dietz 2011; Zheng, Flynn, and Swanson 2013). While strategies such as FAST DRAW and SOLVE provide students with a set process to solve specific types of problems, they do not help students to determine what approach a math problem calls for or to decide how to solve it.

Jitendra's (2007; Jitendra and Star, 2011) schema-based instruction is a problem-solving strategy particularly suited to advanced mathematics, including ratio, proportion, and percent; it can be used for word problems and algebra problems. It is useful when the student needs to discern what the math question is as well as how to solve for it. Students employ a problem-solving heuristic that requires thinking about how it applies to a range of math problem types. The strategy, known by its mnemonic FOPS (Jitendra and Star 2011), guides students in how to recognize the problem and then to organize the solving task and determine the answer. Students use schematic representations and select from among multiple solution possibilities:

Find the problem type.
Organize the information in the problem using a schematic diagram.
Plan to solve the problem.
Solve the problem. (Jitendra 2007)

Within each step students learn to make decisions about the problem-solving task. Schema-based instruction and the FOPS strategy are evidence-based practices for students with HI (Jitendra, Petersen-Brown, Lein, Zaslofsky, Kunkel, Jung, and Egan 2015; also see, for example, Schwab, Tucci, and Jolivette 2013).

General Approaches to Math Instruction

Two general instructional approaches have been documented as particularly effective for teaching mathematics to students with HI, and are featured in other chapters of this book as well. The following are applications of PALS and Direct Instruction (DI) to mathematics teaching.

PALS. The PALS (Peer-Assisted Learning Strategies) peer-tutoring approach was developed based upon Greenwood, Carta, and Maheady's (1991) classwide peer tutoring (CWPT) model. Both approaches are rooted in curriculum-based measurement (C-BM). The primary difference between PALS and CWPT is that PALS prescribes instructional procedures related specifically to, in this case, mathematics. The CWPT procedures involve more generally effective teaching practices (see Greenwood, Delquadri, and Carta [1999] for CWPT instructional materials). Math PALS has been found effective in increasing the quality and amount of computation that students with HI are able to perform at both the elementary (Fuchs et al. 1994) and secondary levels (Calhoon and Fuchs 2003).

In Math PALS, students are assigned to tutor–tutee pairs based on ability level or specific math topics they need to address (Calhoon and Fuchs 2003; Fuchs and Fuchs 2001). After rank-ordering the ability levels of all students in the class, the teacher then divides the roster in half, assigning the highest member of each list as peers, the second-highest to each other, and so on. Following training of the students in PALS procedures, the tutors use scripted lessons to prompt tutees on mathematical calculations. The tutors model and then fade out prompting of procedures for the tutees. When the tutees perform the task correctly, tutors circle the correct response; otherwise, the tutors prompt the tutees to correct a mistake or even to work through the problem again. The scripts and preplanned lesson content help the tutors to provide only accurate feedback. The teacher's job is to circulate around the room to ensure pairs are working appropriately. After a set period of time, the tutors and tutees switch roles and repeat the activities. Setting personal learning goals and graphing progress may be as motivational for secondary-level students participating in Math PALS as are team competitions and rewards for lower-grade students (Calhoon and Fuchs 2003).

Direct Instruction. DI is a specific approach to teaching (Stein, Silbert, and Carnine 1997; see also Chapter 2). There is also a published mathematics curriculum named "Direct Instruction Mathematics" (Stein, Kinder, Silbert, Carnine, and Rolf 2018). Research evidence indicates that students with HI benefit more from DI mathematics instruction than from discovery-oriented approaches (Kroesbergen and Van Luit 2003). The DI approach includes carefully sequenced instruction that is based on task analysis. It calls for systematically checking on students' prior knowledge and reteaching as necessary. **Reteaching** begins with a variety of forms of feedback that include prompting students to try again, telling students the correct response, and reminding students of a strategy for determining the response (Gersten 1992).

DI also calls for explicit teaching of generalizable strategies (Stein et al. 2018). **Explicit instruction** means teaching information overtly in a teacher-directed lesson incorporating some of the principles of DI (review Chapter 2). Accordingly, in DI mathematics curricula (for example, *Connecting Math Concepts*, Englemann, Carnine, Englemann, and Kelly 2002; *Direct Instruction: Corrective Mathematics*, Stein et al. 2018), concepts and skills are taught in a logical sequence. Using the concept of "big ideas" (Harniss et al. 2007) students learn mathematical procedures to mastery.

THINK BACK TO THE CASE **about Felice...**

What specific instructional practices would benefit Felice and her classmates more?

Mr. Truffaut should consider using curricular approaches such as PALS and Direct Instruction. Both he and Ms. Abbott could attend to students as they systematically practice all aspects of the operations they are learning, from conceptual understanding through application to word problems and abstract tasks.

Advanced Mathematics

In addition to showing how mathematics can be applied in daily living, word problems can help prepare students for the tasks required in advanced levels of mathematics. Advanced mathematics in high schools can include geometry, pre-algebra, calculus, trigonometry, and statistics, as well as related courses such as physics. Many states require students to meet algebra standards in order to receive a high school diploma (Dounay 2007).

Handling advanced mathematics requires many skills of basic math and problem solving. Students need to recognize the math question and then transform and reduce an algebraic equation, for example. They must come up with an approach to setting up the problem and solving it. Students who struggle with higher-level mathematics typically have difficulty with basic mathematics skills as well (Geary 2011).

Algebra is a "gateway to abstract thought" (Witzel, Mercer, and Miller 2003) as well as a "gateway to college readiness" (NCTM 2000; National Mathematics Advisory Panel 2008). It requires students to be able to think abstractly. Therefore, most students with HI need instruction in it (Impecoven-Lind and Foegen 2010; Watt, Watkins, and Abbitt 2016). Using algebra, students solve for an unknown that is represented by an abstract symbol ($x + 3 = 7$). Algebraic reasoning encompasses analyzing, recognizing patterns, generalizing, modeling, and justifying quantitative relationships (Dougherty, Bryant, Bryant, Darrough, and Pfannenstiel 2015). For instance, solving $x + 3 = 7$ includes (1) determining the math question (solve for x), (2) recognizing the equation $7 - 3 = x$ and writing it out, and (3) calculating the value of x, using estimating to check the accuracy of the difference and then determining whether the relational value in the original problem (=) has been satisfied.

When algebra problems include multiple steps, including possibly multiple unknowns, fluency (accuracy and speed) in the basic operations and conceptual understanding is essential simply so that students can keep track as they work through the steps of problem solving. Students also need to learn the vocabulary (including print symbols) and rules of algebra. To solve an equation like $x(2) + (4 - 2)(3 + 1) = 12$ they can learn the mnemonic PEMDAS to remind them of the correct order of operations: Parentheses first, Exponents, Multiplication and Division (in left-to-right order), Addition and Subtraction (in left-to-right order). Maccini and Gagnon (2005) found that students with HI benefit from using graphic organizers to visualize the mathematical questions and relationships in algebra problems. Additionally, students need to gradually learn algebraic symbols, such as $<$, $\approx$, and Δ. They can learn these symbols much the same way they learn vocabulary, which is to say they should practice reading and writing the symbol and saying the expression it means, as well as using it in context.

Teaching the skills of algebra should follow the sequence of concrete, to semi-concrete, to abstract instruction and practice (Witzel, Riccomini, and Schneider 2008). When adolescents with LD were taught to solve geometry problems by using manipulatives to represent the problems, they quickly learned the procedures to the point of mastery (Cass et al. 2003). In multiple measures across periods as long as five to six weeks following the instruction to use manipulatives, students were found to have retained the skills they developed. (See Cass et al. for a summary of research on teaching mathematics procedures to students with HI by using manipulatives.)

Attempts to represent abstract problems in concrete forms can be inconsistent with the task some advanced math problems pose (Witzel, Mercer, and Miller 2003). In another experimental study, sixth and seventh graders with LD or who were "at risk" successfully learned algebraic concepts and operations when their math teachers represented the problem with manipulatives, then the students learned symbols to depict the problems in semi-concrete forms, and then the students wrote them in numerical form. (Cass et al. [2003] have questioned whether the semi-concrete stage was truly necessary, however.)

9-3　Mathematics Curricula

As noted previously, students with HI are capable of achieving conceptual understanding and application of mathematical concepts, in addition to skills proficiency (and, therefore, it should be expected of them). Consistent with that, they can participate in and benefit from advanced mathematics instruction. However, historically, replacing "general" or lower-track mathematics classes with inclusive college preparatory math classes has resulted in only marginally improved math achievement for students with HI; they continue to perform below their peers and the levels expected in those classes (Bottge 2001; Gamoran and Weinstein 1998). Further, increases in the challenging standards in inclusive classrooms have not resulted in the positive learning outcomes for students with HI that more explicit mathematical instruction provides (Woodward and Brown 2006). Sadly, the math difficulties many students with HI typically exhibit have not changed as standards and curricula have progressed (Bryant, Bryant, and Hammill

2000). Traditional mathematics curricula are at least partially responsible (Cawley et al. 2001). Despite an emphasis on reform-based mathematics in the Common Core and other state math standards, traditional math, with its emphasis on computation and correct responses, is still found in local schools' curricula and the practices of many math teachers (Schoenfeld 2004). In addition, math teachers' special education counterparts frequently lack sufficient knowledge and skills in mathematics (Maccini and Gagnon 2006). All of these factors can create inconsistent instruction for students with HI.

As we have repeatedly noted, perhaps more so than for any of the other basic skills areas, mathematics curricula at all levels needs to include systematic instruction in specific skills, coordination of the order in which they are taught, and review of prior knowledge and skills (Harniss et al. 2007). For this reason, in addition to using generally effective mathematics instructional practices, mathematics teachers should follow a curriculum in which lessons and units follow a careful sequence. This is true for special educators providing separate mathematics instruction in a pull-out classroom as well. In fact, many school districts adopt mathematics curricula that span several grade levels with this purpose in mind. There is still room for good teachers to use their own effective teaching skills with such curricula.

THINK BACK TO THE CASE   **about Felice...**

Was Mr. Truffaut's approach to teaching both concepts and skills truly focused on students developing proficiency in both areas?

Although Mr. Truffaut was using some effective instructional practices, they were not matched to his students' learning needs. Also, he seemed to be mixing traditional and reform mathematics approaches. Andrea's task analyses of Felice's problem-solving processes revealed that Felice had difficulty with some of the foundational concepts and skills of the four basic operations. Andrea also noted that several students had difficulties with both discerning and solving the algorithms. Felice and the other students needed instruction that also provided practice and support in prerequisite foundational skills. Thus, despite using evidence-based instructional practices, Mr. Truffaut was not meeting the learning needs of some of his students.

The primary source of math curricula has long been textbooks (Ginsburg et al. 2005; Miller and Mercer 1997). Newer textbooks are increasingly influenced by the NCTM and CCSS math standards. However, rigidly progressing through a textbook may not suffice for a comprehensive curriculum, especially in the case of students with HI. Analyses of math textbooks have indicated that they are overly focused on rote learning of computation skills and tend to have low-quality instructional features (Ginsburg et al. 2005; Jitendra, Salmento, and Haydt 1999). Further, math textbooks can overwhelm students with HI by presenting too many concepts, with little or no coordination of the concepts presented (Steen 2007; Stein, Carnine, and Dixon 1998). While the sequence of concepts and skills presented in beginning math textbooks typically follows the prescribed sequence for instruction, the sequences of lessons in popular algebra textbooks may not be tested (Witzel et al. 2003). For these reasons, textbooks are good guides for the mathematics curriculum, but effective teachers should supplement the book's prescribed instruction with the approaches to effective instruction described in this chapter (Gersten et al. 2009) and the NCTM (2000) and CCSS (2010) standards.

As noted previously, Harniss et al. (2007) advocate building mathematics instruction around the "big ideas" behind major mathematical operations. Stressing the importance of mastering both mathematical concepts and procedures, they suggest that a focus on the big ideas will help students appreciate what they are learning. Harniss et al. advocate for drill of mathematical procedures and regular review as well.

Timed drills improve automaticity for students with LD (Burns 2005). However, drills in basic math facts can result in facts mastery but not improved ability to apply the skill for problem solving (see Gersten and Chard 1999). Likewise, a disproportionate emphasis on strategy instruction for facts does not always lead to automaticity (Tournaki 2003). For these reasons, an integration of skill mastery and strategic application is most appropriate (Impecoven-Lind and Foegen 2010). Students with HI benefit from a combination of timed practice drills and strategies for learning facts, more so than from either alone (Woodward 2006). Because EL and minority students may have less proficiency in foundational concepts and skills, they will benefit from mathematics curricula that include a variety of practice opportunities (Cartledge, Gardner, and Ford 2009).

Harniss et al. (2007) advocate the teaching of "conspicuous strategies," or those that have wide applicability. They note that some strategies are so specific that they can only work for a specific operation. Others can be so broad that they seem to be "little more than a broad set of guidelines"; their fit to a given task is hard to discern. A *conspicuous strategy* is one that is applicable to a variety of mathematically related tasks.

In addition to instruction in the big ideas, Fuchs et al. (2008) have recommended "seven principles of intensive intervention," listed in Table 9.3. These principles, which have been addressed throughout this chapter, should be incorporated into any mathematics curriculum and instructional repertoire.

TABLE 9.3 Seven Principles of Intensive Intervention

✓ Ongoing progress monitoring ✓ Drill and practice ✓ Instructional explicitness	✓ Instructional design to minimize learning challenge ✓ Cumulative review	✓ Systematic motivation to promote self-regulation and encourage students to work hard ✓ Conceptual foundation

Reprinted with permission from L. S. Fuchs, D. Fuchs, S. R. Powell, P. M. Seethaler, P. T. Cirino, and J. M. Fletcher, "Intensive intervention for students with mathematics disabilities: Seven principles of effective practice" (*Learning Disability Quarterly*, 2008).

CHAPTER SUMMARY

Students with HI can have a variety of difficulties with learning mathematics. Insufficient understanding of foundational concepts such as number sense may be the root cause of their math difficulties. Students with "math disabilities" and their peers benefit from instruction that sequences from concrete, to semi-concrete, to abstract, for all levels of mathematics. Despite any difficulties with foundational concepts and skills, students with HI may progress to learn the basic arithmetic facts, and then more advanced mathematics. However, careful examination of students' knowledge and skills—typically performed via task analysis—often reveals that their learning "progress" is mostly rote and that they do not comprehend the operations they are performing.

In some cases, the math difficulties that students with HI face relate to the challenges of more advanced mathematics. These students benefit from instruction that takes into account their learning needs (for example, explicit instruction) and that routinely incorporates review of necessary prior knowledge and skills. With supportive instruction that guides students with HI to apply their prior mathematics learning to new tasks, they can learn more advanced mathematics at the same time that they refine their foundational mathematics knowledge and skills. Effective mathematics curricula are designed with these approaches in mind.

KEY TERMS

APPLICATION ACTIVITIES

Using information from the chapter, complete the following activities that were designed to help you apply knowledge that was presented in this chapter.

1. Perform a task analysis on yourself (or, if you are working with a student studying mathematics, you might ask that student). Explain a sample problem that is easy for you to solve at the concrete, semi-concrete, and abstract levels. Then repeat the activity with a problem type that is more challenging. Do you exhibit the same levels of understanding and skill in the two problems?

2. Locate an example of a math practice drill on which a student performed poorly (for example, less than 60 percent accuracy). Perform a task analysis for the skill being drilled. Can you determine the pattern to the student's errors?

3. Review the DRAW/FAST DRAW and Math PALS strategies. By comparing the skills that these strategies emphasize to the NCTM (2000) Mathematics Standards, decide whether or not they satisfy the concept of "conspicuous strategies" that Harniss et al. (2007) advocate teaching.

4. To help you summarize what you have read in this chapter, list one or more instructional activities described per each of the seven recommended principles for mathematics instruction (Fuchs et al. 2008):

   • *Ongoing progress monitoring*
   • *Instructional design to minimize learning challenge*
   • *Systematic motivation to promote self-regulation and encourage students to work hard*
   • *Drill and practice*
   • *Cumulative review*
   • *Conceptual foundation*
   • *Instructional explicitness*

Marmaduke St. John / Alamy Stock Photo

10 Teaching in the Content Areas: Strategies and Techniques

Learning Objectives

After reading this chapter, you will understand:

10-1 Practical teaching practices to facilitate student learning in the content areas
10-2 How to teach in ways that guide students' active participation in content-area lessons
10-3 How to support students in using the basic skills required for content-area learning
10-4 Instructional accommodations and how they are provided

CEC Initial Preparation Standard 3: Curricular Content Knowledge

3-1 Beginning special education professionals understand the central concepts, structures of the discipline, and tools of inquiry of the content areas they teach, and can organize this knowledge, integrate cross-disciplinary skills, and develop meaningful learning progressions for individuals with exceptionalities.

3-2 Beginning special education professionals understand and use general and specialized content knowledge for teaching across curricular content areas to individualize learning for individuals with exceptionalities.

3-3 Beginning special education professionals modify general and specialized curricula to make them accessible to individuals with exceptionalities.

CEC Initial Preparation Standard 5: Instructional Planning and Strategies

5-1   Beginning special education professionals consider individual abilities, interests, learning environments, and cultural and linguistic factors in the selection, development, and adaptation of learning experiences for individuals with exceptionalities.

5-2   Beginning special education professionals use technologies to support instructional assessment, planning, and delivery for individuals with exceptionalities.

5-4   Beginning special education professionals use strategies to enhance language development and communication skills of individuals with exceptionalities.

5-6   Beginning special education professionals teach to mastery and promote generalization of learning.

5-7   Beginning special education professionals teach cross-disciplinary knowledge and skills such as critical thinking and problem solving to individuals with exceptionalities.

Do you think that students with HI should participate in the general education curriculum and are prepared to do so?

Nearly 70 percent of school-age students with learning disabilities spend at least 80 percent of their school day in general education classrooms.[1] However, the percentage of time they spend in general education drops across the secondary school years (U.S. Department of Education 2015). From the elementary to secondary level the curriculum continuously shifts from an emphasis on learning the skills for learning to applying those skills for learning. A widening skills gap is the primary reason for reducing the amount of time in inclusion for some; those who stay highly included tend to achieve at lower levels than their general education peers. In this chapter, we discuss methods to help students with HI participate in and keep up with the general education curriculum, even when they continue to need help with basic skills.

Special education policy requires that all students are provided access to the general education curriculum and are held to the same high standards (ESSA 2015; IDEA 2004). **Access to the curriculum** means providing students with disabilities opportunities to meet the same educational standards to which all other students are held (Hitchcock et al. 2002). In this chapter, you will learn about the challenges that students with HI typically face in content-area curriculums and classrooms (for example, English language arts, foreign language, geography, health, history, mathematics, science), and the corresponding instructional challenges for teachers. You will

CASE 10.1   Ramona's Biology Class

Case Introduction

As you read the following case, ask yourself how students with HI resemble other students in a typical class. Do the tasks that they find challenging also represent challenges to other learners? Also think about their teacher, Ramona. Ask yourself how she can best respond to the tension between her students' learning needs and the expectations for content she will cover. Are there assumptions about how a content-area class should be conducted that need to be considered as well?

At the end of the case, you will find case questions. These questions are meant to serve as points for reflection. Of course, if you can answer them immediately, you should do so, but you may want to wait to answer them until you have read the portion of the chapter that pertains to the particular case question. Throughout the rest of the chapter, you will see the same questions. When you come to them again, try to answer them based upon the portion of the chapter that you just read.

continued

---

[1] Just over 45 percent of those with emotional/behavioral disorders spend that much time in the general education environment. Statistics for those with mild intellectual disability, autism requiring support, and attention-deficit/hyperactivity disorder are not readily calculable, because their categories of disabilities are not separated in the U.S. Department of Education report.

Ramona is a ninth-grade biology teacher who is expected to complete topics featured in all 18 chapters of the textbook and meet the ninth-grade state standards in science by the end of the year. Her class of 23 includes nine students who read and write below grade level, some significantly; five students are enrolled in special education and have IEPs to address difficulties with basic literacy skills, comprehension, or attention; one other student with a disability in the class is currently performing and achieving on grade level thanks to receiving appropriate accommodations specified on her 504 plan. Although the students often do labs and occasional outdoor activities, most class days involve lecture and discussion that Ramona leads, followed by independent or small-group seatwork. The students usually do their weekly reading assignment for homework. They take a quiz each time they finish a chapter and the class activities associated with it.

Ramona is not sure how to meet the learning needs of her multiple learners at once. When she leads lecture/discussions, several seem to have difficulty following along and taking notes. Those with reading difficulties find the textbook very challenging, but in different ways from one another. Also, Ramona has noticed that certain students are consistently among those who do poorly on the quizzes.

Luis, Belle, and Rocco are three of her students with HI.

Luis finds reading the textbook difficult. Directions on handouts and quizzes are almost as hard for him. His IEP states that he reads best at a sixth-grade level; much of the vocabulary he encounters is well above that level, and the sentence structure of the ninth-grade biology textbook is very complex. In addition to reading difficulties, Luis is a very poor speller. Ramona has noticed that he has a hard time learning to spell the weekly vocabulary. He does a little better at remembering the definitions of the words. Ramona thinks that if it weren't for his literacy difficulties, Luis would be "one of the smarter students in the class."

Belle has autism at the "requiring support" level. All of her literacy skills are on grade level with the exception of writing. One of her writing challenges is that she writes so slowly she has difficulty taking notes. This problem is partly grapho-motor: the mechanics of writing, print or cursive, are challenging for her. That problem is compounded by not being readily able to "translate" full sentences into briefer concise points to put in her notes. Also, the notes she does take by hand are difficult for even her to read. The members of her special education team have agreed that there are other more important goals than handwriting, so they have agreed Belle can use a tablet to take notes and do writing assignments in all of her classes. Belle's special education teacher, Alok Saar, helped her learn initial keyboarding skills and she is becoming proficient at that. Belle is still a slow note-taker, so she has incomplete notes and misses some content because she is still focused on taking one note while Ramona has moved on

to the next important point. Belle sometimes expresses frustration with this by sighing, mumbling "this sucks," or blurting out in an angry tone that she wants Ramona to slow down.

Belle's expressions of frustration and other characteristics sometimes common to those with autism at the "requiring support" level also pose challenges for her and Ramona during class. Ramona can't seem to find a lab partner who will put up with Belle insisting on doing things her way or always asserting that whatever she thinks is right as they work together in the lab. Ramona also likes to have the class "turn to your partner" and discuss in small groups as forms of lecture pause during class to help keep the students engaged. She finds the only way for these activities to work peacefully is to find ways to keep Belle busy while everyone else discusses—for example, when she tells everyone to discuss, she will stand next to Belle and then quickly say, "Belle, let's check your notes." But she can't always manage to do that, and when Belle discusses with others there often are "fireworks."

Rocco has difficulty paying attention, but, although Ramona is aware that Rocco has ADHD-inattentive, she seldom notices when he stops paying attention. He is very easily distracted, so she has assigned him a seat in the front of the class, where his classmates cannot distract him and where he can't see out the window into the hallway. However, Rocco still stops paying attention to the lesson or what he is reading when something triggers a distraction. Ramona sometimes notices him staring at his pen, which is fixed at one point in his notes. Ramona's movements or loud voice often call him back to the lesson, but he is never sure of what he has missed.

Ramona has been doing her best to meet the needs of all of her students, including Luis, Belle, and Rocco, by planning carefully and getting support from veteran teachers and her special education colleagues, including guidance from IEPs. Ramona has had some successes; however, she still worries that these three students in particular are not fully benefiting from her class. Ramona is worried that the class is going to get conceptually more difficult as they move from studying anatomy and physiology aspects of biology to cell functioning and DNA.

CASE QUESTIONS

1. What are some ways that Ramona can continue to use a lecture/discussion format but make the information more clear to Belle and her classmates?

2. How can Ramona provide the class with cues as to what information is critical and how to remember it, while also helping Belle and Rocco keep track when they get behind or distracted?

3. How can the students become involved in checking their own knowledge and comprehension during a lesson?

learn about methods you can use to teach content and needed skills simultaneously to those students. You will also learn about how to organize instruction in ways that maximize access so that you meet the needs of all learners in the class. In short, you will learn that it is possible to meet the needs of an academically diverse class without sacrificing either your content or the students.

Ramona is a good biology teacher; she always knew she would teach a diversity of students, including students with a range of interests and abilities for biology. Still, she should have assistance to make sure that she does the best job she can do and that her students all receive the education planned for them. The days of classroom teachers being "locked" in their rooms without any contact with other adults until the end of the school day are behind us (Tickle 2005; also see Goodlad 1984).

When students with disabilities are in the general education content-area classroom, their education is the joint responsibility of the classroom teacher and a special educator. Special educators play varied roles in the content-area classroom. It is rare for the special educator to serve as *the* general education classroom teacher, especially in the case of content-area classrooms. More typically, the special educator collaborates with or supports the general educator in the general education classroom. In limited instances the special educator in a classroom may provide students with HI with curriculum parallel to that of the general education class. Of course, sometimes a student with HI will go to the special educator in a learning center or resource room. In the particular case of content-area teaching, the special educator must balance responsibilities for academic skill instruction and content instruction (Deshler, Schumaker, Lenz, et al. 2001; Zigmond, Kloo, and Volonino 2009). Because the roles of the general education content-area teacher and special educator are intertwined, we address you as a teacher of content in this chapter.

10-1 Facilitating Student Learning in the Content Areas

Students who have trouble understanding content may not have prerequisite knowledge and/or may not have desired academic skills, such as Ramona's student Luis from Case 10.1. Those students need to be taught the prerequisite content and either the necessary skills or how to learn the lesson without primary reliance on those skills.

Of course, for students with HI, learning challenges may also be due to their attention-giving skills or cognitive processing (review Chapter 1); however, problems with learning are rarely entirely due to a student's cognitive limitations. In some instances, students do not understand because they do not know what they are supposed to be learning (the purpose of the lesson). Other times, students do not understand what is expected of them as a participant in the lesson (for example, when to take notes, or the need to estimate or theorize a solution versus find one) (Bulgren et al. 2002). The cause of these problems is that teachers have not clearly communicated what is expected of the learner. These students would have benefited from the teacher devoting a few minutes of class time to explaining why the lesson mattered and what its goal and their process would be.

Cultural and linguistic factors also influence how well students benefit from a lesson. There is ample evidence that many children of color and/or from lower-income families, and/or who are linguistically diverse, receive a weaker education foundation beginning in early childhood, and this has life-long consequences (NCES 2016; Orfield, Losen, Wald, and Swanson 2004). Students of color account for approximately 50 percent of the nation's school population, and 22 percent of those students have disabilities (National Center for Educational Statistics [NCES] 2016). Furthermore, there is a continuing increase in the percentage of students in America who may be considered as English learners. Currently, they represent nearly 10 percent of the school population and are included most often in urban communities (NCES 2016). In some instances English is not the primary language in their home. In contrast to these statistics, only 14 percent of public school educators are culturally and/or linguistically diverse (National Collaborative on Diversity in the Teaching Force 2004). The percentage of students who are both English learners and have a disability is difficult to calculate; however, schools report having difficulty distinguishing between English learner status and learning disabilities (Wagner, Francis, and Morris 2005; see Harry and Klingner 2006). They typically provide inadequate services to support the needs of students who do have this combination (Zehler et al. 2003). In 2014 approximately 20 percent of schoolchildren came from families living in poverty (NCES 2016). Language differences, race and ethnicity, and social class can all lead to lower expectations that, in turn, lead to teachers' differential treatment of students (Ishii-Jordan 2000). Students benefit from culturally and linguistically responsive teaching practices (Neal et al. 2003). Culturally and linguistically responsive teaching practices are not something that is added on to the curriculum (for example, one day where a particular culture's traditions are celebrated); rather, they are ways of teaching that are responsive to how different learners learn.

Lessons should not only be respectful of individual differences, but also address the act of learning in ways that are helpful to students. Think of the difference between the prompts "take notes" and "take notes that include enough detail for you to explain the process when you write your unit reports." Likewise, the content might be too confusing for students to comprehend. For example, think of the barriers to comprehension that your class textbook poses (Box 10.1). Many class lessons pose similar problems for the students.

Teaching is never just the presentation of information. Teaching is the process of helping students to learn. Sadly, an oft-heard complaint from content-area teachers is that "these kids were not properly prepared to be in my class." The implication is that content-area teachers do not have time to devote to teaching academic skills or reviewing what they presume should be prior knowledge. The reality is that students need guidance with the academic skills of reading, writing term papers, tracking data, formulating interesting questions, taking tests, and so on, and not simply because some lower-grade teacher did not adequately prepare them. Traditional content-area instruction can be enhanced to meet the needs of the learners present.

Effective Lecturing

Even though lecturing is more commonly used in the upper grades, elementary-school teachers should not skip this section thinking it does not pertain to them, as they occasionally use lecturing to teach content-area material. Even a 10-minute talk to a second-grade class is as much a lecture as is a 40-minute talk to a 10th-grade class.

BOX 10.1

Problems That Textbooks Pose for Students with HI

- Novel vocabulary
- Assumed prior knowledge
- Complex language
- Lack of transitions
- Few/unhelpful features
- Poor organization

Most teachers use a variety of lesson formats within a single lesson or class period. In addition to lecturing, teachers may have students participate in class-wide discussions, group activities, problem-solving tasks, reading activities, projects, independent investigations, peer tutoring, and more (Hale 2015; Scanlon 2003). Students stay alert and motivated when they receive varied forms of instruction. Certain principles of effective lecturing can be applied to almost any teaching format. Among the principles teachers should know how to use are the following:

- Orient all learners to the lesson topic(s) and goal(s).
- Use effective presentation skills.
- Engage learners in the learning process.
- Check for understanding.

Each of these is addressed in the following sections on teaching content.

However, perhaps the first principle should be *don't lecture*. If you are not an effective lecturer, it is a misconception to think that lecturing is an effective approach. Granted, some lecturing can be an efficient mode of communication. Also, other forms of teaching are not always more appropriate than lecturing, but the truth remains that lecturing is not a very effective form of communication if no one is learning from what you say.

The following principles of effective lecturing help make the material more engaging. These principles are related to a tried-and-true maxim of teaching: *Tell them what you are going to teach, teach them, and then tell them what you taught them.*

Orienting

The very first step of lecturing, or any other form of teaching, is to get the students' attention so that you can "tell them what you are going to teach." Lenz (in Bulgren and Lenz 1996; Lenz et al. 2005) suggests that you start with a "grabber." A **grabber** is anything that provokes your students to (a) attend to and think about the topic and (b) think about the topic in ways you want them to think. A grabber might be in the form of a riddle; it might be a popular song that relates to the topic; it might be an unusual fact that will stun, gross out, or titillate your class; or maybe when the bell rings you appear in a costume relevant to the topic. Because the purpose of your grabber is to grab the students' attention to the topic, you do not want merely to get their attention (for example, scratching your fingernails across the board); be sure your grabber is relevant to the content.

The second important quality of a grabber is that it provokes students to think about the topic in ways you want them to. If you want students to think about why a topic is important (for example, what happens when a DNA chain mutates, why study revolutions), make sure your grabber reflects this approach to the topic, instead of simply having them memorize content.

Once you have your students' attention, your next challenge will be to keep it. To help your students follow your lecture, give them an advance organizer (Allsopp 1999; Gurlitt, Dummel, Schuster, and Nückles 2012) that tells them what you are going to teach them. Think of an **advance organizer** (note the term is not "advanc*ed* organizer") as a "map" to the points you are going to address in your lecture. If Ramona tells her biology students that she is going to teach them about "the DNA structure of chromosomes, how it is replicated, and, finally, how DNA mutations occur," they will know more than that she is going to say something about DNA; they now know the three main points she will make and the probable order of information. This preview will enhance their ability to follow the lesson. An even more effective advance organizer explains how the different topics of the lesson are related (for example, "we are going to discuss mutations after learning how new DNA strands are created because …"). Now the students will know not only what they will be studying, but also why: having a purpose for learning, or a learning goal, helps students to focus on what they should get from a lesson. (See O'Regan Kleinert, Harrison, Mills, Dueppen, and Trailor [2014] for a comparison of the effects of setting learning/academic goals versus other types of goals, such as social, for students with different HIs.) They will have a much better sense of what they are listening to and why, especially if your advance organizer also tells them what you expect of them (for example, take notes, participate by asking questions) and what else you have planned for the class period (after I explain the process to you, you are going to read a little more about it, then each of you will draw a "cartoon" depicting how a normal DNA sequence mutates in the case of Down syndrome). Students should have a sense of where the lesson is going if they are going to remain attentive and get anything out of it.

Advance organizers can be much more powerful than simply providing a "map" or orientation to what will be studied and what you will expect of your students. Advance organizers can also help the students to connect what they already know with what you will be teaching, as well as prepare them to think deeply about what they are learning. The educational psychologist who introduced the concept of advance organizers asserted, "The most important single factor influencing learning is what the learner already knows" (Ausubel 1968, p. vi). At a minimum, an advance organizer helps students to begin thinking about the topic of study, which will help them make connections between what they know and new information. Good teachers begin a lesson by "activating students' prior knowledge," which is what providing an advance organizer does.

Advance organizers can also prepare the student for generative thinking (Greene and Azevedo 2007). That is, even when students do not have much prior knowledge about a topic, being oriented to the topic can help them to think ("generate") about it as the lesson goes on. You will read in Chapter 11 that in strategic note-taking (Boyle and Weishar 2001) students activate their prior knowledge by making notes about what they already know about the topic they are about to study (that is, before taking lecture notes) for this very reason.

Simply telling students information about the lesson at the start of the class constitutes an advance organizer, but it may not be effective if students cannot recall it. You can make ready reference to the advance organizer throughout the lesson and students can independently review it when it is written down. To this end, you might write the day's advance organizer on a corner of the board (Haydon, Mancil, Kroeger, McLeskey, and Lin 2011). Lenz, Marrs, Schumaker, and Deshler (2005) validated the Lesson Organizer Routine in inclusive classrooms, which includes a graphic organizer of the key lesson content and critical questions as an advance organizer for students to keep in mind (review Chapter 2).

Finally, advance organizers do not have to be limited to classroom lessons; they are equally beneficial when used with students in one-on-one instruction.

Either as part of or following your grabber and advance organizer, provide students with some **key questions**. These questions suggest what the students should be thinking about during the lesson. A good key question is not so literal that students merely have to listen during the lecture for the correct answer (Lenz et al. 2005). Instead, a key question provokes synthesis of lecture information and the listener's own knowledge. Good key questions are open-ended and higher-order. Tips on posing effective questions include the following:

1. Focus on essential content.
2. Clearly relate the questions to lesson activities.

3. Relate lesson topics to larger unit topics.
4. Explore conceptual relationships.
5. Use questions that can help to monitor student progress (including student self-assessment).
6. Motivate students.
7. Let students generate some questions (Taymans and Lynch 2004).

A key question does not have to be limited to your immediate lecture; it could relate to an entire unit.

Grabbing your students' attention, providing orientation via an advance organizer, and supplying them with a few key questions can all be done in under five minutes. These activities are investments well worth the short amount of time they take. Please note you do not have to lecture to use any of these instructional practices, but when you do lecture, incorporating them responds to the challenges that your students with HI, and others, may have learning from lectures.

THINK BACK TO THE CASE   with Ramona and her students . . .

1. *What are some ways that Ramona can continue to use a lecture/discussion format but make the information more clear to Luis and his classmates?*

2. *How can Ramona provide the class with cues as to what information is critical and how to remember it, while also helping Belle and Rocco keep track when they get behind or distracted?*

By receiving information about the lesson "up-front" with an advance organizer, Belle and Rocco will be better prepared to know what they should be thinking about. Luis will be able to make more connections to familiar information, and Rocco will have a better sense of where they are in a lesson and how information connects when he finds he needs to refocus on the lecture. Depending on how explicit Ramona's advance organizer is, the students will know what topics will be covered during the lesson, why they are important to learn, and what the expectations are for them.

TIPS FOR GENERALIZATION

Keeping Advance Organizers Handy

Although students will find the information in an advance organizer helpful, they should not expend effort to memorize it. They will appreciate being able to review the advance organizer periodically to remind themselves of unique vocabulary, the learning objectives, and what is still ahead. Rocco from Case 10.1 can also use it like a "program" to remind him of where they are in the lesson. Ramona would do well to refer to the advance organizer periodically as she moves the class between the major topics and activities. Some ways to remind students of the content presented in an advance organizer include:

- Have students keep a personal copy on their desktops.
- Have students keep a copy as a section organizer in their binders.
- Write it in outline form on a corner of the board where it can be easily consulted.
- Begin each class with a one-minute review of the advance organizer, pointing out where the class is today.

The Lesson Organizer Routine (Lenz, Marrs, Schumaker, and Deshler 2005) is a ready source of a tangible advance organizer.

Presenting Effectively

Once you orient students to the lesson, you must keep them engaged and teach in ways that facilitate their access to the curriculum. There is more to teaching than being a persuasive communicator; nonetheless, a few public speaking tips can be useful. The first is to **provide clarity**. If you have ever read a challenging textbook, you have undoubtedly gone back and reread a difficult sentence or paragraph. Many students who listen to lectures wish they could play back the lecture.

There are no formulaic steps to ensure clarity; rather, think about what information is likely to make sense to all of your students. If something will not be clear (for example, "nondisjunction when chromosomes split can result in trisomy 21"), present the material in a way that makes it clear. This process can be as simple as presenting information in an order that is logical to your students. For example, think about which you should teach first, the DNA structure of trisomy 21, the functions of DNA that compose chromosomes, or how chromosomes replicate. To help you determine the best order, think about how each option matters to learning the other concepts.

Also, be sure to explain terms or concepts that may not be clear to the students, even when you think those concepts should be prior knowledge (for example, "Remember, we said *replicate* means to reproduce or make a copy of itself, and chromosomes do this by splitting in half"). Just because you taught new information in yesterday's lesson or even five minutes ago does not mean that your students are ready to use it to learn further information (in this case, follow the replication definition by saying, "The most common way chromosome replication may form the mutation trisomy 21 is when a fertilized egg receives an extra 21st chromosome because one parent donated it"). You can also use repetition to reinforce information (for example, "An extra 21st chromosome results in trisomy 21. And as we just said, *trisomy 21* means 'three pairs of the 21st chromosome instead of the usual two'"). You can also ask students to do the repeating (for example, "Who can tell us what we said *trisomy* means? Look to see what your notes say, or think about the prefix of the word, *tri*").

To aid clarity, effective teachers often use **visuals** or other props when speaking. Effective visuals can serve as backdrops to your presentation; they might list key points you are going to make, supply definitions for important terms, display processes, or depict the organization of information (Boyle and Yeager 1997; Ciullo and Reutebuch 2013; Dexter and Hughes 2011). You may keep a visual up for the duration of your lecture. Students can hear you explain a point and see an example of it. When teachers use technologies such as PowerPoint and SMART Boards (see Chapter 12), students may receive copies of the material presented to the class.

If you want students to attend to your visual, you should wait to display it until the appropriate time, lest they be distracted by it while you are talking. A student like Rocco could easily lose focus on the class while inspecting a visual; you may need to monitor such students periodically to see if you need to prompt them to pass the visual along or make a connection back to what you are discussing. Also, if your visual is complex (for example, a map or chart), you can help focus your students by pointing to the relevant areas. You have undoubtedly been in a class or lecture where the wording is so dense on a presentation slide that you cannot both read it and attend to what the teacher is saying, and taking notes at the same time becomes impossible. So, remember, the visual should support the lecture or the lecture should support the visual, but they should not compete with each other for attention or importance.

Visuals can enhance your lecture, but they can also detract from it. Inappropriate visuals or inappropriate presentation of them, such as described in the preceding paragraph, can confuse students. To enhance your lecture, visuals must be consistent with what you say or demonstrate. Contradictory spoken and displayed terminology can confound students, even when the terminologies are synonyms.

Another way to provide clarity in your lecture is to incorporate cueing. When you use **cueing**, you signal to your students what to pay attention to (Bond 2007). Berry (1999) identified three important forms of cueing: *mannerisms*, *organizational*, and *emphasis*. The three forms often overlap (also see Titsworth and Kiewra 2004).

Mannerism cues include counting off key points by holding up your fingers, and gesturing by pounding your fist or signaling thumbs up or thumbs down, for example.

Organizational cues include counting; stating, "the most important thing for you to know is . . ."; or stating, "what these three features have in common is . . ." A cue is organizational as long as it somehow indicates how information is related (organized), be it linear, hierarchical, contrasting, or proportional, for example.

Finally, *emphasis cues* signal relevance by highlighting a point. For emphasis you might repeat a point, say "listen carefully to this," and then have a dramatic pause or write a term on the board and underline it. Cueing your students to the importance or relevance of information ensures that they know both that it is important, and how it is important.

In studies of instructional interventions, Carnine and others (Carnine and Carnine 2004; Gleason, Carnine, and Vala 1991) have found that the **pacing** of instruction and **student response rate** impact student learning. Although those studies were of timing between prompts and student response during highly structured Direct Instruction lessons (Stein, Carnine, and Dixon 1998), the same point is important to keep in mind when lecturing. An effective lecture must be presented at an efficient pace. Going too slowly by belaboring points or meandering off onto side topics is distracting and confusing. By the same token, presenting too rapidly and jumbling multiple facts or concepts into a sentence or two without elaboration or cueing can overwhelm listeners. A helpful gauge of whether your pacing is appropriate is to observe what students are doing. If they are taking notes at breakneck speed and rarely have time to look up at you, they are too busy trying to keep up to really pay attention. In contrast, if you are just talking (lecturing) endlessly, you may note that your students are not necessarily being provoked to think, which they would be if you asked a question or otherwise cued them to think actively.

 ## Methods and Strategies Spotlight

Tracking Students' Learning

In a crowded classroom, continuously keeping track of whether all students are paying attention, routinely participating, and learning can be difficult. Many teachers try to estimate how well these things are happening as they conduct their lessons. What these classroom teachers often do is judge whether about half of the class is having success (Scanlon, Schumaker, and Deshler 1994). If so, they continue with the lesson. Although this may seem to be a good way to estimate, it still leaves the other half of the class. Those who are not "getting it" are likely to regularly be in that half.

There is an alternative way to estimate how well a lesson is going that accounts for the range of learners present. Before you begin a lesson, try to think of a student representative of those likely to do well in the lesson, a second student representative of those likely to perform in the average range for the particular lesson, and a third student representative of those likely to have difficulty with the lesson; also think of students who have unique learning demands, such as needing accommodations or English learners. You can use the mnemonic HALO (Bulgren and Lenz 1996; Kissam and Lenz 1994):

H High achievers
A Average achievers
L Low achievers
O Other needs

Granted, these students only approximate their peers in how well you predict they will do, but they do reflect a cross-section of your class. During your lesson, if you observe how well these student representatives are doing, you will have a better sense of how all of your students are doing.

Even those students who are engaged with your lecture will benefit from periodic **lecture pauses**. If you think of your lecture as divided up into a series of key points, you should plan to pause before beginning succeeding key points. Students will be able to review their notes and repair them if need be. Pausing to allow students to review and revise their notes has been found to be more effective than waiting until the end of a lesson to do the same thing. When students participate in lecture pauses they can produce better-quality notes and recall more facts and the relationships among them (Boyle 2010; also see Luo, Kiewra, and Samuelson 2016). Students may do even better when they review and revise notes with others (Boyle 2010; Luo et al. 2016), such as a partner or as a whole class. The same effect has been found with calculation performance during math classes for students with learning disabilities and emotional and behavioral disorders (Hawkins et al. 1994).

To make effective use of lecture pauses, let students know that you are pausing and why; you might say, "Take a moment to go over your notes and make sure everything is clear before we go on." Better yet, say, "Be sure that you have all three mutations that result in Down syndrome explained in your notes." (Note that in this example you would be providing clarity as well as cueing your students.) Pauses are also helpful as you explain an important fact or concept; students should have a moment to "digest" what you just said before moving on, not just enough time to get it in their notes. A short pause can provide students with a "cognitive break" before forging ahead with the lecture.

You may also capitalize on lecture pauses as a chance to guide student reflection. If students do not have any questions for you and seem to be comfortable with their notes, you may want to ask them one of the key questions or simply quiz them on important information that they should have received from your lecture thus far. Remember that recall is not the only goal of a lesson; you might choose to ask students an application, synthesis, or reflection question instead. Finally, a lecture pause can also be a good time to remind students where you are in the list of topics and activities named in the advance organizer.

THINK BACK TO THE CASE with Ramona and her students…

> 3. How can the students become involved in checking their own knowledge and comprehension during a lesson?
>
> Lecture pauses provide students with a chance to reflect. Guiding their reflection helps ensure that the lesson has been a useful experience. Read on to learn ways that you can prompt students to be reflective as they attend to the lecture/discussion, including as they take notes.

Keeping Students Engaged

Another approach to keeping your students oriented to your lecture is to ensure they **interact** with the content. Attentive listening by itself is a very low level of interacting; listening and just taking notes is somewhat higher. However, attending and keeping up can be difficult for students with HI. If your students can ask questions, answer questions, figure something out, share opinions, and perhaps even contribute lecture content while you lecture, they will be far more engaged.

As just noted, teachers have myriad ways to make lectures interactive. You can ask students questions such as, "Based on what I just told you, what would happen if . . . ?" or "What else would you like to know about how chromosomes replicate?" Your questions could serve as prompts to relate new information to already familiar concepts, such as, "Does this remind you of anything else we have learned in this class?" The essential component of an interactive lecture (actually a dialogue) is that multiple participants are sharing information through discussion, in the form of ideas or questions.

Students might respond to you or to contributions from others, or they might test a theory out loud. A tried-and-true technique to do this is Turn to Your Partner (Johnson, Johnson, and Holubec 1993). In Turn to Your Partner, students are instructed to turn to someone sitting next to them and repeat information, explain a point, or ask a question.

Students can also be kept engaged in a lecture by being responsible for **taking notes**. There are a variety of approaches to note-taking (see Chapter 11 for a full discussion of note-taking techniques and how to support them). As previously discussed, taking notes while the teacher lectures represents a low level of interactive engagement by itself. Although note-taking is not a substitute for more interactive lecture practices, variations on note-taking can help it to be more interactive. One such variation involves guided notes. In guided notes, students are given some form of an outline or template for note-taking (see Fig. 11.4), which the student is responsible for completing. By using guided notes, students are cued to what is important and assisted in taking notes that are complete by the teacher's standards. When students with HI have difficulty taking notes (for example, those with intellectual disability may not have the skills to take notes independently, and those with attention-deficit/ hyperactivity disorder (ADHD) may be distracted and miss vital content), peer scribes can provide them with copies of the class notes. To maintain confidentiality about students' disabilities, sometimes the scribes do not know which classmate(s) will receive their notes. Also, when teaching using technology such as a computer projection or a SMART Board, provide copies of the lesson materials directly to the students.

Checking for Understanding

By now you realize that checking for understanding is important for a successful lecture. It is better to find out whether your presentation is effective during the actual lecture than at the end of a unit. Some of the previously mentioned practices incorporate asking your students about their comprehension. This is certainly a valuable and straightforward way to check for understanding.

Teachers have a variety of ways to **check for understanding** within a lecture. As we already noted, you may ask students to demonstrate what they have learned during lecture pauses. This technique can be used to determine the quality of students' notes and to check on their comprehension. Calling on just one or two students to respond can be a good way to keep all students on their toes, especially if they think they *might* be called on next. This method is not especially effective for knowing how the overall class is doing, however, so you might consider calling on HALO students (see the Methods and Strategies Spotlight entitled "Tracking Students' Learning") to better sense how various students are doing. Alternatively, by using response devices, you can efficiently check on how all students are doing during a lesson. Students may simply respond using a show of hands, or there are a variety of low-tech response "devices" to inform you as to whether they think some statement you made is correct or not. They can use response cards, which may be jumbo index cards or individual white boards, to write one- or two-word responses to questions you ask (for example, "write which has a positive charge, a proton or a neutron"). You can quickly see who has the concept right when they hold up their cards. You can also use prewritten response cards; distribute cards reading "proton," "electron," "neutron," for example, or "yes" and "no," which students then hold up at the appropriate times.

Using handheld keypads, more commonly known as "clickers," students can press a button to respond to your yes/no or multiple-choice questions. Using a computer to which the clickers are linked, you can immediately see which students answered the question correctly. You can also display response trends on a screen for all to see. One apparent benefit of clickers over either response cards or hand raising is anonymity. A study of college students found that greater percentages responded to instructor questions using clicker technology (Stowell and Nelson 2007). The study also recorded more "honest" answers, as students were not able to delay their responses until they could first see how their classmates responded.

One additional way to check for understanding is embedded in the process of providing **informative feedback**. In this process, teachers not only check for understanding but reinforce or correct it as need be. Long ago, behavioral theorists confirmed that humans are more likely to remember things for which they are reinforced (for example, praise for knowing) (Snowman and Biehler 2006). Learning theorists have added that information on the accuracy of performance, including when, why, and how to perform a task or use certain information, also improves learning (Borkowski 1992).

A critical quality of informative feedback is that it is *informative*. If a teacher were to say "good job" or "that's not right," chances are that students would not leave either situation with a clear understanding of what the correct response was and why. What was missing was the informative part; simply adding "because . . ." to either of those examples would upgrade them to informative feedback. Informative feedback provides students with useful information for maintaining, enhancing, or correcting performance (Vaughn and Swanson 2015). Thus, the informative piece must have that quality. It should help students know what was right, why it was right, or what was wrong and why that was; it should discuss the process that students need to follow to be correct in the future.

Teachers can ask students if they know if information is correct and why. They can also ask students to paraphrase the informative portion of the feedback. If they cannot paraphrase the information, they may not understand it very well.

Informative feedback is useful to students because it provides them with a gauge of accuracy. Individual students can participate in charting their performance by (a) keeping track of feedback on a particular skill (for example, vocabulary words learned per week) and (b) providing their own informative feedback (that is, evaluating their own performance). Figure 10.1 provides an example of Luis's graph of vocabulary words learned for each biology chapter. The solid lines connected by boxes indicate the number of words spelled correctly (Spell-C) and dashed lines by boxes incorrectly (Spell-I) each week and the solid lines connected by dots indicate the number of words defined correctly (Define-C) and by dashed lines incorrectly (Define-I). With this progress monitoring data, Luis and his teacher can note whether particular studying efforts are having the desired effect and if he is making satisfactory progress. Simply charting his

▶ **FIGURE 10.1**

Luis's Vocabulary Quiz
Performance Graph

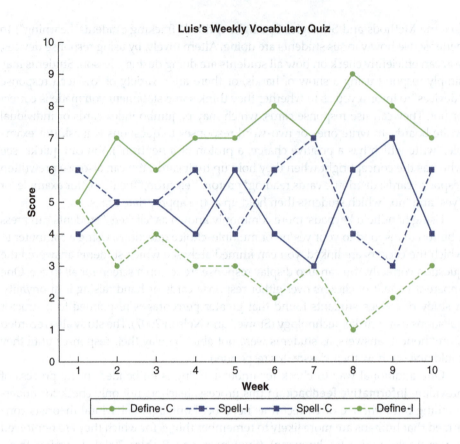

weekly total test score would not be as useful. Reading Figure 10.1, Luis can note that he is doing well on learning word meanings but needs more work on spelling. Without this type of data, Luis could be optimistic and believe he is doing great in vocabulary because he scores so high on the definition parts of the test, or he could be pessimistic because he has the spelling data to prove that he is "no good at learning vocabulary."

Concluding the Lecture

Finally, although many of us use some form of advance organizers in our teaching, we often neglect to extend a similar courtesy to our students at the end of lectures or lessons. A **post organizer** serves to summarize the key points of a lecture (tell them what you taught them), reminds students of how the topic related to things they already knew about, and predicts future uses of the information (Lenz, Ellis, and Scanlon 1996). This informational organizer helps students to reflect on the just-completed lesson, and to match what they learned with what you intended for them to learn. So you might conclude your lecture by stating what your topic was ("I told you three important things about DNA and cell replication"), why it matters ("In addition to the fact that you will need to know this for our next test, you need to understand how chromosomes are structured and how mutations in that structure can cause disabilities as part of understanding where disabilities come from and why"), and predict future lessons ("After we finish studying DNA, we are going to study how the human embryo blastula develops into a fetus, and we will continue to discuss how disabilities develop, so we will see how your DNA sequence determines things like your eye color, how many toes you have, and whether you might have a disability"). Ideally, when you provide a post organizer, you will recall your advance organizer.

PASS and SCREAM

As previously stated, the principles of effective lecturing can be applied to most forms of teaching. Regardless of the instructional approach, an effective teacher embeds the principles in a broader process of teaching, one that begins with good planning. Remembering the mnemonics PASS and SCREAM can help you remember the overall process (Mastropieri and Scruggs 2002).

As explained in Chapter 2, a lesson actually begins in a preplanning phase, during which you consider the content and skill standards for the lesson topic, students' individualized education program (IEP) plans, your resources, and your own skills. In this systematic way to think about effectively teaching an academically diverse class, the first step is to *Prioritize objectives*. This step reminds you to plan taking into account the varied skills required to complete an activity and determine how to help students with disabilities who must complete them, as well as to eliminate others that are unnecessary. The second step is to *Adapt instruction, materials, or the environment*, which is a reminder to be prepared to provide students with individually appropriate accommodations as needed. The third step of PASS reminds you to use *Systematic instruction* by incorporating the SCREAM variables. Finally, the fourth step, implement *Systematic evaluation procedures*, encourages you to conduct ongoing evaluations of individual students' progress toward the lesson goal(s), and reminds you to carefully observe your practices and student learning to be fully informed on how effective your lessons are and whether you may need to adjust your plans and teaching practices (for example, use the curriculum-based measurement [C-BM] procedures outlined in Chapter 2 and other chapters).

The SCREAM variables remind you to incorporate certain principles of effective instruction into your lesson: structure, clarity, redundancy, enthusiasm, appropriate pace, and maximized engagement (Mastropieri and Scruggs 2002). Although SCREAM is a useful mnemonic, we encourage you to incorporate all of the principles of effective lecturing whenever you can.

All of the effective lecturing principles just described reflect evidence-based practices that are responsive to the needs of students with HI and their peers. Read on to learn about another set of content teaching procedures that are based in effective special education practices and that have been found effective for the diversity of learners in content-area classrooms.

10-2 Helping Students Make Sense of Lesson Content

In any classroom, on any given day, there will be variation in how students learning the same content or skill come to understand it. The challenge for teachers is to clearly communicate the critical content of a lesson to an academically diverse room of learners. If students fail to appreciate key concepts fully or their relationships to bigger ideas (for example, the lesson or unit topic), the lesson will not be a success for them. Although effective lecturing is essential for clear communication of important concepts, students also need assistance in thinking about the concepts, so that they may comprehend them.

Because our materials and lessons are not always as clear as they could be, and our students vary in their preparedness to learn, teachers need to know how to:

- Relate current lessons to past and future lessons,
- Differentiate learning goals from learning activities,
- Guide students to engage actively in considering new concepts,
- Guide students to comprehend individual concepts,

- Guide students to form relationships among concepts, and
- Ask questions that prompt clarification and in-depth learning.

Content Enhancement

As the name suggests, content enhancement is an approach for enhancing the presentation of critical content in a lesson. Take a moment to review Box 10.1, which lists examples of the faults of many textbooks. If you think about your own experiences in the classroom, the examples parallel faults of many classroom lessons. Using content enhancement, teachers anticipate that learners will not comprehend all concepts in a lesson and use specific practices to clarify those concepts as part of the lesson (other content-enhancement routines are focused on supporting student work completion). Content-enhancement routines, therefore, provide access to the curriculum (IDEA 2004) for an academically diverse group of students.

Content enhancement incorporates the following four instructional conditions:

1. Both group and individual needs are valued and met.
2. The integrity of the content is maintained.
3. Critical features of the content are selected and transformed in a way that promotes learning for all students.
4. Instruction is carried out in a partnership with students (Lenz, Deshler, and Kissam 2004).

Content-enhancement instructional approaches incorporate instructional routines, devices, and procedures (Bulgren et al. 2009; Bulgren, Deshler, and Lenz 2007). The teacher leads the class through a routine and uses a visual device to help students organize the information. The *routines* involve some classroom teacher and student behaviors common to all content-enhancement approaches and others specific to the one being used. The *visual device* is some type of a graphic organizer that visually depicts the organization or relationship among concepts the students are studying. It also helps to cue cognitive actions, such as comparing or relating concepts. The completed device can be saved as a permanent record of the information learned during the content-enhancement lesson. Finally, all content-enhancement routines include *procedures* to (a) inform the students about using the routines and devices, (b) explicitly teach content, (c) orchestrate student interaction, and (d) co-construct learning (Bulgren et al. 2009). In the language of content enhancement, the combination of behaviors engaged in and the visual device used is collectively referred to as a "content-enhancement routine" (Bulgren 2006; Bulgren et al. 2007). Read on to learn how to use a content-enhancement routine specifically designed to help students explore key concepts.

The Concept Mastery Routine. The Concept Mastery Routine was developed by Bulgren, Schumaker, and Deshler (1993), three of the scholars who initially developed content enhancement. Instead of stopping the lesson to go over a difficult concept or relegating it to a weekly vocabulary word list and hoping more complex learning ensues, the class uses the Concept Mastery Routine to study the concept in relation to other content in the lesson. Using the routine, students develop an understanding of the meaning of the concept at the same time they learn how it relates to other important information (Bulgren and Scanlon 1997; 1998). A visual device called the concept diagram (Fig. 10.2) is used to guide the routine.

Each step of the routine is cued by following the circled numbers on the diagram. In place of following the numbers, students can instead learn the mnemonic CONCEPT, which cues each of the seven steps.

▼ **FIGURE 10.2**

Concept Diagram for
Revolution

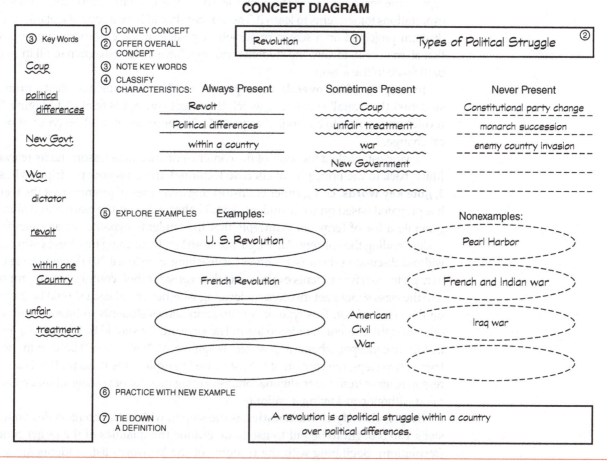

Source: J. A. Bulgren, D. D. Deshler, and J. B. Schumaker. *The Concept Mastery Routine*. (Lawrence, KS: Edge Enterprises, Inc., 1993).

Methods and Strategies Spotlight

When Is It a Strategy or a Routine?

A *strategy* is a process that cues specific cognitive activities, such as the steps or procedures of the ISM strategy. Students can perform most strategies alone, but a small group or the whole class could perform a strategy collaboratively.

Routines are teacher-led activities designed to enhance the presentation of content. Routines typically include visual devices such as the concept diagram.

When a teacher leads a group of students through the steps of a strategy, it may become a routine. Not all routines can easily be transformed into strategies, however. For this to happen, the embedded cues for cognitive processing that the teacher provides when leading a routine would have to be made overt and transferred to the student, perhaps using a mnemonic cueing device (for example, CONCEPT).

In **step 1, convey the concept**, the teacher identifies the concept to be explored by the class and writes it in the box numbered 1 (*revolution*). Alternatively, the teacher could name several representative conflicts and ask students to identify what the concept is. The teacher may explain why this concept is centrally important or may state expectations for students to learn it. The teacher should have a copy of a blank concept diagram projected on a screen or somehow posted in the classroom in such a way that all can see it. Ideally, the students will each have a blank diagram to fill in as they participate in the lesson.

In **step 2, offer overall concept**, the teacher explains (or elicits from the students) the overall concept to which the target concept is related. In Figure 10.2, revolution is going to be studied as part of a larger lesson or unit on types of political change.

Having established the topic of the content-enhancement lesson and its relevance (think back to the principles of effective lecturing), the class now participates in **step 3, note key words.** Using either brainstorming or a series of prompts that the teacher has prepared based on what students should already know, the teacher and students generate a list of terms and concepts that the students hypothesize are relevant to understanding the concept. Although traditional brainstorming involves posting ideas without discussing them (see Center for Teaching Excellence 2011), here the teacher may prefer to have students explain why they consider their contribution appropriate, and the class should get involved in deciding whether or not each should be included on the keyword list. This type of conversation allows students to interact with each other and the content in order to learn. The keyword list should be limited to approximately 10 concepts, whenever possible (Bulgren et al. 1993). As will be seen in the following two steps, the content of the list is used to explore the concept. This is another reason to stray from the traditional brainstorming practice of posting all that comes to mind without considering it critically.

Step 4, classify characteristics, is the step in which the thoughts developed in steps 1 to 3 begin to be put to use to determine the qualities of the target concept (revolution). Beginning with the contents of the keywords list, students are asked to list characteristics of the concept that are *always present*, *sometimes present*, or *never present*. The discussion will almost certainly provoke the students and teacher to come up with additional information to be included on the diagram. Precisely how these activities are done is at the discretion of the teacher, but the class should develop a set of routines across multiple instances of using the Concept Mastery Routine so that they become highly familiar with the expectations for their participation. Students could convene in small groups at this point or hold a spirited class-wide discussion (Bulgren et al. 1993), for example. Although the teacher leads the students through the routine, it should be clear that the teacher does not simply present the content to the learners; in content enhancement, the learners are actively engaged in reflecting on what they know and making predictions that are investigated. All of this necessarily involves making rich connections among familiar and new concepts.

Following step 4, students progress to **step 5, explore examples**, as a test of the characteristics they have classified. Students should list multiple examples of the concept that satisfy the various conditions of *always present*, *sometimes present*, and *never present*. Also, they should list non-examples, because students who have not mastered the content can better comprehend the limits of a concept and its examples when they can identify instances that might reasonably be mistaken for an example (Scanlon 2002). This is a true test of students' ability to comprehend the concept being diagrammed. One of the many options in how to complete the CONCEPT steps is for the teacher to provide the examples and non-examples prior to steps 1 to 4 and guide the students to determine that content inductively (Bulgren et al. 1993).

Step 6, practice with a new example, requires teachers to be prepared with an item not discussed in the routine thus far, which may be an example or a non-example. This new item can be written in the blank "proving ground" space on the diagram between the examples and non-examples bubbles. The students are then challenged to determine whether or not it is an example of the concept. For example, the teacher could write "The Syrian War" in Figure 10.2. Using practice examples becomes a test of both the accuracy of the concept diagram and the students' learning. Of course, any time the students realize they need to refine the content on some section of the diagram, they should be able to discuss it and do so.

Finally, students define the concept in **step 7, tie down a definition**. The definition should name the concept and incorporate all of the *always present* characteristics. Using the Concept Mastery Routine, students will have thoroughly investigated the concept in question and considered related important information. This particular content-enhancement routine can be used to begin a lesson, as a central learning activity of a lesson, or as a way to summarize and evaluate learning.

Other Content-Enhancement Routines. Several other content-enhancement routines are available, some of which are intended to help teachers in their planning and to share that planning with their students (review Chapter 2 for the purposes and benefits of sharing planning with students). Others are designed to help students explore and apply key concepts of a lesson. Content-enhancement routines can be categorized into four domains:

1. Routines for planning and leading learning help teachers to identify critical content and activities at the course, unit, and lesson levels (for example, Lenz et al. 1998, 2005). They include routines and graphic devices to help students understand connections among lessons and to keep track of learning goals and assignments (review Fig. 2.3 for an example).
2. The second domain includes routines for exploring text, topics, and details; these guide students and their teachers through processes for clarifying concepts that are confusing and abstract. For example, the Framing Routine (Ellis 1998) guides students to transform abstract main ideas into concrete representations. The ORDER Routine (Scanlon, Deshler, and Schumaker 2004) helps students reflect on lesson content to understand how discrete concepts relate to one another.
3. The third domain consists of routines for teaching concepts, including the Concept Mastery Routine and Concept Comparison Routine, which guide students through a process of identifying critical similarities and differences between concepts (for example, opposing political parties, protons and electrons).
4. The fourth domain comprises routines for increasing performance. These include the Quality Assignment Routine (Rademacher et al. 1998) featured in Chapter 11, as well as the Recall Enhancement Routine (Schumaker et al. 1998), which helps students to recall critical lesson content; its validated benefits include significantly improved performance on class tests.

These various content enhancement routines are especially beneficial because they are easily integrated into the inclusive classroom environment (Bulgren 2006; see also Little and Hahs-Vaughn 2007).

Research into the effectiveness of various content-enhancement routines has found them to be effective for students with and without HI, and to be readily used by their inclusion classroom teachers (Bulgren and Lenz 1996; Little and Hans-Vaughn

CASE 10.2	Students with Comprehension Difficulties

Case Introduction

Now that you have worked through the first case in this chapter, you should feel comfortable addressing issues in a second case. In Case 10.1, you considered effective instructional practices for the content-area classroom (the inclusion classroom). Those practices were discussed in relation to lecture/discussion instructional activities, but, as stated, they can be appropriate practices for any of the myriad of ways a teacher might lead a lesson. In this case, you will meet another teacher, a special educator named Alok. He is particularly concerned with how to help his students to read challenging texts. As you read the case, think about the ways Alok's challenges resemble Ramona's.

Alok is co-teaching U.S. history with Selma Bean. So that their students can take historical perspectives, they have them read original documents in addition to using the district-adopted textbook. They plan to have the students rely heavily on original documents to help them understand both the unfolding causes of the American Revolution and the sentiments of colonists and others at that time. Alok and Selma want students to develop their own theories of cause, which they will then compare to those presented in the textbook. Although the students don't know it yet, Alok and Selma plan to use this same approach a little later in the school year when they turn their attention to the Civil War.

Alok and Selma co-teach following the alternative teaching approach, where one teacher works with the large class and the other works intently with a few who have particular learning needs. Luis is one of Alok's students. Luis has many of the same problems that he has in Ramona's biology class. He reads below grade level, but the history text is written at grade level. The original documents are sometimes even more challenging for him, as some are written in outdated language styles, and others were written for certain audiences that do not include current-day

ninth-grade students. These texts are even less considerate than the textbook in helping readers to think about the main ideas and how those relate to other topics in the lesson or unit.

Selma wondered if they should excuse Luis from all of the activities involving the original documents. Alok proposed the alternative teaching approach instead as a way he could work directly with Luis and a few others intensively supporting their reading.

Belle, who is also a student in Alok's group, seems to have particular difficulty with the concepts read and discussed in class. Although she is seldom off task, Alok and Selma feel she often isn't understanding what the class is talking about; sometimes Belle lets them know this by heavy sighs or other inappropriate expressions. Alok has stopped asking Belle questions in front of the group because Belle is embarrassed to reveal how confused she is. Belle records very little information in her notebook, even though Selma has started modeling how to write notes on the board and using lecture pauses as parts of her lectures. Alok finds that he needs to go over everything with Belle in detail after Selma's whole-class lectures. Selma finds teaching Belle unrewarding because she has so little success, and Alok sometimes feels that way too, because Belle is never able to articulate what she needs help understanding.

CASE QUESTIONS

1. How can Alok help Luis and other students in comprehending often-challenging original documents?
2. What are some accommodations that Alok could try with Luis instead of excluding him from certain lessons or sending him to the learning center?
3. How can Alok and Selma determine effective accommodations for Belle?

2007). In an overview of published research on "procedural facilitators," Baker, Gersten, and Scanlon (2002) reported that content-enhancement routines and related instructional interventions were effective when they included graphic or mnemonic supports for performing cognitive processes and were taught in an instructionally supportive routine.

In the case of the Concept Mastery Routine, Bulgren et al. (1993) report that secondary students with and without learning disabilities performed better on tests and at comparable rates to one another in inclusive social studies and science classes. The students' enhanced performance was likely due to their improved quantity and quality of note-taking during the routine. Finally, Bulgren et al. report that teachers improved in their cueing of critical content.

Other Lesson Formats

As you have read, lecture-based teaching does not have to mean that you speak at your students while they sit and listen, nor should it. You can use a variety of lecturing techniques to assist your students' engagement (for example, using visuals and cueing). Also, there are a variety of ways to punctuate lecturing to actively involve your students with the content; content-enhancement routines are excellent examples of this. Many of the lecturing practices we have described, and most content-enhancement practices, are rooted in explicit instruction, which (as explained in Chapter 2 and throughout this book) has one of the strongest evidence bases as being effective for students with HI. However, explicit instruction is not the only way to teach effectively; those who say it is have misunderstood the research. When explicit instruction practices are incorporated into other instructional approaches, those other approaches can be effective for students with HI too.

Many teachers like to use project-based learning, inquiry, and constructivist approaches. Also, computer-based instruction and "flipped" classrooms, where students study foundational information online or for homework before the class lesson and then engage in concept exploration or application activities in the classroom (Staker and Horn 2012), are gaining in popularity. In a flipped classroom a teacher may actually have more time to engage one on one with a student (Staker and Horn 2012). Also, students participate in structured activities to practice or apply content they are learning.

Whether students are doing projects, inquiry, or problem solving, among other approaches, ensure that you incorporate effective practices to prepare them to engage with the content, to guide them on how to participate and what to attend to, and to allow you and them to check on their learning progress. The same is necessary for effective constructivist learning. Students with HI have difficulties with memory, attending, metacognition and executive function, and abstract reasoning, in addition to a range of literacy skills. When you incorporate evidence-based instructional practices such as explicit instruction into these other approaches, students with HI can and do learn effectively (Steele 2005; Woodward 2001; also see Gerber 1994).

10-3 | Student Skills Commonly Required for Content-Area Learning

A student's full participation and learning in a classroom takes a variety of skills. In one study (Scanlon 2003), middle-school teachers from a variety of content-area and special education classrooms collectively identified the skills students need to be successful in content-area classes. The teachers identified a range of skills, including traditional academic skills involved in reading, writing, and comprehension, and skills for participating in a classroom that incorporates a variety of learning activities (see Fig. 10.3 and Fig. 10.4). Some skills needed for success in the content-area classroom are unique to content learning; some are even specific to particular content areas.

In all grade levels, all students, regardless of disability, can stand to improve upon their learning skills; however, for students such as Luis and Belle from the chapter cases, improvement is essential for their success. Typically, students with HI are among those who must develop more proficient skills if they are to be successful in the classroom. Without sufficient study skills, students can have difficulty accessing the curriculum. The following are challenges common for students and teachers in content-area teaching and learning.

▼ **FIGURE 10.3**

Study Skills Needed as
Identified by Middle-School
Social Studies Teachers

Strategy Requirements of Social Studies Curricula			

Study groups
Social skills
 	
Organization
Put items in order
Have a plan—"This is
  how I'm going to . . ."
 	
Probing questions
 	
Formulating opinions
	Excellence in homework
	Completion of homework
	
	Read to understand
	Explain in own words
	Pick out most significant
	  characteristics
	Differentiate irrelevant
	Give examples
	Application
	
	Transforming content
	Forming relationships
		Memorize—then apply
		Writing versus memory
		Know the terminology
		
		Understand and use key
		  vocabulary
		
		Note-taking
		Draw it!
		Graph it
		Visually depict information
		Timeline
		Sequencing events
		Think chronologically
			Evaluating
			
			Identify problem and offer solution
			Think ahead of now
			Consider other possibilities
			
			Express themselves
			Vocalize freely
			
			Processing lots of information
			Gather information about issues
			Be able to retrieve information
			Use maps correctly—gather
			  information

Source: D. Scanlon, J. B. Schumaker, and D. D. Deshler. Collaborative Dialogues Between Teachers and Researchers to Create Educational Interventions: A Case Study. (*Journal of Educational and Psychological Consultation* 5(1994):69–76).

▼ **FIGURE 10.4**

Study Skills Needed as
Identified by Middle-School
Team Teachers

Organization Structure long-term projects Time management Follow structured format for notebook ————————— Reading comprehension Reading and following directions How to ask for and seek help	————————— Self control ————————— Peer assessment Portfolio system Connections to prior knowledge ————————— Number skills Vocabulary Number sense	————————— Outlining Logical sequences Time sequences Topic identification Writing/communication/ evaluation	Preferential seating Independent note-taking Studying for tests Group dynamic skills Listening How to use a "tool" Responsibility for personal/ chool material ————————— Summarizing

Source: Scanlon, D. (2003). Learning strategies expected in content-area inclusion. *Developmental Disabilities Bulletin, 31*, 11–41.

Reading

Reading is an essential academic skill for most content-area classes (Leko and Mundy 2012; Vaughn and Wanzek 2014; also see Fisher and Ivey 2005); reading is also the most common skill difficulty for students with HI, such as learning disabilities (Annie E. Casey Foundation Report 2010; Sanford, Park, and Baker 2013).

Classrooms involve a lot of reading. They have posters and bulletin boards, chalkboards, computer programs, schedules, handouts, tests, classmates' notes, handheld PDAs, and original documents, in addition to textbooks. From first grade to 12th grade, students are expected to decode and comprehend these many forms of text.

Content-area reading requires that students recognize and comprehend grade-level-appropriate, and sometimes content-specific, vocabulary (for example, *gigabyte, trilobite, dilute, passage, plot*—notice how these five words share a structural or semantic feature with the preceding and/or following word in the list, are not all key vocabulary in the same disciplines, and sometimes have different connotations by discipline) and phrases (for example, "the measure of a man," "estimate the earth's rotation in rpm," "plot the reaction"). Students need to read in sophisticated ways to acquire information and make connections between new and known information. Thus, content-area students must be able to perform reading skills that include the following:

Basic reading skills (review Chapters 6 and 7)
Vocabulary and concept recognition
Main ideas and key content identification
Main ideas and key content comprehension
Author's perspective interpretation
Other content connections

Review Chapter 7 on Later Reading: Strategies and Techniques, as it contains many useful practices to teach necessary reading skills for the content classroom. The following are a variety of practices that can be used in conjunction with those techniques. These practices differ from those in Chapter 7 in that these not only support good reading practices but are equally focused on learning the content of readings, which is your primary but not exclusive responsibility in content-area teaching.

Begin with Pre-Reading. We are generally more successful readers when we know something about what we are about to read (Palincsar and Duke 2004). (For instance, you benefit from the learning objectives in this book.) Before reading, tell your students a little about the topic about which they are going to read. Even better, also ask them to discuss what they already know about the topic (see the KWL technique in Chapter 3). If the material has chapter questions or a chapter summary, reading those before the main text can also be helpful.

Students should also thumb through the reading to gauge how long it is, and whether they will need to attend to any graphics. If you anticipate difficult vocabulary or concepts, be sure to preview them with the students, so that the terms will not be a hindrance when encountered during reading. This preview should include seeing the word in print, hearing how it is properly pronounced, and establishing what it means (Proctor et al. 2009). Helping your students know why the term is important will aid their reading comprehension.

Use Partnered Reading. Round-robin reading, where students in a circle take turns reading paragraphs aloud, is generally not an effective approach for any member of the group (Gill 2002). Variations where two partners are matched in terms of reading ability can actually be more productive. The two can read and ask each other questions as they go. Ideally, the reading will be close to the weaker of the two readers' comfort reading level. Asking two poor readers to help each other with a difficult text may seem illogical, but it can work if they know some ways to problem-solve their poor reading and to ask for help when needed. Weak readers with autism have been assisted in discussing readings with a partner by imbedding cues to discuss right in the text (Hughes et al. 2013).

That said, matching a weaker reader with a stronger reader is a more typical practice (see paired reading in Chapter 7). This approach requires that the text not be so challenging for one that the other has to do all of the work, and it requires that both readers know how to seek and provide the help they can. Reciprocal teaching (Palincsar and Brown 1984; What Works Clearinghouse 2013), class-wide peer tutoring (Bowman-Perrott 2009; Fulk and King 2001), and peer-assisted learning strategies (PALS) (Calhoon, Al Otaiba, Greenberg, King, and Avalos 2006) are three established approaches to ensuring that reading partners of unequal ability are able to support each other in reading. Students like Belle in Case 10.2 can learn to use these approaches because they do well with learning and following routines.

Motivate the Reader. Students benefit from having a purpose for reading, and the best purpose is motivation to learn. Do what you can to get your students to want to read the assigned material. Previewing the chapter can help to get some students interested; discussions of the chapter topic or why it is important to be studied may be motivating to others. To give the students a purpose for reading, you can provide them with questions (or they can generate their own as part of pre-reading) or guided notes. Looking for information can help readers to stay focused and comprehend (Foorman et al. 2016).

Find an Alternative. Students should learn to read and should be supported in reading as a part of your class. On occasion, it may be more practical, however, to find an alternative to reading. Could you show a video or use a demonstration instead? Why not use a content-enhancement routine in place of a challenging reading to introduce new concepts? Could students do some kind of a project to learn the same information? Maybe you will need to present material with supplemental information. You may be able to find an alternative version of the text that uses simplified vocabulary and sentence structure, or that incorporates helpful graphics. Perhaps the students could listen to the text instead of reading it themselves; struggling readers can read more fluently and comprehend more when they read along with a text that is read aloud (Smolkin and Donovan 2003; see Chapter 7 also for more about this). In addition to recorded books, you can use interactive technologies, including devices that "read" printed text aloud (for example, Kurzweil 3000, Readingpen®; see Chapter 12 for other text-to-speech options).

Select the Best Text. Whenever you have a choice among texts, select the one that has useful reading features. These features include guiding questions, a chapter introduction and/or summary, margin notes, highlighted vocabulary, graphics that support the written text, plenty of white space on a page, and features such as appendices, glossaries, and reference lists. See Crawford and Carnine (2000), Dzaldov and Peterson (2005), and Stein et al. (2001) for guidelines on qualities of texts.

As stated, these good reading practices can be used to help students like Luis and his classmates to read and learn necessary content. A teacher who was to implement a responsiveness to intervention (RTI) model in Alok and Selma's classroom could use many of these practices as part of the tiers of intensified reading instruction (review Chapter 1).

THINK BACK TO THE CASE **with Alok's U.S. history class...**

1. *How can Alok help Luis and other students in comprehending often-challenging original documents?*

Many of the reading comprehension practices presented in Chapter 7 can be used in Alok and Selma's classroom. Alok can also use the practices just described in this section in his general education classroom. His students can use some of these practices together, regardless of their individual reading abilities.

Using the Reading Process to Integrate Reading Skill Development and Content Learning

There is more to reading than finishing a text in a timely manner and answering some recall questions correctly. Good reading begins with pre-reading activities that orient readers toward the topic, providing a chance to think about the topic and prepare for what is ahead. The act of reading the text itself involves reading with a purpose, such as having an interest or seeking specific information. Good readers also think carefully about main ideas and which information is important. They also consider how their prior knowledge relates to what is being presented in the text.

Following reading, good readers reflect on what they have read, thinking carefully about whether their opinions about main ideas, important details, and connections to prior knowledge are accurate, and whether pre-reading questions were sufficiently answered once the reading is complete.

Because the complete reading process actually has a number of steps, students will benefit from an organized strategy to help them complete each stage of the reading process successfully (Foreman et al. 2016) (see, for example, Scanlon, Duran, Reyes, and Gallego 1992).

10-4 Accommodations

Students with disabilities should receive a different curriculum than other students only when it is unrealistic for them to benefit from the general education curriculum (IDEA 2004). This does not mean that the only choices are full participation in the general curriculum with no individualization versus participation in some wholly separate curriculum. Students with HI should receive accommodations that enable them to participate in the regular curriculum. The U.S. Department of Education explicitly endorses the use of accommodations (Box 10.2). Providing accommodations is a primary way of ensuring access to the content-area curriculum for students with HI.

Some students have such poor skills in test taking, essay writing, or interpersonal communication, for example, that a teacher may assume they do not know

---

BOX 10.2

U.S. Department of Education, Office of Special Education Programs, Endorsements of Accommodation Practices

Children with disabilities are included in general state and district-wide assessment programs, with appropriate accommodations, where necessary.

> —*Individuals with Disabilities Education Improvement Act* 2004 [Sec. 612 (a) (16) (A)]

Teachers ensure that students work toward grade-level content standards by using a range of instructional strategies based on the varied strengths and needs of students. Providing accommodations during instruction and assessments may also promote equal access to grade-level content.

> —*Accommodations Manual: How to Select, Administer, and Evaluate Use of Accommodations for Instruction and Assessment of Students with Disabilities*, 2nd ed. (Thompson et al. 2005; http://www.ccsso.org/Resources/Publications /Accommodations_Manual_-_How_to_Select_Administer_and_Evaluate_Use _of_Accommodations_for_Instruction_and_Assessment_of_students_with _Disabilities.html).

the content, when in reality they would have little difficulty learning and performing with accommodations. Students who are slow to formulate answers may appear to be struggling to come up with the answer. The reason they are struggling may only be the pressure of time, however. Unless a fast response is necessary for accuracy (for example, capping a chemical reaction in chemistry lab, doing a timed math drill, debating), allowing a longer response time or a more comfortable response format will allow students to show their abilities. These are examples of accommodations. Other examples include being allowed to use a dictionary app or not being graded on spelling, being provided guided notes, and reading an alternative version of the required text. Accommodations are appropriate whenever they are "reasonable" (IDEA 2004; Thompson et al. 2005); that is to say, they must not be too cumbersome to provide, the student should be able to make use of them, and they must not substantially alter the content of the lesson or methods the teacher or student uses (Thompson et al. 2005).

Defining Accommodations

The terms *accommodations*, *adaptations*, *alterations*, and *modifications* have been used inconsistently, leaving educators confused. We will adhere to the definitions that most closely align with the 2004 Reauthorization of the IDEA (our source, Thompson et al. 2005, is posted as a downloadable PDF on the Council of Chief State School Officers website under the "resources" tab). Hence, the following are the currently used terms and their meanings.

Accommodation is a minor change in how content or material is presented to the student and/or in how the student participates in the lesson. An accommodation does not significantly alter the method of learning or learning outcomes; that is, students are held to the same expectations as others but meet those expectations in alternate ways.

Modification is a significant change in how content or material is presented to a student and/or in how the student participates in the lesson. Although not an entirely different curriculum, a modification has the student learn similar content or the same content but with different expectations for learning compared to others. Sometimes modifications are so extensive that the student learns a **parallel curriculum**, which means she or he studies the same content-area curriculum but learns significantly different content or skills (for example, a high-school student in a class studying the history of cartography and its relation to predicting revolutions who instead learns how to follow her class schedule through the school building).

To add to the terminology confusion, accommodation is used as the label to name the overall category of practices that include accommodations and modifications (as well as the more outdated terms *adaptations* and *alterations*), just as we are using the term in both capacities in this book. What's more, many of the effective teaching practices presented in this book can function as accommodations or modifications. It depends on the particular lesson and its objectives. Remember, accommodations are minor changes and modifications are significant changes, and in either case they are provided specifically to meet the needs of individual students. Even when you elect to apply the accommodation to the whole class (for example, using guided notes, providing assignment directions orally and in writing), it is still an accommodation because you are doing it to meet the needs of a particular student(s).

At this point, you would probably like definitions for "minor" and "significant" changes, but that distinction is a subjective judgment. There are always going to be examples that cause experts to disagree, but think of *minor* changes as altering performance (the teacher's or the student's) but not the standards for learning, and *significant* changes as altering expectations.

Providing Accommodations

To provide accommodations, teachers need to do the following:

- Be familiar with the concepts of "accommodation" and "modification."
- Understand the content being taught and the purpose of the instructional practice(s) being used.
- Know a variety of possible accommodations.
- Collaborate with other educators and the student to identify suitable accommodations.
- Adjust classroom instruction so that one or more students can participate via accommodations.
- Evaluate the effectiveness of accommodations, including the learning that results.

The list of possible accommodations is as endless as the imagination. The IEP team has the responsibility for identifying any accommodations a student with HI may need to have available. They should be listed on the IEP, and, as appropriate, the team can specify the contexts and classes for which specific accommodations are allowed. Instead of generating the longest list the team can brainstorm, educators who know the student's classes and learning demands should identify those that will actually be used. The student must know how to use them, the teachers must know how to support them, and the accommodations must actually be "minor" changes in the contexts for which they are planned. Long lists of accommodations leave educators and students confused as to which to use and can result in none being used (Scanlon and Baker 2012).

There is one more important consideration for identifying appropriate accommodations for a student: standardized assessments. Most standardized tests have lists of approved accommodations, and only those accommodations are allowed on that test. This is not considered a violation of the student's disability-related rights because they are the only ones allowed in order to maintain the psychometric integrity of the test. Therefore, when a team knows a student will be expected to complete a standardized assessment (for example, the PSAT, the home state's high-stakes exam required for matriculation, the National Assessment of Educational Progress [NAEP], or other annual achievement assessments), the approved accommodations listed on the IEP should match those allowed on the exam. Of course, the student should be practiced at using those particular accommodations if they are going to be of use on exam day.

IEP teams (of which classroom teachers and special educators are members) identify appropriate accommodations by considering all the possible ways a student with HI may need to be accommodated. Accommodation needs may be thought of as falling into one of the following four categories:

- *Presentation accommodations* allow students to access information in ways that do not require them to read standard print visually. These alternate modes of access are auditory, multisensory, tactile, and visual.
- *Response accommodations* allow students to complete activities, assignments, and assessments in different ways or to solve or organize problems using some type of assistive device or organizer.
- *Setting accommodations* change the location in which a test or assignment is given or the conditions of the setting.
- *Timing and scheduling accommodations* increase the length of time allowed to complete an assessment or assignment and perhaps change the way the time is organized (Thompson et al. 2005).

See Table 10.1 for a sample list of possible accommodations.

TABLE 10.1 Examples of Accommodations for Students

Adjustable lighting	Advance organizers
Checklist for assignments	Color-code keys on computer or calculator
Computer with speech recognition	Duplicate set of texts at home
Background noise elimination	Extra time
Fidget objects	Guided notes
Manipulatives	Pen or pencil grip
Texts rewritten	Rocking chair
Study carrel	Visual cues
Writing templates	Written copy of oral directions

THINK BACK TO THE CASE   with Alok and Luis . . .

2. *What are some accommodations that Alok could try with Luis instead of excluding him from certain lessons or sending him to the learning center?*

As already noted, the list of possible accommodations is as long as your imagination. In this chapter, you have read about a variety of instructional activities to support struggling readers in the content-area classroom. Alok and Selma could use many of those practices or features of them as accommodations for Luis. They are already using a setting accommodation by having Luis work in a small group with Alok. They might also try a presentation accommodation such as transcribing the original documents into easily readable fonts, and even updating the language if that won't violate the lesson.

The test of an accommodation's appropriateness should consider three factors: lesson integrity, student appropriateness, and manageability. To maintain **lesson integrity**, an accommodation cannot significantly alter the learning standard (content) or method of performance, and a modification can do those things but must remain true to the lesson topic. The learning standard is relatively easily judged: if the accommodation results in lower proficiency than should be acceptable for a student studying the topic, then the accommodation may not be appropriate. The catch is that proficiency is related to what is necessary for the student to learn the lesson, not for simply how you would like the student to do so.

For example, Luis from the two cases in this chapter reads significantly below grade level, so whenever there is a reading assignment he either listens to the book on tape or reads a text presenting the same information but written at a lower reading level. When the class is reading the original text of documents supporting the American Revolution (for example, *Common Sense*, the Declaration of Independence), Luis finds their complex language too challenging to read, so he reads modernized and simplified versions of the same text. He is fully able to participate in the lesson and learn about the principal positions espoused in each document. His accommodations have enabled him to participate in the lesson and to be held to the same learning standards as others. On the other hand, if the goal of the lesson were to learn how to read the original source documents and independently determine their principal positions, Luis should not read modernized and simplified versions of the texts; he could still listen to recordings of them, however. This accommodation would cross the line to becoming a modification only if the lesson goal included reading the original documents in print format only for some reason.

> **THINK BACK TO THE CASE** about Alok's U.S. history class...
>
> *3. How can Alok and Selma determine effective accommodations for Belle?*
>
> Belle might be a good source of information as to what accommodations might be effective for her. If Alok and Selma cannot come up with effective ideas on their own or in collaboration with Belle, they could consult other teachers, including the building's Student Study Team (review Chapter 2). Importantly, they should keep data on how well the accommodations they try work. Accepting that it will take some time for any accommodation they try to become a comfortable routine for Belle, they can plot her skill at employing the accommodation as well as her learning gains following C-BM charting procedures (review Chapter 2).

Belle has trouble with writing fluently. Whenever a task involves writing a lot of information, she has tremendous difficulty and often fails. Her memory deficits also tend to cause her to take longer to recall and perform the steps of a skill she has learned (for example, the steps involved in multiplication that involve carrying), although she can usually perform the skills given an occasional prompt and enough time. In Belle's math class, the teacher gives a speed quiz every Friday. Students earn points for both the percentage of problems correct and the percentage attempted. The math teacher acknowledges that speed is a desirable skill for solving equations, but not an essential one, so Belle is allowed to complete the same quiz as everyone else, but she takes it untimed. Because the scoring system for the quiz incorporates the number of problems attempted, the teacher must also alter how Belle's quiz is graded. Thus, to be accommodated on speed quizzes in math class, Belle must be allowed to be quizzed only on the essential skill of solving problems and not be held to evaluation standards that are inconsistent with her accommodation (in this example the accommodation would unfairly advantage Belle).

As you can judge from the examples of Luis and Belle, **student appropriateness** means that the accommodations provided match what the student needs and that the student can benefit from them. Luis has difficulties with the visual process of reading; if he had a more general comprehension problem, recording grade-level books on tape may not be an appropriate accommodation for him. Simply put, to be appropriate, an accommodation should be matched to what the student can do.

Finally, **manageability** means that providing the accommodation does not unduly tax the student, classmates, teacher, or environment. If an accommodation requires a student to use a heavy piece of equipment that cannot be transported into the chemistry lab, for example, other accommodations should be tried before modifying the one student's chemistry curriculum to exclude labs. An accommodation is manageable as long as it does not impede the lesson. Most claims of accommodations not being manageable can be overcome by thinking creatively about how to provide the accommodation. A paraprofessional or peer tutor may need to assist the student with an accommodation (for example, a student needs to verbalize the steps of a procedure to someone in order to perform them), the student may need to be trained in using the accommodation before it is employed in the classroom (for example, Luis operating a tape recorder, or a student who is allowed to use a template for planning the content of writing assignments), or the classroom configuration may need to be permanently altered so that using the accommodation does not disrupt the routine (for example, for a student who must sit in the front row or move to a study carrel in order to read without distractions). When a particular accommodation truly is unmanageable, an alternative accommodation can be found in most cases.

Selecting Accommodations

Here again, decisions about accommodations require intuition instead of matching to some checklist. Possible accommodations should be suggested on an IEP. Thus, the list of possible accommodations should take into account your curriculum and classroom routines. In some cases, students have very few recommended accommodations. This may be because the student cannot benefit from a great variety of accommodations—although, as we noted above, creative thinking almost always results in devising more accommodations that are appropriate. More often, you will be able to select from a menu of appropriate accommodations, depending on the task and the student's needs in that particular situation (for example, Luis may be accommodated some days by working in a small group where the other students read aloud to him, but on other occasions he may need to use a modified text or an audio-recorded book).

The student should be a helpful resource in selecting the accommodation to use and when to use it. Asking students which accommodation they think best to use helps you to make an informed decision; at the same time, it helps students to exercise control of their own learning skills. To build facility with accommodations, the student should use the same repertoire whenever possible instead of using an endless array of different ones.

Evaluating Accommodations

Students and teachers both might have favorite accommodations, but these may not always be the ones that best fulfill the purposes of accommodations. Just as with any instructional practice or student performance, an accommodation should be evaluated to make certain it has its desired effects. After providing accommodations, if a student does not seem to benefit from a particular lesson, the teacher should look into whether the accommodation is being used correctly, whether it truly matches the task, and whether it is effective for meeting the performance/learning goal (having satisfied the first two conditions). As always, evaluation should not just occur when the lesson is over; observe the accommodation in practice to assess how it is going. If it is not going well, perhaps there are ways to "troubleshoot" its use; otherwise, you can determine how to transition into an alternate accommodation in the hopes of saving the lesson. The observations that you and the students make about accommodations in practice can be used to update the list of suggested accommodations supplied to you and future teachers via the IEP.

CHAPTER SUMMARY

Academic diversity is present no matter how homogeneous a classroom seems. Students with disabilities are full-fledged members of the classroom, regardless of whether they are held to different curricular standards and may require accommodations or other adjustments in a lesson. Teaching and learning in the content-area classroom are shared responsibilities. Teachers must attend to their learners and not unquestioningly to their content; students must use appropriate learning skills and work with their teachers to learn those skills.

In planning and teaching a lesson, teachers must be mindful of the students who are present. They can use a variety of effective lecturing techniques to ensure effective communication of information for learning. Teachers who incorporate these practices into their teaching are being thoughtful about their content and about how their students are receiving it. Content-enhancement routines can be used to further bridge teaching and learning processes; using these routines, teachers coach students to attend to critical concepts.

Students can become active in the learning process by being supported in learning and applying good practices in the classroom. Research evidence indicates that students benefit from learning how to learn as part of content lessons in ways they do not when they first learn skills in isolation (Scanlon, Cass, Amtzis, & Sideredis 2009; Scanlon, Deshler, and Schumaker 1996). Students should be informed as to the importance of attending to how to learn. Teachers should remember that even students in the upper grades still need to learn how to learn, not just to be reminded to use skills they may not have fully mastered. Students who are actively engaged in content learning can participate in initiating, monitoring, evaluating, and improving their own learning performance.

KEY TERMS

Access to the Curriculum, 320
Accommodation, 344
Advance Organizer, 324
Check for Understanding, 330
Cueing, 328
Grabber, 324
Informative Feedback, 331

Interact, 330
Key Questions, 325
Lecture Pauses, 329
Lesson Integrity, 346
Manageability, 347
Modification, 344
Pacing, 328

Parallel Curriculum, 344
Post Organizer, 332
Provide Clarity, 327
Student Appropriateness, 347
Student Response Rate, 328
Taking Notes, 330
Visuals, 327

APPLICATION ACTIVITIES

Using information from the chapter, complete the following activities that were designed to help you apply knowledge that was presented in this chapter.

1. If you have ever created a lesson plan, write notations into it "scripting" your role and your students' roles for each component of effective lecturing.
2. Develop a concept diagram for the content from one lesson or reading you recently completed.
3. Together with a content-area teacher colleague, discuss (a) a lesson plan from the general educator's content class and (b) the learning needs of a student with a HI in that class (hint: consult the student's IEP). Then, separate and each devise lists of at least four accommodations (or modifications if more appropriate) for the student and the lesson. Compare lists and discuss your opinions as to what constitutes an accommodation versus a modification.

Lopolo/Shutterstock.com

11 Organization and Study Skills: Strategies and Techniques

Learning Objectives

After reading this chapter, you will understand:

11-1 The types of organizational skills students with HI need for success in the content-area classroom

11-2 How students can efficiently plan and follow study schedules

11-3 The roles teachers and students play in students completing assignments

11-4 What is involved in taking good notes and making use of them

11-5 Test-taking skills that enable students to demonstrate what they know, along with test-giving skills teachers can use for more accurate testing

CEC Initial Preparation Standard 3: Curricular Content Knowledge

3-1 Beginning special education professionals understand the central concepts, structures of the discipline, and tools of inquiry of the content areas they teach, and can organize this knowledge, integrate cross-disciplinary skills, and develop meaningful learning progressions for individuals with exceptionalities.

3-3 Beginning special education professionals modify general and specialized curricula to make them accessible to individuals with exceptionalities.

CEC **Initial Preparation Standard 4: Assessment**

4-1   Beginning special education professionals select and use technically sound formal and informal assessments that minimize bias.

4-2   Beginning special education professionals use knowledge of measurement principles and practices to interpret assessment results and guide educational decisions for individuals with exceptionalities.

4-4   Beginning special education professionals engage individuals with exceptionalities to work toward quality learning and performance and provide feedback to guide them.

What ways of being organized are difficult for you? What study skills do you need to improve? How do those needs for improvement affect you as a learner?

Most students need help with organization and with learning the skills for learning. They need to learn how to have the right materials on hand, plan and perform learning tasks, manage time, and coordinate all that is expected of them. As you can recall from your own career as a student, the organizational demands placed upon students evolve as they progress through schooling levels; even "highly organized" students continually face new demands.

In this chapter, you will learn about the organizational needs of students with HI and how you can teach them needed skills. Organization and study skills can be particularly challenging for students with attention difficulties and weak memory, which are common for those with HI. Those students often need explicit teacher cueing to use appropriate skills. Organization and good study skills are essential to academic success. In addition to learning how to teach students to be organized and use good study skills, you will learn ways to integrate organization into *your* assignments, tests, and classroom routines.

11-1   Students' Organizational Needs

One key to successful functioning is organization. Without organization, students do not follow schedules or find materials they need. Lack of organization also interferes with efficient performance of tasks, and that can be a problem for completing work, as well as for planning and executing long-range projects. Although organizing is a central trait of cognitive processing for encoding, recalling, and expressing information (Snowman and Biehler 2006), having organizational skills is not automatic. Most students must be taught these skills.

Students of all ages and ability levels need to learn skills for organizing. The specific skills they need to learn depend on both the skills they already have and the demands of their classrooms. You can be relatively confident, however, that they will all need to learn to set, read, maintain, and follow schedules; complete assignments; and study and take tests. All of those activities rely on organization. Students with HI have the compound effect of having life experiences (for example, missing periods of school due to emotional or behavioral disorders) and cognitive processing deficits that make organization particularly challenging (for example, students with attention-deficit/hyperactivity disorder [ADHD] are easily distracted; those with autism spectrum disorder (ASD) "requiring support" are not flexible thinkers and may be resistant to trying new skills of organization).

For students like Jeremy, the first problem of the day is getting to school. Teens are notorious for their poor sleep habits. Many stay up as late as they can at night, and most have a problem with getting out of bed in the morning. Medical research findings indicate that teens typically need 9.2 hours of sleep per night, and even those who get that amount can still expect bouts of tiredness throughout the day (Carskadon and Acebo 2002; Wolfson and Carskadon 2003). Rapid physical development during puberty is a key factor in their routine state of exhaustion (Carskadon and Acebo 2002). The

CASE 11.1   A School Day in the Life of Jeremy

Case Introduction

As you read the following case about Jeremy, you may recognize many of your students; you may even recognize yourself. Maybe you won't see all of the forms of disorganization that Jeremy must contend with in a single individual, but you will see some familiar traits. As you read, ask yourself why Jeremy persists in some of these forms of disorganization. Also ask yourself what the consequences may be.

At the end of the case, you will find case questions. These questions are meant to serve as points for reflection. Of course, if you can answer them immediately, you should do so, but you may want to wait to answer them until you have read the portion of the chapter that pertains to the particular case question. Throughout the rest of the chapter, you will see the same questions. As you see them, try to answer them based upon the portion of the chapter that you just read.

In many regards, Jeremy is an average teenager: he would rather stay in bed than go to school in the morning, and his constant nodding off in first period is proof that he has trouble waking up. Academically, he has good days and not-so-good days when he seems distracted and disgruntled. Sometimes his work is good, and sometimes it is sloppy in both appearance and quality. Sometimes he's late or he simply fails to do his work, and his explanation for this is usually, "I forgot." Although these are characteristics of many teens, they are more constant and more difficult for Jeremy to manage because of his ADHD-inattentive.

This past Thursday, Jeremy got out of bed late, ran downstairs, skipped breakfast, and hurriedly filled his backpack with books and papers until it was overflowing. Once at school, he held up the first-period math teacher while he dug his homework out of his backpack and scribbled his name on it before handing it in. Seeing his incomplete science lab observation sheet from Tuesday, he quickly filled it in so it would be ready to attach to the report they would be finishing today. Between becoming distracted in class, jotting down his lab "observations," and nodding off once or twice, Jeremy didn't have a very successful first period, although he didn't realize just how much he had not fully attended to. Jeremy's attempts at multitasking did not work out very well.

He grabbed the wrong notebook from his locker for period two, but only because he couldn't find the right one. (According to Jeremy's logic, he could either transfer the notes later or just remember to use both notebooks when he studied for that class.) Second, third, and fourth periods all went well, except that he neglected to copy the assignment off the board in period three, and his notes from period four were disorganized and missing some vital content.

After lunch, he met with his study skills tutor for period five; she was teaching him how to sort out when to reduce while converting mixed fractions. He couldn't seem to remember the rule. He arrived at his next class, science lab, late, because he had forgotten the order of his schedule for the week, something he does periodically. When he got to science lab, he didn't follow the directions quite right, in part because he didn't understand everything and in part because he wasn't paying attention. Rather than ask for help, he simply completed the week's lab report in the same reckless fashion that he had filled in his observation sheet earlier. This created a problem for his lab partner, who couldn't keep up with what Jeremy was writing and the questions he was asking (for example, "I'm putting that after we added the catalyst . . . wait, what did you put the catalyst was in the first box?").

For homework, Jeremy will need three of the four sets of books and notebooks that he hastily shoved into his backpack before running for the bus. When and if he remembers to do his civics homework tonight, he will discover that he grabbed the wrong notebook. To top things off, he almost missed the bus. Once on the bus, he discovered that he had neglected to bring home one other notebook he needed. In this case, it was due to his poor attention in period three English class, because he didn't realize that students were assigned to make a timeline of events in the play they are reading. Also, he won't realize that he should have read the final act of the play and written a summary of it until Monday morning, the day it is due.

Once home, he surfed the Internet for about an hour while instant messaging friends and got in trouble for not peeling some potatoes, which he was instructed to do in the note to him on the kitchen counter. After dinner, Jeremy denied having much homework. This was half a lie (he wanted more time on the Internet) and half what he thought was the truth (he didn't know about several of his assignments). The missing assignments included remembering to study for the weekly math quiz, which his teacher had decided not to remind him about today in class.

CASE QUESTIONS

1. What types of organizational skills are expected of students at different levels of schooling?
2. What can students like Jeremy do to remind themselves of their schedules?
3. How can Jeremy both keep track of his assignments and have a plan for completing them on time?

fast-paced life of today's teen, which includes multiple demands on time and over-scheduling, may also be factors contributing to their daily fatigue (see Carskadon, Vieira, and Acebo 1993; Crowley, Acebo, and Carskadon 2007; also see Fuligni and Hardway 2006). In addition, being unable to detach themselves from technology at night can interrupt students' sleep cycles (Zimmerman 2008). It may not be only exposure to lit screens just before bedtime or taking a phone to bed that is the problem; day-time and evening television watching and electronic device use can also interfere with sleep cycles for children and adolescents (Nuutinen, Ray, and Roos 2013). Students with autism and intellectual disability are already prone to poor sleep that interferes with their school performance (Stores and Wiggs 2001). Getting insufficient amounts and quality of sleep is also pronounced for those who experience overt or subtle discrimination during the day, such as ethnic minorities (Huynh and Gillen O'Neel 2016).

Organization in the Early Years

Organization skills develop across the lifespan. As toddlers develop cognitively, they gain memory skills that help them to recall things like names, events, and places. They also begin to learn concepts such as order (for example, by learning about proportions, numbers, and sequences) and classification (for example, by naming and grouping like objects). These rudimentary concepts and skills are the cognitive foundations for learning how to be organized. Most toddlers also begin to learn about and participate in daily routines. For example, many come to expect that their mornings begin with being dressed and whisked out of the home to go to day care, and they more or less know what is expected of them at meal times.

Despite their preschool backgrounds, children entering elementary school typically still have a lot to learn about organization, schedules, and routines. To learn about them, particularly in the lower elementary grades, they practice lining up, sitting silently, putting crayons where they belong, and only using them at designated times. The teacher creates the organizational schemes and teaches the students how to conform to them. The students need prompting and practice to learn them. Learning to be organized takes time, including the shift to being responsible for organizing. Consequently, organizational skills are a central tenet of the elementary-school curriculum, as much so as basic literacy skills.

THINK BACK TO THE CASE   about Jeremy . . .

1. *What types of organizational skills are expected of students at different levels of schooling?*

As students progress through the elementary grades, they learn more advanced organizational skills. They are also increasingly expected to take responsibility. Whereas a first-grade teacher might tell students when to stop working on an assignment, for example, a third-grade teacher might announce, "Watch the clock; you have only three minutes left." Customarily, elementary teachers expect that students graduating to middle or junior high school should be ready to take the initiative at employing a variety of organizational skills to be successful students. They are right.

The Organizational Skills Teachers Expect of Students

In the United States, the elementary-school curriculum gradually changes from a focus on learning basic skills to a focus on applying skills to learn content. Typically, a major shift away from basic skills and toward acquiring content knowledge occurs in fourth grade (Reid and Lienemann 2006) (see the Common Core State Standards, for example [www.corestandards.org]). However, in this era of standards and account-ability, that shift may be occurring at lower grades.

By junior high or middle school, those who are unable to perform skills for learn-ing face major challenges in keeping up with the curriculum. In 1994, Scanlon, Schu-maker, and Deshler asked middle-school general education teachers to identify the priority academic areas in which their inclusive classroom students need to learn learning strategies. As shown in Table 11.1, the teachers named a variety of areas that almost all require organization. Although "organizing" is explicitly named in only one of the areas, "creating visual devices," "note-taking," and "creating relationships" also require students to organize information.

A more recent study (McMullen, Shippen, and Dangel 2007) again found that mid-dle-school teachers expect students with HI to possess organizational skills. Accord-ing to that study, the top skills that students with learning disabilities should have include turning in homework, starting working immediately, requesting help when needed, finishing work, copying homework assignments, bringing a pencil to class, and attending to the teacher—each of which requires some degree of organization.

In addition to acquiring and using organizational skills in school, students need to manage their time and energies to ensure a proper balance between their in-school and out-of-school activities. Students with HI, like Jeremy in Case 11.1, are often frus-trated by their constant disorganization, and they may express that frustration in var-ied ways, including being confused, angry, defensive, or exhausted. Obiakor (2007) states that students with disabilities from minority groups often lack motivation to improve their organizational skills because of the history of sociocultural problems they face. That is, they feel overwhelmed and sometimes even defeated. He suggests that it is particularly important to provide minority students with structured opportu-nities to succeed, along with affirming feedback.

Learned, Dowd, and Jenkins (2009) recommend an instructional conferencing approach to helping students with HI to activate organizational and study skills when they are having difficulty during a lesson. In instructional conferencing, you, as the special educator, should check in with the student as she or he works. When the stu-dent appears to be having difficulty, ask the student if she or he knows what aspect of

TABLE 11.1 Teachers' Strategic Requirements of Middle-School Social Studies Students

Strategy Requirements of Social Studies Curricula			
Study groups Social skills Organization Put items in order Have a plan—"This is how I'm going to … Probing questions Formulating opinions	Excellence in homework Completion of homework Read to understand Explain in own words Pick out most significant characteristics Differentiate irrelevant Give examples Application Transforming content Forming relationships	Memorize—then apply Writing versus memory Know the terminology Understand and use key vocabulary Note-taking Draw it! Graph it Visually depict information Timeline Sequencing events Think chronologically	Evaluating Identify problem and offer solution Think ahead of now Consider other possibilities Express themselves Vocalize freely Processing lots of information Gather information about issues Be able to retrieve information Use maps correctly—gather information

Source: D. Scanlon, J. B. Schumaker, and D. D. Deshler. Collaborative Dialogues Between Teachers and Researchers to Create Educational Interventions: A Case Study (*Journal of Education and Psychological Consultation*, 5(1994): 69–76).

BOX 11.1

Instructional Conferencing Practices and Strategies

Practice 1: Understand the curriculum and the classroom teacher's goals

Build a working relationship with the general education teacher.

Understand the curriculum.

Get up to speed on requisite pedagogy.

Practice 2: Motivate and build students' trust

Build relationships with students.

Be mindful of body language.

Make positive presuppositions.

Identify what students have done correctly first.

Practice 3: Help students organize and begin tasks

Teach "what to do when you don't know what to do" strategy.

Move quickly from general to specific questions.

Note students' receptivity to help.

Set mini-goals and check on progress.

Optimize the learning environment.

Practice 4: Strategic questioning and tutoring

Use a variety of questions to promote thinking.

Allow wait time.

Teach students to make comparisons to a model.

Think aloud.

Teach performance evaluation.

Source: Learned, J. E., Dowd, M. V., & Jenkins, J. R. (2009). Instructional conferencing: Helping students succeed on independent assignments in inclusive settings. *TEACHING Exceptional Children, 41*(5), 46–51.

---

the task is difficult and if she or he knows a way to resolve it (that is, a strategy to use). Help the student think of a skill or strategy she or he knows (such as the ones you will read about in this chapter). Then set "mini-goals" with the student—small steps of progress, such as completing the first portion of the assignment within a certain number of minutes. And, very importantly, check back with the student periodically to ensure she or he is on track for success; provide corrective feedback on strategy performance as needed. Learned et al. reported that instructional conferencing can be motivating for students with HI, helping them to use the skills they have for success and feeling positive about their performance. Note that you are conferencing with the student to determine an approach to overcome the learning challenge; although you may model effective practices, you are not just telling the student what to do.

Box 11.1 lists four "practices" and their accompanying "strategies" that you should use for effective instructional conferencing. Note that they address how you interact with both the general education teacher and your students with HI.

11-2 Student Schedules

Students' schedule use involves much more than just getting from class to class. It includes knowing due dates, prioritizing tasks, and updating schedules as events are added, completed, or changed. Proper use of a schedule tells the student not only the desired outcome (for example, where to go next, what is due today) but also how to achieve it. Students who truly comprehend their schedules know to bring books for period two along to period one to avoid making an unnecessary trip back to their locker. A student who has a 10-page paper due should have a plan for doing the research, writing sections of the draft, and proofreading that does not include pulling an all-nighter.

Teaching Students About Schedules

Students with organizational and memory difficulties cannot be told a schedule once and be expected to remember it. Whenever a new schedule is instituted, you and the students should go over it together. Begin by making sure the students can read and understand a printed copy of the schedule. Being able to read a schedule is a form of reading comprehension, and comprehending a schedule's graphic layout is not always straightforward; if students miscomprehend a schedule, they will not follow it accurately. Illegible handwriting, cryptic and incomplete information, noting it in the wrong place, and not automatically saving on electronic devices can all lead to problems. Just as is done with error analysis (see Chapter 9), you can identify which of these common problems routinely occur for individual students with HI so you can help them to monitor and overcome them.

A common characteristic of students with HI is that they require multiple learning trials to learn new information or skills (Fuchs and Fuchs 2015; Swanson and Deshler 2003). Therefore, even after you and a student declare a schedule "mastered," the student is still going to need reminders. Therefore, students should have their schedules readily accessible. Elementary-school students can tape it to a corner of their desk. They can also begin to learn to keep an **assignment notebook** (Anderson, Munk, Young, Connley, and Caldarella 2008). Older students can post their schedule inside a locker door.

However, think about your students' needs: are those the places where they need their schedule to be? Maybe instead of or in addition to those spots, the schedule should be pasted inside the cover of a binder or inside each and every subject notebook the student uses. Students who routinely use an electronic scheduler or app (including any online organizer) throughout the school day might maintain their schedule in those locations for quick consulting. You and the student should experiment with options to find out which ones the student will actually use and find beneficial.

Methods and Strategies Spotlight

Selecting the Right Type of Organizer

Having the right tools is essential to being organized. Students who bring a flashy notebook that has no pockets for collecting handouts could be in trouble if a teacher frequently supplies handouts. Likewise, in classes where teachers expect notes to be turned in for checking and then placed back in a notebook for future reference, a three-ring binder would work much better than spiral-bound notebooks.

Some teachers consider the choice of notebooks and other materials to be so important that they communicate to parents over the summer what types of materials students should buy for the coming school year (Scanlon 2003). Unless their choices are dictated, students will have to experiment to find out what kind of notebook works best for them. The following are some factors to consider when determining what type of notebook is appropriate for your students:

- The advantage of a three-ring binder is that materials may be easily added or removed; however, students must learn to place things where they belong for the binders to be effective.

- Individual subject notebooks might be more practical for some students. If each notebook is clearly labeled by subject area, the students can easily grab what they need.

- The best of both worlds might be individual subject notebooks that are three-hole punched so that they can be stored in a three-ring binder. Students will need to develop a routine of returning removed notebooks to the binder collection as soon as possible.

- For other students, a laptop computer or a tablet is the most efficient way to take and keep notes, as well as to keep assignments and related materials. Students will need to develop an organized system of folders and files so they can reliably store and locate needed content. (Using search functions may not always work if students cannot remember key words.)

Students with HI who use some type of planner have much higher success at following schedules than students who do not (Anderson et al. 2008; Rademacher, Schumaker, and Deshler 1996). Book-style calendars are helpful for schedule planning, and the calendar can be in the same book that the student uses to record assignments (students can experiment to determine whether weekly or monthly planners work better for them, as well as whether pocket-size or notebook-size planners are more functional). Using a planner or calendar, students can write down both the due dates and critical interim "production deadlines." For example, in Figure 11.1, Jeremy has drawn lines so that he has a visual reminder on a daily basis of what he should be working on. He has also noted dates by which he should complete certain tasks, so that he can keep on task.

THINK BACK TO THE CASE   about Jeremy . . .

2. What can students like Jeremy do to remind themselves of their schedules?

Some students carry a designated assignment notebook with them, and all assignments for the day are written in this one notebook. Even though a student may have a separate notebook for each class, the assignment notebook is a unique book in which only assignments are written. Each page can be marked with the day's date. The advantage of using a notebook for this purpose is that detailed information can be recorded into the book (for example, all of the details provided on the procedure to follow and what kind of content is expected). Also, each teacher can sign the assignment notebook at the end of class to ensure that the assignment has been recorded correctly. A parent could be asked to sign the notebook each evening, which is a way to inform parents that the student has homework and encourage them to monitor the student's work habits at home.

However, a student such as Jeremy is likely to lose his assignment notebook. So although a planner that fits in his backpack seems ideal, all of the moving around it will do poses a risk. If Jeremy can afford an electronic device such as a smartphone or tablet, he will be able to enter assignments as he receives them (assuming their use is allowed in school). Information entered into certain apps can then be synced with or retrieved on other electronic devices. Students who bring electronic devices to class will have a centralized system for organizing assignments and most of their materials as well. Some students may use apps or computer software to create schedules on the computer, and even rely on the computer to help them determine efficient pathways to meeting production deadlines. Students with HI as young as sixth grade have been found to be adept at using devices to integrate their assignment-recording and assignment-completion activities, as well as to independently find apps and programs that match their organization and learning needs (Bauer and Ulrich 2002) (Box 11.2).

continued

SUNDAY	MONDAY	TUESDAY	WEDNESDAY	THURSDAY	FRIDAY	SATURDAY
1	2 Work	3 Study Vocab. → Work	4 Eng.–Vocab. quiz Finish lab report → Work	5 Study → Math HW due Science lab due	6 Math quiz Civics HW due	7 Work
8 Work	9 Draft outline →	10 Study–Vocab. → Draft Outline ~~Begin essay~~ ^ →	11 Eng.–Vocab. quiz Begin essay ~~Finish essay~~ ^ →	12 Study → Finish & proof ~~Proof essay~~ ^ → Work	13 Math quiz Eng.–essay due	14 Work
15 Work	16 Work	17 Study Vocab. → Work	18 Eng.–Vocab. quiz Finish Lab Rep. → Work	19 Study → Span. Translate play Science lab due	20 Math quiz Span-proof translation →	21 Work
22 Work Span. rehearse lines →	23 Span. Rehearse lines →	24 Study Vocab. → Spanish play Work	25 Eng. Vocab. quiz	26 Work	27 Math–no quiz! Study civics →	28 Study civics →
29 Review civics →	30 Civics–exam Work	31 Study Vocab. → Work	Eng.–Vocab. quiz			

FIGURE 11.1
Jeremy's Production Deadline Calendar

BOX 11.2

Electronic Devices: Pros and Cons

The "digital revolution" is here to stay; indeed, you might argue it's over and digital won. Although economic divides remain in terms of who owns and keeps up to date with the array of electronic devices that have become a part of everyday life for many (Dolan 2016), most school students use electronics on a daily basis, at least outside of school if not also during the school day (Madden, Lenhart, Duggan, Cortesi, and Gasser 2013).

As with almost anything, there are advantages and disadvantages to the use of devices. Here are three considerations that have particular bearing on students with HI.

MULTITASKING

Having devices nearby entices us to interact with them at the same time we are doing something else. We can check to see who a message is from, we can do surreptitious "pocket texting," and we can look up something that is being discussed, for example. We even "switch" across functions while using electronics. Two generations ago students were warned not to watch television or listen to the radio while studying, but now our devices are with us almost constantly.

Young people protest that they can turn their attention momentarily, or multitask, with no problem, and it is true that multitasking may actually help to build some executive function skills (Baumgartner, Weeda, van der Heijen, and Huizinga 2014). But the reality is that children and adolescents who multitask do not concentrate as well, they end up taking longer to complete a task, and they achieve at lower levels than if they had attended to their task more carefully (Sparks 2012). Further, the effects appear to extend to functioning on everyday life tasks (Baumgartner et al. 2014).

Given their challenges with memory, organization, and strategic thinking, multitasking may be particularly detrimental to students with HI (Mackinlay, Charmin, and Karmiloff-Smith 2006), and they likely may not realize how it affects them.

DIGITAL NATIVE GENERATIONS

There is a perception that every new generation is even more intuitive about technology than the generations that came before it. Technology evolves quickly, and its applications to schooling and everyday life do seem to grow exponentially. But that still does not mean that students today somehow automatically "get" how technology fits the learning process, and it certainly does not mean they know how to use it all. Make sure your students have not only the access to the technologies that you assume they do, but also the skills to use them appropriately. This requires reviewing procedures for using technology and providing explicit instruction just as you would for any other skill. Of course, this can also mean setting rules for using technology, such as blocking certain programs or sites and avoiding multitasking.

POLICIES AND APPROPRIATENESS

Given how tempting it can be to use technology, and the fact that many students consider it an integral part of their daily functioning, teachers may need to temper their impulse to use technology. Many schools have policies about what devices can be used and when. This has to do not only with equality of opportunity (Dolan 2016) but also with safety and appropriateness. Devices can be hacked, personal information can be inadvertently exposed or shared, and harassment and exposure to inappropriate material can happen easily via electronic media. Also, portable devices are easily misplaced or stolen. Almost all schools have policies about technology use in school and for assignments outside of school. It is important that teachers are familiar with those policies before planning to incorporate technology into instruction.

Although you might think these details of organization are minor, they are the intricacies that prevent many students from being organized. In addition to having the right tools of organization, students must know how to use them properly. Teaching students with HI to use skills and tools for organization is typically most effective when they are taught explicitly (Anderson et al. 2008), just as is the case when teaching them academic content and skills.

Managing Schedules

Students rarely get to set their own schedules for due dates. Consequently, their good intentions to study hard for tomorrow's vocabulary quiz might be thwarted by an unexpected homework assignment in another class and the sudden realization that a project has to be completed for yet another class. Therefore, even students who plan production schedules need to be able to manage their schedules. Managing a schedule means that they need to be able to set a schedule; record, read, and comprehend it; coordinate production deadlines; and revise their plans as new activities are added and deadlines are missed.

THINK BACK TO THE CASE   *about Jeremy...*

3. *How can Jeremy both keep track of his assignments and have a plan for completing them on time?*

Using a planner notebook that includes a week-at-a-glance or month-at-a-glance calendar is ideal. Jeremy should begin by writing down the due date. He should next carefully consider the intermediate tasks that need to be accomplished to complete the assignment (Hughes et al. 2002). Does it involve library or Internet research? Does a draft have to be handed in? After he has determined what must be done to accomplish the task, he should carefully think about how long it will take to do each intermediate task and the logical order in which to do them. All of this can then be marked on a production timeline right in the planner or calendar.

On Jeremy's production timeline in Figure 11.1, he did not get his draft essay outline done on time because he lost track of time while keeping up on social media on Monday, so he moved his intermediate tasks forward a day. He still has a plan to complete the assignment on time, but he is now going to have to work longer and harder on the days remaining to make it all work.

The management plan has to suit the needs of the planner, not just impose deadlines. Jeremy enjoys his friends and tries to socialize with them whenever he can. He also has an after-school job at a fast-food restaurant, and his schedule changes from week to week. Thus, if Jeremy is going to be successful at managing his school schedule, he is going to have to plan for his out-of-school life too. If he keeps one calendar for his school assignments, he would be wise to keep his social and job schedule on that same calendar. This way he will be sure to work around his social schedule as much as possible.

As his teacher, you will need to teach Jeremy how to plan and modify his schedule. Start by making a list with Jeremy of every assignment that he knows he has coming up. Organize that list by due dates. Then for each assignment, one at a time, discuss what production deadlines it will entail. A disorganized student like Jeremy is likely to find this to be a novel question; you will have to guide him to think about what goes into writing an essay or preparing for a quiz. Then show Jeremy how to plot his production deadlines so that he will complete the assignment on time. Be sure to do this in pencil, because you will next plot Jeremy's second assignment, then third, and so on. In this process, he will see that he has to adjust production deadlines based on other assignments. With the experience of matching his draft production schedule to reality, he will be able to realize that he needs to plan well in advance. There are many calendar functions on electronic devices that will allow Jeremy to maintain a production calendar electronically.

11-3   Completing Assignments

In an average school day, students are given a variety of assignments. They can include quick tasks, practice activities, small-group work, culminations of lessons, major projects, and homework. In a flipped classroom (Schmidt and Ralph 2016) it is important for students to complete an assignment before coming to the class where it will be studied. Assignments are an important component of the learning process. They are also major factors in determining grades, particularly at the secondary levels (Cooper, Robinson, and Patall 2006; Munk and Bursuck 2001; Van Voorhis 2011).

How well a student does on an assignment is one indicator of how well she or he has mastered the content of a lesson. Completing assignments to accurately reflect what a student knows can be challenging for students with HI. When a student is challenged in completing an assignment, it can create an unclear impression of how well she or he has learned the material. Challenges for students with HI can occur in every stage of the assignment process, from receiving the assignment to remembering to turn it in, even if they have completed it and brought it to class on time (Bryan, Burstein, and Bryan 2001).

When a student has difficulty completing an assignment, often both the teacher and the student have contributed to the problem. How you give an assignment, including how you explain it, may be the problem on your side. How the student receives the assignment and how she or he approaches doing it are the problems on the student's side.

| CASE 11.2 | Better Ways of Teaching, So Students Can Demonstrate Their Learning |

Case Introduction

Now that you have worked through the first case in this chapter, you should feel comfortable addressing issues in a second case. You are going to read about how a special educator and her inclusive classroom co-teacher improved their students' performances on assignments, including homework and tests. They taught the students specific skills, but they also adopted some new practices for themselves to improve their students' performance.

Berta Strauss is a middle-school special education teacher who co-teaches a few periods a day. She is pleased with the learning her students are doing in their general education classrooms. After being frustrated last year by the fact that her students were not demonstrating their learning on typical classroom assignments and tests in health class, she and her co-teacher set a "self-improvement" goal over the summer of learning how to get their students to perform better on those tasks. They learned that, in addition to teaching the students specific skills, they would have to change some of their own practices as well.

Things are going much better this year for both the special education and general education students. To begin with, the two teachers have been much more thoughtful about the assignments they give their students. In the past, they sometimes used assignments that came with commercially prepared curriculum materials, even though they weren't teaching from those materials; other times, they made up assignments at the last minute. They still rely on prepared assignments, and occasionally come up with an assignment in haste, but they have improved at relating the assignments to the lessons they teach and at considering their students' potential to complete the assignments successfully.

One of the things they realized over the summer was that they were treating assignments like tests, instead of extensions of the lesson. In fact, in the past, they sometimes planned assignments by saying, "Let's see if they can . . ." Now they think critically about why they want to give assignments.

The two teachers also realized that the ways they gave assignments in the past were often inadequate. Often, assignments were hurriedly shouted out as the students began to pack up in anticipation of the bell ringing. Berta barely had time to ask her special education students if they wrote the assignment down and what they needed to do. Because time was tight, she had to take their word for it.

The students with HI had worse records than their classmates at both completing assignments and doing quality work; however, the general education middle schoolers were not

continued

consistently strong at these skills either. To address this class-wide problem, Berta took responsibility for teaching the whole class to record assignments and check what they had written down for accuracy and comprehension before leaving class. This year, completion rates and quality have improved greatly.

Berta has noted that although her special education students are better at the skills of receiving and completing homework, they still have difficulties with applying content that she is sure they comprehended in class. She is beginning to examine the quality of notes they take during class. She has come to realize that they have trouble discerning what information to write down; consequently, they try to write so much that they can't get it all in their notes and keep up with the class. She is wondering if she and her co-teacher could

more clearly cue them as to what to record, without actually saying, "Now write . . ."

CASE QUESTIONS

1. How can teachers, and their students, be sure that students are clear on their assignments?
2. Why might students with disabilities who are clear on an assignment nonetheless have difficulty completing it successfully?
3. Although all middle-school students have to learn how to take notes, what particular difficulties will Berta likely observe for students with HI?

How to Assign

Logically, how you present an assignment has a lot to do with how well your students know what is expected of them, and with how they respond. Making assignments clear and meaningful can enhance the rates at which students with disabilities attempt, complete, and succeed at them.

You may be surprised by how often your students assume the reason for getting an assignment is either that you are trying to keep them busy or that it is a de facto test. Even when they realize that an assignment is a form of practice or an extension of a lesson, they may have no appreciation for what they are supposed to learn from it (Anderson et al. 2008; Rademacher, Schumaker, and Deshler 1996). In Chapter 10, we addressed the importance of using advance organizers to give students an idea of what is expected of them in a lesson and why. The same principle applies here: when students know why they are asked to do an assignment and what is expected of them, they find doing a good job easier.

Giving Assignments. Rademacher, Schumaker, and Deshler (1996) reviewed the professional literature on giving assignments to identify effective practices. They then involved more than 270 middle-school students with and without HI and 22 of their general education teachers in identifying the practices they believed to be effective. Next, they tested the effectiveness of those practices on students attempting, completing, and succeeding on assignments. They also researched how satisfied the students and teachers were. The subset of students and their teachers who participated in that follow-up research identified nine assignment-giving behaviors as important. Interestingly, all three groups (students with and without HI, and their teachers) concurred that all nine are important, with mostly minor variations in their priority rankings. Table 11.2 compares the relative rankings by the three groups.

Based on their research, Rademacher et al. (1996) developed a routine that teachers may follow to be sure they are effective in giving assignments. Teachers can use the mnemonic ASSIGN to remember the routine. Each step cues an important quality assignment-giving activity. According to these researchers (p. 172), to give an assignment effectively, you should do the following:

Activate the assignment-completion process by completing the lesson and alerting students to use their REACT steps [provided later in this chapter].

TABLE 11.2 Student and Teacher Ranking of Assignment-Giving Behaviors

Explanation Factors	Teachers			Students with Learning Disabilities			Students Without Learning Disabilities		
	M	SD	GR	M	SD	GR	M	SD	GR
Give Clear Directions	6.58	.79	1	6.41	1.01	1	6.31	1.15	1
State Purpose/Completion Benefits	6.32	.84	2	5.73	1.29	7*	5.61	1.08	6
Provide Models/Examples	6.34	.84	3	5.85	1.28	5	5.57	1.38	5
Consider Time Factors	6.51	.89	4	6.18	1.29	3	6.11	1.27	3
State Quality Work Criteria	6.04	1.02	5	5.78	1.49	9	5.85	1.20	9
Provide Social Interaction Direction	5.78	1.15	6	5.90	1.20	*	5.40	1.29	8
Provide Student Choice	5.73	1.18	7	6.11	1.15	2	6.18	.93	2
Encourage Creative Expression	5.75	1.04	8	5.70	1.38	6	5.83	1.18	7
Name Available Resources	5.93	1.02	9	5.89	1.10	4	5.68	1.48	4

Note:
M = mean rating, SD = standard deviation; GR = group rank according to respondent votes.
*These explanation factors were tied with regard to group ranking.

Source: J. A. Rademacher, J. B. Schumaker, and D. D. Deshler. Development and Validation of a Classroom Assignment Routine for Inclusive Settings (Learning Disability Quarterly 19(1996): 163–178).

State clear directions that were created [during planning].
Stop (that is, pause 15 to 30 seconds) for students to use their REACT steps.
Investigate student understanding by asking students specific questions about the assignment information.
Guarantee work time in class for beginning the assignment, and offer help as needed.
Note the due date, expectations for students to do quality work, and assistance for anyone who needs it outside of class.

Inclusive middle-school students and teachers validated the effectiveness of these steps as the teachers used the routine in their classrooms.

In the following section, we describe a quality assignment in terms of how the teacher produces it. First, however, we consider the product of assignment giving, which is students receiving the assignment.

Students Receiving Assignments. When you give an assignment, you should have clear ideas of how you expect the students to complete it as well as of the content and appearance of their finished product. Your students' conceptions of the finished product can easily differ from what you think it should be. Also, consider what a good time frame would be for completing the assignment and the resources that students should use (or not use).

Students need to learn how to receive an assignment, as well as how to plan to and actually complete it. This is as important a school skill as learning to follow schedules.

Rademacher et al. (1996, p. 172) validated the five REACT steps that students should follow to ensure they receive and perform assignments correctly:

Record the assignment as the teacher gives verbal directions.
Examine the requirements and choices offered by the teacher.
Ask questions to better understand the directions.

Create a written goal for improving or matching performance on a similar assignment that may have been completed in the past.

Target a time to begin, finish, and evaluate the assignment for quality before turning it in to the teacher.

Students with HI who learn and use assignment-completion routines show improved performance and satisfaction with their assignment completion (Hughes, Ruhl, Schumaker, and Deshler 2002). Also, students with HI have been found more likely to use assignment-completion routines when the routines are taught and supported in the whole class instead of with them individually (Ness, Sohlberg, and Albin 2011).

THINK BACK TO THE CASE about Berta and her co-teacher . . .

> *1. How can teachers, and their students, be sure that students are clear on their assignments?*
>
> It will help you to consider what a student must go through to be a successful assignment recipient. You can (a) make sure your assignment-giving strategy is responsive to the process students should follow and (b) troubleshoot when students struggle to master the process. As the REACT steps indicate, the first thing students should do when receiving an assignment is to be sure to record it, and then immediately check to make sure they have fully and accurately recorded and understood what they should do.

The first REACT step indicates that assignments should be given orally. You may increase the clarity of your presentation if you also write the assignment on the board. This way, students will have plenty of time to copy it down. You can also point to parts of the assignment as you discuss them, even underlining parts for emphasis or numbering the steps or components. Also, you can hand out an assignment with the directions printed on it. This can be a way to ensure that students who have difficulty recording information get the correct assignment in the first place. If you have a classroom webpage the instructions can be posted there as well for students who do not keep track of their materials, such as Jeremy from Case 11.1.

Still, Rademacher et al. (1996) are correct: you should provide oral instructions even if you also provide a print or electronic version. By speaking the directions you can offer emphasis and state the same point in multiple phrasings, which may help.

Questioning your students to make sure they understand the assignment (including its purpose) is important. Your students should also learn to question themselves. When you give an assignment, require your students to record it, and then require them to check the assignment to make sure they understand it (this is similar to the lecture pause described in Chapter 10). Students can check their assignment notes by doing the following:

1. Explaining the assignment to a partner,
2. Checking a partner's assignment notebook,
3. Listing the steps they must follow to complete the task,
4. Stating what they are supposed to get out of the assignment, and
5. Explaining why the particular assignment should contribute to #4.

The challenges students with HI have with organization, using effective study skills, and motivation can all impede successful homework completion (Bryan, Burstein, and Bryan 2001; also see Xu 2009). Teaching skills for homework completion and being thoughtful about how homework assignments are given and supported can enable students with HI to succeed.

The Nature of Effective Assignments. Rademacher et al. (1996, pp. 167–168) also asked their middle-school students and teachers to identify the characteristics of "quality assignments." Twelve characteristics were identified:

1. **Clear, well-organized directions** so that students will know how to do the work,
2. **An understood purpose** so that students will understand how completing the work will benefit their learning,
3. **A set of product evaluation criteria** so that students will know how their finished work will be judged,
4. An **optimal challenge** so that students will not become bored or frustrated,
5. **Personal relevance factors** so that students can relate assignment completion to the social, learning, behavioral, and cultural characteristics of their lives,
6. **Assignment completion feedback** so that students know what they did correctly and what they need to do to improve their work,
7. **A variety of formats** so that assignments do not always seem "the same."
8. **Resource lists** available for doing the work,
9. **Creative expression opportunities** so that students can use their imagination in some ways,
10. **Interpersonal or social actions** so that students can work with others,
11. **Completion time considerations**, such as giving students time to work in class, and
12. **Student choices** in terms of the assignment itself and how it is to be completed.

Interestingly, the students with and without disabilities did not differ meaningfully from each other in terms of how they ranked the 12 they considered most important, but they did differ from their teachers. Teachers ranked "student choices" lowest, but students ranked it highest. However, all three of the groups ranked "clear, well-organized directions" among the very highest (first or second). Table 11.3 shows the groups' rankings.

TABLE 11.3 Characteristics of Effective Assignments

Assignment Characteristics	Teachers			Students with Learning Disabilities			Students Without Learning Disabilities		
	M	SD	GR	M	SD	GR	M	SD	GR
Clear, Well-Organized Directions	6.69	0.55	1	6.65	0.72	1	6.66	0.70	2
Understood Purpose	6.11	0.87	2	6.34	0.99	9	5.93	1.32	8
Product Evaluation Criteria	6.21	0.98	3	5.80	1.48	11	5.81	1.27	10*
Optimal Challenge	5.94	0.79	4*	5.66	1.64	8	6.04	1.13	6
Personal Relevance Factors	5.85	0.94	4*	4.87	1.59	10	4.79	1.49	12
Assignment Completion Feedback	6.30	0.93	6*	6.10	1.12	12	6.20	1.03	10*
Format Variety	5.59	1.37	6*	5.73	1.37	7	5.77	1.19	7
Available Resource Lists	5.90	1.04	8	5.97	1.37	5	6.01	1.19	9
Creative Expression Opportunities	5.59	1.20	9	5.68	1.16	4	5.83	1.08	4*
Interpersonal/Social Interactions	5.65	1.17	10	5.47	1.37	3	5.55	1.31	3
Completion Time Considerations	5.62	1.06	11	6.17	1.33	6	6.50	0.85	4*
Student Choices	4.90	1.39	12	6.17	1.01	2	6.17	1.10	1

Note:
M = mean rating, SD = standard deviation; GR = group rank according to respondent votes.
*These characteristics were tied with regard to group ranking.

Source: J. A. Rademacher, J. B. Schumaker, and D. D. Deshler. Development and Validation of a Classroom Assignment Routine for Inclusive Settings (*Learning Disability Quarterly* 19(1996): 163–178).

More recently, Vatterott (2010) identified five characteristics of effective homework for general education students that echo the list compiled by Rademacher et al.: purpose, efficiency, ownership, competence, and aesthetic appeal.

Homework: A Particular Type of Assignment

While some studies have found students have more homework than ever before, including students with HI (Jakulski and Mastropieri 2004; Shumow 2011) and younger students (Hofferth and Sandberg 2000), other studies claim the rates of homework have been stable for recent decades and that there is only a slight increase in the amount of time per night as students enter higher grade levels (for instance, Center for Public Education 2003; National Education Association 2008). Regardless of how much is actually assigned, homework is an important part of academic learning. In fact, it is estimated to account for approximately 20 percent of students' academic work.

More than 50 percent of students with HI report that they have difficulty with homework and spend more time on it than their general education peers (Cooper 2007; Vatterott 2003). As might be expected, their challenges with homework (and other types of assignment) are often related to memory challenges and executive functioning, or their ability to think and act strategically (Biederman et al. 2004), as well as the fact that they lack proficiency in the necessary skills.

Homework can be a useful teaching and learning activity when it is used wisely. When students do homework, they can develop skills and apply information that they have been learning; depending on the nature of the homework assignment, they may discover new things. Homework is a way for students to learn responsibility for meeting expectations. It requires personal accountability, as students must have some degree of self-discipline to take it home and complete it, and it helps students learn that learning is not merely something they do during school hours (Jakulski and Mastropieri 2004; Ramdass and Zimmerman 2011).

The relationship between homework completion and achievement is strongest at the junior/middle-school and high-school levels (Cooper, Robinson, and Patall 2006). However, as early as elementary school, students who receive homework assignments begin to develop beneficial work habits (Cooper 2007). In fact, high-school dropouts have reported that among the factors that led to their dropping out was teachers not assigning or expecting them to complete homework (Bridgeland, Diluleo, and Morison 2006).

Homework and Students with HI. When used properly, homework can be a way to equalize learning opportunities among those with and without disabilities, and to extend the amount of time a student with a disability devotes to studying a particular skill or concept. However, students with disabilities typically do not manage the homework process well when it involves skills affected by their disabilities (Hughes et al. 2002; Kerr and Nelson 2002). Students from low-income families may be less able to complete homework successfully because they may have time-consuming responsibilities or irregular schedules at home, there may be less parental supervision, and they may not have the work space and resources to complete homework (Bennet and Kalish 2006; Kralovec and Buell 2000).

All of these factors can be mitigated by planning that is responsive to the student's individual needs (see Bennett-Conroy [2012] for several suggestions). The outcome can be positive learning benefits for a range of learners (Epstein and Van Vorhiss 2001; Redding 2000).

THINK BACK TO THE CASE   **about Berta and her co-teacher . . .**

2. *Why might students with disabilities who are clear on an assignment nonetheless have difficulty completing it successfully?*

The problems that students with learning disabilities or emotional and behavioral disorders have with homework range from correctly receiving the assignment all the way to remembering to turn in completed work. Students with learning disabilities have difficulties with homework success because they are likely not to bring home the appropriate materials. Even when they do take the appropriate materials home, some of the problems they exhibit in school are the same ones that inhibit homework performance. Trouble with reading, concentration, or remembering the steps to a calculation all go home with the student. Other problems due to a disability that may be managed during the school day can be a greater problem at home. For example, students who have a highly structured school routine due to distractibility may not have the same kinds of structure and monitoring available at home. They may be using social media while attempting to concentrate on homework. Also, students may not have needed supports at home. Some students come from households where English is not commonly spoken. Some parents may not have the academic skills necessary to help their child with homework, or at least not be confident that they do; this is more likely to be the case in low-income households (Kohn 2006). Even parents who try to participate in their child's homework may not know the routines to help their child with difficult readings or to remember how to organize an essay answer, for example.

Different Purposes for Homework. The different types of homework assignments relate to the kind of learning experience homework is intended to be. See Aloia (2001) for information on how general and special education teachers view homework. The following are the major types of homework and their purposes.

Homework can be a form of *preparation*. That is, if your students need some background information or experience before you launch a new lesson, you might be able to have them acquire it via homework. You might have them review or look at new information that is easily comprehended and that will be checked at the beginning of the new lesson. By completing homework for preparation, they should be ready to begin the lesson that will follow. Because students with HI may have difficulty with homework, you should be ready to address their learning needs, which may show up as failing to complete the assignment or having significant trouble with it.

Homework as preparation could also be a form of a *grabber* (review Chapter 10; Lenz, Marrs, Schumaker, and Deshler 2005). You can grab students' attention at the start of a lesson with some stunt or challenge that provokes them to start thinking about the topic. To grab their interests via homework, you might give an assignment that previews a topic you will begin studying the next day (for example, you can ask students to come prepared with first impressions from the homework or questions to share), or you might give some exciting or fun assignment, such as a puzzle to solve that motivates them.

Homework can be *practice*. This type of homework extends the amount of time available to a teacher and students for practice. Being taught how to parse a sentence, multiply fractions, or evaluate the moral underpinnings of a government policy is not going to be very effective if students cannot try out their skills. Homework can provide an opportunity to apply (practice) what was just studied. Indeed, because homework is removed from the teaching episode, it is a chance for students to recall skills and content instead of only performing them immediately after they are introduced in class. As long as your students have had enough instruction to practice with some degree of accuracy and success, homework can be a good way to ensure they get the practice they need. (Recall the G step of ASSIGN: *Guarantee work time in class for beginning the assignment.*)

Homework is also a way to *extend a lesson.* When students learn the basics of a new skill or information, they can be sent home with the task of figuring out the rest of it. Of course, this use of homework will require that you prepare them to be able to do that, and that you check on the results, with the intention of correcting mistakes. Therefore, homework that extends a lesson may have an element of practice, but this type of homework also gives students the opportunity to learn more original content. That makes it different from only practicing what they have begun to learn. Importantly, when you assign homework as an extension of a lesson, you should have confidence that your students are prepared to be successful (Vatterott 2010).

Slightly different from extending a lesson is homework for *completing a lesson.* The school day rarely goes exactly as planned. For any number of reasons, lessons do not always end before the bell rings. If you were able to get far enough into the lesson that students should know how to complete it with success, the students can finish activities at home. You can then start your next lesson with a homework check and then proceed exactly as you had planned.

Homework is also a way to *connect parents to what is going on during the school day.* Parents can be asked to check that students bring home and complete their assignments, if that is a problem for a student. Also, parents can be asked to help with their child's work. This is a great way to show parents what you are teaching and for them to have direct insights into their child's learning strengths and weaknesses. It is also a great way for students to receive immediate feedback as they practice. In addition, you can spend less time in parent–teacher conferences just bringing parents up to speed on what their child is studying. Be aware, however, that parents and families in some cultural traditions consider it their role to stay out of what the teacher and their child are studying (Salas et al. 2005).

Just about the worst form of homework is that assigned so students can *learn original information* on their own. Of course we value students becoming independent learners, and we should never assume they are never up to the task, but some direction and checking are in order when something new is being learned. As much as students may need to know how to learn on their own, in school, teachers tell, demonstrate, describe, model, monitor, provide feedback, reinforce, and regulate complexity, among many other teaching activities. We do these things because students need that guidance to learn effectively. Teaching research and problem-solving skills and encouraging students to follow their interests to learn more about topics that motivate them are more productive ways to teach independent learning.

Effective Homework for All Students. In light of the unique challenges homework can present for students with HI, success may depend on the type of homework assigned. The most effective form may be practice homework. Cooper and Nye (1994) found that students with disabilities were more successful with homework when it was intended to reinforce learning that had been established in the classroom. Thus, extension and completion homework could also be successful for students with HI, but most likely in cases where the basic knowledge and skills required have been well learned during the in-school portion of the lesson. According to Cooper and Nye, two other important factors for homework success are that the assignment (a) is brief, so that tedium and frustration are less likely to set in, and (b) focuses on only one or a few topics and is supported by parents who communicate effectively that homework is valued (that is, they show it is important but do not turn it into a punishment) and who can provide some supervision that includes academic help and feedback.

Homework should also be relevant to students with disabilities. If they understand why they are given a particular assignment, they will be more likely to value attempting it and the academic expectation is more likely to make sense to them. Effectiveness in giving homework assignments is not much different from giving assignments effectively in the classroom. Review the methods for providing accommodations in Chapter 10, and remember that it is important to use accommodations for homework assignments too.

Learning from Your Students' Homework. Bryan and Burstein (2004) suggest that you treat homework performance as a form of data (also see Rademacher et al. 1996). How homework is done, how well it is done, and the consequences of homework can all be tracked; this data can inform you on just how effective your homework-giving practices are, in addition to your students' homework-completion practices. Start by assessing how well your estimates of time and effort required for homework match your students' reality. Write down how long you expect it will take your students to complete a particular assignment, and then ask them to write on a corner of the page how long it actually took. Your findings could tell you whether your estimates are on or off, as well as whether individual students are uniquely over- or under-challenged by certain assignments. Ask students to rate how easy or difficult an assignment is; you can give them a rating scale so that they all answer in the same format. That information can be very useful in determining if the pace and requirements that are appropriate for the majority of general education students in the class are consistent with what is appropriate for individual students with HI.

Bryan and Burstein also suggest having students graph their own homework performance. Figure 11.2 shows how students can graph their rates of turning in assignments on time, turning them in but late, and not completing them. You can use the graph to discuss their homework skills and habits with them, to communicate to parents about homework performance, or as the basis for incentives to improve performance (Trammel, Schloss, and Alper 1994).

Doing the Homework. Because students can have difficulty with getting homework done, the skill of doing homework should be taught and valued. To help make it meaningful, you can set homework contracts with your students. Students can agree that they will meet some kind of performance standard for homework assignments, based on the number of assignments completed over time or timeliness. Some teachers allow students to cash in points for a "homework-free night." The contracted standards for amount, timeliness, or quality should reflect homework success skills that

▶ **FIGURE 11.2**

Jeremy's Math Homework Completion Graph

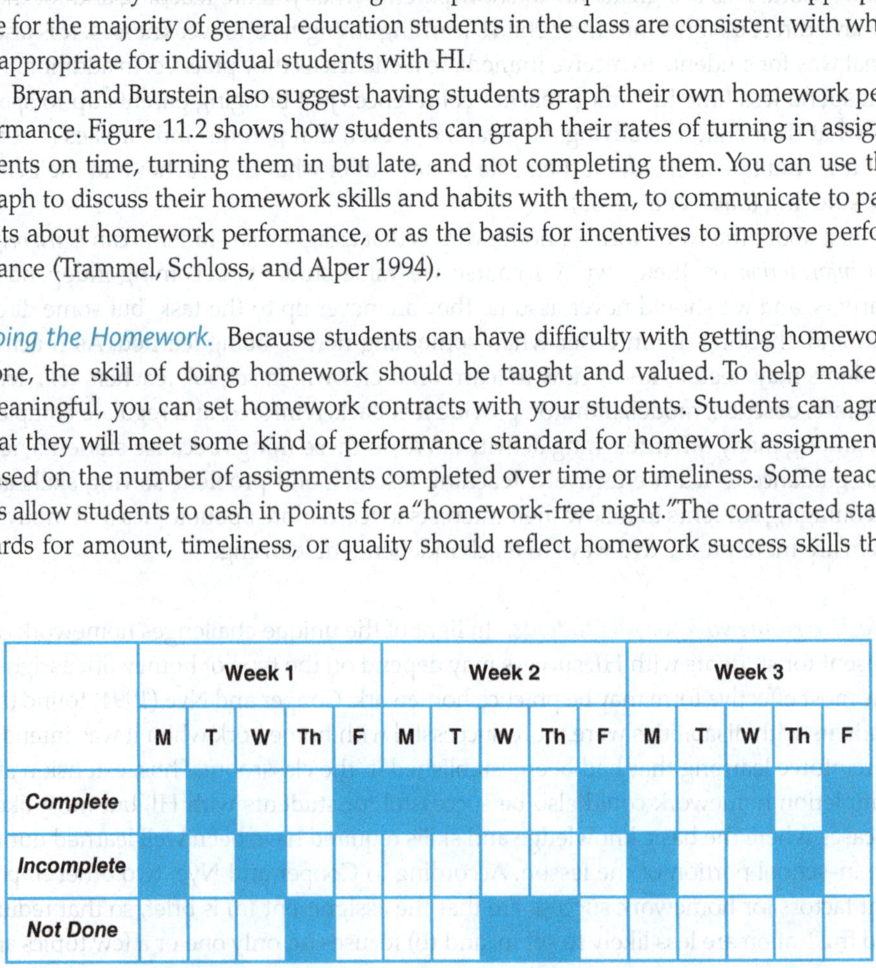

	Week 1					Week 2					Week 3				
	M	T	W	Th	F	M	T	W	Th	F	M	T	W	Th	F
Complete		■		■		■	■		■				■	■	■
Incomplete	■		■							■	■	■			
Not Done					■			■							

are important to build. Over time the standards for satisfying contracts can be gradually increased. Eventually, students need to learn to manage their own homework processes (Hughes et al. 2002). Using contracts is a way to cultivate independence skills.

Once you get students to bring assignments home and know what they are supposed to do, you still have to get your students to do them. One form of help is to have parents sign homework assignment books (or initial individual assignments) as proof that they saw the assignment; even better is if parents sign the assignment after their child explains the homework to them. Keep in mind that homework is not just about having the discipline to sit down and do the work, but also about the students' ability to complete the assignment correctly.

Parents may not always be able to help with assignments. As an effective alternative, establish **homework buddies**. These are students who are assigned to be available to each other at homework time. If they live in the same community or can connect by phone or on the Internet, they can be ready resources if one of them has a question. Just as is the case with cooperative learning groups (see Chapter 2), these students must be able to work well together. Buddies need to establish a common time during which they can be contacted if help is needed.

O'Melia and Rosenberg (1994) have suggested that students form **cooperative homework teams**. These teams should be formed following some of the same principles as used to create homework buddies; members of the team should know how to help each other when they have questions about an assignment. Each buddy has to understand how to articulate a need for help. Thus, team members need to be taught the skills of peer tutoring to be effective (see Chapter 2). In the cooperative homework teams model, team members begin by turning in their work to the team's "checker." That individual is responsible for grading the work based on a scoring guide that the teacher provides. Specific errors should be marked (as opposed to simply marking the item as incorrect). Team members can then help each other to correct their errors; that process that might take up to 10 minutes of class time. (The checker can be responsible for checking and marking the corrected work, but with different-colored ink, which would be helpful for a busy teacher.) Next, the assignments are turned in to the teacher, who can see how well students performed both before and after the team members assisted one another. The students with HI who participated in cooperative homework teams in O'Melia and Rosenberg's (1994) study improved in both the amount of homework completed and the overall accuracy of their work.

11-4 Note-Taking

There is an expectation that students with HI in the general education classroom will be able to access, learn, and master information from the general education curriculum. As we noted in Chapter 10, even in elementary classrooms short "lectures" are commonly used. To succeed, students must be able to attend to the lecture, use selective listening skills, decide which lecture points are worthy of recording, and record those points using an efficient note-taking technique whereby they can simultaneously record notes and listen to the lecture. Unfortunately for students with HI (particularly students with learning disabilities or autism), executive function difficulties often hinder their use of efficient strategies during complex academic tasks like note-taking (Rosen, Boyle, Cariss, and Forchelli 2014). Students with HI have reported that the most difficult aspects of note-taking are writing fast enough, studying notes, deciding what is important to record, making sense out of their notes after the lecture, and understanding what the teacher is talking about during the lecture (Boyle, Forchelli, and Cariss 2015).

The challenge of coordinating careful listening with thinking and writing even occurs in lower-grade classrooms when teachers are simultaneously giving instructions on how to take notes and what to write. In Putnam, Deshler, and Schumaker's (1993, p. 340) investigation of general education classroom demands, teachers reported that "their lectures were the major source of information [upon] which test questions were based"; they also noted that almost half of a student's grade is derived from performance on tests in secondary content classes. Even when classrooms are not dominated by lecture formats, students are still expected to take notes during class-wide discussions, group work, and in-class independent work. In some of these contexts, teachers use less cueing to guide the note-taking process.

THINK BACK TO THE CASE　about Berta and her co-teacher . . .

3. *Although all middle-school students have to learn how to take notes, what particular difficulties will Berta likely observe for students with HI?*

Unfortunately, students with HI exhibit a number of listening and attending deficits that interfere with their ability to learn information from lectures (for example, see Ward-Lonergan, Liles, and Anderson 1998) and other instructional activities. They may pay attention to irrelevant parts of tasks rather than focusing on the most important parts, for example. They may also have information-processing problems that interfere with their ability to receive information and/or "translate" it into notes (Ward-Lonergan, Liles, and Anderson 1998).

Researchers have consistently documented written language deficits in students with learning disabilities, from basic writing skills such as spelling, punctuation, and legible writing (Hughes and Smith 1990) to more complex skills such as detecting writing errors and planning for writing (Ellis and Colvert 1996; Englert et al. 2007; Graham and Harris 1993). Not only do spelling and handwriting deficits interfere with the act of note-taking, but difficulties with these rudimentary skills also create later problems when students review and study their incomplete and illegible notes for tests. Their incomplete notes can be difficult to decipher and comprehend.

In addition to written language deficits, students with learning disabilities exhibit deficits in specific note-taking skills. Suritsky (1992) observed that these students often take notes in a verbatim fashion, despite the fact that this word-by-word method of recording notes is the least effective for learning content information. Students reported that they had difficulty deciding what information was the most important to record, as well as difficulty maintaining attention to the lecturer. Hughes and Suritsky (1994) confirmed students' self-reports; for example, when compared to their nondisabled peers, students with learning disabilities produced fewer units of recorded information (that is, more incomplete notes), even when given explicit instructor cues for important information to record. Missing cued information and recording incomplete notes have immediate repercussions not only with understanding lecture information, but also with later recalling information for tests.

Appropriate Notes

The skill of taking notes begins with being prepared to take notes, and with attending and knowing what information to include or exclude from notes. Then, notes must be organized and transcribed in a format that will prove useful to the student. Specific skills of note-taking include deciding what is important to note; efficiently telegraphing the information while continuing to monitor the lecture, discussion, or other instructional activity; organizing the content of the notes; reviewing and modifying them; and studying them.

Teaching Note-Taking Skills

Note-taking activities occur before, during, and after a lesson, and different note-taking strategies emphasize these different phases.

Strategic note-taking (Boyle 1996; Boyle and Weishaar 2001) was developed based on the premise that students with learning problems are passive learners while taking notes. Therefore, teachers can give students written "cues" on note-taking paper to prompt them to use metacognitive skills during lectures (that is, to organize information and to combine new with prior knowledge), thereby increasing active engagement (Fig. 11.3).

In the first portion of strategic note-taking, before the lecture (or other activity) begins, students quickly identify the lecture topic and relate the topic to their own prior knowledge. By identifying a relationship to prior knowledge, the students make the information more meaningful (see the discussion of advance organizers in

◀ **FIGURE 11.3**

Abbreviated Strategic Note-Taking Form

Fill in this portion before the lecture begins.

What is today's topic? *Human cell parts & functions*

Describe what you know about the topic.

Odd shapes, has nucleus, contains genes

As the instructor lectures, use these pages to take notes on the lecture.

Today's topic? *Nucleus functions*

Name three to seven main points with details of today's topic as they are being discussed.

Store genes on chromosomes.

Organize genes into chromosomes to allow cell division.

Produce messenger ribonucleic acid (mRNA) that code for proteins.

Organize DNA uncoiling, to replicate key genes.

Summary—Quickly describe how the ideas are related.

Important for cell division. Store genes on chromosomes and ensure replication during division.

New Vocabulary or Terms: MRNA, uncoiling, replication

Page 2

Name three to seven _new_ main points with details as they are being discussed.

New Vocabulary or Terms:

Summary—Quickly describe how the ideas are related.

Page X

Name three to seven _new_ main points with details as they are being discussed.

New Vocabulary or Terms:

Summary—Quickly describe how the ideas are related.

Last Page

At End of Lecture

Write five main points of the lecture and describe each point.

Source: Reprinted with permission from J. R. Boyle. "Learning from Lectures: The Implications of Note-Taking for Students with Learning Disabilities" (*Learning Disabilities: A Multidisciplinary Journal*, 14(2006), 91–97).

Chapter 10). In the next step, students cluster three to seven main points with details as they are presented in the lecture. Categorizing ideas can help the student encode and recall the information (Snowman and Biehler 2006). At the bottom of each page, students are asked to summarize the lecture information, again, to assist in encoding the information. The steps of naming three to seven new main points and summarizing immediately after naming the points are repeated until the lecture ends. The last step, completed at the end of the lesson, involves writing five main points and describing each. This step is intended to serve as a quick review of the lecture.

Strategic note-taking is more effective than conventional note-taking for students with HI in terms of the number of notes recorded, immediate recall, long-term recall, and comprehension of content (Boyle 1996, 2010; Boyle and Weishaar 2001).

Guided notes are outlines or sentences corresponding to a lecture presentation that include blanks where students should fill in key content from the lecture. To construct guided notes, identify the main points from your lecture notes prior to a lesson. List those main points on prepared notepaper, leaving space for the student to fill in details during the lecture (Fig. 11.4).

Using guided notes gives students an outline that lists and structures the main ideas. These main ideas serve as anchors to which to connect related ideas. Guided notes can also be developed using lecture slides from presentation software such as PowerPoint. In doing so, teachers can leave the slide blank, using only the slide title, or use the slide title plus the main points associated with it (Austin, Lee, and Carr 2004; Boyle and Rivera 2012). Teachers can then provide students with handouts of the slides, or students can simply use the structure from the slides to record their own notes.

Research indicates that students who are trained to use guided notes record more notes than with conventional note-taking and earn higher scores on tests and quizzes (Austin, Lee, and Carr 2004; Sweeney et al. 1999). Gains were shown for students with HI in content classes when they use guided notes in conjunction with a review period.

Columnar format is a student-directed technique useful for organizing written materials (for example, textbook information). Information is visually organized according to the type of information to be recorded. The columnar format uses two to four columns to assist with note-taking. One way to use the columnar format is to divide a sheet of paper into three sections or columns (Fig. 11.5). The first column is about five inches wide and is labeled "Basic Ideas." The second column is about two inches wide and is labeled "Background Information." The third column is about

▶ **FIGURE 11.4**

Student Copy of Guided Notes

Comparison of Mars and Earth
I. Similarities: Mars and Earth
    A.
    B.
II. Differences: Mars and Earth
    A. Mars
    B. Earth
III. Effects of an atmosphere on planets
    A.
    B.
    C.
    D.

Source: Adapted from B. Lazarus. Guided Notes, Review, and Achievement of Secondary Students with Learning Disabilities in Mainstream Content Courses (*Education and Treatment of Children*, 14(1991), 112–127.

Topic Sentence

Basic Ideas	Background Information	Questions

one inch wide and is labeled "Questions." Also at the top of the page is a line for "Topic Sentence." The teacher might complete the topic sentence for the lecture or direct students to copy the topic sentence from the board. During the lecture, students complete the first section and write down any important facts that might be needed for future study. After the lecture, students complete the "Background Information," where they note anything of interest or areas in which they have prior knowledge. This section guides students to make connections between the new information and prior knowledge, thereby increasing their comprehension. In the last column, students write questions or information that is not clear. The columnar format is effective at increasing comprehension when used by students as they read passages (Horton, Lovitt, and Christensen 1991).

Teachers can use a variety of approaches before, during, or after a lesson to increase the amount and quality of notes students record. Some other easy, unobtrusive practices teachers can use on a daily basis include providing better cues, using a pause procedure, and allowing students time to review notes.

Lecture Cueing. Lecture cuing involves calling attention to important lecture points. Three efficient types of lecture cues are mannerism, organizational, and emphasis cues (Berry 1999). **Mannerism cues** signal students via gestures that information is important. You could say, "There are three important things to remember" while holding up one, two, and then three fingers as you note each. Gesturing or pounding a fist for emphasis and pointing to important information are also mannerism cues. **Organizational cues** are given for points in a cluster of related information. For example, the cue "there are six components to a plant cell" informs students to record the category "components of a plant cell" and at least six points about a plant cell. **Emphasis cues**, on the other hand, are meant to call attention to a critical lecture point. For example, the cue "it is important to remember that . . ." calls attention to a point that may later show up on a test. Writing notes on the board is another type of cue that increases the probability that students will record the information.

The Pause Procedure.   Another guide to good note-taking, the **pause procedure**, was first investigated as a promising practice with college students in the 1970s and 1980s (Rowe 1976, 1980). Later, Ruhl et al. (Ruhl, Hughes, and Gagar 1990; Ruhl, Hughes, and Schloss 1987; Ruhl and Suritsky 1995) began to assess its effects with students with HI and found that it benefited students' short-term and long-term recall of lecture information. You will recognize this as an approach to lecturing described in Chapter 10. The pause procedure requires a two-minute discussion (pause) at least three times during each lecture. During the two-minute pause, students may pair up to review or discuss notes and/or lecture content since the last pause. When the two minutes have ended, the teacher may ask questions related to the notes before moving on to new material. The pauses are placed at random intervals or at logical breaks in the lecture content (for example, before beginning a new topic). Results from a number of studies indicate that students with HI who use the pause procedure perform significantly better than students not using the procedure in terms of immediate and long-term free recall and total information recorded in notes (Ruhl, Hughes, and Gagar 1990; Ruhl, Hughes, and Schloss 1987; Ruhl and Suritsky 1995).

Review Time.   Finally, **review time** is an important skill for all students, especially those with HI. Having students review their notes can be beneficial for increasing recall on tests. A "brief review" can allow students to correct and elaborate on their notes and fill in gaps (Suritsky and Hughes 1996). Reviewing notes serves an important function because students tend to focus on the highest level of information in a lecture during note-taking (Kiewra et al. 1991), leaving little time for filling in the details. Moreover, in reviews of note-taking research (see Boyle and Rivera 2012), students who reviewed their notes had higher achievement on performance tests than those who were not permitted to review their notes. Many review procedures are built into note-taking techniques or strategies, such as the pause procedure. There is not much benefit to taking notes if students never review them. Lazarus (1991) found that, when students were instructed to review their guided notes six times (that is, read them from top to bottom) and subsequently place a checkmark in each of six boxes provided on the notes page, they improved more than when just using guided notes alone.

11-5   Test Giving

As already suggested in this chapter, students with HI perform many academic skills poorly (for example, following schedules, doing homework, taking notes) until they are taught how to do them correctly. Test taking is like any other academic skill; students with HI often lack effective test-taking skills (Scruggs and Mastropieri 1992). As is the case with any other type of skill, students who lack sufficient test-taking skills need to learn and practice them.

Many times students perform poorly on tests because they do not prepare adequately. This may mean either they did not study, or they did not know how to study appropriately. In addition, poor test performance might reflect difficulties with specific skills that influence the outcome, and not just what the student knows about the content. Those test-taking skills range from time management to deduction to accurate expression. Inefficient test-taking skills are a major factor in poor test performance for students with HI (Lewandowski, Berger, Lovett, and Gordon 2016). Successful

TABLE 11.4 The Testing Continuum

Teacher's Role	Student's Role
Preparing for the Test	
1. Decide if you need to give a test.	
2. Determine how you wish to test.	
3a. Ask what is a fair testing situation.	
3b. Consider test-taking skills.	
4. Prepare a fair test.	
5. Prepare the student.	A. Prepare for the test.
Giving/Taking the Test	
6. Make sure the setting is appropriate.	
7. Establish a routine for taking tests.	
8. Plan for a stress-free test.	
9. Administer the test correctly.	
10. Be respectful of accommodations.	
	B. Start by preparing to take the test.
11. Take notes of circumstances during the test.	C. Use common sense.
	D. Check your work.
Assessing Performance on Tests	
12. Use test results as instructional data.	
13. Provide feedback.	
	E. Learn from the test.

test-taking skills encompass preparing for the test, comprehending the test instructions and purpose, self-monitoring test performance, expressing oneself clearly, and reviewing work and test performance.

Not having mastered the content sufficiently to pass a test is also a factor in test performance, but in this section we are focusing on the skills of test taking and giving.

Testing is ideally thought of as a continuum of activities (Table 11.4). First, both the students and the teacher prepare for the test. Then there is the test itself. The test you use, how you administer it, and how the student approaches taking the test all impact the testing experience. Also important is what happens after the test; this includes how the test results are interpreted, how they are used, and what type of benefits the student reaps.

Preparing for the Test

Why test students at all? One obvious reason is to determine what they have learned. A second reason is to "encourage" them to study. Also, tests are often required as one part of report card grades. Elementary and Secondary Education Act (ESEA) regulations call for periodic testing of students in various areas, which is often "high stakes" as a condition for promotion and matriculation. The ESEA requirements for curriculum standards also include an expectation to assess student-learning outcomes. Tests may also be used to evaluate teachers' performances (Birman et al. 2007–2008; Schoen and Fusarelli 2008). But no matter what your reasons are for testing, you should plan to capitalize on the situation by thinking about the productive use you can make of the test.

The first step in the testing continuum is to *decide if you actually need to give a test.* Again, common reasons for testing include finding out what students have retained, as well as how students respond when directly questioned, or how students apply information instead of being directly questioned, and having data to calculate a term grade and report as part of progress monitoring requirements (review Chapter 2). Once you have determined that you want to (a) see what your students know or can do, (b) figure out how they compare to one another or some standard, or (c) encourage them to study, you *may* have your reason for testing. Ask yourself if you really need to test to accomplish this goal. You could construct *portfolios* with the students that document what you want to know. More informal than portfolio construction, you could *sample* the students' work periodically; that is, you could examine the students' performance of a skill (or application of knowledge) from in-class or homework assignments every so often (see "Tips for Generalization").

The second step of the testing continuum is to *determine how you wish to test* your students. Do you require a demonstration, or could they just tell you how to do a task? Under what conditions would they make their demonstration—individually, under time constraints, with a resource guide available, being told what the product should look like, one time or several times, all at once or in parts, while narrating the how and why of the process, on identical or successively more difficult examples? The answers to such questions relate to the original question: *Why do you want to test?*

The third step of the continuum, which covers the form of testing to be given, has two parts. The first is to *ask what is a fair testing situation* for your students. Once you know what you would like to do to test your students, ask yourself what you *should* do. This means asking yourself if how you would like to assess your students will actually be an accurate way to measure what they know. For example, take a math teacher who wants to test problem-solving skills by giving several word problems. The teacher is not going to get very accurate results from students for whom reading is a challenge, even if they are skilled problem solvers. Unless a skill (in this example, reading) is integral to the task, teachers are not accurately assessing their students' knowledge or skill when test performance is incumbent upon it; that is to say, the test may not be psychometrically valid. Therefore, test for what you want to find out.

A simple way to do this is to assess the same knowledge or skills in multiple formats. At a minimum, it is a good idea to have more than one "make-it-or-break-it" test item to evaluate what students know. Remember this principle when constructing end-of-unit, end-of-quarter/semester tests, or final exams that cover a high volume of content.

Next, *consider test-taking skills*. Test taking is a skill too. Students' knowledge of what is actually being tested is just one of two aspects of fair testing, and different test formats require different test skills. Answering questions by filling in the blanks is different from answering multiple-choice questions, and both are different from matching. Distinguishing the right choice from three or four others (multiple choice) or from provided clues (fill in the blank, matching) is different from recalling without cues or prompts. And all of these variations differ from application questions such as asking for a narrative explanation or watching a student apply knowledge or skill in a real-life context. In addition to the differences in cognitive demands, testing that involves prolonged sitting and writing is different from actively demonstrating. The question here is not, "How would I like to test my students?" Rather, it is, "For what forms of testing are my students prepared?"

The fourth step on the testing continuum is to *prepare a fair test*. Some tests simply do not test what they are supposed to. For example, asking, "What factors led up to the Montgomery bus boycott?" is not a good way to find out if students know why so many African-American citizens committed to participating in the boycott. Construction of individual test items might be the problem, or it might be the entire testing format.

TIPS FOR GENERALIZATION

Alternatives to Tests for Data Collection

A *portfolio* is a collection of students' work samples that demonstrates their skills. Typically collected over time, portfolios show how students perform the skills (or apply the knowledge) in question in a variety of contexts. When added to over time, portfolios can also trace students' progress in learning. Some portfolios only contain positive examples of the students' work. Students can actively participate in selecting materials for the portfolio and may even submit their own commentaries on their contributions. In addition to contributing to grading, students can use portfolios to observe their own learning progress and to set goals. Further, portfolios can be shared with parents and can be a useful data source in the process of developing an IEP. Portfolios may be a folder or a box, depending on the type of work samples being collected, or they may be electronic.

Teachers may periodically collect the students' work to see how they are performing the skills (or applying knowledge) in question. *Sampling* may help to monitor the learning process, or to ensure the students are maintaining skill proficiency over time. Whenever you believe you need updates on how students are doing, you can sample a current piece of work where the skill should have been applied. Be sure the work is from a representative task, and bear in mind that a single sample may not be representative of students' true abilities. Depending on the nature of the task, you might sample by having students periodically repeat a specific task (for example, a drill sheet in math or a response to the same essay topic in social studies). Review the discussions of curriculum-based measurement (C-BM) in Chapters 2 and 5 for a more systematic and formalized approach to sampling.

This fourth step is seemingly obvious. Although the previous steps that covered the format of the test also address the fairness of a test, there is more to it; you have to construct one that actually is fair. A fair test satisfies certain psychometric properties, or else it cannot be a fair test, no matter how well you have matched it to your students' skills and knowledge.

There are two central concepts to test fairness: reliability and validity. These terms are often heard in relation to formal and standardized tests, but the principles of reliability and validity can and should be applied in all test construction. To be reliable means simply that a test can be relied upon to measure what it is intended to. The most common way to think of reliability is to question whether the test would yield the same results if given twice. If not, excepting a reasonable margin of error, the test cannot be relied upon. (This is known as **test-retest reliability**.) You can assess tests for reliability for all students in your class or for individual students. If you are new at test construction, you might actually observe how reliable a test is by administering the same test twice (say, with one day off between administrations and without any additional content teaching in between). You can also assess reliability by giving an exam to a subset of your students as a pilot test and asking them afterward what they thought various items asked them. Although this will not tell you whether they would consistently answer the same way, it does provide insight into why they responded as they did.

Sometimes the whole test is not problematic, but rather just a few of the test items are. This can have to do with **item reliability**. If you give a test to a whole class and many students have a problem with an item (a test question), this may indicate that it is not very reliable. The beauty of giving a test with multiple items that assess the same or related information is that you can compare performance across items to see if the students' performance is more a function of an item than of what they actually know.

It is important to test consistently and accurately for what you are measuring. **Validity** means that a test is valid, or accurate, for what it is purported to measure.

For example, if a test of fraction skills presents all of the fractions in decimal form but the students learned them in the traditional numerator/denominator format, the test will not be a valid test of whether your students have learned what you taught them. A clearer violation of validity would be to test skill at reducing fractions by presenting mixed fractions (for example, $1\frac{7}{10}$) as an assessment of whether students know how to convert unreduced fractions (for example, 17/10).

Step 5 in the continuum is to *prepare the student*. Students need a range of testing skills to be successful. Pointing to a correct choice might be a low-level skill, whereas synthesizing information in order to apply it would be a high-level skill. Thinking about the difficulty level of required skills can be useful when planning how sophisticated to make a test, but always take into account the unique needs of individual students when estimating test complexity. For a student with limited motor control, pointing to a correct answer could be a difficult task. The inappropriateness of such a testing demand is obvious, and you surely would come up with an alternate format. Not all testing challenges are as obvious, however. For students with attention difficulties or other cognitive disabilities, tasks such as discerning between alternatives on multiple-choice questions might outweigh the possible benefit of having to recognize the correct answer versus, say, recall it without any clue. Such unique testing needs are individual; they are not uniformly tied to a specific disability. When a particular testing format is important to your content, or to a high-stakes exam, and a student is not skilled at that format, teaching those test-taking skills is imperative.

We continue to address what teachers must do before addressing a student's role, but you will learn about how students should prepare for a test as well when you read ahead. We hope that you are getting the picture that testing is not something that you do separate from the lesson. Even testing mandated by others (for example, reading, mathematics, and science assessments required for ESEA compliance) should be linked somehow to what you teach and how you have prepared your students to succeed (Thurlow and Thompson 2003).

Giving the Test

Just as preparing for an appropriate testing experience is important, so is actually having an appropriate test. Many factors contribute to testing being fair and accurate. You can probably recall experiences when something prevented you from showing all you know on a test. An obvious distraction would be a work crew using a jackhammer right outside the classroom window. Many other factors are not so apparent but can have an equal impact on the testing experience.

Step 6 on the testing continuum is to *make sure the setting is appropriate*. Before you begin the test, thinking of the needs of your students with special needs can be a good way to help you prepare the environment. If some students are going to require extra attention from you, they should be seated in a place where you are easily accessible to them. Using noticeable accommodations during a test might be cause for students to take it in a different location or at a separate time (Baker and Scanlon 2016). Those using common accommodations in the general classroom may be seated together so that the teacher can easily administer the common accommodation, so they or their classmates are not distracted by having alternative formats or procedures, and so that they will not stand out as different any more than necessary.

You can prevent disruptions from outside the classroom by coordinating with other teachers, posting a "no interruptions" sign, and closing the door. Ensure the lighting is bright enough for reading. If students are going to need reference materials, make sure they are out and accessible in ways that will not disturb classmates. Likewise, if students need to look at information posted on the board, be sure that all are able to see it.

Step 7 on the continuum is to *establish a routine for taking tests*. Students with HI benefit from routines: they come to know what is expected of them, and that is one less thing to confuse them. However, you may need to remind your students of the routine. Make certain the setting and the students are prepared before you distribute the test. Remind the students to read directions (see below for more information on student test-taking skills). To minimize disruptions, you might tell students who have questions to raise their hand instead of coming to you. Tell students how long they have for the test, and experiment with individual students to determine if periodically prompting them on how much time is left is helpful or anxiety provoking. Options for appropriate routines are nearly endless and depend a good bit on your unique students and setting. As these examples make clear, you must consider the factors that could influence test performance and minimize their potential to interfere.

Step 8 on the testing continuum is to *plan for a stress-free test*. If you know students have a major project due soon, this is not a good time for them to focus on your test. Unless completing the test within an allotted time is necessary (think of the concept of test validity), plan for what will happen with students who need extra time, and let students know that plan in advance. This will be particularly helpful to students with anxiety or low self-confidence; it will also be helpful to students such as those with ASD requiring support, who may presume rigid test-taking rules that provoke frustration.

As noted, experiment with your students to find appropriate testing formats before you actually give tests. That information will be useful for identifying accommodations on an individualized education program plan (IEP) as well. Taking a practice test, or at least being exposed to the test format and item style in advance, can be helpful in anticipating the test (Hughes 1996).

Step 9 is to *administer the test correctly*. Suffering through a standardized test can involve practices like listening to the teacher reading word-for-word instructions from an administration booklet, and everyone starting exactly when the second hand reaches the hour. Although these might be anxiety-provoking practices, they are important to ensure the reliability of standardized tests. Be sure that students have everything they will need (and have put away what they should not have, so taking it away later does not become a disruption).

Make sure everyone understands the directions. You might ask students to paraphrase the directions back to you, or at least ask if anyone has any questions about what is expected. In standardized testing this may not be allowed, so having a general conversation about the test before you actually begin may be helpful—for example, "Remember, you are going to be told you have to mark your answers on a bubble sheet, so let's review how you will avoid losing your place."

Check in with your students with special needs as soon as the test begins. A common characteristic of students with HI is to act before planning (Harris, Reid, and Graham 2004); thus, they may need to be reminded to review all components of the directions or to think about and make notes about what they know before responding. Observe to be sure that they are actually doing behaviors consistent with following the directions correctly; you might even quietly ask those students to paraphrase the expectations to you.

Step 10 is to *be respectful of test accommodations*. This means being sure that you allow accommodations (see Chapter 10) and monitor their proper usage. Students with disabilities are entitled to test accommodations in order to have an equal testing opportunity (Thurlow and Thompson 2003). The time to discern what accommodations are needed is not at the beginning of the test (for example, "Leon, do you need to use your calculator today?"). You should know in advance what accommodations may be used and be sure that the student (a) knows how to use them and (b) expects to use them or at least to decide on the spot whether they are needed. Preparing the environment includes making sure materials are on hand for possibly needed accommodations. The most effective test accommodations are those that are consistent with accommodations provided during instruction (Thurlow and Thompson 2003).

Step 11 is to *take note of circumstances during the test*. In addition to being vigilant during testing to see if you can prompt or otherwise assist students, you should also watch to see how well your test is working. Make note of circumstances during testing that may have been disruptive. Notice if students seem confused about one of the test items, if needed materials are late in arriving, and so on. Also, pay attention to individuals. Note particular cases of nerves. Watch to see if students with ADHD are particularly distracted or if others appear frustrated or just need a lot of time to perform one part of the test. That information can be considered during scoring and can be useful for teaching students to improve their test-taking skills in the future.

Assessing Performance on Tests

When you are scoring a test, be sure to consider the data you collected during test taking. Take into consideration whether a test was fair for individual students. Also check to see if a particular item was problematic for multiple students; if it was, you may need to make amends by adjusting your scoring.

Step 12 in the testing continuum is to *use the test results as instructional data*. This next-to-last step of the teacher's side of the testing continuum applies to both teachers and students. Students know why they took the test: because you made them. You need to remember the pedagogic reason why you gave the test (steps 1 and 2). Use the results as intended. Alter your upcoming lesson plans accordingly and be sure to reteach anything that was not well learned. Also make note of the testing and learning needs of individual students. Students should make good use of the test results too—but in order for them to do that, you must provide feedback.

Step 13, the final step, is to *provide feedback*. The final score is what everyone wants to know, but there is much more that they should know. Be sure to explain to students why each answer is right or wrong. Simply identifying whether a response was right or wrong is *consequated feedback*. Students will benefit more from *differentiated* or *informative feedback*, which also helps them to understand why responses were correct or incorrect. (Review Chapter 1 for descriptions of different formats for feedback.)

11-6   Test Taking

Just as teachers have a continuum of actions for preparing, administering, and evaluating testing, students also have their continuum of actions for test preparation, test taking, and review (see Table 11.4).

Preparing for the Test

First, students *prepare for the test*. As already stated, students need to know in advance what they will be tested on and when, including what is expected of them to do well. They should also know the format of the test in advance, so they can prepare accordingly. Being able to define vocabulary or major concepts is different from explaining or demonstrating their application, for example. With advance information, students can coordinate a study plan.

Earlier in this chapter, we addressed the organizational skills that students need in order to study in a timely fashion and to prepare for approaching assignments and homework. Much of that information also applies to preparing for tests.

In addition to having a good study plan, a useful way for students to prepare for a variety of testing scenarios is for them to assess their test-taking skills. They should not wait until an important test is coming up to assess their skills; rather, they should do it immediately, so that they are prepared when testing situations arise. You may need to direct them on this task. Indeed, it may not even occur to them that varied skills are called for depending on the test format. One simple way for students with a few years of schooling experience to assess their compatibility with different test formats is to reflect carefully on previous test performances. Old test banks (from your files, from published curricular materials no longer used, or found in the back of a textbook) can be used to try out test-taking skills. To provide an accurate indication of test-taking abilities, these sample tests should test information on which the student is reasonably informed. That way, the students can focus on what was difficult or not about the testing format. From there, you and the students can work together on learning the appropriate skills for particular testing formats, as needed.

The most helpful test-taking skills are those that help students to understand what the test is asking and to understand how to respond effectively, not tips that help the test taker to "out-strategize" the test writer. Take the example of multiple-choice test items. Many students learn sometime in their careers that the most commonly correct answer is C (or is it B?), and that "all of the above" and "none of the above" are never the right answer unless only one or two items on the whole test feature them—in which case they are *always* the right answer. Also, students are sometimes told to look for response options that are grammatically inconsistent with the stem (the multiple-choice question) and to rule those out as foils (options that are incorrect), the logic being that the teacher probably came up with them in a hurry (Hughes, Salvia, and Bott 1991). Although these can, actually, be useful tips, they are not skills that will help students demonstrate what they know in most testing situations. It would be far more useful for students to learn to eliminate the least probable choices and weigh the probability of what remains, for example (Hughes 1996). At least they are attending to the content of the test instead of trying to guess their way to success.

Of course, an important aspect of test preparation is studying and remembering necessary content. Students can use the FIRST-letter mnemonic strategy (Nagel, Schumaker, and Deshler 2003) to remember and recall lists of information for tests. Even when a test calls for application of information (instead of strictly recalling information to fill in a blank, for example), this recall strategy can be useful. The strategy consists of two parts: FIRST and LISTS (Box 11.3). The FIRST steps are followed to create a memorable cue word (for example, forming a word that prompts recall by drawing on keywords from a selected list). The purpose of the cue word is the same as when students are taught to remember the Great Lakes by using the familiar mnemonic device HOMES (Huron, Ontario, Michigan, Erie, and Superior). The LISTS steps are then used to create study cards by selecting lists of words from instructional materials and making them memorable by creating a FIRST device (Hughes 1996).

FIRST. To begin, students are taught to create a mnemonic by following the FIRST steps:

1. In Step 1, *Form a word*, they write down the first letter of words from a list they need to be able to recall (for example, names of the Great Lakes). They use capital letters and write the letters horizontally (for example, HOMES for the Great Lakes) to create a "real" word or memorable nonsense word.
2. If students cannot form a word using the F step, they then use the second step, *Insert a letter(s)*, to insert lowercase letters (one or two at the most) to try to form

> **BOX 11.3**
>
> ### First-Letter Mnemonic Strategy
>
> F _F_orm a word.
> I _I_nsert a letter(s).
> R _R_earrange the letters.
> S _S_hape a sentence.
> T _T_ry combinations.
> L _L_ook for clues.
> I _I_nvestigate the items.
> S _S_elect a mnemonic device using FIRST.
> T _T_ransfer information to a card.
> S _S_elf-test.

a word. For example, when trying to remember the names of the planets, the student could list their first letters, MVEMJSUN (Mercury, Venus, Earth, Mars, Jupiter, Saturn, Uranus, and Neptune), and then try inserting letters such as MoViEM _ _ _ _.

3. If unsuccessful, the student is taught to use the third step, _Rearrange the letters_, to form a word (for example, SUN _ _ _ _ _).
4. If still unsuccessful at forming a memorable mnemonic, the student will _Shape a sentence_ to form a memorable sentence. This can be useful if the order of the words cannot be changed. For example, the student trying to remember the order of the planets in relation to the sun might create the sentence, _My Very Educated Mother Just Served Us Noodles._
5. Finally, if still unsuccessful with the list of words, the student could _Try combinations_ of the F, I, R, and S steps (for example, _MoViEs of Mars versus Jupiter play on SUNdays_).

LISTS. In the next stage, LISTS, students are taught to locate information that could be used to create lists from school materials (for example, notes or textbooks), write those lists down on paper, use FIRST to create a mnemonic device, transfer the mnemonic to cards, and then review the cards.

1. In the _Look for clues_ step, students look for different types of clues (word clues, importance clues, or other clues) that might indicate some part of the material that should be used to create a list. For example, they might look for "word clues" such as _there are six parts to a cell_ (1, 2, 3, 4, 5, 6) or _there are four types of cells_. "Importance clues" refer to study guide questions or information the teacher says to study for an upcoming test. "Other clues" are highlighted, bolded, or italicized words, or illustrations that are labeled.
2. Once students have identified a list in the L step, they create a heading that is concise yet accurate for the items that will be placed in the list. In the _Investigate the items_ step, students write down a short yet related list of items under the heading.
3. Next, students _Select a mnemonic device using FIRST_. They choose one or more of the steps for the list and form a mnemonic.
4. After they form a mnemonic (a word, sentence, or combination of the two), they _Transfer the information to a card_. On one side of an index card, they write down the heading (for example, Great Lakes); on the other side, they write the mnemonic word using capital letters (HOMES) in the upper left-hand corner and the items in the center of the card (Huron, Ontario, Michigan, Erie, and Superior).

5. Finally, students *Self-test* by looking at the heading and trying to remember the mnemonic and the items for that mnemonic, quizzing themselves until they no longer have to flip the card over to remind themselves of the terms.

Students who used the first-letter mnemonic strategy improved test scores by 30 points on average (Hughes 1996). Deshler and Schumaker (2006), reporting the results of Nagel's study, indicated that students with average baseline scores of 53 percent accuracy on ability-level tests and 51 percent on grade-level tests improved to averages of 95 percent on ability-level tests and 85 percent on grade-level tests after using this strategy.

Taking the Test

Just as students can employ many skills to study for a test, they can learn a variety of test-taking skills in advance and use them during a test. In the 1980s and 1990s Hughes et al. conducted a number of investigations of testing demands and the test-taking skills of students with disabilities. They created a useful learning strategy aptly titled the *Test Taking Strategy* (Hughes et al. 1988), but better known to many special education students as PIRATES (Fig. 11.6).

The first step is to *start by preparing to take the test*. The test-taking strategy begins at the beginning. Students with disabilities such as learning disabilities or ADHD are often easily spotted in a testing situation because they are the first ones to start writing or filling in answer bubbles (see, for example, Harris, Reid, and Graham 2004). Although their initiative may seem impressive, it is actually a problem, because the other students are remembering to write their names, check the instructions, preview the entire test, establish a plan for completing the entire test within the allotted time, and think about their responses before making them.

Performing these preliminary steps can guide students to avoid test-taking problems down the line. Students with disabilities often have a particular need to check the instructions carefully, as well as each question before they answer it. They should get in the habit of underlining the question and circling the expected response format (Box 11.4). This simple action will force them to attend to what the question is actually asking. Also, it will make reviewing the test before handing it in easier (see the later

---

TIPS FOR GENERALIZATION

Three Activities to Promote Improved Test-Taking Skills

Give a *practice test* to familiarize students with the format of an upcoming test and to provide practice on responding to the types of test items you will be including on the test. You can discuss together the demands of the test, instead of the content covered on it.

Positive thinking can help students to perform better on homework assignments or tests (Barron et al. 2006). Teach students to identify a positive attribute that will be helpful to success on homework assignments (for example, "I know who to call if I find I need help") or tests (for example, "I know how to eliminate unlikely foils on tests").

The *ANSWER strategy* (Hughes 1996; Hughes, Schumaker, and Deshler 2005) is a six-step procedure for efficiently and effectively responding to essay test questions:

A **A**nalyze the situation (scrutinize what the question is asking and estimate the time needed to respond).

N **N**otice requirements.

S **S**et up an outline.

W **W**ork in details.

E **E**ngineer your answer (plan and follow your plan).

R **R**eview your work.

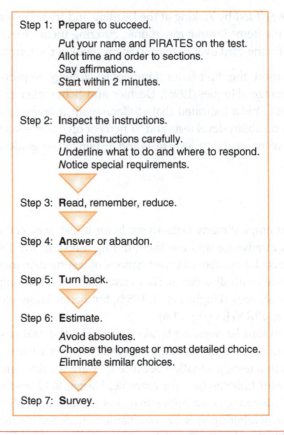

Step 1: **P**repare to succeed.
  Put your name and PIRATES on the test.
  Allot time and order to sections.
  Say affirmations.
  Start within 2 minutes.

Step 2: **I**nspect the instructions.
  Read instructions carefully.
  Underline what to do and where to respond.
  Notice special requirements.

Step 3: **R**ead, remember, reduce.

Step 4: **A**nswer or abandon.

Step 5: **T**urn back.

Step 6: **E**stimate.
  Avoid absolutes.
  Choose the longest or most detailed choice.
  Eliminate similar choices.

Step 7: **S**urvey.

Source: Reprinted with permission from C. Hughes (1995). "Memory and Test-Taking Strategies." In *Teaching Adolescents with Learning Disabilities*, ed. D. D. Deshler, E. S. Ellis, and B. K. Lenz, 2nd ed. (Denver: Love Publishing, Figure 5.15, p. 25).

step "check your work"). In addition to these *Prepare to succeed steps*, students with HI benefit from making a positive affirmation before they begin a test (Barron et al. 2006).

The second step is to *use common sense*. Although we advocate teaching skills for effective studying along with skills for understanding and completing tests over tips for out-strategizing the test writer, Hughes (1996) suggests that using common sense *in addition* to other good test-taking skills can make the difference in the final grade a student earns. He found tips such as ruling out grammatically incorrect foils to be effective for students with HI. Remember, however, that following tips alone is not likely to result in good test performance, so students need to be cautioned explicitly not to overly rely upon them.

Students can use common sense when answering questions, though. Hughes, Salvia, and Bott (1991) reviewed 100 teacher-made and published tests to identify clues that students with disabilities can use to effectively determine how to answer items correctly. They found that 75 percent of the tests included one or more clues. The most

BOX 11.4

Examples of Marked-Up Test Directions and Items

Circle the best answer to each question.

Convert the fraction 21/3 into a whole number.

List three causes of the Industrial Revolution.

State whether a virus is living or not, and explain your answer.

frequent clue was found on items that presented response options (for example, for multiple choice): they found that the longest option was usually the correct choice. Behind that, they found that questions (stems) grammatically cued the answer (for example, "The horse's favorite fruit is an: (a) apple, (b) banana, (c) kumquat").

Students should also reduce their options to those that are the most reasonable, and this skill is not limited to forced-choice test items; they should be willing to let go of answers that they brainstorm for open-ended questions but begin to realize are not quite right. This may be particularly challenging for those with ASD requiring support who are not practiced at being flexible thinkers or those with learning disabilities who tend not to question their work. If they are just not sure about an answer, they should move on and come back (Hughes 1996). Moving on will ensure that they complete as much of the test as they can first; they might get lucky and find a hint to the correct answer somewhere else in the test.

The fourth step is to *check your work*. Students often work on a test until the bell rings—sometimes they even work on it as they slowly approach the teacher's desk to turn it in. Instead, they should check their work before turning in the test. Certainly they want to be sure that their name is on the test and that they have attempted to answer all of the questions they were expected to (the PIRATES steps encourage them to do these things at the start of the test so they are not neglected). They should also glance at their responses. If they marked up the directions and individual questions to indicate how they should respond, this will help speed the checking process. As they read over their answers, they might be tempted to self-doubt. A good skill to learn is to review answers objectively. Are they responding to the question asked? Are the answers reasonable? Are they complete? Students should learn that, if so, they should not change their answers unless absolutely certain they now know what the correct answer is, and this is different from only being sure "I must be wrong" (Hughes 1996).

Performing this step requires the student having time to check her or his work. One way to provide for this is to allot longer testing times than the students need to answer all of the questions. That can be hard to estimate, but getting to know your students and how well they have been learning the test content, as well as how they typically perform on today's test format, should help. You can also announce when there is a suitable amount of time left (for example, five minutes) that "in two minutes it will be time to begin checking your work."

The final step is to *learn from the test*. Just like their teachers, students should learn from the test once it is returned. Students should review their responses, especially those that were wrong, to see if they now understand the information on which they were tested. Carefully reviewing the test takes time. Ideally, the students will read over each item and revisit what is appropriate/inappropriate about various response options. As you can imagine, it will help if a teacher is present to guide the review. Reviewing will cause students to reengage with content actively. With this step, testing can be part of the learning process.

Do Test-Taking Skills Make a Difference?

A history of research has indicated that students with HI tend to have poorer test-taking skills than their peers (see Hughes 1996 for a discussion). Among the test-taking skills found to be problematic for these students are comprehending the task, time management, and clear expression. Of course, academic skill deficits such as reading and numeracy difficulties are also deterrents to good test performance. Most useful test-taking skills that can be taught to students are not tricks such as discerning the correct multiple-choice option by analyzing the grammar of the item; rather, they are methods to work efficiently and effectively. Hughes (1996) reports that students with learning disabilities who are taught the PIRATES mnemonic experience an average of 10 percent improved performance on tests. That is easily a change of a whole letter grade on most tests. Other researchers have reported similar positive gains for students with HI learning test-taking skills (see Hughes 1996).

CHAPTER SUMMARY

Successful participation in school requires organization. As students progress through grade levels, they are increasingly expected to be responsible for their own organization. Getting to the right class on time and having the appropriate materials can be a challenge for students with HI, because the nature of their disabilities includes difficulties relating and organizing information, attending to details, and remembering, among other challenges to organization.

To be organized effectively, students need to learn systems for organization. They can learn how to keep schedules for their in-school and out-of-school daily routines; they can also learn to keep track of assignments by establishing routines for using assignment notebooks or other systems (possibly including electronic devices). Likewise, they can learn to create production schedules so that they can manage all that is expected of them. As we discussed in this chapter, teachers can also employ specific practices to create appropriate assignments and give them in ways that are effective.

Homework is a particular type of assignment. Most appropriately, it is given to extend or reinforce what was taught in a lesson. Students need to be prepared for completing homework; they need skills that range from writing down the assignment and bringing the materials home, to having a schedule for completing it.

Beginning no later than the middle/junior high school years, the skills of note-taking are essential to classroom learning. Students can learn specific procedures for taking notes efficiently. These procedures are consistent with those teachers can use to cue students effectively about the information that they should include in their notes. Just as is the case with note-taking, students can learn skills for efficient test taking. Those skills begin with preparing for being tested and extend through making good use of test results. Following a testing continuum, we have outlined the stages teachers should use in deciding to test and determining the nature of a test, as well as how to teach their students to be effective test takers, to administer tests, and to make the findings educational. There is a companion continuum of student test-taking skills.

In this chapter we have identified how critical organization is to success in school as well as effective practices for teachers and their students with HI.

KEY TERMS

APPLICATION ACTIVITIES

Using information from the chapter, complete the following activities that were designed to help you apply knowledge that was presented in this chapter.

1. If you have access to a classroom, watch for a student who appears to have trouble with an assignment (alternatively, you can work with a classmate who is completing a project assignment). Conduct an instructional conference to help the student. Use as many of the strategies and practices from Box 11.1 as you can. Remember to check back with the student and provide corrective feedback, if needed.

2. Using a lesson plan you have created (or a sample you can find), make a set of notes that would match an ideal set of notes you would like your students to take for the lesson. Translate the notes into at least two of the different forms of note taking described in this chapter.

3. Using the notes from Application Activity #2, modify your lesson plan from Application Activity #2 to include cueing your students and instructing them in the note-taking process.

4. Along with a classmate, construct several items to test what a reader should have learned from this chapter. Instead of answering one another's test, present an analysis of why you do or do not believe each item is part of a fair test.

FatCamera/E+/Getty Images

12 Technology and Teaching

LEARNING OBJECTIVES

After reading this chapter, you will understand:

12-1 Technology skills that are important for students

12-2 The different types of technology that students can use to access text and produce written products

12-3 Different types of technology that teachers can use to improve their own teaching and time management

CEC **Initial Preparation Standard 5: Instructional Planning and Strategies**

5-2 Beginning special education professionals use technologies to support instructional assessment, planning, and delivery for individuals with exceptionalities.

What are the implications of technology growth in the past decade?

The Internet is the fastest-growing tool of communication ever. It took radio broadcasters 38 years to reach an audience of 50 million; television, 13 years; and the Internet, just 4 years (Learningpartnership.org). The number of Internet users has grown tremendously over the short time it has been in existence. In 1995, there were an estimated 20 million users. In 2000, the number jumped to 400 million users. In 2008, there were an estimated 1.4 billion Internet users (Internet World Stats 2008). Today, technology is an integral part of our lives. From laptops to mobile devices and apps, we find it difficult to separate ourselves from our technology.

What does this growth in technology mean for students? According to the U.S. Department of Labor (2000), nearly 75 percent of tomorrow's jobs will require the use of computers or other forms of technology. This prediction means that educators must keep up with the latest technology. Teachers need to know how to support their students in their technology use because even teachers who consider themselves to be members of the digital age can have trouble keeping up with the technologies that their students take for granted.

A word of caution: The rapid development and evolution of technology over the past half-century is quite amazing (Bouck 2016). However, this rapid pace of change has inadvertently created a gap between various types of technology and the evidence supporting their use for students with HI (Kennedy and Deshler 2010: Marino 2010). In the race to create new technology for the market, researchers have few opportunities to conduct rigorous studies and publish results before the particular technology tool has become obsolete (Kennedy and Boyle 2017; Musti-Rao, Lynch, and Plati 2015). An unintended consequence of the short tech development cycle is that students are often taught using tools that have not been subjected to rigorous research (Kennedy and Boyle 2017; Kennedy, Deshler, and Lloyd 2015). Hence, it is often incumbent on teachers to assess the effectiveness of technology tools on student learning and behavior "in vitro."

In this chapter, you will learn about technology skills for students with HI. We will present information about technology standards, technology for students to use in the classroom, and technology for teachers to use to teach students with disabilities. Before you begin reading about technology skills, read Case 12.1 to gain a perspective on issues that teachers face when deciding how to incorporate technology into the classroom.

CASE 12.1   Writing Pains

Case Introduction

In this case, you will read about two teachers who co-teach 10th-grade English and encounter problems with a student. Think about the problems that the student exhibits with writing, and think about how you could use technology with this student to improve her written compositions.

At the end of the case, you will find case questions. These questions are meant to serve as points for reflection. Of course, if you can answer them immediately, you should do so, but you may want to wait to answer them until you have read the portion of this chapter that pertains to the particular case question. Throughout the rest of the chapter, you will see the same questions. As you see them, try to answer them based upon that portion of the chapter that you just read.

Cecilia's assignment for the weekend was to write an essay about an influential person in her life and why that person is influential. Now in 10th grade, she is expected to turn in an essay that contains at least 1,000 words and is void of mechanical errors such as punctuation and spelling. The other requirement is that it should not contain any incomplete sentences (that is, fragments). Cecilia's teacher added this last requirement because her students this year are having problems forming complete sentences in their writing.

Cecilia sat down on the couch in her living room and began writing her essay in her notebook. Her paper looked like this:

My favorit person is Shakira. Shakira was born in Columbia and wanted sign when young. She would sing all the time. Even go kicked out of school quior because her singing was loud. Her voice

continued

drowneded out others who were singing. Best song ever is Underneaf Your Clothes. She is also good at dacing and her videos are cool to see. Great albus also Oral Fixation and Off the Record. Can't wait to get het new album Oral Fixation.

Cecilia knew that this English paper would not be an easy paper to write. She hated to write and was doing poorly in Mrs. Lilia Mena's English class. Mrs. Mena has taught English for the past five years at Estefon High School. She has been co-teaching with the special education teacher, Nancy Barton, for the past three years. Cecilia is one of Mrs. Barton's students and was diagnosed with learning disabilities (LD) in seventh grade. Cecilia's most problematic areas are reading and, this year, English.

Estefon High School is located in a poor section of Los Angeles. It was once a prominent school in the 1970s; however, as more people moved out of that portion of the city, housing prices and city revenue declined. Because of the lack of revenue and maintenance, the school has become rundown, and many of the classrooms are in poor shape. Teachers often lack resources such as books and paper to teach students. The students themselves come from poor housing developments, and the majority of students are on the school's free-lunch program. Despite these conditions, the school does have a well-stocked computer lab, and teachers often have at least one computer in their classroom. Thanks to the benevolence of Los Angeles native Calesto Ferazzi, who owns a chain of famous restaurants, this school has plenty of technology resources.

Cecilia turned in what she wrote to her teacher, Mrs. Mena. As Mrs. Mena went through students' papers, she came across Cecilia's and began to mark it up. She was surprised with the poor quality of her paper and decided to ask Mrs. Barton about it.

"Nancy, weren't you working with Cecilia on her English paper this week?" asked Mrs. Mena.

"Lilia, I asked her to work on it at home and then I would take a look at it before she handed it in," responded Nancy. "I even offered to let her use the computers in your class, but she said she didn't need to use them."

"It seems that she needs to use a word-processing program to help her hand in a legible paper and one that is much better than this one," said Lilia, handing Nancy Cecilia's paper. "Cecilia also complained that she types too slowly to use a computer for composing her paper."

Nancy looked at the paper and shook her head at the poor quality of writing. "We really need to do something to help her write better. What do you think we should do?" asked Nancy. "Many of these problems are mentioned in her IEP."

Nancy and Lilia then sat down and reviewed Cecilia's writing goals for the year. Among the goals were writing longer papers (at least 1,000 words), writing in complete sentences, and using better organization in essays and compositions. With these goals in mind, Nancy and Lilia developed a plan to teach her these skills, which included teaching her a composition strategy and teaching her to use a word-processing program to compose essays.

CASE QUESTIONS

1. What technology skill or skills would you remediate with Cecilia?

2. What are two types of technology or software that you could use to assist Cecilia with writing?

Cecilia's lack of technology skills affected her writing. Although technology alone will not help her writing skills, Cecilia can improve her writing skills when technology is combined with teaching her writing skills and strategies. The first step for teachers is determining where to begin at teaching technology skills to students. A good starting point would be to examine technology standards and then determine which skills students need.

12-1 Technology Standards and Universal Design for Learning

Technology skills are important for all students, but just what skills should be taught? The International Society for Technology in Education (ISTE) (2017) has established technology foundations (standards) for students (Table 12.1). These broad standards simply provide a framework for states to develop specific technology skills for students. States have yet to fully integrate these standards into their state standards; however, many states have taken earlier standards and refined them as specific skills (for example, proficiency at using a word-processing program) and as general skills (for example,

TABLE 12.1 Technology Foundation Standards and Indicators for Students

Empowered Learner

- Students articulate and set personal learning goals, develop strategies leveraging technology to achieve them and reflect on the learning process itself to improve learning outcomes.
- Students build networks and customize their learning environments in ways that support the learning process.
- Students use technology to seek feedback that informs and improves their practice and to demonstrate their learning in a variety of ways.
- Students understand the fundamental concepts of technology operations, demonstrate the ability to choose, use and troubleshoot current technologies and are able to transfer their knowledge to explore emerging technologies.

Digital Citizen

- Students cultivate and manage their digital identity and reputation and are aware of the permanence of their actions in the digital world.
- Students engage in positive, safe, legal and ethical behavior when using technology, including social interactions online or when using networked devices.
- Students demonstrate an understanding of and respect for the rights and obligations of using and sharing intellectual property.
- Students manage their personal data to maintain digital privacy and security and are aware of data-collection technology used to track their navigation online.

Knowledge Constructor

- Students plan and employ effective research strategies to locate information and other resources for their intellectual or creative pursuits.
- Students evaluate the accuracy, perspective, credibility and relevance of information, media, data or other resources.
- Students curate information from digital resources using a variety of tools and methods to create collections of artifacts that demonstrate meaningful connections or conclusions.
- Students build knowledge by actively exploring real-world issues and problems, developing ideas and theories and pursuing answers and solutions.

Innovative Designer

- Students know and use a deliberate design process for generating ideas, testing theories, creating innovative artifacts or solving authentic problems.
- Students select and use digital tools to plan and manage a design process that considers design constraints and calculated risks.
- Students develop, test and refine prototypes as part of a cyclical design process.
- Students exhibit a tolerance for ambiguity, perseverance and the capacity to work with open-ended problems.

Computational Thinker

- Students formulate problem definitions suited for technology-assisted methods such as data analysis, abstract models and algorithmic thinking in exploring and finding solutions.
- Students collect data or identify relevant data sets, use digital tools to analyze them, and represent data in various ways to facilitate problem-solving and decision-making.
- Students break problems into component parts, extract key information, and develop descriptive models to understand complex systems or facilitate problem-solving.
- Students understand how automation works and use algorithmic thinking to develop a sequence of steps to create and test automated solutions.

Creative Communicator

- Students choose the appropriate platforms and tools for meeting the desired objectives of their creation or communication.
- Students create original works or responsibly repurpose or remix digital resources into new creations.
- Students communicate complex ideas clearly and effectively by creating or using a variety of digital objects such as visualizations, models or simulations.
- Students publish or present content that customizes the message and medium for their intended audiences.

TABLE 12.1 *(Continued)*

Global Collaborator
• Students use digital tools to connect with learners from a variety of backgrounds and cultures, engaging with them in ways that broaden mutual understanding and learning.
• Students use collaborative technologies to work with others, including peers, experts or community members, to examine issues and problems from multiple viewpoints.
• Students contribute constructively to project teams, assuming various roles and responsibilities to work effectively toward a common goal.
• Students explore local and global issues and use collaborative technologies to work with others to investigate solutions.

Source: https://www.iste.org/standards/standards/for-students.

using content-specific tools, software, and simulations to support learning and research) (Burke 2001). Earlier technology standards (ISTE 2007) have been incorporated into state standards, as in Virginia, yet in other states, such as Texas, the standards are integrated directly into the curriculum. Teachers should check their own state and school district standards and curricula to find specific technology standards or specific technology skills that students should be taught across different grade levels.

Technology used within a **universal design for learning (UDL)** framework can provide a powerful tool that allows students with HI to access the general education curriculum. Using UDL within the general education curriculum means that students can access materials more easily and teachers can teach and assess students more effectively. For many students with disabilities, accessing the general education curriculum through traditional means has proven to be a challenge. Without accommodations and modifications, and specially designed instruction for most, students with HI typically have difficulty accessing reading materials (for example, basal readers, worksheets, and textbooks) because a disability prevents them from processing and remembering text information. Not only do their disabilities prevent them from accessing text materials effectively, but the implications carry over to classroom learning and affect academic achievement. For example, students who cannot learn efficiently from printed text truly lack access to and participation in the general education curriculum (Hitchcock et al. 2002). To help with access problems, teachers can present text information digitally; text containing vocabulary terms linked to definitions and examples are particularly effective for helping students comprehend the information (Higgins and Boone 1990; Higgins, Boone, and Lovitt 1996).

Teachers who do not take advantage of technology are limiting their teaching in terms of pedagogy used and assessment of learning. Teaching effectively is often a matter of using good pedagogy. UDL approaches that incorporate technology allow teachers to be more flexible in their teaching. The use of technology allows teachers to highlight critical features and provide multiple examples more easily than they could through traditional lecturing methods (Hitchcock et al. 2002). For example, using PowerPoint with accompanying notes, teachers can present complex topics in a more manageable way. Because of space restrictions, the PowerPoint (or Prezi) slides often limit how much content teachers can type in per slide, with teachers usually presenting three to six lecture points per slide. This chunking of information helps students learn content in "parts" and benefits student comprehension of lecture content (Stephenson, Brown, and Griffin 2008).

Like pedagogy, teachers can use technology to monitor student progress and embed technology within learning activities so that teachers do not have to administer a separate assessment of information that students have just learned (Bryant and Bryant 2012). For example, digital books contain stories that have questions embedded with them. After students read a portion of a story, the program would ask students a question, check for accuracy, and then prompt the students to return to that portion of the story from which the question was drawn. *Thinking Reader* (Scholastic; Tom Snyder Productions) is a research-based reading program that presents students with a story that contains hyperlinks for vocabulary, as well as other prompts and supports (for example, use of a reading strategy, such as predicting, summarizing, and clarifying). Periodically, students are given a quick comprehension check through the text to assess comprehension. Moreover, teachers can monitor student performance through a reading log that keeps track of students' responses (for example, strategy use or performance on reading quizzes).

As you will see, teachers can incorporate technology into a variety of lessons and activities to assist students with disabilities before, during, and after learning. Many of these technologies incorporate the principles of UDL by allowing for multiple means of representation of information to students, expression and action by students, and engagement for students with disabilities.

THINK BACK TO THE CASE   **about Cecilia's writing skills...**

What technology skill or skills would you remediate with Cecilia?

Cecilia should be working on improving her skills with word processors. In particular, she should be taught how to use all of the functions of a word-processing program such as cut-and-paste functions for revising and spelling and grammar checks for editing. These functions should help her improve the quality of her papers. Over time, her teacher can help her with other aspects of writing, such as planning and drafting.

12-2   Technology and Learning

The development and use of technology for people with disabilities is not new. The history of technology and disabilities goes back to the invention of the telephone by Alexander Graham Bell (note: others have also been credited with this invention) in 1876. His earlier experiences working with his mother who was deaf led to his interest in acoustics, and later experiences training teachers who worked with deaf people strongly influenced his life's work. Today, technological inventions have helped countless individuals with disabilities by improving the quality of their lives. Those inventions range from assistive and augmentative technologies to different types of technology that teachers use to improve their own teaching.

Assistive technology devices serve to improve the communication skills of students with disabilities. More specifically, they represent "a wide variety of technology applications designed to help students with disabilities learn, communicate, and otherwise function more independently by bypassing their disabilities" (Friend and Bursuck 1996). Many of these technologies include augmentative or alternative communication devices, as well as assistive technology.

Assistive Technology for Accessing the Curriculum

Certain types of technology were developed to allow students with disabilities to have better access to the curriculum. These devices do this by allowing students to hear written words, to write from their own words, or to learn from simulations of events. In other words, technology allows students with disabilities to circumvent their disability so that they can successfully complete classroom tasks, thereby allowing them greater access to the curriculum. Although such technological devices help students gain greater access to the curriculum, teachers must balance these technologies with their usefulness and accessibility once students complete school and move on to the work world or post-secondary education. For example, although a spell-checking or grammar-checking app is helpful for students in school, it may be more of a hindrance than help in the workplace. Math teachers in the 1970s sought this same balance when handheld calculators became widely available. Then, as now, they had to decide what skills and knowledge to teach students before introducing them to this new technology.

A number of technologies have been developed that translate text on a screen or scanned text into speech. Many of these **text-to-speech (TTS) programs** are meant for students to use as read-aloud or read-along programs. These programs use either synthesized speech or digitized speech. Essentially, these programs convert text to phonemes and then convert the phonemes into synthesized speech.

The two biggest factors for determining the usefulness of TTS programs are the *intelligibility* and *naturalness* of the speech. Intelligibility refers to the correct pronunciation of words, and naturalness refers to the tone, rhythm, pitch, and intonation of words, as well as proper chunking of clauses and phrases. Many TTS programs offer options for students, such as highlighting text as it is read, allowing the reading rate to be adjusted, choosing from different voices, altering the background and highlight colors, and saving the TTS file as an MP3 or WAV file that can be transferred to digital recorders (Hecker and Engstrom 2005). A number of different TTS programs are available, such as *Browsealoud, TextAloud, HELP Read, ReadPlease!, AspireREADER 4.0,* and *Kurzweil 3000*. These programs work to read electronic documents, including documents that have been scanned into files. Some programs are free, and others are available at a cost for the user. Those that are available at a cost often have more options.

Although TTS programs can be useful, students with disabilities might not benefit from this type of technology if they become passive learners as the software reads aloud the words. If the computer simply reads text from a screen and the student is not actively involved by reading the text on the screen and comprehending the information, it is questionable whether such a program should be used. In fact, when students with disabilities read the text and simultaneously listened to it being read, research results were either inconclusive (Davis, Caro, and Carnine 2006) or contradictory (Leong 1995; Strangman and Hall 2003). However, when students interacted with the text by periodically stopping to answer comprehension questions or discuss them with a partner, their comprehension was much improved (Kim et al. 2006; Torgesen, Dahlem, and Greenstein 1987).

Still, TTS can be useful to assist students while reading. In one study, Coleman and Heller (2010) used repeated readings with computer modeling. The student read the passage aloud for the first, third, and fifth time; in the second and fourth readings, the computer, via the Kurzweil 3000 software, read the passage aloud as the student read along silently on the computer screen. When the student read the passage aloud, any errors made while reading were corrected. In the first and fifth reading, the student was also asked comprehension questions. The advantage of incorporating software into the intervention was that each word was highlighted as the computer read it aloud (i.e., computer modeling). According to the researchers, students who used the repeated reading procedure with computer modeling increased their reading fluency, accuracy, and comprehension from the first to the fifth reading. In addition, most of the students demonstrated slight increases in reading fluency on novel passages.

Source: Wizcom Technologies Ltd.

▲ **PHOTO 12.1**

The Readingpen®2

Despite the promise of TTS technology, technical aspects may make it a frustrating experience for students. For example, the voice may be robotic and difficult to understand or the program may read the text too quickly or slowly. Teachers should always assist students when using these programs until students can adjust the programs according to their needs and use them fluently. Moreover, when TTS programs are used with reading, teachers should ensure that students are actively engaged in reading the electronic text, asking or answering questions, or using comprehension strategies.

The Readingpen® (Photo 12.1) is a handheld device that optically scans text and translates it into speech. The reading pen not only converts the text to speech but also displays the meaning of the word on its screen, shows syllabication, and spells the word. The reading pen is meant to be a compensatory device to help individuals with reading disabilities bypass their deficits by hearing the printed text and thereby comprehending the text (Higgins and Raskind 2005).

Hypertext is another alternative for students who have difficulty understanding vocabulary used in text. Hypertext, sometimes referred to as hypermedia, allows students to access additional text, data, graphics, or audio bites as they read electronic text. By clicking on embedded links, students can hear the pronunciation of the word, read the definition of it, read background information about the concept, see a picture of the word, or be prompted with a strategy (Strangman and Hall 2003). The interactive features of using hypertext with electronic text allow students to elaborate on their knowledge of the word or concept.

Several studies (Higgins and Boone 1990; Higgins, Boone, and Lovitt 1996; Horton, Boone, and Lovitt 1990; MacArthur and Haynes 1995) have examined the use of hypertext and hypermedia to allow students with LD to interact with passages in a nonlinear fashion. Rather than read from start to finish, using hypertext study guides, students were encouraged to access hypertext links when they needed assistance. The hypertext was linked to strategies, definitions, or graphics that supplemented the student's reading. Results from these studies showed that hypertext and hypermedia study guides were more effective than traditional learning for students with LD. Despite these positive results, others (Davis, Caro, and Carnine 2006; Strangman and Hall 2003) have cautioned that although hypertext and hypermedia electronic text show potential for students with HI, more research is needed.

Electronic books, commonly known as *e-books*, are electronic texts that are available on CD-ROM or other special disks, or can be downloaded from the Internet. Typically, e-books include enhancements such as hypertext (for example, for word definitions), illustrations, or animation that complement the text (Holum and Gahala 2001). Some e-books are embedded with speech software so that students can either listen to the story as they read along with it (sometimes referred to as talking books). Advantages of using e-books are that they support and coach students as they read, provide accurate pronunciations of unknown words, increase motivation to read, aid comprehension of text, and improve decoding skills (Holum and Gahala 2001). Despite these advantages, the current research is mixed as to whether talking books are any better than traditional print storybooks (Strangman and Hall 2003), particularly for students with disabilities. What is known is that, like other forms of multimedia and technology, students must be trained to use e-books in order to access the hypertext and other components of the book (pronunciation clues and other supports). For students with disabilities, this training requires explicit instruction with feedback. Teachers should model aspects of e-books that might be useful to the students. For example, teachers should stop when they come to a hypertext link for a vocabulary word and click on the link to see what information it describes (for example, pronunciation and definition). When finished, teachers should reread the sentence that contained the link and check for comprehension.

Assistive Technology for Writing Tasks

Word processors have dramatically changed the way we write. They have helped poor writers to become good writers, and good writers to become better. Word processors and their built-in tools have encouraged otherwise hesitant writers to sit down at the computer and not have to worry about spelling or grammar. Other features, such as "cut-and-paste," have greatly helped with the revision process, and spelling and grammar checkers have helped shorten the stages of writing. Even the use of electronic files has helped with transferring them to publishers so that student newspapers can come out in print faster. Although these advances have been good for writing and composing, in the end, students still need to be instructed in writing skills and still need to be given strategies and specific directions on how to use computers to get the most out of their writing. Moreover, despite these advances, students with disabilities can still benefit from other advances in technology to compensate for processing and motor problems when writing. Some of these advances include **speech-to-text (STT) programs**, brainstorming programs, idea organizers, word predictors, spelling checkers that use phonetic rules, and homonym checkers.

Using the process approach to writing (that is, brainstorm, draft, revise, edit, and publish; review Chapter 8), there are software programs for every stage in the process. In the initial stage of writing, several programs are available that help students brainstorm and map out ideas for their writing project. *Kidspiration, Inspiration, coggle,* and *Draft:Builder* are programs that can help students to map out their ideas and organize them before writing. Using these programs, students are able to arrange ideas as they think of them in interrelated maps or outlines that help with organizing prior to the drafting stage. In many cases, students can transform an organizer into an outline and check their choice of words using a dictionary (with word meanings) and thesaurus.

Just as software for translating text to speech is available, voice-recognition software that translates speech to written text is also available. Often used during the drafting stage of writing, these programs can fairly accurately transcribe the user's spoken words into text. Although it may not make students better writers in terms of organization or mechanics, it may allow them to turn more ideas into text. Most voice-recognition programs require some training to interpret words correctly from the owner's voice. For students with disabilities, this requirement is no different; however, once trained, students with disabilities can use it fairly accurately (MacArthur and Cavalier 2004). Using this type of software has other potential issues: some programs confuse homonyms (for example, Chile, chili, or chilly), and others have problems with the extraneous background noise commonly found in classrooms. Regional and ethnic accents, as well as speech impediments, can also be challenging for some software programs to "hear." However, for students with writing problems who have strong oral composing skills and clear articulation, the programs might be a viable alternative to typing words into a word processor.

Source: Microsoft Corporation

▶ FIGURE 12.1
WordQ

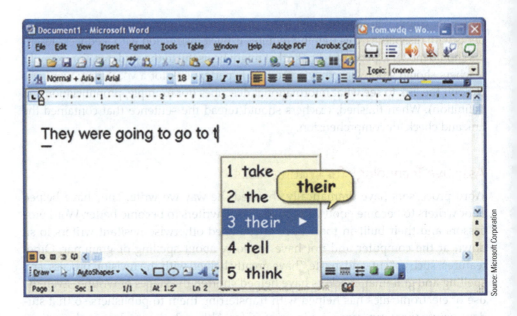

Prominent speech-recognition programs that enable students to use their voice to write on the computer are *Dragon NaturallySpeaking* and *Siri*. In addition, PCs and Macs have this function (see www.howtogeek.com/178636/use-voice-dictation-to-speak-to-your-mac/ for more information about STT capabilities). These programs allow students to dictate words directly into the computer and convert them to text. Other programs, such as word predictors, spelling checkers, and writing assistance programs, can help students as they compose stories. For example, *WordQ* (Fig. 12.1) is a software program that predicts words for students to use. It is used along with standard word processors. It suggests the spelling of words based upon the word that the student is currently typing, and it also makes predictions (in the form of suggestions) about which word might come next in a sentence. In addition, students can use the "read" function to have the software read back what they have just written, similar to other TTS software. Some students enjoy using this function during the editing and revising stages of writing because hearing text read aloud allows them to catch errors or other compositional features they would like to revise.

Another innovation for improving the writing skills of students with disabilities is the use of word-prediction software (see Peterson-Karlan [2011] for a full review of technology to support writing for students with disabilities). Word-prediction software offers the user a list of word choices that appears after the first letter of the word is typed. Most programs also contain a read-back function (via TTS software) for students to check spelling and grammar (Grant 2009). Several studies (Evmenova, Graff, Jerome, and Behrmann, 2010; Handley-More, Deitz, Billingsley, and Coggins, 2003; Mirenda, Turoldo, and McAvoy, 2006) that have examined the effectiveness of word-prediction software for improving the writing skills of students with writing disabilities and of students with physical disabilities have found positive effects on performance. Evmenova et al. (2010) compared the effects of three word-prediction software programs (*WordQ*, *Co-Writer*, and *WriteAssist*) against word processing alone (i.e., baseline condition). In this study, the researchers found that, regardless of the word-prediction software, students with mild disabilities showed improved written spelling accuracy. When using any one of the three programs, students also increased the total number of words produced and the rate at which they composed, though increases varied according to the program. Some of these programs say and spell words so students can hear them being spelled if the spelling checker does not provide the correct suggestion. Finally, during the last stage of the writing process—

publishing—students can save their work as a TTS MP3 file or as a podcast they can listen to, or they can use publishing software such as *PageMaker* to save the document as an unchangeable file.

A number of studies have examined the use of technology on the written language skills of students with disabilities. Overall, word processors appear to be beneficial for students with disabilities in terms of quality of written products and fluency of writing (Graham and MacArthur 1988; MacArthur et al. 1990). In addition, studies indicate that spelling checkers (Graham and MacArthur 1988; Hetzroni and Shrieber 2004) and speech synthesizers reduce the number of spelling errors students with disabilities make in papers (Raskind and Higgins 1995). With respect to whether word processors can be credited with helping students produce written products that are longer or contain more words, the results from studies appear to be mixed (Hetzroni and Shrieber 2004). Some researchers found that students who use word processors do produce longer documents (Bangert-Drowns 1993). MacArthur and Cavalier (2004) found that students with LD who used STT software (that is, dictating into speech-recognition software) via a word processor produced better-quality essays than students who only wrote them. Finally, word processors are helpful at organizing and structuring written products for students with disabilities (Hetzroni and Shrieber 2004).

THINK BACK TO THE CASE about Cecilia's writing skills . . .

What are two types of technology or software that you could use to assist Cecilia with writing?

As described in this section, a number of software programs could be used to assist Cecilia with her written language skills. For example, *Write:OutLoud* offers TTS functions for students who have problems typing text quickly. In addition, this program offers (1) the Franklin spelling checker that suggests words as well as displays and speaks words and definitions, (2) a homonym checker that searches the document for homonyms, and (3) teacher editing tools (for example, marking up text) that could assist Cecilia as she writes. Another program that could help Cecilia is *WordQ*. This program can be used with any word-processing program (for example, *Microsoft Word*) that the student already uses. This program works by predicting words that the student may want to write and displays a list of words for the student to choose from. When she is finished writing a sentence, Cecilia could use the playback function to have the software program read it back to her so that she could hear if she made any mistakes in what she wrote.

Methods and Strategies Spotlight

Useful Apps for Teachers*

Kahoot (**website**): allows the teacher to create interactive informal assessments and quiz reviews; teacher access: www.getkahoot.com

Socrative (**app**): a quizzing/polling app to push out informal assessments to students (teacher and student versions)

ZipGrade (**app**): allows the teacher to create answer sheets for students to complete with their multiple-choice tests; can scan answers for item analyses

* Special thanks to Amy DeProspo for suggesting these apps.

30/30 (app): a visual timer that can be customized with colors and labels for self-regulation and appropriating independent or instructional working time

Piktochart (website and app, but website works better on a desktop or laptop): allows the teacher to create infographics for content with charts and preset templates; https://piktochart.com/

Spark Video (app): allows the teacher to pair pictures and/or text with audio narration to create a short movie

Popplet (app): allows the teacher to create word maps and word webs

abCursive (app): allows students to trace their letters and words in cursive with guided practice

Stick Pick (app): allows teachers to add students' names to virtual popsicle sticks for cold calling, guiding questions, and sentence starters aligned with levels of Bloom's Taxonomy

Explain Everything (app): allows teachers to create presentations with drawing tools, text, images, and more with a real-time voiceover function. Great for students who have difficulties with presenting in front of the class. Another app that has virtually the same functions is *ShowMe*.

Thinglink (app and website): allows teachers to create interactive images with text, images, YouTube videos, and others

Book Creator (app): allows teachers to create virtual books with pictures, images, drawing tools, and audio recording functions to use and record on each page

Canva: allows teachers to create virtual posters and presentations with images, graphics, and a variety of fonts

---

CASE 12.2 | Textbook Problems

Case Introduction

Now that you have worked through the first case in this chapter, you should feel comfortable addressing issues in a second case.

Ruby is a junior at Howell Senior High School, and her homeroom teacher is Larry Kingman. Mr. Kingman teaches sections of a class in current events for most of the morning and history in the afternoons. Mr. Kingman has worked at Howell for 15 years and has only recently begun collaborating with the new special education teacher, Suzie Wetzman. In the class on current events, students discuss everyday news events. Mr. Kingman requires his students to read stories from the newspaper and *Newsweek* magazine prior to coming to class. Class discussion then centers around current news events from these materials. Because a presidential election is coming up in a few months, most of their discussions have been about candidates and their views.

For Ruby, learning has been tough. Since she was assigned the label "emotionally disturbed" (ED) in third grade, she has always been in classes for students with disabilities, and she has struggled to learn new content and knowledge. Her emotional problems, anxiety and depression with resultant behavioral problems, have interfered with her learning. Despite these problems, her high aptitude has kept her academically competitive in mainstream classes (in her younger days) and in inclusion classes more recently. Although she does have serious emotional problems, many of her teachers believe

that she also has a learning disability, particularly in the area of reading. To complicate matters, her psychotropic medications often leave her tired, further complicating her learning problems. Now in 11th grade, Ruby struggles with many of her reading assignments.

Ruby's problems in the current events class stem from her difficulty on her reading assignments, particularly in reading articles that use vocabulary above her head. She often becomes frustrated and then either quits reading the materials or becomes angry and behaves inappropriately. Similarly, she has problems reading her chemistry book. Her poor completion of reading assignments often puts her in jeopardy of failing classes. Her teachers have tried to help compensate for her reading problems by having another student in the class read to her, but they know that this is not the best solution.

During one recent co-planning session, Mr. Kingman and Mrs. Wetzman discussed Ruby's problems. Mrs. Wetzman mentioned her problems and offered to brainstorm with Mr. Kingman.

"Hey, Larry," she starts, "Ruby really needs some help with her reading assignments. What would you think about sending home some scripted notes of the articles?"

Larry, hesitant about taking on more work, responds, "Well, Suzie, last time we tried modifying her assignments, she really didn't take advantage of it."

"Yes," Suzie agrees, "but she needs to pass as many courses as possible if she has any hopes of going to Ben Franklin Community College."

continued

Larry remains quiet because he feels that he has given Ruby enough chances. Then he speaks, "If you want to develop these 'scripted notes,' then go ahead. But this year I am already overwhelmed with the increased documentation that I have to do for the SFS (Standards for Success) and the new lesson plans that old man Varina (the new principal) has us doing."

Suzie did not quite get the support that she wanted from Larry, but even half-hearted support was better than none, she thought. "OK. I understand," she replied. "Well, do you think there may be something that we could do to use technology to help her?"

"Well, we are supposed to be getting new computers in a few weeks and funds to purchase software," Larry replied.

CASE QUESTIONS

1. Describe one technology skill that Ruby needs to be taught.
2. What are two types of technology or software that you could use to assist Ruby with her reading problems?
3. Name and describe a reading technique or strategy that you could teach Ruby to improve the quality of her reading as she uses technology.

12-3 Technology to Enhance Teaching and Management Skills

Teachers can use different types of technology to enhance their teaching of students with and without disabilities. PowerPoint presentations, newsletters, websites, whiteboards, digital video, electronic IEPs, and electronic gradebooks all can add to a teacher's repertoire of skills and lead to enhanced presentation, communication, and management. These software tools and technology allow teachers to present information in an enhanced and motivational format and allow them to manage day-to-day paperwork issues such as writing up IEPs and keeping track of grades.

PowerPoint

PowerPoint is a software tool for presenting information in a slideshow format. PowerPoint uses text, charts, graphs, sound effects, and video to present new information to students. Whether in a classroom lesson or a parent meeting, PowerPoint allows you to make a powerful impression on your audience, using both visual and audio formats. When used along with handouts of a presentation, PowerPoint-enhanced lessons represent a form of universal design that benefits everyone in the classroom. Handouts of the slides can serve as guided notes for students and assist in their learning. When handouts are presented as "partial notes," student have a guide for being engaged in the lecture. Because information is typically presented in a category with three to six points per slide, students are presented with small chunks of information, a format that aids learning (Stephenson, Brown, and Griffin 2008). Finally, when presented with handouts, students have a permanent product they can use to study for tests and quizzes.

"The Basics of PowerPoint" by Amy Gaimaro (www.techlearning.com/article/2144) offers information about creating PowerPoint presentations for students. *Kahoot* and *Poll Everywhere* allow teachers to create games, polls, or quizzes to assess student knowledge and can often be integrated with PowerPoint.

Classroom Website

Another form of technology to enhance teachers' communication is the development and use of a classroom website. A classroom website serves many purposes. It is a great way to keep the lines of communication open between teachers and parents.

Classroom websites provide parents with news about activities in their child's classroom. Teachers can link parents to the curriculum that is being used in the class. For example, if students are learning about the American Revolution, teachers can post links to websites about the Revolution they are using and parents can see directly the information their children are learning. The website can contain information about long-term projects or units. For example, the fifth-grade class might be doing a project on how caterpillars grow into butterflies. On the website, parents, students, and the teacher can keep track of the changes over time. The website can also serve as the weekly newsletter for parents. Often, teachers spend time during the day catching up on classroom news; for some teachers, the time can be spent inputting information into the website. Links can also lead to other school websites such as those of the PTA, the principal, the district, or other teachers who interact with the class (for example, physical education and art).

TIPS FOR GENERALIZATION

Effective Electronic Presentations

The following tips will help teachers make electronic presentations for the classroom:

- Focus on content. Don't forget that the purpose of a presentation is to present content.
- Limit the amount of information on each slide to three to six points.
- Keep each point brief (distill a sentence into one to three key words). During the lecture, elaborate on each point.

- Use a consistent format in your presentation; jumping from one color or texture to another is distracting.
- Limit sound, graphics, and animation; although these are fun to use, they may be distracting to the learner.
- Before using your presentation, preview it, check for errors (particularly spelling errors), and practice with it.
- Be sure students can read the slides from the back of the room.

When students are sick or miss school, classroom websites are a good way for them to find out what happened in the classroom. The website can serve as a place for teachers to post homework assignments and other important activities such as field trips so that parents can make sure they and their child have not missed anything. Permission forms and other forms can also be posted on the website in case students lose them on the way home from school.

Classroom websites also allow grandparents and other relatives a chance to keep up on students despite the distance between them. Classroom websites give students opportunities to work, to read, and to post writings from their classes. In many cases, a website can serve as the publishing stage of the writing process.

Teachers are cautioned, however, that classroom websites are public spaces, even when password protected, and students' identities and personal information should not be posted to them. This warning extends to not using streaming videos or still pictures that capture students' images or voices.

Interactive Whiteboard

An interactive whiteboard is an electronic presentation device that interfaces with a computer. It is useful in many of the same situations as is a chalkboard, creating a space that multiple people can see, refer to, or interact with, and on which one can write and erase. The teacher can use a special pen or highlighter to write and add information to the board. The digital images displayed on the board (for example, lesson notes) can then be captured by a computer, printed out, and distributed to the class. The teacher can also control software from the board by simply using a finger as a mouse to click buttons. Similarly, a whiteboard on a computer class website can be used during a computerized teleconference, a speaking or chat (typed text) session when students are in remote locations. If used in this way, everyone can see what is being written on the whiteboard. Typically, the teacher controls what is written on the whiteboard; however, students can also write on the whiteboard area that everyone participating in the chat or voice teleconference session sees.

According to Bell (2002), an interactive whiteboard has many useful functions for teachers, such as the following:

- Whether used to demonstrate software or to point out important features, the electronic whiteboard is great in allowing live demonstrations.
- A whiteboard allows teachers to present in color and to highlight important information.
- Classrooms that have only one computer can utilize the whiteboard so that multiple students can access technology.
- The large whiteboard area allows students, particularly those with motor disabilities, to run programs easily by tapping on the board rather than using a mouse.
- A computerized whiteboard can be used with other digital devices such as cameras or video players to display objects (for example, a cell) that can then be labeled on the board.

Whiteboards are good for lessons in which you would like to distribute copies of what is written or drawn on the board.

Digital Video

Although analog video has been around for years, it has been used mostly to support classroom learning and is often limited in its format. Digital video, on the other hand, has the potential for interactivity and integration (Thornhill, Asensio, and Young 2002). Digital video can be manipulated by slowing its pace, fast-forwarding to specific scenes, or showing sections in short segments (Okolo 2006). Likewise, digital video can be integrated and directly linked to the content of the lessons or PowerPoint presentations. Digital video can include DVDs, CD-ROM, or streaming video clips from websites. Various organizations and government entities provide video clips that can be downloaded, some for a small fee (for example, Discovery Channel website) or others for free (for example, National Oceanic and Atmospheric Administration [NOAA]).

In content-area instruction, integrating clips into content lessons is particularly useful to break up large sections of lecture content. For example, if a teacher is presenting science content about atmospheric conditions and the formation of hurricanes, the teacher could easily download a clip from NOAA's National Hurricane Center that shows a radar loop of Hurricane Katrina or a NASA image of Hurricane Wilma. Okolo (2006) offers the following tips for teachers using digital video clips in content-area instruction:

- Show the video in short segments that focus on key concepts.
- Help students to integrate the video with other sources on information (for example, textbook or lecture notes).
- Encourage students to take notes during the video so that they can recall key points.
- If the concept is important, view the video clip more than once. Multiple viewings of a video will allow students to learn it well and record it accurately in their notes.

- After viewing the video clip, discuss it to help students understand it.
- Pause the video clip at points and ask students to make predictions (for example, "What will happen when the hurricane moves from water to land?").
- Pause and have students examine certain features of the video clip.

Electronic IEPs

Teachers have known for some time that preparing handwritten IEPs can be a very time-consuming process, and research has documented this fact (Price and Goodwin 1980). In addition to being time-intensive, writing an IEP requires knowledge of pedagogy, school curricula, and state standards (Wilson, Michaels, and Margolis 2005) that teachers will have to research prior to writing or have available while writing the document. Teachers must also know how various components pertain to the development of the IEP (for example, regarding the IDEA: how progress of objectives will be monitored; state and local laws: accommodations permitted for state tests; and school district policy: extent of participation in district-wide tests). Moreover, because teachers are taught to write goals, objectives, and other components differently, written IEPs may lack conformity and standardization (Margolis and Free 2001).

One solution to address many of the shortcomings of handwritten IEPs is to ask teachers to produce electronic IEPs. Electronic IEPs allow for conformity and standardization because the computer programs require teachers to write standard components and often have uniform goal and objective statements, which can be slightly modified for each student's needs but result in similar appearance in terms of goals, objectives, and other IEP components. Although electronic IEPs may not address all of the problems associated with handwritten IEPs, they should meet the need for efficiency and consistency, can be personalized for each child, and allow for the integration of IEPs into databases that can be used for state and federal reports (Margolis and Free 2001).

According to Margolis and Free (2001), there are three main types of IEP technology: *stand-alone systems*, *distributed network systems*, and *centralized network systems*. Using *stand-alone systems*, teachers write IEPs on their own computers that are not networked to other computers or databases. The IEP software typically has a selection of statements (for goals, objectives, modifications, aids, and services), required fields for all IEPs, options to modify statements, and other options to help create professional IEPs. Using this type of software, teachers can prepare IEPs on a computer, make changes as needed, and then print out a finished copy upon completion of the IEP meeting.

Teachers using *distributed network systems* also prepare IEPs on their own computer; however, these computers are networked together and are connected via a secure connection to a central server that contains student information, as well as IEP templates. Using this system, teachers can easily access previous IEPs and student information to prepare or update IEPs. Despite the convenience, schools may require that teachers go through training to transfer content appropriately and maintain confidentiality standards.

Finally, the third type of system is a *centralized network*. In this system, teachers typically have to travel to one or more central locations to work on the IEPs or have to submit coded forms that are fed into the system. When all of the information has been filled out via coded sheets, the information is entered and the IEP is printed. (We used this type of system several years ago when we were teachers developing IEPs for our own students.) Of course, the downside of using such a system is lack of convenience and additional forms to fill out.

Some of the IEP software programs that are available include *IEP Anywhere* by Smart Solutions Inc., *Encore IEP* software by Spectrum K12 School Solutions, *SEAS—Special Education Management Systems* by Computer Automation Systems Inc., and *IEP Team Software* by Teachers' Pet Productions.

Electronic Gradebooks

As technology becomes more accessible, teachers often take the lead in using different types of management tools, such as electronic gradebooks. Electronic gradebooks provide ease and expediency when recording scores and keeping running totals of students' grades. In addition, electronic gradebooks can weigh categories, average, and print out students' scores in an easily readable format at a moment's notice (Vockell and Fiore 1993). These reports can then be presented to principals, parents, or other teachers who request progress reports for a student with HI. Vockell and Fiore (1993) point out several other time-saving features that electronic gradebooks have over traditional gradebooks, including their ability to alphabetize class lists, produce progress reports, display distributions, and perform other analyses (for example, calculating means and standard deviations, and item analysis). In one study (Tetreault 2005) that examined the use of electronic gradebooks by teachers, the author reported that the four biggest uses were (1) tracking student attendance, (2) monitoring student grades on individual assignments and tests, (3) calculating students' cumulative grades, and (4) producing progress reports.

Despite the convenience of using these types of gradebooks, teachers should always double-check the accuracy of information that has been entered into gradebooks because it is easy to transpose or omit numbers when entering scores and grades.

Some examples of electronic gradebooks include *Pinnacle Gradebook* by Excelsior Software, *iRespond Gradebook* by iRespond, *ClassMate Gradebook* by ClassMate Software, and *E-Z Grader Gradebook* by E-Z Grader Company. There are also free gradebooks that can be accessed through websites or apps, such as *Jumprope*, *Thinkwave*, and *LearnBoost.*

THINK BACK TO THE CASE about Ruby . . .

1. *Describe one technology skill that Ruby needs to be taught.*

2. *What are two types of technology or software that you could use to assist Ruby with her reading problems?*

Taking these questions one at a time, Ruby should be taught how to access textbooks using a TTS program such as Kurzweil. To use this technology, the text first has to be scanned into a usable format (for example, *Microsoft Word* or a PDF [portable document file]). The program works with most scanned files, as well as electronic files. Therefore, one of the first skills that Ruby could learn would be how to use a scanner. Next, Ruby should be taught how to use the Kurzweil software program to read scanned files.

Ruby could also learn to use a reading aid such as the reading pen. Using the reading pen, Ruby would simply scan printed text and the device would read it aloud. This may help students such as Ruby with unknown vocabulary words or possibly with reading comprehension.

12-4 Research Evidence

We have described a variety of technology resources in this chapter. Their utility for teaching students with HI has been carefully researched. The following are examples of findings from such research on specific devices and software.

Reading Pens

Students who used reading pens while silently reading passages outperformed students who silently read passages without any assistance on reading comprehension questions (Higgins and Raskind 2005). In addition, students who used reading pens required very little assistance and created few distractions.

Speech-to-Text Software

Using speech-recognition software to dictate compositions offers promise for students with HI. MacArthur and Cavalier (2004) have shown that, for the most part, students with HI can be taught to use speech-recognition software accurately. Moreover, students who used speech-recognition software, via dictation to a computer, composed essays of better quality and with fewer spelling errors than handwritten essays (MacArthur and Cavalier 2004).

Word-Prediction Software

Word-prediction software programs have been shown to increase the accuracy of words spelled in journals among students with HI. MacArthur (1998) compared student performance when students used a word processor during the baseline phase to their performance using a word processor with word-prediction software and speech synthesis during the treatment phase. He found the students with HI were able to increase legibility of words and correctly spelled words in dialogue journals. A similar study found that students with physical disabilities who used word-prediction software improved not only their spelling accuracy and legibility but also their writing quality on 10-minute writing samples (Mirenda, Turoldo, and McAvoy 2006).

THINK BACK TO THE CASE   **about Ruby...**

Name and describe a reading technique or strategy that you could teach Ruby to improve the quality of her reading as she uses technology.

In terms of using a strategy with technology, it seems reasonable that Ruby could be taught to integrate the paraphrasing strategy (review Chapter 7) with either of the technologies described. Of course, her teacher would have to provide explicit instruction in how to integrate the strategy while using the technology.

CHAPTER SUMMARY

Remember, "technology does not obviate the need for work on the part of the learner. It is not yet possible to download knowledge and experience directly into the brain. To understand something we must engage with it" (Finnis 2004, p. 2). Students with disabilities must be taught how to use technology, just as with other learning tasks, and teachers still have to determine which skills to teach to students with HI.

Although teachers may use a number of different technologies in the classroom, ISTE standards serve as a framework for determining the areas in which students need technology. Students with HI should be able to master the use of technology (for example, a computer), productivity tools such as a word processor, presentation software such as PowerPoint, communication tools such as email, and research tools such as the Internet to find materials. Likewise, students with HI can be taught to use a variety of software programs to improve their written essays or compositions, reading comprehension and fluency, and understanding of concepts in content areas. We have reviewed a number of technologies that could be used in each of these areas.

In addition, teachers can incorporate different technologies into lessons, depending upon the skill or content being taught. If teaching content, PowerPoint and whiteboards are useful technologies to help students record notes, and teachers can copy their notes directly from a PowerPoint presentation or whiteboards and distribute those to students.

Finally, teachers should use explicit training with feedback to ensure that students can access and efficiently use all of the components of software or hardware. A software program is only as good as the student's knowledge about how to use it. A software program is no good if students are unsure how to use it accurately. Just as we need practice to become better at using new devices (for example, a GPS mapping system or cellphone), students also need explicit instruction and practice to be able to use new devices and technologies effectively and efficiently.

KEY TERMS

Assistive Technology Devices, 396

Electronic Books, 398

Hypertext, 398

Speech-to-Text (STT) Programs, 399

Text-to-Speech (TTS) Programs, 397

Universal Design for Learning (UDL), 395

APPLICATION ACTIVITIES

Using information from the chapter, complete the following activities that were designed to help you apply the knowledge that was presented in this chapter.

1. Visit a website that offers assistive technology and view a demo, or find out more about one specific product and describe how it can assist students with HI.

2. Visit www.cast.org and read about how technology can improve the lives of students with disabilities.

3. Create a PowerPoint lesson for a content area you will one day be responsible for teaching that can be used to teach students in an inclusive classroom.

References

Achieve. (2010). *Comparing the Common Core State Standards in Mathematics and NCTM's Curriculum Focal Points.* Washington, DC: Author.

Ackerman, P., Holloway, C., Youngdahl, P., & Dykman, R. (2001). The double-deficit theory of reading disability does not fit at all. *Learning Disabilities Research & Practice, 16,* 152–60.

Ackerman, P. L., & Cianciolo, A. T. (2002). Ability and task constraint determinants of complex task performance. *Journal of Experimental Psychology: Applied, 8*(3), 194–208.

ADA Amendments Act of 2008. Public Law no. 110–325, 122 Stat. 3553.

Adams, M. J. (1990). *Beginning to read: Thinking and learning about print.* Cambridge, MA: MIT Press.

Al Otaiba, S., & Fuchs, D. (2002). Characteristics of children who are unresponsive to early literacy intervention: A review of the literature. *Remedial and Special Education, 23*(5), 300–316.

Al Otaiba, S., & Rivera, M. (2006). Individualized guided oral reading fluency instruction for students with emotional and behavioral disorders. *Intervention in School and Clinic, 41,* 144–149.

Albert, L. R., & Ammer, J. J. (2004). Lesson planning and delivery. In B. K. Lenz, D. D. Deshler, & B. R. Kissam (Eds.), *Teaching content to all.* Boston, MA: Allyn & Bacon.

Aljunied, M., & Frederickson, N. (2011). Cognitive indicators of different levels of special educational support needs in autism. *Research in Autism Spectrum Disorders, 5*(1), 368–376.

Allbritten, D., Mainzer, R., & Ziegler, D. (2004). Will students with disabilities be scapegoats for school failures? *Educational Horizons, 82,* 153–160.

Allington, R. L. (2002). What I've learned about effective reading instruction. *Phi Delta Kappan, 83,* 740–747.

Allsopp, D. H. (1999). Using modeling, manipulatives, and mnemonics with eighth-grade math students. *Teaching Exceptional Children, 32*(2), 74–81.

Aloia, S. (2003) Teacher assessment of homework. Academic Exchange Quarterly, 7, 71–77.

American Psychiatric Association. (2013). *Diagnostic and statistical manual of mental disorders* (5th ed.). Washington, DC: American Psychiatric Association.

American Speech-Language-Hearing Association. (2006). *2006 Schools Survey report: Caseload characteristics.* Rockville, MD: Author.

Americans with Disabilities Act of 1990. Pub. Law no. 101–336, 104 Stat. 327.

Amundson, S., & Weil, M. (1996). Prewriting and handwriting skills. In J. Case-Smith, S. Allen, & P. N. Pratt (Eds.), *Occupational therapy for children* (pp. 524–41). St. Louis, MI: Mosby-Year Book.

Anderson, D. H., Munk, J. H., Young, K. R., Conley, L., & Caldarella, P. (2008). Teaching organization skills to promote academic achievement in behaviorally challenged students. *TEACHING Exceptional Children, 40*(4), 6–13.

Anderson, J. (1990). *Cognitive psychology and its implications.* San Francisco: Freeman and Company.

Andrews, S. P., & Slate, J. R. (2002). Public and private prekindergarten programs: A comparison of student readiness. *Educational Research Quarterly, 25*(5), 974.

Annie E. Casey Foundation. (2010). *The 2010 KIDS COUNT data book, 2010, State trends in child well-being.* Baltimore, MD: Author.

Annie E. Casey Foundation. (2014). *KIDS COUNT data book, 2014, State trends in child well-being* (25th ed.). Baltimore, MD: Author.

Applegate, M., Quinn, K., & Applegate, A. (2002). Levels of thinking required by comprehension questions in informal reading inventories. *The Reading Teacher, 56,* 174–180.

Aram, D. M., & Hall, N. E. (1989). Longitudinal follow-up of children with preschool communication disorders. *School Psychology Review, 18,* 487–501.

Arends, R. I. (1998). *Learning to teach.* Boston: McGraw-Hill.

Arndt, S. A., Konrad, M., & Test, D. W. (2006). Effects of the "self-directed IEP" on student participation in planning meetings. *Remedial and Special Education, 27*(4), 194–207.

Aronson, E., Blaney, N., Stephan, C., Sikes, J., & Snapp, M. (1978). *The jigsaw classroom.* Beverly Hills, CA: Sage.

Association for Childhood Education International. (2000). Elementary Education Standards and Supporting Explanation. Association for Childhood Education International. http://www.hunter.cuny.edu/school-of-education/ncate-accreditation/electronic-exhibit-room/conceptual-framework/repository/files/national-standards/ACEI%20Elementary%20Standards.pdf (accessed August 21, 2017).

Association on Higher Education and Disability (AHEAD). (2008). AHEAD Best Practices: Disability Documentation in Higher Education. http://www.ahead.org/resources (accessed May 8, 2008).

Austin, J. L., Lee, M., & Carr, J. E. (2004). The effects of guided notes on undergraduate students' recording of lecture content. *Journal of Instructional Psychology, 31*(4), 91–96.

Ausubel, D. (1963). *The psychology of meaningful verbal learning.* New York: Grune & Stratton.

Ausubel, D. P. (1968). *Educational psychology: A cognitive view.* New York, NY: Holt, Rinehart, and Winston.

Ausubel, D., Novak, J. D., & Hanesian, H. (1968). *Educational psychology: A cognitive view* (2nd ed.). New York: Holt, Rinehart, & Winston.

Ayers, W. (2006). Hearts and minds: Military recruitment and the high school battlefield. *Phi Delta Kappan, 87,* 594–599.

Baca, L. M., & Cervantes, H. T. (2003). *The bilingual special education interface* (4th ed.). Upper Saddle River, NJ: Prentice Hall.

Baddeley, A. (2000). The episodic buffer: A new component of working memory? *Trends in Cognitive Sciences, 4*(11), 417–423.

Baddeley, A. D. (2006). Working memory: An overview. In S. Pickering (Ed.), *Working Memory and Education* (pp. 1–31). New York: Academic Press.

Baddeley, A. D., Hitch, G. J., & Allen, R. J. (2009). Working memory and binding in sentence recall. *Journal of Memory & Language, 61,* 438–456.

Bailey, D. B., Bruder, M. B., Hebbeler, K., Carta, J., Defosset, M., Greenwood, C., Kahn, L., Mallik, S., Markowitz, J., Spiker, D., Walker, D., & Barton, L. (2006). Recommended outcomes for families of young children with disabilities. *Journal of Early Intervention, 28,* 227–251.

Baker, D., & Scanlon, D. (2016). Student perspectives on academic accommodations. *Exceptionality, 24*(2), 93–108.

Baker, S., Gersten, R., & Scanlon, D. (2002). Procedural facilitators, cognitive strategies: Tools for unraveling the mysteries of comprehension and the writing process and providing meaningful access to the general curriculum. *Learning Disabilities Research & Practice, 17,* 65–77.

Baker, S. K., Simmons, D. C., & E. J. Kame'enui. (1998). Vocabulary acquisition: Research bases. In D. C. Simmons, & E. J. Kame'enui (Eds.), *What reading research tells us about children with diverse learning needs: Bases and basics* (pp. 83–218). Mahwah, NJ: Erlbaum.

Baltodano, H. M., Harris, P. J., & Rutherford, R. B. (2005). Academic achievement in juvenile corrections: Examining the impact of age, ethnicity and disability. *Education and Treatment of Children, 28,* 361–379.

Bandura, A. (1977). *Social learning theory.* Upper Saddle River, NJ: Prentice Hall.

Banks, T., & Obiakor, F. E. (2015). Culturally responsive positive behavior supports: Considerations for practice. *Journal of Education and Training Studies, 3*(2), 83–90.

Bargh, J. A., & McKenna, K. Y. A. (2004). The Internet and social life. *Annual Review in Psychology, 55,* 573–590.

Barkley, R. (2000). *Taking charge of ADHD: The complete, authoritative guide for parents.* New York: Guilford Press.

Barkley, R. A. (2006). *Attention-deficit hyperactivity disorder: A handbook for diagnosis and treatment* (3rd ed.). New York: Guilford.

Barkley, R. A., Fischer, M., Smallish, L., & Fletcher, K. (2006). Young adult outcome of hyperactive children: Adaptive functioning in major life activities. *Journal of American Academy of Child and Adolescent Psychiatry, 45,* 192–202.

Barron, K. E., Evans, S. W., Baranik, L. E., Serpell, Z. N., & Buvinger, C. (2006). Achievement goals of students with ADHD. *Learning Disability Quarterly, 29,* 137–158.

Barsch, R. (1967). *Achieving perceptual-motor efficiency.* Everett, WA: Special Child Publications.

Basil, Carmen. (1992). "Social Interaction and Learned Helplessness in Severely Disabled Children." *AAC: Augmentative and Alternative Communication, 8*(3), 188–199.

Bateman, B. (2011). Individualized education programs for children with disabilities. In J. Kauffman & D. Hallahan (Eds.), *Handbook of Special Education.* Routledge.

Bauer, A. M., & Shea, T. M. (1999). *Inclusion 101, How to teach all learners.* Report no. ED432843. Baltimore, MD: Paul H. Brookes Publishing Co.

Bauer, A. M., & Shea, T. M. (2003). *Parents and schools: Creating a successful partnership for students with special needs.* Upper Saddle River, NJ: Merrill/Prentice Hall.

Bauer, A. M., & Ulrich, M. E. (2002). 'I've got a palm in my pocket': using handheld computers in an inclusive classroom. *Teaching Exceptional Children, 35*(2), 18–22.

Baumgartner, S. E., Weeda, W. D., van der Heijden, Li. L., Huizinga, M. (2014). The relationship between media multitasking and executive function in early adolescent. *Journal of Early Adolescence, 34*(8), 1120–1144.

Beder, H., & Medina, P. (2001). *Classroom dynamics in adult literacy education* (NCSALL Report #18). Cambridge, MA: National Center for the Study of Adult Learning and Literacy.

Bennett, S., & Kalish, N. (2006). *The case against homework: How homework is hurting our children and what we can do about it.* New York, NY: Crown.

Bennett-Conroy, W. (2012). Engaging parents of eighth grade students in parent–teacher bidirectional communication. *School Community Journal, 22*(2), 87–110. Retrieved from http://www.schoolcommunitynetwork.org/SCJ.aspx

Benton, L., & Johnson, H. (2014). Structured approaches to participatory design for children: Can targeting the needs of children with autism provide benefits for a broader child population? *Instructional Science: An International Journal of the Learning Sciences, 42*(1), 47–65.

Berch, D. B. (2005). Making sense of number sense: Implications for children with mathematical disabilities. *Journal of Learning Disabilities, 38,* 333–339.

Berkeley, S., Bender, W., Peaster, L. G., & Saunders, L. (2009). Implementation of Response to Intervention: A snapshot of progress. *Journal of Learning Disabilities, 42,* 85–95.

Bernad-Ripoll, S. (2007). Using a self-as-model video combined with social stories to help a child with asperger syndrome understand emotions. *Focus on Autism and Other Developmental Disabilities, 22*(2), 100–106.

Berninger, V., & Amtmann, D. (2003). Preventing written expression disabilities through early and continuing assessment and intervention for handwriting and/or spelling problems: Research into practice. In H. Swanson, K. Harris, & S. Graham (Eds.), *Handbook of learning disabilities* (pp. 323–44). New York: The Guilford Press.

Berninger, V., Vaughan, K., Graham, S., Abbott, R., Abbott, S., Brooks, A., & Reed, E. (1997). Treatment of handwriting problems in beginning writers: Transfer from handwriting to composition. *Journal of Educational Psychology, 89,* 652–66.

Berninger V. W., & Gans, B. M. (1986). Language profiles in nonspeaking individuals of normal intelligence with severe cerebral palsy. *Augmentative and Alternative Communication, 2,* 45–50.

Berninger, V. W. (2003). Preventing written expression disabilities through early and continuing assessment and intervention for handwriting and/or spelling problems: Research into practice. In H. L. Swanson, K. R. Harris, & S. Graham (Eds.), *Handbook of learning disabilities* (pp. 345–63). New York: The Guilford Press.

Berninger, V. W., Abbott, R. D., Whitaker, D., Sylvester, L., & Nolen, S. B. (1995). Integrating low- and high-level skills in instructional protocols for writing disabilities. *Learning Disability Quarterly, 18,* 293–309.

Bernstein, D., & Tiegerman-Farber, E. (1997). *Language communication disorders in children.* Boston, MA: Allyn & Bacon.

Berry, G. C. (1999). Development and validation of an instructional program for teaching post-secondary students with learning disabilities to take and study notes. Ph.D. dissertation, University of Kansas, from Dissertations & Theses: Full Text database, no. AAT 9946088 (retrieved May 22, 2008).

Beveridge, S. (2004). Pupil participation and the home-school relationship. *European Journal of Special Needs Education, 19*(1), 3–16.

Bhattacharya, A. (2006). Syllable representation in written spellings of sixth and eighth grade children. *Insights on Learning Disabilities, 3,* 43–61.

Bhattacharya, A., & Ehri, L. C. (2004). Graphosyllabic analysis helps adolescent struggling readers read and spell words. *Journal of Learning Disabilities, 37,* 331–348.

Biederman, J., Monuteaux, M. C., Doyle, A. E., Seidman, L. J., Wilens, T. E., Ferrero, F., Morgan, C. L., & Faraone, S. V. (2004). Impact of executive function deficits and attention- deficit/hyperactivity disorder (ADHD) on academic outcomes in children. *Journal of Consulting and Clinical Psychology, 72,* 757–766.

Biggs, E. E., & Carter, E. W. (2016). Quality of life for transition-age youth with autism or intellectual disability. *Journal of Autism and Developmental Disorders, 46*(1), 190–204.

Binger, C. & Light, J. (2007). The effects of aided AAC modeling on the expression of multisymbol messages by preschoolers who use AAC. *Augmentative and Alternative Communication, 23,* 30–43.

Birman, B. F., Le Flock, K. C., Klekotka, A., Ludwig, M., Taylor, J., Walters, K., Andrew, W., & Kwang-Suk Yoon. (2007–2008). *State and local implementation of the* No Child Left Behind Act. *Volume II—Teacher quality under* NCLB: *Interim report.* Washington, DC: U.S. Department of Education, ERIC Documents Reproduction Services, no. 497 970.

Bisaillon, J., & Clerc, I. (1999). A computer writing environment for professional writers and students learning to write. *Journal of Technical Writing & Communication, 29,* 185–203.

Blachowicz, C., & Fisher, P. (2000). Vocabulary instruction. In M. Kamil, P. Mosenthal, P. Pearson, & R. Barr (Eds.), *Handbook of reading research* (pp. 502–523). Mahwah, NJ: Lawrence Erlbaum Associates.

Blalock, G., Kochhar-Bryant, C., Test, D., Kohler, P., White, W., Lehmann, J., Bassett, D., & Patton, J. (2003). The need for comprehensive personnel preparation in transition and career development: DCDT position statement. *Career Development for Exceptional Individuals, 26,* 207–226.

Boardman, A., Vaughn, S., Buckley, P., Reutebuch, C., Roberts, G., & Klingner, J. (2016). Collaborative Strategic Reading for students with learning disabilities in upper elementary classrooms. *Exceptional Children, 82*(4), 206–217.

Bond, N. (2007). Questioning strategies that minimize classroom management problems. *Kappa Delta Pi Record.* Fall, 18–21.

Borkowski, J. G. (1992). Metacognitive theory: A framework for teaching literacy, writing, and math skills. *Journal of Learning Disabilities, 25,* 253–257.

Bos, C. S. (1988). Process-oriented writing: Instructional implications for mildly handicapped students. *Exceptional Children, 54,* 521–527.

Bos, C. S., & Anders, P. (1987). Semantic feature analysis: An interactive strategy for facilitating learning from text. *Learning Disabilities Focus, 3,* 55–59.

Bos, C. S., & Anders, P. (1990). Effects of interactive vocabulary instruction on the vocabulary learning and reading comprehension of junior high learning disabled students. *Learning Disability Quarterly, 13,* 31–42.

Bos, C. S., & Anders, P. L. (1992). Using interactive teaching and learning strategies to promote text comprehension and content learning for students with learning disabilities. *International Journal of Disability, Development, and Education, 39,* 225–238.

Bos, C. S., Anders, P., Filip, D., & Jaffe, L. (1989). The effects of an interactive instructional strategy for enhancing reading comprehension and content area learning for students with learning disabilities. *Journal of Learning Disabilities, 6,* 384–390.

Bottema-Beutel, K., Mullins, T., Harvey, M., Gustufson, J., & Carter, E. (2016). Avoiding the "brick wall of awkward": Perspectives of youth with autism spectrum disorder on social-focused intervention practice. *Autism, 20*(2), 196–206.

Bottge, B. A. (2001). Reconceptualizing mathematics problem solving for low-achieving students. *Remedial and Special Education, 22*(2), 102–112.

Boulineau, T., Fore, C., Hagan-Burke, S., & Burke, M. (2004). Use of story-mapping to increase story-grammar text comprehension of elementary students with learning disabilities. *Learning Disability Quarterly, 27*, 105–121.

Bowler, D. M., Gardiner, J. M., & Berthollier, N. (2004). Source memory in adolescents and adults with asperger's syndrome. *Journal of Autism and Developmental Disorders, 34*(5), 533–542.

Bowman, M., & Treiman, R. (2002). Relating print and speech: The effects of letter names and word position on reading and spelling performance. *Journal of Experimental Child Psychology, 82*, 305–340.

Bowman-Perrott, L. (2009). Classwide peer tutoring: An effective strategy for students with emotional and behavioral disorders. *Intervention in School and Clinic, 44*(5), 259–267.

Boyle, J. (1996). Thinking while note taking: Teaching college students to use strategic note taking during lectures. In B.G. Grown (Ed.), *Innovative learning strategies: Twelfth yearbook* (pp. 9–18). Newark, DE: International Reading Association.

Boyle, J., & Hughes, C. (1994). Effects of self-monitoring and subsequent fading of external prompts on the on-task behavior and task productivity of elementary students with moderate mental retardation. *Journal of Behavioral Education, 4*, 439–57.

Boyle, J. R. (1996). The effects of a cognitive mapping strategy on the literal and inferential comprehension of students with mild disabilities. *Learning Disability Quarterly, 19*(2), 86–98.

Boyle, J. R. (2006). Learning from lectures: The implications of note-taking for students with learning disabilities. *Learning Disabilities: A Multidisciplinary Journal, 14*, 91–97.

Boyle, J. R. (2010). Note-taking skills of middle school students with and without learning disabilities. *Journal of Learning Disabilities, 43*, 530–40.

Boyle, J. R., Forchelli, G. A., & Cariss, K. (2015). Note-taking interventions to assist students with disabilities in content area classes. *Preventing School Failure, 59*(3), 186–195.

Boyle, J. R. & Rivera, T. Z. (2012). Note-taking techniques for students with disabilities: A systematic review of the research. *Learning Disability Quarterly, 35*(3), 131–143.

Boyle, J. R. & Seibert, T. (1998). The effects of a phonological awareness strategy on the reading skills of elementary students with learning disabilities. *Learning Disabilities: A Multidisciplinary Journal, 8*(3), 145–153.

Boyle, J. R., & Weishaar, M. (1997). The effects of expert-versus student-generated cognitive organizers on the reading comprehension of high school students with learning disabilities. *Learning Disabilities Research & Practice, 12*(4), 228–235.

Boyle, J. R., & Weishaar, M. (2001). The effects of a strategic note-taking technique on the comprehension and long term recall of lecture information for high school students with LD. *Learning Disabilities Research & Practice, 16*(3), 125–133.

Boyle, J. R., & Yeager, N. (1997). Blueprints for learning: Using cognitive frameworks for understanding. *TEACHING Exceptional Children, 29*(4), 26–31.

Bradley, D., & Switlick, D. (1997). From isolation to cooperation in teaching. In D. Bradley, M. King-Sears, & D. Tessler-Switlick (Eds.), *Teaching students in inclusive settings: From theory to practice* (pp. 225–51). Boston: Allyn & Bacon.

Brandenburg, J., Klesczewski, J., Fischbach, A., Schuchardt, K., Büttner, G., Hasselhorn, M. (2015). Working memory in children with learning disabilities in reading versus spelling: Searching for overlapping and specific cognitive factors. *Journal of Learning Disabilities, 48*(6), 622–634.

Bray, N. W., Fletcher, K. L., & Turner, L. A. (1997). Cognitive competencies and strategy use in individuals with mental retardation. In W. W. Maclean (Ed.), *Ellis' handbook of mental deficiency, psychological theory, and research* (3rd ed., pp. 197–217). Mahwah, NJ: Erlbaum.

Bremer, C., Clapper, A., & Deshler, D. (2002). *Improving word identification skills using Strategic Instruction Model (SIM) strategies.* Minneapolis, MN: National Center on Secondary Education and Transition.

Bridgeland, J. M., Dilulio, J. J., & Morison K. B. (2006). The Silent Epidemic: Perspectives of High School Dropouts. Retrieved from: http://www.civicenterprises.net/pdfs/thesilentepidemic3-06.pdf

Brodzinsky, D. M., Patterson, C. J., & Vaziri, M. (2002). Adoption agency perspectives on lesbian and gay prospective parents: A national study. *Adoption Quarterly, 5*(3), 5–23.

Brown, A. S. (1990). A review of recent research on spelling. *Educational Psychology Review, 2*, 365–397.

Bruner, J. (1983). *Child's talk.* New York: W.W. Norton & Co.

Bryan, T., & Burstein, K. (2004). Improving homework completion and academic performance: Lessons from special education. *Theory Into Practice, 43*, 213–219.

Bryan, T., Burstein, K., & Bryan, J. (2001). Students with learning disabilities: Homework problems and promising practices. *Educational Psychologist, 36*(3), 167–180.

Bryant, D., Bryant, B., & Hammill, D. (2000). Characteristic behaviors of students with LD who have teacher-identified math weaknesses. *Journal of Learning Disabilities, 33*, 168–177.

Bryant, D. P., Bryant, B. R., Roberts, G., Vaughn, S., Hughes, K., Porterfield, J., & Gersten, R. (2011). Effects of an early numeracy intervention on the performance of first-grade students with mathematics difficulties. *Exceptional Children, 78*(1), 7–23.

Bryant, D. P., Goodwin, M., Bryant, B., & Higgins, K. (2003). Vocabulary instruction for students with learning disabilities: A review of the research. *Learning Disability Quarterly, 26*, 117–128.

Bulgren, J. A. (2006). Integrated content enhancement routines: Responding to the needs of adolescents with disabilities in rigorous inclusive secondary content classes. *Teaching Exceptional Children, 38*(6), 54–58.

Bulgren, J., Deshler, D. D., & Lenz, B. K. (2007). Engaging adolescents with LD in higher order thinking about history concepts using integrated content enhancement routines. *Journal of Learning Disabilities, 40*(2), 121–133.

Bulgren, J. A., Deshler, D. D., & Schumaker, J. B. (1993). *The concept mastery routine*. Lawrence, KS: Edge Enterprises, Inc.

Bulgren, J., Deshler, D., Schumaker, J., & Lenz, B. K. (2000). The use and effectiveness of analogical instruction in diverse secondary content classrooms. *Journal of Educational Psychology, 92*, 426–441.

Bulgren, J., & Lenz, B. K. (1996). Strategic instruction in the content areas. In D. D. Deshler, E. S. Ellis, & B. K. Lenz (Eds.), *Teaching adolescents with learning disabilities: Strategies and methods* (2nd ed., pp. 409–73). Denver, CO: Love Publishing.

Bulgren, J. A., Lenz, B. K., McKnight, M., Davis, B., Grossen, B., Marquis, J., Deshler, D., & Schumaker, J. B. (2002). *The educational content and outcomes for high school students with disabilities: The perceptions of regular education teachers.*

Bulgren, J. A., Marquis, J. G., Deshler, D. D., Schumaker, J. B., Lenz, B. K., Davis, B., & Grossen, B. (2006). The instructional context of inclusive secondary general education classes: Teachers' instructional roles and practices, curricular demands, & research-based practices and standards. *Learning Disabilities: A Contemporary Journal, 4*(1), 39–65.

Bulgren, J. A., Marquis, J. G., Lenz, B. K., Schumaker, J. B., & Deshler, D. D. (2009). Effectiveness of question exploration to enhance students' written expression. *Reading & Writing Quarterly, 25*(4), 271–289.

Bulgren, J. A., & Scanlon, D. (1997/1998). Teachers' instructional routines and learning strategies that promote understanding of content-area concepts. *Journal of Adolescent & Adult Literacy, 41*, 292–302.

Bull, R., Johnston, R. S., & Roy, J. A. (1999). Exploring the roles of the visual–spatial sketchpad and central executive in children's arithmetical skills: Views from cognition and developmental neuropsychology. *Developmental neuropsychology, 15*, 421–442.

Bull, R., & Scerif, G. (2001). Executive functioning as a predictor of children's mathematics ability: Inhibition, switching, and working memory. *Developmental Neuropsychology, 19*, 273–293.

Burks, M. (2004). Effects of classwide peer tutoring and the number of words spelled correctly by students with LD. *Intervention in School and Clinic, 39*(5), 301–304.

Burns, E. (2006). *IEP-2005*. Springfield, IL: Thomas.

Burns, M. (2005). Using incremental rehearsal to increase fluency of single-digit multiplication facts with children identified as learning disabled in mathematics computation. *Education and Treatment of Children, 28*, 237–249.

Burns, M. K., & Ysseldyke, J. E. (2009). Reported prevalence of evidence-based instructional practices in special education. *The Journal of Special Education, 43*, 3–11.

Butler, D. (1998). The strategic content learning approach to promoting self-regulated learning: A report of three studies. *Journal of Educational Psychology, 90*, 682–697.

Butler, F., Miller, S., Crehan, K., Babbitt, B., & Pierce, T. (2003). Fraction instruction for students with mathematics disabilities: Comparing two teaching sequences. *Learning Disabilities Research & Practice, 18*, 99–111.

Cain, K., & Oakhill, J. V. (1999). Inference making and its relation to comprehension failure. *Reading and Writing, 11*, 489–503.

Cain, K., Oakhill, J., & Lemmon, K. (2004). Individual differences in the inference of word meanings from context: The influence of reading comprehension, vocabulary knowledge, and memory capacity. *Journal of Educational Psychology, 96*, 671–681.

Calderon, M. (2007). *Teaching reading to English language learners, grades 6–12, A framework for improving achievement in the content areas*. Thousand Oaks, CA: Corwin Press.

Calhoon, M. B., & Fuchs, L. S. (2003). The effects of peer-assisted learning strategies and curriculum-based measurement on the mathematics performance of secondary students with disabilities. *Remedial and Special Education, 24*, 235–246.

Calhoon, M. B., Al Otaiba, S., Greenberg, D., King, A., & Avalos, A. (2006). Improving reading skills in predominately Hispanic Title 1 first-grade classrooms: The promise of peer-assisted learning strategies. *Learning Disabilities Research & Practice, 21*, 261–272.

Callahan, J. F., Clark, L. H., & Kellough, R. D. (1998). *Middle and secondary school students: Meeting the challenge. Teaching in the middle and secondary schools* (6th ed.). Frontin, NJ: Simon and Schuster Company.

Cameron, L., & Bartel, L. (2009). The researchers ate the homework! Perspectives of parents and teachers. *Education Canada, 49*(1), 48–51.

Cantrell, R. J., Fusaro, J., & Dougherty, E. (2000). Exploring the effectiveness of journal writing on learning social studies: A comparative study. *Reading Psychology, 21*, 1–11.

Carlson, Lauri. (1981). Aspect and Quantification. In Philip J. Tedeschi & Annie Zaenen (Eds.), *Syntax and Semantics* (vol. 14). Academic Press, New York, NY, 1981.

Carnine, D. (2000). *Why education experts resist effective practices (and what it would take to make education more like medicine)*, no. ED442804. Washington, DC: Thomas Ford Foundation.

Carnine, L., & Carnine, D. (2004). The interaction of reading skills and science content knowledge when teaching struggling secondary students. *Reading & Writing Quarterly, 20*, 203–218.

Carnine, D. W., Silbert, J., Kame'enui, E. J., & Tarver, S. (2009). *Direct instruction reading*. (5th ed.) Upper Saddle River, NJ: Merrill/ Prentice Hall.

Carnine, D. W., Silbert, J., Kame'enui, E. J., Tarver, S. G., & Jungjohann, K. (2006). *Teaching struggling and at-risk readers: A direct instruction approach.* Upper Saddle River, NJ: Prentice Hall.

Carr, E., & Ogle, D. (1987). K-W-L plus: A strategy for comprehension and summarization. *Journal of Reading, 30,* 628–631.

Carskadon, M. A., & Acebo, C. (2002). Regulation of sleepiness in adolescents: Update, insights, and speculation. *Sleep, 25,* 606–614.

Carskadon, M. A., Vieira, C., & Acebo, C. (1993). Association between puberty and delayed phase preference. *Sleep, 16*(3), 258–262.

Carter, E. W., Lane, K. L., Pierson, M. R., & Glaeser, B. (2006). Self-determination skills and opportunities of transition-age youth with emotional disturbance and learning disabilities. *Exceptional Children, 72,* 333–346.

Cartledge, G., Gardner, R., & Ford, D. Y. (2009). *Diverse learners with exceptionalities: Culturally responsive teaching in the inclusive classroom.* Upper Saddle River, NJ: Merrill.

Cass, M., Cates, D., Smith, M., & Jackson, C. (2003). Effects of manipulative instruction on solving area and perimeter problems by students with learning disabilities. *Learning Disabilities Research & Practice, 18,* 112–120.

Casas, A. M., Ferrer, M. S., & Fortea, I. B. (2013). Written composition performance of students with attention-deficit/hyperactivity disorder. *Applied Psycholinguistics, 34*(3), 443–460.

Catts, H. W., & Kamhi, A. G. (2005). *The connections between language and reading disabilities.* New York: Lawrence Erlbaum Associates.

Causton-Theoharis, J., Ashby, C., & Cosier, M. (2009). Islands of loneliness: exploring social interaction through the autobiographies of individuals with autism. *Intellectual and Developmental Disabilities, 47*(2), 84–96.

Cavendish, W. (2014). Academic attainment during commitment and postrelease education-related outcomes of juvenile justice-involved youth with and without disabilities. *Journal of Emotional and Behavioral Disorders, 22*(1), 41–52.

Cavendish, W., & Hodnett, K. (2017). Current practice alert: Collaborative Strategic Reading. Division of Learning Disabilities ALERT Series: A publication of the Council for Exceptional Children's Division for Learning Disabilities and Division for Research. *Alert, 26,* 1–6.

Cawley, J., Parmar, R., Foley, T. E., Salmon, S., & Roy, S. (2001). Arithmetic performance of students: Implications for standards and programming. *Exceptional Children, 67,* 311–328.

Center for Public Education. (2007). *Research Q & A: Homework.* Retrieved from http://www.centerforpubliceducation.org

Center for Teaching Excellence, VCU (accessed July 14, 2011). Modified from: Center for Teaching Excellence, VCU. Activities to Engage Students. http://www.vcu.edu/cte /resources/active_learning.htm (accessed July 14, 2011).

Chalk, J., Hagan-Burke, S., & Burke, M. (2005). The effects of self-regulated strategy development on the writing process for high school students with learning disabilities. *Learning Disability Quarterly, 28,* 75–87.

Chall, J. S. (1983). *Stages of reading development.* New York: McGraw-Hill.

Chall, J. S., & Stahl, S. A. (1982). Reading. In H. E. Mitzel (Ed.), *Encyclopedia of educational research* (5th ed., pp. 1535–59). New York: Free Press.

Chambers, D. L. (1996). Direct modeling and invented procedures: Building on students' informal strategies. *Teaching Children Mathematics, 3*(2), 92–95.

Chard, D., & Dickson, S. (1999). Phonological awareness: Instructional and assessment guidelines. *Intervention in School and Clinic, 34,* 261–270.

Christensen, C. A. (1999). Learning disability: Issues of representation, power, and the medicalization of school failure. In R. J. Sternberg & L. Spear-Swerling (Eds.), Perspectives on Learning Disabilities: Biological, Cognitive, Contextual. Boulder, CO: Westview Press.

Ciullo, S., & Reutebuch, C. (2013). *Learning Disabilities Research & Practice, 28*(4), 196–210.

Clarke, L. S., Haydon, T., Bauer, A., & Epperly, A. C. (2016). Inclusion of students with an intellectual disability in the general education classroom with you. *Preventing School Failure, 60,* 1, 35–42.

Clarke, L. S., Haydon, T., Bauer, A., & Epperly, A. E. (2016). Inclusion of students with an intellectual disability in the general education classroom with the use of response cards. *Preventing School Failure, 60*(1), 35–42.

Cobb, R. B., & Alwell, M. (2009). Transition planning/ coordinating interventions for youth with disabilities: A systematic review. *Career Development for Exceptional Individuals, 32,* 70–81.

Cobb, B., Sample, P. L., Alwell, M., & Johns, N. R. (2006). Cognitive-behavioral interventions, dropout, and youth with disabilities: A systematic review. *Remedial and Special Education, 27*(5), 259–275.

Coleman, M., & Webber, J. (2002). *Emotional and behavioral disorders: Theory and practice* (4th ed.). Boston, MA: Allyn & Bacon.

Common Core State Standards Initiative. (2010). Common Core State Standards for mathematics. Retrieved from http://www.corestandards.org/assets/CCSSI_Math%20 Standards.pdf

Compton, D. L., Fuchs, L. S., Fuchs, D., Lambert, W., Hamlett, C. L. (2012). The cognitive and academic profiles of reading and mathematics learning disabilities. *Journal of Learning Disabilities, 45,* 79–85

Cook, B., & Cook, L. (2017). Do research findings apply to my students? Examining study samples and sampling. *Learning Disabilities Research & Practice, 32*(2), 78–84.

Cook, B. G., & Cook, S. C. (2013). Unraveling evidence-based practices in special education, *Journal of Special Education, 47*(2), 71–82.

Cook, L., & Friend, M. (2000). *Interactions: Collaboration skills for school professionals* (3rd ed.). New York: Addison Wesley Longman.

Cook, B., & Semmell, M. (1999). Peer acceptance of included students with disabilities as a function of severity of disability and classroom composition. *Journal of Special Education, 33*, 50–61.

Cooper, H. (2007). The Battle Over Homework: Common Ground for Administrators, Teachers, and Parents. Thousand Oaks, CA: Corwin Pres.

Cooper, H., & Nye, B. (1994). Homework for students with learning disabilities: The implications of research for policy and practice. *Journal of Learning Disabilities, 27*, 470–479.

Cooper, H., Robinson, J. C., & Patall, E. A. (2006). Does homework improve academic achievement? A synthesis of research, 1987–2003. *Review of Educational Research, 76*(1), 1–62.

Cortese, S. et al. (2013). Practitioner review: Current best practice in the management of adverse events during treatment with ADHD medications in children and adolescents. *Journal of Child Psychology and Psychiatry, 54*(3), 227–246.

Cortiella, C. (2006). *IDEA parent guide: A comprehensive guide to your rights and responsibilities under the Individuals with Disabilities Education Act* (IDEA 2004). New York: National Center for Learning Disabilities.

Costa-Guerra, L., & Costa-Guerra, B. (2016). Understanding vocabulary use by Native American students and the relationship with special education. *Cogent Education, 3*(1), Article 1180737.

Council for Exceptional Children (CEC). (2007). *Federal outlook for exceptional children: Fiscal year 2008*. Arlington, VA: Council for Exceptional Children.

Council for Exceptional Children (CEC). (2015). CEC knowledge and skill base for all entry-level special education teachers of students with exceptionalities in individualized general curriculums. *What every special educator must know: Ethics, standards, and guidelines for special educators*, 6th ed. Arlington, VA: Council for Exceptional Children.

Council of Chief State School Officers. (2017). *CCSSO principles of effective school improvement systems*. Washington, DC: Author.

Coutinho, M. J., Oswald, D. P., & Best, A. M. (2006). Differences in outcomes for female and male students in special education. *Career Development for Exceptional Individuals, 29*(1), 48–59.

Craig, F. I., & Lockhart, R. S. (1972). Levels of processing: A framework for memory research. *Journal of Verbal Learning and Verbal Behavior, 11*, 671–684.

Cramer, R. L. (2004). *The language arts*. Boston, MA: Allyn & Bacon.

Cratty, J. (1994). Inspiration—On the way to better ideas. *Computer, 27*, 81–82.

Crawford, D. B., & Carnine, D. (2000). Comparing the effects of textbooks in eighth-grade U.S. history: Does conceptual organization help? *Education and Treatment of Children, 23*, 387–422.

Crawford, L., Helwig, R., & Tindal, G. (2004). Writing performance assessments: How important is extended time? *Journal of Learning Disabilities, 37*, 132–143.

Creaghead, N. (1992). *Classroom language intervention: Developing schema for school success*. Buffalo, NY: Edcom Associates.

Crowley, S. J., Acebo, C., & Carskadon, M. A. (2007). Sleep, circadian rhythms and delayed phase in adolescence. *Sleep Medicine, 8*, 602–612.

Crutchfield, M. D. (2003). What do the CEC standards mean to me? Using the CEC standards to improve my practice. *Teaching Exceptional Children, 35*(6), 40–45.

Cuenca-Carlino, Y., & Mustian, A. L. (2013). Self-regulated strategy development: Connecting persuasive writing to self-advocacy for students with emotional and behavioral disorders. *Behavioral Disorders, 39*, 3–15.

Cummings, R., Maddux, C. D., & Casey, J. (2000). Individualized transition planning for students with learning disabilities. *The Career Development Quarterly, 49*, 60–72.

Cunningham, P. (1980). Applying a compare/contrast process to identifying polysyllabic words. *Journal of Reading Behavior, 12*, 213–223.

Cunningham, P. M. (1987). Polysyllabic word strategies for content-area reading. *Clearing House, 61*, 42–45.

D'Antonio, M. (2004). *The state boys rebellion*. New York: Simon & Schuster.

DaDeppo, L. M. W. (2009). Integration factors related to the academic success and intent to persist of college students with learning disabilities. *Learning Disabilities Research & Practice, 24*(3), 122–131.

Daneman, M. (2001). Learning disabled individuals show deficits on working memory tasks: The question is why? *Issues in Education, 7*, 79–85.

Davila, R., Williams, M., & MacDonald, J. (1991). U.S. Department of Education, Office of Special Education and Rehabilitative Services. *Clarification of policy to address the needs of children with attention deficit disorder within general and/or special education*. Memorandum of September 16, 1991.

de Jong, T. (1991). Learning and instruction with computer simulations. *Education & Computing, 6*, 217–229.

De La Paz, S. (1997). Strategy instruction in planning: Teaching students with learning and writing disabilities to compose persuasive and expository essays. *Learning Disability Quarterly, 20*, 227–248.

De La Paz, S., & Graham, S. (2002). Explicitly teaching strategies, skills, and knowledge: Writing instruction in middle school classrooms. *Journal of Educational Psychology, 94*, 687–698.

De Valenzuela, J. S., & Baca, L. (2004). Procedures and techniques for assessing the bilingual exceptional child. In L. M. Baca & H. T. Cervantes (Eds.), *The bilingual special education interface* (4th ed., pp. 184–203). Upper Saddle River, NJ: Pearson.

Dehn, M. J. (2008). *Working memory and academic learning assessment and intervention*. New Jersey: John Wiley & Sons, Inc.

Deno, S. (1985). Curriculum-based measurement: The emerging alternative. *Exceptional Children, 52*, 219–232.

Deno, S. (1992). The nature and development of curriculum-based measurement. *Preventing School Failure, 36*(2), 5–10.

Deno, S. (2003a). Curriculum-based measures: Development and perspectives. *Assessment for Effective Intervention, 28*(3–4), 3–12.

Deno, S. (2003b). Developments in curriculum-based measurement. *Journal of Special Education, 37*(3), 184–192.

Deno, S., Marston, D., & Mirkin, P. (1982). Valid measurement procedures for continuous evaluation of written expression. *Exceptional Children, 48*, 368–371.

Deshler, D. D., Alley, G. R., Warner, M. M., & Schumaker, J. B. (1981). Instructional practices for promoting skill acquisition and generalization in severely learning disabled adolescents. *Learning Disability Quarterly, 4*, 415–421.

Deshler, D., & Schumaker, J. (2006). *Teaching adolescents with disabilities: Accessing the general education curriculum*. Thousand Oaks, CA: Corwin Press.

Deshler, D. D., Schumaker, J. B., Bulgren, J. A., Lenz, B. K., Jantzen, J. E., Adams, G., Carnine, D., Grossen, B., Davis, B., & Marquis, J. (2001). Making learning easier: Connecting new knowledge to things students already know. *Teaching Exceptional Children, 33*(4), 82–85.

Deshler, D. D., Schumaker, J. B., Lenz, B. K., Bulgren, J. A., Hock, M. F., Knight, M. J., & Ehren, B. J. (2001). Ensuring content-area learning by secondary students with learning disabilities. *Learning Disabilities Research & Practice, 16*, 96–108.

Dewey, D., Crawford, S. G., & Kaplan, B. J. (2003). Clinical importance of parent ratings of everyday cognitive abilities in children with learning and attention problems. *Journal of Learning Disabilities, 36*, 87–93.

Dexter, D. D., & Hughes, C. A. (2011). Graphic organizers and students with learning disabilities: A meta-analysis. *Learning Disability Quarterly, 34*, 51–72.

Diana v. State Board of Education, Civil Action, no. C70 37RFP (N.D. Cal. January 7, 1970 and June 18, 1973).

Dickinson, D. L., & Verbeek, R. I. (2002). Wage differentials between college graduates with and without LD. *Journal of Learning Disabilities, 35*, 175–185.

Dieker, L. A. (2001). What are the characteristics of "effective" middle and high school co-taught teams for students with disabilities? *Preventing School Failure, 46*(1), 14–23.

Dieker, L. A., & Murawski, W. W. (2003). Co-teaching at the secondary level: Unique issues, current trends, and suggestions for success. *The High School Journal, 86*, 1–13.

Division for Early Childhood. (2014). DEC recommended practices in early intervention/early childhood special education 2014. Retrieved from http://www.dec-sped.org/recommendedpractices

Dixon, R. C. (1991). The application of sameness analysis to spelling. *Journal of Learning Disabilities, 24*, 285–310.

DoD Instruction 1304.26. (2015). *Qualification standards for enlistment, appointment, and induction*. http://www.dtic.mil/whs/directives/search.htm (accessed April 3, 2017).

Dodge, E. P. (2004). Communication skills: The foundation for meaningful group intervention in school-based programs. *Topics in Language Disorders, 24*, 141–150.

Dolan, J. E. (2016). Splicing the Divide: A Review of Research on the Evolving Digital Divide among K-12 Students. *Journal of Research on Technology in Education, 48*(1), 16–37.

Dolch, E. W. (1936). A basic sight vocabulary. *The Elementary School Journal, 36*, 456–460.

Dolch, E. W. (1939). *A manual for remedial reading*. Champaign, IL: Garrard Press.

Donahue, M., Pearl, R., & Bryan, T. (1980). Learning disabled children's conversational competence: Responses to inadequate messages. *Applied Psycholinguistics, 1*, 387–403.

Dougherty, B., Bryant, D. P., Bryant, B. R., Darrough, R. L., & Pfannenstiel, K. H. (2015). Developing concepts and generalizations to build algebraic thinking: The reversibility, flexibility, and generalization approach. *Intervention in School and Clinic, 50*, 273–281.

Dounay, J. (2007). High school graduation requirements: Mathematics. Denver, CO: Education Commission of the States. http://mb2.esc.org/reports/Report.aspx?id=900.

Dowhower, S. (1989). Repeated reading: Research into practice. *The Reading Teacher, 42*(7), 502–507.

Dowker, A. (2003). Young children's estimates for addition: The zone of partial knowledge and understanding. In A. J. Baroody & A. Dowker (Eds.), *The development of arithmetic concepts and skills* (pp. 243–65). Mahwah, NJ: Erlbaum.

Drame, E. R. (2002). Sociocultural context effects on teachers' readiness to refer for learning disabilities. *Exceptional Children, 69*, 41–53.

Dunlap, G., Kincaid, D., Horner, R. H., Knoster, T., Bradshaw, C. P. (2014). A comment on the term "Positive Behavior Support". *Journal of Positive Behavior Interventions, 16*(3), 133–136.

Dunn, L. M. (1968). Special education for the mildly retarded—Is much of it justifiable? *Exceptional Children, 35*, 5–22.

Dunn, C., Chambers, D., & Rabren, K. (2004). Variables affecting students' decisions to drop out of school. *Remedial and Special Education, 25*, 314–323.

DuPaul, G., Arbolino, L., & Booster, G. (2009). In M. J. Mayer, J. E. Lochman, & F. Gresham (Eds.), Cognitive-behavioral interventions for attention-deficit/hyperactivity disorder. In *Cognitive-behavioral interventions for emotional and behavioral interventions for emotional and behavioral disorders. School-based practices* (pp. 295–327). New York: Guilford Press.

Dzaldov, B., & Peterson, S. (2005). Book leveling and readers. *Reading Teacher, 59*, 222–229.

Eden, S., & Heiman, T. (2011). Computer mediated communication: Social support for students with and without learning disabilities. *Educational Technology & Society, 14*(2), 89–97.

Edens, K., & Potter, E. (2007). The relationship of drawing and mathematical problem solving: "Draw for Math" tasks. *Studies in Art Education: A Journal of Issues and Research in Art Education, 48*, 282–298.

Edgar, E. (2005). Bending back on high school programs for youth with learning disabilities. *Learning Disability Quarterly, 28*(2), 171–173.

Education of the Handicapped Act Amendments of 1983. Pub. Law no. 98–199.

Edyburn, D. (2010). Would you recognize Universal Design for Learning if you saw it? *Learning Disability Quarterly, 33*(1), 33–41.

Ehri, L. (1995). Phases of development in learning to read words by sight. *Journal of Research in Reading, 18,* 116–125.

Ehri, L. (1998). Grapheme-phoneme knowledge is essential for learning to read words in English. In J. Metsala & L. Ehri (Eds.), *Word recognition in beginning literacy* (pp. 3–40). Mahwah, NJ: Lawrence Erlbaum.

Ehri, L. (2004). Teaching phonemic awareness and phonics. In P. McCardle & V. Chhabra (Eds.). *The voice of evidence* (pp. 153–186). Baltimore, NY: Paul Brookes.

Ehri, L. C. (2003). *Systematic phonics instruction: Finds of the National Reading Panel.* Paper presented at the invitational seminar organized by the Standards and Effectiveness Unit, Department for Education and Skills, British Government (March).

Ehri, L. C., Nunes, S., Stahl, S., & Willows, D. (2001). Systematic phonics instruction helps students learn to read: Evidence from National Reading Panel's meta-analysis. *Review of Educational Research, 71*, 393–447.

Ehri, L. C., & Robbins, C. (1992). Beginners need some decoding skill to read words by analogy. *Reading Research Quarterly, 27*, 13–26.

Eisenman, L. T. (2007). Self-determination interventions: Building a foundation for school completion. *Remedial and Special Education, 28*, 2–8.

Elkins, I., Malone, S., Keyes, M., Iacono, W., & McGue, M. (2011). The impact of attention-deficit/hyperactivity disorder on preadolescent adjustment may be greater for girls than for boys. *Journal of Clinical Child & Adolescent Psychology, 40*(4), 532–545.

Elksnin, N., & Elksnin, L. (2001). Adolescents with disabilities: The need for occupational social skills training. *Exceptionality, 9*(1–2), 91–105.

Ellis, E. S. (1989). A metacognitive intervention for increasing class participation. *Learning Disabilities Focus, 5*, 36–46.

Ellis, E. S. (1992). *The vocabulary LINCing routine.* Lawrence, KS: Edge Enterprises.

Ellis, E. S. (1998). *The framing routine.* Lawrence, KS: Edge Enterprises.

Ellis, E. S., & Colvert, G. (1996). Writing strategy instruction. In D. D. Deshler, E. S. Ellis, & B. K. Lenz (Eds.), *Teaching adolescents with learning disabilities: Strategies and methods* (2nd ed., pp. 61–125). Denver, CO: Love Publishing.

Ellis, E. S., Deshler, D. D., Lenz, B. K., Schumaker, J. B., & Clark, F. L. (1991). An instructional model for teaching learning strategies. *Focus on Exceptional Children, 23*(6), 1–24.

Ellis, E. S., & Graves, A. W. (1990). Teaching rural students with learning disabilities: A paraphrasing strategy to increase comprehension of main ideas. *Rural Special Education Quarterly, 10*, 2–10.

Ellis, E. S., & Lenz, B. K. (1990). Techniques for mediating content-area learning: Issues and research. *Focus on Exceptional Children, 22*(9), 1–16.

Engelmann, S., Carnine, D., Engelmann, O., & Kelly, B. (2002). *Connecting Math Concepts.* DeSoto, TX: SRA/McGraw-Hill.

Englert, S. E., Heibert, E. H., & Stewart, S. S. (1985). Spelling unfamiliar words by an analogy strategy. *Journal of Special Education, 19*, 291–303.

Englert, C., & Mariage, T. (1990). Send for the POSSE: Structuring the comprehension dialog. *Academic Therapy, 25*, 472–487.

Englert, C. S., & Mariage, T.V. (1991). Making students partners in the comprehension process: Organizing the reading "POSSE." *Learning Disability Quarterly, 14*, 123–138.

Englert, S. E., & Mariage, T.V. (1991). Shared understandings: Structuring the writing experience through dialogue. *Journal of Learning Disabilities, 24*, 330–342.

Englert, S. E., & Raphael, T. E. (1988). Constructed well-formed prose: Process, structure, and metacognitive knowledge. *Exceptional Children, 54*, 513–520.

Englert, S. E., Raphael, T. E., Fear, K. L., & Anderson, L. M. (1988). Students' metacognitive knowledge about how to write informational texts. *Learning Disability Quarterly, 11*, 18–46.

Englert, C. S., Zhao, Y., Dunsmore, K., Collings, N.Y., & Wolbers, K. (2007). Scaffolding the writing of students with disabilities through procedural facilitation: Using an Internet-based technology to improve performance. *Learning Disability Quarterly, 30*, 9–29.

Ennis, R. P., & Jolivette, K. (2014). Using self-regulated strategy development for persuasive writing to increase the writing and self-efficacy skills of students with emotional and behavioral disorders in health class. *Behavioral Disorders, 40*(1), 26–36.

Epstein, J. L., & Van Voorhis, F. L. (2001). More than minutes: Teachers' roles in designing homework. *Educational Psychologist, 36*(3), 181–193.

Every Student Succeeds Act (ESSA) (2015). Public Law no. 114–95.

Evmenova, A. S., Graff, H. J., Jerome, M. K., & Behrmann, M. M. (2010). Word prediction programs with phonetic spelling support: performance comparisons and impact on journal writing for students with writing difficulties. *Learning Disabilities Research & Practice, 25*(4), 170–182.

Fabiano, G., Pelham, W., Gnagy, E., Burroww-MacLean, L., Coles, E., Chacko, A. et al. (2007). The single and combined effects of multiple intensities of behavior modification and methylphenidate for children with attention deficit hyperactivity disorder in a classroom setting. *School Psychology Review, 36,* 195–216.

Fasko, S.N., & Fasko, D. (2010). "A preliminary study on sight word flash card drill" Does it impact reading fluency? *Journal of the American Academy of Special Education Professionals,* 61–69.

Faulkner, H. J., & Levy, B. A. (1994). Fluent and nonfluent forms of transfer in reading: Words and their message. *Psychonomic Bulletin and Review, 6,* 111–116.

Federal Register. 71(156), August 14, 2006. Rules and Regulations.

Feldman, D., Kinnison, L., Jay, R., & Harth, R. (1983). The effects of differential labeling on professional concepts and attitudes toward the emotionally disturbed/behaviorally disordered. *Behavioral Disorders, 8,* 191–198.

Fenton, A., & Krahn, T. (2007). Autism, neurodiversity, and equality beyond the 'normal'. *Journal of Ethics in Mental Health, 2*(2), 1–6.

Fergusson, D. M., Horwood, L. J., & Lynskey, M. T. (1993). The effects of conduct disorder and attention deficit in middle childhood on offending and scholastic ability at age 13. *Journal of Child Psychology and Psychiatry, 34,* 899–916.

Ferri, B. A., Gregg, N., & Heggoy, S. J. (1997). Profiles of college students demonstrating learning disabilities with and without giftedness. *Journal of Learning Disabilities, 30*(5), 552–559.

Figueroa, R. A. (2005). Dificultades o desabilidades do aprendizaje? *Learning Disability Quarterly, 28,* 163–167.

Fisher, D., & Frey, N. (2015). Teacher modeling using complex informational texts. *Reading Teacher, 69*(1), 63–69.

Fisher, D., & Ivey, G. (2005). Literacy and language as learning in content-area classes: A departure from "every teacher a teacher of reading." *Action in Teacher Education, 27*(2), 3–11.

Fitzgerald, N. S., Miller, S. P., Higgins, K., Pierce, T., & Tandy, D. (2012). Exploring the efficacy of online strategy instruction for improving the reading abilities of students with learning disabilities. *Journal of Special Education Technology, 27*(1), 33–47.

Fixsen, D. L., Blase, K. A., Horner, R., & Sugai, G. (2009). *Scaling-up evidence-based practices in education, Scaling-up brief #1.* Chapel Hill: The University of North Carolina, FpG, SiSep. http://sisep.fpg.unc.edu/resources/scalingbrief -1-scaling-evidence-based-practices-education.

Flavell, J. (1976). Metacognitive aspects in problem solving. In *The nature of intelligence.* Hillsdale, NJ: Erlbaum.

Fletcher, J., Lyon, G. R., Fuchs, L., & Barnes, M. (2007). Learning disabilities: From identification to intervention. New York: The Guilford Press.

Flood, A. M., Hare, D. J., Wallis, P. (2011). An Investigation into Social Information Processing in Young People with Asperger Syndrome. *Autism: The International Journal of Research and Practice, 15*(5), 601–624.

Flower, L. (1985). *Problem-solving strategies for writing.* New York: Harcourt Brace.

Foegen, A. (2008). Algebra progress monitoring and interventions for students with learning disabilities. *Learning Disability Quarterly, 31,* 65–78.

Foley-Nicpon, M., Fosenburg, S. L., Wurster, K. G., Assouline, S. G. (2017). Identifying high ability children with DSM-5 autism spectrum or social communication disorder: Performance on autism diagnostic instruments. *Journal of Autism and Developmental Disorders, 47*(2), 460–471.

Foorman, B., Beyler, N., Borradaile, K., Coyne, M., Denton, C. A., Dimino, J., Furgeson, J., Hayes, L., Henke, J., Justice, L., Keating, B., Lewis, W., Sattar, S., Streke, A., Wagner, R., & Wissel, S. (2016). *Foundational skills to support reading for understanding in kindergarten through 3rd grade (NCEE 2016-4008).* Washington, DC: National Center for Education Evaluation and Regional Assistance (NCEE), Institute of Education Sciences, U.S. Department of Education. Retrieved from the NCEE website: http://whatworks.ed.gov.

Ford, D. (2012). Culturally different students in special education: Looking backward to move forward. *Exceptional Children, 78*(4), 391–405.

Frank, A. R., Wacker, D. P., Keith, T. Z., & Sagen, T. K. (1987). The effectiveness of a spelling study package for learning disabled students. *Learning Disabilities Research, 2,* 110–117.

Frazier, T. W., Youngstrom, E. A., Glutting, J. J., & Watkins, M. W. (2007). ADHD and achievement: Meta-analysis of the child, adolescent, and adult literatures and a concomitant study with college students. *Journal of Learning Disabilities, 40*(1), 49–65.

Freeman, B., & Crawford, L. (2008). Creating a middle school mathematics curriculum for English-language learners. *Remedial and Special Education, 29,* 9–19.

Friel-Patti, S. (1999). Specific language impairment: Continuing clinical concerns. *Topics in Language Disorders, 20,* 1–13.

Friend, M., & Bursuck, W. (2006). *Including students with special needs: A practical guide for classroom teachers* (4th ed.). Boston: Allyn & Bacon.

Friend, M., & Cook, L. (2002). *Interactions: Collaboration skills for school professionals* (4th ed.). New York: Longman.

Froese, T., Stanghellini, G., & Bertelli, M. O. (2013). Is it normal to be a principal mindreader? Revising theories of social cognition on the basis of schizophrenia and high functioning autism-spectrum disorders. *Research in Developmental Disabilities: A Multidisciplinary Journal,34*(5), 1376–1387.

Fry, E., Fountoukidis, D., & Polk, J. (1985). *The new reading teacher's book of lists.* Englewood Cliffs, NJ: Prentice Hall.

Fuchs, L. S., Compton, D. L., Fuchs, D., Paulsen, K., Bryant, J. D., & Hamlett, C. L. (2005). The prevention, identification, and cognitive determinants of math difficulty. *Journal of Educational Psychology, 97,* 493–513.

Fuchs, L., & Fuchs, D. (2005). Peer-assisted learning strategies: Promoting word recognition, fluency, and reading comprehension in young children. *Journal of Special Education, 41*, 93–99.

Fuchs, L. S., & Fuchs, D. (2001). Principles for sustaining research-based practice in the schools: A case study. *Focus on Exceptional Children, 33*(6), 1–14.

Fuchs, L. S., & Fuchs, D. (2004). Determining adequate yearly progress from kindergarten through grade six with curriculum-based measurement. *Assessment for Effective Instruction, 29*(4), 25–38.

Fuchs, D., & Fuchs, L. S. (2015). Rethinking service delivery for students with significant learning problems: Developing and implementing intensive instruction. *Remedial and Special Education, 36*, 105–111.

Fuchs, D., Fuchs, L. S., & Compton, D. L. (2012). Smart RTI: A next generation approach to multilevel prevention. *Exceptional Children, 78*(3), 263–279.

Fuchs, L. S., Fuchs, D., Finelli, R., Courey, S. J., & Hamlett, C. L. (2004). Expanding schema-based transfer instruction to help third graders solve real-life mathematical problems. *American Educational Research Journal, 41*, 419–445.

Fuchs, L. S., Fuchs, D., Hamlett, C. L., Philips, N. B., & Bentz, J. (1994). Classwide curriculum-based measurement: Helping general educators meet the challenge of student diversity. *Exceptional Children, 60*, 518–537.

Fuchs, L., Fuchs, D., Hamlett, C., Walz, L., & Germann, G. (1993). Formative evaluation of academic progress: How much growth can we expect? *School Psychology Review, 22*, 27–48.

Fuchs, D., Fuchs, L. S., Mathes, P. G., & Martinez, E. A. (2002). Preliminary evidence on the social standing of students with learning disabilities in PALS and no-PALS classrooms. *Learning Disabilities: Research & Practice, 17*(4), 205–215.

Fuchs, D., Fuchs, L., Mathes, P. H., & Simmons, D. C. (1997). Peer-assisted strategies: Making classrooms more responsive to diversity. *American Educational Research Journal, 34*, 174–206, no. EJ545455.

Fuchs, L. S., Fuchs, D., Powell, S. R., Seethaler, P. M., Cirino, P. T., & Fletcher, J. M. (2008). Intensive intervention for students with mathematics disabilities: Seven principles of effective practice. *Learning Disability Quarterly, 31*, 79–92.

Fuchs, D., Mock, D., Morgan, P., & Young, C. L. (2003). Responsiveness-to-Intervention: Definitions, evidence, and implications for the learning disabilities construct. *Learning Disabilities Research & Practice, 18*, 157–171.

Fuligni, A. J., & Hardway, C. (2006). Daily variation in adolescents' sleep, activities, and psychological well-being. *Journal of Research on Adolescence, 16*, 353–378.

Fulk, B., & King, K. (2001). Classwide peer tutoring at work. *Teaching Exceptional Children, 34*(2), 49–53.

Fulk, M., & Stormont-Spurgin, M. (1995). Spelling interventions for students with disabilities: A review. *The Journal of Special Education, 28*, 488–513.

Gagne, E. (1985). *The cognitive psychology of school learning.* Boston: Little, Brown and Company.

Gallagher, D. (2010). Hiding in Plain Sight: The Nature and Role of Theory in Learning Disability Labeling. *Disability Studies Quarterly, 30*(2), 4–17.

Gallagher, D. J. (2004). Educational research, philosophical orthodoxy, and unfulfilled promises: The quandary of traditional research in U.S. special education. In G. Thomas & R. Pring (Eds.), *Evidence-based practices in education* (pp. 119–132). Columbus, OH: Open University Press.

Gammill, D. M. (2006). Learning the write way. *The Reading Teacher, 59*, 754–762.

Gamoran, A., & Weinstein, M. (1998). Differentiation and opportunity in restructured schools. *American Journal of Education, 106*, 385–415.

Gardynik, U. M., & McDonald, L. (2005). Implications of risk and resilience in the life of the individual who is gifted/learning disabled. *Roeper Review, 27*(4), 206.

Garmston, R. (1997). *The presenter's fieldbook: A practical guide.* Norwood, MA: Christopher-Gordon Publishers.

Garrison, L., Amaral, O., & Ponce, G. (2006). Unlatching mathematics for English language learners. *National Council of Supervisors of Mathematics, 9*(1), 14–24.

Gartner, A., & Lipsky, D. K. (1987). Beyond special education: Toward a quality system for all students. *Harvard Educational Review, 57*(4), 367–395.

Gaskins, I. W. (2005). *Success with struggling readers: The benchmark school approach.* New York: Guilford Press.

Gately, S. E., & Gately, F. J. (2001). Understanding coteaching components. *TEACHING Exceptional Children, 33*(4), 40–47.

Gathercole, S. E., & Alloway, T. P. (2008). Working memory and classroom learning. In K. Thurman & K. Fiorello (Eds.), *Cognitive Development in K-3 Classroom Learning: Research Applicants.*

Gathercole, S. E., Alloway, T. P., Willis, C. S., & Adams, A. M. (2006). Working memory in children with reading disabilities. *Journal of Experimental Child Psychology, 93*, 265–281.

Gathercole, S. E., Durling, M., Evans, S., Jeffcock, E., & Stone, S. (2008). Working memory abilities and children's performance in laboratory analogues of classroom activities. *Applied Cognitive Psychology, 22*, 1019–1037.

Gathercole, S. E., Lamont, E., Alloway, T. P. (2005). Working memory in the classroom. In S. Pickering (Ed.), *Working Memory and Education.* Elsevier Press.

Gathercole, S. E., Tiffany, C., Briscoe, J., Thorn, A. S. C., & the ALSPAC Team. (2005). Developmental consequences of phonological loop deficits during early childhood: A longitudinal study. *Journal of Child Psychology and Psychiatry, 46*, 598–511.

Geary, D. (2004). Mathematics and learning disabilities. *Journal of Learning Disabilities, 37*, 4–15.

Geary, D. C. (2011). Consequences, characteristics, and causes of mathematical learning disabilities and persistent low achievement in mathematics. *Journal of Developmental & Behavioral Pediatrics, 33*(30), 250–263.

Geary, D., Hoard, M., Byrd-Craven, J., & DeSoto, M. (2004). Strategy choices in simple and complex addition: Contributions of working memory and counting knowledge for children with mathematical disability. *Journal of Experimental Child Psychology, 88*(2), 121–151.

George, C. L. (2010). Effects of response cards on performance and participation in social studies for middle school students with emotional and behavioral disorders. *Behavioral Disorders, 35*(3), 200–213.

Gerber, M. M. (1994). Postmodernism in special education. *Journal of Special Education, 28*(3), 368–378.

Gerber, P. J., Price, L. A., Mulligan, R., & Shessel, I. (2004). Beyond transition: A comparison of the employment experiences of American and Canadian adults with LD. *Journal of Learning Disabilities, 37*, 283–291.

Gersten, R. (1991). The eye of the beholder: A response to "Sociomoral atmosphere . . . A study of teachers' enacted interpersonal understanding." *Early Childhood Research Quarterly, 6*, 529–537.

Gersten, R. (1992). Passion and precision: Response to "Curriculum-based assessment and direct instruction: Critical reflections on fundamental assumptions." *Exceptional Children, 58*, 464–467.

Gersten, R., & Chard, D. (1999). Number sense: Rethinking arithmetic instruction for students with math difficulties. *Journal of Special Education, 33*, 18–28.

Gersten, R., Chard, D., & Baker, S. (2000). Factors enhancing sustained use of research-based instructional practices. *Journal of Learning Disabilities, 33*, 445–457.

Gersten, R., Chard, D., Madhavi, J., Baker, S., Morphy, P., & Flojo, J. (2009). Mathematics instruction for students with learning disabilities: A meta-analysis of instructional components. *Review of Educational Research, 79*(3), 1202–1242.

Gersten, R., Fuchs, L. S., Compton, D., Coyne, M., Greenwood, C., & Innocenti, M. S. (2005). Quality indicators for group experimental and quasi-experimental research in special education. *Exceptional Children, 71*, 149–164.

Gersten, R., Fuchs, L., Williams, J., & Baker, S. (2001). Teaching reading comprehension strategies to students with learning disabilities. *Review of Educational Research, 71*, 279–320.

Gersten, R., Jordan, N., & Flojo, J. (2005). Early identification and intervention for students with mathematics difficulties. *Journal of Learning Disabilities, 38*(4), 293–304.

Gettinger, M., Bryant, N. D., & Fayne, H. (1982). Designing spelling instruction for learning disabled children: An emphasis on unit size, distributed practice, and training for transfer. *The Journal of Special Education, 16*, 439–448.

Gibb, G. S., & Dyches, T. T. (2016). *IEPs: Writing quality individualized education programs* (3rd ed.). Boston, MA: Allyn & Bacon.

Gibbs, D., & Cooper, E. (1989). Prevalence of communication disorders in students with learning disabilities. *Journal of Learning Disabilities, 22*, 60–63.

Gilabert, R., Martinez, G., & Vidal-Abarca, E. (2005). Some good texts are always better: Test revision to foster inferences of readers with high and low prior background knowledge. *Learning and Instruction, 15*, 45–68.

Gill, S. R. (2002). Responding to readers. *The Reading Teacher, 56*, 119–121.

Gillies, R. M., & Ashman, A. F. (2000). The effects of cooperative learning on students with learning difficulties in the lower elementary school. *Journal of Special Education, 34*(1), 19–27.

Ginsburg, A., Leinwand, S., Anstrom, T., & Pollock, E. (2005). *What the United States Can Learn From Singapore's World-Class Mathematics System (and what Singapore can learn from the United States)*. Washington, DC: American Institutes for Research.

Gleason, J. B. (2009). The development of language: An overview and a preview. In J. B. Gleason (Ed.), *The Development of Language* (7th ed., pp. 1–36). Boston, MA: Pearson.

Gleason, M. M. (1999). The role of evidence in argumentative writing. *Reading & Writing Quarterly, 15*, 81–106.

Gleason, M., Carnine, D., & Vala, N. (1991). Cumulative versus rapid introduction of new information. *Exceptional Children, 57*(4), 353–358.

Gonzalez, N., Andrade, R., Civil, M., & Moll, L. (2001). Bridging funds of distributed knowledge: Creating zones of practices in mathematics. *Journal of Education for Students Placed at Risk, 6*, 115–132.

Good, T., & Brophy, J. (1994). *Looking into classrooms*. New York: Harper Collins College Publishers.

Good, T. L., & Brophy, J. E. (2003). *Looking in classrooms* (9th ed.). Boston, MA: Allyn & Bacon.

Good, R. H., Simmons, D. C., & Kame'enui, E. J. (2001). The importance and decision-making utility of a continuum of fluency-based indicators of foundational reading skills for third-grade high-stakes outcomes. *Scientific Studies of Reading, 5*(3), 257–288.

Goodlad, J. (1984). *A place called school*. New York: McGraw-Hill.

Goodman, J. I., & Duffy, M. L. (2007). Using "BUGS" to increase student participation. *TEACHING Exceptional Children Plus, 3*(4) Article 3. http://excholarship.bc.edu/education/tecplus/vol3/iss4/art3 (accessed June 21, 2007).

Gordon, C., & Braun, C. (1983). Using story schema as an aid to reading and writing. *The Reading Teacher, 37*, 116–121.

Gordon, J., Vaughn, S., & Schumm, J. S. (1993). Spelling interventions: A review of literature and implications for instruction for students with learning disabilities. *Learning Disabilities Research & Practice, 8*, 175–181.

Graham, S. (1999). Handwriting and spelling instruction for students with learning disabilities: A review. *Learning Disability Quarterly, 22*, 78–98.

Graham, S., Berninger, V., & Weintraub, N. (1998). The relationship between handwriting style and speed and legibility. *Journal of Educational Research, 91*, 290–297.

Graham, S., Bollinger, A., Booth Olson, C., D'Aoust, C., MacArthur, C., McCutchen, D., & Olinghouse, N. (2012). *Teaching elementary school students to be effective writers: A practice guide* (NCEE 2012-4058). Washington, DC: National Center for Education Evaluation and Regional Assistance, Institute of Education Sciences, U.S. Department of Education. Retrieved from http://ies.ed.gov/ncee/wwc/publications_reviews.aspx#pubsearch.

Graham, S., & Freeman, K. R. (1986). Strategy training and teacher- vs. student-controlled study conditions: Effects on LD students' spelling performance. *Learning Disability Quarterly, 9*, 15–22.

Graham, S., & Harris, K. R. (1988). Instructional recommendations for teaching writing to exceptional students. *Exceptional Children, 54*, 506–512.

Graham, S., & Harris, K. R. (1989). Improving learning disabled students' skills at composing essays: Self-instructional strategy training. *Exceptional Children, 56*, 201–214.

Graham, S., & Harris, K. R. (1992). Self-instructional strategy development. *LD Forum, 16*, 15–23.

Graham, S., & Harris, K. R. (1993). Teaching writing strategies to students with learning disabilities: Issues and recommendations. In L. S. Meltzer (Ed.), *Strategy assessment and instruction for students with learning disabilities* (pp. 271–323). Austin, TX: Pro-Ed.

Graham, S., & Harris, K. R. (1996). Self-regulation and strategy instruction for students who find writing and learning challenging. In C. M. Levy & S. Ransdell (Eds), *The science of writing* (pp. 347–60). Mahwah, NJ: Lawrence Erlbaum.

Graham, S., Harris, K., & Loynachan, C. (1994). The spelling for writing list. *Journal of Learning Disabilities, 27*, 210–214.

Graham, S., Harris, K. R., MacArthur, C. A., & Schwartz, S. (1991). Writing and writing instruction for students with learning disabilities: Review of a research program. *Learning Disability Quarterly, 14*, 89–114.

Graham, S., MacArthur, C., Schwartz, S., & Paige-Voth, T. (1992). Improving the compositions of students with learning disabilities using a strategy involving product and process goal setting. *Exceptional Children, 58*, 322–335.

Graham, S., & Perin, D. (2007). A meta-analysis of writing instruction for adolescent students. *Journal of Educational Psychology, 99*, 445–476.

Graham, S., & Santangelo, T. (2014). Does spelling instruction makes students better spellers, readers, and writers? A meta-analytic review. *Reading and Writing, 27*, 1703–1743.

Graham, S., & Weintraub, N. (1996). A review of handwriting research: Progress and prospects from 1980 to 1994. *Educational Psychology Review, 8*, 7–87.

Graham, S., Weintraub, N., & Berninger, V. (2001). Which manuscript letters do primary grade children write legibly? *Journal of Educational Psychology, 93*, 488–497.

Graves, D. H. (1983). *Writing: Teachers and children at work.* Exeter, NH: Heinemann.

Greene, J. A., & Azevedo, R. (2007). A theoretical review of Winne and Hadwin's model of self-regulated learning: new perspectives and directions. *Review of Educational Research, 77*(3), 334–372.

Greenwood, C. R., Arreaga-Mayer, C., Utley, C. A., Gavin, K. M., & Terry, B. J. (2001). Classwide peer tutoring learning management system. *Remedial and Special Education, 22*(1), 34–47.

Greenwood, C., Carta, J., & Maheady, L. (1991). Peer tutoring programs in the regular education classroom. In G. Stoner, M. Shinn, & H. Walker (Eds.), *Interventions for achievement and behavior problems* (pp. 179–200). Silver Spring, MD: National Association of School Psychologists.

Greenwood, C., Delquadri, J. C., & Carta, J. J. (1999). *Together we can! Classwide peer tutoring to improve basic academic skills* (2nd ed.). Frederick, CO: Sopris-West.

Gresham, F., Lane, K., MacMillan, D., & Bocian, K. (1999). Social and academic profiles of externalizing and internalizing groups: Risk factors for emotional and behavioral disorders. *Behavioral Disorders, 24*, 231–245.

Gresham, F. M., Sugai, G., & Horner, R. H. (2001). Interpreting outcomes of social skills training for students with high-incidence disabilities. *Exceptional Children, 67*, 331–344.

Gualtieri, C. T., & Johnson, L. G. (2006). Efficient allocation of attentional resources in patients with ADHD: Maturational changes from age 10 to 29. *Journal of Attention Disorders, 9*(3), 534–542.

Gunning, T. G. (2000). *Creating literacy instruction for all children.* Boston: Allyn & Bacon.

Gurlitt, J., Dummel, S., Schuster, S., & Nückles, M. (2012). Differently structured advance organizers lead to different initial scemata and learning outcomes. *Instructional Science, 40*(2), 351–369.

Haager, D. (2007). Promises and cautions regarding using response to intervention with English language learners. *Learning Disability Quarterly, 30*, 213–218.

Hackney, C. (1993). *Zaner-Bloser handwriting.* Columbus, OH: Zaner-Bloser.

Hale, C. (2015). Urban special education policy and the lived experience of stigma in a high school science classroom. *Cultural Studies of Science Education, 10*(4), 1071–1088.

Hall, K., Sabey, B., & McClellan, M. (2005). Expository text comprehension: Helping primary-grade teachers use expository text to full advantage. *Reading Psychology, 26*, 211–234.

Hallahan, D. P., Lloyd, J. W., Kauffman, J. M., Weiss, M., & Martinez, E. A. (2005). *Learning disabilities: Foundations, characteristics, and effective teaching* (3rd ed.). Boston: Allyn & Bacon.

Halpern, A. (1993). Quality of life as a conceptual framework for evaluating transition outcomes. *Exceptional Children, 59*, 486–498.

Halpern, A. (1985). Transition: A look at the foundations. *Exceptional Children, 51*, 479–486.

Halpern, A. S., Yovanoff, P., Doren, B., & Benz, M. R. (1995). Predicting participation in postsecondary education for school leavers with disabilities. *Exceptional Children, 62*, 151–164.

Hamill, L. B. (2003). Going to college: The experiences of a young woman with Down syndrome. *Mental Retardation, 41*, 340–353.

Handley-More, D., Deitz, J., Billingsley, F. F., & Coggins, T. E. (2003). Facilitating written work using computer word processing and word prediction. *American Journal of Occupational Therapy, 57*(2), 139–151.

Hanich, L., Jordan, N. C., Kaplan, D., & Dick, J. (2001). Performance across different areas of mathematical cognition in children with learning difficulties. *Journal of Educational Psychology, 93*, 615–626.

Hanley-Hochdorfer, K., Bray, M. A., Kehle, T. J., & Elinoff, M. J. (2010). Social stories to increase verbal initiation in children with autism and asperger's disorder. *School Psychology Review, 39*(3), 484–492.

Harbour, W. S. (2004). The 2004 AHEAD survey of higher education disability service providers. Waltham, MA: Association on Higher Education and Disability.

Harniss, M. K., Carnine, D. W., Silbert, J., & Dixon, R. C. (2007). Effective strategies for teaching mathematics. In M. D. Coyne, E. J. Kame'enui, & D. W. Carnine (Eds.), *Effective teaching strategies that accommodate diverse learners* (3rd ed.). Upper Saddle River, NJ: Pearson Prentice Hall.

Harris, K. R. (1982). Cognitive-behavior modification: Application with exceptional students. *Focus on Exceptional Children, 15*, 1–16.

Harris, K., & Graham, S. (1996). Memo to constructivists: Skills count too. *Educational Leadership, 53*(5), 26–29.

Harris, K. R., & Graham, S. (1996). Memo to constructivists: Skills count, too. *Educational Leadership, 53*, 26–29.

Harris, A. J., & Sipay, E. R. (1990). *How to increase reading ability*. New York: Longman.

Harris, K., Reid, R., & Graham, S. (2004). Self-regulation among students with LD and ADHD. In B. Y. L. Wong (Ed.), *Learning about learning disabilities* (3rd ed., pp. 167–95). Orlando, FL: Academic Press.

Harry, B., & Klingner, J. (2006). *Why are so many minority students in special education? Understanding race and disability in schools*. New York: Teachers College Press.

Harry, B., Klingner, J., & Hart, J. (2005). African American families under fire. *Remedial and Special Education, 26*, 110–112.

Hart, D., Mele-McCarthy, J., Pasternack, R. H., Zimbrich, K., & Parker, D. R. (2004). Community college: A pathway to success for youth with learning, cognitive, and intellectual disabilities in secondary settings. *Education and Training in Developmental Disabilities, 39*, 54–66.

Hasbrouck, J. E., & Tindal, G. (1992). Curriculum-based oral reading fluency forms for students in grades 2 through 5. *Teaching Exceptional Children, 24*, 41–44.

Hastings, R. P., & Graham, S. (1995). Adolescents' perceptions of young people with severe learning difficulties: The effects of integration schemes and frequency of contact. *Educational Psychology, 15*(2), 149–160.

Hawking, S. (1988). *A brief history of time*. New York: Bantam Books.

Hawkins, J., Brady, M., Hamilton, R., Williams, R., & Taylor, R. (1994). The effects of independent and peer guided pauses during instructional pauses on the academic performance of students with mild handicaps. *Education and Treatment of Children, 17*(1), 1–28.

Haydon, T., Mancil, G. R., Kroeger, S. D., McLeskey, J., & Lin, W. J. (2011). A review of the effectiveness of guided notes for students who struggle learning academic content. *Preventing School Failure, 55*, 226–231.

Hayes, J. (1996). A new framework for understanding cognition and affect in writing. In C. M. Levy & S. Ransdell (Eds.), *The science of writing* (pp. 1–28). Mahwah, NJ: Lawrence Erlbaum.

Hayes, J. R., & Flower, L. S. (1980). Identifying the organization of writing process. In L. W. Gregg & E. R. Steinberg (Eds.), *Cognitive processes in writing* (pp. 3–30). Hillsdale, NJ: Lawrence Erlbaum.

Hecht, S. A., Vagi, K. J., & Torgesen, J. K. (2007). Fraction skills and proportional reasoning. In D. B. Berch & M. M. M. Mazzocco (Eds.), *Why is math so hard for some children?* (pp. 121–32). Baltimore, MD: Brookes Publishing.

Hehir, T. (2007). Confronting ableism. *Educational Leadership, 64*(5), 8–14.

Hehir, T. (2009). Policy foundations of universal design for learning. In D. T. Gordon, J. W. Gravel, & L. A. Schifter (Eds.), *A policy reader in universal design for learning* (pp. 35–45). Cambridge, MA: Harvard Education Press.

Heitin, L. (2015, July 7). Common-Core materials penetrate every state. Education Week. Retrieved from http://www.edweek.org/ew/articles/2015/07/08/common-core-materials-penetrateeverystate.html?tkn=VLVFT77bcIGGzdl8aKcrAr2HjOW6pFN%2B4KGp&intc=es

Hergenhahn, B. R., & Olsen, M. H. (2001). *An introduction to theories of learning*. Upper Saddle River, NJ: Prentice Hall.

Hernandez, D. A., Su Hueck, & Charley, C. (Fall. 2016). General education and special education teachers' attitudes towards inclusion. *Journal of the American Academy of Special Education Professionals*, 79–93.

Herrero, E. A. (2006). Using Dominican oral literature and discourse to support literacy learning among low achieving students from the Dominican Republic. *International Journal of Bilingual Education and Bilingualism, 9*, 219–238.

Heshusius, L. (1991). Curriculum-based assessment and direct instruction: Critical reflections on fundamental assumptions. *Exceptional Children, 57*, 315–328.

Hetzroni. O. E., & Shrieber, B. (2004). Word processing as an assistive technology tool for enhancing academic outcomes of students with writing disabilities in the general classroom. *Journal of Learning Disabilities, 37*(2), 143–154.

Heward, W. M. (2006). *Exceptional children: An introduction to special education* (8th ed.). Upper Saddle River, NJ: Merrill/ Prentice Hall.

Hiebert, E., & Fisher, C. (2005). A review of the National Reading Panel's studies on fluency: The role of text. *The Elementary School Journal, 105,* 443–460.

Hill, J. W., & Coufal, K. L. (2005). Emotional/behavioral disorders: A retrospective examination of social skills, linguistics, and student outcomes. *Communication Disorders Quarterly, 27,* 33–46.

Hitchcock, C., Meyer, A., Rose, D. H., & Jackson, R. (2002). Providing new access to the general education curriculum. *Teaching Exceptional Children, 35*(2), 8–17.

Hitchings, W. E., Retish, P., & Horvath, M. (2005). Academic preparation of adolescents with disabilities for postsecondary education. *Career Development for Exceptional Individuals, 28,* 26–35.

Ho, K. M., & Keiley, M. K. (2003). Dealing with denial: A systems approach for family professionals working with parents of individuals with multiple disabilities. *The Family Journal: Counseling and Therapy for Couples and Families, 11,* 239–247.

Hodge, J., Riccomini, P., Buford, R., & Herbst, M. H. (2006). A review of instructional interventions in mathematics for students with emotional and behavioral disorders. *Behavioral Disorders, 31,* 297.

Hodgkinson, H. (2002). Demographics and teacher education: An overview. *Journal of Teacher Education, 53,* 102–105.

Hoffman, A., & Field, S. (2005). *Steps to self-determination* (2nd ed.). Austin: PRO-ED.

Hoffman, L., Marquis, J., Poston, D., Summers, J. A., & Turnbull, A. (2006). Assessing family outcomes: Psychometric evaluation of the Beach Center Family Quality of Life Scale. *Journal of Marriage and Family, 68,* 1069–1083.

Hofferth, S. J., & Sandberg, J. F. (2000). *How American Children spend their time.* University of Michigan, Ann Arbor, MI. Retrieved from http://ceel.psc.isr.umich .edu/pubs/papers/ceel012-00.pdf.

Hogan, K., & Pressley, M. (1997). Scaffolding scientific competencies within classroom communities of inquiry. In K. Hogan & M. Pressley (Eds.), *Scaffolding student learning Instructional approaches and issues* (pp. 74–107). Louiseville, Quebec, CA: Brookline Books.

Hohn, R. (1994). *Classroom learning and teaching.* Boston: Allyn & Bacon.

Holdnack, J., Goldstein, G., Drozdick, L. (2011). Social perception and WAIS-IV performance in adolescents and adults diagnosed with asperger's syndrome and autism. *Assessment, 18*(2), 192–200.

Horn, L., Peter, K., & Rooney, K. (2002). *Profi of undergraduates in U.S. postsecondary institutions: 1999–2000.* Statistical analysis report, no. NCES 2002–168. Washington, DC: National Center for Education Statistics, U.S. Department of Education, Office of Educational Research and Improvement. http://www.ncld.org/index.php?option =content&task=view&id=433.

Horner, R., Carr, E., Halle, J., McGee, G., Odom, S., & Wollery, M. (2005). The use of single-subject research to identify evidence-based practice in special education. *Exceptional Children, 71*(2), 165–179.

Horowitz, S. H., Rawe, J., & Whittaker, M. C. (2017). *The State of Learning Disabilities: Understanding the 1 in 5.* New York: National Center for Learning Disabilities.

Horton, S. V., Lovitt, T. C., & Christensen, C. C. (1991). Note taking from textbooks: Effects of a columnar format on three categories of secondary students. *Exceptionality, 2,* 19–40.

Hoza, B., Gerdes, A. C., Hinshaw, S. P., Arnold, L. E., Pelham, W. E., Molina, B. S. G., Wigal, T. (2004). Self-perceptions of competence in children with ADHD and comparison children. *Journal of Consulting and Clinical Psychology, 72,* 382–391.

Hudson, R. F., Lane, H. B., & Pullen, P. C. (2005). Reading fluency assessment and instruction: What, why, and how? *The Reading Teacher, 58,* 702–714.

Huemer, S. V., & Mann, V. (2010). A comprehensive profile of decoding and comprehension in autism spectrum disorders. *Journal of Autism and Developmental Disorders, 40*(4), 485–493.

Hughes, C. (1996). Memory and test-taking strategies. In D. D. Deshler, E. S. Ellis, & B. K. Lenz (Eds.), *Teaching adolescents with learning disabilities* (2nd ed., pp. 209–66). Denver, CO: Love Publishing.

Hughes. R. W., Hurlstone, M. J., Marsh, J. E., Vachon, F., Jones, D. M. (2013). Cognitive control of auditory distraction: Impact of task difficulty, foreknowledge, and working memory capacity support duplex-mechanism account, *Journal of Experimental Psychology: Human Perception and Performance, 39,* 539–553.

Hughes, C., Rodi, M. S., Lorden, S. W., Pittken, S. E., Dereer, K. R., Hwang, B., & Xinsheng, C. (1999). Social interactions of high school students with mental retardation and their general education peers. *American Journal on Mental Retardation, 104,* 533–544.

Hughes, C. A., Ruhl, K. L., Schumaker, J. B., & Deshler, D. D. (2002). Effects of Instruction in an assignment completion strategy on the homework performance of students with learning disabilities in general education classes. *Learning Disabilities: Research & Practice, 17*(1), 1–18.

Hughes, C. A., Salvia, J., & Bott, D. A. (1991). The nature and extent of test-wiseness cues in seventh and tenth grade classroom tests. *Diagnostique, 2–3,* 153–163.

Hughes, C. A., Schumaker, J. B., & Deshler, D. D. (2005). *The essay test taking strategy.* Lawrence, KS: University of Kansas.

Hughes, C. A., Schumaker, J. B., Deshler, D. D., & Mercer, C. (1988). *The test-taking strategy.* Lawrence, KS: Excel Enterprises.

Hughes, M. T., Schumm, J. S., & Vaughn, S. (1999). Home literacy activities: Perceptions and practices of Hispanic parents of children with learning disabilities. *Learning Disability Quarterly, 22,* 224–235.

Hughes, C. A., & Smith, J. O. (1990). Cognitive and academic performance of college students with learning disabilities: A synthesis of the literature. *Learning Disability Quarterly, 13,* 66–79.

Hughes, C. A., & Suritsky, S. K. (1994). Note-taking skills of university students with and without learning disabilities. *Journal of Learning Disabilities, 27,* 20–24.

Hurst, D., & Hudson, L. (2005). Estimating undergraduate enrollment in postsecondary education using national center for education statistics data. Washington, DC: National Center for Education statistics.

Hutchinson, N., Freeman, J., & Berg, D. (2004). Social competence of adolescents with learning disabilities: Interventions and issues. In B. Y. L. Wong (ED.), *Learning about learning disabilities* (3rd ed., pp. 415–38). San Diego, CA: Elsevier Academic Press.

Huynh, V., & Gillen-O'Neel, C. (2016). Discrimination and sleep: The protective role of school belonging. *Youth & Society, 48*(5), 649–672.

Idol, L. (1987). Group story mapping: A comprehension strategy for both skilled and unskilled readers. *Journal of Learning Disabilities, 20,* 196–205.

Idol, L. (1988). Johnny can't read: Does the fault lie in the book, the teacher, or Johnny? *Remedial and Special Education, 9,* 8–25.

Idol, L., & Croll, V. (1987). Story mapping training as a means of increasing reading comprehension. *Journal of Learning Disabilities, 10,* 214–229.

Impecoven-Lind, L. S., & Foegen, A. (2010). Teaching Algebra to students with learning disabilities. *Intervention in School and Clinic, 46*(1), 31–37.

Individuals with Disabilities Education Improvement Act (IDEIA). (2004). Public Law no. 108–446, 118 Stat. 2647 [Amending 20 U.S.C. §§ 1400 et seq.]

Individuals With Disabilities Education Improvement Act. Public Law 108–446, 108th Cong., 118 Stat. 2647 (2004) (enacted).

Institute of Education Sciences. What Works Clearinghouse. (2006). http://www.whatworks.ed.gov (accessed November 18, 2006).

International Reading Association/National Council of Teachers of English. (1996). *Standards for the English Language Arts.* Newark, DE/Urbana, IL: International Reading Association/National Council of Teachers of English.

Isaacson, S. (1989). Role of secretary vs. author: Resolving the conflict in writing instruction. *Learning Disability Quarterly, 12,* 209–217.

Ishii-Jordan, J. J. (2000). Behavioral interventions used with diverse students. *Behavioral Disorders, 25,* 299–309.

ISTE Technology Foundation standards for all students. http://www.iste.org/standards (accessed June 25, 2007).

Jakulski, J., & Mastropieri, M. A. (2004). Homework for students with disabilities. In T. E. Scruggs & M. A. Mastropieri (Eds.), *Research in secondary schools: Advances in learning and behavioral disabilities* (pp. 77–122). Oxford, UK: Elsevier.

Janiga, S. J., & Costenbader, V. (2002). The transition from high school to postsecondary education for students with learning disabilities: A survey of college service coordinators. *Journal of Learning Disabilities, 35,* 462–468.

Jenkins, J. R., Antil, L. R., Wayne, S. K., Vadasy, P. F. (2003). How cooperative learning works for special education and remedial students. *Exceptional Children, 69*(3), 279–292.

Jenkins, J. R., Dale, P. S., Mills, P. E., & Cole, K. N. (2006). How special education preschool graduates finish: Status at 19 years of age. *American Educational Research Journal, 43,* 737–781.

Jenkins, J. R., Fuchs, L. S., van den Brock, P., Espin, C., & Deno, S. (2003a). Accuracy and fluency in list and context reading of skilled and RD groups: Absolute and relative performance levels. *Learning Disabilities Research & Practice, 18,* 237–245.

Jenkins, J. R., Fuchs, L. S., van den Brock, P., Espin, C., & Deno, S. L. (2003b). Sources of individual differences in reading comprehension and reading fluency. *Journal of Educational Psychology, 95,* 719–729.

Jerman, O., Reynolds, C., & Swanson, H. L. (2012). Does growth in working memory span or executive processes predict growth in reading and math in children with reading disabilities? *Learning Disability Quarterly, 35*(3), 144–157.

Jitendra, A. (2002). Teaching students math problem-solving through graphic representations. *Teaching Exceptional Children, 34,* 34–38.

Jitendra, A. K. (2007). *Solving math word problems: Teaching students with learning disabilities using schema-based instruction.* Austin, TX: Pro-Ed.

Jitendra, A., DiPipi, C. M., & Perron-Jones, N. (2002). An exploratory study of schema-based word-problem-solving instruction for middle school students with learning disabilities: An emphasis on conceptual and procedural understanding. *Journal of Special Education, 36*(1), 23–38.

Jitendra, A. K., Edwards, L. L., Sacks, G., & Jacobson, L. A. (2004). What research says about vocabulary instruction for students with learning disabilities, *Exceptional Children, 70,* 299–322.

Jitendra, A. K., Petersen-Brown, S., Lein, A. E., Zaslofsky, A. F., Kunkel, K., Jung, P., & Egan, A. M. (2015). Teaching mathematical word problem solving: The quality of evidence for strategy instruction priming the problem structure. *Educational Psychology, 48*(1), 51–72.

Jitendra, A. K., Salmento, M. M., & Haydt, L. A. (1999). A case analysis of fourth-grade subtraction instruction in basal mathematics programs: Adherence to important instructional design criteria. *Learning Disabilities Research & Practice, 14*(2), 69–79.

Jitendra, A. K., & Star, J. R. (2011). Meeting the needs of students with learning disabilities in inclusive mathematics classrooms: The role of schema-based instruction on mathematical problem-solving. *Theory Into Practice, 50*(1), 12–19.

Johns, J. L. (1981). The development of the Revised Dolch List. *Illinois School Research and Development, 17*, 15–24.

Johnson, D. W., Johnson, R. T., & Holubec, E. J. (1993). *Active learning: Cooperation in the classroom* (6th ed.). Edina, MN: Interaction Book Company.

Jones, T., & Sterling, D. R. (2011). Cooperative learning in an inclusive science classroom. *Science Scope, 35*(3), 24–28.

Jordan, N. C., & Hanich, L. B. (2003). Characteristics of children with moderate mathematics deficiencies: A longitudinal perspective. *Learning Disabilities Research & Practice, 18*, 213–221.

Jordan, N. C., Hanich, L. B., & Kaplan, D. (2003). A longitudinal study of mathematical competencies in children with specific mathematics difficulties versus children with comorbid mathematics and reading difficulties. *Child Development, 74*(3), 834–850.

Jordan, N. C., Kaplan, D., Ramineni, C., & Locuniak, M. N. (2009). Early math matters: Kindergarten number competence and later mathematic outcomes. *Developmental Psychology, 45*(3), 850–867.

Jordan, N. C., & Montani, T. O. (1997). Cognitive arithmetic and problem solving: A comparison of children with specific and general mathematics difficulties. *Journal of Learning Disabilities, 30*, 624–634, 684.

Kalyanpur, M., Harry, B., & Skrtic, T. (2000). Equity and advocacy expectations of culturally diverse families' participation in special education. *International Journal of Disability, Development and Education, 47*, 119–136.

Kame'enui, E. J., Carnine, D. W., Dixon, R. C., Simmons, D. C., & Coyne, M. D. (2002). *Effective teaching strategies that accommodate diverse learners* (2nd ed.). Columbus, OH: Merrill.

Kaplan, J. S. (1995). *Beyond behavior modification: A cognitive-behavioral approach to behavior management in the school* (3rd ed.) Austin, TX: PRO-ED.

Karp, Karen, S., Bush, S. B., & Dougherty, B. J. (2014). "13 Rules That Expire." *Teaching Children Mathematics, 21*(August), 18–25.

Karvonen, M., Test, D. W., Wood, W. M., Browder, D., & Algozzine, B. (2004). Putting self-determination into practice. *Exceptional Children, 71*, 23–41.

Katims, David S., & Harris, S. (1997). Improving the reading comprehension of middle school students in inclusive classrooms. *Journal of Adolescent & Adult Literacy, 41*, 116–118.

Katzir, T., Kim, Y., Wolf, M., O'Brien, B., Kennedy, B., Lovett, M., & Morris, R. (2006). Reading fluency: The whole is more than the sum of the parts. *Annals of Dyslexia, 56*, 51–82.

Kauffman, J. (1997). *Characteristics of emotional and behavioral disorders of children and youth.* Upper Saddle River, NJ: Prentice Hall.

Kauffman, J. (2002). *Education deform: Bright people sometimes say stupid things about education.* Lanham, MD: Scarecrow Education.

Kauffman, J., Bantz, J., & McCullough, J. (2002). Separate and better: A special public school class for students with emotional and behavioral disorders. *Exceptionality, 10*(3), 149–170.

Kauffman, J., & Hallahan, D. P. (2005). *Special education: What is it and why we need it.* Boston: Allyn & Bacon.

Kauffman, J. M., & Landrum, T. J. (2009). *Characteristics of emotional and behavioral disorders of children and youth* (9th ed.). Upper Saddle River, NJ: Merrill/Pearson.

Kavale, K. A., & Forness, S. R. (1999). *Efficacy of special education and related services.* Washington, DC: AAMR.

Kavale, K. A., & Forness, S. R. (2000). What definitions of learning disability say and don't say: A critical analysis. *Journal of Learning Disabilities, 33*, 239–256.

Kavale, K., & Forness, S. (2000). History, rhetoric and reality: Analysis of the inclusion debate. *Remedial and Special Education, 21*(5), 279–296.

Kelford Smith, A., Thurston, S., Light, J., Parnes, P., & O'Keefe, B. (1989). The form and use of written communication produced by nonspeaking physically disabled individual using microcomputers, *Augmentative and Alternative Communication, 5*, 115–124.

Kellogg, R. T. (1996). A model of working memory in writing. In L. W. Gregg & E. R. Steinberg (Eds.), *Cognitive processes in writing* (pp. 57–72). Hillsdale, NJ: Lawrence Erlbaum.

Kenndy, M., & Boyle, J. R. (2017). Technology and academic instruction considerations for students with high incidence cognitive disabilities. In M. Kauffman, D. P. Hallahan, & P. Pullen (Eds.), *Handbook of Special Education.* New York: Routledge.

Kennedy, M. J., & Deshler, D. D. (2010). Literacy instruction, technology, and students with learning disabilities: Research we have, research we need. *Learning Disability Quarterly, 33*(4), 289–298.

Kennedy, M. J., Deshler, D. D., & Lloyd, J. W. (2013). Effects of multimedia vocabulary instruction on adolescents with learning disabilities. *Journal of Learning Disabilities.* Advance online publication.

Kennedy, M. J., Deshler, D. D., & Lloyd, J. W. (2015). Effects of multimedia vocabulary instruction on adolescents with learning disabilities. *Journal of Learning Disabilities, 48*, 22–38.

Kenny, M. E., Gualdron, L., Scanlon, D., Sparks, E., Blustein, D. L., & Jernigan, M. (2007). Urban adolescents' constructions of supports and barriers to educational and career attainment. *Journal of Counseling Psychology, 54*, 326–343.

Kercood, S., Zentall, S. S., Vinh, M., Tom-Wright, K. (2012). Attentional cuing in math word problems for girls at-risk for ADHD and their peers in general education settings. *Contemporary Educational Psychology, 37*(2), 106–112.

Kerr, M. M., & Nelson, C. M. (2002). *Strategies for managing behavior problems in the classroom* (4th ed.). Upper Saddle River, NJ: Pearson Education.

Kiewra, K. A., Mayer, R. E., Christensen, M., Kim, S., & Risch, M. (1991). Effects of repetition on recall and note taking: Strategies for learning from lectures. *Journal of Educational Psychology, 83*, 120–123

Kim, A., Vaughn, S., Wanzek, J., & Wei, S. (2004). Graphic organizers and their effects on the reading comprehension of students with LD: A synthesis of research. *Journal of Learning Disabilities, 37*, 105–119.

King-Sears, M., Mercer, C., & Sindelar, P. (1992). Towards independence with keyword mnemonics: A strategy for science vocabulary instruction. *Remedial and Special Education, 13*, 22–33.

Kissam, B., & Lenz, B. K. (1994). *Pedagogies for diversity in secondary schools: A preservice curriculum.* Lawrence, KS: University of Kansas.

Klingner, J., Vaughn, S., Boardman, A., & Swanson, E. (2012). *Now we get it! Boosting comprehension with collaborative strategic reading.* San Francisco, CA: Jossey-Bass.

Klingner J. K., Vaughn, S., Boardman, A., & Swanson, E. (2012). *Now we get it! Boosting comprehension with collaborative strategic reading.* San Francisco, CA: Jossey-Bass.

Klingner, J. K., Vaughn, S., & Schumm, J. S. (1998). Collaborative strategic reading during social studies in heterogeneous fourth-grade classrooms. *Elementary School Journal, 99*(1), 3–22.

Kloosterman, P., & Lester, F. K. (2004). *Results and interpretations of the 1990 through 2000 mathematics assessments of the National Assessment of Educational Progress.* Reston, VA: National Council of Teachers of Mathematics.

Kochar-Bryant, C., & Izzo, M. V. (2006). Access to post-high school services: Transition assessment and the summary of performance. *Career Development of Exceptional Individuals, 29*, 70–89.

Koegel, R. L. (2007). Social development in individuals with high functioning autism and asperger disorder. *Research and Practice for Persons with Severe Disabilities (RPSD), 32*(2), 140–141.

Koegel, R. L., & Koegel, L. K. (2006). *Pivotal response treatments for autism: Communication, social, and academic development.* Baltimore, MD: Paul H Brookes Publishing.

Kohn, A. (2006). *The homework myth: Why our kids get too much of a bad thing.* Cambridge, MA: De Capo.

Konefal, J., & Folks, J. (1984). Linguistic analysis of children's conversational repairs. *Journal of Psycholinguistic Research, 13*, 1–11.

Kortering, L., Braziel, P., & Tompkins, J. (2002). The challenge of school completion among youth with behavior disorders: Another side of the story. *Behavioral Disorders, 27*, 142–154.

Koscinski, S. T., & Gast, D. L. (1993). Use of constant time delay in teaching multiplication facts to students with learning disabilities. *Journal of Learning Disabilities, 26*(8), 533–44, 567.

Kralovec, E., & Buell, J. (2000). *The end of homework: How homework disrupts families, overburdens children, and limits learning.* Boston, MA: Beacon.

Krinsky, R., & Krinsky, S. (1996). Pegword mnemonic instruction: Retrieval times and long-term memory performance among fifth-grade children. *Contemporary Educational Psychology, 21*, 193–207.

Kroesbergen, E. H., & Van Luit, J. E. H. (2003). Mathematics interventions for children with special educational needs: A meta-analysis. *Remedial and Special Education, 24*(2), 97–114.

Kübler-Ross, E. (1969). *On death and dying.* New York: Touchstone.

Kuder, S. J. (2013). *Teaching students with language and communication disabilities* (4th ed.). Boston, MA: Pearson.

Kuhn, M. R., & Stahl, S. A. (2000). *Fluency: A review of developmental and remedial practices.* Ann Arbor, MI: Center for the Improvement of Early Reading Achievement.

Kulage, K. M.; Smaldone, A. M., Cohn, E. G. (2014). How Will DSM-5 Affect Autism Diagnosis? A Systematic Literature Review and Meta-Analysis. *Journal of Autism and Developmental Disorders, 44*(8), 1918–1932.

Kupzyk, S., Daly, E. J., III. & Andersen, M. N. (2011). A comparison of two flashcard methods for improving sight-word reading. *Journal of Applied Behavior Analysis, 44*, 781–792.

Kutash, K., Duchnowsil, A. J., Sumi, W. C., Rudo, Z., & Harris, M. (2002). A school, family, and community collaborative program for children who have emotional disturbances. *Journal of Emotional and Behavioral Disorders, 10*, 99–107.

Kuusikko, S., Pollock-Wurman, R., Jussila, Kl, Carter, A. S., Mattila, M. J., Ebeling, H., & Mollanen, I. (2008). Social anxiety in high-functioning children and adolescrns with autism and Asperger syndrome. *Journal of Autism and Developmental Disorders, 38*, 1697–1709.

Kytle, R. (1970). Pre-writing by analysis. *College Composition and Communication, 21*, 380–385.

LaBerge, D., & Samuels, S. J. (1974). Toward a theory of automatic information processing in reading. *Cognitive Psychology, 6*, 293–323.

Laing, S., & Kamhi, A. (2003). Alternative assessment of language and literacy in culturally and linguistically diverse populations. *Language, Speech, and Hearing Services in Schools, 34*, 44–55.

Lambros, K., Ward, S., Bocian, K., MacMillan, D., & Gresham, F. (1998). Behavioral profiles of children at risk for emotional and behavioral disorders: Implications for assessment and classification. *Focus on Exceptional Children, 30*(5), 1–16.

Lane, K. L., & Menzies, H. M. (2010). Reading and writing interventions for students with and at risk for emotional and behavioral disorders: An introduction. *Behavioral Disorders, 35*(2), 82–85.

Lane, K. L., Kalberg, J. R., & Menzies, H. M. (2009). *Developing schoolwide programs to prevent and manage problem behaviors: A step-by-step approach.* New York, NY: Guilford Press.

Lane, K. L., Menzies, H. M., Bruhn, A. L., & Crnorbori, M. (2010). *Managing challenging behavior in schools: Research-based strategies that work.* New York, NY: Guilford.

Lardieri, L. A., Blacher, J., & Swanson, H. L. (2000). Sibling relationships and parent stress in families of children with and without learning disabilities. *Learning Disability Quarterly, 23*, 105–116.

Larkin, P., Jahoda, A., MacMahon, K., Pert, C. (2012). Interpersonal sources of conflict in young people with and without mild to moderate intellectual disabilities at transition from adolescence to adulthood. *Journal of Applied Research in Intellectual Disabilities, 25*(1), 29–38.

Larry P. v. Riles. Civil Action, no. 6-71-2270, 343 F. Supp. 1036 (N.D. Cal., 1972).

Lazarus, B. D. (1991). Guided notes, review, and achievement of secondary students with learning disabilities in mainstream content courses. *Education and Treatment of Children, 14*(2), 112–127.

Le Sourn-Bissaoui, S., Caillies, S., Gierski, F., Motte, J. (2011). Ambiguity detection in adolescents with asperger syndrome: Is central coherence or theory of mind impaired? *Research in Autism Spectrum Disorders, 5*(1), 648–656.

Learned, J. E., Dowd, M. V., & Jenkins, J. R. (2009). Instructional conferencing: Helping students succeed on independent assignments in inclusive settings. *TEACHING Exceptional Children, 41*(5), 46–51.

Learning Disabilities Association of America. (1999). Speech and Language Milestone Chart. http://www.ldonline.org /article/6313 (accessed May 1, 2008).

Learning Disabilities Association of Minnesota. (2004). Multi-syllabic instruction. *NetNews, 4*, 2–4.

Lee, H. J., & Herner-Patnode, L. M. (2007). Teaching mathematics vocabulary to diverse groups. (What works for me.) *Intervention in School and Clinic, 43*(2), 121–126.

LeFever, B. G., Villers, M. S., Morrow, A. L., & Vaughn, E. S. (2002). Parental perceptions of adverse educational outcomes among children diagnosed and treated for ADHD: A call for improved school/provider collaboration. *Psychology in the Schools, 39*, 63–71.

Leko, M., & Mundy, C. (2012). Preparing secondary educators to support adolescent struggling readers. *Preventing School Failure, 56*(2), 137–147.

Lenz, B. K., Alley, G. R., & Schumaker, J. B. (1987). Activating the inactive learner: Advance organizers in the secondary content classroom. *Learning Disability Quarterly, 10*, 53–67.

Lenz, B. K., Deshler, D. D., & Kissam, B. R. (2004). *Teaching content to all: Evidence-based inclusive practices in middle and secondary schools.* Boston, MA: Pearson Education, Inc.

Lenz, B. K., Ellis, E. S., & Scanlon, D. (1996). *Teaching learning strategies to adolescents and adults with learning disabilities.* Austin, TX: Pro-Ed.

Lenz, B. K., & Hughes, C. (1990). A word identification strategy for adolescents with learning disabilities. *Journal of Learning Disabilities, 23*, 149–163.

Lenz, B. K., Marrs, R. W., Schumaker, J. B., & Deshler, D. D. (2005). *The lesson organizer routine.* Lawrence, KS: Edge Enterprises.

Lenz, B. K., Schumaker, J., Deshler, D., & Beals, J. (1984). *Learning strategies curriculum: The word identification strategy.* Lawrence, KS: University of Kansas.

Lenz, B. K., Schumaker, J. B., Deshler, D. D., & Bulgren, J. A. (1998). *The course organizer routine.* Lawrence, KS: Edge Enterprises.

Lewandowski, L. J., Berger, C., Lovett, B. J., & Gordon, M. (2016). Test-taking skills of high school students with and without learning disabilities. *Journal of Psychoeducational Assessment, 34*(6), 566–576.

Lewis, R., Graves, A., Ashton, T., & Kieley, C. (1998). Word processing tools for students with learning disabilities: A comparison of strategies to increase text entry speed. *Learning Disabilities Research & Practice, 13*, 95–108.

Liberman, I., Shankweiler, D., & Liberman, A. (1989). *The alphabetic principle and learning to read.* Bethesda, MD: National Institute of Child Health and Human Development.

Lidgus, C., & Vassos, S. (1996). Increasing achievement of at-risk students through the use of metacognitive strategies, no. ED 399704. U.S. Department of Education.

Light, J. (1997). "''Let's Go Star Fishing'': Reflections on the Contexts of Language Learning for Children Who use Aided AAC." *Augmentative and Alternative Communication, 13*(3), 158–171.

Light, J., Collier, B., & Parnes, P. (1985). "Communicative Interaction between Young Nonspeaking Physically Disabled Children and their Primary Caregivers: I. Discourse Patterns." *AAC: Augmentative and Alternative Communication, 1*(2), 74–83.

Lindstrom, L. E., & Benz, M. R. (2002). Phases of career development: Case studies of young women with learning disabilities. *Exceptional Children, 69*(1), 67–83.

Lipsky, D. K. (2005). Are we there yet? *Learning Disability Quarterly, 28*(2), 156–158.

Lipson, M., & Wixson, K. (1997). *Assessment and instruction of reading and writing disability: An interactive approach* (2nd ed.). Reading, MA: Addison Wesley, Longman.

Little, M. E., & Hahs-Vaughn, D. L. (2007). The implementation of content enhancement routines for improved content literacy for middle and secondary social studies students. *Journal of Personnel Evaluation in Education, 20*, 261–280.

Liu, Y. (2015). An empirical study of schema theory and tts role in reading comprehension. *Journal of Language Teaching and Research, 6*(6), 1349–1356.

Lott, B. (2001). Low-income parents and the public schools. *Journal of Social Issues, 57,* 189–206.

Lott, B. (2003). Recognizing and welcoming the standpoint of low-income parents in the public schools. *Journal of Educational and Psychological Consultation, 14,* 91–104.

Louick, R. A. (2017). *The relationship between motivation, self-perception, and literacy among adolescents with learning disabilities* (Doctoral dissertation). Retrieved from ProQuest Dissertations & Theses Global. (10265044)

Lovett, B. J., & Lewandowski, L. J. (2006). Gifted students with learning disabilities: Who are they? *Journal of Learning Disabilities, 39*(6), 515–527.

Lovett, M. W., Lacerenza, L., & Borden, S. L. (2000). Putting struggling reading on the PHAST track: A program to integrate phonological and strategy-based remedial reading instruction and maximize outcomes. *Journal of Learning Disabilities, 33,* 458–476.

Lowery-Corkran, E. (2006). *Academic experiences of students with learning disabilities at private, highly selective liberal arts institutions.* Doctoral Dissertation. Chestnut Hill, MA: Lynch School of Education, Boston College.

Luo, L., Kiewra, K. A., & Samuelson, L. (2016). *Instructional Science: An International Journal of the Learning Sciences, 44*(1), 45–67.

Lustig, D. C. (2002). Family coping in families with a child with a disability. *Education and Training in Mental Retardation and Developmental Disabilities, 37,* 14–22.

MacArthur, C. (1988). The impact of computers on the writing process. *Exceptional Children, 54,* 536–542.

MacArthur, C. A., & Cavalier, A. (2004). Dictation and speech recognition technology as accommodations in large-scale assessments for students with learning disabilities. *Exceptional Children, 71,* 43–58.

MacArthur, C. A., & Haynes, J. B. (1995). Student assistant for learning from text (SALT), A hypermedia reading aid. *Journal of Learning Disabilities, 28*(3), 50–59.

MacArthur, C., & Graham, S. (1987). Learning disabled students' composing under three methods of text production: Handwriting, word processing, and dictation. *The Journal of Special Education, 21,* 22–42.

MacArthur, C., Schwartz, S., & Graham, S. (1991). Effects of a reciprocal peer revision strategy in special education classrooms. *Learning Disabilities Research & Practice, 6,* 201–210.

Maccini P., & Gagnon, J. C. (2005). Mathematics and technology-based interventions for secondary students with learning disabilities. In D. Edyburn, K. Higgins, & R. Boone (Eds.), *The handbook of special education technology research and practice* (pp. 599–622). Winston-Salem, NC: Knowledge By Design.

Maccini, P., & Gagnon, J. C. (2006). Mathematics instructional practices and assessment accommodations by secondary special and general educators. *Exceptional Children, 72,* 217–234.

Maccini, P., Mulcahy, C. A., & Wilson, M. G. (2007). A follow-up of mathematics interventions for secondary students with learning disabilities. *Learning Disabilities Research & Practice, 22,* 58–74.

Mackinlay, R., Charman, T., & Karmiloff-Smith, A. (2006). High functioning children with autism spectrum disorder: A novel test of multitasking. *Brain and Cognition, 61*(1), 14–24.

MacMillan, D., & Siperstein, G. (2001). *Learning disabilities as operationally defined by schools. Executive summary.*

Madaus, J. W. (2006). Employment outcomes of university graduates with learning disabilities. *Learning Disabilities Quarterly, 29,* 119–131.

Madaus, J. W., Banerjee, M., Merchant, D., & Keenan, W. (2017). Transition to Postsecondary Education. In J. Kauffman, D. Hallahan, & P. Pullen (Eds.), *Handbook of Special Education* (2nd ed.). Routledge.

Madaus, J. W., Bigaj, S., Chafaleous, S., & Simonsen, B. (2006). What key information can be included in a comprehensive summary of performance? *Career Development for Exceptional Individuals, 26,* 90–99.

Madaus, J. W., & Shaw, S. F. (2006). The impact of the IDEA 2004 on transition to college for students with learning disabilities. *Learning Disabilities Research & Practice, 21,* 273–281.

Madden, M., Lenhart, A., Duggan, M., Cortesi, S., & Gasser, U. (2013). *Teens and technology 2013.* Pew Research Center, Washington, DC: Pew Research Center's Internet & American Life Project. Retrieved from http://www.pewinternet.org/files/old-media//Files/Reports/2013/PIP_TeensandTechnology2013.pdf

Mahone, E. M., & Wodka, E. L. (2008). The neurobiological profile of girls with ADHD. *Developmental Disabilities Research Reviews, 14*(4), 276–284.

Mann, L., & Sabatino, D. (1985). *Cognitive processes in remedial and special education.* Rockville, MD: Aspen Publications.

Mann, P. H., Suiter, P. A., & McClung, R. M. (1992). *A guide to educating mainstreamed students* (4th ed.). Boston: Allyn & Bacon.

Maras, P., & Brown, R. (2000). Effects of different forms of school contact on children's attitudes toward disabled and non-disabled peers, *British Journal of Educational Psychology, 70,* 337–351.

Margalit, M., & Al-Yagon, M. (2002). The loneliness experience of children with learning disabilities. In B. Y. L. Wong, & M. Donahue (Eds.), *The social dimensions of learning disabilities* (pp. 53–75). Mahwah, NJ: Lawrence Erlbaum.

Mariage, T. (2001). Features of an interactive writing discourse: Conversational involvement, conventional knowledge and internalization in "Morning Message." *Journal of Learning Disabilities, 34,* 172–196.

Marino, M. T. (2010). Defining a technology research agenda for elementary and secondary students with learning and other high-incidence disabilities in inclusive science classrooms. *Journal of Special Education Technology, 25*(1), 1–28.

Marston, D., Muyskens, P., Lau, M., & Canter, A. (2003). Problem-solving model for decision making with high-incidence disabilities: The Minneapolis experience. *Learning Disabilities Research & Practice, 18*(3), 187–200.

Martin, J. E., Marshall, L. H., Maxon, L., & Jerman, P. (1996). *ChoiceMaker self-determination curriculum.* Longmont, CO: Sopris West, Inc.

Martin, J. E., Marshall, L. H., Maxon, L. M., & Jerman, P. L. (1999). The self-determined IEP. Longmont, CO: Sopris-West.

Massetti, G. M., Lahey, B. B., Pelham, W. E., Loney, J., Ehrhardt, A., Lee, S. S., Kipp, H. (2008). Academic achievement over 8 years among children who met modified criteria for Attention-Deficit=Hyperactivity Disorder at 4–6 years of age. *Journal of Abnormal Child Psychology, 36,* 399–410.

Mastropieri, M., & Scruggs, T. (1997). Best practices in promoting reading comprehension in students with learning disabilities. *Remedial and Special Education, 18,* 197–213.

Mastropieri, M. A., & Scruggs, T. E. (2002). *Effective instruction for special education* (3rd ed.). Austin, TX: Pro-Ed.

Mastropieri, M. A., & Scruggs, T. E. (2007). *The inclusive classroom: Strategies for effective instruction* (3rd ed.). Columbus, OH: Prentice Hall/Merrill.

Mastropieri, M., Scruggs, T., & Fulk, B. (1990). Teaching abstract vocabulary with the keyword method: Effects on recall and comprehension. *Journal of Learning Disabilities, 23,* 92–107.

Mastropieri, M., Scruggs, T., & Graetz, J. (2003). Reading comprehension instruction for secondary students: Challenges for struggling students and teachers. *Learning Disability Quarterly, 26,* 103–116.

Mather, N. (1992). Whole language reading instruction for students with learning disabilities: Caught in the cross fire. *Learning Disabilities Research & Practice, 7,* 87–95.

Matuszny, R. M., Banda, D. R., & Coleman, T. J. (2007). A progressive plan for building collaborative relationships with parents from diverse backgrounds. *Teaching Exceptional Children, 39*(4), 24–31.

Mayer, R. (1987). Learnable aspects of problem solving: Some examples. In D. E. Berger, K. Pezdek, & W. P. Banks (Eds.), *Applications of cognitive psychology: Problem solving, education, and computing.* Hillsdale, NJ: Erlbaum.

Mayer, R. (2004). Should there be a three-strikes rule against pure discovery learning? The case for guided methods of instruction. *American Psychologist, 59,* 14–19.

Mayes, S., Calhoun, S., & Lane, S. (2005). Diagnosing children's writing disabilities: Different tests give different results. *Perceptual and Motor Skills, 101,* 72–78.

McDonnell, J., & Laughlin, B. (1989). A comparison of backward chaining and concurrent chaining strategies in teaching community skills. *Education and Treatment in Mental Retardation, 24,* 230–238.

McEwan, R. C., & Downie, R. (2013). College success of students with psychiatric disabilities: Barriers of access and distraction. *Journal of Postsecondary Education and Disability, 26*(3), 233–248.

McMaster, K. L., & Fuchs, D. (2002). Effects of cooperative learning on the academic achievement of students with learning disabilities: An update of Tateyama-Sniezek's review. *Learning Disabilities Research & Practice, 17,* 107–117.

McMaster, K. L., Fuchs, D., & Fuchs, L. S. (2006). Research on peer-assisted learning strategies: The promise and limitations of peer-mediated instruction. *Reading & Writing Quarterly, 22*(1), 5–25.

McMullen, R. C., Shippen, M. E., & Dangel, H. L. (2007). Middle school teachers' expectations of organizational behaviors of students with learning disabilities. *Journal of Instructional Psychology, 34*(2), 75–80.

McNamara, D. S., & Kintsch, W. (1996). Learning from texts: effects of prior knowledge and text coherence. *Discourse Processes, 22,* 247–288.

McNamara, J., Vervaeke, S., & Willoughby, T. (2008). Learning disabilities and risk-taking behavior in adolescents: A comparison of those with and without comorbid attention-deficit/hyperactivity disorder. *Journal of Learning Disabilities, 41,* 561–574

McNaughton, D., Hughes, C. A., & Clark, K. (1994). Spelling instruction for students with learning disabilities— implication for research and practice. *Learning Disability Quarterly, 17,* 168–185.

McPartland, J. (1994). Dropout prevention in theory and practice. In R. Rossi (Ed.), *School and students at risk: Context and framework for positive change* (pp. 255–76). New York: Teachers College Press.

Medcalf-Davenport, N. (2003). Questions, answers, and wait-time: Implications for assessment of young children. *International Journal of Early Years Education, 11,* 245–253.

Meese, R. L. (2001). *Teaching learners with mild disabilities: Integrating research and practice* (2nd ed.). Belmont, CA: Wadsworth/Thomson Learning.

Meichenbaum, D. (1977). *Cognitive-behavior modification: An integrated approach.* New York: Plenum Press.

Mellard, D., & Lancaster, P. (2003). Incorporating adult community services in students' transition planning. *Remedial and Special Education, 24*(6), 359–368.

Mellard, D., McKnight, M., & Jordan, J. (2010). RtI tier structures and instructional intensity. *Learning Disabilities Research & Practice, 25,* 217–225

Mellard, D., Scanlon, D., Kissam, B., & Woods, K. (2005). Adult education instructional environments and interaction patterns between teachers and students: An ecobehavioral assessment. *Literacy and Numeracy Studies, 14,* 49–68.

Meltzer, L. ed. (2007). *Executive Function in Education: From theory to practice.* New York: Guilford Press.

Meltzer, L. ed. (2010). *Promoting executive function in the classroom.* New York: Guilford.

Meltzer, L. (2014). Teaching executive function processes: Promoting metacognition, strategy use, and effort. In J. Naglieri & S. Goldstein (Ed.), *Executive Functioning Handbook* (pp. 445–474). New York: Springer.

Meltzer, L., & Bagnato, J. S. (2010). Shifting and flexible problem solving: The anchors for academic success. In L. Meltzer (Ed.), *Promoting executive function in the classroom* (pp. 28–54). New York: Guilford.

Meltzer, L., & Krishnan, K. (2007). Executive function difficulties and learning disabilities: Understandings and misunderstandings. In Lynn Meltzer (Ed.), *Executive function in education: From theory to practice.* New York: Guilford Press.

Meltzer, L., Katzir-Cohen, T., Miller, L., & Roditit, B. (2001). Impact of effort and strategy use on academic performance: Student and teacher perspectives. *Learning Disability Quarterly, 24,* 85–98.

Menzies, H. M., & Lane, K. L. (2011). Using self-regulation strategies and functional assessment-based interventions to provide academic and behavioral support to students at risk within three-tiered models of prevention. *Preventing School Failure: Alternative Education for Children and Youth, 55*(4), 181–191.

Mercer, C. D., & Pullen, P. D. (2005). *Students with learning disabilities.* Upper Saddle River, NJ: Prentice Hall.

Mikami, A., Jack, A., & Lerner, M. (2009). Attention-deficit/hyperactivity disorder. In J. L. Matson (Ed.), *Social behavior and sills in children* (pp. 159–185). New York: Springer.

Miller, G. A. (1956). The magical number seven, plus or minus two: Some limits on our capacity for processing information. *Psychological Review, 63,* 81–97.

Miller, P. W. (2005). Body language in the classroom. *Techniques: Connecting Education and Careers, 80*(8), 28–30.

Miller, S. P. (1996). Perspectives on mathematics instruction. In D. D. Deshler, E. S. Ellis, & B. K. Lenz (Eds.), *Teaching Adolescents with Learning Disabilities* (2nd ed., pp. 313–67). Denver, CO: Love Publishing.

Miller, A. D., Hall, S. W., & Heward, W. L. (1995). Effects of sequential 1-minute time trials with and without intertribal feedback and self-correction on general and special education students' fluency with math facts. *Journal of Behavioral Education, 5,* 319–345.

Miller, J. F., Heilmann, J., Nockerts, A., Iglesias, A., Fabiano, L., & Francis, D. J. (2006). Oral language and reading in bilingual children. *Learning Disabilities Research & Practice, 21,* 30–43.

Miller, S. P., & Hudson, P. J. (2006). Helping students with disabilities understand what mathematics means. *TEACHING Exceptional Children, 39,* 28–35.

Miller, S. P., & Mercer, C. D. (1991). *Addition facts 0–9.* Lawrence, KS: Edge Enterprises.

Miller, S. P., & Mercer, C. D. (1991a). *Addition facts 0–9.* Lawrence, KS: Edge Enterprises.

Miller, S. P., & Mercer, C. D. (1991b). *Subtraction facts 0–9.* Lawrence, KS: Edge Enterprises.

Miller, S. P., & Mercer, C. D. (1993). Using mnemonics to enhance the math performance of students with learning disabilities. *Intervention in School and Clinic, 28,* 105–110.

Miller, S. P., & Mercer, C. D. (1997). Educational aspects of mathematics disabilities. *Journal of Learning Disabilities, 30*(1), 47–56.

Mills, C. J., & Brody, L. E. (1999). Overlooked and unchallenged: Gifted students with learning disabilities. *Knowledge Quest, 27*(5), 36–40.

Milsom, A., & Hartley, M. T. (2005). Assisting students with learning disabilities transitioning to college: What school counselors should know. *Professional School Counseling, 8,* 436–441.

Mithaug, D. E., Mithaug, D., Agran, M., Martin, J., & Wehmeyer, M. (2003). *Self-determined learning theory: Predictions, prescriptions, and practice.* Mahwah, NJ: Erlbaum.

Moje, E. B., Ciechanowski, K. M., Kramer, K., Ellis, L., Carrillo, R., & Collazo, T. (2004). Working toward third space in content area literacy: An examination of everyday funds of knowledge and discourse. *Reading Research Quarterly, 39,* 38–70.

Moll, I. (2004). Towards constructivist Montessori education. *Perspectives in Education, 22,* 37–49.

Moll, L. C., Amanti, C., Neff, D., & Gonzalez, N. (1992). Funds of knowledge for teaching: Using a qualitative approach to connect homes and classrooms. *Theory Into Practice, 31*(2), 132–141.

Monsen, J. J., Ewing, D. L., & Kwoka, M. (2014). Teachers' attitudes towards inclusion, perceived adequacy of support and classroom learning environment. *Learning Environments Research, 17*(1), 113–126.

Montague, M. (2003). Teaching division to students with learning disabilities: A constructivist approach. *Exceptionality, 11,* 165–175.

Montague, M., & Bos, C. S. (1986). The effect of cognitive strategy training on verbal math problem-solving performance of learning disabled adolescents. *Journal of Learning Disabilities, 19,* 26–33.

Montague, M., & Bos, C. S. (1990). Cognitive and metacogntive characteristics of eighth-grade students' mathematical problem solving. *Learning and Individual Differences, 2,* 371–388.

Montague, M. M., Enders, C., & Dietz, S. (2011). Effects of cognitive strategy instruction on math problem solving of middle school students with learning disabilities. *Learning Disability Quarterly, 34*(4), 262–272.

Montague, M., & van Garderen, D. (2003). A cross-sectional study of mathematics achievement, estimation skills, and academic self-perception in students of varying ability. *Journal of Learning Disabilities, 36*(5), 437–448.

Morgan, P. L., Farkas, G., Hillemeier, M. M., & Maczuga, S. (2009). Science achievement gaps begin very early, persist, and are largely explained by modifiable factors. *Educational Researcher, 45*(1), 18–35.

Morgan, P., Farkas, G., Hillemeier, M., & Maczuga, S. (2016). Science Achievement Gaps Begin Very Early, Persist, and Are Largely Explained by Modifiable Factors. *Educational Researcher, 45*(1), 18–35.

Morgan, P. L., Farkas, G., Hillemeier, M. M., Mattison, R., Maczuga, S., Li, H., & Cook, M. (2015). Minorities are disproportionately underrepresented in special education: Longitudinal evidence across five disability conditions. *Educational Researcher, 44*(5), 278–292.

Morgan, P. L., & Sideridis, G. D. (2006). Contrasting the effectiveness of fluency interventions for students with or at risk for learning disabilities: A multilevel random coefficient modeling meta-analysis. *Learning Disabilities Research & Practice, 21*(4), 191–210.

Morningstar, M., Trainor, A., & Murray, A. (2015). Examining outcomes associated with adult life engagement for young adults with high incidence disabilities. *Journal of Vocational Rehabilitation, 43*, 195–208.

Mortweet, S. L., Utley, C. A., Walker, D., Dawson, H. L., Delquadri, J. C., Reddy, S. S., Greenwood, C. R., Hamilton, S., & Ledford, D. (1999). Classwide peer tutoring: Teaching students with mild mental retardation in inclusive classrooms. *Exceptional Children, 65*, 524–536.

Mull, C. A., & Sitlington, P. L. (2003). The role of technology in the transition to postsecondary education of students with learning disabilities. *The Journal of Special Education, 37*, 26–32.

Mull, C., Sitlington, P. L., & Alper, S. (2001). Postsecondary education for students with learning disabilities: A synthesis of the literature. *Exceptional Children, 68*, 97–118.

Mulrine, C. F., Prater, M. A., & Jenkins, A. (2008). The active classroom: Supporting students with attention deficit hyperactivity disorder through exercise. *TEACHING Exceptional Children, 40*(5), 16–22.

Munk, D. D., & Bursuck, W. D. (2001). Preliminary findings on personalized grading plans for middle school students with learning disabilities. *Exceptional Children, 67*, 211–234.

Murphy, J., Hern, C., & Williams, R. (1990). The effects of the copy, cover, compare approach in increasing spelling accuracy with learning disabled students. *Contemporary Educational Psychology, 15*, 378–386.

Murray, C., Goldstein, D., Nourse, S., & Edgar, E. (2000). The postsecondary school attendance and completion rates of high school graduates with learning disabilities. *Learning Disabilities Research & Practice, 15*(3), 119–127.

Murray, C., & Naranjo, J. (2008). Poor, black, learning disabled, and graduating: An investigation of factors and processes associated with school completion among high- risk urban youth. *Remedial and Special Education, 29*, 145–160.

Muscott, H. S. (2002). Exceptional partnerships: Listening to the voices of families. *Preventing School Failure, 46*, 66–69.

Musti-Rao, S., Lynch, T. L., & Plati, E. (2015). Training for fluency and generalization of math facts using technology. *Intervention in School and Clinic, 51*(2), 112–117.

Nagel, D., Schumaker, J., & Deshler, D. (2003). *The FIRST-letter mnemonic strategy* (2nd ed.). Lawrence, KS: Edge Enterprises.

Nathan, R. G., & Stanovich, K. E. (1991). The causes and consequences of differences in reading fluency. *Theory Into Practice, 30*, 176–184.

Nation, K. (2005). Connections between language and reading in children with poor reading comprehension. In H. W. Catts & Alan. G. Kamhi (Ed.), *The connections between language and reading disabilities* (pp. 41–54). Mahwah, NJ: Lawrence Erlbaum Associates.

Nation, K., & Snowling, M. (1997). Assessing reading difficulties: The validity and utility of current measures of reading skill. *British Journal of Educational Psychology, 67*, 359–370.

National Center for Education Statistics. (2013). The Nation's Report Card: A First Look: 2013 Mathematics and Reading (NCES 2014-451). Institute of Education Sciences, U.S. Department of Education, Washington, DC.

National Center for Educational Statistics. (2016). *The Condition of Education.* Washington, DC: Author.

National Collaborative on Diversity in the Teaching Force. (2004). Assessment of diversity in America's teaching force: A call to action. http://ww.nea.org/teacherquality /images/diversityreport.pdf (accessed November 6, 2008).

National Council of Teachers of English and the International Reading Association. (1996). *Standards for the English Language Arts.* Newark, DE and Urbana, IL: National Council of Teachers of English and the International Reading Association.

National Council of Teachers of Mathematics. (1991). *Professional standards for teachers of mathematics.* Reston, VA: NCTM.

National Council of Teachers of Mathematics. (2000). *Principles and standards for school mathematics.* Reston, VA: NCTM.

National Early Literacy Panel. (2008). A synthesis of scientific research on young children's early literacy development. Ohio Department of Education, Early Childhood Conference. http://www.famlit.org/site/c .gtJWJdMQIsE/b.2133427 (accessed November 23, 2008).

National Education Association. (2006). *The twice-exceptional dilemma.* Washington, DC: Author.

National Education Association. (2008). *Teaching Research Spotlight: Homework.* Retrieved from http://www.nea.org /teachexperience/homework08.html

National Immigration Law Center. (2004). *Facts about immigrant participation in the military.* Washington, DC: National Immigration Law Center.

National Institute of Mental Health. (2006). Attention deficit deficit-hyperactivity disorder. http://www.nimh.nih.gov /healthinformation/adhdmenu.cfm (accessed June 26, 2006).

National Joint Committee on Learning Disabilities [NJCLD]. (2016). National Joint Committee on Learning Disabilities Definition of Learning Disabilities. Retrieved on August 20, 2017 from www.ldonline.org/njcld

National Joint Committee on Learning Disabilities. (2007a). Learning disabilities and young children: Identification and intervention. *Learning Disabilities Quarterly, 30,* 63–72.

National Joint Committee on Learning Disabilities. (2007b). The documentation disconnect for students with learning disabilities: Improving access to postsecondary disability services. *Learning Disability Quarterly, 30,* 265–274.

National Mathematics Advisory Panel (2008). The Final Report of the National Mathematics Advisory Panel. Washington, DC: U.S. Department of Education.

National Mathematics Advisory Panel Foundations for success: Findings and recommendations from the National Mathematics Advisory Panel (2008b[brochure]). Retrieved August 20, 2017, from https://www2.ed.gov/about /bdscomm/list/mathpanel/nmp-brochure.pdf

National Reading Panel. (2000). *Teaching children to read. An evidence-based assessment of the scientific research literature on reading and its implications for reading instruction.* Washington, DC: National Institute of Child Health and Development.

National Research Council. (1996). *National science education standards.* Washington, DC: National Committee on Science Education Standards and Assessment, National Research Council.

Neal, L. I., McCray, A. D., Webb-Johnson, G., & Bridgest, S. T. (2003). The effects of African American movement styles on teachers' perceptions and reactions. *Journal of Special Education, 31,* 49–57.

Ness, M., Sohlberg, N., & Albin, R. (2011). Evaluation of a second-tier classroom-based assignment completion strategy for middle school students in a resource context. *Remedial and Special Education, 32*(5), 406–416.

Newman, L., Wagner, M., Cameto, R., & Knokey, A. M. (2009). *The post-high school outcomes of youth with disabilities up to 4 years after high school: A report from the National Longitudinal Transition Study-2 (NLTS2) (NCSER 2009-3017).* Menlo Park, CA: SRI International.

Newman, L., Wagner, M., Cameto, R., Knokey, A.-M., & Shaver, D. (2010). *Comparisons across Time of the Outcomes of Youth With Disabilities up to 4 Years after High School. A Report of Findings From the National Longitudinal Transition Study (NLTS) and the National Longitudinal Transition Study-2 (NLTS2) (NCSER 2010-3008).* Menlo Park, CA: SRI International.

NLTS2. (2004). *Transition Planning for Students with Disabilities. A Special Topic Report from the National Longitudinal Transition Study-2 (NLTS2).* Menlo Park, CA: SRI International.

No Child Left Behind Act. U.S. Code 20 (2001), U.S.C. § 6301 et seq.

Nodine, B., Barenbaum, E., & Newcomer, P. (1985). Story composition by learning disabled, reading disabled, and normal children. *Learning Disability Quarterly, 8,* 167–179.

Norman, D. A. (1982). *Learning and memory.* New York: W. H. Freeman and Company.

Nowicki, E. A., & Sandieson, R. (2002). A meta-analysis of school-age children's attitudes towards persons with physical or intellectual disabilities. *International Journal of Disability, Development and Education, 49,* 243–265.

Nuutinen, T., Ray, C., & Roos, E. (2013). Do computer use, TV viewing, and the presence of the media in the bedroom predict school-aged children's sleep habits in a longitudinal study? *BMC Public Health, 13*(684), 8. https://dx.doi.org/10.1186/1471-2458-13-684

O'Conner, R., Jenkins, J., Leicester, N., & Slocum, T. (1992). *Teaching phonemic awareness to young children with disabilities: Blending, segmenting, and rhyming.* Paper presented at the American Educational Research Association annual conference in San Francisco (April).

O'Melia, M. C., & Rosenberg, M. S. (1994). Effects of cooperative homework teams on the acquisition of mathematics skills by secondary students with mild disabilities. *Exceptional Children, 60*(6), 538–548.

O'Shea, L., Sindelar, P., & O'Shea, D. (1985). The effects of repeated readings and attentional cues on reading fluency and comprehension. *Journal of Reading Behavior, 17,* 129–141.

Obiakor, F. E. (2007). *Multicultural special education: Culturally responsive teaching.* Upper Saddle River, NJ: Merrill Prentice Hall.

Odom, S., Brantlinger, E., Gersten, R., Horner, R., Thompson, B., & Harris, K. (2005). Research in special education: Scientific methods and evidence-based practices. *Exceptional Children, 71*(2), 137–148.

Ogle, D. (1986). K-W-L: A teaching model that develops active reading of expository text. *The Reading Teacher, 39,* 564–570.

O'Keefe, Bernard M., & John Dattilo. (1992). "Teaching the Response-Recode Form to Adults with Mental Retardation using AAC Systems." *AAC: Augmentative and Alternative Communication, 8*(3), 224–233.

Olmeda, R. E., Thomas, A. R., & Davis, C. (2003). An analysis of sociocultural factors in social skills training studies with students with attention deficit/hyperactivity disorder. *Multiple Voices, 6,* 58–62.

O'Regan Kleinert, J., Harrison, E., Mills, K., Dueppen, B., & Trainor, A. (2014). Self-determined goal selection and planning by students with disabilities across grade bands and disability categories. *Education and Training in Autism and Developmental Disabilities, 49*(3), 464–477.

Orfield, G., Losen, D., Wald, J., & Swanson, C. (2004). *Losing our future: How minority youth are being left behind by the graduation rate crisis.* Cambridge, MA: Civil Rights Project at Harvard University.

Osgood, D. W., Foster, E. M., Flanagan, C., & Ruth, G. R. (2005). Introduction: Why focus on the transition to adulthood for vulnerable populations? In D. W. Osgood, E.M. Foster, C. Flanagan, & G. R. Ruth (Eds.), *On Your Own without a Net: The Transition to Adulthood for Vulnerable Populations,* Chicago, IL: University of Chicago Press Books.

Ostad, S. A. (1997). Developmental differences in addition strategies: A comparison of mathematically disabled and mathematically normal children. *British Journal of Educational Psychology, 67,* 345–357.

Ostad, S. A. (1999). Developmental progression of subtraction strategies: A comparison of mathematically normal and mathematically disabled children. *Mathematics Cognition, 4,* 1–20.

Palincsar, A. S., & Brown, A. L. (1984). The reciprocal teaching of comprehension-fostering and comprehension-monitoring activities. *Cognition and Instruction, 1,* 117–175.

Palincsar, A. S., & Duke, N. K. (2004). The role of text and text-reader interactions in young children's reading development and achievement. *Elementary School Journal, 105,* 183–197.

Panacek, L. J., & Dunlap, G. (2003). The social lives of children with emotional and behavioral disorders in self- contained classrooms: A descriptive analysis. *Exceptional Children, 69*(3), 333–348.

Pardo, L. S. (2004). What every teacher needs to know about comprehension. *The Reading Teacher, 58,* 272–280.

Parmar, R. S., Cawley, J. F., & Frazita, R. R. (1996). Word problem-solving by students with and without mild disabilities. *Exceptional Children, 62,* 415–429.

Passolunghi, M. C., Cornoldi, C., & De Liberto, S. (1999). Working memory and intrusions of irrelevant information in a group of specific poor problem solvers. *Memory & Cognition, 27*(5), 779–790.

Passolunghi, M. C., & Pazzaglia, F. (2004). Individual differences in memory updating in relation to arithmetic problem solving. *Learning and Individual Differences, 14*(4), 219–230.

Paxton-Burrsma, D., & Walker, M. (2008). Piggybacking: A strategy to increase participation in classroom discussions by students with learning disabilities. *Teaching Exceptional Children, 40,* 28–34.

Pearson, P. D., & Johnson, D. D. (1978). *Teaching reading comprehension.* New York: Holt, Rinehart, & Winston.

Perfetti, C. (1985). *Reading ability.* New York: Oxford University Press.

Perfetti, C., & Marron, M. (1995). *Learning to read: Literacy acquisition by children and adults.* Philadelphia, PA: National Center on Adult Literacy.

Perie, M., Grigg, W., & Dion, G. (2005). *The nation's report card: mathematics 2005,* no. NCES 2006-453. U.S. Department of Education, Washington, DC: U.S. Government Printing Office.

Pew Research Center. (December 17, 2015). *Parenting in America: Outlook, worries, aspirations are strongly linked to financial situation.* Washington, DC: Author.

Pfifner, L., Barkley, R., & DuPaul, G. (2006). Treatment of ADHD in school settings In R. A. Barkley (Ed.), *Attention-deficit hyperactivity disorder. A handbook for diagnosis and treatment* (3rd ed., pp. 122–183). New York: Guilford Press.

Phillips, L. M. (1988). Young readers' inference strategies in reading comprehension. *Cognition and Instruction, 5,* 193–222.

Pierangelo, R., & Giuliani, G. A. (2009). *Assessment in special education: A practical approach* (3rd ed.). Upper Saddle River, NJ: Pearson.

Pikulski, J., & Chard, D. (2005). Fluency: Bridging between decoding and reading comprehension. *The Reading Teacher, 58,* 510–519.

Pinnell, G., Pikulski, J., Wixson, K., Campbell, J., Gough, P., & Beatty, A. (1995). *Listening to children read aloud: Data from NAEP's integrated reading performance record (IRPR) at grade 4.* Washington, DC: Office of Educational Research and Improvement, US Department of Education.

Poehlmann, J., Clements, M., Abbeduto, L., & Farsad, V. (2005). Family experiences associated with a child's diagnosis of fragile X or Down syndrome: Evidence for disruption and resilience. *Mental Retardation: A Journal of Practices, Policy and Perspectives, 43*(4), 255–267.

Polloway, E. A., & Smith, T. E. C. (2000). *Language instruction for students with disabilities.* Denver, CO: Love Publishing Co.

Popham, W. J. (2006). Content standards: The unindicted co-conspirator. *Educational Leadership, 64,* 87–88.

Poplin, M. (1988). Holistic/constructivist principles of teaching/learning: Implications for the field of learning disabilities. *Journal of Learning Disabilities, 7*(21), 401–416.

Poplin, M. (1988). Holistic/constructivist principles of teaching/learning: Implications for the field of learning disabilities. *Journal of Learning Disabilities, 7*(21), 401–416.

Poplin, M., & Rogers, S. M. (2005). Recollections, apologies, and possibilities. *Learning Disability Quarterly, 28*(2), 159–162.

Porter, J. (1974). Research report. *Elementary English, 51,* 144–151.

Powell, S., & Fuchs, L. S. (2010). Contribution of equal-sign instruction beyond word problem tutoring for third-grade studetns with mathematics difficulty. *Journal of Educational Psychology, 102,* 381–394.

Prescott-Griffin, M., & Witherell, N. (2004). *Fluency in focus.* Portsmouth, NH: Heinemann.

Pressley, M. (1991). Can learning disabled children become good information processors? How can we find out?

In L. Feagans, E. Short, & L. Meltzer (Eds.), *Subtypes of learning disabilities* (pp. 137–62). Hillsdale, NJ: Erlbaum.

Pressley, M. (2002a). Metacognition and self-regulated comprehension. In A. E. Farstrup & S. J. Samuels (Eds.), *What research has to say about reading instruction* (3rd ed.). Newark, DE: International Reading Association.

Pressley, M. (2002b). *Reading instruction that works* (2nd ed.). New York: The Guilford Press.

Price, L., Gerber, P., & Shessel, I. (2002). Adults with learning disabilities and employment: A Canadian perspective. *Thalamus: The Journal of the International Academy for Research in Learning Disabilities, 20,* 29–40.

Prior M. (2003). Is there an increase in the prevalence of autism spectrum disorders? *Journal of Pediatrics and Child Health, 39,* 81–82.

Proctor, C. P., Uccelli, P., Dalton, B., & Snow, C. E. (2009). Understanding depth of vocabulary andimproving comprehension online with bilingual and monolingual children. *Reading & Writing Quarterly, 25*(4), 311–333.

Putnam, J. W. (1993). *Cooperative learning and strategies for inclusion: Celebrating diversity in the classroom.* Baltimore, MD: Paul H. Brookes Publishing Company.

Putnam, M. L., Deshler, D. D., & Schumaker, J. S. (1993). The investigation of setting demands: A missing link in learning strategy instruction. In L. S. Meltzer (Ed.), *Strategy assessment and instruction for students with learning disabilities* (pp. 325–54). Austin, TX: Pro-Ed.

Quinn, M. M., Rutherford, R. B., Leone, P. E., Osher, D. M., & Poirier, J. M. (2005). Youth with disabilities in juvenile corrections: A national survey. *Exceptional Children, 71,* 339–345.

Rack, J. P., Snowling, M. J., & Olson, D. (1992). The nonword reading deficit in developmental dyslexia: A review. *Reading Research Quarterly, 27,* 28–53.

Rademacher, J. A., Schumaker, J. B., & Deshler, D. D. (1996). Development and validation of a classroom assignment routine for inclusive settings. *Learning Disability Quarterly, 19,* 163–178.

Rademacher, J. A., Schumaker, J. B., Deshler, D. D., & Lenz, B. K. (1998). *The quality assignment routine.* Lawrence, KS: Edge Enterprises.

Rafoth, M. A., & Foriska, T. (2006). Administrator participation in promoting effective problem-solving teams. *Remedial and Special Education, 27*(3), 130–135.

Ramasy, J. (2010). *Nonmedication treatments for adult ADHD: Evaluating impact on daily functioning and well-being.* Washington, DC: American Psychological Association.

Ramdass, D., & Zimmerman, B. J. (2011). Developing self-regulation skills: The important role of homework. *Journal of advanced Academics, 22*(2), 194–218.

Randolph, J. J. (2007). Meta-analysis of the research on response cards: Effects on test achievement, quiz achievement, participation, and off-task Behavior. *Journal of Positive Behavior Interventions, 9*(2), 113–128.

Rasinski, T. (2003). *The fluent reader.* New York: Scholastic.

Rasinski, T., & Padak, N. (2004). *Effective reading strategies: Teaching children who find reading difficult* (3rd ed.). Upper Saddle River, NJ: Pearson.

Raskind, M. H., Goldberg, R. J., Higgins, E. L., & Herman, K. L. (1999). Patterns of change and predictors of success in individuals with learning disabilities: Results from a twenty-year longitudinal study. *Learning Disabilities Research & Practice, 14,* 35–49.

Raskind, M. H., Margalit, M., Higgins, E. L. (2006). "My LD": Children's voices on the Internet. *Learning Disabilities Quarterly, 29,* 253–268.

Rea, P. J., McLaughlin, V. L., & Walther-Thomas, C. (2002). Outcomes for students with learning disabilities in inclusive and pullout programs. *Exceptional Children, 68,* 203–222.

Redding, S. (2000). *Parents and learning.* Geneva: UNESCO Publications. Retrieved from http://www.ibe.unesco .org/publications/EducationalPracticesSeriesPDF /prac02e.pdf

Reese, L., Garnier, H., Gallimore, R., & Goldenberg, C. (2000). A longitudinal analysis of the ecocultural antecedents of emergent Spanish literacy and subsequent English reading achievement of Spanish-speaking students. *American Educational Research Journal, 37,* 633–662.

Rehabilitation Act, U.S. Code 29 (1973, as amended), § 794 (Section 504).

Reis, S. M., Baum, S. M., Burke, E. (2014). An operational definition of twice-exceptional learners: Implications and applications. *Gifted Child Quarterly, 58*(3), 217–230.

Reid, R., & Johnson, J. (2011). *Teacher's guide to ADHD. What works for special-needs learners series.* New York, NY: Guilford Publications.

Reid, D. K., & Knight, M. G. (2006). Disability justifies exclusion of minority students: A critical history grounded in disability studies. *Educational Researcher, 35,* 18–23.

Reid, R., & Lienemann, T. O. (2006). *Strategy instruction for students with learning disabilities.* New York: Guilford.

Reiser, B. (2004). Scaffolding complex learning: The mechanisms of structuring and problematizing student work. *The Journal of the Learning Sciences, 13,* 273–304.

Research report, ERIC Documents Reproduction Services, no. ED469287. University of Kansas, Institute for Academic Access.

Reutzel, R. D., & Cooter, R. B. (2004). *Teaching children to read: Putting the pieces together* (4th ed.). Upper Saddle River, NJ: Prentice Hall.

Reutzel, R. D., & Cooter, R. B. (2005). *The essentials of teaching children to read: What every teacher needs to know.* Upper Saddle River, NJ: Prentice Hall.

Riccomini, P. J. (2005). Identification and remediation of systematic error patterns in subtraction. *Learning Disability Quarterly, 28*(3), 233.

Rinaldi, C., & Samson, J. (2008). English language learners and response to intervention: Referral considerations. *Teaching Exceptional Children, 40,* 6–14.

Ritchey, K., & Goeke, J. (2006). Orton-Gillingham and Orton-Gillingham-based reading instruction: A review of the literature. *The Journal of Special Education, 40,* 171–183.

Rivera-Flores, G. W. (2015). Self-instructional cognitive training to reduce impulsive cognitive style in children with attention deficit with hyperactivity disorder. *Electronic Journal of Research in Educational Psychology, 13*(1), 27–46.

Roberts, C. D., Stough, L. M., & Parrish, L. H. (2002). The role of genetic counseling in the elective termination of pregnancies involving fetuses with disabilities. *The Journal of Special Education, 36,* 48–55.

Roberts, J., & Zody, M. (1989). Using the research for effective supervision: Measuring a teacher's questioning techniques. *NASSP Bulletin, 73,* 8–14.

Robinson, C. S., Menchetti, B. M., & Torgesen, J. (2002). Toward a two factor theory of one type of mathematics disability. *Learning Disabilities Research & Practice, 17,* 81–89.

Rojewski, J. W. (2002). Career assessment for adolescents with mild disabilities: Critical concerns for transition planning. *Career Development for Exceptional Individuals, 25,* 73–95.

Rojewski, G., & Gregg, N. (2017). Career decision-making and preparation, transition, and postsecondary attainment of work-bound youth with high incidence disabilities. In J. Kauffman, D. Hallahan, & P. Pullen (Ed.), *Handbook of Special Education* (2nd ed.) Routledge.

Rosen, S. M., Boyle, J. R., Cariss, K., & Forchelli, G. A. (2014). Changing how we think, changing how we learn: Scaffolding executive function processes for students with learning disabilities. *Learning Disabilities: A Multidisciplinary Journal, 20*(4), 165–176.

Rosenblum, S., Weiss, P., & Parush, S. (2004). Handwriting evaluation for developmental dysgraphia: Process versus product. *Reading and Writing: An Interdisciplinary Journal, 17,* 433–458.

Rowe, M. B. (1980). Pausing principles and their effects on reasoning in science. *New Directions for Community Colleges, 8*(3), 27–34.

Rowe, M. B. (1986). Wait-time: Slowing down may be a way of speeding up! *Journal of Teacher Education, 37,* 43–50.

Rowe, M. B., ed. (1976). The pausing principle—two invitations to inquiry. *Journal of College Science Teaching, 5,* 258–259.

Royer, J., & Walles, R. (2007). Influences of gender, ethnicity, and motivation on mathematics performance. In D. B. Berch, & M. M. M. Mazzocco (Eds.), *Why is math so hard for some children? The nature and origins of mathematical learning difficulties and disabilities.* Brookes Publishing Company.

Rubin, A., & Bruce, B. (1985). *Learning with QUILL: Lessons for students, teachers, and software designers.* Reading Report no. (60). Washington, DC: National Institute of Education.

Ruhl, K. L., Hughes, C. A., & Gajar, A. H. (1990). Efficacy of the pause procedure for enhancing learning disabled college students' long and short-term recall of facts presented through lecture. *Learning Disabilities Quarterly, 13,* 55–64.

Ruhl, K. L., Hughes, C. A., & Schloss, P. J. (1987). Using the pause procedure to enhance lecture recall. *Teacher Education and Special Education, 10,* 14–18.

Ruhl, K. L., & Suritsky, S. (1995). The pause procedure and/or an outline: Effect on immediate free recall and lecture notes taken by college students with learning disabilities. *Learning Disability Quarterly, 18,* 2–11.

Rusch, F. R., & Loomis, F. D. (2005). The unfulfilled promise of special education: The transition from education to work for young adults with disabilities. *Exceptional Parent, 35*(2), 72–74.

Ryan, J. B., Hughes, E. M., Katsiyannis, A., McDaniel, M., & Sprinkle, C. (2011). Research-based educational practices for students with autism spectrum disorders. *TEACHING Exceptional Children, 43*(3), 56–64.

Saenz, I. M., Fuchs, L. S., & Fuchs, D. (2005). Peer-assisted learning strategies for English language learners with learning disabilities. *Exceptional Children, 71,* 231–247.

Safer, N., & Fleischman, S. (2005). How student progress monitoring improves instruction. *Educational Leadership, 62,* 81–83.

Salas, L., Lopez, E. J., Chinn, K., & Menchaca-Lopez, E. (2005). Can special education teachers create parent partnerships with Mexican American families? Si se pueda! *Multicultural Education, 13,* 52–55.

Salend, S. J., & Rohena, E. (2003). Students with attention deficit disorders: An overview. *Intervention in School and Clinic, 38,* 259–266.

Salvia, J., & Hughes, C. A. (1990). *Curriculum-based assessment: Testing what is taught.* New York: Macmillan.

Samuels, S. J. (1979). The method of repeated readings. *The Reading Teacher, 50*(5), 376–381.

Samuels, S. J. (1994). Toward a theory of automatic information processing in reading, revisited. In R. B. Ruddell, M. R. Ruddell, & H. Singer (Eds.), *Theoretical models and processes of reading* (4th ed., pp. 816–837). Newark, DE: International Reading Association.

Samuels, S. J. (2002). Reading fluency: Its development and assessment. In A. E. Farstrup & S. Samuels (Eds.), *What research has to say about reading instruction* (pp. 166–83). Newark, DE: International Reading Association.

Sanford, A. K., Park, Y., & Baker, S. K. (2013). Reading growth of students with disabilities in the context of a large-scale statewide reading reform effort. *Journal of Special Education, 47*(2), 83–95.

Sansosti, F. J., & Powell-Smith, K. A. (2006). Using social stories to improve the social behavior of children with asperger syndrome. *Journal of Positive Behavior Interventions, 8*(1), 43–57.

Sarkisian, N., Gerena, M., & Gerstel, N. (2007). Extended family integration among Euro and Mexican Americans:

Ethnicity, gender, and class. *Journal of Marriage and Family*, 69, 40–54.

Scanlon, D. (1996). Social skills strategy instruction. In D. D. Deshler, E. S. Ellis, & B. K. Lenz (Eds.), *Teaching adolescents with learning disabilities*. Denver, CO: Love Publishing.

Scanlon, D. (2002). PROVE-ing what you know: Using a learning strategy in an inclusive classroom. *Teaching Exceptional Children*, 34, 48–54.

Scanlon, D. (2003). Learning strategies expected in content-area inclusion. *Developmental Disabilities Bulletin*, 31, 11–41.

Scanlon, D. (2013). Specific learning disability and its newest definition: Which is comprehensive? And Which is insufficient? *Journal of Learning Disabilities*, 46(1), 26–33.

Scanlon, D. in press. Introduction to the issue: Tools that support (2009) education. *Reading & Writing Quarterly*, 25(4), 247–249.

Scanlon, D., & Baker, D. (2012). An accommodations model for the secondary inclusive classroom. *Learning Disability Quarterly*, 35(4), 212–224.

Scanlon, D., Cass, R., Amtzis, A., & Sideridis, G. (2009). Procedural facilitation of propositional knowledge in the content-areas. *Reading & Writing Quarterly*, 25, 290–310.

Scanlon, D., Deshler, D., & Schumaker, J. B. (1996). Can a strategy be taught and learned in secondary inclusive classrooms? *Learning Disabilities Research & Practice*, 11(1), 41–57.

Scanlon, D., Deshler, D., & Schumaker, J. (2004). *The ORDER routine manual*. Lawrence, KS: Edge Publications.

Scanlon, D. J., Duran, G. Z., Reyes, E. I., & Gallego, M. A. (1992). Interactive semantic mapping: An interactive approach to enhancing LD students' content area comprehension. *Learning Disabilities Research & Practice*, 7, 142–146.

Scanlon, D., Gallego, M., Duran, G., & Reyes, E. (2005). Interactive staff development supports collaboration when learning to teach. *Teacher Education and Special Education*, 28, 40–51.

Scanlon, D., & Mellard, D. F. (2002). Academic and participation profiles of school-age dropouts with and without learning disabilities. *Exceptional Children*, 68, 239–258.

Scanlon, D., Patton, J., & Raskind, M. (2017). Transition to daily living for persons with high incidence disabilities. In J. Kauffman, D. Hallahan, & P. Pullen (Eds.), *Handbook of Special Education* (2nd ed.). Routledge.

Scanlon, D., Saenz, L., & Kelly, M. P. (2017). The effectiveness of alternative IEP dispute resolution practices. *Learning Disability Quarterly*. DOI: https://dx.doi.org/10.1177/0731948717698827

Scanlon, D., Schumaker, J. B., & Deshler, D. D. (1994). Collaborative dialogues between teachers and researchers to create educational interventions: A case study. *Journal of Educational and Psychological Consultation*, 5, 69–76.

Scarborough, H. S. (2005). Developmental relationships between language skills and learning to read. In H. W. Catts & Alan G. Kamhi (Eds.), *The connections between language and reading disabilities* (pp. 55–76). Mahwah, NJ: Lawrence Erlbaum Associates.

Schaefer Whitby, P. J., & Mancil, G. R. (2009). Academic achievement profiles of children with high functioning autism and asperger syndrome: A review of the literature. *Education and Training in Developmental Disabilities*, 44(4), 551–560.

Schatschneider, C., Carlson, C. D., Francis, D. J., Foorman, B. R., &Fletcher, J. M. (2002). Relationship of rapid automatized naming and phonological awareness in early reading development: Implications for the double deficit hypothesis. *Journal of Learning Disabilities*, 35, 245–256.

Scheeler, M. C., Ruhl, K. L., & McAfee, J. K. (2004). Providing performance feedback to teachers: A review. *Teacher Education and Special Education*, 27, 396–407.

Schmidt, S. M. P., & Ralph, D. L. (2016). The flipped classroom: A twist on teaching. *Contemporary Issues in Education Research*, 9(1), 1–6.

Schoen, L., & Fusarelli, L. D. (2008). Innovation, NCLB, and the fear factor: Leading 21st-century schools in an era of accountability. *Educational Policy*, 22, 181–203.

Schoenfeld, A. (2002). Making mathematics work for all children: Issues of standard, testing, and equity. *Educational Researcher*, 31, 13–25.

Schoenfeld, A. H. (2004). The math wars. *Educational Policy*, 18, 253–286.

Schreiber, P. (1991). Understanding prosody's role in reading acquisition. *Theory Into Practice*, 30, 158–164.

Schreiner, M. B. (2007). Effective self-advocacy: What students and special educators need to know. *Intervention in School and Clinic*, 42, 300–304.

Schuchardt, K., Gebhardt, M., & Maehler, C. (2010). Working memory functions in children with different degrees of intellectual disability. *Journal of Intellectual Disability Research*, 54(4), 346–353.

Schumaker, J. B., Bulgren, J. A., Deshler, D. D., & Lenz, B. K. (1998). *The recall enhancement routine*. Lawrence, KS: University of Kansas.

Schumaker, J. B., Denton, P., & Deshler, D. (1984a). *The learning strategies curriculum: The paraphrasing curriculum*. Lawrence, KS: University of Kansas.

Schumaker, J., Denton, P., & Deshler, D. (1984b). *The Paraphrasing strategy*. Lawrence, KS: Edge Enterprises Inc.

Schumaker, J. B., & Deshler, D. D. (2006). Teaching adolescents to be strategic learners. In D. D. Deshler & J. B. Schumaker (Eds.), *Teaching adolescents with disabilities: Accessing the general education curriculum* (pp. 121–156). Thousand Oaks, CA: Corwin Press.

Schumaker, J. D., Deshler, D., Alley, G., Warner, M., Clark, F., & Nolan, S. (1982). Error monitoring: A learning strategy for improving academic performance. In W. M. Cruickshank & J. W. Lerner (Eds.), *Coming of age* (pp. 170–83). Syracuse, NY: Syracuse University Press.

Schumaker, J. D., & Sheldon, J. (1985). *The sentence writing strategy.* Lawrence, KS: Edge Enterprises Inc.

Schumaker, J. D., Nolan, J. B., & Deshler, D. D. (1985). *The error monitoring strategy: Instructor's manual.* Lawrence, KS: University of Kansas.

Schunk, D. (2004). *Learning theories: An educational perspective* (4th ed.). Upper Saddle River, NJ: Pearson.

Schwartz, R., & Raphael, T. (1985). Concept of definition: A key to improving students' vocabulary. *The Reading Teacher, 39,* 198–205.

Schwab, J, R., Tucci, S., & Jolivette, K. (2013). Integrating schema-based instruction and response cards for students with learning disabilities and challenging behaviors. *Beyond Behavior, 22*(3), 24–30.

Scorgie, K., & Sobsey, D. (2000). Transformational outcomes associated with parenting children who have disabilities. *Mental Retardation, 38,* 195–206.

Scruggs, T. E., & Mastropieri, M. A. (1990). Mnemonic instruction for students with learning disabilities: What it is and what it does. *Learning Disability Quarterly, 13,* 271–279.

Scruggs, T. E., & Mastropieri, M. A. (1992). *Teaching test-taking skills: Helping students show what they know.* Cambridge, MA: Brookline Books.

Scruggs, T. E., Mastropieri, M. A., & McDuffie, K. A. (2007). Co-teaching in inclusive classrooms: A metasynthesis of qualitative research. *Exceptional Children, 73*(4), 392–416.

Scruggs, T., Mastropieri, M., & Levin, J. (1986). Can children effectively reuse the same mnemonic pegwords? *Educational Communication and Technology, 34,* 83–88.

Searcy, S., & Maroney, S. A. (1996). Lesson planning practices of special education teachers. *Exceptionality, 6*(3), 171–187.

Searlman, A., & Herrmann, D. (1994). *Memory from a broader perspective.* New York: McGraw-Hill.

Sears, N. C., & Johnson, D. M. (1986). The effects of visual imagery on spelling performance and retention among elementary students. *Journal of Educational Research, 79,* 230–233.

Seethaler, P. M., & Fuchs, L. S. (2006). The cognitive correlates of computational estimation skill among third-grade students. *Learning Disabilities Research & Practice, 21*(4), 233–243.

Seidenberg, M. S. (1997). Language acquisition and use: Learning and applying probabilistic constraints. *Science, 275,* 1599–1603.

Shankweiler, D., & Crain, S. (1986). Language mechanisms and reading disorder: A modular approach. *Cognition, 24,* 139–168.

Shannon, P. (1993). Letters to the editor: Comments on Baumann. *Reading Research Quarterly, 28,* 86.

Shannon, T. R., & Polloway, E. A. (1993). Promoting error monitoring in middle school, students with LD. *Intervention in School and Clinic, 28,* 160–164.

Share, D. L., & Stanovich, K. E. (1995). Cognitive processes in early reading development: A model of acquisition and individual differences. *Issues in Education: Contributions from Educational Psychology, 1,* 1–57.

Shefelbine, J., Lipscomb, L., & Hern, A. (1989). Variables associated with second, fourth, and sixth grade students' ability to identify polysyllabic words. In S. McCormick & J. Zutell (Eds.), *Cognitive and social perspectives for literacy research and instruction.* Chicago: National Reading Conference.

Sherin, B., & Fuson, K. (2005). Multiplication strategies and the appropriation of computational resources. *Journal for Research in Mathematics Education, 36*(4), 347–395.

Shore, S. (2003). My life with Asperger syndrome. In R.W. Du Charme & T. P. Gullotta (Eds.), *Asperger syndrome: A guide for professionals and families* (pp. 189–209). New York: Kluwer Academic/Plenum.

Shriberg, L. D., Paul, R., McSweeny, J. L., Klin, A., Cohen, D. J., Volkmar, F. R. (2001). Speech and prosody characteristics of adolescents and adults with high-functioning autism and asperger syndrome. *Journal of Speech, Language, and Hearing Research, 44*(5), 1097–1115.

Shumow, L. (2011). Homework and study habits. In S. Redding, M. Murphy, & P. Sheley (Eds.), *Handbook on family and community engagement* (pp. 77–80). Charlotte, NC: Information Age. Retrieved from http://www.schoolcommunitynewwork.org/Default.aspx (see "FACE Handbook")

Sibley, M. H., Altszuler, A. R., Morrow, A. S., Merrill, B. M. (2014). Mapping the Academic Problem Behaviors of Adolescents with ADHD. *School Psychology Quarterly, 29*(4), 422–437.

Siegel, L. S. (2012). Confessions and reflections of the black sheep of the learning disabilities field. *Australian Journal of Learning Difficulties, 17*(2), 63–77.

Siegel, L. S., & Ryan, E. B. (1989). The development of working memory in normally achieving and subtypes of learning disabled children. *Child Development, 60*(4), 973–980.

Siegler, R., Carpenter, T., Fennell, F., Gearly, D., Lewis, J., Okamoto, Y., … Wray, J. (2010). *Developing effective fractions instruction for kindergarten through 8th grade: A practice guide (NCEE No. 2010-4039).* Washington, DC: National Center for Education Evaluation and Regional Assistance, Institute of Education Sciences, U.S. Department of Education.

Sileo, T. W., & Prater, M. A. (1998). Preparing professionals for partnerships with parents of students with disabilities: Textbook considerations regarding cultural diversity. *Exceptional Children, 64,* 513–528.

Siperstein, G. N., Glick, G. C., & Parker, R. C. (2009). Social inclusion of children with intellectual disabilities in a recreational setting. *Intellectual and Developmental Disabilities, 47*(2), 97–107.

Siperstein, G., Leffert, J., & Wenz-Gross, M. (1997). The quality of friendships between children with and without learning problems. *American Journal on Mental Retardation, 102,* 111–125.

Skiba, R. J., Simmons, A. B., Ritter, S., Gibb, A., Rausch, M. K., Cuadrado, J., Choon-Guen, G. (2008). Achieving equity in special education: History, status, and current challenges. *Exceptional Children, 74,* 264–288.

Skinner, B. F. (1957). *Verbal behavior.* Edgewood Cliffs, NJ: Prentice Hall.

Skinner, M. E. (1998). Promoting self-advocacy among college students with learning disabilities. *Intervention in School and Clinic, 33,* 278–283.

Skinner, M. E., & Lindstrom, B. D. (2003). Bridging the gap between high school and college: Strategies for the successful transition of students with learning disabilities. *Preventing School Failure, 47,* 132–137.

Skrtic, T. M. (2005). A political economy of learning disabilities. *Learning Disabilities Quarterly, 28*(2), 149–155.

Slavin, R. E. (1990). *Cooperative learning: Theory, research, and practice.* Englewood Cliffs, NJ: Prentice Hall.

Slavin, R. E. (1991). Synthesis of research on cooperative learning. *Educational Leadership, 48*(5), 71–82.

Smith, G. (1999). Teaching a long sequence of behavior using whole task training, forward chaining, and backward chaining. *Perceptual and Motor Skills, 89,* 951–965.

Smith, S. W. (2001). *Involving parents in the IEP process.* ERIC Digest E611. Arlington, VA: ERIC Clearinghouse on Disabilities and Gifted Education (ED 455658).

Smith K. A., Ayres, K. M., Alexander, J. L., Ledford, J. R., Shepley, C., Shepley, S. B. (2016). Initiation and generalization of self-instructional skills in adolescents with autism and intellectual disability. *Journal of Autism and Developmental Disabilities, 46,* 1196–1209.

Smith Myles, B., Hilgenfeld, T. D., Barnhill, G. P., Griswold, D. E., Hagiwara, T., & Simpson, R. (2002). Analysis of reading skills in individuals with asperger syndrome. *Focus on Autism and Other Developmental Disabilities, 17*(1), 44–47.

Smith, C., & Hofer, J. (2003). *The characteristics and concerns of adult basic education teachers.* NCSALL Report No. (26). Cambridge, MA: National Center for the Study of Adult Learning and Literacy.

Smith, T. S., Manuel, N., & Stokes, B. R. (2012). Comparisons of high school graduation rates of students with disabilities and their peers in twelve southern states. *Learning Disabilities: A Multidisciplinary Journal, 18*(2), 47–59.

Smith, T. J., & Wallace, S. (2011). Social skills of children in the U.S. with comorbid learning disabilities and AD/HD. *International Journal of Special Education, 26*(3), 238–247.

Smolkin, L. B., & Donovan, C. A. (2003). Supporting comprehension acquisition for emerging and struggling readers: The interactive information book read-aloud. *Exceptionality, 11,* 25–38.

Snowling, M. J. (2005). Literacy outcomes for children with oral language impairments: Students' vocabulary. *The Reading Teacher, 39,* 198–205.

Snowman, J., & Biehler, R. (2006). *Psychology applied to teaching* (11th ed.). Boston: Houghton Mifflin.

Sparks, S. (2000). Classroom and curriculum accommodations for Native American students. *Intervention in School and Clinic, 35,* 259–263.

Sparks, S. D. (2012). New research on multitasking points to role of self-control. *Education Week, 31*(31), 1.

Spencer, T., Biederman, J., & Wilens, T. (2010). Medications used for attention-deficit/hyperactivity disorder. In M. Dulcan (Ed.), *Dulcan's textbook of child and adolescent psychiatry* (published on line). Americian Psychiatric Publishing. Retrieved from http://www.psychiatryonline.com/content.askx?aid-468068.

Stacy, R. (2001). *Complex responsive processes in organizations: Learning and knowledge creation.* London: Routledge.

Stahl, S. (2006). Understanding shifts in reading and its instruction. In K. Dougherty Stahl & M. McKenna (Eds.), *Reading research at work: Foundations of effective practice* (pp. 45–75). New York: Guilford Press.

Staker, H., & Horn, M. (2012). *Classifying K–12 blended learning.* San Mateo, CA: Innosight Institute. Retrieved from http://www.christenseninstitute.org/wp-content/uploads/2013/04/Classifying-K-12-blended-learning.pdf

Stanovich, K. E. (2005). The future of a mistake: Will discrepancy measurement continue to make the learning disabilities field a pseudoscience? *Learning Disability Quarterly, 28,* 103–106.

Stecker, P. M. (2006). Using Curriculum-based measurement to monitor reading progress in inclusive elementary schools. *Reading & Writing Quarterly, 22,* 91–97.

Steele, M. M. (2005). Teaching students with learning disabilities: Constructivism or behaviorism? *Current Issues in Education, 8*(10). Retrieved from http://cie.asu.edu/ojs/index.php/cieatasu/article/view/1607

Steele, M. M. (2007). Teaching calculator skills to elementary students who have learning problems. *Preventing School Failure, 52*(1), 59–62.

Steen, L. A. (2007). Facing facts: Achieving balance in high school mathematics. *Mathematics Teacher, 100*(1), 86–95.

Stein, M., Carnine, D., & Dixon, R. (1998). Direct instruction: Integrating curriculum design and effective teaching practice. *Intervention in School and Clinic, 33,* 227–234.

Stein, M., Kinder, D., Silbert, J., Carnine, D. W., & Rolf, K. (2018). *Direct instruction mathematics* (5th ed.). Boston, MA: Pearson.

Stein, M., Silbert, J., & Carnine, D. (1997). *Designing effective mathematics instruction: A direct instruction approach* (3rd ed.). Upper Saddle River, NJ: Merrill/Prentice Hall.

Stein, M., Stuen, C., Carnine, D., & Long, R. (2001). Textbook evaluation and adoption. *Reading & Writing Quarterly: Overcoming Learning Difficulties, 17,* 5–24.

Stevenson, J. (2003). Best wishes, Ed. *Reading,* grade 2. Hightstown, NJ: McGraw-Hill.

Stodden, R. A., & Dowrick, P. (2000). The present and future of postsecondary education for adults with disabilities. *Impact, 13*(1), 4–5.

Stores, G., & Wiggs, L. (Eds.) (2001). *Sleep disturbance in children and adolescents with disorders of development: Its significance and management.* Oxford, United Kingdom: MacKeith.

Stowell, J. R., & Nelson, J. M. (2007). Benefits of electronic audience response systems on student participation, learning, and emotion. *Teaching of Psychology, 34,* 253–258.

Strickland, T. K., & Maccini, P. (2013). The effects of the concrete-representational-abstract-integration strategy on the ability of students with learning disabilities to multiply linear expressions within area problems. *Remedial and Special Education, 34*(3), 142–153.

Stubbe, D. E. (2000). Attention-deficit/hyperactivity disorder overview: Historical perspective, current controversies, and future directions. *Child & Adolescent Psychiatric Clinics of North America, 9,* 469–479.

Sturm, J. M., & Clendon, S. A. (2004). Augmentative and alternative communication, language, and literacy: Fostering the relationship. *Topics in Language Disorders, 24,* 76–91.

Sturm, J. M., & Clendon, S. A. (2004). Augmentative and alternative communication, language, and literacy: Fostering the relationship. *Topics in Language Disorders, 24,* 76–91.

Sugai, G., & Horner, R. H. (2002). Introduction to the special series on positive behavior support in schools. *Journal of Emotional and Behavioral Disorders, 10,* 130–135.

Summers, J. A., Hoffman, L., Marquis, J., Turnbull, A., Poston, D., & Nelson, L. L. (2005). Measuring the quality of family- professional partnerships in special education services. *Exceptional Children, 72*(1), 65.

Suritsky, S. K. (1992). Note taking approaches and specific areas of difficulty reported by university students with learning disabilities. *Journal of Postsecondary Education and Disability, 10*(1), 3–10.

Suritsky, S. K., & Hughes, C. A. (1996). Notetaking strategy instruction. In D. D. Deshler, E. S. Ellis, & B. K. Lenz (Eds.), *Teaching adolescents with learning disabilities* (2nd ed., pp. 267–312). Denver, CO: Love Publishing Company.

Swanson, H. L. (1999). Reading comprehension and working memory in learning disabled readers: Is phonological loop more important than the executive system? *Journal of Experimental Child Psychology, 72,* 1–31.

Swanson, H. L. (1999). Sentence span measure (SSM). In N. Frederickson & R. J. Cameron (Eds.), *Psychology in Education Portfolio: Memory and Listening Comprehension* (pp. 25–6). Winsor, England, NFER-Nelson.

Swanson, H. L. (2003). Age-related differences in learning disabled and skilled readers' working memory. *Journal of Experimental Child Psychology, 85*(1), 1–31.

Swanson, H. L., & Beebe-Frankenberger, M. (2004). The relationship between working memory and mathematical problem solving in children at risk and not at risk for serious math difficulties. *Journal of Educational Psychology, 96,* 471–491.

Swanson, H. L., Cooney, J. B., O'Shaughnessy, T. (1998). Learning disabilities and memory. In B.Y. L. Wong (Ed.), *Learning about learning disabilities* (2nd ed., pp. 107–62). San Diego: Academic Press.

Swanson, H. L., & Deshler, D. (2003). Instructing adolescents with learning disabilities: Converting a meta-analysis to practice. *Journal of Learning Disabilities, 36,* 124–135.

Swanson, H. L., & Hoskyn, M. (1998). Experimental intervention research on students with learning disabilities: A meta-analysis of treatment outcomes. *Review of Educational Research, 68,* 277–321.

Swanson, H. L., & Hoskyn, M. (2001). Instructing adolescents with learning disabilities: A component and composite analysis. *Learning Disabilities Research & Practice, 16,* 109–119.

Swanson, H. L., Hoskyn, M., & Lee, C. (1999). *Interventions for students with learning disabilities: A meta-analysis of treatment outcomes.* New York: Guilford Press.

Swanson, H. L., Howard, C., & Sáez, L. (2006). Do different components of working memory underlie different subgroups of reading disabilities? *Journal of Learning Disabilities, 39,* 252–269.

Swanson, H. L., & Jerman, O. (2006). Math Disabilities: A preliminary meta-analysis of the cognitive literature. In T. Scruggs, & M. Mastropieri (Eds.), *Special Issue Methodology: Learning and Behavioral Disabilities.* Bristol, Eng: Elsevier LTD.

Swanson, H. L., & Jerman, O. (2006). Math disabilities: A selective meta-analysis of the literature. *Review of Educational Research, 76*(2), 249–274.

Swanson, H. L., Jerman, O., & Zheng, X. (2009). Math disabilities and reading disabilities: Can they be separated? *Journal of Psychoeducational Assessment, 27,* 175–196.

Swanson, H. L., & Saez, L. (2003). Memory difficulties in children and adults with learning disabilities. In H. L. Swanson, S. Graham, & R. Harris (Eds.), *Handbook of learning disabilities* (pp. 182–198). New York: Guilford.

Swanson, H. L., Sáez, L., & Gerber, M. (2004). Do phonological and executive processes in English learners at risk for reading disabilities in grade 1 predict performance in grade 2? *Learning Disabilities Research & Practice, 19,* 225–238.

Swanson, H. L., Saez, L., Gerber, M., & Leafstedt, J. (2004). Literacy and cognitive functioning in bilingual and nonbilingual children at or not at risk for reading disabilities. *Journal of Educational Psychology, 96*(1), 3–18.

Sweeney, W. J., Ehrhardt, A. M., Gardner, R., III, Jones, L., Greenfield, R., & Fribley, S. (1999). Using guided notes with academically at-risk high school students during a remedial summer social studies class. *Psychology in the Schools, 36*(4), 305–318.

Tang, S. (1995). A comparison of trends in living arrangements for white and black youth. *Western Journal of Black Studies, 19,* 218–223.

Tanweer, T., Rathbone, C. J., Souchay, C. (2010). Autobiographical memory, autonoetic consciousness, and identity in asperger syndrome. *Neuropsychologia, 48*(4), 900–908.

Tatayama-Sniezek, K. M. (1990). Cooperative learning: Does it improve the academic achievement of students with handicaps? *Exceptional Children, 56*, 426–437.

Taymans, J. M. (2012). Legal and definitional issues affecting the identification and education of adults with specific learning disabilities in adult education programs. *Journal of Learning Disabilities, 45*(1), 5–16.

Taymans, J., & Lynch, S. (2004). Developing a unit planning routine. In B. K. Lenz, D. D. Deshler, & B. R. Kissam (Eds.), *Teaching content to all* (pp. 162–94). Boston, MA: Allyn & Bacon.

Terrill, M. C., Scruggs, T. E., & Mastropieri, M. A. (2004). SAT vocabulary instruction for high school students with learning disabilities. *Intervention in School and Clinic, 39*, 288–294.

Terry Gandell, & Ann Sutton (1998). Comparison of AAC interaction patterns in face-to-face and telecommunications conversations. *Augmentative and Alternative Communication, 14*(1), 3–10.

Test, D. W., Fowler, C. H., Brewer, D. M., & Wood, W. M. (2005). A content and methodological review of self-advocacy intervention studies. *Exceptional Children, 72*(1), 101.

Test, D. W., & Neale, M. (2004). Using the self-advocacy strategy to increase middle graders' IEP participation. *Journal of Behavioral Education, 13*, 135–145.

Therrien, W. J. (2004). Fluency and comprehension gains as a result of repeated readings: A meta-analysis. *Remedial and Special Education, 25*, 252–261.

Thomas-Presswood, T. N., & Presswood, D. (2008). *Meeting the needs of students and families from poverty: A handbook for school and mental health professionals.* Baltimore, MD: Paul H. Brookes.

Thompson, S. J., Morse, A. B., Sharpe, M., & Hall, S. (2005). *Accommodations manual: How to select, administer, and evaluate use of accommodations for instruction and assessment of students with disabilities* (2nd ed.). Washington, DC: Council of Chief State School Officers.

Thurlow, M. L., Lazarus, S. S., Thompson, S. J., & Morris, A. B. (2005). State policies on assessment participation and accommodations for students with disabilities. *Journal of Special Education, 38*, 232–240.

Thurlow, M., & Thompson, S. (2003). *Inclusion of students with disabilities in state and district assessments.* ED, no. 480 047, 18 pp.

Tickle, L. (2005). The crucible of the classroom: A learning environment for teachers or a site of crucifixion? In D. Beijaard, P. C. Meijer, G. Morine-Dershimer, & G. Tillema (Eds.), *Teaching professional development in changing conditions* (pp. 61–77). Netherlands: Springer.

Titsworth, B. S., & Kiewra, K. A. (2004). Organizational lecture cues and student notetaking as facilitators of student learning. *Contemporary Educational Psychology, 29*, 447–461.

Tolar, T. D., Fuchs, L., Fletcher, J. M., Fuchs, D., & Hamlett, C. L. (2016). Cognitive profiles of mathematical problem solving learning disability for different definitions of disability. *Journal of Learning Disabilities, 49*, 240–256.

Topping, K. J. (2005). Trends in peer learning. *Educational Psychology, 25*, 631–645.

Torgesen, J. K. (1982). The learning disabled child as an inactive learner: Educational implication. *Topics in Learning and Learning Disabilities*, April, 45–52.

Torgesen, J. K., Alexander, A. W., Wagner, R. K., Rashotte, C. A., Voeller, K. K. S., & Conway, T. (2001). Intensive remedial instruction for children with severe reading disabilities: Immediate and long-term outcomes from two instructional approaches. *Journal of Learning Disabilities, 34*, 33–58.

Torgesen, J., Morgan, S., & Davis, C. (1992). Effects of two types of phonological awareness training on word learning in kindergarten children. *Journal of Educational Psychology, 84*, 364–370.

Toste, J. R., Bloom, E. L., & Heath, N. L. (2014). The differential role of classroom working alliance in predicting school-related outcomes for students with and without high-incidence disabilities. *Journal of Special Education, 48*(2), 135–148.

Tournaki, N. (2003). The differential effects of teaching addition through strategy instruction versus drill and practice to students with and without learning disabilities. *Journal of Learning Disabilities, 36*(5), 449–458.

Tracey, D. H., & Morrow, L. M. (2012). *Lenses on reading: An introduction to theories and models* (2nd ed.). New York, NY: Guilford.

Trainor, A. (2005). Self-determination perceptions and behaviors of diverse students with LD during the transition planning process. *Journal of Learning Disabilities, 38*, 233–249.

Trammel, D. L., Schloss, P. J., & Alper, S. (1994). Using self-recording, evaluation, and graphing to increase completion of homework assignments. *Journal of Learning Disabilities, 27*(2), 75–81.

Troia, G., & Graham, S. (2002). The effectiveness of a highly explicit, teacher-directed strategy instruction routine: Changing the writing performance of students with learning disabilities. *Journal of Learning Disabilities, 35*, 290–305.

Troiano, P. T. (2003). College students and learning disability: Elements of self-style. *Journal of College Student Development, 44*, 404–419.

Tseng, M., & Cermak, S. (1993). The influence of ergonomic factors and perceptual-motor abilities on handwriting performance. *American Journal of Occupational Therapy, 47*, 919–926.

Turnbull, R., Huerta, N., & Stowe, M. (2006). *The Individuals with Disabilities Education Act as amended in 2004*. Upper Saddle River, NJ: Pearson.

U.S. Department of Education. (2015). *To assure the free appropriate public education of all children with disabilities: Thirty-seventh annual report to Congress on the implementation of The Individuals with Disabilities Education Act*. Washington, DC: Office of Special Education Programs.

U.S. Department of Education, Institute of Education Sciences, National Center for Education Statistics, National Assessment of Educational Progress (NAEP), *2011 Writing Assessment*.

U.S. Department of Education, National Center for Education Statistics. (2016). *Digest of Education Statistics, 2014* (2016–006).

U.S. Department of Education, Office of Special Education Programs. Washington, DC: ERIC Documents Reproduction Services (ED 458 759).

U.S. Department of Education, Institute of Education Sciences, National Center for Education Statistics. (2003). *The nation's report card: Writing 2002*, NCES 2003–529, by H. R. Persky, M. C. Daane, & Y. Jin. Washington, DC: U.S. DOE.

U.S. Department of Education, Institute of Education Sciences, National Center for Education Statistics. (2017). *National Assessment of Educational Progress* (NAEP), various years, 1990–2015 Reading Assessments.

Uberti, H. Z., Scruggs, T. E., & Mastropieri, M. A. (2003). Keywords make the difference! Mnemonic instruction in inclusive classrooms. A classroom application. *Teaching Exceptional Children, 35*(3), 56–61.

Udwin, O., Yule, W. (1991) A cognitive and behavioural phenotype in Williams syndrome. *Journal of Clinical Experimental Neuropsychology, 13*, 232–244.

Udwin, O., & Yule, W. (1990). Expressive language of children with Williams syndrome. *American Journal of Medical Genetics, 37*(S6), 108–114.

Van Balkom, H., & Welle Donker-Gimbrere, M. (1996). A psycholinguistic approach to graphic language use. In S. von Tetzchner & M. Jensen (Eds.), *Augmentative and alternative communication: European perspectives* (pp. 153–170). London: Whurr.

Van der Molen, M. J., Van Luit, J. E. H., Van der Molen, M. W., & Jongmans, M. J. (2010). Everyday memory and working memory in adolescents with mild intellectual disability. *American Journal on Intellectual and Developmental Disabilities, 115*(3), 207–217.

van Garderen, D., & Scheuermann, A. (2014). Diagramming word problems: A strategic approach for instruction. *Intervention in School and Clinic, 50*(5), 282–290.

Van Reusen, A. K., Bos, C. S., Schumaker, J. B., & Deshler, D. D. (2002). *The self-advocacy strategy: For education & transition planning*. Lawrence, KS: Edge Enterprises.

Van Reusen, A. K., Bos, C. S., Schumaker, J. B., & Deshler, D. D. (2007). *The Self-Advocacy Strategy*, revised. Lawrence, KS: Edge Enterprises.

Van Voorhis, F. L. (2011). Costs and benefits of family involvement in homework. *Journal of Advanced Academics, 22*(2), 220–249.

Vatterott, C. (2003). There's something wrong with homework. *Principal, 82*(3), 64.

Vatterott, C. (2010). Five hallmarks of good homework. *Educational Leadership, 68*(1), 10–15.

Vaughn, S., Bos, C. S., & Schumm, J. S. (2000). *Teaching exceptional, diverse, and at-risk students in the general education classroom* (2nd ed.). Boston, MA: Allyn & Bacon.

Vaughn, S., & Fuchs, L. S. (2003). Redefining learning disabilities as inadequate response to instruction: The promise and potential problems. *Learning Disabilities Research & Practice, 18*, 137–146.

Vaughn, S., Gersten, R., & Chard, D. J. (2000). The underlying message in LD intervention research: Findings from research syntheses. *Exceptional Children, 67*(1), 99–114.

Vaughn, S., Reiss, M., Rothlein, L., & Hughes, M. (1999). Kindergarten teachers' perceptions of instructing students with disabilities. *Remedial and Special Education, 20*, 184–191.

Vaughn, S., & Swanson, E. A. (2015). Special education research advances knowledge in education. *Exceptional Children, 82*(1), 11–24.

Vaughn, S., & Wanzek, J. (2014). Intensive interventions in reading for students with reading disabilities: Meaningful impacts. *Learning Disabilities Research & Practice, 29*(2), 46–53.

Veenendaal, N. J., Groen, M. A., & Verhoeven, L. (2015). What oral text reading fluency can reveal about reading comprehension. *Journal of Research in Reading, 38*(3), 213–225. Retrieved from http://ezproxy.fiu.edu/login?url=http://search.proquest.com/docview/1720064499?account id=10901

Veit, D., Scruggs, T., & Mastropieri, M. (1986). Extended mnemonic instruction with learning disabled students. *Journal of Educational Psychology, 78*, 300–308.

Vellutino, F. R., Scanlon, D. M., & Lyon, G. R. (2000). Differentiating between difficult-to-remediate poor readers: More evidence against the IQ-Achievement discrepancy definition of reading disability. *Journal of Learning Disabilities, 33*, 223–238.

Venable, G. P. (2003). Confronting complex text: Readability lessons from students with language learning disabilities. *Topics in Language Disorders, 23*, 225–240.

Verschaffel, L., & de Corte, E. (1997). Teaching realistic mathematical modeling in the elementary school: A teaching experiment with fifth graders. *Journal for Research in Mathematics Education, 28*, 577–601.

Visser, S. N., Blumberg, S. J., Danielson, M. L., Bitsko, R. H., Kogan, M. D. (2013). *State-Based and Demographic Variation* in *Parent-Reported Medication Rates for Attention-Deficit/Hyperactivity Disorder, 2007–2008*. [Erratum appears in Preventing Chronic Disease 2013;10. http://www.cdc.gov/pcd/issues/2013/12_0073e.htm.] Prev Chronic Dis 10, 20073. DOI: http://dx.doi.org/10.5888/pcd9.120073

Visser, S. N., Danielson, M. L., Bitsko, R. H., Holbrook, J. R., Kogan, M. D., Ghandour, R. M., Perou, R., & Blumberg, S. J. (2014). Trends in the Parent-Report of Health Care Provider- Diagnosed and Medicated Attention-Deficit/Hyperactivity Disorder: United States, 2003–2011. *Journal of the American Academy of Child & Adolescent Psychiatry, 53*(1), 34–46.

Vygotsky, L. (1978). *Mind and society: The development of higher psychological processes*. Cambridge, MA: Harvard University Press.

Wagner, M., & Blackorby, J. (2002). Disability profiles of elementary and middle school students with disabilities. SEELS (Special Education Elementary Longitudinal Study), no. ED 00CO0017. U.S. Department of Education.

Wagner, M., & Cameto, R. (2004). The characteristics, experiences, and outcomes of youth with emotional disturbances. A report from the national longitudinal Transition Study-2, 3(2). *NLTST Data Brief* 3(2). National Center of Secondary Education and Transition, University of Minnesota.

Wagner, R. K., Francis, D. J., & Morris, R. D. (2005). Identifying English language learners with learning disabilities: Key challenges and possible approaches. *Learning Disabilities Research & Practice, 20*(1), 17–23.

Wagner, M., Marder, C., Blackorby, J., Cameto, R., Newman, L., Levine, P., & Davies-Mercier, E. (2003). *The achievements of youth with disabilities during secondary school. A report from the National Longitudinal Transition Study-2 (NLTS2)*. Menlo Park, CA: SRI.

Wagner, M., Newman, L., Cameto, R., Garza, N., & Levine, P. (2005). *After high school: A first look at the postschool experiences of youth with disabilities. A report from the National Longitudinal Transition Study-2 (NLTS2)*. Menlo Park, CA: SRI International. Retrieved from ERIC database. (ED494935).

Wagner, M., Newman, L., Cameto, R., Levine, P., & Garza, N. (2006). *An overview of findings from Wave 2 of the National Longitudinal Transition Study-2 (NLTS2)*. National Center for Special Education Research, Menlo Park, CA: SRI International.

Walker, H. M., & Sprague, J. R. (2007). Early evidence-based intervention with school-based behavior disorders. Key issues, continuing challenges, and promising practices. In J. B. Rocket, M. M. Gerber, & T. J. Landrum (Eds.), *Achieving the radical reform of special education. Essays in honor of James M. Kauffman* (pp. 37–58). Mahwah, NJ: Erlbaum.

Walther-Thomas, C., Korinek, L., McLaughlin, V. L., & Williams, B. T. (2000). *Collaboration for inclusive education*. Boston: Allyn & Bacon.

Walton, P., Walton, L., & Felton, K. (2001). Teaching rime analogy or letter recoding reading strategies to prereaders: Effects on prereading skills and word reading. *Journal of Educational Psychology, 93*, 160–180.

Ward-Lonergan, J. M., Liles, B. Z., & Anderson, A. M. (1998). Listening comprehension and recall abilities in adolescents with language learning disabilities and without disabilities for social studies lectures. *Journal of Communication Disorders, 31*, 1–32.

Washington, J. A. (2001). Early literacy skills in African-American children: Research considerations. *Learning Disabilities Research & Practice, 16*, 213–221.

Watt, S. J., Watkins, J. R., Abbitt, J. (2016). Teaching Algebra to students with learning disabilities: Where have we come and where should we go? *Journal of Learning Disabilities, 49*(4), 437–447.

Weaver, C. (2002). *Reading process and practice*. Portsmouth, NH: Heinemann.

Webb-Johnson, G. (2002). Are schools ready for Joshua? Dimensions of African-American culture among students identified as having behavioral/emotional disorders. *International Journal of Qualitative Studies in Education, 15*(6), 653–671.

Wehmeyer, M. L (2000). Assessment of self-determination—Negotiating the minefield: A response to Baker et al. *Focus on Autism and Other Developmental Disabilities, 15*(3), 157–158.

Wehmeyer, M. L. (2007). Self-determination. In M.F. Giangreco & M. B. Doyle (Eds.), *Quick-guides to inclusion: Ideas for educating students with disabilities* (2nd ed., pp. 61–74). Baltimore, MD: Paul H. Brookes Publishing Co.

Wehmeyer, M. L., Agran, M., & Hughes, C. A. (2000). A national survey of teachers' promotion of self-determination and student-directed learning. *Journal of Special Education, 34*, 58–68.

Wehmeyer, M. L., Palmer, S. B., Agran, M., Mithaug, D. E., & Martin, J. E. (2000). Promoting causal agency: The self-determined learning model of instruction. *Exceptional Children, 66*, 439–453.

Weintraub, F. E. (2005). The evolution of LD policy and future challenges. *Learning Disability Quarterly, 28*(2), 97–99.

Weiss, M. P. (2004). Co-teaching as science in the schoolhouse: More questions than answers. *Journal of Learning Disabilities, 37*, 218–233.

Weiss, M. P., & Brigham, F. J. (2000). Co-teaching and the model of shared responsibility: What does the research support? In T. E. Scruggs & M. A. Mastropieri (Eds.), *Advances in learning and behavioral disabilities: Educational interventions* (vol. 14, pp. 217–45). Oxford, UK: Elsevier.

Welch, M. (1992). The PLEASE strategy: A metacognitive learning strategy for improving the paragraph writing of students with mild disabilities. *Learning Disability Quarterly, 15*, 119–128.

Welsch, R. (2007). Using experimental analysis to determine interventions for reading fluency and recalls of students with learning disabilities. *Learning Disability Quarterly, 30,* 155–129.

Weyandt, L. L. (2009). Executive functions and attention deficit hyperactivity disorder. *The ADHD Report, 17*(6), 1–7

What Works Clearinghouse. (2013). *Intervention Report: Reciproal Teaching.* Washington, DC: Institute of Education Sciences.

White, T. (2005). Effects of systematic and strategic analogy-based phonics on grade two students' word reading and reading comprehension. *Reading Research Quarterly, 40,* 234–255.

White, B., & Frederiksen, J. (2005). A theoretical framework and approach for fostering metacognitive development. *Educational Psychologist, 40,* 211–223.

Wiener, J. (2004). Do peer relationships foster behavioral adjustment in children with learning disabilities? *Learning Disability Quarterly, 27*(1), 21–30.

Wiig, E. H., & Semel, E. M. (1984). *Language assessment and intervention for the learning disabled.* Columbus, OH: Merrill.

Wilby, P. (2004). Teach the language of tolerance. *Times Educational Supplement,* Issue: 4588, 23.

Will, M. C. (1984). Let us pause and reflect—but not too long. *Exceptional Children, 51*(1), 11–16.

Will, M. C. (1986). Educating children with learning problems: A shared responsibility. *Exceptional Children, 52,* 411–415.

Williamson, P., McLeskey, J., Hoppey, D., & Rentz, T. (2006). Educating students with mental retardation in general education classrooms. *Exceptional Children, 72,* 347–361.

Willoughby, S. S. (1990). *Mathematics education for a changing world.* Alexandria, VA: Association for Supervision and Curriculum Development.

Wilson, B. (1996). *Instructor manual: Wilson reading system.* Milbury, MA: Wilson Language Training Corporation.

Wilson, C. L., & Sindelar, P. T. (1991). Direct instruction in math word problems: Students with learning disabilities. *Exceptional Children, 57,* 512–519.

Winter, S. M. (2007). *Inclusive early childhood education: A collaborative approach.* Upper Saddle River, NJ: Prentice Hall.

Witzel, B. S., Mercer, C. D., & Miller, M. D. (2003). Teaching algebra to students with learning difficulties: An investigation of an explicit instruction model. *Learning Disabilities Research & Practice, 18,* 121–131.

Witzel, B. S., Riccomini, P. J., & Schneider, E. (2008). Implementing CRA with secondary students with learning disabilities in math. *Intervention in School and Clinic, 43,* 270–276.

Wodrich, D. L. (2000). *Attention-deficit/hyperactivity disorder: What every parent wants to know* (2nd ed.). Baltimore, MD: Paul H. Brookes Publishing Co.

Wolf, M. (2007). *Proust and the Squid: The story and science of the reading brain.* New York: Harper Collins.

Wolf, M., & Bowers, P. (1999). The "Double-Deficit Hypothesis" for the developmental dyslexias. *Journal of Educational Psychology, 91,* 415–438.

Wolfson, A. R., & Carskadon, M. C. (2003). Under-standing adolescents' sleep patterns and school performance: A critical appraisal. *Sleep MedicineReviews, 7,* 491–506.

Wong, B. Y. L. (1991a). Assessment of metacognitive research in learning disabilities: Theory, research, and practice. In H. L. Swanson (Ed.), *Handbook on the assessment of learning disabilities* (pp. 265–84). Austin, TX: PRO-ED.

Wong, B. Y. L. (1991b). *Learning about learning disabilities.* San Diego, CA: Academic Press.

Wong, B. Y. L. (1996). *The ABCs of learning disabilities.* San Diego, CA: Academic Press.

Wong, B. Y. L. (1997). Research on genre-specific strategies for enhancing writing in adolescents with learning disabilities. *Learning Disability Quarterly, 20,* 140–159.

Woodward, J. (2001). Constructivism and the role of skills in mathematics instruction for academically at-risk secondary students. *Special Services in the Schools, 17*(1–2), 15–31.

Woodward, J. (2006). Developing automaticity in multiplication facts: Integrating strategy instruction with timed practice drills. *Learning Disability Quarterly, 29,* 269–289.

Woodward, J., Beckmann, S., Driscoll, M., Franke, M., Herzig, P., Jitendra, A., … Ogbuehi, P. (2012). *Improving mathematical problem solving in Grades 4 through 8, A practice guide [NCEE 2012–4055].* Washington, DC: National Center for Education Evaluation and Regional Assistance, Institute of Education Sciences, U.S. Department of Education.

Woodward, J., & Brown, C. (2006). Meeting the curricular needs of academically low-achieving students in middle grade mathematics. *Journal of Special Education, 40,* 151–159.

Woodward, J., & Howard, L. (1994). The misconceptions of youth: Errors and their mathematical meaning. *Exceptional Children, 61,* 126–136.

Woodward, J., & Montague, M. (2002). Meeting the challenge of mathematics reform for students with LD. *Journal of Special Education, 36,* 89–101.

Wraga, M., Helt, M., Jacobs, E., & Sullivan, K. (2006). Neural basis of stereotype-induced shifts in women's mental rotation performance. *Social Cognitive and Affective Neuroscience.* (Dec. 8).

Xu, J. (2009). School location, student achievement, and homework management reported by middle school students. *School Community Journal, 19*(2), 27–44.

Yampolsky, S., & Waters, G. (2002). Treatment of single word oral reading in an individual with deep dyslexia. *Aphasiology, 16,* 455–471.

Yopp, H. K., & Yopp, H. (2000). Supporting phonemic awareness development in the classroom. *The Reading Teacher, 54,* 130–155.

Yuill, N. M., Oakhill, J., & Parkin, A. J. (1989). Working memory, comprehension ability and the resolution of text anomaly. *British Journal of Psychology, 80*, 351–361.

Zehler, A. M., Fleischman, H. L., Hopstock, P. J., Pendzick, M. L., & Stephenson, T. G. (2003). *Descriptive study of services to LEP students and LEP students with disabilities,* no. 4. Arlington, VA: U.S. Department of Education, Office of English Language Acquisition (OELA).

Zentall, S. S. (2007). Math performance of students with ADHD: Cognitive and behavioral contributors and interventions. In D. B. Berch & M. M. M. Mazzocco (Eds.), *Why is math so hard for some children?* (pp. 219–43). Baltimore, MD: Paul H. Brookes.

Zhang, C., & Bennett, T. (2003). Facilitating the meaningful participation of culturally and linguistically diverse families in the IFSP and IEP process. *Focus on Autism and Other Developmental Disabilities, 18*(1), 51–59.

Zheng, X., Flynn, L. J., & Swanson, H. L. (2013). Experimental intervention studies on word problem solving and math disabilities: A selective analysis of the literature. *Learning Disability Quarterly, 36*(2), 97–111.

Zigmond, N., Kloo, A., & Volonino, V. (2009). What, where, and how? Special education the climate of full inclusion. *Exceptionality, 17*, 189–204.

Zimmerman, F. J. (2008). *Children's media use and sleep problems—Issues and unanswered questions. Research Brief.* Washington, DC: Kaiser Family Foundation.

Zionts, L. T., Shellady, S. M., & Zionts, P. (2006). Teachers' perceptions of professional standards: Their importance and ease of implementation. *Preventing School Failure, 50*, 5–12.

Zoino-Jeannetti, J. A. (2006). *"It would turn the lights on in your head": Perceptions and experiences of learning of women enrolled in an adult education program.* Doctoral Dissertation, UMI Microform no. 3238850. Chestnut Hill, MA: Boston College.

Index

Note: The letter 't' 'b' 'f' and 'case' followed by numbers represents 'table' 'box' 'figures' and 'case' respectively.

CEC Initial Preparation Standards	Chapters
STANDARD 1: Learner Development and Individual Learning Differences Beginning special education professionals understand how exceptionalities may interact with development and learning and use this knowledge to provide meaningful and challenging learning experiences for individuals with exceptionalities.	
1.1 Beginning special education professionals understand how language, culture, and family background influence the learning of individuals with exceptionalities.	1, 3, 4
1.2 Beginning special education professionals use understanding of development and individual differences to respond to the needs of individuals with exceptionalities.	1, 2
STANDARD 3: Curricular Content Knowledge Beginning special education professionals use knowledge of general and specialized curricula to individualize learning for individuals with exceptionalities.	
3.1 Beginning special education professionals understand the central concepts, structures of the discipline, and tools of inquiry of the content areas they teach , and can organize this knowledge, integrate cross-disciplinary skills, and develop meaningful learning progressions for individuals with exceptionalities.	9, 10, 11
3.2 Beginning special education professionals understand and use general and specialized content knowledge for teaching across curricular content areas to individualize learning for individuals with exceptionalities.	9, 10
3.3 Beginning special education professionals modify general and specialized curricula to make them accessible to individuals with exceptionalities.	2, 9, 10, 11
STANDARD 4: Assessment Beginning special education professionals use multiple methods of assessment and data-sources in making educational decisions.	
4.1 Beginning special education professionals select and use technically sound formal and informal assessments that minimize bias.	11
4.2 Beginning special education professionals use knowledge of measurement principles and practices to interpret assessment results and guide educational decisions for individuals with exceptionalities.	11
4.3 Beginning special education professionals in collaboration with colleagues and families use multiple types of assessment information in making decisions about individuals with exceptionalities.	2, 3
4.4 Beginning special education professionals engage individuals with exceptionalities to work toward quality learning and performance and provide feedback to guide them.	3, 11
STANDARD 5: Instructional Planning and Strategies Beginning special education professionals select, adapt, and use a repertoire of evidence-based instructional strategies to advance learning of individuals with exceptionalities.	
5.1 Beginning special education professionals consider an individual's abilities, interests, learning environments, and cultural and linguistic factors in the selection, development, and adaptation of learning experiences for individual with exceptionalities.	1, 2, 3, 10
5.2 Beginning special education professionals use technologies to support instructional assessment, planning, and delivery for individuals with exceptionalities.	5, 6, 7, 8, 9, 10, 12
5.3 Beginning special education professionals are familiar with augmentative and alternative communication systems and a variety of assistive technologies to support the communication and learning of individuals with exceptionalities.	6
5.4 Beginning special education professionals use strategies to enhance language development and communication skills of individuals with exceptionalities.	5, 6, 7, 8, 10
5.5 Beginning special education professionals develop and implement a variety of education and transition plans for individuals with exceptionalities across a wide range of settings and different learning experiences in collaboration with individuals, families, and teams.	1, 2, 3, 6
5.6 Beginning special education professionals teach to mastery and promote generalization of learning.	5, 6, 7, 8, 10
5.7 Beginning special education professionals teach cross-disciplinary knowledge and skills such as critical thinking and problem solving to individuals with exceptionalities.	5, 6, 7, 8, 10
STANDARD 7: Collaboration Beginning special education professionals collaborate with families, other educators, related service providers, individuals with exceptionalities, and personnel from community agencies in culturally responsive ways to address the needs of individuals with exceptionalities across a range of learning experiences.	
7.1 Beginning special education professionals use the theory and elements of effective collaboration.	2
7.3 Beginning special education professionals use collaboration to promote the well-being of individuals with exceptionalities across a wide range of settings and collaborators.	2